ISLAMIᴄ...

Manifestations of Islamic Martyrology

Islamikaze

Manifestations of
Islamic Martyrology

RAPHAEL ISRAELI

FRANK CASS
LONDON • PORTLAND, OR

First published in 2003 in Great Britain by
FRANK CASS PUBLISHERS
Crown House, 47 Chase Side, Southgate
London N14 5BP

and in the United States of America by
FRANK CASS PUBLISHERS
c/o ISBS, 920 NE 58th Avenue, Suite 300
Portland, Oregon, 97213-3786

Website: www.frankcass.com

British Library Cataloguing in Publication Data

ISBN 0-7146-5491-4 (cloth)
ISBN 0-7146-8391-4 (paper)

Israeli, Raphael.
  Islamikaze: manifestations of Islamic martyrology
  1. Martyrdom – Islam 2. Terrorism – Religious aspects – Islam
  3. Suicide – Religious aspects – Islam 4. Islam and politics
  I. Title
  297.2'72

Library of Congress Cataloging-in-Publication Data

Israeli, Raphael.
  Islamikaze: manifestations of Islamic martyrology / Raphael Israeli.
    p.cm.
  Includes bibliographical references and index.
  ISBN 0-7146-5491-4 (cloth) ISBN 0-7146-8391-4 (pbk.)
    1. Martyrdom – Islam. 2. Terrorism – Religious aspects – Islam.
  3. Islamic fundamentalism. 4. Islam and culture. 5. Islam and
  politics. I. Title.

BP190.5.M3I85 2003
297.7'2–dc21

2003043926

Typeset by in 10.5/12pt Palatino by FiSH Books, London
Printed in Great Britain by MPG Books Ltd., Bodmin, Cornwall

To my children
Shlomit, Avi and David
and my grandchildren
Tal and Dan
whose painful physical absence
makes them ever more present

Contents

List of Abbreviations

AFP   French News Agency

AWADS   Alliance of Western and Democratic States

CAIR   Council of American–Islamic Relations

CIA   Central Intelligence Agency

DFLP   Democratic Front for the Liberation of Palestine

ETA   Euzkadi ta Askatsuna (Basque Nation and Liberty)

FBI   Federal Bureau of Investigation

GIA   Groupes Islamiques Armés (Armed Muslim Groups)

GOP   Grand Old Party (US Republican Party)

HIV   Human Immune Virus

IIF   International Islamic Front Against Jews and Crusaders

IRA   Irish Republican Army

MEMRI Middle East Media Reports

NATO   Northern Atlantic Treaty Organization

OIC   Organization for the Islamic Conference

PFLP   Popular Front for the Liberation of Palestine

PLO   Palestine Liberation Organization

POW   Prisoner of War

UNRWA   United Nations Relief and Works Agency

Acknowledgements

This project, which has been lying in abeyance since the completion of my 1997 article on the Islamikaze (*Journal of Terrorism and Political Violence*),[1] like many other things in our lives, received a tremendous impetus following the axial events of 11 September 2001 in New York and Washington, which not only pushed the battle against Muslim terrorism to the forefront of international concerns and agendas, but also dramatically increased worldwide eagerness to understand this phenomenon and what makes this new brand of ruthless terrorist tick.

Texts had been collected over the years that were cited as lending Muslim juridical justification to this sort of senseless violence, but were shelved and left to accumulate dust due to their incredulous nature and unrealizability. But then, after long years of a steady but relatively meagre stream of violence in the name of Islam, on 11 September, this long-contained current of hatred and violence gushed out with unexpected force and fury, causing imagination to challenge reality and making it recoil. It was time to retrieve the texts from the shelves, dust and air them, and prepare them in context for the scrutiny of the dazed Western public.

In view of the initial jubilant reactions to this horror throughout the Muslim world, it seems that expectation had been growing there that such horrendous feats would succeed in toppling Western pride and blunting US dominance over the world as the only surviving mega-power in the new century and millennium. Thus it became imperative to explain both the disarray and disbelief in the Western world as well the almost messianic Muslim expectations, which seemed to have been realized, even for some of the most educated and 'moderate' among them. Later pathetic attempts made by Muslim rulers, intellectuals and clerics to retract some of their initial instinctive pronouncements, or to quell the spontaneous joy of the populace, cannot efface without questioning the vast support those acts of terror enjoyed.

I am indebted, first and foremost, to Batsheva Hetzroni, who helped in collecting and interpreting some of these texts more than a decade ago, and to my home base, the Truman Institute for the Advancement of Peace at the Hebrew University of Jerusalem, which paid for Batsheva's efforts and granted me the office space, the library and other generous services that made this project possible. I am also grateful to a host of colleagues for their remarks, and to my wife Margalit for her patience in accepting the long hours of daily and nightly work, which by necessity came at her expense.

For my mistakes in interpretation and misapprehension of facts, I remain, however, solely responsible. I apologize for my failures to understand, my pretence to have understood, and my arrogance in imparting to others my own beliefs and errors.

Jerusalem, Autumn 2002

NOTE

1.   'Islamikaze and Their significance', *Journal of Terrorism and Political Violence*, Vol. 9, No. 3 (Autumn 1997), pp. 96–121.

Introduction

Atrocious acts of terror have occurred during the last decades of the twentieth century, ranging from hijackings of aeroplanes, boats and other means of ground transportation, to the kidnapping of civilians for ransom or political blackmail, the blowing up of buildings, malls, restaurants, airports, aeroplanes in mid-air and trains and buses, and gun attacks on individuals and groups. Atrocities of this sort were practiced in and around the Middle East from the late 1960s onwards, but they soon spread to other areas of the world, until no continent or country was immune from them. During those years, terrorist groups, which leaned toward Marxist-prone 'revolution' of some kind or other, mushroomed in practically all parts of the world, from the Red Army in Japan, to the Symbionese Liberation Army in the United States, the Red Brigades, the Action Directe, the ETA, IRA, and the Bader-Meinhoff in Europe, the Shining Path in Peru and the various Palestinian rival groups of the PLO, the PFLP, the DFLP, the Abu Nidal group and their clones and splinter groups.

Notwithstanding their different motivations, goals, scope of action, diffusion, means and targets of action, all these groups either sought to sow fear amidst their enemy and humiliate and intimidate him into surrendering to their demands; or undertook a long-term military struggle in order to weaken the enemy by guerilla warfare and constant bleeding; or tried to capture the attention of the world media in order to air their grievances and attain their redress; or tried simply to obtain by terrorist means objectives which they could not achieve in the arena of the battlefield. But although all these groups and organizations often collaborated and aided each other (for example, the Bader-Meinhoff involvement in the hijacking of the Air France plane to Entebbe in 1976, or the Japanese Red Army's role in the rampage at the Ben-Gurion Airport in 1972), they never constituted branches or arms of the same international networks. Moreover, while these acts of terrorism were often daring and required sophistication in planning and execution, they had always been the business of small groups and were calculated to extract a payment from, or to inflict pain and damage on, the enemy, while the perpetrators were planning and hoping to get away.

In most of the cases cited above, either the ideologies have faded over the years, or the members of the terrorist cells have mellowed with age and change of status, or have shifted tactics and adopted peaceful means of achieving their goals, or have been driven into oblivion due to effective eradication campaigns launched by the states concerned. Notable exceptions are those cases, such as in Kashmir, Xinjiang, the Philippines and the Middle East, where residual, unresolved ethno-national problems have complicated the issues at hand and contributed to their prolongation. At the same time, however, a new type of terrorism has emerged over the past two decades, triggered and nurtured by a certain interpretation of the creed of Islam, usually dubbed 'fundamentalist', which has lent new twists to the entire idea of terrorism. Now it was no longer the followers of an ideological splinter group who purported to produce 'revolution' by terrorist means, but the adepts of one of the largest and most successful universal religions, which is the established faith in some 56 Islamic countries across the world (namely about one-third of the total) spanning mainly the continents of Asia and Africa, but also counting among its 1.2 billion membership (that is, one-quarter of the world population) large minorities around the rest of the globe.

The massive return to Islam during the past two or three decades – whose roots and modalities have been discussed elsewhere – has by necessity coloured both the domestic struggle for legitimacy of governments within Muslim countries, and the lingering ethno-national strife between those countries and the rest of the world. Thus, on the one hand, one observes Muslim rule taking root in countries such as Saudi Arabia, Iran, the Sudan and Afghanistan, or struggling for the upper hand, *inter alia* through terrorism, in other countries such as Algeria, the Palestinian Authority, Lebanon or Egypt ; while, on the other hand, one cannot help but notice that some of the international conflicts in which Muslim groups or countries are involved, such as in the Middle East, Kashmir, the Philippines or Xinjiang, have also been tinged by Islamic ideology. The implications are vast: if, thus far, conflicts have been mediated and settled by negotiation and compromise, namely by quantitative means, once they are pushed to the religious domain they become qualitative and not given to negotiation and compromise and become that much more difficult to resolve.

The Muslim groups and countries that have embraced this way, those we customarily call 'fundamentalists', prefer the language of 'victory' over 'compromise', 'Holy War' (jihad) over negotiation, rejection over acceptance, exclusion over tolerance, the absolute Truth of Allah over human reasoning, and zeal over accommodation. In this state of affairs, terrorism, in the name of Allah, in His Path and for His Sake, becomes not only permissible due to the unmatchable forces of the Western Satan and his underlings, but indeed inevitable. Only the vocabulary changes in this setting: jihad is never terrorism, but lawful battle, and the enemy's counter-attack is never legitimate self-defence or counter-measure, but always 'aggression', 'state terrorism', violation of the Divine Will, rebellion against the Divine Order. In this setting, when conventional terrorism is no longer efficient enough to deal the enemy painful blows, and the necessity arises for unhindered access for the terrorist to strike his lethal blow at the enemy, then 'suicide bombers' move into the picture, not to commit suicide, but to annihilate the enemy in earnest.

The misnomer 'suicide bombers' will be discussed below, because it is pertinent to our analysis of Islamic terrorism. Here, suffice it to mention that this mode of terrorism is not unique to Islam; the Japanese kamikaze at the end of the Pacific War (1944–45) had acted likewise. We have also seen Indira Gandhi and then her son, Rajiv, die at the hands of such terrorists, as well as a number of other cases where the perpetrator was courageous/desperate/ motivated enough to lose his life in the process of eliminating his valuable target. But it is in the Shi'ite Islamic precedent of the 'Assassins' in the Middle Ages where this form of self-sacrifice finds its roots. It is no coincidence that it was among the Shi'ites of Lebanon that this lethal tradition resurfaced in the 1980s, in the context of the Lebanese War, first against the American marines who landed in that quagmire to guard the peace, and then against the Israelis. Few in the West suspected that a generalization of this method, both in terms of the perpetrators and their victims, would soon drag into the fray the Sunnite Hamas and Islamic Jihad, who have also embarked along this route, with Western civilization in general as the prime target.

This is what dramatically changed the world scene on 11 September 2001, when it suddenly dawned on people that this ill-understood 'treatment' by 'suicide bombing' was not reserved for the Jews and Israelis, nor was it limited to the Middle East and the Arab–Israeli conflict, but was a well-thought out, patiently contrived and cunningly devised all-out war against the West, the Great Satan, for its 'corrupting' effect on the youth of the world, notably the Muslims who were being led astray by the glamour of American material culture and tending to drift into the Western orbit of misdeed and mischief. Furthermore, the tragedy of the World Trade Center attested to an undreamt-of new reality where the 'suicide bombers' were not individuals who acted foolishly on the spur of the moment, but a coterie of several determined individuals who acted in unison to carry out a simultaneous series of hijackings for which they had been groomed for years, and had even precisely and cautiously programmed their harrowingly cold-blooded act of terror to coincide, in time, scope, space and horror, with the simultaneous and equally horrendous acts perpetrated by their like-minded fellow 'suicide bombers'.

This drama has shown not only that the perpetrators of these murderous acts did not need the pretext of the Intifadah (which began to unfold long after the preparations for the Twin Towers were under way) and the Palestinians (who currently plan and carry out their own 'suicide bombings', without waiting for Osama Bin-Laden), but also that the myth that used to link 'suicide bombings' with economic under-development did not have a leg to stand on. Neither Bin-Laden nor his operatives, who could afford to study engineering and piloting in Europe and the United States, were exactly the impoverished types who, out of despair, depression or personal grievance, would embark on this most horrible (and complicated) of atrocities. Explanations have, therefore, to be sought elsewhere, for example, in the powerful grip of Islamic ideology in general and its fundamentalist teachings in particular.

It is true that it is not Islam as such that has declared war on the United States and the West. For one thing, there is no single papal-like authority that can make such declaration in the name of all Muslims. It is also true that one can cite verses of peace or war from any holy book, and manipulate holy scriptures, religious tenets, vocabulary and symbols to fit tailor-made arguments. But one must also face several puzzling quandaries and attempt to resolve them:

1. Is it pure coincidence that all the hijackers and perpetrators of these horrors are Arabs/Muslims? And are the papers found on some of them, pointing to Muslim fundamentalist training and attachment, actually relevant?
2. If this horror has nothing to do with normative Islam, as we

often hear it said, do we find in any other contemporary faith or system of belief any individual or organization which has launched or made common cause with a scheme of this scope and of this horrendous cruelty and inhumanity?

3. Why is it that Islam has given rise to so many groups of 'suicide bombers', and to so many 'spiritual' leaders who openly condone this practice and lend legitimacy to it: Bin-Laden in Afghanistan, Sheikh Yassin in Gaza, Sheikhs Fadlallah and Nasrallah in Lebanon, and so on? Why is it that those adulated personalities condemn acts of terror in general, but not those of their own doing or inspiration?

4. Why is it that most armed conflicts in the world today, and most acts of terrorism throughout the globe, are caused by, or connected to, Islam of one brand or another: from the Abu Sayyaf group in the Philippines, which kidnaps foreigners and holds them to ransom; to recurring arson attacks on churches in Indonesia, Nigeria, the Sudan and Egypt; the ongoing genocide against the Blacks in southern Sudan; the war in Kashmir; the Hamas, Islamic Jihad and Hizbullah connection of the Arab–Israeli conflict; the civil war in Afghanistan and Central Asia; the heinous slaughter of civilians in Algeria and Egypt; and the new wave of terrorism in the United States and Western Europe, and so on? What is in fundamentalist Islam that is so bellicose and uncompromising as to sanction conflict, terrorism and 'suicide bombing'?

These are some of the questions we will be tackling in the following pages, not only through examining their historical sources and their modern manifestations, but also by referring to some of the texts that have become hallowed in the modern Islamic world and are being consulted and cited as 'justifications' for these horrors. We have repeatedly heard the argument that those are 'un-Islamic' deeds performed by 'un-Islamic' zealots, and yet they all say and write, and are indoctrinated to believe, that they act in the name of Islam, for the sake of Allah. Are we then talking about a different Islam? If so, then how do we explain the vast popularity of the deeds and their perpetrators among the Muslim populace, after due lip service is paid, of course, to the 'deep trauma' that many Muslims say they feel in the aftermath of the Twin Towers carnage? If the trauma were genuine, why is it that in previous, smaller-scale murders of this sort, no outright condemnation was forthcoming from Muslim leaders?

In the wake of the Twin Towers horror, an almost universal cry of condemnation of this horrendous act was heard across the globe. One would have noticed, however, that except for the United States and certain of its closest allies, almost no one dared to condemn the perpetrators, under the pretext that 'clear evidence' is needed before one hurries to indict. When this argument is advanced by law-abiding regimes, one could still perhaps understand; but when it is particularly emphasized by the world of Islam, which does not count among its 56-nation membership even one regime ruled by law, this sounds more like a rather flimsy pretext to avoid the need to act against the culprits. This is the reason that while almost all Muslim countries rushed to take cover by swearing allegiance to the United States, for fear of its wrath, none of them has been accommodating in terms of joining the battle itself, or at least making its facilities freely available to the United States' fighting units.

Here, a paradox arises: had the Muslim countries been so certain, as they claim, that no Muslim element was involved in the anti-American onslaught, then why were they reluctant to join the battle against the perpetrators? In fact, they know exactly where the terrorists came from, that all those involved were Muslims, their doctrine Muslim, their financing from Muslim sources, their constituencies Muslim and their goal Muslim. It is the same Muslim governments who have fought the terrorism that threatened them (Mubarak against the *Gama'at*, Assad against the Muslim Brothers, Arafat against the Hamas), but when the same terrorism was directed against Israel, the United States or the West, they did not act against it, and often even harboured it (Egypt – the hijackers of the *Achille Lauro*; Syria – the Islamic Jihad and the Hizbullah; Iran – all the Islamic terrorist organizations; and the Palestinian Authority – the Hamas and Islamic Jihad, who day in, day out terrorize Israeli cities. Saudi Arabia and Libya subsidize the Hamas and other terrorist groups, and the Yemen refused to turn in the saboteurs of the US Navy ship in Aden.)

A spade must be called a spade, and terrorism must be identified not according to its victim, but according to its perpetrator and mode of action. Whenever an organization trains, indoctrinates and dispatches groups or individuals to engage in the wanton killing of civilians, for any purpose, it is a terrorist organization pure and simple, and one that has to be pursued and eliminated. No national or religious grievance, justified as it may be, can explain away or provide 'understanding' for acts of terror, and those who tolerate any kind of terrorism are bound to see it turned against themselves. There are civilized ways to struggle against 'injustice', 'oppression', 'occupation' and 'exploitation', which involve armed struggle against the armed forces of the enemy, if negotiations should fail; similarly, it is the duty of any country witnessing terrorism in the making to take all necessary measures to avert it, through legal means if possible, but also through elimination of the culprits if necessary, after all precautions have been taken to minimize collateral damage to innocent civilians.

It will be the contention of the present work that while acts of violence that clearly take on the characteristics of terrorism have to be identified and eradicated, one ought also to detect and recognize the ideological infrastructure which permits them to take a stronger hold in certain societies than in others. While there are widespread acts of injustice, domination and inequality of opportunity around the globe which generate terrorist movements (ETA, IRA and the like), they are bound to recede when these grievances are laid to rest. What characterizes the latest wave of Islamic terrorism in the United States is that no specific demands were attached to it – such as the payment of ransom, adoption of a certain policy, relinquishing a certain territory, or releasing hostages. It was not unleashed as a warning or to establish a bargaining position, or to enforce a list of demands, the fulfilment of which would resolve the crisis and avert the horror, but as an irreversible punishment to be exacted, an expression of anger to be vented. This calls for investigation and clarification, and this is what we shall attempt in the following pages.

1. Sampling Muslim Reactions to the New York and Washington Horrors

Unlike their governments, which lack legitimacy for the most part and do not reflect their public opinion, much of the populace in most Muslim countries reacted with jubilation to the disaster that befell the West following the attack against the Twin Towers and the Pentagon on 11 September 2001. This is, of course, not necessarily indicative of the Islamic doctrine as such, or of the interpretation the Muslim masses lend to it in the world today, but it certainly reflects the depth of hostility towards the West, its wealth and values. Much of this hostility can be imputed to the fashion in which the policies, way of life and economic prosperity of the West are perceived by the unfortunate multitudes who live under oppression, misery, disease and illiteracy in those lands; but there is no doubt that a crude popular perception of Islamic doctrine has also played a significant role in this view of the world.

There is no way, of course, to gauge the predominant sentiment among the masses throughout the length and breadth of the entire Islamic world, but judging from press write-ups, and public demonstrations where pictures of Bin-Laden were displayed, slogans were brandished or shouted, and US (and Israeli) flags and effigies were trampled and then burned by crowds in delirium, and the attacks against US institutions or businesses, one can not mistake the intensity of feeling. Sometimes, it was evident from the support manifested for the Taliban or for Bin-Laden, or from the waving of Islamic slogans, that the angry populace was transmitting a Muslim message of vindication, but at other times the virulent grievances sounded generally anti-Western and anti-American. In either case, it is certain that since Islam has remained the main focus of identity among Muslim societies, the anti-Western vitriol voiced among the masses will almost always retain Islamic under- or overtones. There is also little doubt that educated,

Westernized and less-bigoted Muslims would feel and express sadness and horror at the sight of the tragedy, but still the seemingly prevailing mood among those societies was not one of mourning or identification with the victims and their families.

This should come as no surprise when one bears in mind, on the one hand, the harsh, even fanatic, reaction of Muslims worldwide to what they perceive as the profanation of their holy sites or any slur on their culture, or the enthusiastic and self-assured way they go about spreading their faith and imposing it on others; and on the other, the unbearable ease with which they deny others' religious rights, and even step in to obliterate the religious heritage of other faiths. Similarly, it escapes no one's scrutiny that those who die in their clashes with non-Muslims are immediately dubbed *shahid* (martyr), their funerals are tumultuous, emotional, vindictive and replete with demands for revenge, even when the deceased had engaged in a visibly aggressive and unprovoked act of terrorism; while the death and destruction of others is jubilantly celebrated by dance, distribution of sweets and outright delight in the misery and havoc they have wrought on others. It is as if human happiness were a zero-sum game, where someone's glory must come at the expense of others' misfortune, and where any success of the West is regarded as a Muslim failure, and vice versa.

Mosques can be, and are, erected throughout the Christian and Jewish worlds, Muslim clerics are invited to officiate in national ceremonies of Western countries, as a matter of course, but no church can be built anywhere in Saudi Arabia or Afghanistan, Buddhist symbols are torn down by the Kabul government, and existing churches are torched or blown up in Indonesia, Egypt, the Sudan, Kosovo and elsewhere in the Islamic world, where the state religion is invariably Islam and therefore no provision is allowed or possible for other faiths. Moreover, Muslims around the world have grown accustomed to the fact that their rampages against other faiths go unpunished, and this encourages their belief that persecuting others is the natural state of affairs. For example, during the first year of the al-Aqsa Intifadah (2000–1), Muslim immigrants in Western democracies were involved in hundreds of cases of vandalism, desecration and assaults against Jewish sites and Jewish individuals and worshippers, the scope of which has been unprecedented in Europe since *Kristallnacht*. Since not much was done to deter the vandals, it took a full year to calm tempers there, although in the Middle East itself Jewish sites continued to be desecrated.

In short, there is a world of difference between Western values and Muslim ones, at least those articulated by the fundamentalists among them. While, for the West, terrorism is terrorism, and under no circumstances can there be any justification for the loss of life of innocent civilians, Muslim fundamentalists, and one suspects also other Muslims around them, have found ample ideological rationalization for the wanton killing of civilians. Among the Palestinians, for example, though the Hamas supporters constitute no more than one-third of the Palestinian constituency, polls among the populace show some 80 per cent support for acts of terror against Israeli civilians. This accurately reflects the numbers of the people who have celebrated in the streets of the West Bank and Gaza, and for that matter in the other Muslim cities and towns across the world, the New York and Washington horror. Years prior to this horrendous act of terror, Absallah Shami, the Head of the Islamic Jihad group in Gaza, when questioned by an Israeli journalist about indiscriminate 'suicide bombing' of civilians, answered thus:

> We do not possess the military hardware our enemy possesses. We do not have planes, missiles, or even a cannon with which we can fight injustice. The most effective tool to inflict damage and harm with the least possible losses is operations of this nature. This is a legitimate method based on martyrdom. The martyr gets the privilege of entering Paradise and frees himself from pain and misery.[1]

In these terms, not only does the killer have no qualms about killing anyone, by any method, due to his lack of arms, but he also delights in taking the shortcut to Paradise by doing so. And since the wanton murderer is 'privileged' to be dubbed a 'martyr', killing becomes 'legitimate'. This is the world of the values of these terrorists, and this is the Islamic rationalization of these values. These notions, which are cultivated by entire networks of ruthless terrorists, as we have seen and heard following the Twin Towers tragedy, are also backed by the crowds who cannot resist the temptation to publicly express their jubilation. Worse, they are incited by politicians, journalists, clerics and intellectuals, who have no compunction about voicing their distorted and inhuman worldview in public, both in writing and in speech. The following selection will exemplify this horrific state of mind, which allows this type of assassin to flourish and operate among a sympathetic population.

Maybe the most telling broadside against the United States, while it was still in shock, just one day after that horror unfolded, came from the Hamas movement in the Palestinian territories; those same people who murder civilians in restaurants, blow up school buses, re-enact those atrocities in public and then brag about them. Typically for this brand of terrorist, the accusation is directed at the victim themself, which means not only that the act of terror and mass-murder are justified in their eyes, but that they expected more to follow and that they might participate themselves in future butcheries of this sort. What is particularly sad and disillusioning about this is that one author, Atallah Abu-al-Sabah, boasts the title of PhD, indicating that he is a well-educated man, supposedly versed in the humanities and perhaps trained to honour human life and human values as they are cultivated in the West. Here are some excerpts from his 'Letter to America' which he published in the organ of the Hamas in Gaza, *Al-Risala* (The Message, The Mission):

> I am confident that you will be facing for a long time to come the mirror of your history. Thus, you will be able to realize how oppressive, corrupt and sinful you have been, how many entities you have wiped out and how many states you have destroyed. Do you remember what you did in Korea and Vietnam? Do you recall how you turned Hiroshima and Nagasaki into piles of radioactive rubble, which contain death for the two destroyed cities, now and in the future? Not one single human being was left in those two cities that the fire has not deformed, nor a baby who was not torn to pieces, nor a bird that was not drowned in a sea of flames!!!
>
> Oh America, the sword of oppression, arrogance and crime!! Do you remember how you smashed man's humanity? Do you remember how you mistreated the Blacks under your aegis? Can you describe for us the humiliation, disgust and contempt you meted out to those unfortunate people, whose only sin was that they were born to black parents? It was your white son who chained their necks in slavery, after he had hunted them down in Africa's forests and along its coasts. They were born free, but were enslaved in your virgin land...
>
> Did you ever ask yourself about what you did to the original inhabitants of your land, the Apache Indians? You trampled them under your white feet, and then used their

name, the Apache, for the helicopter that carries death, destruction and annihilation to owners of rights, who dared to clamour for their rights. This is a heinous and destructive conduct, which made us hate the Apache, before we could realize that they were themselves victims, just like us...

Did you ever ask yourself what was the sin of the children of al-Amariya[2] or Kana,[3] or the reason for the continuous injustice you have been bringing down on Baghdad,[4] Jerusalem and Jenin[5] and on all those who do not see eye to eye with you, or refuse to walk the road of those sycophant and emasculated [Arab] rulers that you treat as 'excellencies' and 'majesties'? America, did you ever ask yourself why do you produce cluster bombs, nuclear and hydrogen bombs, biological weapons for mass killings, and F-16 planes? Even should we accept the contention that you do it for your own war preparedness, why do you put these weapons in the hands of every murderer, war criminal, and enemy of humanity, such as [Serbian war commander] Karadzic, [Prime Minister] Shamir and [Prime Minister] Sharon?

America, have you ever tasted horror, pain and affliction? These have been our lot for a long time, and they have filled our hearts, torn our guts and burned our skin. This has become daily routine for us, and carried out by your favourites with high proficiency. They indeed destroy our shacks in Jenin, and what has happened to us tonight there, is no different from what has happened to you...

Every so often Dick Cheney and his girlfriend, Condolezza Rice, set out to calumniate us, to castigate us, to incite against us. And we lined up and asked Allah to let you sip from the cup of humiliation, until Heaven responded. Now, America, consider whether you are able to forgo your fanaticism, your arrogance and your vanity...While we have accepted your mediation for the sake of peace...you have opened the gates of the Pentagon for every Jew to acquire a knife in order to slaughter us...You have planted yourself the seed of hatred for you...You did not think that the roots of those plants would grow to poke your eyes, even as they were placed on top of the World Trade Center...Those plants have also grown to hit at the heart of the Pentagon, the most heavily guarded facility on earth...Can you not see that the outgrown roots have reached the very eyes of your strong Secretary of

Defence, Donald Rumsfeld, who thought he was immune to revenge for what he did?

America, why did you evacuate the Sears Building, the way we do every night in order to flee your laser-eyed missiles? Are you scared, just like us? Do the giants also experience fear and run for their lives just as the oppressed do?...It turns out that you are weaker than the weak, and miserable like all the refugees whom you forced out of their villages on the Palestine seashore, together with their wives, children and torn clothes...America, where is your famous CIA which can detect even ants on a rock? You did not see the grievances of those who have struck you...for your blindness could only see through the eyes of traitors and spies...America, where is your second eye, the Mossad, which you always made us believe could detect anything?...

Can we expect that this time you will reconsider and avoid attacking a drug factory in Khartoum, or in Libya? Or will the appetite for revenge again blind your sight and lead you to discharge your wrath again on Al-Amariya or Bet Hanun [in the Gaza Strip]? What good did your Navy or ballistic missiles and nuclear reactors do to you? How have your satellites and AWACS, NATO and world leadership, come to your help? All those were paralyzed when the sword of vengeance got to your neck, in this unprecedented feat in world annals...You surely understand, that unless you repent from your corruption, you are bound to be hit once and again by the same perpetrators...

America, re-examine your decisions to cast hundreds of veto votes [at the Security Council of the UN], with a view of denying humanity its rights. Look at your humiliated face, and check whether it is not due to those votes. This will teach you to stand by justice and the righteous, even if they are weak, and then perhaps the dust of humiliation will be removed from your sad face.[6]

Much along the same lines, the editorial of the same journal, also written by an educated and enlightened Dr Ghazi Hamad, calls the United States to task, stressing the rule that 'the punishment fits the crime', and wondering why the United States had not learned any lessons from the killing of her marines in Lebanon, the destruction of her headquarters in the Khobar Towers in Saudi Arabia, the bombing of her two embassies in Africa, the incapacitation of the USS *Cole* in the Yemen and the attacks against her forces in Japan and the Gulf. Thus, says the editorial, the United States was bitterly 'reaping today what she had sown in the hearts of millions'.[7] These first projections of the blame on the victim, which showed no signs of sympathy for the families of the dead, and were probably boosted by the atmosphere of jubilation in the Palestinian streets, soon gave way to denials that Arabs or Muslims could have had anything to do with the horrendous destruction. So, on the one hand, the Arabs were not displeased by the disaster that befell the United States, but on the other hand, when they began to grasp the gravity of the horror and to fear the wrath of US response, they ran for cover: they had neither seen nor heard; it was all the fault of others: the United States itself, Israel and all sorts of evil powers-that-be.

A columnist in the London-based Arabic *Al-Sharq al-Awsat* put the blame squarely on President Bush and Secretary Powell. Bush, because he was 'hardly elected' to his post, and he needed the drama to draw behind himself the bi-partisan support of the United States, and Powell due to his military background which conditions him to conduct war, not diplomacy.[8] The next hypothesis was of course Israel/Zionism/the Jews, they being the 'most likely to benefit' from the slaughter. The Jews/Zionists, who 'control the world media, economy and politics', wished to press NATO and the Americans to 'surrender even more thoroughly to Zionist ideology', and to further promote the 'Zionist slogan of Islamic terrorism'.[9] World Zionism was accused by other Arab and Muslim journalists, who could see the imprint of the US–Zionist–Israeli 'holy alliance' on this affair, though they implied that the 'perpetrators' rushed to accuse 'international terrorism', by which they meant Arab and Islamic. One columnist advocated a firm stand by the Arabs to wash their hands clean of any accusation, and to transcend their defensive stand and move to the offensive.[10]

With Israel found to be the culprit, the act of terrorism becomes horrible, inhuman and unthinkable, epithets that fit in with 'legendary Zionist cruelty'. Another Arab writer claimed that only the Jews themselves would not be afraid to be caught, because no one 'would dare accuse them and incur the danger of being blamed for bringing upon them a new Holocaust'. Therefore, they are the only people who 'hide their crimes and are sure that no one would ask them to account for their deeds'.[11] The author did not explain, however, why the Jews needed to hide their deeds if they were not held accountable in any case. Another Jordanian columnist was 'personally certain that no Arabs or Muslims stood behind this act', because it was the Zionist organizations who were interested in perpetrating the crime in order to preoccupy the world while they destroy the Aqsa Mosque[12]; while a compatriot imputed the deed to either Christian fundamentalist groups who support Israel or the Israeli Mossad, which reputedly pursues 'evil and dangerous avenues'.[13] The organ of the Muslim Brothers, *Afaq 'Arabiyya*, after exclaiming that 'no one in the East has shed tears for the Americans', castigated the United States for 'wishing to teach the world who is Allah', and for

> preferring the monkeys [the Jews] over other humans whom they mistreated, for supporting homosexuals and interest [in banking, which is prohibited by Islam], and forgetting that no one can escape Allah's punishment, and He indeed came from an unexpected direction and struck their hearts with fear.[14]

A Syrian columnist advanced the theory that this was a belated vengeance by the Japanese for Hiroshima and Nagasaki.[15] A Palestinian author, who admitted that there were many potential candidates for this act of terror, who had suffered, like the Palestinians, from US and Western policy, nevertheless counselled the Americans to look for the perpetrators far afield from the Middle East, because 'not all those interested to counter American policy have also the means to perpetrate an act of this sort'.[16] Not a word of sympathy or compassion for the victims, just an expression of Arab helplessness in carrying out such a feat due to the scarcity of wherewithal at their disposal. A Lebanese reporter raised the idea that young computer hackers may have taken over the computerized air-control system and 'directed the aeroplanes to painful targets'.[17] Another reached the conclusion that since the Arabs did not stand to gain anything from the horror, they were not the likely perpetrators, but that others, like the Israelis, the Mafiosi, the Russians or the Chinese, who oppose the US anti-missile defence programme, or perhaps a fundamentalist group in the United States, must have concocted it.[18]

A pro-Arab British journalist, Patrick Seal, who is considered the court-biographer of Hafez al-Assad, also joined the chorus of denials in the Arab media. Set against his doubt that Arabs or Muslims could have perpetrated this act, he posits the many 'massacres' committed in the past by the United States and Israel. He also embraced the theory that 'ecological terrorists' might have mounted the plot to deter the process of globalization. He elected to put aside the question of the immorality of 'suicide terrorism', and confine himself to inquiring about their efficacy, and evinces some understanding to acts of terrorism which impel desperate and oppressed people to seek vengeance, and to establish a 'balance of terror', which means that, for example, Palestinians threaten to kill Israelis, if the latter kill Palestinians, and that is an act of deterrence. Therefore, says he, there is no doubt that the perpetrators of the Twin Towers atrocity meant to establish a balance of terror with the Americans. He did not elaborate, however, upon whether Bin-Laden was appointed by the Vietnamese or the Japanese dead, or the Palestinians for that matter, to avenge them.[19]

The state-controlled Egyptian press, with some exceptions, condemned the attacks against the United States and also the Arabs and Muslims who had expressed joy at the misfortune that had befallen America, but it also used the occasion to call upon the United States to alter its policy in the Middle East. At the same time, many members of the Egyptian media, including those toeing the government line, spoke about 'American and Israeli terrorism' and predicted the 'fall' of the United States from her superpower position. Ahmed Ragab, a columnist from mainstream *Al-Akhbar*, who had in the past shown support for Hitler, could not contain his joy over the disaster. He wrote: 'I know a person, extremely wealthy, scaringly influential, who rules like a tyrant, imposes his will but loses everybody's love. Suddenly, out of the dark, he was painfully struck on his behind. He turned around but only saw ghosts.'[20]

The opposition press, which does not toe the line, but would not dare publish, for example, a personal critique of Mubarak, took the opportunity to overtly explode in delight, as if human compassion had nothing to do with political opposition to any rule :

> Let me state things directly and honestly: I am happy about what has happened to America, and I am elated about the high rate of casualties there. They can accuse me however they wish, but this will neither change nor diminish one iota the happiness and delight that have taken me over, and no one can cause me to take back my words under any circumstances and for whatever reasons. All those innocent

dead are the victims of the 50-year-long American barbarism and terrorism…Just count the numbers of the victims of American weapons around the world and compare them to the figure of the killed in the United States now, and you will discover that the latter is hardly one per cent of the former. Therefore, I have the right to be happy, I have the right to be joyful, for the Americans have finally tasted the bitter flavour of death.[21]

The editor of that harrowing 'columnist' also insisted on his 'right' to celebrate, because that was the first step 'in the 1,000 mile journey towards the rout of America by knock-out'.[22] Another columnist, this time a woman whom one would have expected to show more sensitivity to human suffering, also expresses her elation in no uncertain terms:

I cannot hide my feelings, nor restrain my joy. For the first time in my life I can observe with my own eyes the collapse of American arrogance, tyranny, vanity and evil. For the first time in my life I am asking myself: Has Allah finally listened to the prayers of mothers and the supplications of the victims in Palestine, Iraq and Libya…Am I expected to be hypocritical, like all the others, condemn the killing of civilians, express my sorrow about the American and other victims, and pray and donate blood for them? Why are we trying to satisfy the Master in the White House of our innocence? Throughout history we have never been caught red-handed with the blood of the innocent: Indians, slaves, Vietnamese, Palestinians, Iraqis. I want no alliance with America, I have had enough with the shame brought upon us in Iraq. I wish neither to pray for the Americans nor donate my blood to them. I do not want to condemn what has happened. It is America that killed them, as it had killed us in Iraq, and as it is continuing to slaughter us in Palestine.[23]

Other columnists called upon the United States to 'withdraw from the world, both as thieves and as policemen', and to choose between 'respecting other nations or dying'. There were writers who stated that they were not happy about the death of civilians, but about the fact that 'America's honour had become a mop to trample upon'.[24] The peak of jubilation came, ironically, in the organ of the Egyptian

'Liberal' Party, which rejoiced over the rout that the United States suffered which demonstrated that she was a 'paper tiger'.[25] Very tellingly, one such 'liberal' author complained about the pressures exerted on him and his likes by the powers-that-be to contain his joy:

> We were banned from demonstrating the happiness and delight we feel so as not to hurt American feelings, although in this case, expressions of joy are a national and religious obligation. For America is Israel's protector, and when we watch her crumble instantly, and her heroes run away in horror, to prohibit public jubilation is an unbearable burden. But we were deprived of it and forced to show sympathy to our executioners.[26]

Some writers resorted to sarcasm in order to 'expose the hypocrisy of those who are now whining for the American losses'. One of them suggested that he could have hired the services of a professional weeper, but no one would agree 'even if he paid her $100 for each tear'. How could a columnist, asks he, who believes that 'America got what she deserved for sucking the blood of other nations', escape the lies of the hypocrites who 'volunteer to shed tears, to donate blood and to put their intelligence apparatus in the service of their cardboard Master'? And furthermore: 'If you are killed by a thug, that is unfortunate; but if you are forced to attend his funeral, that is the peak of humiliation. Sorry, America, we have no tears left to participate in your sorrow.'[27] These unbearably horrific words were surpassed by another writer who described his watching the horror live as:

> ...moments of a beautiful and glamorous hell, the best and dearest of my life. I saw the towers, the walls, those symbols of power which constituted a modern and scary monster, penetrated by a courageous hornet... The hornet stung that mythological monster, who looked horrific as he cried, shouted and collapsed like a hell. All the media who ply to America, broadcast once and again those pictures, that all the past and future generations will envy us for having been privileged to witness.[28]

These harrowing remarks were not criticized by anyone of stature in the Arab or Islamic worlds, because all those were busy containing similar outbursts of callous rage and furious indecency in their own countries, lest their 'national interest' be harmed by the exposure of those statements to international scrutiny. Many decent Muslims were certainly mortified by what had happened, but not all necessarily because of the human tragedy involved. Any number of them are embarrassed that so much killing has been occasioned in the name of their faith, or that so many violent movements across the Muslim world purport to represent Islam or to urge the Believers to jihad against non-Muslims; others fear that the tragedy might backfire on them, elicit international hatred of Islam or lead to a negative blanket judgement being passed on it. And if this is the situation in the countries most closely associated as 'allies' of the United States, how much more so in environments overtly hostile to it – such as Iran, Iraq, the Sudan, Libya and Afghanistan – where words of compassion, or of criticism of the popular mood are not even allowed; and among any number of other Muslim and Arab countries and organizations, notably Muslim fundamentalist groups, where hostility to the West is very deeply embedded.

Sheikh Yussef al-Qardawi, one of the senior spiritual leaders of the Muslim Brothers, and an authoritative doctor of the Holy Law in Sunni Islam in general, who was one of the first to sanction 'suicide bombing', had argued that the martyr who goes to his death for the sake of Islam wages jihad as an active agent who seeks the extermination of the enemy of Islam, and therefore he is justified in launching his attacks even though he might kill himself in the process. However, while in previous bombing incidents against Israel he was more permissive of wanton killing of the enemy in general, the horror of 11 September apparently prompted him to effect some fine-tuning to this rule: he said that the Shari'a (the Holy Law of Islam) was against indiscriminate killing, and that only enemy combatants who carried weapons were legitimate prey for the Muslim jihad fighter, while innocent civilians were to be spared. He even stated that those who committed this sort of atrocity could not be called Muslims. Nonetheless, this ruling was mitigated by so many caveats as to make it ineffective, or at the very least questionable. His main points were:

1. It is the West who has turned Islam into its enemy since the Crusades, by coveting Muslim lands and resources, while Islam, in his words, did nothing to justify its enemy status.

What about the Islamic conquests in the Middle Ages, which threatened Europe and the entire civilized world at the time, or the present-day onslaught on Christians throughout the Muslim world, or the multitude of wars and acts of terror perpetrated in the name of Islam? He did not elaborate.

2. If the West attacks Muslim countries we cannot enter into any alliance with it, unless it is proven that they authored or sponsored the act of terrorism. Just to harbour terrorists does not mean that the harbouring country can be accused of participating in the murder. Just as one cannot attack Egypt or Algeria just because Sheikh Abdul-Rahman or some Algerian have done something, so Afghanistan cannot be attacked.

3. This attack against the United States is the fruit of hatred, whose roots have to be investigated, for if Bin-Laden is killed, another 1,000 like him will emerge. Is this what the world desires? Besides, neither the Taliban nor Bin-Laden could have had any involvement in this.

4. The Shari'a forbids collaboration with non-Muslims against other Muslims. Such collaboration is a sin and an act of aggression. Moreover, the Shari'a obliges every Muslim country to rush to the help of any other Muslim state under attack, with money and fighters.

5. It is also prohibited by Islamic Law to surrender a Muslim to non-Muslims, for this opposes common sense, since Islam does not recognize any geographic borders, race, colour or language differences between Muslims. They are all one *umma* (nation) dwelling in *Dar al-Islam* (Abode of Islam), united in its belief in Islam and in its Islamic fraternity.

6. It makes no sense that Pakistan should assist foreigners to invade its Muslim neighbour, no Muslim scholar would countenance such a prospect, and I do not understand why the Pakistani scholars of the Holy Law can allow this to pass.

7. If Bin-Laden should be proved guilty, I having no objection to having him handed over to Muslim justice in Egypt or Saudi Arabia. But who can prove that he recruited, trained, financed and dispatched the culprits? This would be very difficult, for terrorists exist all over the world and it is not inevitable that Bin-Laden or al-Qa'ida should be involved.

8. There is no doubt that the Zionist entity is the one who stood to gain most from this crime; the United States supports Israel, and Israel is the greatest terrorist in the world.

9. There are two lines of terrorism: the one pursued by people who defend their rights and homeland, which is sanctioned by the Qur'an, as the Believers are enjoined to 'cast fear'[29] in the enemy's heart; this is the kind of terrorism practiced by the Hamas, the Fat'h and other Palestinian movements who defend their land. If this is terrorism, then this is the best kind of terrorism, because it is a jihad for the sake of Allah. The other kind of terrorism, which is illegitimate, is Israel's terror which kills illicitly and desecrates Muslim holy sites. But even though the United States supports this Israeli terrorism, we should not attack civilians in the United States. We could, instead, boycott the United States and compel it to retreat as we did in Durban.

In other words, terrorism in the eyes of the venerated Sheikh, who is looked up to in vast sections of Sunni Islam, is not a mode of operation that is absolutely forbidden under any circumstances, but it all depends on who does the killing and against whom: when Muslims fight for their 'rights', which they alone are authorized to determine, then a 'human bomb' is permissible even among innocent civilians; if the enemy of Islam defends itself against Muslim onslaught, it is he who is the terrorist, even when he uses more discriminatory modes of fighting than the Muslims would adopt. In either case, the definition of who is the terrorist, what is the subject matter that can be deemed as justifying Muslim 'suicide bombing', what is the criterion for morality, right, justice, crime and so on, are all determined at the discretion of Muslim Law, and not matters of universal human rights, justice, or internationally agreed definitions and conventions.

What is appalling is that these points of view are not only shared by journalists who shape public opinion or are shaped by it, and Muslim fundamentalists in the Arab and Islamic worlds whose uncompromising anti-Western stance we have explored, but also by people who have intellectual pretences, such as writers and politicians who set the tone of discourse in their societies. As has already been pointed out above, many Arab and Muslim leaders who nominally joined the US coalition, or have been knocking at its door, due to the promises it may hold, have set themselves on a collision course with their peoples and in the long run may have undermined their own regimes. But the others, who either openly loathe the United States and its coalition, or see no prospects of joining it, do not mince their words when they analyse their perception of the 11 September events. So much so that an Egyptian movie critic, Samir Farid, wrote that he was 'ashamed of the commentaries I read in the Egyptian press...in towns and villages of Egypt processions marched exclaiming the abominable slogan "We shall redeem you with our soul and blood, O Bin-Laden!"'[30]

Thus, the Chair of the Arab Writers Association found no other place than the *Literary Weekly* (Damascus) to give vent to his disturbing trend of thought, which was found to merit depiction in harrowing detail in a supposedly humanistic artistic journal:

> I ache for the death of innocent people, but the day the power symbols of America collapsed on 11 September reminded me of the daily funerals of so many innocent people in occupied Palestine...of the day of the American–British aggression against Tripoli (Libya), when they tried to destroy the house of its leader while he was asleep, but they only succeeded in burying his daughter under the ruins; of the oppression of peoples in Korea and Vietnam...So, my soul was filled with disgust and bitterness towards a country which failed to register anything but a history of oppression and support to the racism of Nazi Zionism and apartheid in South Africa, a country which has itself founded its 'civilization' on the robbery of other nations and the imposition of tyranny, in the name of fighting tyranny...
>
> The American Administration, which is ruled by Zionist decisions and supports the occupation and racist deeds of the 'Israelis', has numbed my feelings. The American Administration has contaminated my soul, and when I saw the multitudes running away in terror, in the streets of New York and Washington, I was telling myself: 'let them taste from the cup they have forced upon all nations and upon us in particular...'
>
> When the Twin Towers collapsed...I felt as if I were extricated from the bottom of a tomb, as if I were hovering over the arrogant mythological symbol of American imperialism, which has covered up the crimes it had committed...My lungs filled with pure air, and I breathed deeper than ever before...Even when I thought about the innocent who were buried under the rubble...I was sorry that my humanity had been soiled by Zionist America and world Zionism...But minutes later I learned new facts from the

media: that Arabs and Muslims are accused as the culprits, and threats were voiced calling for revenge against them...

This has returned me to the spiritual tomb where I was submerged by the aggression, arrogance and distortion of facts. But my inner stamina which saved me from drowning, enabled me to breathe again over the surface: we shall live, be victorious and bring justice to the world, because we are ready to sacrifice ourselves for our existence, our rights, justice and the world's humanity... The American people has to wake up to the image that his policy has created of him, that is the dirty policy that does not bring respect to its initiator... That moment of 11 September has to produce a re-examination of policy, strategy and ideas... Maybe even the American brain will understand that military and economic power deprives it of true humanity...

Americans have to understand that their commitment to support racist Zionism and its Nazi deeds... causes the entire Arab nation to rejoice when America suffers death and destruction... The symbolism of destroying one of the five wings of the Pentagon, and of killing one thousand people there, is far more important than the fact that it continues to exist and to threaten other nations and especially Afghanistan and Bin-Laden. This means that it is enough that one person has decided to die for his honour, rights, nation, faith and civilization, in order to attain his goal even against a superpower and in the heart of its territory... Consequently, if nations wake up and evince this kind of will power, and set out to resist tyranny, dictators, racists, arrogance and imperialists who drink their blood... then it is easy to imagine what will happen then...

American policy causes hatred in support of racist occupiers, whose entire history is shameful, bloody, destructive, scandalous and full of plots against others. The hands of their leaders are soaked in the blood that was spilled by their racist policy of collaboration with the Nazis. The [Jews] distort history, religious faith and facts. They despise Gentiles and Prophets, crucify them, and treat other humans like animals which were born in human shape in order to serve the Jews...

Something has collapsed in America, and this is the beginning of America's collapse as the sole superpower...

This collapse will be followed by the building of a new base for the victory of the oppressed and miserable people, for all tyranny will come to an end, force will be routed by force, and there will be no limit to human will when it determines to take on the arrogance of force...

Sure as I am that many of the victims do not deserve compassion, due to their belonging to the blood suckers of other people, one should not rejoice at the loss of human life. My humanity, that American and Zionist policy have attempted to numb, gains the upper hand in the final analysis over hatred and hostility.[31]

In the face of these explosions of inhumanity, which were rather popular among the Arabs and Muslims, in contrast to the reserve of their rulers who huddled to be embraced by the US coalition, the isolation and illegitimacy of the rulers grows ever more acute, in so far as they do not represent their public opinion on the one hand, and are unable to contain it in the long run, on the other, to the point of reaching the brink of being swept away when it erupts in earnest. One of their devices for walking the tightrope between popular resentment and their inability to respond to the American challenge to join the world war against terrorism is their attempt to draw distinctions between various kinds of terrorism. Theirs is considered, of course, 'national liberation', while moves of self-defence by the United States, Israel, or any country that does not toe their line, is 'state terrorism', or simply 'true terrorism'. Even those who recognize the United States' legitimate anger are afraid lest it retaliate in 'illegitimate terms', thus hurting its own and others' interests.[32] All this rhetoric can be simply construed, however, as the third stage in Arab and Islamic reactions to the horror of 11 September.

The first stage was of unlimited joy and a bursting sense of revenge at the sight of what seemed a defeated and hapless United United States of America. Then, as the voices of harsh retribution rose among the US administration and public, and growing evidence unfolded of Arab and Islamic involvement in the disaster, denial set in: suddenly, the Arabs knew nothing and heard nothing, and all insinuations about their possible connection were categorized as 'biased' against them. Finally, when the culprits were named, and concrete plans started to crystallize regarding the targets for retaliation, differences between various kinds of terrorism were found, according to who performed them, not to the mode of their execution. In this fashion, the grotesque situation arose where some of the champions of terrorism began to condemn it (not its perpetrators), meaning the terrorism of others, and so they thought that they could gain the status of 'coalition members', and see themselves removed from the terrorist list of the State Department.

Because of that sequence of events, the Arabs and Muslims have been pressing for UN involvement, where they have an automatic command of one-third of the votes, to re-define terrorism and to sponsor any international measure taken against the perpetrators of the New York and Washington acts of terrorism. They do not hide their hope that if their position is adopted they would be able to indict Israel for her 'crimes', which amount to terrorism in their eyes, while their brand of terrorism against her would gain international legitimacy, since in their view it is the Arabs who have 'always fought against terrorism'. Therefore, according to this logic, it would be futile to search for Arab or Muslim culprits. For even if Bin-Laden threatened the United States, this does not make him any more susceptible in their eyes than, say, Prime Minister Netanyahu of Israel, who had once, in their view, 'threatened to burn Washington'.[33] The attempt to distract world attention from the arrested Arab and Muslim suspects in the United States, and from the direct indictment of Afghanistan and Bin-Laden, naturally put many Arab and Muslim leaders on the 'Israeli track', claiming that since the Zionists stood to gain the most from 'blackening the faces of Muslims across the world', they were the primary suspects as perpetrators of that horror, not Bin-Laden or Afghanistan.[34]

When the picture began to clear with regard to the violent reactions in the Arab and Muslim streets to the US reprisals against Afghanistan, all the above dilemmas became more acute: the distance between Muslim rulers and the ruled grew larger and more bitter; the onslaughts against the Jews, who 'invented terrorism', as compared to Islam, which 'has always denounced it',[35] gained momentum; and, most importantly, the accusations against the United States were scaled up for its perceived brutality, terrorism, arrogance, support of Israel, aggression, anti-Islamic sentiment and policy, and so on. What has not changed is the one-sidedness of the 'values' which the Muslims stand for: they clamour for justice, that is, the justice they favour, namely that the West should respond to all their demands; they are all against terrorism, that is, any use of force against them, while the force they use against others, including terrorism, is fully justified; regardless of coalitions, accusations, culprits and indicted terrorists, they are reluctant to have any Muslim country act against any other Muslims, even if they are proved to be terrorists or harbouring terrorists; they are convinced that the United States deserved the punishment meted out to her in retribution for her misdeeds; they are determined to extract from the West all the possible concessions and quid pro quo's they can, in return for nothing, for pure talk, or for promises they do not intend to fulfil in any case.

In sum, President Bush was right in not only declaring a world war against terrorism, but also in coining a whole new vocabulary for dealing with it: its initiators were 'wanted', like in the old West; they were to be 'smoked out of their hiding holes'; they were to be targeted, sought out and destroyed; their protectors who harboured them were to be punished, collateral damage and casualties not-withstanding; the war against them was to be sustained, protracted, determined and all-encompassing until they were caught, defeated, eliminated or brought to justice, and their bases destroyed, their finances dried up, their front-organizations disbanded and their supporters punished or otherwise coaxed to abandon them.

But that kind of policy cannot succeed unless it is global not only in its goals and means, but also in its definitions, norms, standards and modalities. It is impossible to win, for example, if other acts of terrorism that do not directly concern the United States are dubbed 'local' (ETA in Spain, Corsica against the French, the IRA against Britain or the Hamas, the PLO, the Hizbullah or the *Tanzim* against Israel), and therefore unworthy of the global fight against terrorism. It is also impossible to win if some acts of terror are accorded 'understanding' and various 'justifications'. Terrorism is a violent activity against civilians, for whatever reason; therefore, while one can 'understand' the struggle of the IRA or ETA against the security forces of Britain and Spain, whom they perceive as the occupiers of their countries, the moment they blow up car-bombs in the middle of Londonderry or San Sebastian, wantonly killing and maiming civilians, they become terrorists who should be relentlessly combated.

Terrorism will not be successfully defeated if the vocabulary devised by the President of the United States is made invalid in places other than the US. The United States has been rightly targeting the heads of al-Qa'ida, using aeroplanes to bombard their bases, sending forces into their territory to 'smoke them out', cutting off their sources of financing and supplies. However, when it puts down and condemns the exact replicas of those actions, when pursued by others, as 'assassinations of leaders', as resorting to 'disproportionate force', as 'invading others' territory', or as 'depriving others of their lawful income', this does not sound like a universal war, which is launched on universally agreed standards, according to universal criteria. If the war is indeed one of good against evil, then evil cannot be allowed to masquerade as good, nor terrorism as a 'war of liberation'. If the clear and iron-clad definitions voiced by President Bush are allowed to erode because of short-term considerations, then the moral basis of the entire US campaign will grow so slim and shaky as to arouse domestic and international opposition to it.

When the United States searches for allies in its worldwide endeavour, the staunchest of them can only be found among democracies whose committed leaders have a staying power based on their legitimacy in government. Tyrants, monarchs, military juntas, who have no popular base to their rule, not only cannot pledge a long-standing and unrelenting support to the United States, but their very collaboration with the West arouses the opposition to both their 'participation' in the war effort, and also to their personal hold on government. The fact that the only committed allies of the United States are democracies, while the others shrink from 'attacking fellow Muslim states', demand 'evidence' of Bin-Laden's culpability, insist on novel definitions of terrorism which would sanction theirs (for example, the Islamic terror against Kashmir or Israel), only reinforces this trend of thought. Instead of President Bush categorizing the countries of the world into 'with us or against us', something that caused all of them to scramble for shelter under the wings of the virtual 'coalition', he ought to invite all the countries which fought terrorism and eradicated it to join in, while cautioning the others which did not to clean up their act, or else... There would have been no stronger incentive for them to conform and to embrace the US definitions of terrorism.

The fact that almost all terrorist movements in the world today are Muslim, and all the universal organizations and networks among them are the produce of fundamentalist Islamic thought, ought to cause us to review not the 'root reasons' for this terrorism, as the Saudi Prince suggested to the brave Mayor of New York who refused to sell out his principles but to review the childish, uninformed and untruthful declaration by many Western leaders that 'Islam is a religion of peace'. If it is peaceful, why are so many atrocities committed in its name? Every Muslim and Western leader repeats the mantra that 'the acts of terror are un-Islamic'. If they knew something about the division of the world into *Dar al-Harb* (the Abode of War) and *Dar al-Islam* (The Abode of Islam), that is brandished by the Muslim fundamentalists today to justify their jihad (Holy War, including terrorism) against the non-Muslims, maybe they would shudder at the thought that this core concept is part and parcel of political Islam, not a new fundamentalist invention.

At the same time that Muslims across the globe trample US flags and intimidate US citizens with horrific acts of terrorism, long queues are formed in the Muslim world to apply for student visas to the West or ask for outright immigration there (yes, that hated West). But those who grant the visas are not aware, or pretend not to understand, that those young students and the rest of the migrants, while they may innocently wish to study or to better their lot economically, are the very people that will turn their acquired knowledge against the countries that were courteous enough to dispense it to them, and the very masses who will go on the rampage against the democratic governments that gave them shelter. In the year of the Intifadah, for example, hundreds of cases were recorded in all Western democracies of desecration of Jewish sites, of torching synagogues and destroying cemeteries. Those same Muslim migrants, if not checked, will turn against their new governments and compatriots, as the events of 11 September have shown.

NOTES

1. Israel TV, Channel 1 (in Hebrew), 9 December 1994, 18:00 GMT.
2. The hundreds of civilians who were accidentally killed in a bomb shelter in Baghdad during the US bombings of the Gulf War (January 1991).
3. The hundred or so civilians killed by a stray Israeli bomb in southern Lebanon during the Israeli operation there in spring, 1996.
4. The continued bombings by the United States and Britain of Iraqi targets in the no-flight zone established there in the aftermath of the Gulf War.
5. The retaliatory raids by Israel, using American-made weapons, against Palestinian targets.
6. *Al-Risalah*, 13 September 2001. Cited (in Hebrew) by *MEMRI, Terror in America* , No. 1. The *MEMRI* series, *Terror in America*, began on 11 September 2001.
7. Ibid.
8. *Al-Sharq al-Awsat*, London, 14 September 2001. Cited by *MEMRI* (Hebrew), *Terror in America*, No 4.

9. *Al-Dustour* (Jordan), 13 September 2001. Ibid.
10. Ibid.
11. Ibid.
12. *Al-Ra'i* (Jordan), 13 September 2001, ibid.
13. *Al-Dustour* (Jordan), 13 September 2001, ibid.
14. *Afaq 'Arabiyya* (Egypt), 19 September 2001.
15. *Tishrin* (Syria), 13 September 2001, ibid.
16. *Al-Ayyam* (Palestinian Authority), 13 September 2001, ibid.
17. *Al-Safir* (Lebanon), 12 September 2001, ibid.
18. *Al-Sharq al-Awsat*, 13 September 2001, ibid.
19. *Al-Hayat* (London), 13 September 2001, *MEMRI, Terror in America*, No. 5.
20. *Al-Akhbar* (Egypt), 17 September 2001, *MEMRI, Terror in America,* No. 8.
21. *Al-Arabi* (Egypt), 16 September 2001, ibid.
22. Ibid.
23. Ibid.
24. Ibid
25. *Al-Ahrar* (Egypt), 14 September 2001, *MEMRI* (Hebrew), *Terror in America*, No. 8.
26. *Al-Ahrar*, 17 September 2001, ibid.
27. *Al-Usbu'* (Egypt), 17 September 2001, ibid.
28. Ibid.
29. The Arabic term is *irhab*, which translates as the modern word 'terror'.
30. *Al-Hayat* (London), 3 October 2001.
31. *Al-Usbu' al-Adabi* (The *Literary Weekly* – Damascus), 15 September 2001, *MEMRI, Terror in America*, No. 10.
32. See, for example, the article by Dr Adnan 'Amran, the Syrian Minister of Information, in *Al-Dustour* (London), 21 September 2001, *MEMRI, Terror in America*, No. 11.
33. Ibid.
34. One of the most outspoken accusations of Israel was voiced by the Syrian Minister of Defence, Mustafa Tlas, who cited as 'evidence' the 'fact' that the Jewish employees of the World Trade Centre had been forewarned of the impending massacre so as to save their lives.
35. Saudi Prince Mamduh Ibn abd-al-Aziz, in *Al-Hayat* (London), 29 September 2001.

2. Muslim Terminology and World of Discourse

The stunningly obtuse vocabulary that we have seen above, used by common people, leaders, clerics and intellectuals throughout the Islamic world, raises the question whether humankind, in its large variety of cultures, resorts to the same words and notions to describe the same phenomena, or whether we have to inquire about the meaning of each word when uttered by a member of a different civilization and make sure that what we hear or read is what is meant. In fact, people use the same words to signify different meanings and notions, because each word, which had developed in its socio-cultural environment to respond to a local cultural need, has been borrowed, often by default, and moulded into a different mindset, in which it necessarily carries a whole gamut of significances which are culturally different to the culture from which they were borrowed.

Thus, non-Western cultures, for example, such as the Muslim cultures, can claim that they had invented (or created) limitations on the use of violence or terrorism, tolerance, freedom, democracy, socialism, human rights and so forth, well before those ideas became the hallmark of the West. But when one examines their content one discover that they are a far cry from what is meant in the Western cultural context. Moreover, non-Westerners often call the West to task for having departed from those norms, even as they attempt to impose their own ways, for example, Islam, as the only way to create 'just and equal societies', which would bask in freedom and democracy, while they vilify other cultures, for example, Christian and Jewish, and express their inherent hostility to Western values and norms.

Had Western writers been aware of these cultural differences, and of the uses made by Muslim societies to define terms such as terrorism, democracy, tolerance, co-existence, pluralism, and so on, they would have been less stupefied by the statements they hear from Muslim fundamentalists the world over, such as the call by a radical Muslim leader that President Bush should convert to Islam, or by Bin-Laden's accusation against him of assuming the leadership of the Infidels. This specifically Muslim terminology – which is not admittedly put into operation by most Muslim countries, mainly due to their inability to apply it, and also in consequence of the illegitimacy of their rulers who are themselves menaced by Muslim fundamentalism – has nevertheless become the conventional discourse in practically all Muslim fundamentalist movements across the globe, be they in government, as in Iran, Sudan, Saudi Arabia and Afghanistan, or in strong opposition to it, as in Egypt, the Palestinian Authority, Lebanon, Indonesia, Algeria, Pakistan and the rest.

It would not go amiss, therefore, if we were to carefully examine the most important terms that are tossed around by Muslims in this clash of worldviews and this war of misunderstandings. Analysing each term in its Muslim context would certainly spare us aggravations and recriminations when we debate with them as this would help us realize that our cherished democracy is not something they aspire to; that justice for them means Muslim justice; tolerance to them is not unconditional acceptance of the other; terrorism is what the others do; pluralism is altogether unheard of; ending a conflict can only be done through victory, not compromise; sovereignty belongs to Allah, not to the people; legislation is not the prerogative of humans but of the Divine Will; Western values amount to corruption; logic and reason must follow the Muslim ways of thinking; they expect respect for Islam but dispense contempt for others; they regard their own shouting and rampaging as a show of force, and their foes' dignified quiet and restraint as evidence of weakness; everybody owes them everything, but they owe nothing to anyone; and they view any attack on others as legitimate and lawful, while any act of self-defence by non-Muslims is nothing but aggression.

These notions, which were well-known and often directly experienced by the West in its 'medieval' violent encounter with Islam, were forgotten and often ignored in the modern world, as they were no longer valid or practicable when Islamic countries were conquered, colonized, trampled upon and subjugated and the West reigned supreme. However, the rising wave of Islamic fundamentalism over the past few decades, which has occasioned the reaffirmation of these ideas, thus challenging the hegemony of Western political and social theory, has allowed their restatement and facilitated their diffusion. And since Islamic ideas have occupied the public arena in Arab and Muslim countries, where most of the existing regimes are illegitimate, the Muslim discourse has gained the upper hand as the only viable alternative that is able and willing to contend for predominance and power.

This mode of thinking naturally sets the Islamists a world apart from the accepted norms of deliberation, exchange of ideas and conduct both domestically in their own countries and externally *vis-à-vis* other nations and cultures. This is a world where relativism is obscured by absolutes, and scepticism by certainties; a world of qualitative ideas that are to be taken or left, not quantities that could be negotiated and compromised on. In other words, seeking understanding and accommodation for these Islamists, who presume they embrace the only valid truth, so much so that they expect their rivals to see the light and embrace their faith, is tantamount to betraying their own bedrock of creed and commitment, and surrendering to the physical force of their enemies or, worse, to the lure and false glamour of their convictions.

Almost since its inception, Islam has recognized the division of humanity into three categories of people: the Muslims, the People of the Book (initially Jews and Christians, and then extended to include others), and the pagans who knew no God; the lands of the globe were divided into basically two domains: the *Dar al-Islam* (the Abode of Islam) and *Dar al-Harb* (the Abode of War). While, for practical purposes, these categories are no longer operative because they would otherwise throw international relations into chaos, in the circles of Muslim fundamentalists, both those in power and those in opposition, this terminology has been revived and widely used to analyse internal and external affairs in accordance with the requisites of the Shari'a, that is, the Holy Law of Islam.

One has to realize that the religion of the Muslim fundamentalists is one and the same as the Islam of old, not a new one. Therefore, when they or their deeds are condemned by other Muslims as 'non-Islamic', this is merely a blanket statement calculated to skirt the embarrassment caused by the excesses of their co-religionists. Since Shari'a submits only to eternal laws and cannot be abrogated or amended at the whim of anyone, either it is applied more or less and strictly, as do the Islamists, or it is, partly or wholly, ignored by a multitude of Muslims who have elected to succumb to the requirements of modernity. The difference is then only in the degree of enforcement: the Muslims in general, while aware of, and caring about, the tenets of their creed, may be lax about the implementation of some of them, insistent as they may be on their Muslim identity and commitment; the Islamists, or fundamentalists, however, impatiently display their burning passion for full implementation here and now at almost any cost.

Like fundamentalist Christians, who give precedence to the holy texts over latter-day interpretations, so do Muslim fundamentalists, who revere the text of the Holy Qur'an, the Word of Allah and the supreme manifestation of His Will, and the Hadith, the traditions referring to the life of the Prophet who, as the most perfect of beings, had set for all generations to come the model of piousness and conduct to be emulated. Other sources of the Shari'a, such as analogy and consensus, widely resorted to by non-fundamentalist 'ulama' (scholars of the Holy Law), are discarded as human (therefore susceptible to failure) reasoning. In consequence, the fundamentalist sheikhs are usually at odds with established Islam, which is subservient to the rulers whom they despise and seek to unseat; something that posits them as opposition forces in their countries and often violently so.

Because they are feared by the authorities, on the one hand, and ruthlessly persecuted, on the other, these fundamentalist groups often form their own enclaves within their societies which set them apart spiritually, if not physically, from their environment, and facilitate the cultivation of their vocabulary and peculiar way of life. When possible, and as long as they play by the restraining rules of manifesting themselves only religiously and socially but not politically, they occasionally throw their gauntlet into the public arena, openly criticize the rulers as un-Islamic, and preach their Muslim way as the 'solution', the 'alternative', or the 'truth'. But then, when they act violently and menace the governments in place, they are eliminated by the regime and they seek asylum elsewhere, either in the West, where democracy affords them the opportunity to undermine it from within – for example, the Islamic movements in the United States (with Egyptian Sheikh Abdul Rahman as their head), Britain and the rest of Europe – or in like-minded fundamentalist countries, such as the Sudan or Afghanistan, which lend them protection, as in the case of the Saudi Bin-Laden in Afghanistan.

In their sheltering countries, the fundamentalists experience an existential contradiction: they are enjoined by the Shari'a to live under Islamic rule, which alone theoretically meets the definition of the Abode of Islam, where Islam is freely practised and even defines the socio-political and religio-cultural contours of their living environment. However, paradoxically, that is the environment that they had to run away from, in order to be able to implement, in full freedom, the tenets of Islam. Thus, the Abode of War, that is, the Domain of the Infidel, is found to be more accommodating to the Islamists than most Islamic countries which constitute the Abode of Islam itself. This anomaly is rationalized either by claiming that *Dar al-Islam* lies wherever freedom of worship is permitted, or by bragging about the gains and inroads they make into their host societies and winning converts to Islam. As long as they can build their mosques, practise their religion, establish their Muslim institutions, raise money under the cloak of charity, demonstrate for the cause of Muslims in other parts of the world, and even achieve positions of influence in the host society, all of which allow them to pursue their active support to their movements in their countries of origin or worldwide, all seems well. But it is not.

It is not, because these movements by definition either seek to subvert the rule in their native countries, which often maintain good relations with their countries of asylum; or they act violently in their host countries against policies not to their liking, pursued by the local governments; or they attack other minorities, such as the Jews, which are perceived as inimical to Muslim interests. The fact that the perpetrators of the Twin Towers horror in the United States were, for the most part, Arabs who had won access to that country as immigrants is a case in point. There are numerous other ethnic and religious groups who came to the United States to improve their lot over the centuries of immigration into that country, and who now constitute a melting pot of multi-culturalism and ethnic and religious pluralism. But once they tied their fate with their new land, they became part of its social fabric and committed to its values. No other cultural or religious group – not even the most underprivileged, disinherited, disaffected and exploited among them, such as the descendants of the black slaves, nor the offspring of the American Indians who escaped extermination – have given rise in their midst to such horrendous cold-blooded murderers, of such ruthless cruelty, and on such a staggering scale.

This means that while most Arabs and Muslims who have settled in the United States over the years seek to improve their lives and internalize the values that America has been imparting to them, the fundamentalists among them, be they newcomers or old-timers who were swayed by the radical cause, insist on their own interpretation of the dichotomic partition of the world between the Abode of Islam where Shari'a should reign, and the Abode of War which is ruled by non-Muslims. Their temporary dwelling in the latter does not mean that they accept its norms and rules, and their using its facilities and protective rule of law does not signify that they have come to identify with it. It does mean that they find it much more expedient, certainly more so than in their countries of origin, to exploit the open democratic system in order to undermine it from within. In this sense, the Muslim fundamentalists who seek refuge in the West, or are native there, are not necessarily susceptible to becoming more moderate, grateful to their hosts, or pro-Western, but quite the contrary, like the great luminaries of modern Muslim radicalism – Sayyid Qut'b of Egypt and Hasan Turabi of Sudan, who were educated in the West and knew it intimately – they grow to become its greatest and most sworn detractors and enemies.

Many of those Muslim fundamentalists who found shelter in the West regard their stay there as the equivalent of the Prophet's move from Mecca to Medina in AD 622, in order to effectuate a mental as well as spatial migration (*hijra*) from the land of 'ignorance' and godlessness (*jahidiyya*), to construct a new base of power and then launch the decisive assault against their native land in order to rescue it and reintegrate it within a purified *Dar al-Islam*. Their Western asylum is, in this context, the convenient base in which they can freely prepare to remove their own illegitimate rulers, and in so doing they widen and solidify their base of power by winning over converts, indoctrinating their followers, collecting funds, and illegally stocking up on weapons (evidence of which has been surfacing in the United States and Western Europe). But when the process becomes frustratingly slow, and the West does not seem to weaken fast enough to succumb before their ideas; or the hated regimes in their native countries appear to hold on to power ever more strongly with the help of Western powers; or perceived enemies of Islam and Muslim populations (Russia in Chechnia, the Serbs in the Balkans, India in Kashmir, China in Xinjiang, Israel in the Middle East, and now the United States in Afghanistan) seem to persist in their onslaughts on Islam, then outbursts of Islamic fury are bound to occur.

Under such circumstances, the head-on collision between the fundamentalist guardians of *Dar al-Islam* and its Western rivals comes into the open as of old, in the form of Holy War, the only war sanctioned by Islam, that is called jihad. Jihad is not only the tool that served the Prophet to conquer all Arabia and enforce Islam on it by the sword during the early decades of the seventh century, as well as enabling his successors to spring out of the desert peninsula and go for the conquest of the world, it has also remained the religious rationale for any war waged by Muslims against non-Muslims, and often even against other Muslims. For example, all the wars of conquest of Islam were termed jihad for the purpose of Fat'h (conquest, and also the name of the main group within the PLO today), as were all the Arab wars against Israel and many campaigns in Asia and Africa against European colonizers. The Egyptian incursion into the Yemen in the 1960s was a jihad as was the Iraq–Iran war in the 1980s. The Hamas and Hizbullah are waging jihad against Israel today, as is al-Qa'ida against the United States and Britain. Jihad against non-Muslims is *ipso facto* justified as the combat of *Dar al-Islam* to expand its domain, to defend it, and/or to fight *Dar al-Harb* into submission.

Etymologically, jihad was meant to designate an intellectual 'striving', and by extension also a physical striving, for a cause. In Islamic Shari'a, however, jihad has principally one meaning: a military action by *Dar al-Islam* or elements thereof against *Dar al-Harb* or any entity defined as such. The idea is founded on the notion that Islam is not simply one of the revealed religions, but the prevailing faith which has come to replace the other monotheistic religions; it being the latest and therefore the most updated, as it were, and they being forgeries of the original Divine Message whenever and wherever they differ from the latest Muslim version thereof. Hence the call of the Hamas, the Hizbullah and al-Qa'ida upon President Bush and other world leaders to convert to Islam and thus resolve their misunderstandings of, and rifts with, it.

It is incumbent upon Islam, as this classical faith viewed things in the past and the fundamentalists still view it today, to extend its rule all over the world by peaceful means if possible, by war if necessary. Jihad is usually viewed as a collective duty (*fard kifaya*), binding the Muslim community at large, the *umma*, as a whole. Namely, when the Muslim authorities-that-be pursue jihad, every Muslim individual is thereby viewed as having discharged his duty. The duty to fight jihad is universal and perpetual until the entire world comes under Muslim dominion. However, because Muslim countries have desisted in practice, under various theological and practical considerations, from this idea, which otherwise would have permanently pitted them against the rest of the world, Muslim fundamentalists have come to take this duty as a personal one (*fard 'ayn*), and so have consecrated any struggle of theirs against Unbelievers as a pursuit of that holy duty. Let us listen to what the Hamas group has to say in this regard: a call which is echoed throughout all Muslim groups:

> When our enemies usurp our Islamic lands, jihad becomes a duty binding on all Muslims. In order to face the usurpation of Palestine by the Jews, we have no escape from raising the banner of jihad. This would require the propagation of Islamic consciousness among the masses on all local, Arab and Islamic levels. We must spread the spirit of jihad among the Islamic *umma*, clash with the enemies and join the ranks of jihad fighters.[1]

Admittedly, various interpretations were given to jihad in the modern world, intended to emphasize the spiritual aspects thereof, and are drummed up today throughout the Muslim establishment in the world, and by some latter-day 'experts on Islam' who have an axe to grind when belittling the impact of the jihad spirit. There is no doubt, however, that the most prevailing interpretation, especially among Muslim radicals, is the violent one. It would be ludicrous to claim that while the Hizbullah, the Hamas or al-Qa'ida inflict horrendous acts of violence, murder and terror on innocent civilians, and while they attack the military and institutions of countries they regard as hostile, they mean to promote a 'spiritual jihad'. Quite the contrary, in their public calls for 'sacrifice', 'battle', 'fighting' and 'elimination' of the perceived enemy, and much more so in their murderous attacks against civilians, the military and installations of other countries, they consecrate the use of violence. In fact, one suspects that this sentiment is so widespread among the populace in the Muslim world – if one is to judge by the manifestations of jubilation described in the previous chapter in the face of such horrendous acts – as to make it universal, transcending the confines of the radicals.[2]

The message of jihad is universally attractive – in spite of the pathetic attempts made today, in self-defence, to present the Qur'an and other Islamic teachings as 'peace-loving' – due to the repeated injunctions in the Qur'an which urge the Believers to engage in the Holy War, which are also echoed in the Hadith, and are routinely cited as a matter of course by Doctors of the Holy Law of all brands of Islam. When the Hamas states, for example, that it is 'one of the links in the chain of jihad in the confrontation with the Zionist invasion',[3] or the luminaries of the Muslim Brothers urge the Believers to fight the West, or Bin-Laden proclaims jihad against America and launches it violently and lethally, and few voices are heard in the Muslim world denouncing those terms or outlawing them, it is hard to see what kind of 'gentle', 'peaceful' and 'spiritual' Islam we are talking about. 'Waging jihad against the enemy, when he sets foot on the land of Muslims... is an individual duty binding on every man and woman', as stated by the Hamas Charter,[4] means that any territory that Muslims would care to identify as Muslim land (that is, *Dar al-Islam*) – for example the Iberian Peninsula or Israel, Kashmir or Western China, or the Caucasus and the Lower Volga – are legitimate targets for jihad (violent, not spiritual), as current events show daily. Moreover, even if land is not contested, jihad can be brought over to the domain of the Unbelievers who hamper Muslim conquests elsewhere, to punish them for their refusal to submit to the policies, logic and rule of the *Pax Islamica*.

The total rejection of objective, universal and rational non-Muslim criteria to judge between Muslim *versus* non-Muslim contenders, and the reliance exclusively on Muslim terms of reference, make jihad an ever-more potent tool of arbitration in the hands of Muslim radicals. For example, when they proclaim that the problems of Kashmir or Palestine can only be solved by jihad;[5] this means that all tools of peaceful negotiations are rejected, due to the Qur'anic injunction[6] not to let Unbelievers arbitrate Muslim affairs – all the more so since fundamentalist movements in Islam cultivate the idea that jihad had been effective in the past in thwarting the Crusaders and the Tartars in Palestine, therefore it can repeat the same feat today against the Western 'New Crusaders', notably the Americans and the Zionists, who have 'invaded' Muslim lands in dangerous and profane proximity to the Muslim Holy Places of Arabia and Palestine. All it takes is a daring new Saladin who would follow the example of that legendary Muslim fighter who had extirpated the invaders from Muslim lands in the Middle Ages. Saddam Hussein was often put forward as a possible leader among Muslim radicals as a tool of the fury of Allah against the new invaders, even though the Iraqi dictator was not exactly a pious Muslim in their eyes.

This is the reason why jihad has become the rallying slogan of many of these radical movements, as in 'Allah is the goal, the

Prophet, the model, the Qur'an the Constitution, jihad the Path, and death for the cause of Allah the most sublime creed'.[7] Death in the course of jihad becomes, then, an expected, even desirable outcome, especially when jihad is taken as the explanatory motive of history. Indeed, radical Islamic movements regard the present generation's struggle in the Path of Allah as only one link in the chain of continuous jihad, inasmuch as preceding fighters/martyrs had opened the path, and the living in each generation must follow in their footsteps, 'whatever time it might take'.[8] In fact, the Muslim Brothers' symbol comprises a copy of the Qur'an surrounded by two swords; their explication being that force (jihad by the sword) defends 'justice' as encapsulated in the Qur'an. The present-day national flag of Saudi Arabia also consists of the *shahadah* (the vow of submission to Allah and the Prophet) and a sword to defend it, in white against the Prophet's favourite green background.

Hence the powerful appeal of jihad, and of death in jihad if necessary, is reinforced by the Islamic legal prescription that all are liable to jihad, except for the blind, the handicapped and the old, who cannot expend the requisite effort in the battlefield. In the macho-prone youth of the Islamic world, going to jihad is proof that one is not afflicted by those inabilities, Allah Forbid! Islamists, like the Muslim Brothers in Egypt and elsewhere, call upon the jihad fighters to brandish the banner of the Holy War until all Islamic lands are liberated and the universal Islamic state is restored. Similarly, Hamas leaders have repeatedly emphasized the importance of jihad by according to it the validity of a 'Sixth Pillar'.[9] In a fatwa (religious verdict) circulated in the Palestinian territories, Muslim leaders have indeed determined that jihad is a personal duty binding on each and every individual 'until the usurper has been removed from the land by force of the sword'. They rejected peace with Israel, if only because that would amount to cessation of the jihad and the obstruction of the road of jihad which lay before the coming generations.

When taken to task for the aggressive and universalistic message of fundamentalist Islam today, Muslim apologists repeat that military jihad is allowed only in 'self-defence'. The problem is that the definition of 'self-defence' is left to the discretion of the Muslims themselves to determine. For example, the United States deserves to be countered by jihad, to their mind, not because she occupies Muslim territory and needs therefore to be thwarted, but because she is perceived as having aided others in that endeavour, or because her subversive culture has undermined Muslim tradition and civilization. Similarly, India has no standing in claiming her right over Kashmir, because the latter belongs to *Dar al-Islam*, and certainly Palestine is Muslim territory, thus the Jews have no claim to it. Even the historical claim of the Jews to Temple Mount, which is documented and confirmed by Christian history which acknowledges Jesus' peregrinations to that holy space, is rejected by Muslims altogether, because Jews and Christians, in their eyes, had 'forged' the Holy Scriptures, thus forfeiting any claim of theirs to sanctity in any Muslim Holy Place. Only Muslim history, documents, fatwas and Holy Scriptures are valid and authentic, while all the rest have to be discarded as forgeries. Thus, Muslims have the right, indeed the duty, to wage military jihad in 'self-defence' against the Unbelievers who dare to dispossess or challenge the Muslim version of sovereignty over any land, or who are considered as subversive to Islamic values. In short, for any reason or pretext that one can imagine, Muslims would feel 'justified' in launching jihad, and its prospective victims have either to submit to its interpretations and demands or face war, terror, violence and the like, all under the banner of jihad.

No matter how the United States and its allies attempt to blunt the acuity of the jihad directed at them by denying that it is one, the Muslims – even the mainstream among them – regard the confrontation in those terms. Many Muslims across the world view President Bush's declaration of a 'crusade' against terrorism as a replay of the medieval Crusades, something that in itself necessitates mobilization of the Islamic world in jihad against the West. Let us listen to a few authoritative voices coming from Al-Azhar University dons, who represent the most 'moderate' trend of the Muslim establishment and are themselves exposed to onslaughts from the fundamentalists who despise them:

> We are in the midst of a fateful confrontation [between the United States and Islam], whether we like it or not. This confrontation was declared by our rivals, and we are all its target. Muslims will be attacked everywhere in the world, because the target of American attacks is our faith. They are fighting our faith under all kinds of headings such as terrorism, cultural hostility and [Muslim] rebellion [against the West]. The bottom line is that the target is Islam...The West sensed that they are threatened by Islam, therefore they

formed a coalition against it...Why don't we unite too around the slogan 'there is no God but Allah and Muhammed is the Messenger of Allah'?[10]...Allying with America is an act of apostasy,[11] therefore the Afghan opposition ought not to collaborate with America, they must go hand in hand with their compatriots and co-religionists, lest they be cursed by Allah and His Angels.[12]

America could have been a friendly state if she had behaved fairly with us and returned our rights to us. But when she attacks us, our lands and our Islam, and eliminates innocent Muslims, how can she be considered a friendly state? There is no doubt that we are talking about a hostile state which is fighting against us, therefore we have to oppose it...Our resistance could use any possible means, war included. When the enemy sets foot on one inch of Islamic soil, we have to fight him. In this [jihad] war, a son can join without permission from his father, a wife without her husband's consent...a slave without his master's agreement. Islam enjoins us to join jihad for the sake of Allah until one of two positive alternatives is gained: martyrdom or victory...When Islam is attacked, there are no boundaries. In this case jihad is a duty binding on all Muslims.[13]

This war [against Afghanistan] is a criminal attack that resembles the medieval Crusader wars launched by the West under the pretext of defending Christian pilgrims, but in fact it targeted Islam and the Muslims. Today, America has launched a war against Afghanistan under the pretext of fighting terrorism, while indeed targeting Islam in order to wipe it from the face of the earth...The Islamic world must stand by the oppressed and fulfil its duties towards Islam and Muslims. If Muslim armies do not fulfil their duty in the face of this invasion of Islam, they had better be disbanded.[14]

America cannot make use of American Muslims in her war, because she would suspect their loyalty...Those Muslims who issued the fatwa permitting American Muslim participation in the war could have saved their vain effort...for those soldiers are prohibited from fighting alongside the Americans, even if this should cause them harm, for this harm would be much lighter than the harm they would incur by waging a war against an entire nation. Any drawback a few thousand soldiers might suffer is far less significant than the collapse of a state, the annihilation of a nation and the killing of its children, women and the old.[15]

Another religious scholar, Dr Abd-al-Sabur Shahin, says that, based on the Qur'an, the word *irhab* (terror) carries a positive connotation inasmuch as it urges the Believers to sow terror in the hearts of the enemies of Allah, while modern-day terror is a sort of destructive madness carried out by individuals and has nothing to do with nations. Therefore, accusing Islam of terrorism is mistaken, the Muslims being the 'symbol of peace in the world, and the Muslim *umma* had never attacked a neighboring nation'.[16] If so, Dr Shahin would have a hard time showing why and how Islam had expanded through conquest since its inception, unless, of course, we accept the argument that those nations had refused to surrender peacefully to the rule of Islam, therefore Islam had to occupy them in 'self-defence'. Moreover, it would be impossible for him to explain why, when Islam is accused of terrorism, he advances the claim that terrorism is individual and therefore cannot be imputed to states; but at the same time, any nation fighting that terrorism is itself accused of 'state terrorism', as in Mat'ani's affirmation that 'America is leading a campaign of world terrorism against the weak'.[17]

A differentiation is therefore evolving between jihad and terrorism, according to Dr Shahin. Jihad, he posits, is an act of war that only the leadership can declare, and never the province of an individual. Therefore, says he, the jihad (namely terrorism) launched by the Palestinians is legitimate since it aspires to defend Muslim Holy Places, as is the jihad declared by the Afghan people in self-defence against aggression.[18] In other words, terrorism or 'state terrorism' is the combat of those who resist Islamic terror, like the Americans, the Israelis and the Indians, while the combat of Muslims, even when it is terrorism against non-Muslims, as in those three cases, is in any case jihad: that is, a legitimate battle in 'self-defence'. The notion that terrorism is defined according to the mode of combat and its targeted victims, not by who wages it and against whom, simply escapes the Muslim minds. Indeed, another Al-Azhar scholar, Dr 'Abd-al-Hayy al-Farmawi, insists on typifying the US operation in Afghanistan, not the Bin-Laden horror, as 'terrorism, oppression, travesty of justice, barbarism and hooliganism' and urges his co-religionists to 'wake up before the American Crusaders reach us'.[19] Other Muslim scholars therefore draw the fateful conclusion that the 'war is against Islam and

Muslims' and that the Muslims 'must declare jihad against Americans', for the 'international crime performed by America and the West' is bound to encompass the rest of the Islamic world.[20]

Theoretically, after the jihad resulted in conquest and the expansion of *Dar al-Islam*, the Muslim ruler faced three kinds of people under his realm: the Muslim conquerors, who were the elite and the chosen people by virtue of their submission (*Islam*) to Allah; the Scriptuaries, or the People of the Book, that is the Christians and Jews who were accepted and protected by the Muslim rulers, and were allowed to keep their faith and their rituals, provided they submitted to Muslim rule and paid a special poll-tax (*jizya*) in return for their protection (*dhimma*); and the idolaters who must either convert to Islam or perish by the sword. This is only theoretical, because the vertiginous pace of the Muslim conquests was always much faster than the generations it always took for subjugated peoples to adapt to their conquerors and convert to the Islamic faith, out of conviction, interest, or under duress. Therefore, Muslim societies, unlike their European contemporaries, were seemingly much more open and accepting of non-Muslims in their midst than Christendom of non-Christians, something that produced the myth of Muslim 'tolerance' which we shall tackle below.

The attitude towards the People of the Book in Islam was always ambivalent. On the one hand, their Holy Books were accepted as the Divine Message and their historical heroes (like the Patriarchs, Moses and Jesus) as Prophets; but on the other hand, they did not consider Islam as one of the three monotheistic faiths which branched out from each other: it was rather taken as the latest, and therefore the most updated, as it were, dispensation of Allah's Will to humanity, through the latest and last Prophet of God – Muhammed. Furthermore, since the Qur'an, the Word of Allah, differs in many details from the Old and New Testaments, the latter, which came earlier, were regarded as 'forged' by their followers who are still dubbed the 'forgers' of the Holy Scriptures, with all the attendant mistrust and suspicion that this view inspires. Hence 'toleration' of them as long as they dwell in the lands of Islam, are kept under its control, and do not challenge it. However, when they refuse to live under Islam, or pretend to be its equal or even superior, and defy its sovereignty and way of life, they are no better than idolaters and, as such, deserve to be fought by jihad.

Dhimmitude, the term coined by the foremost writer on Jews and Christians in Islamdom,[21] was not only a subservient second-class status in political, social, economic and judicial terms, conferred on Jews and Christians in lands of Islam, from which they could not disengage unless they converted to Islam, but it also became a state of mind. This state of mind, which dictated caution, surreptitious manoeuvring in order to survive and a self-humiliating sycophancy towards the Muslim ruler in the hope of gaining his favour, amounted in the final analysis, after many centuries of oppression and contempt by the rule of Islam, to a self-diminution of the *dhimmis*, a loss of their confidence in themselves, self-flagellation that they did not stand up to the standards set for them by their rulers, and a total distortion of their self-image and the image of their oppressors. So much so, that many Christians and Jews, years after being liberated from dhimmitude, continued to think and act as *dhimmis*, namely to hold themselves grateful to their Muslim masters who beat, humiliated and mistreated them.

What is more, the spirit of dhimmitude has been adopted, or taken over, by many Western societies today which, for reasons hard to understand or explain, pretend not to hear or comprehend Muslim threats, smile, and evince 'understanding' in the face of those threats, and seem to be marching foolishly towards spiritual and cultural capitulation and enslavement. Take, for example, the regime of self-defence and of intruding into the privacy of the air-passengers, which has been imposed in airports all over the world in the past two decades due to Arab and Muslim terrorism. Instead of persecuting it and eliminating it at its roots, the West surrendered to it and adopted, at considerable financial, human and moral cost, measures to live with it, not to fight it, in what has amounted to submission to a mammoth collective punishment of innocents. Or consider the economic boycott of Israel by Muslim and Arab countries for the past half-century, to which most Western societies surrendered due to their perceived commercial interests; or the horrendous acts of hostage-taking, at times accompanied by blackmail and executions of innocent civilians, by Muslim and Arab groups over the past decades, which were not countered in a concerted fashion by the entire civilized world. All these acts of wanton hostility towards the West were often launched in the name of Islam and justified in terms of jihad. For, as the famous Muslim historian of the fourteenth century, Ibn Khaldun, said:

> In the Muslim community the holy war is a religious duty, because of the universalism of the Mission and [the

obligation] to convert everybody to Islam, either by persuasion or by force. Therefore, caliphate and royal authority [namely religion and politics] are united, so that the person in charge can devote the available strength to both of them at the same time.[22]

That injunction has never been cancelled or revised, and it remains only a question of practicability whether it is enforced or postponed to better days. Not much has changed since, at least in the purview of Muslim fundamentalists. More recently, Bat Ye'or wrote prophetically:

> The jihad, which the Islamist trend is waging against the West, is a many-sided, multi-dimensional struggle which cannot be defined precisely. It emerged in the terrorism of...certain states (Iran, Iraq, Syria, Libya), in economic pressure or threats (the oil weapon) and in psychological conditioning...
>
> Hostage-taking is a classic tactic of the jihad. At the theological–juridical level, it is legal and moral. The hostage – a *harbi* [from *Dar al-Harb*] prisoner – represents a military asset for the exchange of prisoners or for obtaining a ransom to finance the war effort. In both cases, the *harbi* (American, European or any other) becomes a dehumanized object, deprived of the inalienable rights attached to any human being...
>
> Modern terrorism is linked to the border raid. The means of transport now available allow the contemporary [terrorist] to sow death in the very heart of *Dar al-Harb*, as their ancestors used to massacre the inhabitants of border villages. In recent times it fell to Palestinian Arab terrorists to revive the glory of the old *ghazis* who set ambushes in order to attack civilians...At a historical level, the jihad, whether it be anti-Israel or anti-Western, only represents two interdependent and interactive facets of the same battle against the People of the Book...
>
> The resurgence of traditionally Islamic policies is certainly not a passing phenomenon. These patterns of behavior are rooted in thirteen centuries of history and develop in accordance with permanent realities of an ideological, religious, demographic and political nature. The last jihad advance was halted at Vienna in 1683. Yet, the stabilization of

frontiers barely interrupted the Islamization process of those territories originally populated exclusively by non-Muslims. As in the earlier Arab conquests, the processes whereby the original *Dar al-Harb* was transformed into *Dar al-Islam*, stretched over many centuries and extended the aims of jihad to domestic policies...

Although a number of Muslim governments – Turkey, Egypt, Morocco, Tunisia and others – are trying today to fight Islamic trends, this effort cannot succeed without a complete recasting of mentalities, the desacralization of the historic jihad, and an unbiased examination of Islamic imperialism. Without such a process the past will continue to poison the present and inhibit the establishment of harmonious relationships. When all is said and done, such self-criticism is hardly exceptional. Every scourge, such as religious fanaticism, the Crusades, the Inquisition, slavery, apartheid, colonialism, Nazism and, today, communism, are analyzed, examined, and exorcized in the West...It is inconceivable that Islam, which began in Mecca and swept through three continents, should alone avoid a critical reflection on the mechanisms of its power and reflection.[23]

From the Muslim point of view, jihad, whether in its peaceful or, more frequently, forceful manifestation, is calculated to bring 'justice' and 'peace' to the world; naturally, Muslim justice and peace that can only be dispensed by the Muslim legal system within the *Pax Islamica*. Hence, the current clamour of Muslims for justice, or for the construct of 'peace with justice', when they fight the United States, India, Israel or any power, namely those who stand in the way of their enforcing Muslim justice and prevent Muslim justice from reigning. Now, just like wisdom and beauty, justice and peace are in the eye of the beholder. However, while Western legal and moral tradition has developed a certain vision of peace and justice, partly based on biblical prophecies of 'beating swords into ploughshares' so that nations would wage no war any longer, and partly on the Roman concept of *justicia* and *pax*, in Islam there is no concept of equality between a multitude of nations, for the only prevailing one is the *umma* of Islam, the 'elected nation of Allah', whose divine mission is to propagate the Word of Allah among nations until they 'see the light' and convert, then peace and justice would be served.

This belief in Islamic superiority goes hand in hand with the abysmal contempt Muslim fundamentalists feel towards non-Muslims, especially Christians and Jews, whom they perceive as the direct challengers to Muslim hegemony, the former due to the potency of the Christian West in all walks of life worldwide, the latter in view of the ongoing confrontation between them and much of the Muslim world in the Middle East. This contempt is fed by the inexplicable gap between their inferiority, which has been cast upon them by Allah Himself, and the injunctions to fight them,[24] on the one hand, and their rather stunning success as advanced, rich and powerful in the modern world, in spite of the fact that they are vastly outnumbered by Muslims, on the other. Particularly incomprehensible and unacceptable to the Muslim fundamentalists is the status of the Jewish communities in the West, especially in the United States, where they enjoy a far greater influence in the economic, cultural, scientific and political domains than their small numbers would warrant. Especially humiliating to them is the fact that the Muslim communities there, with their large Arab component, surpass in numbers, and in years of existence in some cases, their Jewish counterparts, but are nevertheless nowhere near them in terms of impact.

Hence, the doubly violent reactions of the Muslims to this reality: a propensity to lump Christians and Jews together as an object of attack and target of terrorist acts, such as burning churches in Egypt, Pakistan and Indonesia, and prohibiting new ones from being erected in Saudi Arabia, Iran, the Sudan and Afghanistan, and synagogues in the West Bank and across the Western world, from Sydney to Berlin and from New York to Sao Paolo; and, at the same time, perceiving Israel as an arm of the West and its long arm in the Middle East, something that is symbolized by the perennial and ritual burning of the US and Israeli flags and effigies together throughout the world – Muslim and Western alike – whenever grievances are aired against either of them. It is as though Muslim justice is meted out this way on the symbolic level as long as it is impracticable in the real world.

Muslims have yet to overcome the reversal of their fortunes, especially when compared to the West, which was able to modernize, develop and gain power, while their successive caliphates, who reached their peaks in the early Middle Ages and then in the early modern era under the Ottomans in the Middle East and the Moghuls in the Indian sub-continent, have declined and fallen. It is they who were colonized by Western powers, not the other way round, and most of their efforts to Westernize, namely to adopt Western values, technologies and institutions, have failed dismally. So much so, that not only were they unable to catch up with the West and revive their past glory, but the gap between them and modernity continues to yawn. This creates in their minds a strong resentment of the West which they were unable to imitate, and they have come to the conclusion that only its demise can allay their humiliation in view of their painful backwardness. Hence, their clear decision to hurt it and bring about its downfall rather than make the sustained effort to rise to its level. Because acknowledging their aspiration to Westernize means recognizing the gap separating them from the West, they would rather adopt the strategy of denial by harking back to their past glory, castigating the West for its 'materialism', 'corruption', 'injustice' and inevitable decay, and aggrandizing themselves by promising a return to Islam which will bring them victory and revenge.

This mode of thinking, though it is more typical of Muslim fundamentalists who find the chasm between their faith and the realities around them most insulting and mortifying, is quite current among mainstream Muslims and even 'secularists' among them who strive for modern, Western-like statecraft in their midst. The day will come, they believe, or make-believe, when their civilization must prevail and they thereby justify to themselves and to others the causes of their own lagging behind, and also kindle the hope, indeed certainty, that the future is theirs. Consider what a Palestinian textbook for children, unwittingly financed by donations from the European Union, puts forward as regards the prospects that await their benefactors in the West:

> In the present period...of unprecedented material and scientific advances...scientists in the West are perplexed by the worrying increase in the number of people suffering from nervous disorders...and the statistics from America in this matter are a clear indication of this...
>
> Western civilization flourished, as is well-known, as a consequence of the links of the West to Islamic culture, through Arab institutions in Spain, and in other Islamic countries where Muslim thinkers and philosophers took an interest in Greek philosophy...
>
> Western civilization, in both its branches – the Capitalist and

the Communist – deprived man of his peace of mind, stability, when it turned material well-being into the exemplary goal… his money leading him nowhere, except to suicide…

There is no escape from a new civilization which will rise in the wake of this material progress and which will continue it and lift man to the highest spiritual life alongside material advancement…Is there a nation capable of fulfilling such a role? The Western world is incapable of fulfilling it…There is only one nation capable of discharging this task, and that is our nation…No one but we can carry aloft the flag of tomorrow's civilization…

We do not claim that the collapse of Western civilization and the transfer of the center of civilization to us will happen in the next decade or two, even in 50 years, for the rise and fall of civilization follow natural processes, and even when the foundations of a fortress become cracked it still appears for a long time to be at the peak of its strength. Nevertheless [Western civilization] has begun to collapse and to become a pile of debris…We awoke to a painful reality and to oppressive Imperialism, and we drove it out of some of our lands, and we are about to drive it from the rest…[25]

It would seem that in light (or rather obscurity) of the 11 September events, Bin-Laden, not content with waiting for 'natural processes' to unfold, decided to force Allah's hand by short-circuiting the long, frustrating and painful expectation that the West would collapse under its own volition, and has even lived to see the piles of debris for himself, smiled under his moustache and promised some more. Indeed, since 11 September 2001, and following on the successful example of the battle against the Jews that had been launched decades earlier with the unwitting complicity of much of the West (which was searching for ways to satisfy Muslim justice), fundamentalist Islam has now determined to lump both the Christian West and Jewish Israel together and fight them both simultaneously: car-bombs, biological and chemical warfare, kidnappings of soldiers and terrorizing of civilians, all calculated to make life untenable in Western cities and towns, until they are reduced to dhimmitude once again. Thus will Islamic justice be established.

These manifestations of hostility throughout the Western world are facilitated by the increasingly burdensome issue of the Islamic penetration via illegal immigration. Already in early November 2001, four weeks into US bombardments of Afghanistan, the Taliban threatened that the pressure of the wave of Muslim immigrants to Australia would not recede until the latter desisted from her support for the US war against terrorism. This means that the demographic balance will be affected in the long run, especially in countries of immigration such as the United States, Canada and Australia; exactly as it already is in Western Europe, where the local birth rate is at an all-time low, on the one hand, while on the other hand, it accords asylum to refugees from Islamic countries. In France, Belgium, Germany, and certainly the United States, some of those 'refugees' have already been caught red-handed in ideological crime, fund-raising under front-names of charity organizations, stockpiling arms and explosives and even training underground operatives against their host states. These Muslim migrants, both the long-established and the newcomers, including the illegal among them, also import to their countries of shelter their hatred of Israel and the Jews, and use the openness of these democracies to act violently and criminally against the local, and usually peaceful and prosperous, Jewish communities which they envy and detest.

In our days, the globalization of information has caused the universalization of Arab and Muslim solidarity. In a paradoxical way, the local media in each Islamic country provides immediacy and helps break the local siege on information which is typical of autocratic regimes. International Arab and Islamic concerns have thus been hijacked by radical groups who not only instantly transmit messages regarding the perceived oppression of other Muslims across the world (like the Uighurs by the Chinese, Moros by the Philippines, Palestinians by Israel or Kashmiris by India) and decry the take-over or mistreatment of Muslim Holy Places by non-Muslims, but also raise funds, urge co-religionists to demonstrate, violently if necessary, in support of these causes, and even provide instructions on where to report for 'volunteer' work, how to join terrorist lodges or to concoct explosives. Thus, what happens in Xinjiang, Gaza, Srinagar or Mindanao has immediate reverberations in the streets of Melbourne and London, not to speak of the Arab streets from Rabat to Baghdad, or the Islamic streets from Teheran to Jakarta.

Unable to attain the level of the West and to attack it on the open battle field, Muslim fundamentalists try to destabilize and terrorize it from within, by sowing chaos, fear and disorder that will erode its edge. Shooting, bombing, threatening jihad, pledging Islamic justice and spreading germs certainly thwart tourism, disrupt production and paralyse normal life; and in the prosperous, modern and industrious West, which needs to maintain its standards of living and stability, these disruptions are bound to cause irreparable damage to the whole political, economic and societal system. The terrorists have detected precisely the characteristics of the Western 'soft states', which seem no longer willing to defend their strategic and cultural assets if they levy too heavy an economic and human price, thus giving top priority to immediate short-term 'peaceful' gains at the expense of the long-term existential interests of Western civilization. Therefore, the more the Muslim radicals, joined by others in the Third World, decried their falling victim to globalization, economic exploitation and the 'selfishness' of the West, and clamoured for justice, the more the West proved willing to 'understand', to make compromises and concessions, increase its aid and so forth, in a plea to reassure the Muslims and their allies and assuage their fears. This typically *dhimmi*-like behaviour of the West indicated to the radicals that their diagnosis of Western weaknesses was sound, and therefore it was time to strike.

Moreover, the Muslim and other countries have suddenly become aware of the 'injustices' in the distribution of wealth between nations, while they themselves maintain the same, and even more extreme, injustices at home. They are also furiously jealous of the West as, due to their own incompetence, which is tainted with corruption, they are unable to achieve parity with Western development. The more the West exhibits prosperity, freedom and democracy, the more they feel exposed and threatened by their citizenry which clamours for the same. Therefore, only if they wreak havoc on a West they cannot emulate lest they lose their hold on power can they remove this menacing – because more successful and appealing – looming alternative. There is no basis to the worn-out assumption that economic development in the Islamic world will blunt fundamentalism and make the West more acceptable. The hypothesis which posits that economic development could override ideological and doctrinal considerations is not only incorrect but also patronizing and condescending, and does more harm than good. Saudi Arabia, perhaps the most fundamentalist Islamic regime apart from the Taliban, and Bin-Laden, who elected a life of hiding in caves rather than live in luxury in his country or in the West, all in the service of his jihad for the cause of Islamic justice, are cases in point.

The term in Arabic for 'justice' is *'adalah*, or *'adl*, and it is linked in the Arab mind to the notion of balance between the two humps on the camel's back, without which the camel cannot march for long periods across the desert.[26] Justice is also connected to honour, and the maintenance of honour hinges on the ability to protect one's property and women, and a proven capacity to retrieve them if they are violated. Otherwise, a man's reputation is irretrievably stained and compromised. Thus, one's honour is constantly on the line, and it is tested by one's daring in the service of this honour. An Arab or Muslim following that tradition will not rest until the wrong done to him is redressed and his property is recovered. Only then is justice is done, and one can go back to functioning normally. There are no objective criteria to examine the feeling of right and wrong, or the parameters of encroachment on one's honour; they hinge on the subjective sense of the wronged individual or tribe or society.

Chief among the Muslims' burning reasons for establishing justice is their feeling that they have fallen victim to conspiracies and plots around them. True, their paranoia does not mean that they have no enemies, as the old adage goes, but when they create fantasy in order to explain away things, and concoct the most absurd claims in order to justify their demands for 'justice', then we transcend the realm of rationality. It was Sayyid Qut'b who, in the early 1950s, identified the Jews as the enemies of Islam and humanity, and the arm of the West in the Islamic world. In his book *Our Campaign Against the Jews*,[27] he, the great Master of the Muslim fundamentalists, warned against the universal subversion of Islam by the Jews, and took them to task for rebelling against the Divine Will, for concocting revolutions and trouble everywhere, for instigating war and destruction, and so on. He accused them of being egotistical and ungrateful, of having forged their holy scriptures, and claimed that their innate hatred towards Islam stemmed from their hostility to the Angel Gabriel, who transmitted the Holy Revelation of the Qur'an to the Prophet of Islam.[28]

No amount of discussion could have changed the mind of that illustrious man, who believed in the combined evil of the Jews and the West, not even all the attempts to show that throughout history it was the Muslims who lambasted the Jewish (and Christian) minorities under their aegis, or that it was the Jews who sought the protection of the Muslim empires and therefore had no reason to hate them, or that the Angel Gabriel remains as holy in Christianity and Judaism as in the Muslim tradition. Qut'b's thinking was picked up by the Hamas, which numbers among his ardent followers:

> The enemies have been scheming for a long time...They accumulated a huge and influential material wealth which they put to the service of implementing their dream: to take control of the world media and news agencies, the press, publishing houses, broadcasting and the like...They stood behind the French and Communist Revolutions and most of the revolutions we hear about. They used their money to establish clandestine organizations which are spreading around the world in order to destroy societies and carry out Zionist interests. Such organizations are: the Free Masons, Rotary Clubs, Lions Clubs, Bnai Brith and the like. All of them are subversive spying organizations. They also influenced imperialistic states and made them colonize many countries in order to exploit the wealth of those countries and spread their corruption therein.[29]

This is not a page from any history book: just plain and repulsive fantasies that could not stand the test of Western justice, had a suit for libel been brought to a court of law in any civilized country. No wonder that Bin-Laden and his peers can recite the same mantras today against the West and Israel, and convince multitudes in the Muslim world of their veracity. Indeed, as we have seen, Jews and Zionists have already been accused throughout the Muslim world of having blown up the Twin Towers, and as a 'proof', a story was trumped up that all the thousands of Jewish employees at the site had been forewarned to evacuate the complex prior to the explosion. Similarly, the Islamic world has believed for years that Israel is entertaining the ambition to rule 'from the Nile to the Euphrates', and they cite as 'proof' the Israeli flag which portrays two blue stripes 'representing the two rivers', while in fact it depicts the Jewish prayer shawl; they spread the Protocols of the Elders of Zion and the Blood Libel as true facts of history; they impute US support for Israel to the 'Zionist grip on the corridors of power' in the White House and the Congress, even though, except for the existence of corridors in both locations, no one could corroborate that claim; and, best of all, they are fond of accusing Israel and the

Jews, with US support to boot, of all manner of poisoning campaigns to destroy humanity: Palestinian girls are poisoned in the West Bank in order to 'harm their reproductive organs'; HIV is passed on to Palestinian youth as part of 'genocide against the Palestinian people'; Egyptian lands are poisoned by Israeli farming experts in order to 'ruin Egyptian agriculture'; and, most tragic-comically, chewing gum is sold across the Muslim world which incites the sexual passion of women so as 'to corrupt them beyond decency'.

To fight these conspiracies becomes, then, a moral imperative and part of redressing justice before the virus of corruption invades the Muslim societies too deeply and brings them to the brink. To achieve this, the 'invaders', be they Israelis in Palestine, Americans in Arabia, Christians in Indonesia and Nigeria, or the Indians in Kashmir, must be extirpated from Muslim lands so that the balance be redressed and justice done. In other words, regardless of what others might advance as a disclaimer in historical, legal, political, logical or human terms, all is irrelevant as long as the Muslims lay claim to a territory, a resource or an asset, and they will not be satisfied until and unless justice – that is their justice – is done. The whole notion of negotiation and compromise does not come into play, because for something to be yours, you must obtain it first. All Israeli peace 'partners', from Sadat to Hizbullah, have demanded a total Israeli withdrawal before the negotiations could proceed, not because, as some diplomats have thought, the Muslims wanted to obtain the result of the negotiations before they even begin, but in order to signal that their property and belongings, their rights and justice, are not negotiable. It is theirs. Period. The West will encounter similar demands and attitudes from its Muslim 'allies' as the crisis persists.

Islamists often cite 'moral' arguments in order to encourage guilt among Western intellectuals and civil rights activists who are sensitive to human issues. They invoke notions of democracy, freedom, humanity, equality and compassion, which ring familiar bells in Western ears, and produce an inordinate amount of self-flagellation, remorse and self-inflicted guilt among naive and well-meaning souls who do not comprehend that these very terms and notions mean different things to those who utter them, and are used only to subvert Western conscience. This tactic works, because there are not a few Westerners who cultivate their sense of guilt to the point of adopting the Muslim point of view lock, stock and barrel, militate for it even at the detriment of their own national interest, apologize for their own existence, express dismay at their governments' policies and unwittingly mobilize their authority and sensitivity in the service of the enemies of their own civilization, country and interests. They begin to speak of their own governments as 'imperialistic', their economy and international trade as 'exploitative', their culture as 'arrogant', and of their sworn enemies as 'kind', 'co-operative' 'underdogs' who deserve sympathy, 'victims' who merit redress, and members of a worthy but misunderstood civilization. This is precisely dhimmitude at its 'best', namely taking blows and punches and showing sycophantic gratitude for them.

Naturally, Muslim militants not only find solace and encouragement in these words of support from within their perceived enemies, but also view them as 'proof' that their messages are being absorbed by their detractors and that the time will come when the latter will see the light and convert to Islam. Instructive in this regard are the words of Dr Fatihi, a member of the faculty of the Medical School at Harvard University who, following the 11 September drama, reported to the Arabic press, *inter alia,* the following:

> From day one, the media began hinting that Muslim and Arab hands were behind this event. We convened an emergency meeting of the Islamic Center in Boston and decided to organize blood donations, to be covered by the media...We all tried to hang on to any bit of information that would distance this criminal act from Islamic and Arab hands...for we wanted to prove our humanity as we were attacked on all sides, and we were afraid that our preaching for Allah was set back 50 years in the US and the entire world...
>
> On Saturday the 15 of September I took my wife and children to the largest church in Boston at Copley Square, to represent Islam there, at the invitation of Boston Senators... We were welcomed as if we were foreign ambassadors...The senior priest defended Islam in his sermon and introduced me to the audience as the representative of the Muslim Association of Boston. Following his sermon, I read a statement of the heads of the Muslim religion which condemned the events...and explained the principles of Islam and its sublime teachings...
>
> After that, I read translations into English of verses from the Qur'an...Those were moments I shall never forget, because

the entire audience broke in tears when they heard the Words of Allah...One of them told me: 'I do not understand Arabic, but what you said certainly sounded like the Words of Allah'. Another woman left a note in my hand upon leaving the church in tears. It said: 'Forgive us for our past and present. Please continue to sermonize to us.' Another person, also in tears, stood at the gate of the church and said: 'You are just like us, nay, better!'...

On Sunday, 16 September, we issued an invitation to the public to visit the Islamic Center that lay between Harvard and MIT. We expected 100 visitors, but we got 1,000... including university professors, priests...who were invited to speak, and all of them expressed solidarity with Muslims... There were many questions from the public who wanted to understand the teachings of Islam, not one of them was hostile. Quite the contrary, they were in tears when they heard about the lofty principles of Islam...Many of them had only heard of Islam through the incitement of the media...I was invited to repeat the same at another gathering in the church the same day, and the sights were the same...

On Thursday a delegation of 300 professors and students from Harvard, accompanied by the American Ambassador to Vienna, undertook a visit to the Islamic Center. They sat on the floor of the mosque...We talked to them, explained Islam and cleared it from the suspicions that had been attached to it. I once again read from the Qur'an and their eyes filled with tears. Many of them were so excited that they asked to participate in the weekly classes that the Center holds for non-Muslims. Friday, the 21 of September, a Muslim delegation convened for a closed meeting with the Governor of Massachussetts, when the introduction of Islam into school curriculi was discussed, so as to avert racism against Islam which originates from American ignorance of the Islamic faith...

This is an example of what is happening today in Boston and other American cities. Our proselytizing not only was not set back 50 years as we had feared...quite the contrary, those 11 days that elapsed since 11 September were the equivalent of 11 years of proselytizing. I am writing to you today with full confidence that Islam will expand all over America and the entire world, by the Will of Allah, much faster than at any time in the past, because the world is all too eager to know Islam.[30]

So far so good. But the same Dr Fatihi, who praised the lofty principles of Islam and bragged about his successes, like the Prophet, in bringing non-Muslims to tears, could not retain for long his feelings of obscene bigotry towards the Jews, and started boasting – he who acted for understanding and harmony – about destroying the Christian–Jewish dialogue. Again, let this eminent intellectual and champion of Islamic-style fraternity speak for himself:

> In spite of the campaigns of distortion launched by the Zionist lobby, which mobilizes many of the media to his service, there are signs that our intensive educational campaign is bearing fruit. For example, the number of converts has doubled since 11 September...and many non-Muslims have evinced solidarity with Muslims in American universities. For example, dozens of non-Muslim female students at Wayne University have worn the veil in solidarity with Muslim students on campus and elsewhere...
>
> Jewish organizations have called upon us to open dialogue with them, because they are afraid of the Christian–Muslim dialogue in the churches, mosques and campuses...There are already positive fruits to the Christian–Muslim dialogue: a radio station has broadcast a sympathetic programme about the suffering of the Palestinians...something that angered the Jews and they decided to boycott it, which in turn increased the pro-Muslim coverage...For example, the station interviewed young American female students who converted to Islam, through the efforts of the Boston Islamic Association... They hold advanced degrees from Boston and Harvard Universities, spoke about the greatness and might of Islam and about the sublime status of women in Islam, which prompted their conversion into Islam...
>
> Thus, the Muslim community in America in general, and Boston in particular, has become perplexing to the Zionist lobby. In fact, what the Qur'an said about them is true: 'They will be humiliated wherever they are found, unless they are protected under a covenant with Allah, a covenant with another people. They have incurred Allah's wrath and they have been affected with misery. That is because they continuously rejected the Signs of Allah and were after slaying the Prophets without just cause, and this resulted from their disobedience and their habit of transgression'.[31]

In his prudent decision not to attack the Jews directly, in order not to detract from the appeal that Islam is allegedly enjoying among Christians in the United States, this author refers to the Zionist Lobby, knowing full well that the subsequent quote from the Qur'an denigrates Jews, not Zionists. Incidentally, the cited passage from the Qur'an, which promises humiliation to the Jews unless they are 'protected under a covenant with Allah', is precisely the *dhimmi* status that traditional Islam has reserved for them, and for the Christians as well. In other words, unless all Christians and Jews convert to Islam – and that is what Muslim missions in the West have been working on – they can still come temporarily under Islamic rule as *dhimmis* as their only alternative. This enlightened author, who operates at the heart of Western intellectual endeavour and does not hide his desire to see all of the United States Islamized, predicts at the end of his vitriol against the Jews that their seemingly strong ties to Christian America are much weaker than they think and will be severed, thus ending the main source of their sustenance.[32] Now, this is not a Bin-Laden or a medieval obscurantist, but a professor of medicine, trained in the West and enjoying the religious freedom which allows him to convert Americans to Islam, to maintain Islamic institutions within his tolerant host-society that he wants to transform, and to hate the Jews, under the guise of anti-'Zionism', whom he wants to push back to dhimmitude. This is not fanaticism or extremism, this is mainstream Islam which is spoken loud and clear throughout the Islamic world day in, day out, including in Egypt, which made peace with the Jews more than two decades ago.[33] This is mild stuff compared with what Muslim radicals have in mind and express in rhetoric and writing, for they also strive to apply by force those beliefs contrary, one should hope, to more civilized Muslims such as Dr Fatihi and his like.

The Islamic hierarchical view of the world and humanity, where Muslims are at the apex, the Scriptuaries (Christians and Jews) are 'protected' *dhimmis* and the rest must embrace Islam or perish, also dictates and defines what they regard as 'tolerance'. Certainly, compared with medieval Christianity, which rejected non-Christians, Muslims were much more open to accepting Christian and Jewish minorities or even local majorities such as in Spain, as long as they recognized the superiority of Islam and accepted their subservient *dhimmi* status. This is not to be confounded with pluralism in societies composed of many theoretically equal groups. Indeed, in Western terms, a tolerant society is a pluralistic one when everyone is equal under the sun, and no one's culture, belief, race or political conviction makes one superior over all others. But in Islamic terms, toleration of the other, that is the *dhimmi,* means his acceptance in spite of his or her inferiority. Thus, while the Western concept of tolerance does not pass any value judgement on the tolerated, the Muslim does: we have seen the appeal to others to convert to Islam in order to 'resolve all problems', the conviction of the inevitability of such prospect, and the thrill at the sight of non-Muslims being reduced to tears when they discover the redeeming Word of Allah.

This understanding of tolerance not only is not likely to produce an egalitarian and pluralistic society, but is sure to perpetuate a patronizing condescension towards non-Muslims. This is precisely the socio-political framework into which the Muslims, who aspire for world conquest, would like to fit the Jews and the Christians, if they could. The massive conversions to Islam in the United States and the West generally, whether they are real or imagined, certainly lend encouragement to this dream. In this regard, the Muslims in Western democracies view the well-established Jewish communities there as their rivals, and therefore they strive not only to sever the link between them and the economic, cultural and political establishment there, where they have achieved great gains out of proportion to their numbers, but also to scare the Jews into submission. The large waves of Muslim anti-Semitism which have exploded since October 2000 in the West, concurrently with the Palestinian Intifadah, in fact exported the Arab–Israeli conflict into those liberal democracies and signalled to the Jews that their prominence in Western societies was no longer guaranteed.

This view of non-Muslims certainly does not promote modern Western ideas of democracy either. Even without non-Muslims in their midst, not one of the existing 56 Muslim countries has succeeded in adopting the pure Western model of liberal democracy to rule its own people. Though some Muslim countries clamour for their 'democracy', or at the very least believe sincerely that they are on their way to 'democratization', whatever that may mean, others, and especially Muslim radicals, reject Western democracy as inadequate for their purposes, and brandish their own Muslim models of benevolent rule, which is a far cry from democracy as we understand it. All compose lofty constitutions, but with few exceptions, rulers put them aside to rule by diktat. Parliaments are elected, but are subservient to the ruler. The frequency of new 'constitutions' goes apace with the coups mounted by new rulers against their predecessors and demonstrates the will of the ruler to have his own writ of legitimacy to cover his uncertain grip on power, rather than fulfilling the country's need for a basic iron-clad set of principles to restrict government. In the West, constitutions provide stability and predictability by their very continuity in the face of constant changes in government; in Islamic countries, constitutions are, for the most part, the expression of instability and unpredictability.

In most Islamic countries, the ultimate locus of power is the ruler. Even Turkey, until recently the only borderline case of a functioning democracy, has known in our lifetime three military takeovers, and the ousting of a democratically elected Islamist Prime Minister (Erbakan) under military pressure in the late 1990s. In non-Islamized Muslim countries, which are ruled by military juntas, monarchies or other illegitimate rulers, Islamic legitimacy is deemed threatening to the regimes in place, and therefore shunned, discarded and feared because of its potency and popular appeal. That does not make the illegitimate government legitimate, even though it may be considered an ally of the West and a worthy member of Western coalitions. It does make it the source of Islamist opposition wrath in every one of those countries against both their illegimate rulers and the West which supports them (Pakistan, Egypt, Syria, Jordan, Morocco, Saudi Arabia and all the rest). Yet, all those illegitimate rulers claim that they represent their people and regard the fact that they have 'elections' (rigged for the most part) as a sure sign of their 'democracy'.

Opposition may exist in those countries, but only if it is 'loyal' and does not cause 'division'. When the opposition takes its duty seriously, it is often branded an 'enemy of the people' undermining the state and the regime, and treated accordingly. In Algeria, free elections were permitted for the first time in 1992, but when the victory of the Islamists became apparent, the results were reversed and a military junta took over power. A 'democratic' regime, such as Mubarak's Egypt or King Hussein's Jordan, for example, does not permit the Islamists as such to run for election – even the more placid among them, such as the Muslim Brothers – for fear that an Algerian scenario might unfold. The Islamists, on their part, paradoxically clamour for democracy, human rights, freedom, free elections, multi-party systems, as the only way both to gain access to power and to attract sympathy from the outside. But, when their voices are not heard in the West, they accuse it of hypocrisy in the face of the oppression they are subjected to, in their own countries, by their illegitimate rulers who are usually supported by the West. However, their democratic language has often gained political asylum for their leaders and their mouthpieces in the West (for example, 'Umar Abdul Rahman in the United States and the *Filastin al-Muslima*, the organ of the Hamas, in the United Kingdom), and enables them to collect funds under the cover of charitable front organizations, to publish pamphlets and magazines banned in their countries of origin, and expose those regimes. In turn, rulers of those countries recognized by the West as legitimate accuse the West of sheltering the dissidents who seek their downfall.

In this maze of 'democratic' pronouncements and counter-pronouncements, Western societies have a hard time comprehending the 'democratizing' processes that they are told are taking place in Muslim countries. The 'elections' in some of those countries are covered by Western media and are nonchalantly commented upon in terms of percentage points, majorities and minorities, party affiliation and ideological platforms, as if they were describing elections in the American mid-West or in Yorkshire. Terms like democracy, pluralism and multi-party elections are aired carelessly, disregarding the fact that they have quite different meanings when votes are rigged and everyone knows it, parties are banned, candidates are prevented from running, at best, or imprisoned or worse, in less favourable circumstances. The West has been conversing with the Islamic world in a language it does not understand, or show any propensity to learn. Thus the West is failing and, furthermore, losing: it is not consistent in its support of democracy and therefore attracts the wrath of the fundamentalists who could win democratically if they were given the chance; but at the same time it provokes frustration among the illegitimate regimes it supports when it gives shelter to the opponents of their rule; and on top of all that, the Muslim 'victims' of persecution whom it harbours very often become the hard core of the Islamists who undermine it from within and bring disaster upon it.

Finally, we need to look at some more terms that the Muslim world uses profusely when it confronts the West, which if not taken with a huge pinch of salt or carefully tested against reality can, and indeed do, confuse the candid viewer, distort facts and events and embark on exaggerations, sometimes fabrications, of events which cannot be substantiated. Parts of these utterings, when examined in context and verified, provide only indications of the Muslim psyche, projections onto the enemy of what they would have done or how they would have acted in similar circumstances. This projection is sufficient for them to accuse their enemies of acts never committed or even intended. This is generated, at least in part, by the generally total blindness to others' misery, by the conviction that whoever is not Muslim does not deserve compassion, by the lack of almost any sign of sympathy for, or will to share with, others. One can see the untold billions squandered on palaces and obscene luxury by Muslim princes, but seldom will any of them engage in donations to people elsewhere who are hunger-stricken or war-ravaged, or are suffering in the aftermath of some natural disaster, except if they are either Muslim or if it would serve some political or personal purpose. The 'generous' cheque sent by the Saudi prince to the people of New York, under the watchful eye of the media, was a case in point, as was Mayor Giuliani's Western-bred disgust at that cheap attempt to score political points at the expense of people struck by disaster.

Very seldom, however, will one catch a Saudi prince, or the Saudi State for that matter, allocating aid to the hungry of Ethiopia or Rwanda, or the war victims of the Sudan, or the flood-ravaged but unglamorous people of Bangladesh – not even a fraction of the $100 million they disburse every year to the Hamas, or the billions they spend on their orgies of weapon-purchasing or palace-building or extravagant spending in the West. The same is true of Iran, which expends billions to export the Islamic Revolution and arm the Hizbullah to sow terror and destruction, but will not come to the help of fellow humans. Libya, Brunei and other money-wielding dictatorships in the Muslim world act, or rather refrain from acting, likewise. Take, for example, the perennial problem of the Palestinian refugees, who have been rotting in squalid camps for three generations in constant expectation of sacks of flour financed by the United Nations, or by the generosity of Western powers, foremost of whom is the hated United States; but the Saudis or other Muslims, far from contributing to alleviating the plight of their 'brothers' that unite them with the rest of the Muslims in politics and propaganda, hardly lift a finger for them and rather perpetuate their misery in order to draw some political 'gains' or questionable 'benefits' for themselves.

Muslims seldom care for world affairs or for humanitarian

efforts. Unlike countries in the West, which allocate part of their wealth to foreign aid, and endeavour to raise the standard of living of the poor by extending technical assistance to them, rich Muslim states such as Saudi Arabia or Libya only use their money for either the acquisition of weapons by belligerent Muslims who are too poor to afford them; for Muslim purposes such as the construction of mosques and Islamic centres in foreign countries for the glory of Islam and the donor; or for buying 'protection' from violent militant groups who would otherwise endanger the giver; or for financing terrorist groups which export violent Muslim or Arab activism abroad. They are much more consumers of Western technology, prosperity, development and standard of living, than contributors to it; but, except for the minority of truly Westernized and educated Muslims who either live in the West or are attempting in vain to promote Western values from within their societies, the majority of their co-religionists only wish to borrow from the West its technology and assets, and persist in rejecting its values which they cannot match or even comprehend, for example: openness, equality, a state of law, freedom of individuals and of collectives, alternation in government, pluralism, toleration, democracy, social solidarity, right of dissent, and so on.

Indeed, those values, which are not applied anywhere in the Muslim world, permit the growth of abominable concepts and practices among them: their enemy, for example, be it the United States or Israel, are so demonized and de-humanized in the state-controlled media, which usually does not accord 'equal time' to the rival to respond, as to make them easy prey and legitimate targets of violence. That is the reason why Muslim societies are so violence-prone; domestically, they often elect bullets over ballots, and externally they would opt for terrorism to demean the rival and undermine him from within. Should he dare to defend himself, he would be dubbed an 'aggressor'; any counter-attack against Muslims would be termed 'racism', any battle waged against them would be labelled 'genocide', 'ethnic cleansing', 'state terrorism', the 'arrogance of power', 'massacre of innocent civilians' and so on. They are always the innocent victims, for the foreigner cannot be right and therefore should not counter-attack. The terrorists among them take innocent hostages, hijack aeroplanes, blow up public places, murder civilians, impose collective punishment on entire populations, mutilate the bodies of their victims, refuse to give any details about their captives despite the supplications of the grieving families, burn flags and effigies of their rivals, re-enact in public their horrendous acts, sow jubilation in the streets at the sight of those horrors or of the enemy's losses, and believe that their behaviour is justified and beyond reproach.

True, these patterns of mind-boggling and inhuman conduct are, one should hope, the domain of the terrorist minority, but judging from the vast scenes of popular joy, interest and enthusiasm, in which adults and children partake equally, one is entitled to question the validity of this generous assumption. These patterns do not come from nowhere; they are the result of persistent and sustained incitement in school textbooks and the media, and the promotion of ignorance and callous de-humanization of others. Until 11 September, these horrors were perpetuated against Israel 'only', therefore little attention was paid to them by the West. Muslim extremists have therefore felt encouraged to persist, as no one has stopped them, and their poisonous message has been permitted to filter through to the populace and become mainstream thinking. If, in November 2001, two months after the 11 September disaster and during Ramadan to boot, 'moderate' Muslim states in the Gulf were able to entertain their television viewers with a series that depicted the Jews as 'drinkers of Arab children's blood', this is because, for decades, other Muslim countries, such as 'moderate' Egypt and 'straightforward' Syria, have been denying Jewish history, promoting the idea of the Blood Libel, using some of their choice 'scholars' to rationalize it, and repeating it *ad nauseam*, while the West watches and responds with only a dismissive smile.

Hitler also began his mad designs by accusing the Jews, and the Western powers reacted by letting down the Jews and selling out Czechoslovakia, thereby hoping to quench the hatred of the tyrant and end his quest for world dominion. Only when he turned against them did they wake up, but by then it was too late. Now, the Muslim radicals have already risen against the West, who for years has ignored the impending disaster, despite the fact that the writing was on the wall. It is their Garaudys, Faurissons and Irvings, and their peers who denied the Holocaust in Europe, and who have been welcomed as heroes in the Muslim world, whom they taught to speak and act likewise. As a consequence, unlike in Europe, *Schindler's List* was banned throughout most of the Muslim world because no counter-evidence to their anti-Semitic convictions could be tolerated. A good example of their famous 'tolerance'. But, instead of exerting pressure on them, battling with them, boycotting them and forcing them into compliance with the basic rules of human conduct, the West looked the other way, until the lives of its own people were on the line. Muslims have kidnapped hostages in the Philippines, in Lebanon, in Kashmir and elsewhere. But instead of standing up to the terrorists and fighting them in their hide-outs, every country bought back its hostages, occasionally bowing to the extravagant demands of the kidnappers.

No wonder, then, that what looks to us an abominable pattern of discourse and action became the routine *modus operandi* of those uncontrolled gangs of Muslim terrorists who are bent on destroying civilization. The West did wake up, but for a long time was not alerted to the fact that what begins with Jews spills over to Western civilization in the final analysis. In fact, the very reproaches to Israel as she has been desperately fighting terrorism, such as 'targeted killing', 'exaggerated use of force', 'killing innocent civilians', 'resolving issues through negotiations', 'there is no military solution to terrorism' and 'addressing the root reasons for terrorism', all collapsed once the United States contravened all of them, with the vocal or silent quiescence of its allies. What should be of concern to civilized society today is the harrowing prospect of watching these terrorists wield means of mass destruction, bringing down with them the entire world as we know it, including themselves. But they are not concerned, for they have cultivated over the years a new type of dedicated fighter who not only does not fear death, but is often eager to take the short-cut to their Paradise by committing massive acts of murder and sacrificing themselves in the process.

NOTES

1.   Article 15 of the Hamas Charter. For the full text see R. Israeli, 'The Charter of Allah: the Platform of the Islamic Resistance Movement', in Y. Alexander (ed.) *The 1988–9 Annual of Terrorism,* Amsterdam: Martinus Nijhoff, 1990, pp. 99–134.
2.   See, for example, Surat al-Nisa, verse 74; Surat al-'Imran, verse 169; Surat al-Saf, verse 4; Surat Muhammad, verse 4.
3.   Article 7 of the Hamas Charter, see R. Israeli, 'The Charter of Allah', p.112.
4.   Article 12 of the Hamas Charter, ibid. p. 114.
5.   Article 13 of the Hamas Charter, ibid. p. 115.
6.   Sura 2 (the Cow), verse 120, says: 'And the Jews will not be pleased by thee, nor will be the Christians, till thou follow their creed. Say "Lo, the guidance of Allah Himself is the guidance". And if you should follow their desires after the knowledge which has come unto thee, then you would have from Allah no protecting friend nor helper.'
7.   Article 8 of the Hamas Charter, ibid. p. 112.

8. Article 7 of the Hamas Charter, ibid.
9. After the normative Five Pillars (*arkan*) of Islam: the *shahadah* (vow of creed), Prayer, fast, alms and the Hajj (Holy Pilgrimage to Mecca).
10. This is the *shahada*, or statement of faith, that is the first of the *arkan* (see n. 9 above).
11. Apostasy (*ridda*) is punishable by death without appeal.
12. Sheikh Ali abu-al-Hassan, the Head of the Fatwa Council, 11 October 2001. Extracted from Al-Azhar Internet Site by *MEMRI, Terror in America*, No. 28, p. 1.
13. Sheikh Abu-al-Hassan, 18 October 2001, ibid.
14. Dr 'Abd-al 'Adhim al-Mat'ani, a lecturer at al-Azhar, 11 October 2001, ibid. p. 2
15. Dr Mat'ani, 22 October 2001, ibid., p. 3.
16. Dr Shahin, 15 October 2001, ibid.
17. Ibid.
18. Ibid.
19. 11 October 2001, ibid.
20. See, for example, Dr Yihya Isma'il, the Spokesman of the Azhar Doctors of the Holy Law, Sheikh Yussef al-Badri, a popular preacher, and Dr Zaki 'Uthman, a lecturer in the *Da'wa* (Mission) Department of al-Azhar. 11 and 22 October 2001, ibid. pp. 3–4.
21. See Bat Ye'or, *The Dhimmi*; and *The Decline of Eastern Christianity Under Islam*, both published by Fairleigh Dickinson University Press, Madison and London, 1985 and 1996, respectively.
22. Ibn Khaldun, *The Muqaddimah: An Introduction to History*, Princeton NJ: University Press, 1958 (3 vols, Vol. 1). Translation by Franz Rosenthal, London 1967, Vol. 1, p. 183.
23. Bat Ye'or, *The Decline*, pp. 217–20.
24. See, for example, the Qur'anic Sura (9:29): 'Fight against those to whom the Scriptures were given [Jews and Christians], who believe not in Allah nor in the Last Day, who forbid not what Allah and His Apostle have forbidden, and follow not the true faith, until they pay the tribute out of hand [the *jizya* mentioned above] and are humbled.'
    Sura 5:51: 'O you who believe! Take not the Jews and the Christians as friends. They are friends to one another. Whoever of you befriends them is one of them. Allah does not guide the people who do evil.' Sura 9: 30–31: 'The Jews say "Ezra is the son of Allah" and the Christians say "The Messiah is the son of Allah". Those are the words of their mouth, conforming to the words of the unbelievers before them. Allah, attack them! How perverse they are! They have taken their rabbis and their monks as lords besides Allah, as so too the Messiah son of Mary, though they were commanded to serve but one God. There is no God but He. Allah is exalted above that which they deify beside Him.'
25. *Outstanding Examples of Our Civilization for 11th Grade*, pp. 3–16. See R. Israeli, 'Education, Identity, State Building and the Peace Process: Educating Palestinian Children in the Post Oslo Era', in *Terrorism and Political Violence*, Vol. 12, No. 1 (Spring 2000), p. 87.
26. See the insightful article by Clinton Bailey, 'A Note on the Bedouin Image of 'Adl as Justice', *Muslim World*, Vol. 66, No. 2, 1976.
27. *Ma'rakatuna ma'a al-Yahud*, 7th edition, Beirut, 1986.
28. Ibid., especially pp. 20–38.
29. Article 22 of the Hamas Charter. See also R. Israeli, *Muslim Fundamentalism in Israel*, London: Brassey's, 1993, pp. 101–8.
30. Article by Dr Fatihi in *Al-Ahram al-'Arabi* (The New York Times of the Arab world, Cairo), 20 October 2001. It is noteworthy that this motif of 'tears when one hears the sublime verses of the Qur'an' goes back to early Islamic history, which relates that the Christians of Najran in southern Arabia burst into tears when they heard the Prophet reciting to them the Word of Allah, and they converted on the spot. See Report No. 36 (Hebrew) by *MEMRI*.
31. Sura 3, Verse 113 from the Holy Qur'an. The article was published in *Al-Hayat* (London), 11 November 2001. See *MEMRI*, ibid.

32. Ibid.
33. See, for example, R. Israeli, *Peace is in the Eye of the Beholder*, Berlin and New York: Mouton, 1985. and R. Israeli, *Arab and Islamic Antisemitism*, Tel Aviv: Ariel Center for Policy Research, 2001.

3. *Fida'i, Shahid* and Islamikaze

One of the most puzzling aspects of Islamic terrorism, which has almost no parallels in other cultures, is the readiness of the perpetrators to blow themselves up in the process of destroying their enemy, in what has mistakenly come to be called 'suicide bombing'. This amazing example of self-sacrifice in the service of a cause is all the more stupefying in view of the normative Muslim prohibition on taking one's life, since it belongs to Allah, its Creator, and no human can override His Will. Suicide (*intihar*) is therefore looked down upon, shunned and discouraged in Muslim tradition, and consequently provokes reactions of horror, disbelief, fear, outrage, dismay and anger, especially when it is performed *en masse*, like on 11 September, with 19 murderers co-ordinating their harrowing act of terrorism-cum-self-immolation and producing a slaughter never previously equalled of thousands of innocent civilians.

In spite of the fact that murders and other targeted killings have happened before, some of them to attain political goals, the world had never seen wanton murder on this scale of people who had nothing to do with the sick hallucinations of the perpetrators, or with their pathological sense of revenge, or the murderous character of their ideology. So much so, that governments and peoples have raised their hands in despair; tried to appease the murderers instead of fighting them, under the excuse that 'against mad, sneaky and unpredictable assassins there was nothing that could be done'. Many attempts were pursued, in vain, to draw up a profile of the so-called 'suicide bomber' in order to be able to predict the likely person to put his life on the line, of his own volition, in order to achieve a goal he is made to believe in. But it turned out that people of almost all ages, socio-economic backgrounds, education, family situations and walks of life could be drawn into this kind of murderous web.

The murderer is not necessarily a poor, psychologically unstable being who finds himself in dire straights, when he has the stamina, forebearance, talent, means and motivation to study long years of engineering and piloting, or hide in caves when he could easily enjoy his 'normal' life elsewhere, just in order to attain what looks to us an insane pursuit. In other words, why would young men, sometimes with a promising future ahead of them, apparently sane and healthy in every respect, put themselves in jeopardy and volunteer for units, and for tasks, which are likely to put an end to their dreams and unfulfilled lives? They could, for example, join a high-risk combat unit if all they desired was to serve a collective goal for their nation and at the same time satisfy their sense of adventure or their machismo inclinations. But here, it seems that they are pushed towards death by some mysterious latent impulse. Or, is it the rosy promise full of delight and clear of worry, awaiting them in the hereafter, which kindles their passion? After all, the so-called 'suicide bombing' is not a natural death, nor is it the sort of 'running away' from the vagaries of life as we perceive them that occurs in Western culture.

To remove any doubt regarding the motivations of these murderers, one ought to consider the parameters which, from the point of view of Western psychiatry, define the requisite steps of the regular and 'normal' suicide type[1]:

1. A thought about killing oneself.
2. The presence of a plan – how to proceed, what are the precise steps to be taken, their sequence and timing and so forth – all concocted in solitude and single-handedly.
3. The suicidal individual must have a certain energy level, that is, a capacity to carry out the plan.

By contrast, in the case of the terrorist killers we are talking about, it is the determination to kill the perceived enemy which is the driving force; the plan relates to killing others and it is often prepared by the killer's superiors, not independently on his own initiative, because unlike the candidate for suicide he does not carry alone the burden of decision, and therefore he does not have to evince the same high degree of 'suicidal resolve'. According to psychiatrists,[2] the above three cumulative factors are among the most important for providing an indication of the likelihood of a suicidal occurrence. Moreover, they say, suicide can be sudden, as in the case of major depression, or in compulsive individuals under conditions of extreme frustration; or it can premeditated, as in a long-standing major depression where the individual has perhaps crafted a careful plan and meticulous preparations, such as giving away his most precious belongings, or may sometimes have written a note on his impending suicide. This certainly cannot be said about the terrorists, who are a part of a larger scheme for which they are trained and prepared, together with others who share their convictions, and are prepared for arduous and long-term studies and physical and mental training and preparations.

The mass murderers of al-Qa'ida, the Hamas and their like, never go for a 'sudden death'; it is always premeditated and carefully planned, though not necessarily by them personally. However, while it is difficult to cite individual depression, frustration or compulsion in all these cases – because otherwise it is hard to envisage how this kind of individual could enroll in an all-volunteer programme designed by others with a strategic goal to attain – it is also not unthinkable that some of these individuals may entertain their own private goal of quitting this world and moving on to the next. The person who commits self-immolation usually causes embarrassment after the fact to his friends and family, who are ashamed to be related to such a weak character who was unable to confront his problem and elected to run away from it. The terrorist killers, by contrast, are models of adulation; their loved ones are proud of them as they join the gallery of martyrs, and are usually rewarded financially by the organizations which had sent them to their death; unlike suicidal types who often abandon their families in need and add economic difficulty to the sorrow of separation.

These higly motivated terrorists do write 'suicide notes' – in our days in the form of video-tapes – and may also pre-distribute their belongings, both signs of suicidal intentions, but in this case the interpretation of these signals ought to be vastly at variance with the classic suicidal syndrome. When a self-immolating terrorist writes or records a note or a tape or a video, it is not usually geared to vindicate his act, to ask for clemency from the bereaved relatives and friends, or to 'punish' them by disappearing and causing them disarray and embarrassment. Quite the contrary, the messages left behind are 'educational' in essence, formulated so as to provide role models and positive examples to other youth who might be recruited after them. In any case, the recording session is orchestrated by the operators, who then undertake the duty of propagating the 'legacy' of the deceased. In fact, all those terrorists killed in action become martyrs and heroes, they are celebrated and receive citations in their community, and their relatives, far from evincing grief outwardly, on the contrary exalt with pride the honour that the departed has imparted to them. When the terrorist is killed in operation, what is left to distribute after him is a 'pension' disbursed to the family by the operating organization. In other words, this is not a *pre*-death parting with belongings that is typical to the suicidal type, but a promise to the family that they would not be forgotten *after* the death of the martyr. Due to their generally young age, these martyrs very seldom leave any property behind, but when they do, their belongings – such as pictures, items of clothing, written notes and so forth – achieve the status of 'relics' which may become the object of worship-like adoration.[3]

The prevailing terms for a self-sacrificing Muslim devotee, who dies for the sake of Allah or of Islam has been traditionally distilled into the two notions of *shahid* and *fida'i*, both connoting death in the course of a worthwhile act, usually the jihad discussed above. But, not only is there a difference between these two terms, but also in the nuances when either of them is used. *Shahid* can have three varying meanings: a martyr who died for the sake of Allah; the fallen in the jihad; or a Muslim who experienced suffering before a tragic death. In spite of the various nuances attached to each meaning, they are all founded on a religious concept connected to death in the process of performing a worthy act recommended by the Faith. The Holy Book of Islam, in fact, attests to such a death, even if the use of the term *shahid* there refers often to a 'witness' of all sorts. *Fida'i*, as Bernard Lewis attests, was the name which the medieval Isma'ili Assassins (*Hashishiyun*) used for themselves. They were considered to be criminal fanatics by their victims, but for their masters they were:

> A *corps d'élite* in the war against the enemies of the Imam; by striking down oppressors and usurpers, they gave the ultimate proof of their faith and loyalty and earned immediate and eternal bliss. The Isma'ilis themselves used the term *fida'i*, roughly devotee, of the actual [operator-] murderer, and an interesting poem has been preserved praising their courage, loyalty and selfless devotion. In the local Isma'ili chronicles of Alamut... there is a roll of honour of assassinations, giving the names of the victims and of their pious executioners... Isma'ili writers see the sect as custodians of secret mysteries to which the Believer could attain only after a long course of

preparation and instruction, marked by progressive initiations.[4]

One will have noticed that, except for the harrowing 'roll of honour', a sort of Hall of Fame nowadays reserved for outstanding sportsmen, or wax-museum for other celebrities, the *fida'i* is very close in mission, state of mind, conduct and training to the Islamist murderers we are talking about. It is no coincidence, therefore, that the Palestinians adopted the same title for their messengers of death back in the 1950s and 1960s, when the *Fidayeen* wrought havoc and terror against Israeli nurseries, schools, roads and other innocent civilian targets. However, while the classical *fida'i* had targeted a person who was considered an oppressor and usurper, today's murderers in the name of Islam execute indiscriminate mass murders against innocent civilians, which have won them the attribute of 'terrorists'. The difference in *modus operandi* may also be imputed to the development of the means of destruction. For while the medieval Assassin had to approach his targeted victim and stab him to death, point blank, something which required considerable courage and a very high motivation, today's murderers carry high explosives on their bodies sufficient to annihilate anyone in sight, without necessarily targeting anyone specifically.

Thus, both *shahid* and *fida'i* are motivated by a profound and numbing religious fanaticism which pushes them to commit acts of self-sacrifice, which we usually refer to as 'suicide attacks', though they have nothing to do with suicide. However, while the *shahid* is a martyr in the sense that he is a serving a cause, the *fida'i* connotes more of a devotion to a leader, be he religious (like Sheikh Ahmed Yassin of the Hamas, Sheikh Fadallah of the Hizbullah or Bin-Laden), or layman (like Arafat or Habash). In current parlance, both these types of murderers are confounded in the world of practise, as we have seen Palestinian killers adopting both appellations in various periods of their activity. In both cases, however, the self-sacrificing hero is assured of martyrdom and of very concrete rewards in the hereafter, not only for himself, but also for his loved ones. It is not uncommon, therefore, to witness hordes of well-wishers coming to the bereaved family of the martyr to express not condolences, but congratulations for the way their relative had paved for them the road to Paradise. In either case, the would-be killers have to be trained and prepared psychologically in such a fashion as to neutralize the normal human instincts for self-preservation, and to be able not only to defy death, but to be eager in the face of it.

The total and unmitigated devotion of the *fida'i* to his leader, to the point of committing acts of murder for him without posing questions or raising doubts, conjures up the legendary loyalty of the Japanese samurai, which has been immortalized in the notion of *junshi*, that is, 'accompanying the lord to his death' by committing suicide after his death, or, more commonly, abiding by the bushido (the samurai code of conduct) which required fighting for the lord to one's death. Anecdotally, one might notice that the samurai dressed up colourfully (contrary to his wont in daily life), cleaned and perfumed himself prior to his battles for his lord, so that he remain 'respectable' in his death, and he often tied a white kerchief around his forehead (*chimaki*), ostensibly to absorb sweat before it leaked into his eyes and irritated them during the battle. Not surprisingly, the Muslim 'suicide bombers' we have all been witnessing have also been known to cleanse themselves and dress up before they launch their horrific acts of terror, so as to be presentable at the entrance gate to the promised Paradise. We have also seen the processions of Hizbullah and Hamas members in the cities of Lebanon and the Palestinian Authority, parading their white (connoting celebration of death), green (the Prophet's favourite colour) or red (the colour of blood) kerchiefs around their foreheads, adorned with scriptures advertising '*Allah Akbar!*' ('Allah is the Greatest' – the war-cry of Muslim fighters, or the *shahada* – the first of the five Pillars of Islam – 'There is no God but Allah, and Muhammed is his Prophet').

Remaining with the Japanese parallel, we may push it still further and consider the most famous Japanese form of ritual or dutiful suicide (as contrasted with the trivial form of 'normal' suicide). In Japanese tradition, this kind of self-immolation could be motivated by a strong sense of protest against an existing order or state of affairs that one is unable to withstand or to alter, or by a desire for revenge on a person or group with which one is disenchanted but from which one cannot disengage. Therefore, one performed hara-kiri, or ritual suicide, which provided a respectful way out to people in such dire need. The most poignant example of the former was the mass hara-kiri performed in front of the Imperial Palace in Tokyo after the Emperor announced his country's capitulation to the Americans at the end of the Pacific War in August 1945. The most important form of hara-kiri, however, was the ritual self-killing that the samurai was ordered to perform by his lord, as an honourable self-inflicted punishment in order to escape a degrading and humiliating execution that he had 'earned' by his misdeeds or misbehaviour. In Islamic 'suicide bombing', the elements of protest against powers-that-be, or of despair in the face of an overwhelming situation one cannot control or change, are certainly there, though it is difficult to isolate them under the rhetoric of bombastic self-righteous proclamations after each bombing horror.

An aspect of the culture of shame has also to be addressed in the context of these murderous bombings. In Japan, one defended ferociously both one's own and the nation's honour, and committed self-immolation to escape humiliation. No other culture has ever made self-immolation, individual or collective, such a lofty ideal which allows an individual and society to save face and avoid facing shame. Countless samurai performed hara-kiri to avoid punishment by their lord; politicians or generals who failed in their duty committed suicide or were assassinated by other Japanese who felt humiliated by their deeds; and many Japanese preferred self-inflicted death to the humiliation of submission to their enemies. Thus, in Japan, suicide of all sorts was undertaken in situations of failure – moral, political, or in the line of duty. The Muslim 'suicide' killers, though they also share with the Japanese a culture of shame, belong to a tradition of vengeance which ties them back to the *lex talionis* that preceded Islam in ancient Arabian society. The humiliated party, whose honour had been trampled upon, would go to the ends of the earth to demonstrate that he would not forgive or forget until the wrong had been redressed. Out of the sense of seeking to redress what had been wronged, including striking the evil-doing enemy where it hurt him most, they would even commit missions of 'suicide bombing' if it were deemed necessary.

However, unlike the hara-kiri performers and others of their kind, the Japanese soldiers who were organized in 'Special Units' and designated to blow themselves up with their enemies during the Pacific War were typically motivated by their devotion to their country and their Emperor, in addition to being influenced by the mental infrastructure of shame in the face of failure. The coupling of protest and hara-kiri had been instilled into them by their culture. This new type of fighter became popularly known as kamikaze – the 'Spirits of the Gods'[5] – and they inflicted casualties, damage and terror on the US forces during the final stages of the Pacific War (1944–45).

These special units, which were trained, indoctrinated and sustained by the Japanese State, were in quite a different category from the hara-kiri in the sense that they were not self-motivated, did not cater to their own personal instincts or needs, and were part of a larger group of like-minded fellows. They felt that in their act they were making an ultimate sacrifice for a cause, which not only had a political-ideological purpose, but also had a strong religious colouring (the 'Spirits of the Gods'); and, in so doing, they were prepared to sacrifice their lives without hesitation.

Typologically, then, the Muslim fundamentalist self-immolating assassins – who have nothing suicidal about them nor ressemble the hara-kiri of either the imposed or the voluntary type – come closest to the kamikaze in organization, ideology, execution of their task, posthumous glory, and historical background of self-effacing loyalty, murderous fanaticism (samurai and *fida'i*, kamikaze and *shahid*) and culture of shame. It is therefore proposed to adopt the appellation of *Islamikaze* to describe them, combining their inner Islamic motivation and vocation with the other outward attributes of their fellow kamikaze. In fact, a report from an Afghan camp where the Islamikaze were being trained in the mid-1990s, and which has come to be known as the 'Kamikaze Barracks', sported a slogan at its main entrance, made of whitewashed pebble and stone, which stated 'Jihad – Istishhad – Paradise – Islamic Kamikaze – Human Bombs',[6] meaning: 'The Holy War of Islam – Death in Martyrdom – The Promised Hereafter – By Means of Muslim Kamikaze – who are Human Bombs'. This is, in essence, the entire story.

It has been customary for the media and governments, until 11 September 2001, to report on Hizbullah and Hamas terrorism in the Middle East, and in recent years also about al-Qa'ida's trouble-making in East Africa, but there was little publicity on the Islamikaze camps in Afghanistan, which were wholly Muslim in both their trainees and instructors, where, in contrast with the dismal development of the country, the latest technologies of death and terror were imparted to Muslim volunteers who had streamed there from all over the Muslim world to prepare for their sinister missions. There are also comparable camps in Lebanon, in Iran, in the Sudan, and in any number of other Islamic countries under conflict which do not attract much attention, but their impact on world terrorism is no less acute. However, Afghanistan, until recently, has been the ideal ground for such camps owing to several factors:

1. Many of the camps are the offshoot of the long-standing intake of immigrants from all over the Arab and Islamic worlds who went to Afghanistan to fight on the mujahedin side in the 1980s, at the instigation of the Americans and the Saudis, in order to undermine the Soviet grip there. Upon returning to their homelands at the end of the war, these battle-hardened, so-called Afghanis often became the spearhead of Muslim oppositions to the illegitimate regimes of their countries. Bin-Laden himself, and the many Arabs and other Muslims who flocked to his call once he moved his al-Qa'ida organization to Afghanistan, are graduates of these camps.

2. During the First Afghan War (1979–89), the Pakistani border city of Peshawar, which had previously been a remote backwater, grew into a major centre which gave shelter to millions of real Afghan refugees. The city also became the staging area for mujahedin counter-attacks against the Soviets and, under Pakistani protection and American connivance, also a teeming centre of international terrorist and other illicit activities: arms smuggling and deals of all sorts, spying grounds, drug traffic and so on. It is in Peshawar that the blind Sheikh Abdul Rahman, ostensibly an Egyptian political refugee from his native country, concocted the first attempt against the Twin Towers in 1993, and then was allowed into unsuspecting America to carry out his scheme.

3. Afghanistan is a country torn by ethnic differences,[7] but after the Soviet invasion in 1979, they were quick to organize, with US and Pakistani backing, a unified movement of mujahedin against the godless Communist invaders. As long as the battles raged and US aid abounded, all factions were kept busy and happy, for all prescribed Islam as their goal and way of life, and all vowed to extirpate the Soviets from the land at any cost and regardless of the time this would necessitate, much to the delight of the Americans and the West in general. But as soon as the Soviets tired of this endless war of attrition, as their casualties mounted and the vanity of the campaign became evident, they also realized that their goal of suffocating radical Islam in Afghanistan, lest it spread to their own Muslim Republics, had backfired on them and had increased its fervour and capacity to resist them. The Soviet withdrawal from Afghanistan signalled the division of the country between local warlords, though there was a nominal central government in

Kabul, and they facilitated the establishment of the Islamikaze camps in their midst due to the benefits they reaped from them.

4. While the foreigners who fought alongside the mujahedin returned home to stir up trouble in their own countries, the Afghani militias deployed their full forces and prepared to take over Kabul. The infighting that ensued left Afghanistan ruined and Kabul half-destroyed in a senseless civil war that lasted from 1992 to 1996 until the Taliban takeover. In that chaos, each militia used any kind of income it could obtain: foreign aid from supportive countries (Iran, Saudi Arabia, Pakistan), drug trafficking, and sponsorship of Islamikaze camps.

5. After the Taliban takeover and the invitation of al-Qa'ida to base itself in Afghanistan, Bin-Laden was not only happy to go back to his militant roots, but also to lend his sponsorship and financial aid to the Islamikaze camps and to encourage old Afghani hands to flock back to him there.

The evidence existing on the Islamikaze camps following the 1996 report of *al-Watan al'Arabi* (the written equivalent of the *al-Jazeera* Televison network today, which should have been heeded but was not), and which was published in 1997 but also not heeded,[8] pointed out all the components of Islamic international terrorism that the West was 'surprised' to awaken to on 11 September 2001. Since the reporters who compiled this survey of the camps were versed in Arab and Islamic affairs, and presumably Arab and/or Muslim themselves, their warnings should have awakened even the dead. They wrote, *inter alia*, the following enlightening remarks:

- The camp, which they saw was located in a remote area in the vicinity of the Afghan–Pakistani border and was the ground for extremely demanding physical training. For example, the trainees would run long stretches of the road every day, carrying bags of rocks and sand on their shoulders. This suggests, of course, that these people were not simply sent to their death, as their misnomer 'suicide bombers' would suggest, but were rather instilled with skills of fighting, survival and resilience.

- The instructors in that particular camp originated from Egypt, Saudi Arabia and the Yemen and were known for the toughness of their character. The Egyptians and Saudis at least came from countries supposedly friendly to the United States, and most of them were probably known to the security services of their native countries.

- The weapons instruction included arms of all sorts and of various origins: Chinese, American, Turkish, even the famous Israeli Uzi sub-machine-gun. The calibre of the weapons spanned the entire gamut: from rifles and pistols to anti-aircraft Stinger missiles. This means that not only an abundance of these weapons was still available as a remnant of the First Afghan War, and obviously irresponsibly distributed into the wrong hands, but, more ominously, that the trainees were taught to handle them to down enemy (and also civilian) aircraft.
- Instruction of the Islamikaze also included urban guerilla combat, sabotage, handling and concocting explosives and installing car-bombs, again a testament to the sophistication of these new terrorists, and to their perception and self-perception as being more war- and death-machines than mere human bombs.
- The trainees were all designated, recruited, indoctrinated, dispatched and financed by their local Islamic organizations. It was the foreign currency poured into Afghanistan to finance these courses, with the collaboration of successive foreign currency-hungry governments, which kept the Islamikaze camps going. The Islamic organizations and their sponsors, either governments or wealthy private benefactors (Bin-Laden was one of them), then determined where the hardened graduates of these courses were to act, under what cover and to what specific tasks they would be assigned. And all this under the soundly snoring noses of the security apparatus of those countries from which the future murderers originated, or where they sought asylum, or planned to infiltrate, including, of course, the United States and other unsuspecting Western democracies.
- Trainees came from not only Arab and Islamic-majority countries, but also from countries where Muslim minorities, or Muslim areas under non-Muslim rule, were deemed to be oppressed. Cases in point: Muslims in France (mainly North Africans), in Germany (mainly Turks), Palestinians (under Israeli rule), Bosnian Muslims, Chechnians, Filipino Moros and others. Only when the West woke up to a reality of the existence of 60 al-Qa'ida bases worldwide, including in Western countries, could it bite its fingers with remorse and regret for having allowed that horror to build-up in their own

societies. This conjures up the concept of the difference between conscience and consciousness: the latter is when one becomes aware of reality, the former is when one wishes he had not.

- Graduates of these courses were found later serving in such Islamic countries as Jordan and Egypt, or they stole across the Pakistan border to help remove Benazir Bhutto from power. Once again, these places are known as close allies of the United States, and their security machines were generally able to disrupt and arrest these sorts of subversive elements before they acted against the regimes in place. Was there a lapse in the state of alertness of those governments involved in these cases, or were they reluctant to unnecessarily infuriate their Muslim radicals as long as they did not threaten them?
- Other graduates arrived in Kashmir to help terrorize the Indians into submission and install a Muslim government there; many of them went to fight in Bosnia against the Serbs, again courtesy of the West who supported the Muslims. The expert saboteurs among them have detonated explosive charges in Delhi, Bahrain and New York, to cite only a few examples. This means that these dedicated fighters of Islam had begun to take up positions in their target-countries well before 11 September.
- The trainees were 16–25-year-old boys. Those who graduated to the upper echelons of training, in preparation for Islamikaze missions, were subject to a particularly testing regime: they did not talk to each other in order to encourage introspection and avert hesitation under the influence of free dialogue. Side by side with taxing their physical endurance, they underwent endless sessions of religious indoctrination, mainly by Egyptian and Saudi 'ulama' (scholars of the Holy Law). The identity of those preachers may indicate that they were reacting specifically to the overly close relationship (to their minds) between their governments and the hated West.
- The camp in question was founded by a Pakistani scholar of this type. This suggests that, like those 'ulama' who groomed the Taliban (literally 'students') until they graduated from Pakistani puritanical madrasa's (religious schools) and were to take over rule in Afghanistan, the Pakistani preachers in the camps were exporting their teachings into the Islamikaze camps in Afghanistan and thence to the entire Islamic world.
- The graduates who were earmarked for Islamikaze missions

were considered by their operators to be of a higher quality and so 'deserving of' the ultimate form of training in preparation for their supreme act of devotion. Their solitary state of meditation was to allow them pave for themselves the last portion of their way to Paradise on their own.

- The internal fighting in Afghanistan, until the Taliban take-over, had enabled foreign trainees to test both their weapons and their methods in real battle in real time, all without any outside interference. This unlike similar camps in Lebanon, Syria, Iraq, Iran, Libya, the Sudan and Algeria, where such camps might be subject to the scrutiny, or literally to the mercy, of the local authorities, who manipulate them for their own needs and interests.

- Each course lasted for a few months and cost approximately US$3,000 per trainee, hence the bonanza of foreign currency for impoverished Afghanistan. But it was reported that both instructors and trainees also engaged in drug trafficking and smuggling, either as personal moonlighting or to ensure the smooth functioning of the camp. Local Afghan warlords, at least until the Taliban takeover, collaborated with the camps in order to obtain some illicit income for themselves, while according, on their part, freedom of operation to the Islamikaze and their mentors. So, all rival parties in Afghanistan, from that of the nominal President Rabbani to arch-rebel Hikmatyar, could count on the camps in their areas of control for foreign currency income. There is no reason to believe that things have changed dramatically under the Taliban or that the new post-Taliban government in Kabul will be able or willing to act to alter this state of affairs.

It seems rather aberrant that countries such as pre-Taliban Afghanistan, Pakistan, Iran, Libya, Jordan, Saudi Arabia, Egypt and the Sudan – which had enjoyed a close relationship with the United States and the West in the past, or are continuing to promote it at the present, at least officially – should turn so violently anti-Western, not only on the rhetorical level but also in the domain of terrorism. But one has to remember that these countries share one common denominator, namely Islam which, *prima facie*, cuts through diverse ethnic, linguistic, national, political and social systems, and facilitates the growth of international, mainly anti-Western and anti-Israeli, terrorism. Moreover, if one takes into account the diffusion of the Afghanis and their like throughout nearly all Islamic countries, including those considered 'moderate' or pro-American, one could come to the erroneous conclusion that Islam equals terrorism, or that Islam, by definition, overrides all other considerations when it comes to international terrorism.

The reality is much more varied and nuanced, and it is tied specifically to local conditions in each country. The Islamikaze stand in most Islamic countries not as part of the established order, but in opposition to it. Although their claim to Islamic legitimacy sounds loud and clear in contrast with their illegitimate rulers, they represent not the mainstream of Islam – which is usually pragmatic and strikes compromises with the rulers in place in accordance with the Sunnite precept of 'better a bad ruler than political chaos' where no Muslim would be able to practice his faith – but more or less marginal groups in Islamic society. These groups may have many sympathizers and supporters, but they themselves thrive on the disoriented, the disaffected, the disenchanted and the dysfunctional strata who cannot catch up with the rapid changes in society and who abhor modernity. They harshly criticize the regimes of their own countries, accuse them, not without good reason, of corruption and submission to subversive and immoral Western values at the expense of Islamic ideals and tradition; and they often urge, and at times even attempt, the toppling of their home regimes. In other words, unlike established Islam which seeks Islamization of society gradually and peacefully, in collaboration with the regime, these radicals want everything here and now, and they are ready to use violence to attain their goals. Their passion is impatient.

The Islamists, as they are sometimes termed in the West, gather their forces, their passion and their deep commitment around charismatic leaders, like Sheikhs Yassin and Fadlallah, or Bin-Laden and Mullah Umar, who usually have an impeccable record of simplicity, modesty and honesty, shun extravagance and waste, and provide their followers with a model of populistic sincerity, paternal devotion and concern, and scholarly wisdom and knowledge. They come to regard their immensely popular leaders as role models and they almost adore them as the epitome of rightfulness and as their source of guidance, not unlike the Jewish hassidim *vis-à-vis* their rabbi. Setting themselves apart from the evil society of sinners which surrounds them, they wholeheartedly and boundlessly follow the word, the example and the hard path traced for them by their leaders as the ultimate interpretation of the Will of

Allah. Wherever the need arises, these leaders can pronounce tailor-made fatwas (religious verdicts) to lend justification to the warranted action. One can understand how, propelled by this kind of relentless drive, enveloped by an approving and supporting environment, and guided by the almost divinely inspired sanction of the leader-generated fatwa, a Muslim radical can also transcend the ordinary into the mystic and magnetic world of the Islamikaze.

In order to cultivate their self-image as the alternative to the existing order, these Islamikaze-prone revolutionaries not only boast their slogans of 'Islam is the Solution!', 'Islam is the Alternative!' and 'Islam is the Truth!', but they also delegitimize the regimes under which they live, and the enemies against whom they are pitted, be they godless communists, the corrupt and corrupting West, aggressive America and Israel, and the like. Rhetorical violence against opponents, enemies or rivals sets the stage for their ultimate elimination. And if they cannot be annihilated by face-to-face confrontation due to their (temporary) superiority in weaponry and technology, then self-sacrifice by way of Islamikaze may be the answer. Once again, it is not the desire of these people to commit 'suicide' that propels them, but the burning and uncontrollable eagerness to destroy the enemy even if it costs them their lives.

To induce a young Muslim to become an Islamikaze his operators must first emasculate the natural fear of death that is innate in any human being. They may fascinate their naïve and adept novice by comparing the promised hereafter, where the would-be martyr is free of concern and pursues a rewarding and eternal material life depicted in lively colour and enveloped in lust and debauchery, with the hardships of his real life, which is full of pitfalls, frustrations and uncertainties, and fleeting in any case. He may be tempted to take a shortcut to Heaven to save himself the vagaries of his actual and temporary stay on earth. In April 1995, a poignant story was published in an Israeli newspaper concerning a young 15-year-old Palestinian boy from Gaza, whose quest to blow himself up among Israeli civilians had been foiled. He said during his police interrogation, 'We are born to die, and our lives are merely a transition to death and eternal life in Paradise...Death is a good thing, not the bad, horrific and ugly thing that we were made to believe.'[9]

Hard to grasp? Indeed! In this rather infrequent case of aborted self-immolation during an act of terrorism, it was possible to obtain *post factum* the statement of the would-be perpetrator. But, as a rule, due to the impracticality of clinical evaluation prior to the act of 'suicide bombing', much less subsequent to it, one is left with little or no basis for the reconstruction of the personality of the martyr or his biography before the act. Even in cases of 'failed' 'suicide bombings', or when the bombing succeeded but the perpetrator escaped death (which in itself invalidates that terminology in the first place), it is perhaps impossible to reconstruct his mindset prior to the act, because his survival, which may have been miraculous or due to some technical quirk, does not diminish one iota from either his self-perception as a hero who has succeeded even though he survived, or who tried at great risk to attain his goal but was foiled by outside forces beyond his control, or from the way others perceive him, not as a martyr if he did not die, but as a hero worthy of emulation. Conversely, the fact that he narrowly escaped death may make him view the world differently, realize that life is worthwhile hanging on to, and revise his instilled attitude towards death. Who knows?

If one could draw up personal profiles of would-be bombers after their recruitment, then perhaps their shared character traits, family backgrounds and socio-economic environments might hint at their predisposition to commit this sort of voluntary martyrdom. But again, since this is not suicide in the conventional sense, no individual can be tested for his intention to kill himself when he had, perhaps, never intended to do so in the first place, or before he in fact did it in the real world and for totally different purposes than suicide. According to conventional wisdom based on collected data to date,[10] it would seem that people most likely to join these missions, or equally dangerous cults or revolutionary groups, share some basic characteristics which, in themselves, do not necessarily indicate psychiatric illness:

1. They are young and therefore have few life responsibilities: career, business, family, material possessions. In the real world, however, there are many exceptions to this rule: Palestinian terrorists in Israel, as well as many involved in al-Qa'ida and the 11 September horror, had families, careers and fortunes to lose, foremost of them Bin-Laden himself (who so far has not shown any propensity to perform an act of martyrdom but lives very dangerously nevertheless), who has more than one wife and a couple of dozen children, but chooses to live in caves and run for his life under constant persecution. Or perhaps he took

all those risks when he did not take seriously US determination to hunt him down? Or perhaps his faith and dedication to the cause of Islam is simply more important to him than money, easy life and family? Who is to know?

2. Many of the would-be martyrs were not particularly successful in their lives: in study, work or interpersonal relations; or they have been relatively shunned by their families/friends/ environments to the point of feeling isolated. Again, we have seen perpetrators among the Palestinians who had a good standard of living, or were employed and enjoyed their family lives, but their call for martyrdom decided their faith. We also know from the 11 September massacre that some of the 19 perpetrators, specifically those who studied engineering and took pilot courses in preparation for their mission, could not be said to have belonged to the poor, to have lacked the requisite qualities to succeed in their careers, or to have failed in their family lives. Consequently, no one can explain why they elected to die.

3. The perpetrators of such acts were usually assumed to be characterized by poor self-esteem. But when we watched those talented young people who planned and executed their attack with such a breath-taking precision against New York and Washington on 11 September, afer long years of patient self-training for the mission, we could not be convinced that they suffered from a low self-esteem. If anything, the contrary was in evidence.

According to this conventional wisdom, people of this sort might have well sought and found an alternative social organization, marginal, persecuted, risky and problematic as it might be, in order to be recognized and accepted, enhanced and appreciated. Their association with the Islamikaze would give them the opportunity to expand their own ego, and the newly acquired comradeship would sustain their self-esteem and self-importance. It is said that these types might be depressed and in search of easy solutions to their problems. Unsuccessful, perhaps self-despising, they would find solace in becoming martyrs, thus almost instantly and mythically transforming frustration into glory, failure into victory, and self-deprecation into public adoration. Perhaps this explanation holds for a certain percentage of these youths, perhaps others are duped as were their *fida'i* predecessors. Perhaps still others are romantics or idealists (whatever that might mean). There is no doubt, however, that in the post-September 11 era, we realize that an entire spectrum of personalities is involved. But from the strategic point of view, the crucial issue is that a highly structured organization is shaping, moulding and using these individuals for its own ambitions and sinister goals.

What is more, while adherents of cults in general find solace for their individual selves in their life and death, the Islamikaze fulfil a societal-family ideal, by preparing the grounds in Paradise for their entire family to follow: something that makes their act bearable, not to say desirable, for their loved and loving ones. Their role as pioneers before their kin makes them precious in the eyes of their public, which views them and their surviving families with awe and admiration: something which can hardly be said about cult or regular suicide victims. Moreover, if one is to summarize the popular songs about these martyrs, which are distributed post-mortem on video, tapes and in brochures and posters; the host of orally transmitted stories of their heroism and self-sacrifice; and the repeated replay on stage of the saga of their martyrdom, much reminiscent of the Shi'ite *ta'zia*,[11] one cannot help noticing the enormous differences between these two kinds of self-inflicted death.

Indeed, in the world of the Islamikaze, the hereafter is lauded not as an escape, but as a desirable fulfilment. Paradise is unexpectedly depicted in exciting, plastic, worldly and pleasurable terms, not in some vague spiritual entity worthy of mystics or saints of other traditions. Sex and wine, the two foremost taboos in traditional Islamic society, are exalted in the Islamikaze popular literature as accessible and permissible in unlimited quantities, because in the hereafter, everything is in abundant and limitless supply and the restrictions of the worldly Shari'a law do not apply. More puzzling is the fact that the public which extols the martyrs stands as an approving, envious and adoring audience in the face of the violation of their worldly Shari'a limitation, not as a traumatized or disgusted public, as in the case of cult-instigated massacres or plain suicide.

The construct 'suicide bomber' has been used by Western media and the political community and, as such, it has had deleterious consequences: minimizing, trivializing and distorting a highly significant phenomenon. 'Suicide bomber' implies a disposition towards madness, yet it has not emanated from psychologically responsible sources. Turning to an Islamic frame of reference for a definition, and perhaps a diagnosis would, then, appear imperative if we are to comprehend the underlying motive for this sort of unparalleled mode of self-sacrifice. As mentioned in Chapter 1, when questioned by a reporter about 'suicide bombing', Absallah Shami, a respected leader of the Islamic Jihad group in Gaza, replied that as long as they did not have access to the same military hardware as their enemy, 'suicide bombing' was the most effective weapon they had. Consequently, he saw it as a legitimate method of operation.[12]

The sheikh is then claiming that only dearth of weapons, or military impotence in general in the face of well-armed and powerful powers-that-be, had caused his movement to use humans instead. He does not idealize or justify 'suicide bombing' as a goal in itself. Moreover, while in conventional suicide the victim wishes to inflict the greatest possible damage on himself in order to make his task 'successful', here there is a reverse prescription to reduce the perpetrators' losses (and presumably to increase the enemy's). However, when loss there is, the perpetrator/victim is assured of life in the hereafter. To reduce the losses also implies that the operators of such acts do engage in 'economic' calculations inasmuch as they strive to decrease the numbers of would-be martyrs for each operation, not in order to increase its efficacy, but in order to diminish the toll of their own casualties, possibly to save them for more operations of this sort. Had death in itself been the ideal, even in the context of eliminating the enemy, then a maximum number of participants in the operation, not the necessary minimum, would have been envisaged. This is similar to the kamikaze, our control group where death for the Emperor, as much as it was idealized and irrational, was still tempered by the rational imperative to manage the available resources economically in order to put them to optimal use.

The build-up of the Islamikaze's ideological commitment is made incrementally of the following three elements: identifying the enemy; strengthening the value of jihad in particular and doctrinal conviction in general against the identified enemy; and then instigating the Islamikaze to show personal valour and self-sacrifice for the attainment of the prescribed goal. While the first two elements will be dealt with in the coming two chapters, some elaboration will be offered below on the question of what makes the Islamikaze tick. The would-be martyrs belong to three concentric circles of identity which coincide with the three societal circles in which they operate: their public at large; their inner circle of like-minded activists; and the innermost nucleus of those ready for the ultimate sacrifice:

1. Exactly as the kamikaze won the support of, and found sympathy among, the wartime Japanese public, so do the Islamikaze in their Islamic environment. Both publics, as we have seen in Chapter 1, were focused on their enmity and hostility towards their sworn enemy, thereby constituting the water from which these guerilla-martyrs sought sustenance. The clear identification of that enemy which they shared with their public, and the equally clear recognition by the martyrs that when they act the public will stand behind them, and will revere them if they should fail and much more so if they die in battle, are the foundations for building the first element of the Islamikaze worldview, high motivation and readiness to perish for the cause.

2. Islamikaze and kamikaze alike belonged to radical, battle-hardened, battle-defiant and highly indoctrinated groups which vowed to serve the cause with unlimited devotion: the Muslim fundamentalists and the Imperial Japanese Armed Forces respectively. For the Muslims, jihad, their tool of fighting for the Path of Allah, as actively interpreted and propagated by their fundamentalist religious leaders, is the rallying point and the chosen path, and death in it promises in itself martyrdom and access to Paradise.

3. Above and beyond the commitment of Muslim radicals to jihad, there is a chosen nobility, the best of the best, who prepare themselves for the superior form of sacrifice: the Islamikaze. Unlike the common jihad fighters who fight in unison, usually as part of the armed forces of an Islamic state and under the religious sanction of its Islamic hierarchy, and seek comfort and courage in each other, the Islamikaze, like the kamikaze, train alone for their mission and prepare themselves in glorious self-isolation and self-purification for their task. Hence the requirement of the ultimate degree of audacity, devotion, piety, consciousness, and the capacity to discard any thought or deed which might interfere with those ultimate qualities.

It is this transition from common jihad fighter to Islamikaze that needs clarification. Let us listen to a widely circulated tape extolling the Islamikaze:

I   Come on brother, join jihad
    Carry your machine-gun from early morning
    And come brother, join jihad. Choose one of the two:
    Either victory and a life of delight
    Or death and a life with a Paradise girl.[13]

    (Refrain)
    Oh brother! Your country calls upon you!
    Stand up and come to liberate her.
    Oh, Aqsa Mosque, we are all mourning
    Your desecration by those cursed by Allah [the Jews].

II But when the Muslims take notice,
    You will bloom again like jasmine.
    Oh brother! We have already endured humiliation
    Look at Sabra and Mia Mia.[14]
    Manhood and zeal are lost
    Unless you pick up your machine-gun and join jihad.[15]

The feeling of 'we have reached the ebb', 'we have nothing to lose' is exactly the impetus for exposing oneself to a certain death, either by self-immolation at the heart of the enemy, or in daring battle without chance of survival. For while 'here' there is only humiliation and suffering, 'there' the promise is great, and still greater is the temptation to take a short-cut and get there as early as possible in one's life. Beyond this, one can detect in the song all three elements of the Islamikaze make-up: delegitimation of the enemy (the desecrators of al-Aqsa, who are cursed by Allah); the call for jihad, which binds all Muslim fighters, more so the fundamentalists who are not waiting for the established community or regime to launch it; and the final step of luring the predisposed to do so, to their death without fear and with great rewards awaiting the strong of heart. Here is another popular song of this sort:

The solution is inherent in your faith, your Islam, your weapons
Oh brother! Persist in your way, with determination and resolve
How sweet to the ear is the voice calling for jihad!
You better sing these lyrics of audacity
While handling the arrows in your quiver.

We shall crush the bastions of injustice
And turn them into ashes.
Then we shall brandish the banner of faith
With pride and fortitude.
We have come to you, the landscape of our country,
Ready to defy death and to cleanse the impurities
Of the Zionist enemies.[16]

The link between self-sacrifice and daring in battle, and the hereafter, had been established by a passage from the Qur'an, where the Prophet, who was instigating his followers not to fear battle, lauded the next world, which is ' incomparably better than this one'.[17] This link is further elaborated in the tradition related to the Angels *Munkir* and *Nakir*, who reportedly interrogate every recently deceased Muslim by making him traverse the purifying fire of Heaven before he is admitted to Paradise.[18] Reputedly, martyrs will have saved themselves from the torments of that horrible interrogation, both upon their arrival to Heaven, since they are directly admitted to Paradise, and on the Day of Resurrection, when all humans will resubmit to that frightening trial. A Hadith, citing the Prophet, specifies that the *shahid*:

> ... will be pardoned [for his sins] by Allah, will take his place in Paradise, will be dressed with the Cloth of Faith, will marry beautiful-eyed young women, will be spared the torments of the tomb, will not submit to the Day of Judgement, and will have one of the world's best precious stones adorn his crown.[19]

After admission into Paradise, the martyrs are blissfully rewarded by acquiring a higher position than all the other dwellers, which enables them to partake of the eternal pleasures and delights that the place has to offer. The Holy Qur'an abounds with exciting descriptions of the Garden of Eden, where the climate is temperate – not a trifle for Arabs originating from the deserts of Arabia – and where they can indulge in drink from silver cups, dressed in expensive silk, adorned with silver jewels amidst gardens where wine flows like rivers.[20] This dream-like living is certainly mind-boggling inasmuch as it provides a never waning source of happiness and bliss, as compared with worldly suffering, uncertainty and deprivation. It was the Prophet himself who urged jihad fighters to distinguish themselves in battle, in view of what was awaiting them in the quickly attainable hereafter.[21] The position of the martyr in Heaven is extolled, for his dwelling surpass all the others, as it is located close to Allah's throne.[22] Many Hadith elaborate on those magnificient descriptions, like the one painting Paradise in terms of a divine blinking light, branches of fragrant trees, flowing rivers, tall palaces, an abundance of fruit, luxurious clothes and exquisite women, which make for eternal, glorious, peaceful and plentiful living.[23]

This mind-boggling mode of life, that is no doubt irresistible to the prospective martyr, also has a spiritual side. The *shahid* is considered a mediator for others to gain admission to Paradise, for after his death he can 'lobby' for others before the highest in Heaven. This striving on behalf of others, known in Islam as *shafa'a*, which for the most part has been reserved as a prerogative of the Prophet himself in Muslim tradition, was expanded to the martyr by scholars like Abu Talib, the Meccan, and the famous scholar and mystic, al-Ghazali.[24] It is precisely this combination of sublime living and superior spiritual power which makes martyrdom a very sought-after and enviable status in normative Islam, let alone among the fundamentalist militants, whose sensitivity and proclivity to these promises makes them so popular and adulated, and role models to follow. If this needs to be stressed once again, this is what elevates the Islamikaze above and beyond regular fighters, and certainly distinguishes them from plain suicidal types or murderers in the eyes of non-Muslim societies. Under these cultural circumstances, martyrdom reads not as a hasty murderous act by a deranged individual who could not find his place in society, but as a supreme act by a worthy and chosen individual, who attains in one stroke what the living, even the most pious among them, cannot achieve by a lifetime of good deeds and saintly practices.

As Fat'hi Shqaqi, the secretary general of the jihad group,[25] explained in a press interview regarding 'suicide bombing', in which he essentially repeated all the elements already discussed above :

> Our battle with the enemy inside Palestine is to open to all possible jihad methods and likelihoods, including martyrdom operations... The enemy thought that by signing the Oslo Accords he had closed the Palestinian file and was about to liquidate it, a fact which demands from us a special effort to

foil the plot. Hence the importance of martyrdom operations at this stage... As to Iranian support, it consists in the main of help to the families of the martyrs and the prisoners... Other than that, the Iranian support is just political and moral...

The young people who started Islamic Jihad in Palestine in the early 1980s were young people from primary and secondary schools... I was one of the young people who felt extreme bitterness and sorrow following the 1967 defeat... It shook us because it threw us into a bottomless pit... During that time, I and others... lost all our balance... We could not do anything then other than cling to Allah as a means of getting out of the impasse and restoring our psychological balance... The idea of Islamic Jihad emerged later and matured during our studies in Egypt in the 1970s...

As to Sayyid Qut'b, his influence on our generation is beyond dispute... The Islamic Jihad movement also works for the unification of the Arab and Islamic efforts towards Palestine while at the same time preaching Islam and its creed, laws, culture and discipline, and the revival of its cultural message to the nation and to mankind alike, and work for its emergence and triumph... These objectives fall within the framework of our realization of the growing link and dialogue between the confrontation with Zionism and imperialism, and the revival of the nation, for it would not be possible for us to accomplish the Islamic revival plan without the question of the liberation of Palestine being the nucleus of such a plan and the ground of its basic battle...

Israel is an imperialist entity... founded on expansionism... It is also an imperialist base and an ally and partner of the West, and helps to facilitate the West's penetration into the Arab and Islamic fold, to dominate it and loot its wealth... It is true that the material balance of power is not in our favor... But this should not prevent us from striking a balance of terror with the enemy. Here lies the significance of the martyrdom operations which prove that the unjust balances of power are not eternal... and that we possess the option of fighting rather than surrendering... Change is undoubtedly coming, for it is a divine law and way. So it is better that change should find us steadfast in our positions, rather than on our knees bearing the document of capitulation before the Zionist entity and NATO.[26]

The above quotes, from Islamic sources or from those directly involved in Islamikaze activities, certainly provide the Islamic rationale for their acts. What is missing is the formal religious-legal sanction lending a stamp of approval to these thoughts, and to the Islamikaze's daring operations in which many innocent victims fall. Such approvals have been pronounced by several scholars of the Holy Law under the form of fatwa (a religiously binding verdict). The next chapter will provide a wide selection of some of those spiritual sponsors of Islamikaze, but here it suffices to cite one of them, Yussef al-Qardawi, who published a 2,000-word dissertation headed by the unequivocal judgement that 'Martyrdom Operations in Occupied Palestine Represent one of the Greatest Forms of Jihad for the Sake of Allah'.[27] The link that was missing for the Islamikaze to launch their acts, namely the fatwa, was necessitated by the fact that Islam usually proscribes suicide, as explained above, since the soul given by Allah cannot be taken away by the unilateral act of a mortal Believer. Qardawi recognizes the Qur'anic injunction, 'Make not your own hand contribute to your destruction.' He also acknowledges the consensus among most Muslim jurists to the effect that near-suicidal attacks by one man against a large number of the enemy are allowed when the perpetrator believes he has a good chance of staying alive, or if he believes he can inflict a substantial loss on the enemy, although his own death is certain. And he concludes :

> Calling these operations suicidal is an erroneous and misleading description. They are sacrificial and heroic, and as martyrdom operations they are totally detached from the concept of suicide. A suicide takes his own life, but this one in question kills himself for the sake of his religion and nation. A suicidal is a person who despaired of himself and of Allah, but this mujtahid is full of faith in Allah's mercy and beneficience.
>
> Israeli society is a military society [hence the permission to strike at it]. Its men and women are soldiers in its army and can be summoned up for service at any moment. If a child or an old person is killed in these operations, this is not intentional but accidental. The necessities of warfare permit [normally] forbidden actions...
>
> All we ask is that these martyrdom operations be carried out after careful consideration. It is best if they are undertaken through the collective intellectual effort [*ijtihad*] of reliable

Muslims. If they decide that there is benefit in going ahead, they should do so and place their trust in Allah.[28]

NOTES

1. For the following discussion I am indebted to my colleague, Dr Daphne Burdman, a Jerusalem psychiatrist, who has been pursuing research on Islamic terrorism.
2. Ibid.
3. For this discussion, see R. Israeli, 'Islamikaze and their Significance', *Journal of Terrorism and Political Violence*, Vol. 9, No. 3, (Autumn 1997), pp. 96–121.
4. Bernard Lewis, *The Assassins*, New York: Basic Books, 1968, p. 48. See also, Ignaz Goldziher, *Muhammedanische Studien*, Halle, 1989, p. 387; A.J. Wensick, 'The Oriental Doctrine of the Martyrs', in Med Akad, *The Martyrs*, Amsterdam, 1921, Series A, No. 6, p. 1; and S.G. Hodgson, *The Order of Assassins*, The Hague, 1955, pp. 133–6.
5. Kamikaze, literally 'Winds of the Gods', was applied to a strong prevailing wind off the Japanese coast. By extension, kamikaze referred to the storms that twice destroyed much of the invading Mongol armadas off the northwestern coast of Kyushu and forced the rest to withdraw back to Korea, in 1274 and again in 1281. To the Japanese, the storms represented divine intervention. The myth of the kamikaze was picked up in World War II to designate the units of human bombers trained by the Japanese army to create disarray in the American armadas of aircraft-carriers and destroyers in the Pacific, which were coming dangerously close to the Japanese Islands, while the Imperial army, navy and airforce lay in tatters and were unable to stop the imminent American invasion. See *Kodansha Encyclopedia of Japan* (Tokyo and New York: Kodansha, 1983), p. 126.
6. See *Al-Watan al-'Arabi*, London, article translated and cited by *Ha'aretz*, 28 June 1996, p. 6b.
7. According to current estimates, the Pashtun (or Patan) make up just about 50 per cent of the total local population of some 20 million, and they occupy the southern part of the country as well as the adjacent border area with Pakistan where several million of them live. In the north it is Tajik country with about 20–30 per cent of the population, and the rest are minorities such as the Shi'ite Hazara, Uzbeks, Turkemans and others. Many of the latter were organized in the Northern Coalition which fought the Taliban Government (1996–2001), and supported the US onslaught on Afghanistan in late 2001.
8. See Israeli, 'Islamikaze and their Significance'.
9. *Kol Ha'ir*, Jerusalem, 20 April 1995, p. 45.
10. See n. 1.
11. *Ta'zia* is the 'Ashura Day acting of the massacre of Hussein, the Third Imam of the Shi'a, and the second son of the Caliph 'Ali, who was assassinated with his retinue by Yazid, the son of Mu'awiyya, the founding father of the Umayyad Dynasty in Damascus, and the challenger of Ali's rule. That event, which occurred in AD 680 in the vicinity of Karbalah, a town in southern Iraq, has triggered the transformation at the end of the seventh century of Shi'ite Islam, from a dissident political group vying for the legitimacy of Ali's rule, into a religious movement. It is important to note that the whole idea of martyrdom via individual acts of self-immolation has ever since been a hallmark of the Shi'ites. The medieval 'Assassins' discussed above were Ismai'li Shi'ites, and the first followers of this tradition in the contemporary world were the Hizbullah Shi'ites, trained and indoctrinated by Shi'ite Iran. Only later did Muslims of the Sunnite majority denomination adopt this sinister idea.
12. Israel TV, Channel 1 (in Hebrew), 18:00 GMT, 9 December 1994.
13. In Islamic folk representation of Paradise, which is often supported by popular religious sheikhs and citations from Islamic sources, the martyr may freely mingle

with the virgins of Paradise (*huriya*), some say as many as 72 of them each, and after each sexual intercourse the girls miraculously regain their virginity in order to afford the martyr a continuous virginal pleasure. So it goes for alcohol, the other major taboo in Islamic society, since Shari'a does not apply in Heaven.

14. Palestinian refugee camps in Lebanon which had suffered during the civil war there (1975–86) and the Israeli incursion in 1982, and thereafter under Israeli reprisals and Palestinian infighting.

15. I am indebted for this text, in its Arabic version, to my colleague Meir Bar-Asher from the Hebrew University, Jerusalem.

16. Like the preceding song, this one was also widely distributed by Hamas sympathizers on audio cassette in 1994–5. See preceding note.

17. See the Repentence Sura, Verse 38. On the attitude of the Prophet to death in battle, see Thomas O'Shaughnessy, *Muhammad's Thoughts on Death*, Leiden: Brill, 1969, pp. 61–6.

18. Ragnar Eklund, *Life Between Death and Resurrection According to Islam*,Uppsala: Brill, 1941, pp. 4–6.

19. See Ibn abi-'Isam, *Kitab al-Jihad* (the Book of Jihad), Al-Madina, 1989, Vol. 2, p. 533 (Hadith No. 204).

20. Adam's Sura; see also the Repentence Sura.

21. See the Repentence Sura, verses 20–22.

22. For Hadith regarding the position of the *shahid* in Paradise, see Wensick, 'The Oriental Doctrine', pp. 2–3 and n. 2; and Eklund, *Life Between Death and Resurrection*, pp. 16–20 and n. 11.

23. Abu Abi-'Asem, op. cit., Vol. 1, p. 128, Hadith No. 1.

24. See Wensick, 'The Oriental Doctrine', p. 5; and also Mahmoud Ayoub, *Redemptive Suffering in Islam*, The Hague, 1978, pp. 197–216.

25. Shqaqi was liquidated in Malta in 1995, and the jihad group of which he was head charged Israel with that murder. He was a Palestinian who graduated in science and mathematics from Bir Zeit college in the West Bank, like many other Muslim fundamentalist leaders. In 1968 he joined the Islamic Movement, and in 1974 he enrolled as a medical student in Cairo, where he was arrested on account of his activity when the Egyptian authorities realized he could be dangerous to them, not only to Israel. In 1981, he returned to the West Bank and worked as a doctor before he was detained and deported by Israel in 1988. Since then he founded and led the Islamic Jihad from Damascus until his assassination.

26. Excerpts from a long interview that Shqaqi gave to the London-based *Al-Sharq al-Awsat* (the Middle East), 17 March 1995, p. 10.

27. See FBIS-NES-96-132, 9 July 1996. Leaders of the Hamas and other like-minded groups also circulated in the West Bank and Gaza similar fatwas, that will be dealt with below.

28 . Ibid.

4. The Doctrine of Islamikaze

Wensinck has demonstrated the resemblance between the Christian and Muslim doctrines of martyrology, down to small details and to the parallel development of the two. He has also shown that the ancient roots of both go back to the Jewish monotheistic concepts of death and martyrdom for the sake of God (*kiddush Hashem*), and also took in philosophical and ascetic elements from Hellenic tradition, all anchored in the pre-monotheistic pagan world.[1] Incidentally, even the etymological transition from the Qur'anic *shahid* as a witness into the self-sacrificing martyr of later times,[2] as already pointed out in Chapter 3, can be traced in Christian tradition as well, inasmuch as the 'witnesses' to the deeds of God in the New Testament developed into martyrs.[3] Even in the rewards of the martyr, both traditions maintain that similarity in so far that in both he is promised an eternal life of bliss in the highest position in Paradise, close to God Himself and above the righteous and regular pious Believers. In both, the martyr is assured of exoneration for his sins and from the torments of the Day of Judgement, and in both, the idea is there of the martyr as the mediator who intercedes before God on behalf of other Believers in order to alleviate the burden of their sins.

Understandably, during the lifetime of the Prophet, and then the expansion of Islam, which sprung out of Arabia and launched the jihad for the conquest of the world (Fat'h – incidentally also the name of the major component faction of the PLO, which set out to conquer Palestine–Israel), the jihad fighters were at their prime and their status in society attained its highest level yet. The martyrs who perished in the battle in consequence acquired precedence over all other Believers. But when the Islamic empire settled down and the fighting zeal receded, at a time when the expansion of Islam was pursued more by Sufi mystics than by illustrious conquerors, the question of martyrdom through other avenues than fighting came to the fore. For example, if the mystic missionary put himself in the service of Islam at great risk, by travelling distances and penetrating uncharted territory, then why was his brand of martyrdom any less than the classic fighter who died in combat? Then, interpretations of martyrdom as the supreme spiritual state of the Believer, who knows how to control his worldly desires and rein in his ambitions and personal interest, began to advance to the forefront as worthy forms of martyrdom. Ghazali, the eminent medieval mystic (d. 1111), was quoted as saying that 'Anyone submitting [Islam = submission to the Will of Allah] totally to Allah in his battle against his desires, is himself a martyr.'[4]

In the contemporary Middle East – due to the vicious conflict opposing the Arab-Muslims to Israel and consequently, in view of the sustaining support the United States of America, and to a lesser extent the rest of the West, are perceived as extending to Israel – there has been a revival of the old notions of martyrdom. It is true that all the Arab casualties of the half-dozen wars that broke out between Israel and its neighbours over the second half of the twentieth century were considered martyrs. However, it was the Hizbullah in Lebanon which gave them the greatest impetus in the last two decades of the century, in the sense that a martyr was no longer a Believer who accidentally died in battle with martyrdom automatically thrust upon him as a mechanical result thereof; a new model of martyrdom was introduced, of the Believer who defied death actively and was ready, if not eager, to die in the process of destroying the enemy: namely the Islamikaze type. The Hizbullah is, of course, the direct product of Shi'ite Islam, the same brand of Islam that rules Iran, therefore one has to look at the trunk in order to comprehend the branches.

Central in Iran as well as in other Shi'ite communities is the re-living of the legendary suffering of Hussein in Karbalah in AD 680, before he was annihilated with his followers by Yazid, the son of the Umayyad founder, Mu'awiyya. The re-enacting of that horror, dubbed *ta'zia*, a sort of passion play, which is performed on 'Ashura Day' by processions of the pious who beat and hurt themselves in an orgy of supreme masochism, is considered the apex of identification with the suffering of Hussein. Suffering as a theme unto itself, including self-inflicted bleeding and death, has become a way of life for the devout Shi'ite: a fashion of expressing selfless sacrifice in honour of the assassinated son of Ali, the first true Imam and successor of the Prophet, who had been neglected by three 'imposter' caliphs who took over power before him. The bitterness of the Shi'ia, the downtrodden and persecuted branch of Islam (in fact, a branch of them in Lebanon called itself the 'downtrodden on Earth', as a sign of distinction, not complaint), is best expressed in the anger and rush toward self-sacrifice, on the one hand, and the posthumous glorification of the martyrs after their death, on the other. Thus, young Iranians were encouraged to clear minefields during the first Gulf War (1980–88), with 'keys to Paradise' hanging on their innocent necks; their parents were congratulated, not consoled, by family friends for the martyrdom of their children, and all those horrendous sacrifices were immortalized in the memorial for the martyrs in Teheran, a water fountain coloured in blood-red, which symbolizes and eternalizes the endless flow of suffering and blood.

Naturally, those groomed in such a culture cannot be expected to recoil from the ultimate act of suffering, that is death. Quite the contrary, the stream of the Islamikaze has never dried up in Iran, and it is diverted to flow in other lands of Islam. The attractive rationale reads:

> The skies are shrouded in black, rivers of tears are flowing, Hussein arrives in Karbalah to sacrifice himself for Allah. This is the 'Ashura story', lend your ears to listen to its sadness, let your tears flow for the King of the Martyrs, because he will bring you to Paradise.[5]

These are lyrics to one of the songs which comprise one of the mourning 'musical-passions' which are re-enacted in Iran and elsewhere to commemorate the martyrdom of Hussein. These re-enactments, and the generally militant demands by the Shi'ites for their rights and for justice, went into abeyance or adopted a low profile for centuries (a state of *intidhar* – namely waiting and expectation), due to the principle of *Taqqiya* (dissimulation), which was adopted after the mysterious disappearance (not death) of the Twelveth Imam (hence Twelver Shi'ia), as a defensive measure of self-preservation in a hostile environment. That state of expectation for the return of the absent Imam provided the entire rationalization and driving power behind Twelver Shi'ism, inasmuch as it encouraged the Believers to suffer and wait, for the more they waited and suffered, the closer was deemed his return (like the 'pangs of the Messiah' in Judaism), but if anyone, at any time, claimed to be the Imam, he was immediately repulsed and condemned as an imposter, and treated accordingly.

The last decades of the twentieth century, however, saw the ideological and political quantum jump effected by the Shi'a, under the revolutionary impulse of Ayatullah Khomeini and his like. The nature of the change, which has taken the Shi'a from passivity and expectation to activity and aggression, namely making the human will predominate over fate or over the 'natural course of events', is indeed nothing short of revolutionary. This is inherent in Shi'ite theology, which recognizes the head of the clerical hierarchy as the *marja' taqlid*, the supreme reference who commands the emulation of the Believers. In fact this major figure, who gains his superior status through his scholarship and religious authority, is the supreme *mujtahid*, the 'striver', to interpret the will of the Hidden Imam who is the actual ruler of the world. The *mujtahid* thus acquires in the Shi'a the power of legislator, and his rulings are the law. This is the reason why Khomeini spoke about *wilayat faqih* (the rule of the jurist), for only such Heaven- and Imam-inspired jurists, who are the upper echelon of the mullahs, could be clairvoyant enough to detect the Truth and pass it on to others. Khomeini himself wrote that 'only the mullahs are able to take people to the streets and motivate them to die for Islam, and bring them to beg that they be allowed to spill their blood for Islam'.[6]

The new activism, brought about by the Islamic Revolution in Iran, has taken up the tragic death of Hussein, which used to be viewed as a murderous and cowardly act sustained by that greatest of martyrs, and remembered throughout the years by the low-profile followers of the Shi'a, and rendered it into an active declaration of war against injustice, which has to be initiated out loud and pursued in earnest by Hussein's followers. In this context, Hussein becomes not someone to be mourned, but a heroic leader in battle and a model worthy of emulation on the way to Paradise. He, the paradigm of martyrdom, will intercede on behalf of his followers to ensure the admission to heaven of the new generations of martyrs. Hence, we learned of the flocking of millions of adults and children to the mosques in Tehran when the war with Iraq broke out, and a call for volunteers to the Front was sounded by the government. The demand for martyrdom by far exceeded the needs of the military. Children were urged to go to the Front without their parents' permission, and were used to clear minefields in a deadly trance that the naive and unsuspecting young and inexperienced minds were easily swept under. They expressed their happiness at 'rushing to Paradise in unison with their friends', under the promise that in Paradise, too, they would be able to unite and pursue their worldly worry-free life.

The eagerness for death through martyrdom in that culture often prompts young Iranian demonstrators to join processions covered by their death shrouds to signify that not only do they defy death, but they are also ready for it. They were swept under the magic rhetoric of their leader, whom some saw as the Imam, that is, an incarnation of the Hidden one, when he said that life was illusory and merely a corridor to the real life in Paradise, therefore it was not worth living. The re-enactment of the martyrdom of Hussein, which in Iran has involved a real change in the *ta'zia* ceremonies on 'Ashura Day', has also transcended Iran's boundaries and been made a model for other Shi'ites, such as in Lebanon where Hizbullah in particular, and the Amal Shi'ites in general, have adopted the same style. Moreover, the Hizbullah, the active long arm of Iran in its quest to internationalize the Iranian Islamic Revolution, has been adopting a militant and aggressive stance in its pursuance. It not only routinely uses violence on the Israeli–Lebanese borders, but is known to aid terrorism across the world against Israeli and Jewish interests, such as blowing up the Jewish Community Centre and the Israeli Embassy in Buenos Aires, or its close co-operation with the Palestinian Intifadah, both in co-ordinating joint operations against Israel and in direct involvement in arms supplies, instruction to violence and terrorist warfare.

Above all, however, the doctrine of the Islamikaze, that is, active death in martyrdom, was revived by the Hizbullah in Lebanon. The first acts were performed in the early 1980s against US and Israeli presence in Lebanon, but as the Israeli presence in the southern part of that country wore on, those operations were intensified until they became the routine trademark of the violent encounters between Israelis and the Hizbullah, usually at the initiative of the latter. It took another decade or so before that mode of action was emulated by other Muslim terrorist groups, most notoriously the Sunnite Hamas, and to a lesser extent, Islamic Jihad. All it took for the transition to take place was for fundamentalist Sunnite scholars, such as Sheikh al-Qardawi, whose doctrine was mentioned above and will be discussed below in more detail, to provide the missing link between the 'natural' vying for suffering that fundamentalist Shi'ism has inherited from the *ta'zia* tradition and practice, and which pushed martyrdom to the top of the individual's striving to emulate the slain Imam Hussein, and the general Islamic hallowed idea of martyrdom and its rewards, not with the goal of self-inflicted pain, but aimed at inflicting damage on the enemy, even at the cost of one's life. The long succession of fatwas delivered to fill this gap, which will be cited and discussed below, has indeed provided the rationalization for the mostly Sunnite Islamikaze groups to launch their deadly attacks.

It is quite amazing indeed to watch the Sunnite fundamentalist groups adopt the Shi'ite ways, not only by embracing the Iranian and Hizbullah mode of operation, something that has been evinced in the collaboration of Iran and the Hizbullah with the Hamas and the Islamic Jihad, and the latter with the al-Qa'ida network, but also by creating their own version of the supreme sacrifice and suffering inherent in the *ta'zia*, only in reverse. In the field of battle and terrorism for the sake of Allah, we have seen 19 members of al-Qa'ida committing collective Islamikaze acts within one hour of each other on US soil, on 11 September 2001. Al-Qa'ida fighters in Afghanistan defied death in the face of US airpower, as do Hamas and Islamic Jihad operatives in the Palestinian Authority, or the fanatic *Gama'at* in Egypt, or the Abu Sayyaf group in the Philippines, or the Muslim terrorists in Kashmir and India Proper, or the fundamentalists in Algeria who slay their own compatriots with the same senseless and blind zeal as they do when they attack foreigners. This universalization of Sunni Muslim terrorism also carries with it a growing daring in the operations, to the extent of its banalization in the face of its frequency and diffusion. Not only the massive Islamikaze attack on 11 September, with probably more to come, but especially the almost daily such attacks in Israel and against its civilians by Hamas and Islamic Jihad, have rendered these harrowing acts routine, to the point that they risk becoming accepted as 'part of life', as if they were God-ordained and impervious to human preventive initiative.

Even more worrisome, however, is that the non-Shi'ite fundamentalist groups do not content themselves with getting closer to the Shi'ites in terms of audacity, sophistication and the spread of Islamikaze worldwide. They are able to capitalize on being Sunnis, like most of their compatriots, in order to draw into the circle of self-sacrificing terrorists other groups, like the *Tanzim* or the Popular Front among the Palestinians, who are not avowedly fundamentalists or Muslim zealots. It is quite extraordinary to watch members of the Marxist-oriented Popular Front talking of jihad and *istishhad* (martyrdom) when they set out for their operations. They realize the high status of the Islamikaze in their society, and since they act against the same enemy as the Hamas, they seem to have no compunction about gaining popularity through the usage of the fundamentalist vocabulary and discourse. The Sunni Islamikaze are edging towards their Iranian model not only ideologically, as we shall see in the following pages, but even in the mores and patterns of behaviour. For example, the headgear around the foreheads of the Hamas people parading in the streets of the Palestinian Authority, under the permissive eyes of its security forces and often in collaboration with it; the video cassettes they leave behind as their will and parting speech on leaving their loved ones, which are often used by their operators as a 'patrimony' to preserve and as an 'educational' tool to recruit others; and the slogans, citations from the Holy Scriptures, and words of praise about martyrdom and the martyrs, are all ominous imitations of the Shi'ite model.

Most intriguing, however, is the counter-example of the Sunnite *ta'zia* in reverse, widely and repeatedly practised by the Hamas, and perhaps by others, too. We have seen that Shi'ite martyrdom was closely associated with suffering and bitterness, first out of passive identification with the supreme martyr – Imam Hussein – and then, even after the Islamic Revolution pushed the protest into the domain of action, and the *ta'zia* grew more aggressive and became a rallying point for the martyrs, it remained essentially a self-pitying, introspective, self-sustained, self-consoling and 'within-the-family' sort of affair. Within the Hamas and the Islamic Jihad, a new pattern has developed to re-play, re-emphasize, boast about and delight in the suffering they inflict on their victims. Indeed, every now and then, especially when the Palestinian Authority allows these acts or fails to intervene for fear of the populace, and especially following major acts of terrorism which left dozens of Israelis dead or maimed, local chapters of the Hamas set up processions to mark the event. With their headgear of the hallowed *shahid*, slogans of martyrdom shouted and brandished, Israeli and US flags burned and puppets representing Israeli and US leaders stabbed by a frantic crowd, they arrive at the end of the procession, during which, invariably, they shoot wildly in the air with the illegal weapons they should not possess or handle in the first place, and then the harrowing orgy of 'celebrations' begins.

We have become 'accustomed' to the horrendous sights of Palestinians, and other Muslims, deliriously and ecstatically exhibiting outlandish eruptions of jubilation when news breaks regarding a 'successful' terrorist attack against the United States (as in the Twin Towers and the Pentagon), against Israel or Jews at large, with no one in sight to rein them in. On those occasions, they distribute sweets, dance in the streets, cry slogans of 'Allah Akbar!!!', the war-cry of Muslims in general, as if to attribute to Him those great deeds against their sworn enemies, or go into the repetitive ritual of burning the flags of their victims or trampling them under their feet. What the demonstrators in person are unable to deal to their enemies, they perform symbolically, praising Allah for His intercession on their behalf. But few outsiders have paid attention to the makeshift stages, erected at the terminal of those processions, which bring to their climax the celebrations. Often, the latest target they destroyed, for example an Israeli bus loaded with dozens of passengers on board, is meticulously reconstructed in paper, cardboard and cloth, painted so as to imitate the original, and then set ablaze to the lunatic cries of delight of the watching crowds. All the while, the perpetrators of the actual horror against the real Israeli bus, or more often their successors, who wished to cultivate the 'heritage' of the deceased Islamikaze, run around the stage in frenzy, shoot long bursts in the air as if possessed by some other-worldly power, shout blood-chilling war cries, repeatedly invoke the Power of Allah, smash the burned carcass of the bus and stab with their bayonets the 'remnants' of the slain 'passengers', whom they, or their fellow kamikaze, had earlier slain in reality.

Even these horrendous scenes, taken from a different reality than the one known to civilized people, can be 'improved upon' by the Hamas. In Nablus, during the Palestinian Intifadah that broke out in October 2000, a most disturbing 'exhibition' was presented to the general public in the city public square, which showed in inhuman detail the replicas of blown-up limbs and body pieces of Israelis who had perished in a restaurant attack by Hamas Islamikaze. It was only the reports of the deeply disgusted foreign correspondents, and the protests of the Israelis who did not want to relive that horror by seeing it replicated on the screens, which convinced the Palestinian Authority to move the exhibition indoors, not to close it down and arrest its promoters. Once again the thermometer was broken, but the fever refused to vanish. It is understood that by widening the scope of the viewers of those scenes among the Muslims, to the point of rendering them a sort of popular street theatre, even among the majority of quietist Muslims, most of whom do not belong to the fundamentalist hardcore, the organizers came to elicit respect and esteem for the deceased heroes, to encourage the *shahids* of tomorrow who are bound to emulate them, and to facilitate recruitment of new Islamikaze in the future.

In other words, unlike the inward-turning stories of suffering re-enacted by the Shi'ites for the sake of commemoration, identification and self-hardening in order to stand the excruciating things to come, the Hamas hardens its crowds and cultivates its audiences by boasting about the gruesome suffering inflicted upon the enemies. This change of focus, or a *ta'zia* in reverse, emanates from the difference between the Shi'ite universal doctrine of *istishhad* as the ultimate way to identify spiritually with Hussein, and the Hamas, whose most urgent goal is to bring down its enemy. In Palestinian thinking, the most atrocious injustice was done to them by Israel by its very birth and continued existence. For its presence in their midst and vicinity exposes their own helplessness and haplessness. They and Israel had begun from the same departure-point half a century ago, but while their sworn enemy has progressed, settled down its refugees, prospered and advanced to the forefront of modernity and technology, they are still rotting in refugee camps for the third generation, the gap between them and Israel continues to widen, and their refugees have remained dependent upon UN flour supplies and foreign aid (ironically US and Western, and less Arab and Islamic).

There is nothing more humiliating for the Palestinians than that. Therefore they hate Israel, who shows to them what they had failed to achieve by not following her example, and they spurn the United States to whom they must turn as beggars to improve their lot. In consequence, rather than striving to equal Israel in order to eliminate their dependence on the United States, they would rather attack them both in order to bring them down and wipe out their constructive model which constantly exposes them to shame. That is the reason why, when the Oslo process was at its hopeful beginnings, it was the fundamentalist Hamas who rejected it, lock, stock and barrel, for fear that it might reinforce and eternalize the superior stature of Israel, which they could neither bear nor reconcile themselves to. The ensuing demonization of Jews, Zionists and Israel, and the legitimization of ruthless attacks against them, as demonstrated in the recurrent Islamikaze onslaughts in Israeli city streets aimed at intimidating the Israelis and wrecking their economy, are part of the mechanism of this externalized *ta'zia* in reverse, which focuses on the suffering inflicted on the enemies, instead of extolling their own suffering and sacrifice. The Twin Towers horror, also inflicted by Sunnite Islamikaze (al-Qa'ida is one of their organizations), can therefore be interpreted in the same vein. Bin-Laden himself, not to mention other Muslims throughout the world (see Chapter 1), was shown delighting in humiliating the United States and helping to bring her down, as he had hoped.

The paradox is that while in Shi'ite Islam, notably after the end of the first Gulf War (1988), acts of Islamikaze were restrained after they had peaked in the 1980s, it was precisely then that they were picked up by the Hamas and other Sunnite groups. In Lebanon, where it all started, the Hizbullah leadership had come to the conclusion that the exaggerated use of over-zealous youth for those acts had often ended in the death of the perpetrator without inflicting enough casualties on the enemy to justify that sacrifice. The head of the movement, Sheikh Fadlallah, has even issued a fatwa allowing acts of Islamikaze only on special occasions.[7] Sheikh Na'im Qassem, the Deputy Secretary of Hizbullah, translated the guideline of his spiritual leader into specific directives, which he issued to the organization and released to the public in a press interview:

> First, one must obtain the authorization of an accredited mufti. Anyone seeking to sacrifice himself, especially by car-bomb or blowing himself up, must first consult with a lawyer of the Holy Law, because the soul is dear and can be expended only for the sake of the Islamic *umma*.
>
> Secondly, after the religious authority delivers its verdict, the political leadership of the movement must deliberate on the political and military merits thereof. For when the same goals can be obtained without self-sacrifice, we do not send any Islamikaze to his death. The Islamikaze act is efficient only when other means are not deemed [by the leadership] to attain the same results.[8]

True, when the Islamikaze martyrdom was adopted by the Palestinians in the 1990s, there were tremendous debates among Palestinian scholars of the Holy Law whether they should be sanctioned. Dr Hamza Mustafa, the Head of the Shari'a College at Al-Quds University, and himself a member of the Jerusalem-based Supreme Islamic Council, was emphatic in a press interview:

Allah has determined that whoever commits suicide will end up in Hell. It is clear that suicide is unreservedly prohibited, because his soul is not his private property but belongs to Allah. There are those who believe that when suicide is committed as part of an act of war against the enemy, it is not forbidden, but most believe that suicide is prohibited in any case.[9]

It was therefore believed at that time that while the tiny Islamic Jihad group did opt for Islamikaze bombings as part of its world-view of self-sacrifice,[10] the larger and more popular Hamas did not encourage its membership to engage in this kind of operation. Sheikh Jamil Tamimi, one of the leaders of the Muslim Movement in the West Bank, for example, was often quoted as totally opposing these acts, not only due to the loss of life involved, but mainly because of the categorical prohibition against self-immolation in Islam. He recognized that some Muslim scholars did permit this sort of operation in the context of war and of struggle against the enemy, though he emphasized that he personally was opposed to this interpretation.[11] At the same time, however, Izz a-Din al-Qassam,[12] a hallowed name and symbol for both the Hamas and the Islamic Jihad, was cited as urging his followers to martyrdom, because 'martyrdom is only the beginning of the road...jihad is either victory or martyrdom'.[13] 'Victory or martyrdom' as a slogan and battle-cry naturally encouraged and led people to sacrifice themselves. Indeed, after the first Islamikaze act against Israelis in Beit Lid in 1994, perpetrated by Islamic Jihad, one of the Gaza mosques' loudspeakers proclaimed: 'Islamic Jihad has announced long ago that we have hundreds of volunteers for martyrdom, ready at any minute to hurt the Zionist enemy and burn the land under his feet.'[14]

So, while no one of authority in Islam permits suicide *per se*, those who allow, indeed urge, the martyr to sacrifice his life use precisely the commonly held view that the soul belongs to Allah and one should facilitate its return to Him. Thus we are not talking here of a suicide, nor of an accidental or incidental death incurred during battle, which is commonly dubbed *istishhad* (martyrdom) even when the martyr did not willingly and by choice embrace it, but of an *'amalyya istishhadiyya* (an act of martyrdom), meaning that the individual has taken the conscious decision to sacrifice his life for the Islamic cause. In this case, the martyr has considered his act as imperative to achieve his goal, he has 'purposely thrown himself to his death, confident that he is rushing to Paradise'.[15] And since he neither wished nor prepared any way of retreat, he has no other choice than to perish together with his targeted, or incidental, victims. Even the above-described Islamic Jihad's eagerness for martyrdom is, however, limited by the prohibition to kill innocent people, and the essence of the matter then becomes the definition of who is right and who is wrong, who is innocent and who is the culprit. At any rate, the struggle of the Islamikaze has become so sustained that differences between Hamas and Islamic Jihad on the one hand, and the nuances distinguishing the innocent from the culprit on the other, have been totally blurred. Moreover, as already pointed out, other Palestinian organizations, which had thus far nothing to do with the Islamikaze, have been joining that effort of martyrdom.

The author of the *Readings in Islamic Martyrology*,[16] which will be extensively dealt with below, indeed addresses himself to these basic dilemmas. He cites Shari'a sources which negate suicide, taken from the Qur'an, through the authoritative collection of Hadith edited by Bukhari, and finally decrees that it is unlawful for any Muslim to commit suicide by poison, by jumping from a high place, by stabbing, by suffocation, by cutting main arteries in the hands or neck, under the threat of punishment in Hell. He determines that Islam prohibits suicide out of despair from life, or to avoid suffering due to illness or injury, or to debt, poverty, fear, disaster, imprisonment or torture. Killing others can only be undertaken 'justly', based on a Qur'anic injunction, namely for adultery, murder or apostasy, and against those who deserted the company of the Believers.[17] By avoiding generalizations and overarching and abstract principles, and keeping strictly faithful to the detailed cases of prohibition mentioned in the sources, the writer of *Qira'a* thus prepares his readers to conclude that everything that is not expressly forbidden is allowed.

The most fascinating aspect of these prohibitions is that they rest on the strict requirement grounded in the Qur'an[18] regarding the sanctity of human life, and the superior role of humans in Allah's creation. It is fascinating because it stands in stark contradiction to the seemingly unbearable facility with which the Islamikaze kill themselves, and much more others. The resolution of this contradiction is the whole innovative import of the new, convoluted interpretations undertaken by fundamentalist Muslim scholars. Man was created, according to the *Qira'a*, with the belief in Allah imprinted in his heart, and all his strength and spirit are devoted to the straightening out of the created world. In order to guide man to follow the right path, Allah sent Prophets, apostles and His Messenger Muhammad, together with the Qur'an and the Sunna. Hence, the purpose of man on earth is to worship Allah (*'ibadat Allah*), which is more important even than human life. However, these two themes of the sanctity of human life and the worship of Allah are not contradictory.

This world is the scene of the struggle between good and bad, between the worship of God and the worship of Satan, the choice between a life of belief and the option of disbelief. The right choice by man of Truth in this world will bring him to eternal life in Paradise. Namely, if man devotes his life in this world to worshipping Allah, he will end up in eternal life in the Hereafter. Thus, the laws of jihad not only do not contradict the prohibitions of self-immolation and of killing others unjustifiably, but are even complementary to them. And this is precisely what makes Islam a perfect religion in terms of its regard for human life: namely, the preservation of human life, on the one hand, but also self-sacrifice for the sake of Allah, on the other. For, contrary to other doctrines which permit killing in the pursuit of material benefit, Islam preaches the value of human life; and, contrary to the theories that regard human life as a supreme value, Islam puts forward value of the worship of Allah. Therefore, in the final analysis, according to this logic, setting human life as the supreme value permits injustice to persist without opposition, thus *eo ipso* violating human dignity. Conversely, the worship of Allah, which applies the tenets of making justice and upholding right (*iqamat al-'adl wa-ihqaq al-haqq*), in itself constitutes the delicate balance, between these two values. This kind of balance, which exists only in Islam, puts it as the supreme human and cultural model in existence.

Naturally, when the author of this dissertation posits the worship of Allah as supreme, and the way of jihad as the superior apex of worship, he inescapably comes to the conclusion that any Believer who follows divine guidance with regard to jihad and emulates the Prophet in this respect must evince his willingness to die for Allah.[19] To support his conclusion, the author refers to a famous Hadith, where the Prophet undertook to die for Allah, come back to life and then die once again.[20] This means that there was no bigger goal in the Prophet's own existence than to die for Allah, and repeatedly so. Therefore, this tenet constitutes, in the author's mind, a divine guideline that applies everywhere at all times. Hence the necessity for Believers to embrace the road of self-sacrifice (*tad'hia*) and spiritual devotion (*badhl a-nafs*) becomes a central motif in the author's concept of jihad. He recounts many episodes from the life of the Prophet where the latter proved his devotion to these themes in his jihad battles against his enemies.[21] This had necessitated the Prophet's readiness, indeed eagerness, to die in the course of jihad, which should be the standard behaviour for all Muslims who seek battle at the highest level of risk, and are eager to take that risk and sacrifice themselves. For this purpose, the author recognizes three kinds of battles, which must be graduated in accordance with the level of risk involved:

1. Where the chances to die or to emerge alive are even. In this case, the surviving fighter would deserve honour (*karama*), and if he should perish, his death would be considered martyrdom (*shahada*). An illustrious Muslim fighter, Khalid ibn al-Walid, was quoted as wondering every day of battle whether he was escaping from the day of *karama* or that of *shahada*. That meant that dying in this fashion was a winning proposition in any case.[22]

2. Where the balance of power is in the Muslims' disfavour, the Muslim fighter needs to display much more audacity to overcome the enemy against all odds. Once again, many of such battles, in which the Companions of the Prophet (*sahaba*) participated, the Messenger of Allah provided a personal example by fighting valiantly and very close to the eye of the storm, in defiance of the dangers the enemy posed to him. Such harsh battles – where some of the *sahaba* made the ultimate sacrifice after they sustained so many multiple wounds that their corpses became unrecognizable[23] – of course set the high standards of combat to be followed by other Believers.

3. A third category of battle is when self-sacrifice is not only hallowed, as in the previous examples, but when it becomes imperative as the only way to win it. This is where the act of jihad, itself highly regarded and lavishly rewarded in Heaven, transcends into the domain of an act of martyrdom (*istishhad*). The difference between standard self-sacrifice and spiritual devotion on the one hand, and this sort of conscious and deliberate act of martyrdom on the other, is that here a special strategy is adopted by a special group of Muslims in order to

rescue the entire Muslim army, or the whole of the Muslim *umma*, from dangerous straits, or with a view to disrupting the enemy's war plans or sow disarray in its ranks, or is geared to hurt the enemy's morale and boost the Muslims', or is likely to bring such a disaster upon the enemy as to increase his losses and decrease the Muslims'.

It is easy to guess that the latter mode of combat is assuredly the highest and most adulated, and conforms typologically to the Islamikaze *modus operandi* that we have been dealing with in this work. We learn from the author of the treatise that he regards Islamikaze not as a current, normal and routine strategy to fight the enemy in the battlefield where massive armies are deployed, but as a tactical device to be used when regular, conventional battles are to no avail or about to be lost, and only when no other avenues are open to the Muslim armies to win the battles. In this context, we may digress to find grounds to interpret the Twin Towers disaster, or the daily attacks by the Hamas and Islamic Jihad against Israel, when the Palestinian Intifadah had failed to bring Israel to its knees. It is also noteworthy that when Yasser Arafat came to the end of his wits, when he realized that his declared campaign against Israel was falling flat on its face and despaired of gaining anything in his campaign of terror, he personally joined the fray by stating before delirious and equally despairing crowds that he was ready to be a *shahid* for the sake of 'liberating' Jerusalem, and he repeatedly urged his followers to launch the jihad to realize the evasive dreams of the Palestinians.[24]

In this ultimate model of self-sacrifice too, it is the Prophet himself or his *sahaba*, who, once again, star personally and make daring self-sacrifices to save the entire Muslim strategy in the battlefield from failure – when sacrifice, namely martyrdom, was necessary in order to attain the victory of the Muslim armies, unless victory could be assured without it. From cases of this sort, drawn from the personal histories of the most worthy Muslims at the time of the Prophet, the author infers implicit permission for Muslim fighters to sacrifice themselves for the public interest.[25] This is the stuff that the present-day Islamikaze hang on to, to justify their acts of martyrdom. The author makes very concrete connections between the two: he says that while today the Islamikaze can carry explosives on their bodies in order to carry out their mission, in the times of the Prophet, the audacious fighter threw himself on the swords of the enemy, but both modes of action are essentially the same. Similarly, exactly as in early Islam, valiant Muslim fighters had to dismount from their horses, which were no match for the elephants of the enemy, and proceeded to face those immense and frightening animals with their bare swords in their hands, even though they were trampled upon and slaughtered. So, today, an Islamikaze can defy, with his body, planes and tanks, and perish under their weight, or blow himself up on a minefield in order to facilitate the passage of his fellow fighters into enemy territory, or their retreat into safety, at the price of sacrificing himself. In both cases, the gates of Paradise were wide open to receive the new martyrs.[26]

Thus, the author of this treatise, which gives license to acts of Islamikaze, builds his argument tier after tier: first, he designates the value of the worship of Allah as above the value of human life; then defines the jihad as the supreme form of worship; and, since the jihad involves self-sacrifice, three levels thereof are identified, the highest and most commendable of which is the act of martyrdom. All these stages are widely and soundly grounded on the precedents set by the Prophet himself or his Companions, whom the Believers hold in high esteem and whose model, posed for all generations to come, they cannot dismiss. Moreover, from the examples from early Islam cited by the author, where self-sacrifice was not absolutely necessary,[27] one can deduce that the very defiance of death in the face of the enemy, in a battle for Islam and for Allah, is seen in itself as a worthy act which allows the deceased fighter through the doors of Paradise. Moreover, as the author quotes the Prophet determining that jihad is the 'top of Islam's honey', he asserts that the martyrdom act is the 'top of jihad's honey', thus concluding that the higher the risk of perishing in such an act, the more precious is the martyr's status in the eyes of Allah.[28] To illustrate his point, the author relates a sprinkling of Hadith which demonstrate that, in the eyes of the Prophet, defying death for its own sake is in itself a worthy act, even when it was not absolutely necessary to achieve victory for Islam. For example, he cites the case of a Muslim fighter in the fateful battle of Badr, who removed his armour before the battle and was killed as a result, but he won praise from the Prophet for his audacity.[29]

The author of the treatise does not avoid confronting the contradiction between his sanctification of death and the Qur'anic injunction to preserve life and escape peril. Once again, precedents from the time of the Prophet and his Companions are cited – for example, of the fighter who brought about his own death when he single-handedly attacked an entire Byzantine column, whereupon a discussion ensued about whether that hero did not throw himself at certain death unnecessarily. For the author, again through a tortuous manipulation of Hadith accounts, the real peril is not death in battle, but in turning one's attention to material life and neglecting jihad activity.[30] The same goes for the explicit Qur'anic prohibition against committing suicide,[31] and the author has to perform an intellectual somersault of sorts in order to circumvent the issue and manipulate it to prove his point. He says that while both suicide and the act of martyrdom require the express act of will of the Islamikaze, what matters is not the act, but the intention (*nia*) of the martyr, which is what determines, in the final analysis, the quality of the act. Once again, the literature of the first Muslims is invoked as example and precedent. A case in point is that of a martyr for Islam who appeared on the Day of Judgement and claimed that he fought for Allah, but Allah reminded him that his courage was displayed only so that it could be said of him that he was courageous, whereupon he was 'dragged away on his face and consumed by the fire of Hell'.[32]

This crux of the argument is extremely important, for it leaves everything to the final judgement to Heaven even when a man performs acts of extreme audacity and is considered by his peers, eye-witnesses and contemporaries as a hero of Islam and a well-deserved martyr, it is up to Allah to scrutinize his intention and decide otherwise. Conversely, a man may be considered by other humans to have committed a despicable suicide, but when Allah examines his intentions, he might be rewarded with the highest degree of martyrdom and of status in Paradise. And this is precisely what sets suicide, a flight from the vagaries of life, apart from an act of martyrdom, which is a human response to the call of Allah to sacrifice oneself for the sake of the religion of Allah and to inflict loss on the enemies of Allah. However, there remains the question of whether martyrdom is the domain of the elected few who can cultivate the requisite pious intention, or whether it is given to the choice of every willing individual Muslim. An analogy is suggested by the author with regard to laws of conversion. Muslims are allowed to renege on their faith outwardly, says the essayist, under duress or threat against their lives, as long as in their hearts they do not budge from their creed.[33] However, insists the author, as against that permission (*rukhsa*), there exists also personal resolve ('*azima*), which is admittedly more difficult to pursue and to experience, and consists in refusing to abandon the faith even in the face of certain death. But those who choose this course out of their own resolve, in spite of the allowance made by the Shari'a in cases of imminent peril, of course attain the highest levels of martyrdom and reward.[34] Also, since in every operation against the enemy there is a danger of death, the whole issue is one of the degree of the threat. Any act of martyrdom of the Islamikaze kind carries with it certain death, though everything is ultimately in Allah's hand, and this is what places it at the apex of martyrdom.

This is, in a nutshell, the Doctrine of Martyrdom as viewed by the author of *Qira'a*. The problem remains to discern the circumstances under which this weapon can be used, and to detect the enemy to be targeted for such lofty operations. First of all, the act of martyrdom is an expression of jihad, but since this act is not necessarily initiated by an Islamic state which would lend it legitimacy, and is often necessitated as an act of defence against an enemy who has invaded the Muslims' homes and territory, it rests with individual Muslims to act by force in order to redeem their rights. Therefore, unlike state-led jihad, which is the duty of the entire Islamic polity, in this case it becomes an individual duty (*fard 'ayn*, already mentioned above), to be performed by the Muslims who are closest to the enemy and have access to him. In the case of Palestine, which is the arena discussed specifically by the author, he focuses on the duty of jihad against the combined Judeo-Western onslaught which constitutes a threat to Islam. There, he says, attacks against Muslims are physical: expulsion, killing, wounding and imprisoning; there is the take-over of Muslim Holy Places to replace them with Jewish ones; the Judaization of Muslim land and the violation of the honour of Muslim women; and, especially, the expansion of [Israel], which serves as a launching pad to conquer more Muslim countries, and to form a Western base to 'diffuse Jewish corruption, Westernization, humiliation, enslavement and exploitation of Muslim society'.[35]

These combined actions by the enemy amount to a declaration of war of annihilation against Islam, something which impels any Muslim to take up jihad without waiting for permission from Muslim authorities which do not exist there. Therefore:

The Zionist enemy must be attacked by all means permitted

by the Shari'a, and all possible efforts ought to be expended to that end, not only by the Palestinians but by the entire Muslim *umma*. For Zionism is not a local enemy, it is a universal one, it is the sword that tears apart this blessed land.[36]

This analysis by necessity leads the author to conclude that the actual battle is of the third category, which makes acts of martyrdom imperative and entails an individual commitment by every Muslim to engage the enemy. The current danger to the Muslim *umma* is great both due to the rifts and splits within Muslims on the one hand, and the combined power of the Zionist enemy and his allies on the other. According to the author, the situation of the Muslims today is worse than in Crusader times, therefore jihad in Palestine acquires its own character and requires acts of martyrdom to take precedence over all other modes of warfare. For him, all the prerequisite conditions to launch such acts exist in Palestine with regard to the Zionist enemy, particularly when all other conventional military avenues have proved insufficient or ineffective, in view of the military superiority of the enemy's tactics, equipment and technology. Even laying explosives in enemy targets would not help due to his vigilance, or due to the random effect on victims who may turn out to be women and children.[37]

On the other hand, says he, in an act of martyrdom the explosive is focused on precise targets that cannot be missed. Moreover, due to the interception of weapons and explosives by Israel before they could be activated, it becomes imperative to use the little there is in the most focused and infallible manner, through the Islamikaze. From these harsh words of the essayist one can draw many sad conclusions:

1. The precise targets chosen for these acts of martyrdom, which are supposed to spare children and women, seem to be ignored by the perpetrators, since most of the victims have been women, children and aged people.
2. The more counter-terrorist attacks succeed in paralysing the terrorist organizations (what we call the infra-structure of terror), such as the Hamas and the Islamic Jihad, the more their members will be pushed to resort to acts of Islamikaze.
3. The more frequent the acts of Islamikaze, the more evident the failure of the organizations in the overall campaign.

Another advantage that the author seems to ascribe to the acts of Islamikaze is their effect on morale, inasmuch as:

> ...by Allah's grace, one or two fighters succeed in breaking into the lines of the enemy, then attack a group of the enemy's forces by an act of martyrdom, thereby inflicting on him heavy damage and tottering his morale in the face of the indestructible fighting spirit of the martyrs.

He also asserts that, by this kind of operation, the entire Islamic *umma* is rescued, inasmuch as it minimizes its own casualties, maximizes the enemy's and weakens his ability to retaliate. For the destruction of any part of its force means the corresponding saving of lives of hundreds of Muslim women, children and the aged, and extricating them from his bloody grip. All this is certainly worth sacrificing a few fighters for. It is imperative, however, that those who embrace this road should do it with *nia*, namely not as an escape from life and its vagaries, but with the intention of jihad for Allah, in order to kill the enemies. This is, in fact, he concludes, the best and most economical possible way to engage in jihad in Palestine under the prevailing circumstances.[38]

To sum up this totally amazing doctrine: it first pays lip service to the value of human life but then posits the value of worship of Allah above it, and then, as the highest degree of worship – jihad. It overlooks, dismisses and banalizes the entire humanistic concept of sanctity of life as it is understood in Western tradition. Even though the injunction to self-sacrifice in jihad is divided into three levels of necessity – unnecessary if there is an equilibrium of forces with the enemy; desirable when the balance of forces is in the Muslims' disfavour; and imperative when extreme danger threatens the community – one cannot escape the impression that this edifice of rationalizations is geared, in the final analysis, to dwarf human life and to make it subservient to religious fanaticism. This is borne out by the fact that the author lauds self-immolation in the process of the act of martyrdom, even for its own sake, and even when it is not needed for the success of the operation, for he seems to say that death for Allah, as long as the intention is there, has a special significance and is considered the highest form of martyrdom. Indeed, he speaks about the sanctity of death, which in a very round about, paradoxical way stems from the basic assumption of the sanctity of life. Noteworthy, however, is his reluctance to bind the Muslims in general with such a harrowingly demanding injunction, and he limits it to the few who have attained such a degree of self-sacrifice as to be able to commit it without hesitation, and who would therefore be rewarded in the higher reaches of Paradise.

Characteristic of this treatise is its fundamentalist approach to the sources and their interpretation, inasmuch as it harks back to the times of the Prophet and his Companions, cites profusely from the Qur'an and Hadith, and almost disregards the 13 centuries of Shari'a developments since. For, had he surveyed the entire span of Muslim Law, it is doubtful whether he would have come to the ultimate conclusion that every 'true Muslim' must be ready, eager and willing to sacrifice his life in the course of jihad. He himself complains in his essay, on more than one occasion, about the attempts made throughout history to 'hide the true meanings of jihad and martyrdom', therefore it was only natural for him to go directly to the early sources and squeeze every bit of them to extract, and justify, his fundamentalist interpretations. For him the 'true Muslims' are those who follow the radical interpretations, in contrast to those who have been spoiled and diluted by Western and modern outside accretions and are no longer faithful to the pure creed.

Even so, the Hadith cited by the author are not always accurate and are sometimes turned around in order to illustrate the point he wants to make, even when it is not certain that the original, or the most authoritative version thereof, had intended to exactly convey that meaning. It would be interesting to draw some comparisons with other versions that appear in books of other scholars, such as Ibn al-Athir, but that is beyond the scope of this study. At any rate, it is clear that, because some radical Muslim movements which have sanctified self-sacrifice are accused of adopting Shi'ite theology, the author is clearly making an effort to stay within the bounds of the Sunna, even if it is the most puritanical and strict interpretation thereof. In the context of universal Muslim combat for survival, which the author describes as the context in which Islamikaze acts are imperative, one is led to believe that without the supreme act of martyrdom, there is no other way to rescue Islam from its demise. Paradoxically, as we have indicated above, it is precisely the perceived impending danger to Islam which forces the martyrs to their fanatical act of self-immolation, and it is their desperate act of self-sacrifice which signals that they failed to transmit their message in some more acceptable and less horrendous way.

NOTES

1. Wensinck, 'The Oriental Doctrine', pp. 1–28.
2. Goldziher, *Muhammedanische Studien*, p. 387.
3. Wensinck, 'The Oriental Doctrine', p. 9.
4. Cited by Wensinck, 'The Oriental Doctrine', pp. 5–6.
5. Amir Taheri (a former pre-revolutionary editor of the daily *Kaihan*), *The Spirit of Allah* (in Hebrew translation), Tel Aviv: Am Oved, 1986, p. 148. See also Mahmoud Ayoub, *Redemptive Suffering in Islam*, pp. 148–58; Emanuel Sivan, *Muslim Radicals* (in Hebrew), Tel Aviv: Am Oved, 1985, pp, 192–5.
6. Amir Taheri, p. 55. See also Hamid Algar, *Islam and Revolution*, Berkeley, CA: University of California Press, 1981, pp. 329–43; and Martin Kramer (ed.), *Protest and Revolution in Shi'ite Islam* (Hebrew), Tel Aviv: Tel Aviv University, p. 29.
7. Report by Guy Bechor, Arab Affairs commentator of *Ha'aretz*, 6 December 1995, p. b2.
8. Ibid.
9. *Ha'aretz*, 23 January 1995, p. 6a.
10. Meir Hatina, *Palestinian Radicalism: The Islamic Jihad Movement* (Hebrew), Tel Aviv: Tel Aviv University, 1994, pp. 79–80.
11. *Ha'aretz*, 23 January 1995.
12. Izz a-Din al-Qassam was the founder and hero of the Islamic movement in Palestine in the 1930s, which engaged in battle both against the British Mandatory forces and the Jewish self-defence groups, until his death in combat in Samaria in 1935. His name was picked up by the Hamas, upon its foundation in 1988, and given to the military arm of the organization.
13. *Hatina*, p. 82.
14. A citation from an Islamic-Jihad distributed leaflet, *Ha'aretz*, 23 January 1995, p. 6a. The leaflet was reportedly headed by a citation from the Repentance Sura in the Qur'an which promises Paradise to those who kill and are killed in the battles of Allah.
15. *Qira'a fi Fiqh al-Shihada* (Readings in Islamic Martyrology), the very subtitle of this work, was published in 1988 as a special addendum to *Al-Islam wa Filastin* (Islam and Palestine) that appears in Nicosia, Cyprus, but has been the ideological supporter of the Islamikaze operations against Israel. See *Al-Islam wa-Filastin*, 5 June 1988, p. 9.
16. See previous n. 15.
17. *Qira'a*, p. 3.
18. The Cow Sura, verses 28–36.
19. *Qira'a*, p. 4.
20. Citing Malik ibn Anas, *Ahadith al-Jami' al'Saghir*, in *Qira'a*, p. 4.
21. Ibid. p. 7.
22. Ibid. p. 8.
23. Ibid pp. 8–9.
24. Palestinian Authority Broadcasting, shown on Israeli Television , 24 January 2002, 20:00 News Bulletin.
25. *Qira'a*, p. 12.
26. Ibid.
27. Ibid. pp. 10–12.
28. Ibid. p. 10.
29. Ibid. pp 10–12.
30. Ibid. p. 10.
31. Qur'an, Women Sura, verse 29.
32. *Qira'a*, p. 6.
33. The Bee Sura, verse 108.
34. *Qira'a*, pp. 10–11.

35. *Qira'a*, p. 7.
36. Ibid.
37. Ibid. pp. 14–15.
38. Ibid.

5. Friends and Foes: Interpretations and Misinterpretations

A great confusion has swept the Arab and Islamic worlds following the events of 11 September, inasmuch as it was difficult to comprehend who was critical of the terrorists and who was supportive, what were the cleavages between governments and populace, what the splits within the bureaucracy and among the clerics, with self-righteousness masquerading as truth, bigotry parading as justice and plain hatred as ideology or religion. The convoluted arguments that we have heard since the New York horror occurred have had a very hard time covering up the disarray that was caused within Muslim societies worldwide and in their international relations. At the end of the day, it was very difficult to cull the significance of the contradictory remarks that were uttered and deeds that were done on all sides. Some of these debates have already been discussed in Chapters 1 and 4, but here we shall group them according to the main players in the Middle East, who were eager to show a friendly face to the United States, on the one hand, but could not control the anger and spontaneous hatred of the crowds or control the statements of the clerics, on the other. Particularly telling are the debates which took place in countries whose governments are allies of the United States – foremost of which are Saudi Arabia and Egypt – but which, due to the illegitimacy of their rule, did not necessarily reflect public opinion and sentiment.

Partly, at least, the apparent meandering and contradictions in the articulated positions of various clerics regarding Islamikaze can be imputed to the idea of *siyyasa shar'iyya* (religious policy), which has been a tool of government in Muslim states and which has been used by the Muslim establishment to churn out elaborate justifications of the government's policies through the mechanism of fatwas.[1] This would explain, for example, the soothing words offered the United States, and even the condemnatory remarks directed against the terrorists, which were pronounced by the supreme sheikhs of Saudi Arabia and Egypt directly after the 11 September disaster; then followed by a reversal and almost open support of the Islamikaze by the same clerics when it suited their internal politics or their struggle for prestige in the inter-Islamic arena. The overarching rationale for the extensive examples of this has been *maslaha* (public interest), usually as judged by the rulers. Thus, for example, while Sheikh Tantawi, the head of Al-Azhar, was sent by his government to participate in the highly visible inter-faith meeting in Alexandria after 11 September, which made unambiguous statements against terrorism and the killing of innocent civilians; the same cleric, when hard pressed by interviewers to justify the Palestinian Islamikaze attacks against Israeli civilians, practically lent them his blessing, as we shall see below.

It is worth noting that well before 11 September, some Arab commentators spoke out in favour of Bin-Laden, claiming that he was not a terrorist but an 'unfortunate man seeking refuge in the high mountains of Afghanistan', hiding from 'a terrorist US which has taken over the world'; therefore, only attacks against US Embassies can resolve the problem of globalization as long as it remains impossible to defeat the Americans in direct combat.[2] The author of these gratuitous words, Mr Atwan, a respectable editor of an Arabic daily which appears in London, who is constantly sought by the major international networks for interviews, pretends to present Arab views on current matters. Three months after the New York tragedy, the same journalist was invited by *Al-Jazeera* television to join a panel to comment on one of the video-cassettes released by Bin-Laden. He lauded Bin-Laden's 'good timing' when he chose to 'criticize America's hypocritical policy which allowed Sharon to act criminally against the defenseless Palestinian people'.[3] He added, *inter alia*:

> The US issued its own judgement and carried out the verdict, and now it is seeking the evidence. It is like executing someone first and then looking for the evidence that he deserved the capital punishment. The US is using huge B-52 bombers and bombs villages and towns. They also used Daisy Cutter bombs, weighing 15,000 pounds each on Tora Bora and the caves...I noticed that in the video-cassette Bin-Laden's left shoulder looked frozen, I hope he is all right and was not hurt...

Whenever an American is killed in the war, they say it was 'friendly fire', and when a helicopter crashes, they say it was a 'technical failure'. Americans never fall as a result of resistance and of Arab and Muslim fire. We have already observed the lies in these statements when we saw the Taliban and al-Qa'ida showing us the downed helicopters with their registration numbers...In Iraq too, the Americans tried to reduce the numbers of their casualties in the war, and no one tells us the true numbers to this day...The US bombed and killed 65 tribal chieftains in Afghanistan who were on their way to greet Qarada'l, but America continues to insist that they were members of al-Qa'ida. This is a lie, a disinformation. Why can't she admit that she killed them erroneously? Errors are always attributed to Arabs and Muslims, but the Americans are always supermen who cannot do wrong, who always hit their targets, and whoever kills them is a terrorist and a criminal...

The fact that Bin-Laden is still alive has spoiled the celebrations of American victory in Afghanistan...The fact that he still is alive has caused the postponement of American aggression against other countries such as Syria, Iraq, the Yemen and Somalia. The fact that he is still alive and got this cassette to al-Qa'ida, which smuggled it via Pakistan to Qatar, means that our brothers in Iraq, Syria, Hizbullah, the Yemen and Somalia must be grateful [for his survival]. Had Bin-Laden been killed at the outset of the war, as the Americans and some Arab regimes, May Allah Forgive them!, had anticipated, it is well possible that the war would have moved to these countries and we would have witnessed bombings of Iraq, Syria, Lebanon, Somalia and the Yemen.[4]

Admittedly, those accusations against the United States did not remain unanswered in the Arab press. For example, an Egyptian columnist, Salah 'Isa, who wrote for the Egyptian weekly *Al-Maydan*, reproached 'Atwan for his consistent support of Bin-Laden which might create the impression that all Arabs and Muslims are consistently on Bin-Laden's side, while there are Muslim clerics who have in fact voiced their reservations about him and his deeds. 'Isa also urged *Al-Jazeera* television, which hosted the talk show, to become aware that it actually served Bin-Laden and tarnished the reputation of other Arabs and Muslims. He concluded that if *Al-Jazeera* was aware of that and nevertheless proceeded with its programmes, that was bad enough, but if it was not aware, the disaster for the Arabs and Muslims was even greater.[5] But those words of reason were countered and in fact cancelled out by the editor of the same journal, 'Issam al-Ghazi, who wrote:

> The entire world is keeping silent and submissive [in the face of American attacks], except for Bin-Laden who has become a legend in the minds of the youth of the world, just like the Che Guevara legend of the 1960s. The pictures of Bin-Laden now appear on the screens of cellular phones, T-Shirts and internet screens used by youth. His pictures appear on many products as a testimony to their high quality, while the pictures of America adorn toilet paper. No one of the youth of the world wishes Bin-Laden to fall into American hands in spite of the US$20 million prize offered for his head...Bin-Laden has become the symbol of resistance to American Imperialism, whose tyranny has caused the destruction of Afghanistani mountains in the search after him. Even if sycophant Arabs regard him as a fundamentalist terrorist, the coming generations will view him as a mythological hero who defeated the strongest nation on earth by hitting the symbols of its power: the Pentagon and the Twin Towers. Everyone will kneel before his memorial monument and take off their hats, even if America thinks he is Satan. Bin-Laden has earned his place as the undisputable hero of the first year of this millennium...
>
> America created Bin-Laden as a thorn in the Arabs' throats, but he has turned out to be a thorn in her own throat.[6]

Another debate of this sort went on between a liberal Tunisian columnist and a Saudi reader, which became a *cause célèbre* in the Arab world because it touched upon the painful process of self-examination that many Arabs and Muslims went through in the wake of 11 September. The Tunisian writer addressed himself to the educational infra-structure in the Arab and Islamic world which produced the phenomenon of Islamikaze, and suggested an overhaul of the existing system by emasculating the very basic concepts of traditional Islam which looked with hostility and contempt upon the others, thus making them legitimate prey for Muslims. Interestingly enough, since within the society and culture he wants to reform he would be rejected and excommunicated, if not worse, were he openly to advocate uprooting its basic vocabulary (see Chapter 2), he had to use Islam itself, and its acknowledged tradition, in order to facilitate and make more palatable the changes he wished to introduce. For example, based on the precedents of 'Umar Ibn al-'As, the renowned conqueror of Egypt for Islam, and other Muslim historical celebrities, he counselled desisting from dividing the world into *Dar al-Islam* and *Dar al-Harb* (see Chapter 2). He also advocated discontinuing the teaching of jihad in schools and replacing it with the teachings of *ijtihad*;[7] that is, the independent interpretation of the Shari'a in order to adapt it to the necessities of the new world.[8]

He spoke courageously about putting an end to dubbing others as 'sons of Satan', which has so far only produced a 'collective religious narcissism' among Muslims, encouraged their self-aggrandizement and the dwarfing of others. He warned that:

> The extrication of religious education from the madness of the centrality of the creed, is something that only contributes to the deepening of self-delusion among the students, and to contempt of the other who is dubbed 'Unbeliever', instead of simply and neutrally terming him 'non-Muslim'. When the other is called 'Unbeliever', he regains the title he used to have in Arabia at the time of the Prophet, namely a *muharib* [a person who has to be fought], who is neither loyal nor can become an ally, nor be associated with diplomatically or commercially, and therefore if he is your compatriot, you may neither shake his hand, greet him nor allow his houses of prayer to be taller than ours...[9]
>
> Can we construct any sense of citizenship based on common values and life, as long as we maintain this racism? Are the Muslims ready to come to some sort of under-standing like the others...? Where is the common denominator between Islamic education and the universal human rights which strive to bring down the ethnic and religious partitions between humans and institute the universal citizenship that philosophers have talked about? If not a universal citizenship, then a least a universal solidarity short of which no country or group of countries can sur-mount the world challenges in the fields of ecology, demography, terrorism, epidemics and others.[10]

The author attacked Iman Zawahiri, Bin-Laden's Egyptian-born religious mentor and deputy, who invoked the 'consensus' among Muslim scholars regarding the illegitimacy of the rulers in the Muslim world who 'alter the rules of the Shari'a' and therefore have to be removed from power. Again, basing himself on traditional Islamic models, he dismisses this 'consensus' as a delusion, and produces precedents whereby great Muslim luminaries, beginning with Caliph U'thman, who adopted some aspects of Byzantine law, and Sanusi and Rashid Rida, who adopted European codes of law, rather than distinguishing between Islam and Unbelief, opted for the distinction between right and wrong. He said that addressing texts without their contexts turned events that occurred in a certain period into anachronistic and detached accounts, took over the students' consciousness and oppressed their critical faculties... Without all these elements, he wrote, school becomes little more than an intermediate institution which preaches violence and war (hot and cold) against the West. He stressed that since the subtle theological arguments are not understood by the Muslim populace, the call for jihad against Israel, which is understood by everyone, has become the rallying point of Muslim fundamentalists. Therefore, the columnist urges Muslim countries to put an end to 'schools of jihad' and turn them into 'schools of *ijtihad*', as a way to abrogate the school curriculi that educate for violence, and drain the marshes of religious fanaticism 'without spilling one single drop of blood'.[11]

This clear and rather unusual message did not go unheeded. A certain Farajallah Ahmed Yussef, of Riyadh in Saudi Arabia, rushed forward with his violent reaction to *Al-Hayat*, decried what were for him the false allegations of the Tunisian journalist, lashed out at his liberal views, and returned the readers of that exchange to the beaten path of Islamic rhetoric:

> Al-Akhdar forgot to described to us the rivers of blood spilled by the Crusaders when they occupied Jerusalem in 1099...He did not mention how rare were Muslim prayers at Al-Aqsa under the Crusader Kingdom, while prayers at the Holy Sepulchre, the Nativity and the Annunciation, as well as in all countries occupied by Islam, never stopped...I counsel al-Akhdar to consult books and dictionaries to learn that the word 'Unbeliever' never carried any sense of contempt...And look who is talking about contempt of others! It is the same al-Akhdar who described on satellite television anti-Zionist

French intellectuals as 'garbage'[12]...I apologize for having to mention this outrageous conduct...

Al-Akhdar's lies reach their peak when he alleges that the relations between Muslims and non-Muslims in Islamdom are based on racism on the Muslims' part. I do not think I have to refute this stupid error on the part of someone whose heart is full of hatred...Is the West's treatment of Muslim prisoners of war at Guantanamo evidence of Western tolerance of the Other, and proof that it does not despise the Other?

France recognized the right of nations to participate in government only after the French Revolution...But in the Arab kingdoms which existed centuries before the birth of Jesus Christ, the right of people to participate in government had been recognized...The Qur'an bears evidence to the fact that when the Queen of Sheba received the letter of the Prophet [= King] Solomon, she convened her consultative council...The West that found its advocate in al-Akhdar's propaganda, finally found out about human rights only in the twentieth century, while we can mention the 'Fudul' at the end of the sixth century as the beginning of human rights legislation in the presence of the Prophet...Thereafter, Islamic Shari'a developed which determined the rights not only of Muslims but also of Jews, Christians and pagans who were the subjects of the Islamic State...

Al-Akhdar has to realize that the banner of jihad will continue to be hoisted until all Muslim lands are liberated from colonialism, regardless of whether it is Zionist or Crusader...[13]

SAUDI ARABIA AND THE GULF STATES

Throughout the rocky history of the 'friendly' relations between Saudi Arabia and the United States, both parties knew that they had to play a double game: US military and diplomatic support for one of the most obscurantist regimes in the world, by a superpower who pledged to promote human rights and democracy; and in return, Saudi insurance of the free flow of oil, on which the kingdom is dependent, and the maintenance of US bases on the Saudi sacred soil, in spite of the resentment that the Western presence causes among the conservative and puritanical clerics who provide the ideological underpinnings of the regime. This is an uneasy balance that is readily upset in times of international crisis, in spite of the declarations of friendship between the parties. When Saudi Arabia was directly threatened by the Iraqis in 1990, it reluctantly accepted US and international intervention to ward off the threats, but immediately after Saddam's defeat, the Saudis insisted upon immediate US withdrawal, as they could not stand the accusations that foreign troops were desecrating the Holy Land of Mecca and Medina. Even after the withdrawal, except for bases where equipment remained pre-positioned in case of another conflagration, anti-US resentment resulted in the attack on the Dhofar Towers, and other attacks against Americans, with the host country hardly collaborating in the investigation.

Following 11 September, especially as many of the Islamikaze who sowed terror in the United States, as well as the head of al-Qa'ida himself, Osama Bin-Laden, turned out to be Saudis, much of that permanent uneasy tension erupted. The Saudis, themselves afraid of becoming the victims of Islamist extremists, rushed to join the coalition of President Bush, and apparently to aid in fighting international terrorism, but they also found themselves in the embarrassing situation of funding terrorist organizations such as the Hamas, or spending huge sums to promote Islamic revivalist groups around the world, some of which have also turned to violence. Hence the ambivalence in Saudi statements and policies thereafter. The Saudi Chief Mufti, Sheikh Abd al-Aziz, who had caused outrage by his moderate statements, remained unflinching in his rhetoric after 11 September, and even lent more vigour to his opposing views of terrorism, under the new circumstances, though his nuanced interpretation of what he meant leaves much to be desired. In an interview to a Saudi daily he stated:

> Our monotheistic faith urges us to respect obligations and warns against their violation...The Prophet had said that those 'who kill allies will never enjoy the scent of Paradise'... Ibn Hajr[14] discusses the allies of the Muslims, either via the paying of *jizya*[15] or *hudna*,[16] or through *aman*[17]...
>
> It is incumbent upon Muslims to fear Allah, to think carefully and not to punish anyone for the faults of others, for our faith is built on justice...One must think carefully, because the consequences of such [terrorist] activity can hurt

Islam and Muslims in the world and the Hereafter... This kind of behaviour is very harmful and tends to generate internecine wars, riots and destabilization of security. To conduct oneself in this fashion is forbidden, due to the obligation to fulfil one's commitments, as stated above, due to the intimidation of Muslims it might provoke, and due to the scaring away of those who would otherwise seek [Muslim] protection.

It is incumbent upon all Muslims to fear Allah inwardly and outwardly, and not to indulge in affairs of which they understand neither their essence nor their ramifications. Whoever possesses scientific knowledge [in Shari'a] must explain the truth and open the eyes of people as to their duty to turn to their rulers and ulama in time of internal strife... It is also incumbent upon scholars of the Holy Law to avoid rushing into discussing these serious matters which concern the entire Muslim *umma*, and to leave them to those better qualified than themselves. The common people must avoid dealing with these affairs which are beyond their comprehension...

We all know that the events in question [11 September], were ordained by Allah, and that Allah determines what is to happen with an immense wisdom, which may or may not be comprehensible to His servants. Due to His wisdom and His complete mastery of what is useful to His servants, Allah may determine a good event that common people abhor, or a bad event that people like... It is incumbent on all Muslims to spread the Religion of Allah in the world, but they must all know that Allah not only preserves this faith, but also ensures that it beats all others... We Muslims must preach for Allah and make sure that current events do not turn us from our mission...

These matters all go back to rulers and Doctors of the Holy Law, because they understand the situation better than all others, master the written sources, know best our interests and the dangers that threaten them, and know best how to attain the most vital interests and thwart the worst dangers. Hence the duty of all individuals to cluster around the ulama and their rulers. For when they say something they know what they are saying, and when they keep silent they know why they keep silent. We must beware not to listen to all the voices we hear that wish only to kindle internal strife but carry with them no benefit.[18]

Not a speck of humanity or sorrow for the victims of 11 September, only an acceptance of the events as acts of Allah, and a warning to the people of Saudi Arabia to abide by the rulings of the established coalition of the country, between the rulers and the ulama, who 'know best'. This moderate sheikh also apologizes to his readership for not being more forthcoming in his interview, because he 'knows when to keep silent'. There were other voices, too. A Saudi columnist, a relative of one of the plane hijackers who triggered the 11 September disaster, was himself in the United States on that day and could not help publishing his feelings, immediately thereafter, under the telling headline, 'The New War: My Clan and Terrorism'.[19] He says that while he was present in the United States when disaster struck, his personal disaster unfolded only later when he saw the list of the hijackers, many of whom were Saudis from the south of the country, where his own clan originated from. To his knowledge, those were well-rooted Arabs who respected sublime values and were religiously moderate. He tried to find the reason for this atypical explosion of extremism among them in socio-economic development, such as the relative impoverishment of the south, but he concluded that his area had achieved in three decades what it took other parts of the world ten millennia to achieve. He found out that modernity and urbanization had invaded that erstwhile, primitive part of the kingdom to the extent that, nowadays, one can find there all the most up-to-date trappings of life. Even service in the security apparatus, which is open, by his own admission, only to the most loyal citizens, was made available to them.

The writer does not have answers, only questions: was it crash modernization that numbed the parents while a new generation of materialistic youth was becoming, under their eyes, easy prey for religious fanatics? He concludes that he will continue to be proud of the achievements of members of his clan and country who pursue an honest life, and excommunicate those 'who put themselves at the service of ignorance'.[20] He cites from the Holy Book: 'Our Lord, we have wronged ourselves. If Thou forgive us not, surely we are of the lost!'[21] A dramatic admission of shame, not of guilt; of helplessness, not of remorse; of fate, not of the need to remedy. This columnist's attitude, which rightly reflected the state of shock and disarray among the Saudis in general, was echoed in the government's own dismay as to what it could do to silence (not to stem) Islamic fanaticism domestically and to attempt to deflect the accusing fingers of the world elsewhere. On 14 November 2001, Saudi Crown Prince Abdallah convened the leading clerics of the country to brief them on his talk with President Bush, including the mufti Sheikh Abd al-Aziz, whom we have copiously cited above. As reported in the Saudi press, that briefing included the following major points:

- You must act with moderation and examine every word you say, as you are responsible to Allah and to the Islamic Nation...
- I counsel you to seek words of logic in order to serve Islam, not to allow emotions to overtake you, and allow no one to provoke you, because each of you is responsible before Allah, his people, his homeland, his family and his honour...
- The Qur'an says 'We have made you a moderate nation...' and 'there should be no extremism in religion'... This is not a matter of give and take [with the US], but of acting with reason and deliberation, as you know what the situation in the world is...
- I hope Allah will spare us the evil of Muslims who pretend to believe in Islam but in fact are not on the path of righteousness. May Allah spare us of their evil... lead us in the path of righteousness, and lead them back to true Islam.[22]

Again, not a word of condemnation of the horror for its own sake, nor of sympathy for the victims, just caution and damage-control. The mufti who attended that meeting, as well as Sheikh Saleh, Chair of the Supreme Judicial Council, echoed the same approach of 'watching our mouths' and 'doing what is in the interest of our country', but no moral judgment on the circumstances that had dictated this new policy of reticence. Sheikh Saleh cautioned his fellow clerics that, exactly as someone who had not studied economics should refrain from discussing economic matters, so those without experience in international affairs ought not to address these matters, and those who did not study religion must not make pronouncements on these topics.[23] In his efforts to quiet down the tempers, the Crown Prince also assembled top officials of the defence and intelligence establishment, on 18 November 2001, to brief them on his talks with the American administration. Details of the briefing seeped out to the local press:

- I wish to remind you of the unjust attack being waged these days by the foreign media against the Saudi Kingdom. I mean foreign papers, and you know who is behind them...These papers, behind whom stands 'you-know-who', criticize your religion, the things most precious to you, your faith and your holy scriptures...There is no choice for them but to understand that you are strong in your faith in Allah the exalted, and in your devotion to your faith, your belief and your loyalty...

- There is a spite against our country because of our enforcement of Islamic religious law, and I am confident that no other country in the world does this...Let this be a source of pride and glory for you...

- The media attacks on Saudi Arabia include curses on Islam, and on all Arabs and Muslims, but on you [Saudis] in particular...However there is a proverb that says 'Let the snake die of its own venom'...They will find from you and from Islam nothing but love, peace and friendship between peoples of the world. Islam is goodness, blessing, glory and honour. Islam will be victorious, come what may.[24]

This rather puzzling attempt to seek friendship and peace via victory, amidst the caution and low profile which characterized Saudi utterances, was somewhat betrayed by more open statements of both clerics and officials of the Saudi regime. A member of the Shura Council, the Consultative Assembly that is supposed to act as a parliament but is appointed by the absolute king, indeed spilled the beans. On 18 January 2002, the *Washington Post* ran an article citing Saudi officials who expressed the desire to see US presence on Saudi soil end after it had become a liability due to the Saudi public's hostility to the United States. A few days earlier, Dr Othman al-Rawwaf, a member of the Shura, had published an article in the Saudi London-based daily, *Al-Sharq al-Awsat*, calling for a shift in the Saudi focus from the United States to Europe. His main points were:

- From their inception, Saudi–US relations were based primarily on mutual strategic interests connected to oil and the transfer of advanced technology to Saudi Arabia. This led to the friendship between the two sides that became closer over time. However, these relations faced, from the outset, two major challenges: the Saudis are opposed to Washington's absolute support for Israel, and the big gap in cultural and political values between their respective societies.

- The US media campaign and commentators from various research institutes in the United States, which have been directed against Saudi Arabia after 11 September, exacerbated that relationship, though the strategic and economic interests remained intact...Some columnists participating in that campaign are known for their pro-Israeli bias and criticism of Arabs and Muslims...They enlist their publications to attack the Arab states that lead the struggle against Israel.
- It goes without saying that in the 1990s, Saudi Arabia sharply objected to normalization with Israel...and led the Arab countries in support of the Intifada and in defence of the rights of the Palestinians...Some of those columnists now want to settle accounts, and they demand that Washington adopt a hostile attitude towards Saudi Arabia...but most of the media attacks are directly linked to the cultural and political differences between the parties...
- What is new in the media attacks is their linking of Wahhabism with violence and their claims that Saudi schoolbooks educate to violence and extremism...But it is known that Wahhabism is a movement of religious reform, not a political movement calling for confrontation and clashes with the West...It is from this movement that the modern Saudi state emerged, which has been described by Europe and America as moderate, wise, and renouncing violence...
- In the 1980s and 1990s, Egypt and Algeria witnessed violent and barbaric acts, perpetrated by extremist groups in the name of Islam...The curricula in both those countries are different from the Saudi one and do not include such an intensive study of religious subjects...So if our curricula are the reason for violence, we should not be seeing so much extremism in Egypt and Algeria...
- Perhaps Saudi Arabia will begin to rely more on Europe than on the United States for economic and strategic partnership... If the United States decides that its main interests link it to Israel at this point, then it would be natural for Saudi Arabia to seek other partners...and the United States will be relegated to second place.[25]

An atypical liberal view from the Gulf States was expressed by Dr al-Ansari, the Dean of Islamic Law at Qatar University. Like other speakers in the name of Islam during the heady days following the attacks on the United States, Ansari chose to publish his articles in the London-based *Al-Hayat*, in full view of his targeted Western readership, not in some obscure Muslim organ of a backwater Arab village. His starting point is a dazzling historical allusion: the Kharijite Uprising, which had erupted after the Battle of Siffin (AD 657), when the rebels turned away from their loyalty to Caliph 'Ali as he agreed to negotiate the fate of the caliphate with his opponent Mu'awiyya instead of deciding it by war. 'Ali turned against them and annihilated most of them at the Battle of Nahrawan a year later, but for centuries they remained subversive *vis-à-vis* the caliphate, and held that anyone of irreproachable character and religious commitment could become a caliph, while the caliphs in place were far from responding to those qualifications and therefore did not deserve the loyalty of their subjects. They also accused other Muslims of being heretics, who held different opinions from their own, and demanded a strict and puritanical interpretation of the Law of Islam. Ansari now claimed that Bin-Laden's forces were the new Khawarij, though they were more 'fortunate' than their predecessors as they acted with 'satellite channels that enabled them to become popular stars' in the Islamic world.[26]

Al-Ansari criticized the host of commentators who supported the 'New Kharijites', and the religious leaders who 'volunteered to issue fatwas demanding that they be heeded', and threatened that any Believers who held back their support would be contaminated by sin. He observed that those who called for jihad against the 'Crusaders' who set off to attack Islam were inciting the mobs against their governments who voiced their support for the United States, and deceiving them into demonstrating and acting against the 'enemies of Islam'. The result was that those who acted hastily were destroyed and their families stricken by tragedy, while the Imams who incited them pursued their lives of tranquility and comfort undisturbed, without being held accountable for the consequences of their incitement. Al-Ansari's conclusion is that declarations of jihad should not be left to any hysterical and irresponsible preacher to utter, but should be confined to the rulers, for otherwise chaos and destruction would ensue and state interest would be harmed. He consciously stated that since the Saudi sheikhs had declared that only the rulers had the right to proclaim jihad, he was obligated to follow suit and concur. The writer argues with those who claim that, in the name of freedom of expression, microphones should be afforded to jihad fighters who bring the Arab Nation to the brink of the precipice.[27]

The problem with this voice of reason and moderation is that it challenges the authority of the religious hierarchy who enjoy, according to his own reckoning based on a poll by *Al-Jazeera*, 83 per cent of public support when they declare that Bin-Laden is a jihad fighter and not a terrorist. That brings dramatically into focus the illegitimacy of the rulers in place who, for transient interests, not for immutable moral reasons, lend their lip-service support to the West and quell the swelling emotions among their publics in favour of the Muslim jihad fighters. He contends that these terrorists have in mind primarily to oust the existing regimes and install puritanical ones in their stead. But since they have failed, they turn against the United States, whom they accuse of having produced these corrupt governments, in order to force it to leave their lands to their fundamentalist mercy. The writer claims that the Muslim soul is naturally disengaged from terrorism, but the fundamentalist incitement falls on receptive ears due to the high profile of fanaticism in Arab societies, which has taken root because of the educational system which has remained impermeable to pluralism. The culture of terrorism, he concludes, can only be fought by education.[28] Like other voices of moderation and self-criticism in the Islamic world, al-Ansari, too, provoked a very heated debate, first with his articles in his Qatar home papers and then throughout the Arab world.

Al-Ansari, who is credited as a 'prominent liberal voice in the Muslim religious establishment', was interviewed for *Al-Raya* daily in Qatar, following his daring remarks in *Al-Hayat*. He proclaimed his commitment to curricular reforms in the Arab and Islamic worlds with a view to 'removing all seeds of hatred, repulsion, and fanaticism towards others, towards women, towards holders of other faiths or those professing different schools of law within Islam'. This audacious statement, which goes a long way to admit the deficiencies in the existing curricula, certainly cannot be made without reference to other great reformers in Islamic history, who had been greatly appreciated and respected, and of whom a fresh interpretation was needed to make them relevant once again for the current crisis that he courageously acknowledged. He invoked the great figures of Sheikh Muhammed al-Ghazali and Sheikh Muhammed 'Abduh who had striven, in his words, to 'eliminate the elements of divisiveness both within the *umma* and between it and the rest of the nations'. He argued that since tolerance reigned supreme in Islam, it was necessary to re-install that notion in school curricula. He cited several examples:

- In Islam, he said, studies focused on those 'who will be saved', that is, the Muslims, to the exclusion of all the others whose inheritance was Hell. He explained that the student who is educated in that vein grows to believe he holds the exclusive Truth while all the others will remain deceivers and ignoramuses.
- Similarly, he claimed, when students are educated in the notion that foreign relations are determined by the differentiation between *Dar al-Harb* and *Dar al-Islam* (see Chapter 2), and the jihad is prescribed as the way of intercourse between them, then aggression becomes possible in the name of jihad. He even asserts that while 'some ideas exist in several religious law books, allowing Muslims to attack non-Muslims', those ideas are wrong. He says that since the Qur'an allows man the right of choice, then anyone can be a Believer or Unbeliever, therefore the rationale of waging jihad by Muslims against non-Muslims is removed.
- He comes out virulently against the 'type of Islam which breeds terrorists', since that in itself is 'a crime against true Islam and the Muslims themselves'. He condemned the schools of thought which produced extremist groups that 'cannot deal with modern reality', and blamed the preachers in mosques who portray the war in Afghanistan as a Crusader battle between Islam and Christianity. He ridiculed those preachers of hate, asserting that if Allah had listened to them and destroyed the Christians, they themselves would not 'have a microphone to preach with, or the air-conditioner or the car they so enjoy'.
- He dubs as 'unfair' the naming of the US counter-attack in Afghanistan as 'terrorism', because to do so would be to confuse terrorism with self-defence, or response with aggression. He says that Arab history is replete with examples where the response to acts of terrorism on the scale committed in the United States had warranted total annihilation of the perpetrators.[29] He commends the United States for trying other avenues before they moved decisively against the Taliban.
- He asserts that even if there is considerable collateral damage during the punitive attacks against the terrorists, and many innocent civilians are killed, the blame lies squarely at the door

of the terrorists who had kindled the reprisals against them. What was done in Afghanistan was named by the author as a 'liberation of our Moslem brothers by the Americans, though unfortunately not by Muslim hands'.

- Al-Ansari maintains that the attraction of the Arab world to Bin-Laden is only the latest link in the long chain of 'liberating heroes, grounded in Arab mentality', beginning with the legendary 'Antara, and then Saladin, 'abd-al-Nasser and Saddam Hussein. For the populace who adored those heroes, it did not matter if they were liars, adventurers, tyrants or terrorists, because 'Arab mentality ascribes to them a sanctity that covers their sins'.
- Al-Ansari links this state of mind of the Arabs to their frustration emanating from their 'political, social and ideological repression, backwardness and inability to change', and the incitement to hate the 'colonialist West' and 'American hegemony'. He particularly berated *al-Jazeera* television for carrying Bin-Laden and his aides' propaganda and incitement, and making them stars, thus lending their screens to murderers to spread their propaganda...
- The author also attacks 'hollow' Arab intellectuals who echo the incited masses by sacrificing the truth and scientific analysis in favour of appeasement of tempers, and by 'hypocritically' linking September 11 to the Palestinian issue, which had never been invoked in al-Qa'ida literature before.[30]

A Kuwaiti columnist, Ahmed al-Baghdadi, embarked on a campaign of painful self-flagellation that echoed, in some respects, the concerns of his Qatari co-religionist, but it also opened new vistas of self-criticism not often heard or allowed in Arab lands. The article, which made its debut in a Kuwaiti daily, *Al-Anba'*, was later picked up by other Arab media, notably the Egyptian magazine *Akhbar al-Yaum*.[31] It should be noted, however, that Baghdadi had already been embroiled with his religious authorities who had sentenced him to one-month's imprisonment for blasphemy. His angle is quite innovative, for by condemning Israel and the West, he actually implied criticism of his country, his countrymen, his co-religionists and his culture. He accused Prime Minister Sharon, for example, of terrorism, but at the same time insisted that the 'Zionist entity' never exercised terrorism against its own intellectuals and never put its writers in prisons, and that its Prime Minister was duly and democratically elected, while the Arab and Islamic world cannot boast of any leader who had likewise attained legitimate power. He also said that not only did Arabs and Muslims commit a horrendous act of killing innocent civilians on 11 September by a group of 'martyrs', but that prior to that, Arab rulers had practiced terrorism towards their own citizenry: something that has no parallel in either Israel or the West.

Baghdadi's list of condemnations of Arab regimes is long: they let Muslim fatwas come to pass, which sanctify the killing of people for their beliefs, something that had not occurred in Europe since the Middle Ages (he even sarcastically suggests that Arabs should be awarded a Nobel Prize for their novel 'invention'); they sue intellectuals in courts for their views and indict them for blasphemy, and in some cases force a couple to separate because one of them was sentenced for heresy, something that amounted to terrorism in his eyes; their intelligence services have executed hundreds of intellectuals and dissidents, a form of terrorism that the Zionists have never adopted; people disappear at the hands of secret apparatuses, a sort of terror never used in the West or in Israel, but in which Arab and Islamic regimes, notably Iraq, excel; Arab Muslims even introduced that hell into Afghanistan and brought about its demise and destruction; Arab Muslims, like Hizbullah and the Palestinians, have invented plane hijacking and sowed terror in the hearts of innocent passengers. In short, he posited the Arabs and Muslims as the masters of terrorism, which began in their domestic policies against their own citizenries, and ended in international terrorism. For that reason, he justified the behaviour of the West, which has been humiliating Arabs and Muslims and rejecting them from its midst. He determines that, while stating that it is a religion of tolerance and Saddam Hussein begins his speeches with a blessing of peace, Islam does not tolerate other's opinions and even undercuts its own intellectuals at a time when the 'heretic' West and Israel do not practice that kind of terror.[32]

Reactions, some of them violent, were not slow in coming. The day after al-Ansari's interview, *Al-Raya* distanced itself from its 'deviant' interviewee, stating that the 'published material reflected the views of Dr Ansari, not those of the paper', but also courageously assumed responsibility and refused to disown the published interview, arguing that Dr Ansari 'can defend his own views'. What was more disheartening were the virulent attacks by readers from all walks of life who heaped personal abuse on the writer, one of them claiming that his words were published 'in preparation for the attack against Iraq'. Many readers and radio listeners were outraged by what they regarded as blasphemy on the part of the writer and demanded that further publication of those views be banned. Others accused al-Ansari of Americanizing Islam to the extent that he encouraged people to perform the pilgrimage to New York rather than to Mecca.[33]

But worse was to come. An editorial in *Al-Raya*, by 'abd al-Halim Qindil, complained that the United States, not content with invading other nations and instigating other governments to wage war on its behalf, has also determined to 'educate other nations' over the heads of their governments. Not content with Sunnite and Shi'ite Islam, she has resolved 'to install a new school of Islam of the Bush brand, depleted of spirit, honour, and the will of jihad. She wants to turn the Arab and Islamic countries into a shameful emulation of the tank-secularism of the Turks', all the while covering her designs under slogans of tolerance , love and democracy.[34] Another writer, Muhammed al-Maliki, made the point that even should the current curricula be turned into non-curricula:

> Islam will remain rooted in our midst for ever, and we shall continue to teach our children that all evil emanates from the West, that Zionists cannot be trusted because they entertain no good intentions toward humanity. We shall continue to cultivate the morality and values that will protect them against openness and permissiveness, and we shall continue to nurture them with honour, force, pride, freedom, struggle, resistance to occupiers and jihad for the sake of Allah.

The writer vowed that should the curricula be altered, the Arabs and Muslims would not submit to the 'perverted will of the West', and would continue to remind their children that the change had been forced on them, thus keeping the old curricula in the minds of generations.[35]

Other writers, such as 'Aisha 'Abidan, a columnist in *Al-Raya*, also attacked al-Ansari for inviting the Americans to tamper with Arab and Muslim school curricula, after they had already taken possession, through globalization, of all the political, social and moral aspects of life. She contends that al-Ansari does not reflect the views of the Muslim majority, and they therefore deserve to be refuted both by preachers in the mosques and intellectuals in order to avert a new US hegemony. For the US aim is to tear the Muslim world apart and encourage its ideological and cultural disintegration; its behaviour in Afghanistan amounts to terrorism, and therefore it should not be allowed to take control of the school curricula or of Muslim civilization.[36] Similarly, but even more vitriolically, Dr Ansari's predecessor as the Dean of Islamic Law at Qatar University, Dr Ali Muhammadi, came out against US subversion of the Islamic *umma* in 'order to destroy it and re-shape it by foreigners and to their tune', and against those who 'elect to live like slaves in US farms, at a time when their Islam assures them of their freedom'. He distinguished between two sorts of Americans: those who follow only greed and material profit and are out in Africa and Asia, trying to impose their material and economic yardsticks of human behaviour; and those who live in their own country, where they promote murder, rape and robbery against their own countrymen. They cause misery to others by their pollution of the earth, their accumulation of weapons of mass destruction, and their tampering with the human genome. Therefore, he concludes, it would be self-defeating to let the likes of Rushdie alter Muslim curricula, which have remained as the last dam against globalization.[37]

Many other columnists, public figures, members of the Muslim establishment and intellectuals joined the fray, with a minority, like Dr Ahmed Bishara from Kuwait, decrying the Islamic takeover of education systems in the Gulf States, which has resulted in 'Arab and Muslim terrorism carried out in the name of Islam, of which the Arabs themselves are now victims'; but the overwhelming majority condemned Ansari out of genuine outrage. For example, Dr Tabtaba'i, the Chair of the Legislative Committee of the Kuwaiti parliament, lashed out at Ansari for aiming to 'drag us to Americanizing our identity and abolishing our Muslim identity'. He reaffirmed that 'Allah was the Guardian of the Islamic Faith, thanks to the mujahedin who have been spreading it all over'. He expressed regret that Ansari, who 'accused Islam of terrorism, was an academic in charge of educating the young in Qatar and the Gulf'.[38] The Egyptian columnist, Hassan al-Harawi, also condemned those who have gone astray by:

> ...supporting Machiavellism and turning us into Indians at the hands of Americans, so that we accept aid and weapons, and in return we alter our curricula, and our Qu'ran and

Sunna, to please America who wants to create a new mixture of Islam and Christianity...We are expected to be tolerant, turn the other cheek and then all other parts of our body.

He insisted that if tolerance is predicated on the respect of the other, then Islam, too, must be allowed to act with tolerance as it understands it, even if this involves the use of force. He explained that there was no logic in a 1,400-year-old faith giving way to one hardly four centuries old, which was constructed 'on the ruins of the Indians, debauchery and tyranny, and is now looking for new Indians'.[39]

Another Egyptian, the fundamentalist, Sheikh Qardawi, who had initially founded the Islamic Law Faculty in Qatar, and whose fatwas we have discussed above, naturally joined Dr Ansari's detractors, and refuted the US desire to:

> ...strike off jihad, doing good and avoiding evil, removing sin by force when persuasion fails, struggle against oppression and resisting tyrants...they do not want us to use the word Unbelievers even when these are aggressors...We can fight easily against colonialism and occupation, but the invasion of our minds via ideological and cultural war is much more dangerous...They want to enslave us, drive us by rods and pull our ears as if we were cattle.

This kind of discourse has prevailed in the Gulf States, supposedly the most open, modern and moderate, as well as being in desperate need of US protection since the explosion of hatred against the United States and the West following the events of 11 September. We have also seen the few daring, dissident voices that spoke out but were almost universally drowned in protest, condemnation and intimidation. There are probably many more moderates who dare not surface for now, but their silence is known to speak volumes. How much more so in other, less open countries.

EGYPT: THE HUB OF OFFICIAL MODERATION AND POPULAR FERMENT

Egypt, perhaps more than any other Arab country, is counted on by the United States as a staunch supporter because, unlike Saudi Arabia, which has petroleum to offer, it is poor and resource-less, and depends considerably upon US military and economic aid. It has strategic assets, such as the Suez Canal and probably the most formidable Arab Army, also US-equipped, but due to the popularity of the Muslim groups that place themselves in opposition to the government and are by definition antagonistic to the United States, it is uncertain how much longer the corrupt and autocratic rulers there can maintain the treacherous balance between their avowed pro-Americanism and the popular sentiment amongst their impoverished, frustrated and oppressed masses. As in the case of Pakistan and other Muslim countries, the events of 11 September have brought into focus that conflict and further widened the gap between rulers and ruled, and therefore further sharpened the dilemmas facing those regimes. This is all the more so since public opinion-makers – intellectuals, professionals, and certainly clerics, especially the fundamentalists among them – contribute to shaping popular resentment of the West, to bolstering support for other Muslims under duress and, in consequence, to cultivating the Islamikaze as national and cultural heroes. So much so that even the regime itself, after paying the usual lip service to moderation and voicing sympathy for the US plight, often slides back into the popular mood.

The core of the matter for Egypt, as for other Arabs and Muslims, is that they lack an accepted definition of terrorism; they do not accept the State Department's notion that the nature of terrorism is determined by its manifest content (harming innocent civilians in order to attain political goals) and not by the identity of its practitioners. They therefore seek refuge in their self-righteousness, which allows the Muslims to act indiscriminately, because that is jihad, or self-defence, while anything done by others, even if it is a thoughtful, discriminating and defensive measure, is dubbed as aggression and terrorism. Mubarak himself, who in the 1980s gave shelter to the Palestinian killers of Mr Klinghoffer – the US national whose boat was hijacked in high seas and his body callously tossed overboard – later made himself the champion of anti-terrorism when he ruthlessly fought the *Gama'at* that challenged his rule, carrying out shootings and executions without any due process and without the West so much as protesting. Thus, four months into the post-11 September era, two months after the counter-attack in Afghanistan began, and at least one month after Bin-Laden was shown on the screens boasting of his Twin Towers 'exploit' and rejoicing publicly over it, Mubarak was not quite sure yet who was to blame. In a speech before his Third Army near Suez, he said:

I cannot say for sure who were the perpetrators of the 11 September events. We leave it to history to determine. This does not mean that I justify anyone. Egypt's stand has been as clear as daylight. We were the pioneers of counter-terrorism, we are opposed to any act of terrorism and we condemn all forms of terrorism. I have always counselled the American party to refrain from attacking terrorism in Afghanistan as long as Israel was carrying out acts of killings and violence against the Palestinians, because the Arabs at large would simply not accept that.[40]

Mubarak was not alone, he just set the tone and nodded in approval. After a break of several weeks, in which the establishment media refrained from attacking the United States following the outrage caused in the West by Egypt's initial virulence (see Chapter 1), the attacks were resumed, as the United States, Egypt's 'ally', was still deeply involved in its battle against the Bin-Laden terrorists:

Four months into the barbaric war, in which America has targeted Afghanistan, the truth has surfaced: the US has been sticking to its double-standard policy, even when dealing with terrorism, which proves its hypocrisy, lies and shallowness... For it turns out that the only reason for the continuation of the American oppressive policy, of turning facts upside down and of abandoning justice, principles and values and ignoring the resolutions of international legitimacy, has been to preserve the vital interests of its client – Israel. This has caused her to regard rebellious and deviant Israel's terrorism and horrendous crimes as a legitimate struggle and 'jihad' in self-defence, but at the same time, Washington who was supposed to protect international legitimacy, resorts to the same lies, distortion, travesty of justice, hooliganism and arrogance to lay the blame on the legitimate Palestinian struggle against [Israeli] terrorism...
According to that same logic, the act of terror perpetrated on 11 September, was legitimate, because it is totally identical with the acts of terror committed by Israel.[41]

The author gave, in great detail, a description of the Israeli actions in Palestinian camps, which were accepted by Secretary Powell as 'self-defence'. This outraged him and the 'killing, destruction, starvation and siege' imposed by the Israelis, seemed to him, an experienced writer, as 'identical', 'exactly similar' to those acts perpetrated by the terrorists of 11 September (who were justified and even praised in many Egyptian media, as we have seen above.) In other words, this editor of an establishment major daily was not out to condemn any act of terror against civilians, but only Israel's actions which were supported by the United States and committed against other Arabs, the inference being that 'who does' is more significant in his mind than 'what is done'. When Powell pronounced himself in support of Israel, he did not condone any act against civilians, contrary to the editorial accusation: quite the contrary. Moreover, he would have condemned these acts outright had they been the result of an unprovoked Israeli initiative, or if civilians had been targeted, even in the case of an Israeli response to a provocation. Israel's acts should have been compared, then, not to the Twin Towers act of terror, but to the US response in Afghanistan. In both cases, indiscriminate acts of terror were perpetrated against innocent and unsuspecting civilians (in buildings, cafés, restaurants, buses, streets and so forth) with a view to maximizing innocent civilian casualties. This triggered, on their part, not revenge or retaliation, as the Arab writers would have it, but acts of punishment against the perpetrators and preventive acts against further terrorist horrors. These are the subtleties that the editor, and many other Arab and Muslim writers, have failed to comprehend.

Faced with acts of indiscriminate terrorism, the victim countries can sit with their arms folded and thus invite more terrorism; can ask for extradition of the perpetrators, or their operators in the case of Islamikaze attacks; or demand that they be arrested and punished by their local authorities; or try to eliminate them by surgical operations that do not involve much collateral damage; or go and get them when all the other alternatives have failed. Getting them is the most costly operation, in moral and human terms, as the perpetrators hide within innocent civilian populations, or holy shrines, or government compounds which give them shelter and where they seek immunity. Therefore, dislodging them not only jeopardizes the party seeking retribution but, unfortunately, innocent civilians too. In other words, despite the intention of the party who acts in self-defence to minimize casualties – and that is the difference between the terrorists and civilized societies who respect the rule of law – unwanted and un-intentional collateral damage is caused in this course of action: innocent people are killed, houses are destroyed if they served as military positions (but after their population is evacuated), and infra-structure that served the terrorists is destroyed. It is the authorities who gave shelter to their terrorists (the Palestinians and the Taliban, in our cases), or even encouraged and sustained them, who are to blame for the collateral damage, not those who acted in self-defence. Another difference between civilized and terrorist societies is that the former apologize, compensate, allow recourse to their court system and investigate, under public scrutiny and pressure, whether any unwarranted harm resulted from abuse or unnecessary zeal by their forces, and punish the culprits; while terrorist societies hold their terrorists as heroes, dispatch them in order to sow death among the innocent in the first place, and indulge in public orgies of jubilation at the sight of the horrors which result from their acts.

If this is the popular mood in those countries, it is not surprising for Arab and Muslim writers to seek fault with others. This mode of behaviour is not new, as the United States and Israel have never enjoyed high marks in the Arabic press. But after the events of 11 September, and in view of the fact that many of the perpetrators were Egyptian, writers in Egypt, like their peers in the rest of the Arab and Muslim world, desperately attempted to displace the attention of their readers onto the evil image of the United States instead of looking in the mirror at their own. The same editor of *Al-Akhbar* not only attacked Israel for its 'horrors and genocide', and the Americans who 'backed them', refusing to look at the niceties separating terror from self-defence, but he tried to 'explain' to his readers why the United States would act so callously and insensitively. The United States is steeped in corruption, as the collapse of Enron has demonstrated, which was linked to the financing of President Bush's election campaign along with those of many senators and congressmen. He wrote:

> Economic corruption is part and parcel of the political corruption that is reflected in Washington's foreign policy and its subservience to the Jewish Lobby who acts on behalf of Israel, itself the foremost state of hatred in the world, and the servant of the dons of the most widespread world corruption...American economic and political corruption have become an industry in themselves. Therefore I am warning American media and politicians: Cease accusing

others of corruption while you yourselves live in a glass-house of corruption.[42]

Similarly, *Al-Ahram*, which prides itself as the '*New York Times* of the Arab world', attacked the United States for her 'double standards' in condoning Israel while herself proclaiming her fight against terrorism. The author, Salameh Ahmed Salameh, accused the United States of having divested its struggle against terrorism from lofty human values, which had helped her elicit Arab support, and then degenerated into submission to Israel once her initial goal against the Taliban had been attained. The author thus invoked the 'moral' principle at the base of Egypt's support for the fight against terrorism, but then blames the United States for forsaking her pledge to resolve the 'Israeli occupation of Palestine' and to refrain from attacking Arab countries in return. Thus, according to this writer, the Arabs had hoped for a utilitarian quid pro quo when they came out in public for the US struggle, and once the Americans did not deliver, the Arabs became justified in turning their backs on them. Being oblivious of the standard definitions of terror in the West, he also accused the Americans of having corrupted the understanding of those definitions by allowing the Israelis to perform war crimes. But that is not enough: now America herself is condemned for her long litany of war crimes: bombing villages in Afghanistan and 'massacring hundreds of innocent civilians', while claiming 'inevitable collateral damage', but at the same time accusing Palestinians of terrorism when 'Israeli civilians and settlers are killed inadvertently, during the acts of martyrdom of the Palestinians'. The Americans were also blamed for their 'barbaric acts against the prisoners of war they captured', by transporting them like animals to Guantanamo, with their 'hands in shackles and their eyes blindfolded and under the effect of drugs...She placed them in closed solitary cells, like seized predatory beasts.'[43]

The Muslim al-Qa'ida and Taliban prisoners of war, who were seized by the United States in Afghanistan, indeed became the topic of much discussion in Egypt and the rest of the Arab world. It was inconceivable to most Arab and Muslim audiences that mujahedin who fought for the cause of Allah, and were considered heroes in those societies, notably in Egypt, where the rejoicing and elation of the press was widespread in the wake of 11 September (see Chapter 1), should be reduced to hapless, shackled and disgruntled prisoners, at the mercy of the United States. Therefore, the Egyptian (and other Arab, for that matter) media ceased talking about the horrors they were accused of and turned the blame on the 'barbaric acts of the Americans', comparing Bush to Hitler, or vilifying him by attaching to him the anti-Semitic attributes of Shylock. The Arab comments on the US President following his State of the Union Address on 29 January 2002, where he lumped Iran, Iraq and North Korea together in an 'Axis of Evil', were particularly vicious. For example:

> I saw the Guantanamo base in Cuba in 1963...It is a nice base. No one expected it to be turned into a base for torturing al-Qa'ida members from Afghanistan, in a way unprecedented in history – worse than what Hitler did to his rivals among Jews and Christians...Hitler's soldiers burned, strangled, and then killed. But America's prisoners were transferred in planes, on a trip lasting over 20 hours...What was done to them is abominable: they were blindfolded, their ears covered and their noses sealed. They could not see, hear or smell; they wore iron masks. Their hands, arms, necks and legs were shackled in heavy chains. Twenty hours of sensory deprivation is sufficient to damage the senses of any man...In the solitary confinement cells the darkness is absolute. Suddenly, the Americans would shine a brilliant light and make aggressive noises for a few moments, and then quiet and darkness are restored. Those moments are enough to leave the prisoners blind, deaf and brain-damaged...Even America's friends have condemned this inhuman treatment...the American Defense Secretary claims that they are not POWs, but criminals who have offended the law by being members of Bin-Laden's gang...These POWs cannot go to American courts because they are not on American soil, but rather at 'Camp X-Ray' which is designed to turn them from men to beasts within hours.[44]

President Bush presented himself in his State of the Union [address] as a leader thirsty for bloodshed and for declaring war on half the world to satisfy a sense of vengeance and in submission to the sick Israeli incitement that stems from the interests of the Hebrew State, even if satisfying these interests comes at the expense of the destruction of the entire world... The 'Triangle of Evil' that he described poses no threats to the

United States, but jeopardizes Israel's aspirations of expansion... Bush's fiery speech reminds us of the speeches of the Nazi Adolph Hitler. His threatening of Iran and Iraq reminds us of Hitler's threatening of Poland and Czechoslovakia... The entire world must act to stop his recklessness before he drowns in destructive wars that will make the First and Second World Wars seem modest...

The American war against terror in Afghanistan has, to date, chalked up only minor victories incompatible with the high price the United States has paid, and perhaps will yet pay to accomplish its goals... President Bush is making threats in order to hide this reality, to cover up the political losses and loss of life in Afghanistan which have not been made public... He tried to terrify Arab and Islamic countries and emphasized Iran because it has the greatest influence in thwarting his conspiracies in Afghanistan... With these idiotic threats, Bush accomplished the miracle of bringing Iran and Iraq together... He created a global front against the unjustified policy of fear that he leads... If the American President has lost his wits because of the acts of one man, such as Bin-Laden, who headed an organization that comprises no more than a few hundred men, what state will he be in if he faces an alliance of Iran, Iraq, North Korea, Syria, Hamas, Islamic Jihad and Hizbullah, all of which have a rich history of struggle etc...?

The American President is playing with fire. He is like an unbalanced man given a rifle, about to go out to the street and start shooting at passers-by. Thus, the intelligent people of the world have to hasten to stop him and take away his gun before it is too late... I felt pain and disappointment at the sight of the Congress applauding his threats... which will lead their country to bankruptcy and perhaps to collapse. The 'Axis of Evil' is not Iraq, Iran and North Korea, but the United States and Israel.[45]

Egyptian clerics – including Sheikh Tantawi of Al-Azhar, who had earlier spoken out decisively against the Islamikaze and even participated in the inter-faith meeting in Alexandria in early 2002, in which voices of moderation were raised against terrorism – joined their fundamentalist colleagues who were cited above and consecrated terrorism, of course of the kind carried out by Muslims against non-Muslims. In an interview with the Egyptian opposition daily, *Al-Wafd*, he confirmed that 'anyone who blows himself up in the midst of his enemies in defence of his rights is a *shahid, shahid, shahid*!!! [martyr]', thus approving that mode of terrorism, though he posited that such acts were legitimate only against oppressors but not against innocent and helpless civilians, because that would contradict the 'nobility of Islam'. He also disagreed with fundamentalist clerics who maintained that since all Israelis are combatants, none of them should be spared, explaining that there are supporters of peace among them who do not fall into the category of warriors.[46] A columnist on religious affairs, Dr Abdallah al-Najjar, commented on the Islamikaze in the mainstream *Al-Gumhuriyya*, the mouthpiece of the regime in revolutionary days:

> The Believers in Allah are not scared by their enemies and are not afraid to engage in jihad...because they regard jihad as a way to sell their lives to Allah, in view of the expectation that victory is theirs since they sacrifice their lives cheaply for Allah...But their enemies safeguard their lives the way criminals do, that is at any price, even at the price of misery and humiliation...It is unfortunate that their quest to safeguard their lives has instigated them to develop science and encourage innovation, so that they can enforce their inferior thinking by the use of their superior weapons, at a time when the people of Truth [that is the Muslims] have neglected that aspect inasmuch as they did not distinguish themselves in science and paid no attention to developing means to overcome the people of Deceit [the enemies of Islam]. Therefore the balance is upside down and the voice of Deceit has overwhelmed the voice of Truth...
>
> But the Believers are not afraid of their enemies, and they do seek to preserve life, for Allah has promised them one of two good things: either victory or martyrdom. Each one of these options is so much imbued with grace and hope that the boundary between them is blurred...Conversely, their enemies preserve their lives like the miser his money. They are so reluctant to sacrifice their lives that they avoid combat and do not rush to martyrdom. This is the secret of the Believers' victory over the Unbelievers, in spite of the fact that the latter are more numerous and better armed and equipped...Allah has already decreed that small groups can overcome large groups with the

> help of Allah... Had military power had any significance, the Qur'an would not have written these words. These are the words of Allah and they constitute the unalterable Truth.[47]

In the wake of Secretary Rumsfeld's decision not to relent on US bombings in Afghanistan during the month of Ramadan (November–December 2001), and the outpouring of sarcasm against him by Muslim scholars who ridiculed his observation that Muslims have always fought during Ramadan throughout their history (for example, the Arab onslaught against Israel in 1973 was launched during Ramadan), an Egyptian scholar from Al-Azhar University clarified the issue. Dr Fuad Mukhaimer, who also chairs the Shari'a Associations of Egypt, made a long survey of Muslim victories throughout history and found out that the month of Ramadan has been particularly propitious for victory, because the discipline of the fast not only prepared the Muslim fighters generally for tough military conduct, but in particular for fighting 'battles of honour' during that holiday which was usually termed 'the month of jihad', the Islamic *umma* was dubbed the *'umma* of jihad', and its moral values became reputed as the 'values of war'. The idea is, as this author confirms it , that 'since the Muslims conquer themselves through the fast, they can also conquer the enemy'. Thus, for this writer, 'the month of Ramadan is the month of victories, education and military training. When the Muslims fast, Allah generates victory for them by overwhelming Satan who tempts the Believers to eat', and in any case, He promises the ultimate victory to Islam, be it during Ramadan or at any other time.[48]

On the same website, another cleric of the establishment Al-Azhar University, Sheikh Muhammed al-Gamei'a, who also served as the Imam of the Muslim Center in New York until he was recalled after 11 September, crowned the US attack in Afghanistan with the title of 'terrorism', predicted that the war would generate the 'end of America', and that 'had the Americans known that 11 September was perpetrated by the Jews, they would do to them what Hitler did'.[49] A few more 'pearls' from the imam's mouth are worth recording:

> Following the incident, Muslims and Arabs stopped feeling safe in sending their wives to the market or their children to school [in the United States]. Muslims do not feel safe even going to hospitals, because some Jewish doctors in one of the

hospitals poisoned sick Muslim children, who then died…

The Muslims are being persecuted by the people and the federal government [in the United States]. This is the result of the bad image created by the Zionist media, and of their presenting Islam as a religion of terrorism. That is the reason why the Americans have linked the recent incidents to Islam…

During my conversations with a group of [American people], it became clear to me that they knew very well that the Jews were behind those ugly acts, while we, the Arabs, were innocent and that someone from among their people was disseminating corruption in the land. Although the Americans suspect that the Zionists are behind the act, none has the courage to talk about it in public…

Those people said that the Zionists control everything and that they also control political decision-making, the big media organizations, and the financial and economic institutions. Anyone daring to say a word is considered an anti-Semite… The Jewish element is as Allah described it when He said 'They disseminate corruption in the land'. We know that they have always broken agreements, unjustly murdered the Prophets, and betrayed the faith. Can they be expected to live up to their contracts with us?…Do you think they will stop spilling our blood? No. You see these people [the Jews] all the time, everywhere, spreading corruption, alcoholism and drugs. Because of them there are strip clubs, homosexuals and lesbians everywhere. They do this to impose their hegemony and colonialism on the world…

We saw these Zionists, just one hour after the event [of 11 September], broadcasting on the BBC that the Arabs and particularly the Palestinians, were rejoicing over the American deaths. To this end, they broadcast a video from 1991 filmed during the invasion of Kuwait. But Allah thwarted them when a Brazilian professor stated that the video was a forgery, because she had a copy of it. These people have the script prepared in advance, and they have the ability to fabricate events in their favour…This is what the Jews plotted and planned and they used Arabs to carry it out…

All the signs indicate that the Jews have the most to gain from an explosion like that. They are the only ones capable of planning such acts. It was found that the automatic pilot was neutralized a few minutes before the flight, and the automatic pilot cannot be neutralized if you do not have command of the control tower. The black boxes were found to contain no information. America has the most powerful intelligence apparatuses. How did the perpetrators manage to infiltrate America without their knowledge? Jews control decision-making in the airports and in the sensitive centres in the White House and the Pentagon. And besides, America has presented no proof incriminating Bin-Laden and al-Qa'ida... Therefore, only the Jews were capable of planning such an incident because it was planned with great precision of which Bin-Laden or any other Islamic organization or intelligence apparatus is incapable...

I advise every Arab and every Muslim not to offer any aid whatsoever to the oppressing superpower in her attack against Muslims, because this is a betrayal of Allah and His Prophet...It was said on the news in the United States that 4,000 did not go to work at the World Trade Center on the day of the incident, and that the police arrested a group of Jews rejoicing in the streets at the time of the incident...This news item was hushed up immediately after it was broadcast...The Jews who control the media acted to hush it up so that the American people would not know. If it became known to the American people, they would have done to the Jews what Hitler did...

An American attack on Afghanistan will constitute terrorism, as the United States did in Iraq and Palestine...I think that this war will be the end of the American oppressor...They have skyscrapers and large factories ..., they are arrogant in their power...but Allah will avenge himself on them...In every trouble there is some good...This incident urges people to come to know Islam, now that it has been proven to the Americans that they were deceived by the Jews...Allah has foiled their plot when they set a trap to try to distort the image of the Muslims, and has proved to the Americans what the truth is. Therefore, I believe that the future of the Muslims in the United States will be glorious.[50]

No wonder, then, that this vitriol, which is widely spread throughout Egypt and the rest of the Arab and Islamic world, has also produced some action. A group of Muslim Brothers, an organization banned in the political arena of Egypt, began to secretly train young people for an Islamikaze role in combat (*Tanzim Ishtishhadiyun*, The Organization of Martyrs), and even presented eight of them live on 18 March 2002 to hundreds of demonstrators at Al-Azhar University. During the demonstration, the students heard a live broadcast of encouragement from the Leader of the Hamas in Gaza, Sheikh Yassin. According to the report, the eight would-be martyrs had their faces covered with black cloth and on their heads were red bands which carried the slogan 'Jihad is our Way'. The eight demonstrated their abilities in martial arts, to free hostages from their captors and carry out surprise attacks against armed soldiers. The *Al-Mustaqbal* reporter also interviewed one of the eight, who said that 'our operations are directed against the Israeli enemy'.[51]

THE PALESTINIAN PARADIGM OF ISLAMIKAZE

The Palestinians, who have been involved in a sharp and escalating violent clash with Israel since their declared 'Al-Aqsa Intifadah' (September 2000), itself pregnant with Muslim symbolism, have brought the use of the Islamikaze tactic to its harrowing apex, and they have become role models for the rest of the Arab and Muslim world. Moreover, while the idea of martyrdom which impels the martyrs to act is Islamic, the concept of self-sacrifice for the sake of Islam seems to have expanded to such an extent that it has transcended the boundaries of fanatic Muslim organizations, such as the Hamas, Islamic Jihad or the Hizbullah, to become a universal tool of terrorism among Palestinian 'secular' organizations, such as the Fat'h and its derivatives: the Tanzim, Force 17, and other groups. In fact, the escalation between Israel and the Palestinians in 2002 has so dramatically increased the numbers of Islamikaze self-immolating bombers that it is evident that the Hamas and the Islamic Jihad would not be able to sustain the pace of two to four acts a day, and that without the infusion of more volunteers for death into this sinister apparatus, the Palestinians would have to either desist from these acts or seek outside volunteers. Therefore, Yasser Arafat's Fat'h stepped in and standardized this mode of action for their own recruits, too. In so doing, they signalled that not only would they be ready for the supreme sacrifice, but that they would not be outdone by their Islamist competitors in public opinion and for popularity in the Palestinian street, which is customarily enthusiastic and overjoyed by each bombing of civilians in the heart of Israel, the perpetrators of which are held as national heroes.

We have, thus, a new situation in which terrorism by Islamikaze, though hitherto solely the trademark of Muslim radicals, and rarely so, has, since 11 September, become an acknowledged universal and common *modus operandi* in and of Muslim societies, as a mind-boggling expression of displeasure about domestic or international politics. On 11 September alone, 19 self-sacrificing young Muslims died in the United States; and since then, about 100 Palestinian terrorists have died in the same fashion, taking with them hundreds of Israelis. The crossover from an extreme act to a current and routine action not only necessitated the widening of the circle of volunteers, so far drawn from young Muslim recruits, but also engendered a new attitude towards the participation of women in this sort of battle. Hitherto, Muslim clerics had frowned upon active military service by women in any of the Muslim countries, and the heads of Hamas and Islamic Jihad have similarly reserved for their women the role of educators and 'manufacturers of men'.[52] The current cross-gender and cross-national universalization of Islamikaze terrorism, however, has opened the door wide for the banalization and routinization of this stunning phenomenon. Because what it requires is not a trained and resolute fighter, with high-class physical skills, battlefield experience, endurance under stress and technical sophistication, but only an ordinary person, male or female, indoctrinated and eager to die for Allah, who knows how to push a button and evaporate instantly into Paradise, while pushing his victims and their loved ones into Hell.

The debate surrounding the 'martyrdom' of Wafa Idris, the first Palestinian woman Islamikaze, who has since been followed by others, is in itself indicative of the new mood. Arafat's 'Al-Aqsa Brigades' took responsibility for Wafa's explosion in the central street of Jerusalem, which killed one woman and maimed dozens of others. Much of the initial debate concerned her motivations for sacrificing herself, and cited personal difficulties.[53] But when fellow Palestinians began to justify her act, quoting the precedents of other renowned Palestinian women-fighters, like Laila Khalid, and predicting that more women might follow suit,[54] the religious aspect of it all broke into the open. Hamas leaders said that jihad was an obligation that applied to women also, and that Islam had never differentiated between men and women in the battlefield based on a precedent of the Prophet, who used to draw lots among women who wished to join the battle.[55] Jamila Shanti, the Head of the Women's Activities of the Palestinian Islamic Movement, concurred with the idea of equality of women in the struggle, provided they avoid inappropriate behaviour. However, the women martyrs are allowed, in her opinion, to relinquish the veil for the occasion in order to 'mislead the enemy'. She believes that since the clerics share a consensus that Islamikaze operations are the highest form of martyrdom, there is nothing wrong with them.[56] The Head of Hamas, Sheikh Yassin, however, had some reservations, stating that while women had a role in jihad and martyrdom, their uniqueness warranted that they must be accompanied by a chaperon,[57] exactly as puritanical Muslims would not allow women to drive or to roam the streets unaccompanied by a brother, a father or a husband.

Yassin, bowing to operational requisites, later amended his position, realizing that the lone operation of the martyr woman would become unfeasible if she were accompanied by someone who would attract attention and might himself die in the attack. Therefore, he stated that only if the woman was to stay out for the day and the night did she need company, while if her absence were shorter, as in the case of martyrdom where she was not supposed to return, she might go alone.[58] But a would-be woman martyr, who was arrested in Israel for attempting to blow herself up and was released on the basis of the Oslo Accords, invoked a Hadith where the Prophet was said to have allowed women to go to jihad even without their husbands' consent in case the land of Islam was invaded, which she thinks was now the case.[59] Thus, for her, as for Yassin, necessity permitted what was usually prohibited. At Al-Azhar University, where disputes converge in expectation of the rulings of Sheikh Tantawi, an internal debate ensued. While Sheikh Abu al-Hassan decreed that the act of jihad by women against Israelis was permissible, especially when the enemy has 'plundered even one inch of Muslim land', in which case they are entitled to 'wage jihad even without their husbands' consent, and the slaves without their masters' permission', Tantawi had ruled in favour of those acts provided that they were not directed against civilians. Abu al-Hassan also quoted precedents from the time of the Prophet, when women were said to have been allowed to fight and kill men from among the enemy Infidels.[60]

Although Yassin explained that women were simply not needed in the Hamas ranks of martyrs for the moment, because more male volunteers were available than his organization could absorb,[61] the debate continued to rage in the Arab world. Egypt's *Al-Sha'b* glorified the woman who could teach all Arab men, rulers, princes and women a lesson in heroic defence of her country in 'the battle of martyrdom which petrified the heart of the enemy's entity, and shocked the enemy with her meager, thin and weak body... when with her exploded all the myths about women's weaknesses, submissiveness and enslavement'.[62] A Jordanian columnist, who prided himself on the 'dignity that women enjoyed in the Arab and Islamic world', accused the Western human rights activists of 'robbing women of their rights to be human, and viewed them as bodies without souls', and stressed that Wafa 'never dreamt of owning a BMW or a cellular phone, and never carried makeup in her bag, but rather explosives to fill the enemy with horror'. He said that it was the West who demanded that Eastern women should become equal to men, and that was the way the martyr Wafa understood equality. 'Oh Wafa Idris!!! Mercy upon you and shame upon us !!!' was his concluding cry.[63] Similarly, *Afaq 'Arabiya*, the mouthpiece of the Muslim Brothers in Egypt, accused the West of wasting money in vain, attempting to 'disrupt the consciousness of the Muslim women and make them believe that their bodies and needs were most important'. The writer, sociologist Dr al-Maghdoub, launched an all-out attack on that Western intervention which invokes women's liberation, equality with men, and 'their right to be prostitutes, to strip, to reveal their charms', and assured that those concepts are doomed to fall on deaf ears.[64] For this 'enlightened' sociologist, those Westernized 'superficial women' served the West by:

> Giving [Arab] countries their drug-addicted young men and women... who have perverse [homosexual] relations, commit rape, theft, and murder... But they are still a minority, even if they make a lot of noise. The majority of young Muslims are still in good shape. It is true that they are silent, but we have seen how the silence of Wafa Idris ended.[65]

In Egypt and the rest of the Arab world, words of support for Wafa Idris also abounded. Dr Samia Sa'd a-Din, a woman herself, proclaimed the end of gender classification in the Palestinian struggle, once Palestinian women have decided to 'write the history of their liberation with their blood and will become time bombs in the face of the Israeli enemy. They will not settle for being mothers of martyrs' any longer', she assures.[66] Another columnist from the same mouthpiece of the regime, *Al-Akhbar*, found it strange that while the Swedish Foreign Minister, Anna Lind, was criticizing the US position, Wafa carried out her act of martyrdom. Lind, too, spoke up 'while men kept silent' and was unafraid of doing so *vis-à-vis* US policy. Thus, one brave woman spoke up while another brave woman acted.[67] For *Al-Ahram* columnist, Zakariyya Nil, Wafa Idris was nothing less than a modern Jeanne d'Arc,[68] and another, 'Abd al-Halim Qandil, of the weekly *Al-'Arabi*, elevated her to new heights, asserting that 'a nation who has in it Wafa Idris can never be defeated' for she became the 'most beautiful of women in the world, and of the world to come, once she rose to Heaven'. He considered her martyrdom as 'a death which instilled life' and 'a chunk of flesh and blood transformed into illuminating spirit and purity for the generations to come'. He praised her beauty when she liberated the Arabs from their sins and 'elevated the humiliated nation to Paradise'.[69] No one, however, went as far as praising her as the Egyptian psychologist, Dr 'Adel Sadeq, the Head of Psychiatry at Cairo's Ein Shams University, who compared Wafa to no less than Jesus Christ. He said that perhaps the Holy Spirit that placed Jesus in the womb of Mary did the same by 'placing a bomb in the heart of Wafa and enveloped her pure body with dynamite', and it was no coincidence for him that 'the enemy in both instances was the same [the Jews]'.[70]

This understanding, even sympathy for the Islamikaze, by intellectuals, professionals and journalists, some of them at the hub of supposedly moderate and pro-Western Arab societies, shows us more about those societies than about the bestiality of the attacks by those hallowed 'martyrs' who indiscriminately blow up innocent civilians. For the voices of sympathy and support are those of public opinion makers, who have a great impact on their crowds through the media. What is particularly puzzling is that those self-righteous 'humanists' and 'enlightened' intellectuals not only have no words of condemnation for those horrendous acts that any civilized person should disown, and certainly no words of condolence for the victims, but in elevating those acts to the level of heavenly missions and national heroism, they thereby contribute to building up the legitimacy of such acts, expectation among the crowds for more, and the motivation among young Muslims to flock to the ranks of the Islamikaze. No wonder then, that those words of encouragement feed the spiral of senseless Islamikaze attacks, and force their victims to adopt harsher defensive measures against them. So, in the final analysis, even according to the logic of these machines of death, they are bound to bring more destruction and bereavement against those very people and supportive audiences who now applaud them.

While it was to be expected that the Palestinian terrorist organizations who dispatched Wafa to her death would eulogize her for her martyrdom,[71] it is much harder to explain in any rational terms the swelling support, symbolic and otherwise, that her act produced throughout the Arab world. For if one can understand the political machinations of Saddam Hussein, when he decided to erect a memorial in her honour, one is aghast when a woman film director, an Egyptian PhD to boot, Amira Abu-Fattuh, writes under the headline 'An Oscar-winning film':

> This is not a movie like all other movies. The heroine is the beautiful, pure Palestinian woman, Wafa Idris, full of faith and willpower. I could find no one better than she, and I could find no film more wonderful than this, that shocked Israel's heart...From Paradise where she is now, she shouts with all her strength: 'Enough glorification of the dead! Enough glorification of the victories of your forefathers!!!' They have played their part, and now it is your turn.[72]

This short-lived but symbol-laden 'Wafa Festival' was triggered by the London-based Arabic daily, *Al-Quds al-'Arabi*,[73] but was immediately picked up, like other sensational issues in the Arab press, and repeated like a mantra by Arab and Muslim writers of all political convictions. It was as if their oppressed frustration and hatred for Israel and the Jews, regardless of the 'peace' accords that their countries (Egypt and Jordan) had signed with Israel at a considerable cost to the latter, were merely a new starting point to force her to disarm, to absorb attacks, and to take evasive action in the face of more at the hand of new heroes like Wafa. She was seen as 'a spark of light and hope in the midst of darkness and courageous in deeds, not words';[74] a Mona Lisa, only more beautiful than the original, with her 'dreamy eyes and the mysterious smile on her lips', and in general 'more beautiful than any picture of a woman painted by any artists';[75] or her suitcase of explosives that carried her to her death as 'the most beautiful prize any woman can possibly win. Her spirit was raging, her heart filled with anger and her mind convinced by the calls of peace and co-existence.'[76] Even the horrifying detail of her act sounded like music in the ears of those columnists:

> She quietly made her decision, sought explosives, went to pray, and then chose her target carefully. She went to a big restaurant with dozens of customers. She asked Allah for a martyr's death and victory...she kissed the soil of the homeland and went calmly to her fate. She inscribed her name on the forehead of history.[77]

What is even more terrifying is the wish of the writer that the number of victims could have been higher, because the assassin killed 'only' one victim, an 81-year-old woman passerby along the main street of Jerusalem, but the over-enthusiastic columnist carried her in his dreams to a 'restaurant with dozens of customers'. This time he was wrong, but at other times, other terrorists like Wafa have killed dozens of unsuspecting civilians, children, and entire families of customers in restaurants, much to the delight, one has to assume, of that zealous writer.

The tragedy inherent in this seemingly total, pan-Arab, unqualified lack of concern for human life, with no 'if', 'because' or 'but', their inability to sympathize with innocent victims, and their self-centred perception of being the victims of the West, have all combined to create this distorted state of mind which enables them to glorify the Islamikaze and to regard it as a 'glowing light' that will lead them somewhere. Where exactly, we do not know. It would seem that it is much more important for them to destroy the West, which they denigrate because they cannot be like it, than to try to rise to its level. They want to destroy it (and Israel) because they cannot help but compare their drab existence and gloomy future with the more attractive alternative they see in their Western neighbours, while remaining unable to appropriate it for themselves. Therefore, they support any violent means likely to destroy that alternative so as not to have to face their own impotence. Because they are incapable of reaching the technological superiority of the West, on which they depend, much to their chagrin, they despise it culturally and claim to have an edge on it. Also, if they cannot face the humiliation of technological inferiority, then they would use the ultimate weapon of Islamikaze terrorism to terrify Western populations, be it in New York or in Tel Aviv. This is the underlying state of mind which not only condones indiscriminate killings of civilians, but sanctifies it and encourages its growth.

Thus, Wafa the martyr was made a model of behaviour in one Arab paper after another, by columnists of all walks and opinions, government and opposition, especially in 'moderate' Egypt, and her act of 'donning the belt of explosives and talking to Israel, America and the world in the only language they understand'[78] was made the ideal for other youth to emulate. A female columnist, Nagwa Tantawi, dismissed Western culture and pledged victory to the superior culture of the Arabs and Muslims. She just forgot to say explicitly whether the values she was boasting about included martyrdom and wanton killing, but one could infer that from her comparison of Wafa with President Bush's daughters:

> Bush, who leads an oppressive campaign to educate the world, cannot even educate his own daughters. Note the difference between Wafa, the daughter of Arabism and Islam, and Bush's daughters. The difference is the same as the difference between our culture, based on beautiful and noble values, and on the values of homeland and martyrdom, and the materialistic culture [of the West]. This proves that whatever developments will be, victory will be ours – because we have culture and values.[79]

The centrality of martyrdom in Palestinian life after the outbreak of their September 2000 Al-Aqsa Intifadah is reflected not only in their writings, broadcasts and the written media, but also by leaflets that are disseminated in the territories under their rule, as well as audio- and video-cassettes that extol acts of Islamikaze, sanctify their perpetrators and cause families who have sacrificed one of their sons to pledge the souls of the rest of them for the sake of Allah. Was it not Arafat himself who, in the heat of the battle against Israel, coined the war cry 'We are coming to Jerusalem, as martyrs in the millions'? Here is one of those poems, ominously addressed to the Israelis, that became popular in the Palestinian street:

> Because I am a Palestinian
> Because I am enamoured of fate
> And my fate is to have my blood

Turned into songs,
That sketch out the road to freedom,
My fate is to become a human bomb,
Because I am a Palestinian.

Oh, lovers of cruelty, we
Inform you in the name of our hopes
Either I will meet Allah by means
of perfume and musk[80]
or I will live on my land in
Freedom and honour.

Much to your distress,
we will not forget Haifa and Acre
To your distress,
all of Palestine is ours
Because I am a Palestinian.

We have nothing for you but death
Plant as many Gharqad trees[81] as you like
Build as many shelters and hiding places as you desire,
And, if you want, create your own artificial peace.

Your history is black and covered
Your ancestry is a tree whose
Branches are corrupt,
Because I am a Palestinian.
And the Arab rulers in this homeland
Lie in a perpetual sleep
Eating from the fruit of your tree
And drinking of your humiliation
As if they were not Muslims.

Because I am a Palestinian,
Because I bear the flag
And long for the memory of Hittin,[82]
I will place the parts of my body as bombs
In your hatred, in your origin
In your accursed fruit
And in spite of you, they will germinate
The most beautiful of flowers

They will germinate the most beautiful Palestine
Because I am a Palestinian.[83]

This petrifying idealization of violence and death that has been
expanding to ever wider circles, beyond the radical Islamic groups
which had adopted it in the first place, and under the instigation of
the Palestinian leadership, religious and otherwise, is rooted in the
wide-ranging and all-encompassing theology that lay at its base; in
the embrace that non-radical Muslim groups have given to this
ideology in order not to be seen as lagging behind their radical
rivals in the national struggle; and in the callous modes of
behaviour adopted by the Palestinians, which lend legitimacy to
the application of this ideology and turn it into a horrifying and
matter-of-course routine. On the theological level, none other than
the Chief Mufti of Jerusalem, Sheikh 'Akrama Sabri, an Arafat
appointee, criticized the Muslim authorities who did not approve of
Islamikaze attacks, and stated that the acts are justified and to be
encouraged. He was referring to Sheikh Tantawi of Egypt, who had
prohibited such attacks in general and then limited the prohibition
to only innocent civilians, and to a Saudi mufti who also banned
this kind of operation. According to the Palestinian mufti, the
rulings of these clerics were the result of international pressure, and
admonished 'those who do not have the courage to speak the truth
to remain quiet and not say things that create confusion'. He added
that 'resistance is legitimate, and those who give up their lives do
not require permission from anyone', and that 'we must not stand
in the way of the Intifadah and jihad. Rather, we must stand at the
side and encourage them.' When asked whether no differentiation
should be made between civilians and fighting personnel, he
clarified:

> Who is civilian and who is military? There have been many
> more Palestinian civilians than fighters killed in the Intifadah.
> Schoolchildren whose bodies were torn to pieces. Pregnant
> women who were prevented from reaching hospitals – many
> times the mother and child died.[84]

If this was the position of the highest cleric of the Muslim
establishment of the Palestinian Authority, how much more so for
the Hamas, which rebels against that authority and has often
virulently accused it of 'collaborating' with Israel against the

martyrs?[85] In fact, the mouthpiece of the Hamas, *Al-Risala*, posited the struggle waged by the jihad martyrs as a veritable clash of civilizations, a statement which it is well worth citing in full:

> The starting point of Islamic civilization is the basic fact that the *umma* is guided in all its deeds in the divine Straight Path, which constantly oppresses the natural propensity of humans towards evil...Conversely, their [Western] civilization, was not blessed with that enlightened aspect which should have oppressed their desire to control others and to rob their resources...Therefore, violence has come to characterize Western civilization throughout its history...Let us respond to some of their false accusations that they try to market...
>
> They accuse us of violence. For example, they take the rapid Islamic conquest of many countries, by the force of the sword in their view, to be the best evidence of violence in Islam. Our response is that the only way to explain the Islamic conquests is that they were in implementation of Divine Will, which charged the Muslims with the responsibility to disseminate it, in consequence obliging Muslims to transmit that message to those who did not receive it yet. When that message reaches non-Muslims, they only face two choices: either to convert to Islam or pay *jizya*[86] to the Muslim government, which today may be interpreted as taking up civil obligations [under the Muslim state].
>
> As to conquest by the sword, Islam does not resort to that means unless it feels impelled to remove obstacles in the way of the Divine Message. If we examined that principle thoroughly, we would find its parallel in modern Western civilization which regards the freedom of speech as a sacred right. Therefore, if no obstacles are put on Islam's road to deliver that Message, it would have no need to use the sword...History proves the peace-loving nature of Islam. Caliph 'Umar captured Jerusalem peacefully, and the inhabitants of the conquered countries were acculturated to the Islamic *umma* and enjoyed the same rights and duties. In other words, Muslims did not go to those countries as colonialists who ousted the native inhabitants and replaced them, as America had done with the Indians and Israel with the Palestinians. For example, when the Muslim armies conquered Samarkand, its inhabitants applied to the Muslim

judge, claiming that they were not given the choice between conversion, paying the *jizya* [dhimmitude], or waging war [to the finish] that the Muslim conquerors had customarily accorded to others. Thus, the Muslim judge had no option but to order the Muslim armies to evacuate the city...How can one then say, that Islam is a violent civilization?

Conversely, Western civilization was profoundly influenced by [Roman] civilization which sanctified force and used to throw gladiators to the arena to fight each other or be swallowed by lions, in order to satisfy their own inferior bestial instincts. The characteristics of this civilization consist of oppressing the other and robbing his resources. It is known for its egotism and arrogance towards the weak. Many wars broke out only to enable it to lay its hands on more wealth. The peak of its appetite was evinced in its kindling two world wars within a quarter-century, in the latest of which nuclear bombs were used that annihilated hundreds of thousands of people.[87]

Under the title: 'The Americans are Digging their own Grave by Invading Afghanistan', another columnist in the same organ attacked the Americans and their underlings in the Arab and Islamic world ('the eunuchs who serve them') for holding the belief that their weapons can bring them victory, while in fact they only hasten the arrival to Paradise of the jihad fighters. He boasted:

> We are eager to get to Paradise, that is our permanent dwelling, it is there that the black-eyed virgins[88] are awaiting us in the garden pavilion, as well as other innocent girls whose virginity had never been violated by any other man or *jinn* (devil). Conversely, the present world where we live today, and which they [the Americans and their servants] think they own, is not worth for us even the wing of a mosquito...The Qur'an has determined that the battle is bound to end in either our victory over the lords of fallacy, or in our gaining martyrdom and entry to Paradise...But those who fight against our faith and oust us from our houses will either be tortured by the Almighty Allah, or He will torture them via us.[89]

This stunning train of thought somehow brings the author from the plastic and luring depiction of the delights of Paradise for the martyrs to 'evidence' of Allah's heavy-handed punishment of the

Unbelievers. The accident where 66 Israeli Jews of Russian origin lost their life over the Black Sea, in October 2001, was seen as precisely such a manifestation of Allah's justice, because those innocent civilians on a trip to their former homes in Russia were 'suspected' in this writer's sick mind of being Zionists, which in itself justifies their killing at the hands of his vengeful Allah. He also praised other Palestinian terrorists who attacked Israeli civilians and 'sent them to Hell, while they themselves paved their way to Paradise'; yet another sign of Allah's intervention by way of His devoted martyrs. Even the accident in the Versailles Halls, where more than two-dozen Israelis were killed during a wedding celebration when the floor collapsed, was reason for rejoicing by that heartless cleric who pretended to guide his followers into the secrets of Allah's designs against Zionists. He ends his words of deviant 'wisdom' with a promise for an apocalypse, once Bin-Laden defeats the Americans in Afghanistan; then, he pledges that the United States will no longer be able to protect the Zionists, and their 'elimination will be easier than a cold drink in the middle of the summer', as Muslims like Bin-Laden have learned from the gospels of Muhammed the Prophet.[90]

On the behavioural level, the perpetrators of these acts of Islamikaze terrorism seem to have adopted the attitude that their mass murders of innocent people are worth not only discussing as a source of 'inspiration' for others, but that they should be enacted and re-enacted in public, not only in order to boast about them and recycle the sadistic enjoyment they draw from them, but also to provide a model for other youth. In September 2001, they re-played on stage the barbarous attack against the Sbarro Pizzeria in Jerusalem, where entire families were blown up while dining by a Hamas Islamikaze who wiped out 15 civilians along with himself. Wearing a military uniform and a black mask, a Palestinian entered a doorway under the replica of the Sbarro restaurant and set off a fake explosion. A Palestinian audience crowded through the doorway to see the recreation of the 9 August bombing, complete with body parts and pizza slices strewn all over. That was part of an exhibition of the Hamas in Nablus. In another room, the visitors looked through dark windows to see figures dressed as Islamikaze, each with one hand on the Qur'an and the other on an automatic rifle, re-enacting the grisly last testament of the Islamikaze before they set out on their 'mission'. The organizers explained to the visitors that that 'struggle' would continue as long as the

Palestinians were occupied, which in Hamas terms means 'as long as Israel exists'. At the end of the exhibit stood a large rock, behind which a hideous cartoon-figure of an Ultra-Orthodox Jew hid, and a recording called out 'Oh Muslim, there is a Jew behind me, come and kill him'.[91] Students who visited the exhibition expressed their identification with its ghastly exhibits.[92]

This means that this thirst for Jewish blood is not the domain of a few sick-minded individuals or of extremist religious radicals, but, as we have seen, it cuts across large sections of Palestinian, Arab and Muslim societies, including intellectuals, the educated, professionals and young people. Moreover, Israel, as a symbol of the democratic West in their midst, is easy prey for their displaced aggression towards the United States and the West, on which they depend and which they cannot attack directly. The concept of Islamikaze, which has been cultivated by the Palestinians and found its most dramatic and gruesome expression among them, was deemed the ultimate weapon to tear Israel apart, and they use it wholeheartedly, not only through lack of choice due to their military inferiority, but as a strategic choice , as a mobilizing force, and an ideal which youth are called upon to emulate. When their political head, Arafat, makes the vow to see 'One million martyrs march on Jerusalem', he not only shows a callous disregard for the lives of his people, never mind the perceived enemy, but he elevates martyrdom to the level of a legitimate political tool to achieve his goal. Worse, when his chief mufti and other clerics brandish martyrdom as a desirable goal in itself because of the Muslims' 'love of death', unlike the Westerners' 'love of life', and thereby justify the indiscriminate annihilation of innocent civilians, then they take one more step towards their exclusion from human kind.[93]

NOTES

1.   See Muhammed 'Atawna, 'Shari'a and Politics in Saudi Arabia: Siyyasa Shar'iyya as a Mechanism to Stabilize Saudi Society and Government' (in Hebrew), *Jama'a*, Beer Sheba, Vol. 8, 2001, pp. 54–83.
2.   Abd-al Bari Atwan, the Editor of *Al-Quds al-'Arabi* (London), in a talk show at *Al-Jazeera* television (Qatar), 10 July 2001. MEMRI, *Terror in America*, No. 45 (Hebrew), p. 1.
3.   MEMRI, *Terror in America*, No. 45 (Hebrew).
4.   Ibid. p. 2.
5.   *Al-Maidan* (Cairo) , cited by *Al-Quds al-'Arabi* (London), 2 February 2002, ibid.
6.   Ibid.
7.   *Ijtihad*, that is, an intellectual striving to find legal answers to problems that are not

dealt with in the Qur'an or the Hadith, had been traditionally pursued by early Sunnite Islam until the four Schools of the Holy Law (*madhahib*) were established, whereupon the 'doors of *ijtihad* were closed', and all a Sunnite Muslim could do thereafter was to observe *taqlid*, namely imitation of the tradition. But due to the special power of the Mullahs in Shi'ite Islam, who maintain relations with the 'Hidden Imam' until his reappearance, *ijtihad* has remained open to them. Paradoxically, many Sunnite fundamentalists today practice *ijtihad* that is only based on the Qur'an and the Sunna, but modern reformists have resorted to the same legal procedure, but making a more liberal use of human reasoning, such as the *Qyas* (analogy) and ijma' (consensus).

8. 'Afif al-Akhdar, *Al-Hayat* (London), 3 February 2002. Cited and translated by *MEMRI* (Hebrew).

9. Under the famous 'Umar Regulations, the *dhimmis* under Islam underwent many limitations as to their professions, clothing, riding of horses, carrying weapons and also building their houses of prayer in Islamdom. And when permitted to build, they were in no event allowed to stand taller than adjoining mosques.

10. *Al-Hayat* (London), 3 February 2002. Cited and translated by *MEMRI* (Hebrew).

11. Ibid. p. 2.

12. In a panel discussion at *Al-Jazeera* television (15 May 2001), Al-Akhdar did indeed dub French Holocaust deniers, such as Roger Garaudy, 'garbage'.

13. *Al-Hayat* (London), 3 February 2002. Cited and translated by *MEMRI* (Hebrew).

14. Ibn Hajr, a commentator on the choice selection of Hadith, edited by the foremost Hadith Authority – al-Bukhari.

15. This is the poll tax that was paid by People of the Book (*dhimmi*) – See Chapter 2.

16. A temporary cease-fire or truce that was declared by the Muslim ruler when he could not overcome his enemies, and was limited to ten years, renewable *ad perpetuum*, following the model of the Prophet at Hudaybiyya (AD 630).

17. Aman is guarantee of protection given to non-Muslims by Muslim rulers.

18. *Al-Riyad* (Saudi Arabia), 24 October 2001. Cited and translated by *MEMRI* (Hebrew).

19. Tarad al-'Amari, *Al-Watan* (Saudi Arabia), 22 November 2001. *MEMRI, Terror in America*, No. 44 (Hebrew), p. 1.

20. Ibid. p. 2.

21. Sura VII (The Heights), verse 23.

22. *Al-Watan* (Saudi Arabia), 15 November 2001. *MEMRI*, Special Dispatch on Saudi Arabia, No. 304, 28 November 2001, p. 1.

23. Ibid. p. 3.

24. *Al-Ayyam* (Palestinian Authority), 27 November 2001, ibid. p. 4.

25. *Al-Sharq al-Awsat* (London), 15 January 2002.

26. *Al-Hayat* (London), 29 November 2001. See *MEMRI*, No. 307, 4 December 2001.

27. Ibid.

28. Ibid.

29. Al-Ansari is probably referring here to President Assad's reaction to acts of terrorism by the Muslim Brothers in Syria (1982), when he razed large sections of the city of Hama (their stronghold), and, by conservative estimates, eliminated over 20,000 of them.

30. See *Al-Raya* (Qatar), 6 January 2002; and also al-Ansari's articles in London-based *Al-Sharq al-Awsat*, 28 September and 25 October 2001. All in *MEMRI*, No. 337, 28 January 2002.

31. 3 November 2001.

32. *Akhbar al-Yaum* (Kuwait), 3 November 2001.

33. *Al-Raya*, 7 January 2002, *MEMRI*, No. 26 (Hebrew).

34. *Al-Raya*, 8 January 2002, ibid.

35. *Ibid.*, 12 January 2002.

36. *Al-Raya*, 12 January 2002.

37. *Al-Quds al-'Arabi* (London), 10 January 2002.

38. Ibid.
39. Ibid.
40. *Al-Quds al-'Arabi* (London), 14 January 2002; and *Al-Ahram* (Egypt), 13 January 2002.
41. *Al-Akhbar* (Egypt), 14 January 2002 (editorial by Galal Duweidar.)
42. *Al-Akhbar*, 16 January 2002.
43. *Al-Ahram*, 17 January 2002.
44. Famous columnist and notorious anti-Semite Anis Mansur, who used to be in Sadat's close entourage and established the journal *October* after the 1973 War. *Al-Ahram*, 26 January 2002.
45. *Al-Quds al-'Arabi* (London), 1 February 2002, in *MEMRI*, No. 341, 5 February 2002.
46. *Al-Wafd*, 8 February 2002.
47. *Al-Gumhuriyya*, 7 October 2001. See also *MEMRI* 289, 19 October 2001.
48. www.lailatalqadr.com, 21 November 2001.
49. www.lailatalqadr.com/stories/p5041001/shtml, 4 October 2001. *MEMRI*, No. 288, 16 October 2001.
50. Ibid.
51. *Al-Mustaqbal* (a Lebanese daily owned by Prime Minister Hariri), whose reporter was invited to cover the gathering, 18 March 2002, in *MEMRI*, No. 358, 22 March 2002.
52. See Articles 17–18 in the Hamas Charter. R. Israeli, 'The Charter of Allah: The Platform of the Islamic Resistance Movement', in R.Israeli, *Fundamentalist Islam and Israel*, Lanham, NY and London: University Press of America, 1993, pp. 144–5.
53. See *Al-Sharq al-Awsat* (London), 2 February 2002; *Al-Ayyam* (the Palestinian Authority), 31 January 2002; *Kul al-'Arab* (Israel), 1 February 2002. All in *MEMRI*, No. 83, 12 February 2002.
54. *Kul al-'Arab*, 1 February 2002.
55. *Middle East News Online*, 28 January 2002; and *Al-Sha'b* (Egypt), 1 February 2002.
56. *Al-Sha'b* (Egypt), 1 February 2002.
57. *Al-Sharq al-Awsat* (London), 31 January 2002.
58. Ibid. 2 February 2002, in *MEMRI*, ibid.
59. *Al-Sharq al-Awsat*, 31 January and 2 February 2002, ibid.
60. *Afaq 'Arabiya* (Egypt), 30 January 2002; *Al-Quds al-'Arabi* (London), 31 January 2002, in *MEMRI*, ibid.
61. *Al-Sharq al-Awsat*, 31 January 2002.
62. *Al-Sha'b*, (1 February 2002), see *MEMRI*, ibid.
63. *Al-Dustur* (Jordan), 5 February 2002, ibid., Part II.
64. *Afaq 'Arabiya* (Egypt), 7 February 2002; *Al-Quds al'Arabi* (London), 8 February 2002, ibid.
65. Ibid.
66. *Al-Akhbar* (Egypt), 1 February 2002.
67. Ibid.
68. *Al-Ahram*, 2 February 2002.
69. *Al-'Arabi* (Cairo), 3 February 2002; and *Al-Quds al-'Arabi* (London), 4 February 2002.
70. *Hadith al-Madina* (Egypt), 5 February 2002; and *Al-Quds al-'Arabi*, 6 February 2002. *MEMRI*, No. 84, part II. Op. cit.
71. *Al-Ayyam* (Palestinian Authority), 1 February 2002. *MEMRI*, No. 85, 14 February 2002.
72. *Al-Wafd* (Egypt), 7 February 2002; *Al-Quds al-'Arabi* (London), 8 February 2002. *MEMRI*, ibid.
73. *Al-Quds al-'Arabi*, 28 January 2002.
74. *Al-Wafd* (Egypt), 3 February 2002.
75. *Al-Ahram* (Egypt), 10 February 2002.
76. *Al-Dustur* (Jordan), 24 February 2002.
77. *Al-Wafd*, see n. 73.
78. *Al-'Arabi* (Egypt), 3 February 2002; *Al-Quds al-'Arabi* (London), 2 and 4 February 2002. See also *Al-Ahram* (Cairo), 3 and 5 February 2002; *Al-Wafd* (Egypt), 1 February

2002; *Al-Gumhuryya* (Egypt), 31 January 2002; *Sawt al-Umma* (Egypt), 3 February 2002. All in *MEMRI*, ibid.

79. *Al-Wafd* (Egypt), 3 February 2002; and *Al-Quds al-'Arabi* (London), 4 February 2002.
80. According to Muslim tradition, the bodies of the martyrs do not putrefy, but give off the scent of musk.
81. According to Muslim tradition, which is incidentally also cited at the end of Article 7 of the Hamas Charter (see R. Israeli, 'The Charter of Allah', p. 137), on the Day of Judgement the Muslims will fight the Jews [and kill them], and the Jews will seek to hide behind rocks and trees, which will cry: 'Oh, Muslims! A jew is hiding behind me! Come on and kill him!!!' This will not apply to the Gharqad, a sort of raspberry bush which is considered a 'Jewish' tree. Rumour among the Arabs has it that Israel has been planting many of those trees in order to avoid the massacre awaiting her.
82. That is the decisive battle in which Saladin routed the Crusader armies in 1187 and evicted them from much of Palestine. In Palestinian and Arab imagery, Israel is often likened to the Crusader Kingdom whose days are numbered.
83. By Ayman al-Skafi, an unknown poet, *Al-Istiqlal* (The Weekly of Islamic Jihad in Gaza), 13 December 2001.
84. *Al-Hayat*, 7 December 2001, cited by *Ha'aretz* (Israel), 9 December 2001.
85. A leaflet distributed in the streets of the major Palestinian cities on 27 November 2001 accused the Palestinian authority of exchanging intelligence with Israel and bringing about the liquidation of many jihad fighters. Citing a verse from the Quran (17:18), the statement promised that its 'truth would smash the Authority's lies', and that the latter would literally be sent to Hell.
86. See Chapter 2. The *jizya* was limited to the Scriptuaries (Jews and Christians), while pagans were subjected to the sword. The payment of *jizya* symbolized the subjugation of the *dhimmis* to Muslim rule, and in return for it they received protection from the Muslim state, the assumption being that no other state was legal.
87. *Al-Risala* (Palestinian Authority), 11 October 2001.
88. According to Islamic law, the martyrs are promised unlimited sexual intercourse with 72 virgins each, who regain their virginity after every sexual act so as for the martyrs to enjoy unlimited and eternal pleasure.
89. *Al-Risala*, 11 October 2001. *MEMRI* (Hebrew).
90. Ibid.
91. See n. 80.
92. Article by Muhammed Daraghmeh, the *Jerusalem Post* (Israel), 23 September 2001.
93. See article by Aluma Solnick, 'The Joy of the Mothers of Palestinian Martyrs', *MEMRI*, No. 61, 25 June 2001; Michael Gove, 'Spare Us More Middle East Peace Plans', *The Times* (London), 2 April 2002; Thomas Friedman, 'Suicidal Lies', *New York Times*, 31 March 2002.

6. Champions of Islamikaze: Their Admirers and (Muted) Detractors

When the Organization of the Islamic Conference (OIC), attended by 54 delegates, concluded its annual session in Kuala Lumpur on 2 April 2002, it failed to reach agreement on the main issue on the agenda, namely the definition of terror. On one topic they were unanimous: whatever Israel does, even when it acts to defend itself against the savagery of terrorist attacks against her citizens, is terrorism by definition. However, on the subject of the Islamikaze, many Muslim countries claimed that it was legitimate for Palestinian 'freedom fighters' to blow themselves up in the middle of civilian populations as part of their 'struggle against occupation', while others maintained that operating against innocent people was considered terrorism. None of them, however, approved of the right of Israel or any other country to take measures against these terrorists. This matter is of capital importance to the whole world, because if the logic of Islamikaze is accepted, then the terrorists have a licence to operate anywhere, at any time, against any target, be it a restaurant in Tel Aviv or the Twin Towers in New York, or a metro station in Paris, or the parliament building in Delhi, or a synagogue in Marseille or Leeds, in order to achieve a political goal.

It is therefore crucial to expose both the literature of hate which is directed against the West in general, and Israel and the United States in particular, and the manufacturers of that literature and its champions. Most of them are radical clerics, but in view of their expanding popularity, which almost no liberal mind in Islamdom dares to contradict, many a secular leader, such as Saddam Hussein, Arafat, Qaddafi, Assad, and certainly the Iranian regime, find themselves unable or unwilling to oppose or fight them, and therefore they join them and adopt terrorism as their policy. Moreover, even in countries such as Egypt, Tunisia, Morocco,

Algeria, Pakistan, Indonesia and Jordan, whose regimes combat the Muslim fundamentalism that threatens them, persistent cores of Muslim fundamentalism exist, centred around charismatic clerics who command the attention and the adulation of the populace more than the governments in place. Agreed, the governments are usually supported by the Muslim establishment in those countries, but as we have seen, established chief clerics, such as Tantawi in Egypt or Sabri in the Palestinian Authority, are often unable to withstand the tide of popular sentiment and toe the line of the extremists. Worse, many intellectuals, professionals and other supposedly enlightened elites, especially newspaper columnists, seem to be carried away far enough by the popular wave of Islamic resurgence and anti-Western phobia as to reflect public opinion rather than shaping it.

THE BIN-LADEN PHENOMENON

While there is no doubt that the personality of Bin-Laden has preoccupied the Western and Muslim media before and after 11 September, a number of talk shows, symposia and interviews with other clerics, Muslim and non-Muslim, intellectuals and journalists, independently issued fatwas by widely recognized ulama, and interviews and reports with and about some of them, have brought into focus the universality of the problem of Islamikaze in particular, and Muslim-sanctioned violence in general. First among them, as in other sensational domains, the Qatar *Al-Jazeera* television programme 'Opposite Direction' aired a talk show two months prior to 11 September, significantly titled 'Bin-Laden: The Arab Despair and American Fear', where two participants with opposite views were invited to participate.The critic of Bin-Laden was exiled Sudanese author, Al-Hatem 'Adlan, also the leader of the banned 'Al-Haqq Democratic Forces Movement', and his opponent was Abd al-Bari 'Atwan, another Arab resident of London, also the editor of the pro-Iraqi Arabic daily, *Al-Quds al-'Arabi* (a widely cited Arab medium), who had previously interviewed Bin-Laden. The latter, together with the host of the programme, Dr Faysal al-Qassem, and most of the show's callers, praised Bin-Laden in awesome and adulatory terms: 'a worthy opponent feared by America, which moves its fleets and puts its army and embassies on highest alert'; who:

...smashed one of its destroyers on the high seas; who fought it in Somalia and caused its troops to run like rabbits; who made its embassies throughout the world like fortresses, where their residents fear even light breezes; and who caused America to yell in pain one hundred times; and who has recently become the No. 1 Arab and Muslim hero.[1]

When 'Adlan said that he perceived the Bin-Laden phenomenon as part of international terrorism which means to 'seize power by violent means', 'Atwan disagreed, saying that while his rival was trying to defend legitimate governments against terrorism, it was the United States who had dropped nuclear bombs on Hiroshima and Nagaski on innocent people, something that casts doubt on the legitimacy of its government, because it has been a terrorist government who has been killing innocent people since 1945. A caller from Amman supported the latter's argument, claiming that Bin-Laden was not a terrorist, because:

> ...in the eyes of Muslims throughout the world, Bin-Laden is fighting a war of jihad for the sake of Allah...America today is arrogant, it is America that sucks the blood of the peoples, and anyone who challenges her or refuses to obey her is persecuted by her judicial system as a terrorist, a violator of human rights and a danger to world peace.

He insisted that Bin-Laden was the 'conscience of this [Muslim] nation...If you were to conduct a poll...you would find that the overwhelming majority of the Muslims of the world support Bin-Laden and consider him their conscience'. The programme's host announced that many faxes were coming in claiming that 'in view of the terrible Arab surrender and self-abasement to America and Israel, many Arabs unite behind this man who pacifies their rage and restores some of their trampled honour, their lost political, economic and cultural honour'.[2]

Those calls were capped by Dr Sa'd al-Faqih, a renowned Saudi Islamist living in London (many of the most celebrated Islamists, who loath the West in their writings, have opted to live in its midst and enjoy its 'decadence', 'oppression' and 'debasement of Muslims'), who went on the air stating:

> The Nation thirsts deeply for someone who would confront

America…not with words and slogans [as he himself did]…
someone who can prove in practice that he is a worthy
opponent. Bin-Laden has become the right man for this
important role in the confrontation with America, the enemy
of the Muslims, which conspires with the Muslim rulers to
hurt and plunder the nation's resources.[3]

Then the discussion veered to the Arab regimes' behaviour as a
factor in the emergence of Bin-Laden. It was emphasized that the
Arab regimes in place had prevented the establishment of political
parties, cancelled or rigged elections, violated human rights, used
torture, ruled by emergency law, and even dictated sermons in
mosques. 'Adlan responded by asserting that the Arab regimes did
not permit the Arab 'Afghani' graduates of the Afghan War to
return to their lands, as a self-defence measure, because those
battle-hardened candidates for repatriation 'returned with
conspiracies to assassinate their presidents, and brought back with
them terrorism, assuming that this was the next stage on their road
to victory'.[4]

Thereafter, the host of the programme began praising the
Hizbullah in Lebanon, which proved to his mind that the jihad
movement against Israel was very effective, claiming that they had
succeeded in 'expelling the Zionists from Southern Lebanon like
dogs – my apologies to the dogs'. He said that judging from the
faxes flowing in from his audiences, exactly as the Hamas and
Islamic Jihad in Palestine made Israel bleed, so the jihad movement
in Afghanistan had made the United States bleed in a way that no
Arab regimes, who deserve only derision, had succeeded in doing.
He complained that in Arab countries, those movements are
destroyed and their members jailed, while they constituted the
'nation's strategic reservoir', according to popular public opinion.
He reiterated that the jihad warrior, Bin-Laden, and his movement
put the United States on the run and struck fear into its heart, which
'shudders at the sound of his name'. He boasted that 'not even a
green fly can get close to an American warship': while Bin-Laden
succeeded in hitting its USS *Cole* and destroying it. While he was
pursuing his litany of praise for Bin-Laden, the spokesman for al-
Qa'ida, Sheikh Suleiman Abu-Gheith, called and was put on the air.
He said:

Osama Bin-Laden is an excellent example of following the

right path in order to escape the pitiful situation and the
nation's subordination [to the West]. We indubitably think
there is a global heresy, disseminated by Jews and Christians,
and headed by America, the spearhead of heresy, which
genuinely occupies Muslim lands, plunders their resources,
exiles their sons, and carries out a series of illegitimate actions
in order to gain control and influence... America occupies the
Arabian Peninsula... which contradicts the religious writings
that command the exclusion of Jews and Christians from
there... Fighting them is an obligation in which there can be
no compromise, until they leave the Arabian Peninsula and all
the Muslim lands they occupy... We sense that Muslim youth
are extremely perturbed by the American presence in the
Peninsula and its unlimited support to the Jews. The Muslim
youth look for ways to remove the Americans from this land,
and this is clearly shown by the Islamikaze operations they
carry out, that undoubtedly constitute the most tremendous
acts of obedience to Allah... The Americans must know that
Bin-Laden is the symbol that the nation has been seeking for a
long time. His ideology has already spread and taken root,
and they must not think that his dying, or that killing him, will
stop the jihad and the resistance.[5]

At the end of the programme, its host announced that, sifting
through the responses of the public, he could not find one opposing
Bin-Laden and all the callers were for him. He also emphasized that
a poll run by a Kuwaiti paper revealed that 69 per cent of Kuwaitis,
Egyptians, Syrians, Lebanese and Palestinians think Bin-Laden is
an Arab hero and a jihad warrior; 65 per cent thought that attacking
US targets was justified in fulfilment of the 'an eye for an eye'
principle, and because the Americans thought that 'Might is Right';
76 per cent affirmed that they would be sorry if Bin-Laden were
caught. He also cited an opinion poll carried on the Internet by *Al-
Jazeera*, the host channel, which found that out of 3,942 people who
voted, a full 82.7 per cent saw Bin-Laden as a jihad fighter, only 8.8
per cent viewed him as a terrorist, and 8.4 per cent did not know.
He concluded that there was a consensus from the Gulf to the
Atlantic in favour of Bin-Laden, adding sarcastically that these
figures were the result of a truly democratic process, not 'like the
percentage points in elections in Arab countries'. He also came to
the conclusion that since the respondents were of the educated class

who used the Internet, 'one could imagine what would be the result among the poor, the persecuted, and those stripped of their rights. Maybe 99.99 per cent!!'[6]

Bin-Laden's thinking, which has increased his popularity following the events of 11 September, especially after the US military action was launched against the Taliban, was revealed, in part, by an Internet site belonging to al-Qa'ida, significantly called 'The Struggle against the Crusader War'. One of Bin-Laden's aides, Abu 'Ubeid al-Qurashi, wrote an article there propounding his master's theory of world wars. More than anything else, the article posited Bin-Laden as a rational strategist, not just a blind fanatic or a merchant of death and destruction, as he was depicted by his detractors, who had a blueprint to overcome the United States and the West by feasible and well-calculated means. Al-Qurashi said that he was dismayed by the defeatism in the Muslim world, heralded by Muslim clerics who saw the shrinking support for the mujahedin and jihad as the result of the perceived imbalance between overwhelming US and Western power and that of the Muslim fighters, which led to the feeling that there was no point in challenging that power by jihad. He claims that the conclusions reached by those clerics were merely the result of ignorance of both the Shari'a and contemporary Western military thinking.[7]

Al-Qurashi, who seemed to have done his homework, even if some of his interpretations and conclusions were slanted, cited five US warfare experts, who had published a joint article predicting fundamental changes in the future of warfare.[8] They had predicted that wars of the twenty-first century would be 'asymmetric wars', or 'fourth generation wars', where not only military objectives would be targeted, but also societies, in order to wear them out from within, destroy their support for the troops fighting on their behalf by using television news, which has become a 'more powerful tool than armoured divisions'. In this type of warfare, the border is blurred between war and peace.[9] This means that those who initiate this type of warfare, for example, by wanton terrorism, would not declare it as such, and would leave it to the defendants to declare their war and be counted as the 'aggressors', while they create atrocities that are sure to attract television coverage and thus strike fear into the hearts of their enemies, and then retreat back to their centres of population. But when the victim strikes back in self-defence, television can again be counted on to show the 'abuses' of the 'aggressor', and gain sympathy for the cause of the terrorists a second time around. The author also cited other Western strategists[10] who disagreed with the above analysis and stressed, instead, psychological pressure on the minds of the enemy's planners, not only in the military field but also in the domain of information and media networks, in order to influence public opinion and the ruling elites.

According to this writer, the second school of military thought has concluded that the fourth generation wars would be small-scale, sprouting in various regions around the globe, against an enemy which 'like a ghost appears and disappears'. The focus of this war would be political, social, economic and military; also national, international, tribal, and even intraorganizational, and might continue to use previously known technologies. Since this sort of war would pose considerable difficulties for Western armies, they would have to alter their concepts and tactics. In this sort of war, says the author, which has in part already been tested in the field, the superiority of the theoretically weak party has already been proven, for in many instances, nation-states have been defeated by stateless people. As a 'proof' of this theory, the author points to the 'fact' that since the victorious Ottoman Empire, the Islamic *umma* has never chalked up so many triumphs, in the short space of 20 years, against the best-trained and best-equipped armies of the world: the Soviet Union in Afghanistan, the United States in Somalia, Russia in Chechnya, and the 'Zionist entity' in Southern Lebanon. These victorious battles were waged by Muslim mujahedin in mountain, desert, hill and urban areas, and in all of them a tribe, small organization or tiny group drove the superior enemy out and attained their goals, while using only light weaponry.[11]

Hence the admission by the writer that on 11 September, al-Qa'ida, following scrupulously the new tactics of the fourth generation wars, had accomplished the destruction of the 'elements of America's strategic defence, which the USSR and other hostile states could not harm'. These elements were enumerated by experts as early-warning, preventive strikes and the principle of deterrence,[12] all of which were said to have been overcome by the al-Qa'ida strike. In early warning, the al-Qa'ida strike surpassed the other cases of surprise attacks, like Pearl Harbor, the German attack against the Soviets in 1941, the Soviet invasion of Czechoslovakia in 1968, or the Egyptian attack across the Suez in 1973, and so on, thus exacting a huge economic and psychological price from the United

States. As far as preventive attack is concerned, even had the United States had early warning, it could not have launched a preventive strike against an organization that moves rapidly and has no permanent bases. Also, in the area of deterrence, it does not work when one party 'seeks to survive and defend its interests', while the other 'does not care about living and thirsts for martyrdom'. The conclusion is, of course, that the Islamic world should re-adjust its strategy to the fourth generation wars and make the necessary military preparations to get there, and proselytize and mobilize public opinion in order to gain political support. The best example of this was the Palestinian Intifadah, which 'wiped out the Zionists' military superiority over the Muslim Palestinian people'.[13]

Another prominent member of al-Qa'ida, Abu Hifz al-Mauritani,[14] who was accused by the United States of having masterminded the attacks against the US Embassies in East Africa in 1998 and was notorious enough to be included in President Bush's listed of 'wanted', had met Bin-Laden in the Sudan and become one of his underlings. After 11 September, he gave an interview to *Al-Jazeera* television. He said that, as so far no one has been convicted, al-Qa'ida also declared that it had nothing to do with the attacks. At the same time, he claimed that the finger should be pointed at the 'oppression, tyranny, travesty of justice and aggression of the United States against the Arab, Muslim and other oppressed peoples'. He said that the United States was to blame because the perpetrators of that massacre trained there, not in Afghanistan, and that the US people should take their country to task for having spent billions of dollars on maintaining its security, intelligence and army apparatus to no avail. However, instead of getting rid of its security heads for their dismal failure, the United States was looking for a scapegoat, and she found one in Afghanistan. He admitted that while his group did not perpetrate the horror, 'hundreds of millions of Muslims could not contain their joy at the sight of America tasting in one stroke some of the pain and bitterness she had inflicted on the Arabs and Muslims for years'. He insisted that although his group was not the author of that disaster, the results thereof were 'good for us and fit in with our interests'.[15]

This arch-terrorist complained during the interview that the United States has hit mainly civilian targets in Afghanistan, which 'proves their cultural and moral values', killed or maimed children in their mothers' bosom, destroyed mosques and burned Qur'an books, and wiped out entire villages. He dubbed the US counter-attack a 'crusade', said that his group's support for the Taliban stemmed from the Qur'anic injunction to support Truth, because the Taliban government who ruled the Islamic Emirate of Afghanistan was the only one that ruled according to the Qur'an, the Sunna (tradition) of the Prophet and the word of the great doctors of the Holy Law. He emphasized that all the mujahedin in Afghanistan, including al-Qa'ida, were under the command of the *Amir al-Mu'minin* (the Commander of the Faithful), that is, Mullah 'Umar, and that all owed him total obedience. He was the man who rejected the US plea to surrender Bin-Laden by asserting that it was easier for him to give up one of the Pillars of Islam than surrender Bin-Laden. He did that, because while the United States had pledged to defeat Afghanistan, it was Allah who promised the Taliban victory, for they would prefer death by jihad than a life of humiliation. The interviewee asserted that while the United States declared that it would root out terrorism in Afghanistan, in fact it was the Afghans who dragged it, humiliated and intimidated, out of its fortresses, into Afghanistan. This was, said he, the sign that the end of the United States was close at hand.[16]

Abu Hifz also claimed that the United States knew that the Taliban and al-Qai'da were innocent, but nevertheless launched the attack against Afghanistan because the US mind was set, initally, on three elements: Israel's security, the free flow of oil and unhindered navigation in international waterways, and to prevent the rise of an Islamic state ruled by true Islam. He affirmed that the United States had planned a war against Afghanistan, even prior to 11 September, in order to wipe out the Islamic regime which was not to its liking, and had simply used those events as a pretext to expedite it schemes. He asserted that the Palestinian problem is the most important for Islam due to the holy places in Jerusalem connected with the biography of the Prophet,[17] and the unprecedented mistreatment of Palestinians by the 'barbaric Jews' under the Crusader instigation of the United States and Great Britain. Thus, it has become incumbent on any Muslim to fight jihad in Palestine, but the access there is blocked by the neighbouring Arab countries who protect those borders against outside intervention. So, al-Qa'ida strikes at Americans and at Jews where it can... This is the reason why Afghanistan, where al-Qa'ida is based, has become the primary target of the 'Crusader–Jewish Alliance'. Therefore, he called any act of killing Americans, or of inciting or waging jihad against them, an 'act of grace', and al-Qa'ida has been the tool to implement that. He said that the higher the price the United States set on the heads of his organization, the higher the honour conferred on them, for America was the most barbaric and tyrannical force in history, who robbed and oppressed people.[18]

His definition of terrorism is no less harrowing than the acts of terror he subscribes to. He said that al-Qa'ida are not terrorists, because only those who killed 'truly innocent people, namely those whom Allah has prohibited to kill, like women, children and the aged, and non-combatants' are. Conversely, he confirmed that 'we worship Allah through jihad against those who deserve to be fought and killed'. He specified: jihad in defence of Holy Places (to Islam), and against those whom Allah has ordered Muslims to fight, such as polytheists who have to be 'killed anywhere you can find them, besiege them and ambush them'. The Qur'anic verse is conjured up, which is precisely at the root of the Arabic use of *irhab*, the modern term for terror: 'Make ready for them whatever force and strings of horses you can, to *terrify* thereby the enemy of Allah and your enemy, and others beside them that you know not; God knows them'.[19] This means that anyone Muslims would care to define as polytheist, or 'enemy of Allah', is by definition also the enemy of Muslims and therefore fair game for the Believers to terrify. He explains: 'to terrorize the enemies of Allah is a divine tenet, and the Muslim thus faces two choices: either he believes in these verses, which are clear, or he disbelieves in them. Muslims have no other option.'[20] He stressed that even though al-Qa'ida was not responsible for the 11 September disaster, there was enough clarification made by eminent ulama that if mujahedin were identified as the authors of that murder, their act was impeccable and without any blemish.[21]

In response to the interviewer's question about innocent civilian casualties caused by that act, he had this to say:

> I have to make a clarification. First, to describe the Pentagon, which the Americans themselves admit is a centre of evil and therefore constitutes the military target par excellence, as an innocent civilian target, is a travesty of the truth. Can those whom Allah and His Prophet allow us to fight against be considered as innocent? Secondly, the World Trade Center has been the world centre of money laundering and the hiding place for the CIA, which now admits that many of its offices

have been destroyed there. How can one describe, then, these obviously military, economic and political centres as innocent targets? I would like to say to all those who shed crocodile tears in mosques in Mecca and Al-Azhar, throughout the Islamic world, over the 'innocents' in America: Where was your condemnation of [American] terrorism in Afghanistan and where are your tears as children and the old are being murdered in Afghanistan? *Al-Jazeera* has aired all the horrible massacres that American planes have perpetrated against children and targets that are indisputably civilians. America has also been overlooking the robbery and rape committed by the [Northern Alliance] opposition in Mazar-a-Sharif. This selectivity and these double standards will cause many mujahedin to launch many more serious attacks than those of 11 September...If the Americans use non-conventional weapons against us they can expect a retribution in kind. We have been waiting for them, with Allah's Will.[22]

EGYPTIAN AND OTHER ULAMA–ESTABLISHMENT AND ANTI-ESTABLISHMENT

Dr Muhammed Tantawi, the Sheikh of Al-Azhar, probably the most heeded jurist of established Islam anywhere, whom we have cited above, is the most duplicitous of the ulama to have pronounced themselves in the context of the Islamikaze killings. For unlike others, who have been either clearly for (and this is the majority), or emphatically against (the minority – see below), Tantawi has attended the inter-faith Alexandria Conference in January 2002, where those acts of terrorism were denounced, and come out strongly against them when they targeted innocent civilians, although his position has been constantly eroded, both when it came to justifying the Wafa Idris case and then when he accepted the indiscriminate attacks against civilians as justified. Tantawi's position is particularly sensitive because, while he responds to the Egyptian establishment and has to toe the official anti-terrorist line of his government which appointed him, he is also in a responsible and prestigious enough position to heed the popular resentment of the masses against the United States and Israel. In his name, the following unambiguous statement was made:

The Great Imam Tantawi, the Sheikh of Al-Azhar, has asked the Palestinian people in its entirety, to step up the [Islamikaze] operations of self-sacrifice against the Zionist enemy, as they meet the highest standards of jihad, and described the young people who commit them as having sold to Allah their dearest. These words were said during a reception the Sheikh held for Israeli-Arab politician and former Knesset member, Darawshe, who confirmed that the Palestinian people stands fast and will pursue its struggle until victory or martyrdom, whichever comes first.[23]

Another officially appointed Egyptian cleric, Sheikh Dr Ahmed al-Tayyeb, the newly nominated Mufti of Egypt, who replaced Sheikh Nasser Wasil recently due to the latter's opposition to Tantawi's initial rulings opposing Islamikaze-style martyrdom, has converted his views to suit the new militant Tantawi. He declared that the 'solution to Israeli terror lies in the proliferation of the *fida'i* acts of martyrdom which strike terror in the hearts of the enemies of Allah. Islamic countries, peoples and rulers alike, must support these martyrdom attacks.'[24] As we have seen, the activities of the Islamikaze against Israel have become accepted as the norm among the Egyptians, and during the 18 March demonstrations at Al-Azhar University, eight students training to carry out these kinds of martyrdom attacks were presented to the cheering public.[25] Neither the clerics, nor public opinion-makers, nor the government acted against that trend, and the clerics, as we have seen, have even encouraged it by their rulings. So much so that Mahmoud al-Zahhar, one of the leaders of Hamas in Gaza, made a stunning statement to the Israeli-Arabic weekly, *Kul al-'Arab*: 'Two days ago, in Alexandria, enrolment began for volunteers for martyrdom operations. Two thousand students from the University of Alexandria signed up to die a martyr's death. This is the real Egyptian people.'[26]

If that is official and mainstream Egypt, what can be expected from extra-establishment clerics and others who support the Muslim radical cause, some of them within Egypt, as we have seen, others from their exile, where they sought refuge for being deemed too dangerous to the regime? Arguably the most outspoken, respected and popular among them is Sheikh Yussuf al-Qardawi who, from his Qatar exile, exerts a tremendous impact on the entire Muslim world. A spiritual leader of the Muslim Brothers, and among the first to uphold Islamikaze actions, he also repeatedly pronounced himself against attacking innocent civilians, but on the question of US retaliation in Afghanistan, he ruled that according to Shari'a, Muslims should be on the Taliban side, not on the US coalition side. Interviewed on *Al-Jazeera* television, this is what he had to say:

> My communiqué condemning the acts of terrorism that killed innocent civilians is not my first. I am against terror as a matter of principle, because this is the position of Islamic law... Since the days of the Crusades, there are some mental conundrums from which the West has not freed itself. It attacked Muslim countries, but Islam triumphed... Perhaps they will attack Afghanistan, the Yemen, the Sudan, Lebanon... It is inconceivable that we, the Muslims, could enter into an alliance against an Islamic state that has not been proven to have done anything. Who says that Afghanistan, as a state, took part in those attacks? What is 'harbouring terrorists' supposed to mean? Should Egypt be attacked just because Sheikh 'Umar abd-al-Rahman is from Egypt? If a group of Algerians do something, should Algeria be attacked?...
>
> Those attacks resulted from hatred of the United States. If they kill Osama Bin-Laden, 1,000 Osama Bin-Ladens will rise. Is this in the world's best interest? The Taliban have nothing to do with this matter, they are preoccupied with their internal problems... I also think that Bin-Laden no longer has the means to carry out something like this... There are religious rules to be observed. A Muslim is forbidden from entering into an alliance with a non-Muslim against another Muslim... Allying with others to kill other Muslims is collaborating in sin and aggression... It is also forbidden to hand over Muslims to others... the Shari'a says that if a Muslim country is attacked, the other Muslim countries must help it, with their souls and money, until it is liberated. Islam treats Muslims everywhere as one nation, and it does not recognize geographical borders or differences of race, colour or language. It sees Muslims as one nation in *Dar al-Islam*, united in Islamic belief and Muslim brotherhood. Co-religionists must not rise against each other for other people's causes, particularly when it is not proven that the crime was carried out by one of those Islamic countries...
>
> How can Pakistan aid and abet invading its neighbour and

co-religionist? How can Pakistan's clerics remain silent? I support the claim that if Bin-Laden is proven guilty, he should be handed to an Islamic court in any Islamic country...like Saudi Arabia or Egypt, but only if he is proven guilty...Can anyone prove that he sent [the Islamikaze] or funded and organized them? There are terrorists all over the world, and they are not necessarily from al-Qa'ida, and they did not necessarily act on Bin-Laden's instructions...

There is no doubt that the one who benefits from this is the Zionist entity, which has exploited it in the media militarily and politically...We must differentiate between two kinds of terrorism: the terror of those defending their homeland and their rights and that is legitimate. The Palestinian factions defending their lands, such as Fat'h, Hamas and Islamic Jihad, are not terrorists; this is jihad for the sake of Allah...Even the United States is guilty in that it supports Israel, but this does not mean that we can attack civilians in the United States, because the civilians there are not guilty. We should fight the Americans militarily when we can, and economically and politically when we cannot. Let us boycott the United States!!! At the Durban Conference all the popular organizations stood against America, until it was forced to withdraw...But Islam does not allow us to kill civilians...

Regarding my fatwa on the martyrs, whom a viewer calls 'suicide bombers', I believe that the viewer is not a Muslim, because a Muslim would not let an Islamic homeland like Palestine, and Jerusalem, remain in the hands of Zionists who plunder it and damage its holy sites, without the owners of the land having the right to defend themselves. I said that the oppressed people have the right to defend themselves and that every man has the right to become a human bomb and blow himself up inside this military society. Israeli society is a military society: anyone who is not currently a soldier is a soldier in the reserves. I issued this religious ruling, and all the Islamic clerics have ruled like me, except for a few... Hundreds of Muslim clerics have ruled that these martyrdom operations are one of the most sublime types of jihad for the sake of Allah. Many have asked me whether it is permitted to carry out operations outside Palestine, and I always say no. I support what Hamas says, that every martyrdom operation must be within the lands of Palestine.[27]

In other words, Qardawi is in favour of battling only non-civilians, except in Israel, where 'everyone is military', including infants and the very old. For him, Israeli civilians are easy prey 'only in Palestine', but his definition of Palestine includes Israel. He says that Muslims are entitled to launch jihad for their rights, but he leaves it to the Muslims to decide what their rights are. His pragmatism, which is tied into the *siyyasa shar'iyya* (see p. 123), goes as far as to avoid fighting the United States militarily, when Muslims are unable to do so, and must instead centre on the Zionists.[28]

Another Egyptian cleric who holds radical views is Abu Hamza al-Masri, whose residence in London, where he serves as the imam of Finsbury Park Mosque, does nothing to mollify his fundamentalism. He heads the *Ansar al-Shari'a* (supporters of the Shari'a), a movement which would have surely been outlawed in Cairo, wherein he propagated for the violent Groupes Islamiques Armés (GIA) who acted in Algeria. Both his native Egypt and the Yemen have demanded his extradition. He emerged from a background of moral corruption, something that is sure to have made him more radical than others, as if he wished to catch up on his 'lost' years.[29] Thereafter, he moved to Afghanistan with his family prior to the Taliban regime at a time when the Islamikaze camps were disseminated in the various domains of the regional landlords.[30] He fought against the withdrawing Soviet forces and was severely injured by a landmine which removed both his hands and destroyed one of his eyes.

In 1994, al-Masri, a civil engineer by training, found refuge in London at a time when the entire West was off its guard with respect to the international Islamic terrorist networks that were being erected in its midst, where he founded his *Ansar al-Shari'a* organization. Reminiscing on that period, he complained that while he had never lived off his hosts' money, those 'infidels' levied heavy taxes on him when he worked for them as an engineer, and therefore that justified his present attacks against the West which had 'plundered the lands of Islam'. He never explained why he chose to live in the land of his alleged 'robbers', unless we take his words at face value: 'I am a cripple, and I use their country to spread good, exactly like the [British] authorities who use it to spread corruption.' In spite of his continuous complaints that he was persecuted by the authorities, his Muslim activity went unhindered, until he was briefly arrested in May 1999 and then released. On his Internet site he claimed that Yemen was the best launching pad after Afghanistan for the Islamic Revolution that was to spread worldwide,[31] and it was there that he directed his attention in 1998, after having left his London mosque to take care of his 'Aden Abyan Muslim Army'. He apparently masterminded an abortive attempt against the life of the Yemeni President, and the kidnapping of foreign tourists. In a press conference that he conducted in London in January 2000, he called for the overthrow of the Yemeni regime and urged foreign visitors to leave Yemeni soil, and in a letter in the London-based Arabic daily *Al-Hayat*, warned the ambassadors of Britain and the United States that they should leave the Yemen, lest a painful strike against 'the enemies of Islam' might be carried out against them. He also attacked Arab monarchs and depicted the deceased King Hussein of Jordan as roasting in Hell.[32]

Al-Masri has also shown aggressive concern for Muslim communities under pressure or threat. He convened a conference in 1999 on the Chechnian Muslims, and incited his crowds against a group of Russian reporters who were on hand to cover the debates. On the same occasion he voiced support for the Chechnian attacks in Moscow in the summer of that year.[33] His choice of the Yemen as the ideal place to start the Muslim Revolution emanated from the fact that it was the only country in the Arabian Peninsula that had not yet 'surrendered to the United Snakes [*sic*] of America', and he was certain that after the takeover of that country by the Islamists, the rest would follow as the domino effect unfolded. He denied in one of his interviews that he had called upon his followers to kill foreigners in the Yemen, specifying that he meant Infidels, unless they converted to Islam, paid the *jizya* (see Chapter 2), or entered into a pact that guaranteed their safety in a Shari'a country. Otherwise, he asserted, their 'blood and wealth are not protected'. He admitted that he had also operated in Algeria and Egypt, but because reform there was impossible from within, due to the corrupt regimes in place, he came to the conclusion that only an outside 'Muslim invasion' would trigger the Islamic Revolution and the warranted change. And that invasion he envisages as stemming from Yemen and fanning out worldwide.[34]

Al-Masri's work consists not only of promoting Muslim terrorism, recruiting volunteers, indoctrinating others and collecting funds for Muslim organizations, but he also launched a campaign to recruit, convert and train British Muslims. For that purpose, he held 'Islamic camps', usually in the grounds of his mosque, offering 'military training for brothers, self-development skills, martial arts, map-reading etc.', and aimed at distracting the 30 young men in attendance from 'television and the obscenity of Christmas'. Incidentally, the website that made the announcement was decorated with a picture of a hand grenade.[35] Some of those trainees found their way to Afghanistan and were killed there but did not come to the media attention until after the horrors of 11 September.[36] In February 1999, during the Second Conference of the Islamic Revival Movements held in London, al-Masri told the gathering of 500 Muslims of a plan to 'blow up civil and military aircraft, so as to challenge Western monopoly of the skies'. He even gave details of 'new flying mines, connected to balloons, currently being experimented on in Afghanistan' and hinted that sometime in the future such an operation would be carried out in Britain or in the United States.[37] There are indications that al-Masri was aware of the plans of 11 September, that he was involved in masterminding a plan to kill President Bush during the G-8 meeting in Genoa two days before the New York and Washington attacks, and that he participated in a meeting at his London mosque on 29 June 2001, where the idea of attack using aircraft was raised.[38]

The most relevant aspect of al-Masri from our point of view, is his encouragement of violence, which has been cultivated and elevated into an ideology in its own right. His advocated use of violence has a two-pronged purpose: to topple regimes in place in the Arab and Islamic world in order to replace them with Islamic governments, and to facilitate the diffusion of Islam in the world. In a gathering in early 1999, commemorating the removal of the last Ottoman caliph by Kemal Attaturk, he openly urged Muslims to resort to the sword to achieve his blueprint domestically and also internationally. One of his supporters, Muhammed Yussuf, seconded his mentor's ideas by urging his followers not only to fight back against the West in the Balkans and the Middle East, but also by establishing a 'strong Fifth Column' within the Western world,[39] something that would explain his own self-imposed 'exile' in London and his cultivation of violent Islam there. In 2001, he became involved in a press debate geared to 'clear' his name from the 'accusation' that he had relinquished the use of violence, something that was, of course, antithetical to the nature of his struggle. Indeed, according to the London-based *Al-Quds al-'Arabi*, *al-Masri* had been accused by another Egyptian fundamentalist ex-patriot, also residing in London, 'Abd-al-Hakim Dyab, of having dismissed a fatwa of the Palestinian radical cleric, Abu Qatada, who had decreed that Muslims should kill the wives and children of Egyptian police and army officers as part of the 'struggle against Arab regimes'.[40]

The accusation was too much of an affront for al-Masri. In his rebuttal in the same paper, he said that he did not recognize the term 'violence', because it had become a weapon used by the world media to dub anyone defending his faith and his honour in the face of the Arab regimes who rule through 'legislative and oppressive measures'. Therefore, the very term 'violence' is deceptive and incompatible, in his eyes, with Islamic religious law and the struggle for the survival of Islam. He said that mujahedin have never recognized that term, because it was used to sustain the monopoly of the regimes in the usage of terrorism, and conversely to eliminate the religious precept of 'doing good and prohibiting the doing of evil'. This is the clearest explanation yet of Muslim terrorism as an act of 'good', and any attempt to fight it as inherently evil. This thinking also helps explain why, for the Muslim radicals, the Western definition of terrorism is not acceptable, as long as it addresses itself to a means of combat or struggle (namely acting against innocent civilians to attain a political goal), instead of addressing the core theme of the struggle, that is Islamic good against Western or anti-Islamic evil. It is instructive to heed al-Masri's own words:

> As a rule, Islam teaches that those with opinions different from one's own should be treated gently and with flexibility, provided that they are willing to listen and comply, and provided that one's tolerant efforts do not lead to a blurring of rights and borders... Treating gently anyone who blocks his ears and forces perversion, heresy, abomination, and humiliation on the Muslims in their own countries by armed forces, is a kind of idiocy and loss of rights and religious precepts... What can be said of Arab regimes who have enacted abominable laws and give licence to carry them out, and use taxes to appoint military personnel to protect the abomination, instead of protecting Jerusalem and its people?... This is the mark of Cain, which is unprecedented in the history of Egypt.[41]

In other words, Islam is 'tolerant', according to this interpretation, only as long as the challenger to its rules ultimately accepts it and complies with it. For Islam alone can define right or wrong, holy and profane, acceptable and abominable, and anyone opposing it is not subject to the 'gentle treatment and flexibility' suggested in the definition of tolerance. Finally, getting to the point of violence, that he had been outrageously accused of having abandoned, he stated:

> My position is clear as the sun, praised be Allah, and it has not changed and will not change...I do not recognize the term 'violence' and will not agree to abandon the jihad or to sign a truce with the regimes of the tyrants. As Allah said: 'Fight them so there will be no internal strife (fitna) and so that their religion will be Allah's religion.' The Muslim Nation to which I belong cannot come to terms with anyone who does not have mercy on and respect for the people...Physical exile far from my homeland is much easier for me and for many like me than the exile of our souls, the slaughter of our faith and of our values, and the amputation of our tongues as the price for returning to our homeland.[42]

And finally, in defence of Islamic violence (jihad) against the West, he had this to say to the *Christian Science Monitor*:

> It was when the Americans took the knife out of the Russians [in Afghanistan] and stabbed it in our back...In the meantime, they were bombing Iraq and occupying the Arabian Peninsula, and then with their witch-hunt against mujahedin, everything became clear: it was a full-scale war...The Americans wanted to fight the Russians with Muslim blood and they could justify that only by triggering the word jihad. Unfortunately for everyone, except the Muslims, when the button of jihad is pushed, it does not come back that easily. It keeps going on and on until the Muslim Empire swallows every existing empire.[43]
>
> I do not condone what happened [on 11 September] nor do I condemn it, because I do not know yet who did it. If somebody has done this just for earthly gain and political advancement then obviously it is a cheap cause. But if it was done because people are desperate and their lives have been threatened, then that is a respectable cause...Then those people who carried out the attacks would be martyrs.

Martyrdom is the highest form of jihad. If you do things for the cause of Allah, losing your life for it is the highest form of faith. This is in the Qur'an. America thinks it comes first, but Muslims believe that Believers come first. When you damage a people, and they have no home and no hope, and their babies and children are killed, then they retaliate. America took decisions to give arms to certain people and take arms away from others. What happened yesterday would be self-defence...

I have sympathy for the victims, but also for Bin-Laden who is the victim of an American witch-hunt, but who is unable to do a thing like this, though he probably has millions of sympathizers [who could have done it].[44]

Sheikh 'Umar al-Bakri, of Syrian origin, who also took refuge in London, is of much the same brand of radical clerics whose co-existence with the Muslim establishment in his country became untenable, and he had to seek the freedom of the West in order to attack it from within. He founded, in London, the local branch of the Palestinian-based *Hizb-al-Tahrir* (the Liberation Party), and also *Jama'at al-Muhajirun* (the Association of Emigrants).[45] He has introduced himself to interlocutors as the spokesman of Osama Bin-Laden's 'International Islamic Front for Jihad against Jews and Crusaders', which is known to have raised funds for the Hamas, Islamic Jihad and the Hizbullah, and recruited volunteers for training in Islamikaze attacks. He left Syria for Beirut following the drowning in blood of the Muslim Brothers uprising in Hamas in 1982. Then, under the name of 'Umar Fistuk, he established his *Muhajirun* group in Jeddah as a front for the Liberation Party, which spread to Europe thereafter (Lille, France and Hannover, Germany); all in all, some 47 Muslim organizations in Western Europe under the umbrella of the Liberation Party, with its headquarters in Hamburg.[46] In 1985, he was evicted by the Saudis and landed in London, where he fell into disagreement with his fellow Islamic party members who wished to focus on the revival of the caliphate, while he meddled in all manner of Muslim organizations.

In 1996, Bakri applied for British citizenship after he had become a legal resident three years earlier. Since then, he has been preaching in London mosques and delivered fiery sermons to Muslim assemblies, the largest of which convened in Trafalgar Square and Wembley Stadium. He founded the *Khilafa* (Caliphate)

Publishing House and claims service in a Shari'a Court of the United Kingdom. In an interview with the *Daily Mirror*, he admitted that he lived on a weekly state allowance of £300 to provide for his family of eight, rationalizing that 'Islam permits me to take the benefits the system offers. I am fully eligible. It is very difficult for me to find a job. Anyway, most of the leadership of the Islamic Movement [in Britain] is on state benefit.'[47] But after seven radical terrorists, some of them Egyptians, were arrested in September 1998, Bakri began attacking his benefactors unabashedly, denouncing Great Britain as the 'spearhead of blasphemy that seeks to overthrow Muslims and the Islamic caliphate'. He explained that the arrested Egyptians were political refugees who were not involved in terrorist activities, and that the Muslims in Great Britain 'condemned the barbaric acts of the British government against innocent Muslims who…were lulled and betrayed into believing they could seek sanctuary in Britain from their corrupt regime'.[48]

This reversal of roles is what will characterize the behaviour of Muslim terrorists who sought refuge in the West that they detest and wish to undermine, for the most part on the run from their home governments that they tried unsuccessfully to topple. Since they are persuaded that they fight for the way of Allah, they certainly do not regard themselves as terrorists, and when they are arrested for terrorist activity within their host countries which had generously, naively and self-defeatingly given them shelter and provided for their needs, they accuse their benefactors and condemn their 'barbaric behaviour'. This mechanism of denial, which posits Western democracy as just a milking cow which owes them sustenance while they owe her nothing, allows them to deny the good and protection they receive and to even mount subversive cells that are liable, as in the cases of the United States and al-Qa'ida branches in Europe, to act in the heart of their countries of refuge as of right, and to cause havoc, death and destruction upon the nations that took them in, and in spite of their commitment to refrain from political or subversive activity as a condition for being accorded the status of 'refugee'.[49] To them, it has become the responsibility of the West to rescue the fundamentalists from their own corrupt regimes, and therefore the host countries which try to battle terrorism are accused when they do not comply with the Islamists' schemes. The democratic countries to which those Muslim radicals streamed, uninvited, now become the 'oppressors' of the 'poor and peaceful Muslims' who had fled from their countries of origin, and are condemned for their 'harsh policy that uses fear and force, like the tyrannical regimes of Saudi Arabia, Iraq, Syria, Iran and so on'.[50]

The tension between Bakri and his peers, on the one hand, and the British authorities, on the other, did not begin with the 11 September events, nor with the awakening of Europe to the danger of international terror that was being posed by the growing, and increasingly radicalized, foreign Muslim population. Already, during the Gulf War in the early 1990s, the British MI5 had interrogated Bakri for his alleged call to assassinate British Prime Minister John Major. Indeed, Bakri was quoted by the British press as declaring that 'Major is a legitimate target. If one gets the opportunity to assassinate him...it is our Islamic duty and we will celebrate his death'.[51] Bakri said that he had been misquoted, specifying that Major would have been a legitimate target only if 'he set foot in a Muslim country', and that applied to Tony Blair, his successor, as well, and he confirmed that, in such a case, he would not condemn the killers.[52] The lenient British, instead of making it clear that they rejected the Islamic way of assassinating rivals as a legitimate comment on current politics, let things go and forgivingly dismissed that threat on their system. But similar Islamic patterns of behaviour were not slow in coming to the surface and persuading even the most diehard liberals to tighten the rules and the supervision of those potentially subversive elements. Indeed, a spokesman for the *Muhajirun* in England, Salim 'Abd-al-Rahman, also announced, after 11 September, that Tony Blair had become a legitimate target for Muslims because of the British attacks on Afghanistan. In his words:

> Now that the Americans, the British and probably the French, have begun to bomb Muslims in Afghanistan, government buildings in Britain, military installations, and No. 10 Downing St, have become legitimate targets. If any Muslim wants to kill him or get rid of him, I would not shed a tear for him. In the Islamic view, such a man would not be punished for his deeds, but would be praised.[53]

In December 2000, Bakri went to Birmingham, under the open eye of the British security apparatus, to preach his brand of Islamic radicalism. He was so sure of himself, and of numbing British indolence at the time, that he gave an interview to the local newspaper and explained that he came to Birmingham to recruit volunteers not only for his *Muhajirun* group, but also to fight for the Muslim cause in such foreign countries as Kashmir, Afghanistan and Chechnya. He said that in Britain there were 'only physical training camps', but that volunteers were sent out from Britain for military training in South Africa, Nigeria, Afghanistan, Kashmir and the United States.[54] This cleric, who depended for his living on the generosity of the British government, admitted in another interview that he was involved in financing the training of volunteers for his 'jihad network', who were sent to the United States, taking advantage of the fact that training with firearms and live ammunition was more readily available there than in Britain. The rationale was: 'When they [the British] started to label us as terrorists when we went to Afghanistan, we now go on to the United States'. He gave some details of that training: the use of firearms and explosives, surveillance and other skills, in order to join jihad fighting in some country, such as Chechnya, Palestine, Kashmir, South Lebanon, and emphasized that the choice of the battle arena depended on each individual fighter. He stressed that the training camps were run by private firms in states like Michigan and Missouri, and the Muslim recruits came from various countries: British, American, Arab and Asian, who had European or American citizenship and therefore did not need visas, stayed there for periods ranging from one week to three months.[55]

With a spirit of nonchalance that could certainly not be adopted in an Arab and Muslim setting, and was born out of the absolute certainty of the Muslims in the West that their citizenship in Western countries gave them the right to subvert their lands of asylum, Bakri explicitly said about his military activities:

> It is not illegal. We are not hiding anything. It should be looked at with an open mind. We are talking purely about helping people who would like to train. The skills they learn are part of the religious obligations every Muslim has. A Muslim must have military training at least once in his lifetime.[56]

But lest the reader should think that only military training *per se* was imperative for Muslims in their lands of dwelling and citizenship, a clarification follows: 'In Muslim countries we can fulfil this obligation by joining our national armies. But some Muslims would not want to join the British or US forces and would rather go to an independent training camp.' An expression of puzzlement spread on his face: 'Why call this terrorist training? All Americans can learn how to shoot – so what happens when this American person happens to be Muslim? Unless, of course, you consider us second- or third-class citizens.'[57] The answer to those rhetorical questions came 15 months later, on 11 September 2001.

In other press interviews, Bakri admitted that the International Islamic Front Against Jews and Crusaders (IIF), created by Bin-Laden, and with which he was himself connected, supported Hamas and Islamic Jihad in Palestine, who were the acknowledged masters of Islamikaze, collected funds for them, recruited 'militiamen', and took care of their propaganda needs in Europe. He said that in October 2000 alone, the month the Al-Aqsa Intifadath was picking up steam in Israel, 160 British 'volunteers' were recruited and sent to Jordan, where 'they awaited opportunities to infiltrate the West Bank and join the Intifadah'. He said that more recruits were sent to Lebanon, who joined training in the Palestinian refugee camps with a view to opening up a new front with Israel in the southern part of the country, and confirmed that his group, the IIF, maintained connections with the Hizbullah and other Islamic movements, such as *Usbat al-Ansar*, which are committed to fight for the 'liberation of Jerusalem'.[58] Bakri is also active on the Asian front. He claimed that it was he who recruited Muhammad Bilal to carry out the Islamikaze attack in Srinagar, in Indian Kashmir, in December 2000, where a number of Indian soldiers were killed, that he also trained Bilal's brothers and cousins for similar operations, and that Bilal's parents were 'proud of their son's sacrifice'. According to him, he also recruited 600 British Muslims in universities and mosques to fight in Kashmir, and some media attributed to him the financing (again he, who lives off British unemployment and social welfare funds) of *Al-Madad* (literally, 'assistance' or 'auxilliary supplies') organization which, together with other groups, has recruited 2,000 other young men across Britain.[59]

Bakri's activities in Asia also encompass the Muslim rebel minority in southern Thailand, where reports surfaced about foreign supporters who 'provided money and training to southern separatists', and about a training farm 20 kilometres from the Malay border linked with 'the Middle East and radical Muslims based in

London', one of whose foreign supporters was Bakri.[60] He voiced his support for aeroplane hijackings and in an interview gave his harrowing judgement on the worth of Muslim blood compared to that of others:

> The Islamic Movement has the right to sacrifice whoever it sees fit. The rule is that children, women and the weak should not be a goal, except in one situation: if it is difficult to win without sacrificing them. So, if hijackers find [Muslim] women, children and elderly people on a [hijacked] plane, they should set them free except if the goal of the hijackers is to free other women, children and elderly people held prisoners in other countries. In this case, they can be kept, because the blood of Muslims is equal, but they can sacrifice foreigners on the plane... If you study Shari'a, you will know that. The ransom (*fidya*) of a Muslim is 12,000 dirham, while that of a *dhimmi* (Christian or Jew) is only 4,000 dirham.[61]

Bakri's renown as 'the leader of the Islamic Movements' is widespread in the Islamic world.[62] Although he denies any organizational or hierarchical link to Bin-Laden, he has repeatedly declared that they were both committed to the same ideology, but he also objected to defining Bin-Laden as a terrorist, explaining that 'if someone supports Muslims against the occupying forces in Somalia or in Arabia, I will never call him a terrorist. I will call him a freedom fighter. I will call him a hero.'[63] After the bombing of US embassies in Saudi Arabia and East Africa in 1998, Bakri insisted that even if it was proven that Bin-Laden was responsible, 'those still remained legitimate acts', because as US troops in the Gulf were there to fight against Muslims and Islam, it was the duty of every Muslim to fight them. He cited the US bombing of Sudan and Afghanistan, the war against Iraq, and United States 'blind support' for Israel as 'acts of war against Allah and his Prophet'.[64] Following that US missile attack against the Sudan and Afghanistan, Bakri read an announcement to the Italian press, allegedly coming directly from Bin-Laden:

> The war has begun. Our response to the barbaric bombardment against Muslims of Afghanistan and Sudan will be ruthless and violent'...Our response could happen in any corner of the world. Retaliation for the US attacks will end

only when the last American soldier has left Saudi Arabia and the Gulf, and when the embargo against Iraq is over... We will not give a truce to America.[65]

In July 1999, Bakri published a letter to Bin-Laden on his *Muhajirun* website, calling upon him to act against the West. And though the letter was removed from the site following US protest, it was read out in mosques in London, Bradford, Sheffield and Leicester. Bakri warned in his letter that the Islamic movements had not used 'the real weapon' yet, and addressed Bin-Laden thus:

> Oh, Osama!... You and your brothers are now breathing new life and dignity 'into the body of the *umma*... Our main mission as Muslims is to carry the Islamic message to the entire world... we are an *umma* of jihad, and beyond doubt we have been chosen by Allah to lead the whole world if we hold to his command... The opportunity is here and we must not pass it by... Our Muslim brothers are firm in their jihad so we must not lose time aimlessly and act now... Oh, Osama, let us hear the good news from you and your brothers, for a new dawn is near at hand.[66]

Allegedly, that letter was heeded by Bin-Laden and answered in a circular read out in mosques in London and Pakistan. Another letter by Bin-Laden to Bakri was faxed in the summer of 1998 and later published in the *Los Angeles Times*. It allegedly contained the four specific objectives for jihad against the United States: 'Bring down their airlines, prevent the safe passage of their ships, occupy their embassies and force the closure of their companies and banks.'[67] Had the West heeded these threats and arrested those dangerous Muslim operatives, instead of sheltering them in its cities and letting them foment incitement and hatred in their midst, the events of 11 September might never have occurred. Journalist Steve Emerson in the United States, and a handful of academic writers who were warning, during those years, against the impending explosion of Muslim radical rage, were dismissed as alarmists, and their cries: 'Wolf!!! Wolf!!!' were glossed over as bouts of hysteria at best, racism and hatred of Islam at worst. Even when a security apparatus in the West knew the facts they misinterpreted them and rejected them in disbelief, thus allowing one of the greatest strategic surprise attacks in modern times to come to pass, while the prosperous, complacent, spineless, hypocritical, short-sighted and sycophant West, with the exception of the United States, looked on indolently and helplessly, although it had unwittingly itself helped breed the catastrophe by naively allowing in the Trojan horse, leaving itself open and vulnerable when the hidden fighters surged forth and attacked.

Bakri, being perhaps the most virulent and dangerous Western-based spokesman of the world war that radical Islam has declared against the West, made no effort to hide his programme. Not only did he side openly with Bin-Laden, and recruit and indoctrinate would-be Islamikaze in the heart of the West and in Islamic countries further afield, but he did not relent from his open campaign of hatred against the Jews, and then the West in general, when the latter did not react decisively to nip it in the bud. He had posters, 'Kill the Jews!', plastered on walls around him, and to escape punishment he claimed that those were the 'words of the Holy Scriptures', not his own.[68] He accused Jews of exploiting the Holocaust to achieve 'hegemony over the Muslims', and insisted that far worse war crimes had been perpetrated by others against Muslims in Chechnya, Kashmir and Palestine than those Muslims were accused of in other parts of the globe.[69] He also said that he had no problems with Jewish communities as such, only against Israel, which was a 'cancer in the heart of the Islamic world', and therefore it must be 'eradicated and removed'. He told his demonstrating audiences in front of the Regent Park's Mosque, on the outbreak of the Al-Aqsa Intifadah, that 'all Israeli targets are legitimate for you. All Israelis must be destroyed.'[70] His campaign of incitement also included the playwright, Terrence McNally, for portraying Jesus Christ as a homosexual in his play *Corpus Christi*, while in Islam He ('*Isa*) was considered a Prophet, and he suggested that all homosexuals ought to throw themselves down from Big Ben.[71]

The most relevant aspect of Bakri's teachings, however, as far as use of violence is concerned, is his reliance on the jihad. In a document entitled 'Jihad', that he posted on the *Muhajirun* website, he offered a lengthy analysis of what he meant:

> Jihad, as a term, cannot be translated as 'Holy War', nor can it be translated as 'struggle'... At best, its legal meaning can be understood as 'using military force where diplomacy fails, to remove the obstacles the Islamic state faces in carrying its ideology to mankind'... The aim of jihad, unlike the Crusades,

past and present, is not forcibly to convert to Islam the inhabitants of other lands. Rather, it is to provide them with the security that comes from the application of Islam, leaving them the choice of adopting Islam or keeping their own religions...History confirms that this is, and always has been, the role of jihad, for it was in Muslim Spain that the Muslims, Christians and Jews could live peacefully under an Islamic authority...The difference between the use of force by the West and that by Islam is that the capitalist West uses force overtly and covertly for the benefit of a few, such as corporations, while Islam uses force openly and justly to carry its mercy to others...jihad is...one of the Pillars of Islam, after *tawhid* [the assertion of monotheistic faith] and *da'wa* [proselytizing]. In fact, jihad is *da'wa* by the Islamic state and its foreign policy.[72]

Unlike his fellow-expatriot, al-Masri, who posited the Yemen as the launching pad for the Islamic revolution, or al-Qa'ida leaders who relied on the Taliban regime to kindle the world fire, Bakri thinks that it must all start in London, thus lending *ex post facto* rationale to his exile there. He aspires to establish a world Islamic caliphate, starting in the United Kingdom, the first Islamic state in a new world order. Thus, he conveniently called the British laws and democracy that allowed him to take refuge there in the first place 'phony rules', made up by the 'monkeys in Parliament',[73] and stated unequivocally to *Le Monde* his intention to 'make the flag of Islam fly high at 10 Downing Street and at the Elysée'. In his view, 'Islam is the supreme ideology facing an immoral West...and all contemporary leaders of the Muslim world, with no exception, are pawns of the West'.[74] In interviews and public lectures by Bakri, he made his doctrine clear and explicit:

> With thanks to Allah, we bring peace to all, and we help the world realize that Islam is the only way of life...Terrorism, according to the West is defined as 'the systematic use of violence to achieve political or religious ends'...*Al-Muhajirun* defines terrorism as 'to attack without the divine right'...
>
> Clinton is a target of jihad, and American forces are a target of jihad wherever they are...The American people must reconsider their foreign policy, or their children will be sent back to them in coffins...Clinton is responsible and he will

pay...The existence of Israel is a crime and must be removed...

Our duty is to work to establish a Muslim state anywhere in the world, even in Britain...Life is protected under us. There will be no minorities or majorities as in America. Anti-Semitism in America is disgraceful. Synagogues and churches will flourish in the Islamic caliphate, as long as they adopt Islamic law...We restored life for the Jews after the Crusades, and we plan to do so again...

What President Clinton and Prime Minister Barak are doing [that is, negotiating a peace] is putting themselves in the position of Allah, therefore they are now at direct war with the people who believe in Allah.[75]

The horrors of 11 September neither surprised Bakri, who had been consistently preaching for similar action, nor generated any remorse in him. Quite the contrary, he regarded them as 'compensation for the atrocities the United States committed against Islam',[76] and warned that should the United States attack the Taliban, the 'verdict of Allah', already issued by Muslim scholars of the Holy Law, had made all US government and military installations legitimate targets. He exhorted all Muslims to unite in the fight, sacrifice themselves and their wealth in order to get to Paradise, and to make clear the difference between 'truth and falshood, Belief and heresy, oppressors and oppressed, the alliance of Satan and that of Allah'.[77] After the US attack began, Bakri issued a fatwa against Pakistan's President Musharraf and other Muslim leaders who let their territories be used by the Americans against a fellow Muslim state. The verdict said:

There is no doubt that America has attacked, and is still attacking, the Muslims in every place and is carrying out massacres against them...It is the obligation of all Muslims to be in a state of war against it. The minimal obligation is a complete boycott, by means of avoiding diplomatic relations...The only ones who claim that diplomatic relations are permitted are the clerics and the treacherous sultans, most of them are donkeys bearing books, and some are like dogs. They have renounced the verses of Allah and become like dogs that should be left to pant, as a place is already reserved for them, surely on the lowest level of the fires of Hell...

Those people…are *murtaddun* (heretics), if they were at all Muslims to start with. They are all involved in the war against Islam and Muslims, and therefore the sentence of *murtadd harbi* (a heretic who should be fought) applies to them, to wit:

1. His blood becomes permissible and he must be killed, as an obligatory punishment, without possibility of forgiveness, because he fights against Allah and his Prophet.
2. His marriage becomes invalid, as does his guardianship of his children and relatives.[78]
3. His property is permissible – he will not be able to bequeath it.
4. He cannot be buried in a Muslim cemetery, because burying Muslims is an honour that is fitting only those who are Muslims…while they [the rulers] are *murtaddun harbiyyun* and are not Muslims.
5. He must be treated with animosity and hatred, exactly like a heretic *harbi* should.
6. There is no difference between man and woman in this verse…The blood of a woman who is a heretic *harbiya* is permissible, even if her fighting is limited to singing… Thus acted the Prophet against the fighting women of the Quraysh tribe. He permitted their blood and ordered them killed, although he generally prohibited killing women.[79]

The fatwa appeared, in its Arabic version quoted above, under the emblem of the 'Shari'a Court of the United Kingdom', and was signed jointly by Bakri himself, under his title of 'Shari'a Court Judge in London', and Muhammed al-Musa'ari, the Secretary General of the Committee for the Protection of Legitimate Rights in Saudi Arabia, which lends to it authority and respectability. Its English version, however, was slightly different, and signed by 'Muslim Jurists from Syria, Lebanon, Kuwait, the Emirates, Saudi Arabia, Pakistan, Afghanistan and the United Kingdom', with the names of the two original signatories, Bakri and Musa'ari, appearing at the bottom, with their telephone numbers for further inquiries. In this version, the passage about 'panting dogs' and 'donkeys' was replaced by the Qur'anic verse threatening that:

The punishment of those who wage war against Allah and his Prophet and strive to make mischief in the land is only this, that they should be murdered or crucified or their hands and their feet should be cut off on opposing sides, or they should be imprisoned.[80]

And the section about the women of Quraysh, who were killed by the Prophet, was replaced by a paragraph that reads

Therefore, we ask Muslims with the capability, especially the armies of Muslim countries, to move quickly and to capture those apostates and criminals involved in these crimes, especially the ruler of Pakistan, King Fahd of Saudi Arabia and Rabbani of Afghanistan, and his followers [in the Northern Alliance].[81]

PALESTINIAN CHAMPIONS OF ISLAMIKAZE

As has already been pointed out in Chapter 5, the Palestinians, being the chief models of Islamikaze, the most active agents in the implementation of the idea, and the ones who have widened the circle of its validity beyond the few Muslim self-sacrificing radicals into a legitimate national form of struggle for the masses, have also provided some of the most pointed and virulent arguments and rationalizations of it.

At first, only the most virulent terrorist organizations among the Palestinians, such as the Hamas and the Islamic Jihad, and then only the hard-core few among them, resorted to Islamikaze tactics inherited, as we have seen, from the Shi'ite Hizbullah. Then, as the Intifadah unfolded, non-Islamic groups, such as Tanzim, the Aqsa Brigades and the Force 17 Presidential Guards, embraced the same means of struggle, capitalizing on the rewards any Muslim would be entitled to if he died as a martyr. Then, after much debate, Palestinian women, also not necessarily affiliated with any Islamic movement, joined the fray, and became heroines and model martyrs. Finally, the peak of the horror was reached when teenagers, as young as 14 or 16, were co-opted and encouraged to join, first as martyrs in shootings and hand-grenade attacks against Israelis, and then, as their martyrdom death becomes an acceptable standard in their society, it is evident that they will also be trained for Islamikaze operations.

This rapid escalation of the rage for martyrdom in Palestinian society, and its growing respectability and centrality as increasing numbers of volunteers swell the ranks, is perhaps the most dramatic development in the Palestinian doctrine of struggle, which will have far-reaching repercussions in the years to come. Because, if the Islamikaze hard core has hitherto been constituted by eccentric individuals, just like their erstwhile Japanese kamikaze counterparts, today, idealizing this mode of fighting, with the active support of the clerics, within the mainstream of society, will only increase Palestinian resolve to oppose Israel at any price, since no price is then high enough. If it is so with Palestinian zeal, indeed enthusiasm, for self-immolation, it is so much more so for indiscriminate killings in the enemy camp. In other words, human life has totally lost its value in their eyes: the enemy's because he deserves to lose it as the price of his 'aggression', and their own because they are eager to attain the rewards of Paradise for their martyrdom.

Although there is a wide variety of clerics debating the issue of Palestinian participation in what the West calls 'terrorism', the Palestinian ulama, who pronounce themselves on this matter, are unified by the theme of what they perceive as a concrete, daily, and all-pervasive national struggle to which they are pushed to provide theological responses; a far cry from the fantasies and wishful thinking of delusionary radicals like al-Masri and al-Bakri, who want to confront the world, bring down the West, kindle a world Islamic revolution, subvert their Western countries of exile from within, or other dreams of this sort. A pertinent place to start would be with the mufti of the Palestinian Authority, Sheikh Akrama Sabri, who was appointed by Arafat (not by the Hamas or some other fanatic group). In early June 2001, just one week prior to the disastrous Islamikaze act against the discotheque in Tel Aviv, where 21 teenagers who were simply having fun were blown to pieces, and as a sinister prophesy of things to come, Sabri gave a Friday sermon in the controversial Al-Aqsa Mosque in Jerusalem. He first praised the Islamikaze martyrs in general, criticized the Saudi mufti who had prohibited these acts (in the meantime, he had qualified his prohibition as explained above) and demanded that the Americans release the four Muslims who were convicted for the first attempt to blow up the Twin Towers in 1993. Then came the text of his sermon:

> Oh Muslims!! Let me begin my sermon with a quote from the words of the Prophet's Companion...in a speech to his army before the battle of Mu'tah,[82] where he said: 'Oh people, I swear by Allah that the thing you hate [meaning death] is

what you are going out to seek today, namely the *shahada'*
[martyrdom]...

We are not fighting with a large army nor with force. We are
fighting only with this religion of Islam with which we have
been blessed by Allah. So, attack and you will gain one of two
blessings: either victory or martyrdom. In the eighth [*sic*,
ought to be seventh] century, the Muslim army consisted of
3,000 fighters while the Romans [*sic*: ought to be Byzantines],
had 100,000...Nevertheless the Muslim commanders decided
to go into the battle...

Oh Muslims! The first Commander of the Muslim Army
sacrificed his life in Mu'tah...so the command was taken over
by another Companion until his right-hand palm was cut-off.
He passed the banner to his left hand until that was severed
too, so he continued to hold the banner with the two stumps
of his severed hands until he was struck down...His body
was cut in two, in his body there were 50 stabbings, but none
of them entered in his back because he did not retreat...That
is the nature of Believers who do not retreat at the time of
assault. I am asking: was his breaking into the ranks of the
enemy called 'suicide'? No!! Allah Forbid!! That was
martyrdom for the sake of Allah! The Prophet then named him
Ja'far (the Flyer), because Allah granted him two wings when
he reached Paradise, in place of his two hands lost in combat.
He persisted in attacking the enemy until he attained
martyrdom...We say this to those who think it is an act of
'suicide'...Be careful with your rulings.[83]...

[Finally, after the pool of commanders was depleted], came
Khalid Ibn al-Walid [later a famous fighter in the conquests of
Islam], who fought fiercely and devised a brilliant plan for
withdrawal, sustaining only minimal casualties...Before the
Prophet sent the army to Mu'tah he gave instructions not to
kill innocent people, women or children, not to uproot a tree
or destroy a house. This is our great Islamic religion. It
encourages good ethics and high morale in peace and in
war...On the other hand, our enemies destroy houses, kill
children...and uproot trees. They prevent pregnant women
from reaching hospitals...They use aeroplanes against
defenceless civilians. Yes, they are occupiers and do not
deserve any sovereignty.

We tell them that as much as you love life, the Muslim loves death and martyrdom. There is a great difference between he who loves the hereafter and he who loves this world. The Muslim loves death and strives for martyrdom. He does not fear the oppression of the arrogant or the weapons of the blood-letters. The blessed and sacred soil of Palestine has vomited all the invaders and all the colonialists throughout history, and it will soon vomit out, with Allah's help, the present occupiers.[84]

This statement of the preference of death over life, citing the precedents of the Companions of the Prophet, not only sanctifies martyrdom and posits it as an *ideal* in itself, not merely a necessity, but also pushes Muslims to fight against all odds, even when they are certain to die, as it posits martyrdom as a worthy alternative to victory. What is interesting is that the venerable sheikh confuses the logic of his own sermon by:

1. Bringing up the precedents of the Prophet who spared the lives of the innocent, but at the same time pushing young people to die indiscriminately, which is in the nature of Islamikaze attacks where the maximization of civilian casualties is an ideal; and
2. While he unremittingly praised the martyrs, who fought against all odds, he also lauded the brilliant act of withdrawal of Kahlid Ibn al-Walid, which is exactly the reverse of martyrdom, namely the admission of the vanity of sacrifice in the face of reality, the praiseworthy abandonment of it and the election of life over death.

If this was the official Palestinian attitude prior to 11 September, how much more so subsequent to it, when the escalation of the Palestinian Intifadah and the total mobilization of the Palestinian people against Israel produced an increase in the resort to Islamikaze acts on a scale, with a frequency and continuity, and with a zealotry and rage never experienced before by Muslims anywhere, deserving of the comparison with the Japanese kamikaze at the end of the Pacific War. However, there was a difference: while the kamikaze aimed at military targets in order to destroy the US fleet in the Pacific, the Palestinian Islamikaze aim primarily at Israeli civilian targets in order to maximize civilian casualties and cause terror, disarray and demoralization among them, something akin to what the perpetrators of the Twin Towers

horror had devised against the United States. True, at first, Yasser
Arafat tried to appear as negating acts of Islamikaze that the world
had rejected with horror after the New York disaster, and he
declared his siding with the war against terrorism. His troops even
killed three jubilating Hamas youths, who could not hide their
delight at the sight of a terror-stricken United States. But soon
thereafter, not only did the Hamas escalate their war of terror
through martyrdom against Israel, but they were joined by Arafat's
own forces, the Aqsa Brigades. In fact, the Fat'h, Arafat's movement
within the PLO, embraced the Hamas concept that the martyrdom
operations had achieved a kind of balance of deterrence of the
Palestinian people in their struggle against Israel, and was an 'act of
self-defence' against what they saw as 'Israel's aggression'.[85]
Consequently, there was an intensification of the incitement to more
Islamikaze attacks by imams throughout the Palestinian Authority.
Sheikh Ibrahim Mahdi, who incidentally doubles up as a lecturer in
ecology at the local Al-Aqsa University, delivered a clear message
to his Palestinian audience in a Friday service at a mosque in Gaza:

> We are convinced of the victory of Allah, we are convinced
> that one of these days we shall enter Jerusalem as conquerors,
> and to Jaffa, Haifa, Ramlah...and all Palestine as
> conquerors...All those who did not gain martyrdom yet will
> wake up in the middle of the night and say: 'My God! Why did
> you deprive me of martyrdom, for the *shahid* lives by
> Allah'...Our enemies now suffer more than we do, because
> we know that our dead go to Paradise while the Jewish dead
> go directly to Hell and to their cruel lot...This is the reason for
> our steadfastness, out of obedience to Allah...The Jews are
> expecting their false Messiah, but we are waiting for our
> Mahdi and for Jesus, Blessed be He...He will kill with his
> own hands the Jewish false Messiah, in Lydda, Palestine.
> Palestine will then be, as in the past, the cemetery for the
> invaders, as it had been for the Tatar, Crusader and the old and
> new colonialist invaders...
> A Hadith says that 'The Jews will fight you, but you shall
> dominate them.' What could be more beautiful than this
> tradition? It will be Allah who would put the Muslim in a
> position of dominance over the Jew...until the Jew hides
> behind the rock and the tree. But the rock and the tree will say:
> 'Oh Muslim, oh servant of Allah!, a Jew hides behind me,

come and kill him!' Except for the Gharqad tree, which is the tree of the Jews...We believe in this Hadith, we are also convinced that this Hadith heralds the spread of Islam and its rule all over the land...

Oh beloved, look to the east of the earth, and you will find Japan and the Ocean. Be assured that these will be owned by the Muslim nation as the Hadith says 'from the Ocean to the Ocean'...

Oh Allah, accept our martyrs in the highest Heavens...

Oh Allah, show the Jews a black day...

Oh Allah, annihilate the Jews and their supporters...

Oh Allah, raise the flag of jihad across the land...

Oh Allah, forgive our sins.[86]

This incessant self-aggrandizement of the Muslims as the future rulers of the entire universe on the one hand, and the incitement for action and glorification of death, which has seeped down into all the crevices of the grassroots of Palestinian society on the other, impel the Palestinian populace to identify instinctively with their martyrs and *eo ipso* to encourage more sacrifices among them. Thus, when visitors come to the homes of the martyrs to greet (not to bring condolences to) the 'delighted' (not bereaved) families of the Islamikaze, the mothers declare to the gatherings, that are well publicized by the official press and television, their vow to send the rest of their boys too, some present, some yet to be born, into jihad and acts of Iskamikaze. Children from kindergarten age on also appear on Palestinian television during their regular 'educational' activities, brandishing weapons and vowing, with visible excitement and joy over something they ill-comprehend, their desire to be martyrs. The constant nurturing of the flames of the Intifadah by this never-ending, even growing, enthusiasm for jihad and martyrdom, which they say is well rooted in Islamic history, is the most revolutionary and lasting contribution of the Palestinian leadership, clerical and political, to the idea of the Palestinian struggle. So much so that when Arafat was confined to his office by the Israeli siege in Ramallah in April 2002, his most cited declaration to the press was that he aspired to become a *shahid* (martyr) himself.

Interestingly enough, though the universal Palestinian jubilation *vis-à-vis* martyrdom has peaked during the Al-Aqsa Intifadah that broke out in October 2000, the Palestinians were 'educated' and prepared for martyrdom long before that. There are tapes of incitement of school children to become martyrs dating back to 1998, though in most of them, martyrdom *per se* is extolled without necessarily encouraging the young to blow themselves up in the process. Indeed, martyrdom is instilled in them as an ideal not only in the context of dramatic and much-hallowed Islamikaze actions, but also as a routine of a grinding confrontation with Israeli troops, where the demonstrating children, instilled with the audacity to face the enemy and provoke him, could end up dying. In that case of passive death too, unlike the active search for death by the Islamikaze, they would be considered martyrs. Clips abound on Palestinian television of young teenagers vowing martyrdom, but the most dramatic and world famous, which was played and replayed by the world media, concerned Muhammed al-Dura. In November 2000, at the very start of the Intifadah, he was killed in crossfire, apparently shot by Palestinians, in an area of confrontation from which children should have been kept away in the first place. But since it is part of the Palestinian strategy to push their children to the frontline and then turn their own cruelty towards their children into a propaganda campaign against Israel, he was led there by his careless father, and the child paid the price with his life. But then the Palestinian machine started operating to glorify Dura at home, to accuse Israel of his death abroad, and to call other Palestinian children to follow his model.

The clip on Palestinian television was re-enacted by actors with the child, Muhammed al-Dura, being shown lying in the field and, interspersed with many violent scenes of battle, he is always shown in beautiful, peaceful places, running along the beach, or through the Plaza of the Al-Aqsa Mosque, or alongside wonderful fountains, flying a kite in a green pasture, approaching a giant ferris-wheel. The soundtrack tells the children that death in conflict with Israel will bring them to a child's Paradise, where Muhammed is tranquil, as we see him playing and waving to the audience of children to 'come, follow me here'. The main lyrics pass up and back from narrator to choir, to 'A'ida, a popular woman singer (whose name incidentally means 'the returnee') with long tresses and dressed in striking flowing red robes. The dead boy, Muhammed, talks to his father, 'till we meet, my father, till we meet! I go with no tears, with no fears, how sweet is the fragrance of the Martyrs!!! I shall go to my place in Heaven, how sweet is the fragrance of the martyrs!!' The narrator continues: 'How sweet is the fragrance of the martyrs, how sweet is the fragrance of the earth, its thirst quenched by the gush of blood flowing from the youthful body'... The screen at this point is filled with two huge roses which are closing in slow motion, accompanying the narrative: 'The earth, its thirst quenched by the gush of blood from the body of youth.' 'Ai'da continues: 'How sweet is the scent of the earth, its thirst satisfied by the gush of blood, flowing from the body of youth.' These refrains are repeated several times, ending with 'Ai'da singing: 'Oh the children of the world say "till we meet, oh Muhammed till we meet!"' The clip closes with the following credit: 'Produced by the Ministry of Information and Culture – the Palestinian National Fund.'

This cynical and cold-blooded exploitation of children, which has become the norm for the Palestinian Authority in its struggle against Israel, has been watched around the globe, with world networks focusing on the dead Muhammed al-Dura and accusing Israel of the killing which, even had it been true, would still have been inadvertent in the middle of an exchange of fire, while few asked the obvious question, what business had that boy, together with many others, in presenting himself at the frontline and putting himself in danger. Only Queen Sylvia of Sweden asked that question, but was quickly hushed by the European governments who were more interested in supporting Arafat than in uncovering the truth. Recent investigations by independent Israeli and German reporters completely exonerated Israel from any wrongdoing in that case, but most of the press in Europe, not to mention in the Arab and Islamic world, pursues its litany of anti-Israeli, baseless attacks on this matter. They refuse to allow any fact to disturb their preconceived ideas of the Israeli–Palestinian dispute, and not for the first time would follow blindly what the Palestinians say, regardless of other facts presented to them.[87] Encouraged by world support, the Palestinians had no reason to mend their ways, and their campaigns of incitement to terrorism against Israel, the killing of innocent civilians, the denial of Israel's right to exist, and martyrdom, including by children, remain entrenched in the Palestinian 'educational' system which has been generously funded by Europe. Thus, the latter unwittingly became a partner in Arafat's harrowing schemes to kill others and sacrifice his own children in the process.

These are harrowing concepts in which the children of Palestinians are indoctrinated on their national television and by their leaders, supported by the clerics of the Palestinian Authority in general, chief among them is the same Akrama Sabri cited above. In an interview given to the Egyptian weekly *Al-Ahrah al-'Arabi*, the sheikh not only laid claim, as a matter of course, to all Israel, but he stressed the need for martyrdom of children in the process of 'liberating' Jerusalem and all the rest of Palestine in order to prove that the 'new generation will carry on the mission with determination'. He said:

> We have not sacrificed enough yet to be worthy of liberating Al-Aqsa...To liberate Jerusalem, Salah a-Din al-Ayyubi made great sacrifices for a long time, and we have to sacrifice until Allah's victory is completed...The land of Palestine is not only Jerusalem. This land stretches from the Jordan River to the sea. The Palestinian problem relates to all this land. We cannot establish a homeland only by liberating Jerusalem. It is true that Salah a-Din did not rest until he liberated Jerusalem, but this does not mean that the rest of this blessed land should be neglected or given up...
>
> Every Palestinian is in fact in a state of jihad. I feel the martyr is lucky because the angels usher him to his wedding in Heaven...There is no doubt that the child martyr suggests that the new generation will carry on the mission with determination...The younger the martyr, the greater and the more I respect him...One wrote his name on a note before he died...It said 'I am Martyr so and so.' In every martyr's pocket we find a note with his name on it. He sentences himself to martyrdom even before he becomes a martyr...The mothers [who cry in joy when they hear of their sons' martyrdom] willingly sacrifice their offspring for the sake of freedom. It is a great display of the power of belief. The mother is participating in the great reward of the jihad to liberate Al-Aqsa. I talked to a young man who said: 'I want to marry the black-eyed women of Heaven.' The next day he became a martyr. I am sure his mother was filled with joy about his heavenly marriage. Such a son must have such a mother...
>
> I am filled with rage towards the Jews. I have never greeted a Jew when I come near one and I never will. They cannot even dream that I will. They do not dare to bother me because they are the most cowardly creatures Allah has ever created...Palestinian children are thus taught, almost from

their birth to hate Jews and to glorify jihad, even to the point of their own death and martyrdom, as an essential part of their culture.[88]

Besides the clerics who encouraged acts of Islamikaze, obviously in response to the huge wave of popular support for that mode of struggle, there were some mainstream professionals, such as Ashraf al-'Ajrami, a columnist in the Palestinian Authority daily, *Al-Ayyam*, who realized the damage that the outrageous procedure of using children causes to national interest and who counselled the Authorities to desist from it. He acknowledged the fact that 'the phenomenon of martyrdom was on the increase, especially among minors', but predictably blames the 'Israeli occupation' for the 'degradation of life which pushes many to disdain life and seek the shortest way to the hereafter'. He also admits, however, that it is the 'honour and esteem that the Palestinian people gives to the martyr that has had a crucial effect on the emergence of this phenomenon'. He also imputed importance in this regard to the 'funerals of the martyrs and the celebrations held in their honour, which have always been accompanied by talks of everlasting life and eternal serenity in Paradise'. Therefore, the rationale goes, why wait through the tribulations of life if one can take a shortcut to Paradise by pressing a button or purposely coming within range of Israeli shooting? At the same time he contends that the enthusiasm among minors for being hailed as heroes and martyrs might encourage their gratuitous exploitation by others. He also concedes that some Gaza children are influenced by mosques and schools, an admission of the ruinous character of the Palestinian textbooks, some funded by the European Union, which cultivate Islamikaze death.[89]

The columnist, who appears to be well updated on the techniques and motivations of the young Islamikaze, delves into terrifying details and counsels Palestinians to desist from this practice, not for the moral burden it puts on the Palestinian leadership but for the damage it causes to Palestinian propaganda:

> Some are willing to arm them for money – with pistols, hand grenades, and readily available pipe bombs that cost only a few shekels. These brainwashed children are imbued with motivation to approach the nearest settlement where they are shot dead by the soldiers of the occupation...
>
> The children's martyrdom promotes the hostile propaganda

of the enemies, particularly in reinforcing their claims that the Palestinians send their children to the front line. These are false claims aimed at justifying the indiscriminate shooting at all the Palestinians...The phenomenon also causes the children to rebel against their parents, in so far as the children threaten their parents that they would martryr themselves if the parents did not meet their demands or did not turn a blind eye to their inappropriate behaviour...Moreover, some of the children have used pipe-bombs during arguments amongst themselves...

Collective efforts should be made to contain this phenomenon...All activities having an ill-effect on the children's emotional stability, pulling them in directions outside the normal matters of children, must be monitored...The security apparatuses should apprehend the arms traffickers and collaborators acting among the youths to make money or to exterminate this generation with its nationalist enthusiasm and its will to fight...It is also important to stop the mosques from engaging in exaggerated political activity and providing ground for anyone who wants to abuse the minds of youth and minors...The Palestinian media also have a role in refraining from broadcasting pictures affecting the emotional state of children, and from exaggerating in reporting tragic news that arouses the children's feelings of frustration and despair.[90]

A rare, courageous Arab voice against the self-immolation of children was raised by a female Arab journalist, Huda al-Husseini, who was incensed at the systematic sacrifice of children in a war they did not initiate and perhaps ill-comprehended:

Some Palestinian leaders...consciously issue orders with the purpose of ending their childhood, even if it means their last breath. I want to know why we, the Arabs, insist on dying rather than living for our homeland. If these children have nothing to lose, and they think the training is a game, are we supposed to continue pushing them with hypocrisy and stupid enthusiasm to actually lose their lives? Have we exhausted all means and used every argument, have we exhausted our brains, having nothing left but to gamble with the lives of children and push them to confront Israel? Or maybe the Palestinian leaders – those who are in the PA or those who get ready to fill a role in it – put their trust in the humanity of Israel? If this is what they do, they are wrong...What kind of independence is based on the blood of children while the leaders are safe and so are their children and grandchildren?...Are only the miserable destined to die in the spring of their lives? Those children who are killed may not, in their short lives, have enjoyed a fresh piece of bread, sleeping in a warm bed, the happiness of putting on a new piece of cloth, or carrying books with no torn pages to school...

The time for Arafat and those around him has reached its dusk...First of all, these children deserve to live, before we push them to find death. But, what are we doing to them? We abuse their innocence, we supply them with tons of stones, while we sit in our offices and commend their death. Then we accept an invitation for a working lunch or dinner and talk about those children who died holding stones, those that died, probably hungry.[91]

But others in the Arab world, including supposedly enlightened academics, and certainly populist, self-made clerics who do not conform to the establishment, as well as non-Palestinian jurists and other notables, remained unflinching in their support of the Islamikaze. For example, Halim Barakat, a Professor at Georgetown University, castigated the Arab states for their oppression of their populations, but credited the Arab peoples for their awakening from their slumber. He created a rule of thumb whereby the 'more technologically advanced the people the less moral and more barbaric it becomes', implying that Western countries like the United States, which has given him asylum, and Israel, are so technologically advanced that they qualify for his definition of barbarism in their actions against the Muslims in Afghanistan and Palestine, thus turning on its head the definition of terrorism: the barbarians are not those who blew up the Twin Towers or the restaurants and buses in Israel, but those who moved decisively to eliminate them.[92]

Another 'enlightened' voice, in the person of the Saudi Ambassador to London, Dr Ghazi al-Gosaibi, a recognized Arab poet, wrote a poem praising the Palestinian Islamikaze, in which he heaped praise on Ayat al-Akhras, the 18-year-old Palestinian girl who blew herself up in a Jerusalem supermarket, killing two Israelis and wounding 25.[93] The respectable Ambassador, who had been serving his country for a decade, and from whom one could have expected some level of diplomacy, wrote that the 'doors of Heaven are opened to her' and that the 'heart of the White House was filled with darkness'. The British Foreign Ministry, which released a statement condemning 'suicide bombing as a form of terrorism', pledged that a senior official would make clear British views to the Ambassador, but did not rebuke the Ambassador nor undertake any other measure against him. The Board of Deputies of British Jews stated that it was 'appalled', but no action was taken to oust the author of that appalling statement.[94]

Another Saudi notable, Dr Ibrahim al-Sa'adat, a columnist in the government-owned daily, *Al-Jazirah*, came out with a campaign of idolization of 'Abd-al-Baset 'Oudeh, who blew himself up in the Netanya Hotel during the Passover Seder, killing 29 people and wounding scores of others, and Ayat al-Akhras, the teenage girl who blew up an Israeli girl of her own age at the entrance to the Jerusalem supermarket. His description of his 'heroes' is almost as horrendous as the acts themselves:

> May Allah have mercy on you, Mujahid [*sic*] and martyr, the quiet hero who infiltrated so elegantly and spoke so gaily. You defended your religion, your homeland, and your people... Courageously, full of willingness to wage jihad...you executed your assignment and sacrificed your pure soul... The Israeli military, armed to the teeth, did not remove a hair of your head...You knew the Zionists do not honour promises, treaties and understand only the language of resistance and jihad...
>
> May Allah have mercy on you, 'Abd-al-Baset, the beloved son of the Arab nation. You evoked hope that had begun to dissipate, you restored life [by killing 29 innocent civilians] that had begun to expire; you revived the Arab pride, chivalry, valour and sacrifice that had begun to die, and you caused pain to the people who had begun to celebrate and sing atop the bodies of the children, youth and mothers of your people...You entered silently, with the faith and the confidence with which Allah inspired you...You reached your destination, you sat down at one of the tables, talked, told a few jokes and laughed with them, and then Allah

decreed for you a martyr's death. What heroism, courage and strength – almost unmatched on the face of the earth!

May Allah have mercy on you Ayat al-Akhras! You left your home for the path of martyrdom and Paradise... You proceeded with a determination, will and strength rarely found, even impossible to find, in a 16-year-old girl[95]...

You did not seek advice with American or Russian governments... you knew that the hand of Allah is supreme, that self-sacrifice is the highest form of jihad. You were not tempted by, nor did you rejoice in the life of this world... Oh, beloved of the Arab Nation of 16 springs. Marriage was before you, you were a girl engaged and looking forward to... [getting] wed; except you chose Allah, Paradise and martyrdom... You taught the Arab nation a lesson never taught in the schools and universities, and you breathed your last and awakened in us the sensations that had begun to disappear... May Allah have mercy on you, you Ayat and all male and female mujahedin. We ask Alllah that the angels welcome you as righteous martyrs, and beseech Allah to give you the highest level of Paradise.[96]

The rewards of the Hereafter after martyrdom are the most concrete promise, indeed certainty, that pushes the Islamikaze to cross fearlessly the last obstacle of hesitation and embark on the martyrdom venture. Therefore, it is within the Palestinian community, which has trained and sent to self-immolating jihad the greatest proportionate numbers of its sons, daughters and children, that these promises are the most vividly described and debated, once they have become a matter of routine, rather than remote, theoretical theology. The debate began not in the aftermath of the 11 September events, but at the end of the 1990s in the context of the Hamas and Islamic Jihad activities within Israel and against Israelis and Jews. On 19 August 2001, barely three weeks before the New York horrors, CBS's '60 Minutes' aired a programme on the Hamas in which one of its operatives, Muhammed Abu Wardeh, was asked to tell of his recruiting activities among would-be Islamikaze. He said, *inter alia*, that part of his technique was to describe to the novices the way Allah would reward them after they became martyrs by 'giving them 70 virgins, 70 wives and everlasting happiness'.[97] Embarrassed by the carnal temptations that were involved in what was meant to be a pure act of self-sacrifice for the sake of Allah, Muslim leaders in the

West (not in the Islamic world, where this doctrine enjoys widespread currency) raised questions about the accuracy of the translation of the interview and tried to discredit CBS, accusing it of 'fabrication' and defamation of their faith, and demanding retraction and apology.[98]

The controversy centred around the translation of *houriya*, a term which all Muslim conventional interpretations are proud to render as 'virgins', usually with the epithet of 'black-eyed', while some Muslim organizations in the West insisted that it was a metaphoric appellation of 'angels' or 'heavenly beings'. While it was much less important to focus on sexual fantasies than on the horrific acts of indiscriminate killing among the innocent perpetrated all the same by the Islamikaze, the newsworthy sexual controversy persisted nonetheless. To counter those denials, Sheikh Palazzi, an Italian Muslim leader, gave references in the Qur'an as well as in Islamic tradition (Sunna or Hadith) where the doctrine of the 72 (not 70) 'black-eyed' 'wives' is elaborated in vivid detail,[99] and took the other Muslim leaders in the West to task for their ignorance of the sources. Among Muslim clerics in the Muslim world there is no equivocation; things are clearly and unabashedly stated. In response to an Australian Muslim query about the reward of female martyrs in Paradise, in comparison with the males who got the black-eyed virgins, the Deputy Director of the authoritative Al-Azhar University, Sheikh 'Abd al-Fattah Jam'an responded:

> The Qur'an tells us that in Paradise Believers get the black-eyed, as Allah [namely the Qur'anic text] has said: 'And we will marry them to the black-eyed'. The black-eyed are white and delicate, and the black of their eyes is blacker than black, and the white [of their eyes] is whiter than white. To describe their beauty and their great number, the Qur'an says that they are 'like Sapphire and pearls',[100] in their values, in their colour and in their purity. And it is said of them: 'They are like well-protected pearls in shells',[101] that is they are as pure as pearls in oysters and are not perforated, no hands have ever touched them, no dust or dirt adheres to them, and they are undamaged. It is further said: 'They are like well-protected eggs',[102] that is their delicacy is as the delicacy of the membrane beneath the shell of an egg. Allah also said: 'the black-eyed are confined to pavilions',[103] that is they are hidden within, safe for their husbands . . .

Most of the black-eyed were first created in Paradise, but some of them are women who acceded to Paradise from this world. And are obedient Muslims who observe the words of Allah: 'We created them especially and have made them virgins, loving and equal in age.' This means that when the women of this world are old and worn out, Allah re-creates them after their old age into virgins who are amiable to their husbands. 'Equal in age' means equal to one another in age. At the side of the Muslim in Paradise are his wives from this world, if they are among the dwellers of Paradise, along with the black-eyed of Paradise...

If a woman is of the dwellers in Paradise but her husband in this world is not among them, as in the case of Asia, the wife of Pharaoh, she is given to one of the dwellers of Paradise who is of the same status. Regarding the woman who was married to more than one man in her lifetime, and all her [former] husbands are dwellers of Paradise, she may choose among them, and she chooses the best of them ... Thus, it is known that women in Paradise also have husbands. Every woman has a husband. If her husband in this world is a dweller of Paradise, he becomes her husband in Paradise, and if he is an Infidel, she is given to one of the dwellers of Paradise who is suited to her in status and in the intensity of his belief.[104]

It is quite understandable that these verses that are attributed to Allah may be taken as folkloric metaphors by some Muslims who are remote from the combat front of the Islamikaze. There is no doubt, however, that for Muslims whose pursuit of jihad is an active and preponderant aspect of their lives, particularly so among the Palestinians, the question of reward in Paradise constitutes a crucial portion role of their worldview and plays a major role in their battle motivation. in the Palestinian press and the death announcements of martyrs, which are usually pre-recorded in person by the Islamikaze and then kept as part of the cultivated patrimony of martyrdom that the Palestinians weave in order subsequently to impart it to their youth, there is no mincing of words; indeed, there is boasting, desire, expectation and impatient eagerness to take the short cut and join in one stroke the pleasures of Paradise. Chilling as the words may sound, such announcements as 'Greetings will be accepted immediately after the burial and until 10:00 pm ... at the home of the martyr's uncle', or 'With great pride the Palestinian Islamic Jihad marries the member of its military wing, the hero Yasser al-Adhami, to the black-eyed', appear prominently in the Palestinian press,[105] and did so even before 11 September.

The Hamas mouthpiece, *Al-Risala*, for example, published the will of Sa'id al-Hutari who carried out the horrendous massacre of 23 teenagers at the Dolphinarium Discotheque in Tel Aviv on 1 June 2001. It said: 'I will turn my body into bombs that will hunt the sons of Zion, blast them and burn their remains...Call out in joy, oh mother! Distribute sweets, oh father and brothers! A wedding with the black-eyed awaits your son in Paradise.'[106] Similarly, the bombing of the Sbarro pizza restaurant in Jerusalem (9 August 2001) was 'celebrated' by the Hamas with the announcement that the Islamikaze, Izz al-Din al-Masri's relatives had 'distributed sweets and accepted their son as a bridegroom who married the black-eyed, not as someone who had been killed and buried in the ground'.[107] Other Palestinian youth announced their preference for the black-eyed rather than marrying 'women of clay' in this world, while their leaders confirm to them that if 'the martyr dreams of a black-eyed, he will get her'.[108] When Jack Kelley of 'USA Today' visited a Hamas school in Gaza, he saw an 11-year-old boy speaking to his class: 'I will make my body a bomb that will blast the flesh of the Zionists, the sons of pigs and monkeys...I will tear their bodies into little pieces and will cause them more pain than they will ever know.' His classmates shouted in response 'Allah Akbar!!', and his teacher shouted: 'May the virgins give you pleasure.' A 16-year-old youth leader in a refugee camp told Kelley: 'Most boys cannot stop thinking about the virgins.'[109] And so on, literally *ad nauseum*, showing the inextricability of the expected heavenly wedding from the senseless death of Palestinian youth in their prime, taking with them to their death and destruction hundreds of innocent civilians and wiping out entire families.

Similarly, Palestinian clerics and 'educators' such as Dr Yunis al-Astal of the Islamic Law Department in Gaza University, the aforementioned Sheikh Sabri and the Palestinian Police Chief Mufti, Abu Shkheydem, spoke chillingly about the weddings of the Islamikaze with the black-eyed in Paradise, and the joy of their mothers. Al-Astal asserted that Paradise was the abode of the martyrs, and in it were 'the black-eyed confined to pavilions, and also women with downcast eyes whose chastity had not been violated before by either man or *jinn'*, and that the world that the Americans and their Arab 'eunuchs', that is, those who supported them, was 'in our eyes, not worth the wing of a mosquito'.[110] As a bonus, the sheikh of the police force, which is probably actively engaged in recruiting those young would-be martyrs, promised them that:

> ...from their first drop of spilled blood, they will not feel the pain of the wounds, and they are forgiven for all their sins; they see their seats in Paradise; they are saved from the torments of the grave; they marry the black-eyed; they vouch for 70 members of their families; they gain the crown of honour, the precious stones of which are better than the entire world and everything in it.[111]

The most prominent Palestinian cleric in Israel, Sheikh Ra'id from Umm al-Fahm, who served as mayor of his town for more than ten years, asserted in no uncertain terms in an interview to the major Israeli daily, *Ha'aretz*, that he 'had proof' that the story of the virgins was true and that was, of course, the writings in the Qur'an and the Sunna. He specified that the *shahid* received from Allah six special gifts, including 70 virgins, no torment in the grave, and the choice of 70 members of his family and his confidants to enter Paradise with him.[112] In the instructions given to the Islamikaze of 11 September, a copy of which was found in Nawwaf al-Hamzi's car, the black-eyed were mentioned twice:

> Do not show signs of uneasiness and of tension; be joyful and happy, set your mind at ease, and be confident and rest assured that you are carrying out an action that Allah likes and that pleases Him. Therefore, a day will come, Allah willing, that you will spend with the black-eyed in Paradise...Know that the gardens of Paradise have been decorated for you with the most beautiful ornaments and that the black-eyed will call to you: 'Come, Faithful of Allah', after having donned their finest garments.[113]

NOTES

1. *MEMRI*, No. 319, 21 December 2001. All information on this media event is based on that report.

2. Ibid.
3. Ibid.
4. Ibid.
5. Ibid.
6. Ibid.
7. www.geocities.com/al_ansar,index.html; and *Al-Quds al-'Arabi* (London), 9 February 2002. Both in *MEMRI*, Special Dispatch, No. 344, 10 February 2002.
8. Captain W. Lind, Colonel K. Nithtenagle, Captain J. Schmitt, Colonel J. Sutton and Colonel G. Wilson, 'The Changing Face of War: into the Fourth Generation', *Marine Corps Gazette*, October 1989.
9. The first type, following the Industrial Revolution, was based on large armies equipped with primitive rifles; the second stage, between the American Civil War and World War I, was fought by exhausting the enemy's economy and using intensive gun-fire to wear the enemy out and inflict on him many casualties by a frontal war of trenches and attrition; the third stage was revealed during World War II, especially by the German *blitzkrieg*, where the enemy was overwhelmed rapidly by tanks and aircraft surprising him in the rear. In the fourth stage, the battle will be scattered and not limited to military targets, but will destroy societies and popular support for the fighters on their behalf . See *MEMRI* , No. 344, 10 February 2002.
10. Colonel Thomas Hammes, 'The Evolution of War: the Fourth Generation', *Marine Corps Gazette*, September 1994.
11. Ibid
12. S. Simpson and D. Benjamin, 'The Terror', *Survival*, Vol. 43, No. 4, January 2002. V. Goulding, 'Back to the Future, with Asymmetric Warfare', *Parameters*, Winter 2000–01. Cited by *MEMRI*, ibid.
13. Ibid.
14. Not to be confused with Abu-Hifz, the Egyptian who was apparently killed during the American bombings in Afghanistan. Abu Hifz (Keeper or Guardian) is apparently a current *nom de guerre* among al-Qa'ida, and the fact that they are differentiated by their countries of origin is indicative of the truly international nature of that organization.
15. The interview was conducted by *Al-Jazeera* correspondent in Qandahar, Yussuf al-Shuli, and published in *Al-Sharq al-Awsat* (London), 27 September 2001. See *MEMRI* No. 42 (Hebrew – No Date).
16. Ibid.
17. According to tradition, the Prophet had effected a nightly journey to Jerusalem (*isra'*) on the back of his mythical horse (*al-Buraq*), whence he ascended to Heaven (*mi'raj*), before he rode back to Mecca.
18. See n. 14.
19. Qur'an, 8:62
20. See n. 14, ibid. p. 8.
21. Ibid.
22. Ibid.
23. www. lailatqadr.com/stories/p4040401.shtml, 4 April 2002, in *MEMRI* , No. 363, 7 April 2002.
24. Ibid.
25. *Al-Mustaqbal* (Lebanon), 19 March 2002, ibid.
26. *Kul al-'Arab* – (Nazareth), 5 April 2002, ibid.
27. *Al-Jazeera* television (Qatar), 16 September 2001. *MEMRI*, No. 277, 26 September 2001.
28. See Amir Weissbrod, *Turabi: A Spokesman of Radical Islam* (Hebrew), Tel Aviv: Dayan Center, 1999, especially pp. 9, 39–40, 64–5, 74, 82–3, 115.
29. For al-Masri's background, see *Al-Ayyam* (Yemen), 8 August 1999; *Christian Science Monitor*, 27 September 2001; www.al-bab.com/yemen/hamza/hamza1.htm. All cited by *MEMRI*, No. 72, a report by Yotam Feldner, 16 October 2001.
30. For a description of the camps, see Israeli (1997), 'Islamikaze and their Significance'.

31. See note 29.
32. Ibid.
33. Online Journalism Review, 15 November 1999, ibid.
34. *Al-Ayyam* (Yemen), 11 August 1999, ibid.
35. *Christian Science Monitor*, 13 January 1999, ibid
36. *Daily Telegraph*, 5 October 2001, ibid.
37. French News Agency (AFP), 28 February 1999, ibid.
38. http://dsc.discovery.com/news/briefs/20010910/abroad.html, ibid.
39. *Middle East Times*, Issue 13, 1999. *MEMRI*, No. 72, 16 October 2001.
40. Al-Quds al'Arabi, 21 July 2001, ibid.
41. Ibid.
42. Ibid.
43. Ibid.
44. *The Radical*, 13 September 2001, ibid.
45. The terminology is very evasive and ambiguous in this instance. While the original *Muhajirun* are those who had emigrated with the Prophet from Mecca to Medina in AD 622, radical Muslims who were forced to emigrate from their countries have sought to equate their emigration with the Prophet's, so as to lend to it an aura of sanctity. In London, for example, it might also signify the ex-patriots who took exile from Arab and Muslim countries where they were banned, or just like the Indian Muslims who migrated to Pakistan after the partition of 1947 and were also dubbed *Muhajirun*.
46. *The Observer*, 13 August 1995; and *Intelligence Newsletter*, No. 295, 19 September 1996. Both cited by *MEMRI*, Yotam Feldner's article No. 73, 24 October 2001.
47. *Daily Mirror*, 7 September 1996, ibid.
48. *Al-Ahram Weekly*, 1 October 2001, ibid.
49. *Executive Intelligence Review*, 4 September 1998, ibid.
50. See n. 48.
51. *Mail on Sunday*, 12 November 1995, ibid.
52. http://artsweb.bham.ac.uk/bmms/sampleissue, January 2001, asp, ibid.
53. AFP, as cited by *Al-Hayat al-Jadida* (Palestinian Authority) 10 October 2001, ibid.
54. See n. 52.
55. Ibid. Incidentally, the details remind one of the camps in Afghanistan described in Israeli (1997), 'Islamikaze and their Significance'.
56. See n. 52 above.
57. CNSNews.com, 24 May 2000, ibid.
58. *Middle East Intelligence Bulletin*, November 2000, citing Milan's *Il Giornale*, of 14 October 2000, ibid.
59. Irfan Hussein, 'The Battle for Hearts and Minds', *Dawn Weekly*, 6 October 2001, citing the *Asian Age Magazine*, ibid.
60. *Periscope Daily Defense News Capsules*, 4 September 1996, ibid.
61. *Roz al-Yussuf* (Egypt), 13 September 1999, cited by www.geocities.com/~lrcc/Women/comment.htm, ibid.
62. *Al-Ahram Weekly*, 19 November 1999, ibid.
63. CNSNews.com, 24 May, 2000, ibid.
64. See n. 62.
65. La Republica (Italy), 24 August 1998, ibid.
66. www.terrorism.com/_trcctforum5/000004b5.htm, ibid.
67. *Los Angeles Times*, 14 October 2001, ibid
68. http;//artsweb.bham.ac.uk/bmms/sampleissuejanuary2001.asp, ibid.
69. Ibid.
70. BBC News, 14 October 2000, ibid.
71. For those fiery speeches and the reactions to them by Britons, see *The Times*, 9 September 1996 and *The Guardian*, 9 September 1996, ibid.
72. www.almuhajiroun.com/islamictopics/islamicissues/jihad.html, ibid.
73. *The Mercury*, cited in http://artsweb.bham.ac.uk/bmms/sampleissuejan2001.asp, ibid.

74. *Le Monde*, 9 September 1998, ibid.
75. *The Jerusalem Post*, 30 May 2000, ibid.
76. *AFP*, 14 September 2001, ibid.
77. www.almuhajiroun.com/press_releases/index.html, ibid
78. Even in relatively moderate Egypt, whose regime is one of the closest to America in the Muslim world, a case became cause célèbre recently when an outspoken woman writer, Nawwal Sa'dawi, who criticized the haj (pilgrimage to Mecca) in Islam as an act of paganism, was declared a heretic by Islamists and her husband was ordered to divorce her. Previously, an academic from Cairo University, Dr Nasir Hamid abu-Zeid, who had been equally accused of heresy, was ordered to divorce his spouse and created a worldwide outrage. He exiled himself to the West rather than submit.
79. www.obm.clara.net/shariacourt/fatwas/fs3.html, ibid.
80. Qur'an, 5:33.
81. See n. 79.
82. In AD 629, after the reoccupation of Syria by the Byzantines, the Prophet sent a 3,000-man expedition to Mut'ah in southern Syria, which made a show of force there. For the general context, see Marshall Hodgson, *The Venture of Islam*, Vol. I, Chicago, IL: University of Chicago, 1974, p. 194.
83. Reference is made, obviously, to the Saudi mufti mentioned above, before retracting his fatwa by qualifying it very heavily.
84. *MEMRI*, No. 226, 8 June 2001.
85. See the announcement released by the Hamas, commenting on Arafat's speech of 17 December 2001 which pledged to close the Hamas down and put an end to terrorism.
86. Palestinian Authority television, 12 April 200. *MEMRI*, 17 April 2002.
87. See, for example, R. Israeli, *Poison: Modern Manifestations of the Blood Libel*, US: Rowman and Littlefield, 2002, where a hoax was fabricated against Israel who claimed the 'occupation' forces had 'poisoned' Palestinian teenagers in order to sterilize them. Even after the hoax was discovered, the world media and International organizations, including the UN, remained on record as accusing Israel and never retracting their accusations.
88. *Al-Ahram al-'Arabi*, 28 October 2000. *MEMRI*, cited by David Kupelian, in 2000 WorldNetDaily.com. See also Gerald Steinberg, *Jerusalem Post*, 27 October 2000.
89. *Al-Ayyam* (Palestinian Authority), 3 May 2002, *MEMRI*, No. 376, 6 May 2002.
90. Ibid.
91. *Al-Sharq al-Awsat* (London), 27 October 2000, ibid.
92. Al-Hayat (London), 4 April 2002.
93. BBC News, 18 April 2002.
94. Ibid.
95. The author here has deducted a year from the girl's age in order to emphasize her youth. Exaggeration is a conventional method adopted by Arab writers in order to stress the point they are making.
96. Al-Jazeera, (Saudi Arabia), 1 April 2002. *MEMRI*, No. 367, 12 April 2002.
97. Cited in print by *MEMRI*, No. 74, 30 October 2001, article by Yotam Feldner.
98. Ibid.
99. There are no less than six references to the virgins and the black-eyed in Paradise that are mentioned or hinted at in the Holy Qur'an, and in massive elaborations on those brief references in the vast literature of the Hadith, Palazzi specifies that those women are available not only to martyrs but to any Believer who accedes to Paradise.
100. Surat *Al-Rahman*, verse 58.
101. Surat *Al-Waqi'a*, verse 23.
102. Surat *Al-Safat*, verse 49.
103. Surat *Al-Rahman*, verse 70.
104. Cited in *MEMRI*, see n. 96 above.
105. *Al-Ayyam* (Palestine Authority), 21 July 2001; and *al-Istiqlal* (Palestine Authority), 4

October 2001.

106. *Al-Risala*, 7 July 2001; another case of such a posthumous 'wedding' was publicized by *Al-Hayat al-Jadida*, also within the Palestinian Authority, 4 October 2001.
107. *Al-Risala*, 16 August 2001.
108. *Al-Hayat al-Jadida*, 17 August and 11 September 2001, *MEMRI*, ibid.
109. 'USA Today', 26 June 2001, *MEMRI*, ibid.
110. *Al-Risala*, 11 October 2001.
111. *Al-Hayat al-Jadida*, 17 September 2001; see also Palestinian Authority television, 17 August 2001.
112. *Ha'aretz*, 26 October 2001.
113. *Al-Sharq al-Awsat* (London), 30 September 2001. *MEMRI*, ibid.

7. Identifying the Enemy: Domestic and External

Evidently, Islamikaze do not seek martyrdom as a purpose unto itself, but only as a means of struggle in order to attain what the martyrs consider as lofty goals, though we have seen that in their zeal to promote their goals, some martyrs, and especially their operatives and mentors, have turned the means into a desirable and highly commended goal in its own right. Let there be no mistake, the founders, leaders, trainers, manipulators and financers of Islamikaze fighters have a vision, distorted and perverse as it may be, which they believe is divinely ordained and which they seek to impose on the world, regardless of the price involved. It must be made clear that while, to us, those visions might sound blurred at best, lunatic at worst, there are enough people who believe in them and are prepared to act upon them to cause the rest of us concern. Moreover, while rationalizations of 'despair', 'frustration', 'self-defence' and 'vengeance' are often bandied around to justify acts of mass-murder, aggression, cruelty, bigotry and account-settling, there is also a normative aspect to what seems to us as madness or foolishness, and that is couched in fundamentalist, revolutionary, totalitarian, unforgiving, brutal and uncompromising terms that unremittingly push the would-be martyrs and their operatives to unflinching irrational, and often horrendous, actions.

The Islamikaze doctrine has been formulated in a violent environment of metal and blood as a result of its failure, by and large, to convince its society to convert to its terms and ideals. Therefore, its policy and vision are founded on violence and aimed at sweeping away all those who oppose or hinder it. The world dominion of Islam which it envisages cannot come about unless both domestic and external forces that bar its way are forcibly removed. Hence the profuse usage of terms such as jihad, fighting *Dar al-Harb* and restoring *Dar al-Islam*; treating the West as Crusaders and Israel as its underling; talking about its opponents in terms of aggressors, oppressors, exploiters, arrogant and godless;

labelling Arab and Muslim leaders who toe the Western line, or are allied to it, as eunuchs, servants, slaves, even as *kuffar* (Infidels) or *murtaddun* (heretics), or simply as incompetent, traitors and the like. Some of those fundamentalists, especially their great spiritual mentors and supporters that we have cited above, would begin their jihad domestically in order to revolutionize their societies from within and then prepare them for world dominion, as Iran, the Sudan, and, for a while, Taliban Afghanistan have done. Others, like al-Qa'ida, would start from the world Islamic revolution before they turn to reform their own societies; still others would act on both fronts simultaneously. Characteristic to all of them, however, is their seeking to establish themselves in the heart of their Western enemy, not only in order to learn about it from within and take advantage of its openness, generosity and democratic freedoms so that they may undermine it, but paradoxically because their native countries do not permit them the same leeway and opportunity to collect funds, recruit followers, train their recruits and launch their attacks. Like Archimedes, who needed a base outside the globe to jostle it with his lever, these arch-supporters of Islamikaze would not be able to wipe out their own regimes unless they had a base from which to gather their strength and then from which to depart.

But, first, identifying the enemy is essential. Do the fundamentalists act only against rulers whom they consider illegitimate? Who is legitimate in the variety of autocratic regimes that rule the more than 56 Muslim countries today? Does Muslim rule have to extend only to Muslim-majority countries, or does it have to include also non-Muslim states, as in Europe and the United States? Is it enough to encourage Muslim immigration into those countries and wait patiently for the critical mass of Muslims to develop before they strike, or should they let Islam impact on their host countries in preparation for taking them over in the long run? Should each 'liberated' Muslim country, such as Iran and the Sudan, join hands with the others to restore the world caliphate of Islam, or should it liberate other countries first, by sustaining their Muslim movements, as a preparation for domestic Islamic revolutions that are bound to burst from within and topple the illegitimate autocrats? How pressing is the need to trigger the Islamic Revolution now, as Bin-Laden has attempted to do, underestimating the United States' resolve to fight back while estimating precisely continental European spineless policy of surrender; or would the Islamists rather prepare the ground for the revolution to ripen? Will the stringent measures to rein in the fundamentalists, in the United States and Britain, precipitate their determination to act before the new restrictions take their toll, or should they adopt a low profile and wait for things to improve?

Many of these questions have been tackled by Muslim fundamentalists worldwide, and new modes of warfare have been studied and discussed, as we have seen, to deal with these realities and dilemmas. Without establishing a specific hierarchy of the priorities which preoccupy the Islamists, we can say with assurance that they are all eager to remove most of the existing Muslim regimes, using the present bases of Iran and the Sudan, and until recently Afghanistan, to achieve their goal. To that end, they destabilize the regimes in place, as in Egypt, Saudi Arabia, Algeria, Jordan, Morocco, Pakistan and the like: precisely those rulers who are supported by the United States, something that incidentally adds to their discredit. They use demonstrations, hate literature and violence, and occasionally the Israeli scarecrow, to alienate the masses from the regime. At the same time, they strive to gain legitimacy within their own country by running for election, by ballots where they are allowed, or by bullets where they are not. Externally, they are set to destroy Western culture, which they regard as subversive to Islam and the Muslim world. Far from being willing to measure up to the West by rising to its level, they would rather fight against it and attempt to bring it down, together with the challenge it poses to them, since they remain fundamentally incapable of reaching its much more rapid advance. The very existence of Israel, which signifies the presence within their heartland of the Western challenge at its best, and which is a daily reminder of their incapacity to be like her, further exacerbates their feelings of outrage and frustration, which they discharge in acts of aggression, hatred and calumny against her and against her Jewish constituents.

The multi-front struggle that the fundamentalists have vowed to lead simultaneously against their corrupt and illegitimate regimes – with the United States being the pinnacle of the hated Western culture and the Jews, both as a faith and as embodied in Zionism in the State of Israel – requires an elaborate strategy of delegitimization in order to turn all those into an open target. The Arab regimes are depicted as corrupt, subservient to the West, and enjoying no popular support, hence the reluctance of the rulers to submit their rule to elections. As such, they are certainly subject to toppling through violence. The United States, needless to say, is the model of success, prosperity, technology, progress and innovation, and since the Muslims can neither resemble nor challenge it, they condemn it as corrupt, arrogant, imperialistic and pro-Zionist; hence the need to destroy it and remove it not only as a positive model of imitation, but also as a negative force that obstructs the way before world Islamic revolution. Since the United States and the West are proud of their prosperity, democracy, Christianity, military and technology, it is precisely those things that should be the targets of the Islamikaze attacks, as the 11 September horrors have illustrated. Jews and Israel, together with world Zionism, being at the epicentre of Western culture, are de-legitimized through gross, coarse and brutal anti-Semitism, which not only plays up the world Jewish conspiracy, as it is profusely recounted in the Protocols of the Elders of Zion (in itself a favourite reference of the Islamists) and the Blood Libel, which has been revived throughout the Arab and Islamic worlds, but also harks back to Muslim writings about the Jews as 'monkeys and apes', as the 'enemy of Allah' and humanity and so on, enough mud-slinging to make the Jews, Zionists and Israel a target of their calumniation. As we know, rhetorical poisoning augurs the imminent use of violent force which trails close behind. Therefore, it is important to micro-document these utterings of virulent condemnations which are, in our case, already being accompanied by acts of terror.

THE DOMESTIC JIHAD

Understandably, most critics and calumniators of the domestic scene in Islamic countries act either from the comfort and safety of their Western exile, where they can exploit the openness of their host countries to attack the regimes they have escaped or, more rarely, when circumstances allow, from within. It is worth noting that there are critiques not only from the right, by the fundamentalist Muslims who are in opposition to their regimes which they seek to topple, but also from the left, by courageous and conscientious liberals who want to implement Western-style reforms in order to stop the Islamists and pull their societies out of the obscurantism that has been reigning there. The reformers' comments are usually countered by others, from within and without, mainly by fundamentalists who are outraged by the attempts at, or even the mere talk about, the much-needed reforms. Some of those controversies, which tie in domestic with external issues, will be illustrated in this chapter. Interestingly enough, Christians are often the targets of Muslim fundamentalists, not only as the preponderant culture and religion of the hated West, but also as an internal problem that has to be battled where Christian minorities still exist in the Islamic world. The legitimacy of the internal struggle against them is often rationalized not only in terms of their commonality of faith with the Western enemy, but also due to their perceived proximity to the Jews and Israel.

The most notorious critics and sworn adversaries, indeed enemies, of the existing regimes in Muslim countries are probably al-Qa'ida and its branches, who have sought asylum either in rogue countries such as Iran, Afghanistan and the Sudan, or in the heart of the West itself. From the safety of their exiles, they not only attack those regimes violently, but also mount formidable terrorist networks, often manned by fanatic Islamikaze, to subvert, fight and destroy those regimes to the finish. The rationale was eloquently and horrendously worded not only in Bin-Laden's now famous fatwa's and declarations, but also in the Training Manual of that organization that was seized and published after the 11 September events:

> After the fall of our orthodox caliphate on 3 March 1924,[1] and after expelling the colonialists, our Islamic nation was afflicted with apostate rulers who took over in the Muslim nation. These rulers turned out to be more Infidel and criminal than the colonialists themselves. Muslims have endured all kinds of harm, oppression and torture at their hands.
>
> These apostate rulers threw thousands of the Islamic Movement youth in gloomy jails and detention centres that were equipped with the most modern torture devices and experts in torture and oppression. Those youth have refused to move in the rulers' orbit... but they opposed the idea of rebelling against the rulers. But the rulers did not stop there; they started to fragment the essence of the Islamic nation by trying to eradicate its Muslim identity. Thus, they started to spread godless and atheistic views among the youth. We found some that claimed that socialism was from Islam, democracy was the *Shura* (religious council), and the Prophet, blessed be He, propagandized communism...
>
> These young men realized that an Islamic government

would never be established except by the bomb and rifle. Islam does not coincide or make a truce with unbelief, but rather confronts it...The confrontation that Islam calls for with these godless and apostate regimes, does not know Socratic debates...but it knows the dialogue of bullets, the ideals of assassination, bombing and destruction, and the diplomacy of the cannon and machine-gun.[2]

Together with Bin-Laden and his associates, the radical expatriate Sheikhs Bakri and al-Masri (see Chapter 6), are probably the most outspoken against their former governments in the Islamic world. Abu Hamza al-Masri, for example, admits that his life prior to his re-birth as a devout Islamist was tantamount to *Jahidiyya*,[3] that is, the era of 'ignorance' which had prevailed in pre-Islamic times, before humanity benefited from the Prophet's divine message. The term 'Jahidiyya', borrowed from the pre-Prophetic era, has been prevalent among Muslim fundamentalist leaders, foremost of them Sayyid Qut'b, the spiritual mentor of the Muslim Brothers in Egypt until he was executed by the Nasserite regime in Egypt in 1966. The use of this vocabulary has far-reaching implications for radical Muslims, because it implies a mode of action following the blueprint of the Prophet himself: first, since he could not bear the *Jahili* environment of his native Mecca, he migrated (the famous hijra that took place in AD 622 and signalled the beginning of the Muslim Calendar) to create a new Muslim milieu; that, of course, justifies the 'migration' of today's radicals to the West once their native lands, under their godless rulers, have made Muslim existence untenable. Secondly, exactly as the Prophet used his base in Medina to conquer his native Mecca and then the world, so would they. They conceive of the generosity and leeway they receive in the West as an Allah-ordained opportunity afforded to them to launch their onslaught for the re-conquest of their lands of Islam from the present corrupt and illegitimate governments.

Thus, following the example of Bin-Laden, who has been acting against his Saudi government from the outside, and his Egyptian deputy, al-Zawahiri, who advanced the cause of Islamic revolution, or Sheikh 'Umar abd-al-Rahman, the mastermind of the first attempt against the Twin Towers in 1993 who, until he was convicted, incited his countrymen against Mubarak and his rule, al-Masri, too, has acted likewise. He encountered Arab mujahedin, who had come to London from the fields of Afghanistan, to seek medical treatment and was taken by their never ending enthusiasm to fight for the cause of Islam, and that just jostled him in some fundamental way . He said to his interviewer:

> When you see how happy they are, how anxious to just have a new limb so they can run again and fight again, not thinking of retiring, their main ambition is to get killed in the cause of Allah...you see another dimension of the verses in the Qur'an.[4]

That experience caused him to move to Afghanistan and work there as an engineer (training for which he received in London), and at the same time he fought with the mujahedin against the Soviet Power and began measuring Muslim regimes worldwide against the yardstick of the pure, zealous, enthusiastic, pristine, devout and disinterested Islam of Afghanistan. That was the reason he moved to the Yemen and decided to make it his launching pad for the world Islamic revolution. He recruited volunteers to the 'Aden Abyan Islamic Army',[5] and was involved in an attempt to assassinate the Yemeni President, Ali Abdallah Saleh. In early 1999, President Saleh accused the Supporters of the Shari'a of plotting to finance, sabotage and launch bombings in his country, and specifically mentioned an incident on 13 October 1998 in which a bomb hidden under a donkey's saddle exploded, wounding a soldier and an officer who were escorting the President. The 'Supporters of the Shari'a' boasted on their website of another attack in November 1998, under the headline 'Yemeni Mujahedin Send a Donkey to Kill a Donkey Officer';, they doubted the claim of the government that it had caught one of theirs, rationalizing that the 'Mujahedin donkey was far too clever for them'.[6] The Yemeni authorities also accused Abu Hamza of involvement in the kidnapping of 16 foreign tourists by the Aden Abyan Islamic Army on 21 December 1998, which was related to the arrest of five Britons and a French Algerian whom Abu Hamza had sent to train in Yemen. Among the arrested was Abu Hamza's son, Muhammed Mustafa Kamel, and his stepson, Muhsin Ghalin. One hour after the kidnapping, Abu Hamza's accomplice in the Yemen, Al-Mihdar, called him in London and informed him that he had kidnapped 'several Infidels'. Three Britons and one Australian were killed in the operation to free the hostages, and al-Mihdar, who was arrested, was later executed.

This *modus operandi* of the Islamists against the authorities that they consider illegitimate has been geared to prove to the world both the incapacity of the governments in place to assert their authority, hence the need for them to be replaced, and to frighten off foreign tourists in order to hurt their government where it hurts most, namely the pocketbook and the reputation of the rulers. That very same stratagem was successfully pursued by the Egyptian Gama'at, who shot tourists by the dozen during the 1990s, until Mubarak ordered their elimination, and by the Islamists in Algeria, who literally cleansed their country of foreign presence. In fact, after his friend, al-Mihdar, was killed, Abu Hamza called a press conference in London in January 2000, and called upon all foreign citizens to leave the Yemen. He also appealed for the toppling of the Yemeni government and signed a document to that effect on behalf of the Supporters of the Shari'a.[7] Two months later, he sent a letter to the London-based *Al-Hayat*, on behalf of the new commander of the Aden Abyan Islamic Army, warning the British and American Ambassadors to leave the Yemen, and threatened that if they stayed, 'the strike against the enemies of Islam would be painful'.[8] Though Abu Hamza has been focusing in Yemen, which he regards as the launching-pad of Islamic revolution, his message is directed to all Islamic countries. When King Hussein of Jordan died, Abu Hamza placed a picture of the deceased on his website under the heading: 'Another One Bites the Dust', and depicted the King with horns on his head and surrounded by animated flames, implying that he was roasting in hell.[9]

As we have already seen, Abu Hamza saw the Yemen as a new cradle of Islam, similar to that of the Prophet in Arabia, where the new Islamic Revolution would be announced and whence it would spread to the entire universe. The choice was made not only because isolated, primitive and mountainous Yemen, just like Afghanistan, was suitable to train Islamikaze, but also because it was the 'only country in the Arabian Peninsula that had not surrendered yet to the United Snakes [*sic*] of America'. The preventive remedy, before Yemen also succumbed, was to 'explode in the face of the snakes', which would create a domino effect in the entire Peninsula.[10] Abu Hamza explained that his fatwa calling for a revolution in Yemen was of general import, because before he became active there he had been involved with the same ideas in Egypt and Algeria. But he had found it difficult to operate within those societies which needed an 'invasion' from the outside, because they did not contain the requisite built-in elements of reform due to their corrupt anti-Islamic policies. Therefore, he declared that the war of invasion, which would start off from the Yemen, would move outwards and all Muslims everywhere were bound to join it. He warned that if the Yemen continued in its secular path, it 'would suffer disintegration, corrosion, destruction and inner strife, with no winner'. However, if matters were restored to 'Allah and the Prophet's hands, and even if some were killed along the way, it would be forgiven, all tongues would be stilled, because when Allah and his Prophet speak, all tongues should be stilled'. He disclaimed any ambition to rule, because what is needed is not the change of a President, but that 'the regime should be changed and Yemen should become Islamic'.[11]

He said that since the existing regimes in Muslim countries monopolized terrorism against their nationals, the term 'violence' cannot be correctly applied to the Islamists who wish to promote the tenet of 'doing good and prohibiting evil'. He insisted that Islam was tolerant towards dissident views, provided they 'listen and comply, and the tolerant efforts do not lead to a blurring of rights and wrongs'. He explained that treating gently those in the Islamic world who 'block their ears and force perversion, heresy, abomination and humiliation of the Muslims in their own countries by armed forces' is an 'act of idiocy' and a loss of religious precepts. Therefore, the Arab regimes who 'enacted abominable laws, give license to carry them out, and use taxes to appoint military personnel to protect the abomination instead of protecting Jerusalem and its people, carry the mark of Cain in Egyptian history'. Hence Abu Hamza's rejection of the accusation that he and his like use violence to alter the domestic scene in the Islamic world, and he stuck to his vow of jihad rather than sign 'a truce with the regimes of the tyrants'. He cited Allah's injunction to 'fight them so that *fitna* (internal strife) is avoided, and so that they might return to Allah's religion', explaining that the Muslim nation 'cannot come to terms with anyone who does not come to terms with Allah and does not have mercy or respect for the people'. He asserted that exile from his native Egypt was much easier to bear than the 'exile of his soul, the slaughter of his faith and values or the amputation of his tongue' as the price of being permitted to return to his homeland.[12]

Sheikh Bakri, also an exile, is not merely an armchair revolutionary. He had experienced violence himself when, in 1982,

Syria's President Assad massacred Muslim Brothers in Hamah who challenged his rule, forcing Bakri to escape. He then tried his hand in Lebanon and Saudi Arabia and Western Europe,[13] where he committed himself to the re-establishment of the caliphate, that is, to the toppling of existing regimes in the Muslim world. He accused his country of asylum, Britain, of 'barbaric acts against innocent Muslims' and of adopting a harsh policy against the 'peaceful Muslim community' using 'force, fear, and the methods of tyrannical regimes such as Saudi Arabia, Egypt, Iraq, Algeria, Syria, Iran and other Middle Eastern governments', leaving no doubts as to his views on those governments. He trained mujahedin to fight in Kashmir, Afghanistan and Chechniya,[14] and in one instance he admitted to having recruited 160 volunteers in Britain and sent them to Jordan, where they awaited opportunities to infiltrate the West Bank and join the uprising against Israel, to having enlisted Palestinians in the refugee camps of Lebanon for the same purpose, and signed up thousands of young Britons, presumably Muslims, to fight against India in Kashmir. Similarly, Bakri supported the Muslim rebels on the Thai–Malay border.[15] Unlike al-Masri, however, who wanted the caliphate to spread out from the Yemen, Bakri maintained the fantasy that it would all start from London and take over the Champs Elysées after taking hold in No. 10 Downing Street.[16]

Apart from the dreams of world dominion that are blatantly declared by Islamists, and the plans they weave to make them happen through the use of violence, either beginning in Muslim countries or outside them, many domestic debates between the fundamentalists and their opponents reveal the deepest concerns of those societies about the ramifications that grow out of the bellicose mood of the Islamikaze and their champions. In these debates, attempts are made to convert jihad, the flagship of the militants, into something more constructive and peaceful, or demands are raised to lend top priority to internal strife, inequities, the status of women and children, education and development, rather than inflame the fire of violence, warfare, killing and destruction. These voices of reason are, for the most part, silenced and not allowed to predominate, but we learn from them, by default, about the ambitions of the Islamists and some of their methods of struggle. Sometimes, the writers of reason feel so intimidated that they write anonymously, for fear of being identified and asked to conform. Such a voice, an 'Arab diplomat', wrote an article in the Saudi-owned and London-based *Al-Sharq al-Awsat*, where he audaciously suggested 'replacing jihad by development': a temerity that could have cost him his life had it been published in a traditional, or even not-so-traditional, Muslim country. He wrote, *inter alia*:

> Now that the second Intifadah has ended, at such a terrible price, the Arabs must try, at least once, to grasp the lesson that they have been taught yet again...And first, we must admit that the ones who pushed the children into the second Intifadah...wanted to thwart any initiative that President Arafat sought to promote...and to make him their and Israel's prisoner...Demonstrations filled the streets of Arab capitals [in support of the Intifadah], reminiscent of the giant demonstrations to defend the honour of Comrade Saddam...Why don't they demonstrate to protest against the deficient or non-existent basic services in their countries? These countries have no health, education or services, and buckle under the poverty line...but they are all preoccupied with the Palestinian issue, and no voice rises above the voice of battle there...
>
> What would happen if every Arab country had, since 1948, turned its attention to building itself from within, without making Palestine its main issue?...What would happen if every country focused on educating its citizens and on improving their physical and emotional health and cultural level? Wouldn't this have made the battle with Israel a cultural one instead of us sinking into religious and military battles?...Moreover, I am amazed at the clerics who raise a hue and cry about jihad against Israel...and compete with each other issuing religious fatwa's on martyrdom attacks, but do not encourage the citizens to wage spiritual jihad. Wouldn't this be more useful to the Nation, which since the turn of the century has been subject to *Nakba*[17] by its own military, and now marches toward a second *Nakba* by its scientists – I refer, of course, to the scientists of religion, and not the scientists of physics, natural science, health or engineering.[18]

Or take, for example, the debates within the Muslim world regarding the very desirability of the Islamikaze phenomenon, which the conventional wisdom among them calls *istishhad*, the respectable and much adulated way to die as a martyr, while all those who dare, as in the West, to dub it 'suicide bombing', or plain 'terrorism' or 'murder' are castigated and humiliated into submission to the accepted norms in their society. The Syrian Minister of Information, a euphemism for the supreme commissar for propaganda or 'national guidance' in those regimes, when interrogated during an inter-Arab symposium on the terminology of martyrdom, retorted:

> Verily, too many Western terms have been invading our media...but more dangerous than them is the infiltration of ideas. A few days ago we heard one of them say that acts of martyrdom against the Zionist enemy are acts of violence and terror. Even if the life of the person who said that is dearer to him than his honour and his country...he must let the *shahid* (martyr) choose to sacrifice his life for the sake of his country; he must let the martyr fulfil his duty...
>
> This is a mistake originating from the West, since Washington has demanded from all Arab countries that they condemn martyrdom. They themselves thereby deny their own history, as we have seen their Hollywood film industry boast about their own suicide missions across enemy lines...Like the Japanese kamikaze in World War II, who blew up American warships in order to gain independence and obtain their legitimate rights, so are the *fida'i*[19] acts of heroism that hurt the Zionist occupier, but for them [the Americans] that is considered a heinous crime...Therefore what we see here is not only contempt for the honour of our nation, but also a devaluation of the values of Western societies themselves.[20]

Predictably, Iran, who opened the way to the Islamikaze phenomenon, has also been its most virulent advocate, though there, too, a few defiant dissidents have dared to disagree and were dealt with accordingly. Ayatollah Muntazari, for example, who has been under house arrest since 1996, is on record as calling upon the Palestinians to desist from acts of martyrdom, in spite of the Supreme Spiritual Leader 'Ali Khamene'i's assertion that those acts were the 'pinnacle of Palestinian Resistance, and of audacity, honour and glory to the *umma*'.[21] He was endorsed by other prominent clerics in Iran, like Ayatollah Nuri Hamadani, Ayatollah

Yazdi and Hujat al-Islam Khurasani,²² who would naturally consider the dissident voices in this regard as inimical to Islam. Others, like Subhi Fuad, the editor of *Al-Masri*, an Arabic journal appearing in Australia, blamed the Egyptian leaders – first Nasser, with his pan-Arab dreams and then Sadat, who introduced Islam into politics – for Egypt's backwardness, and suggested that had a separate Egyptian identity been cultivated, his country would today be developed and advanced.²³ A Sudanese author, writing, like his peers, from the safety of a London-based Arabic paper, said that the enemy lay within the Arab world itself, in the form of 'the mental illness that has affected us since we were defeated by Israel in 1948', and is manifested in the Arab propensity to blame others, not themselves, for their setbacks, and he declared that 'we, the Arabs, are the lawful parents of Bin-Laden, not America'.²⁴ Another Arab columnist accused the Arab corrupt regimes of their internal repression of any signs of protest, hence their proven capacity to silence the Arab masses who would demonstrate against US and Israeli wars in Afghanistan and Palestine. He claimed that 'public opinion', which Arab rulers invoked as threatening their regime, was simply a myth.²⁵

In the context of the events of 11 September and their aftermath, and the internal debates and soul-searching they provoked throughout the Arab and Islamic world, the prevalent mood remained of blaming the United States, the West and Israel for all the malaise that first created and then sprang from the New York disaster, but that was also an opportunity for all sorts of oppressed, dissident, liberal, silenced opposition, exile, minorities or fundamentalists to take a free ride on the general ambiance of criticism and self-criticism to air their concerns. For example, an unnamed Egyptian woman (and that is significant in itself) wrote a lengthy dissertation about the position of women in her country, asserting that her female compatriots were living 'exactly as Afghan women'. She accused the Egyptian press of lauding the liberation of women in Afghanistan after the US attacks there, and of vowing to fight terrorism, while at the same time they disregarded the terror against women in their own country. She was particularly shocked when her son, who grew fanatical under his father's education, was jubilant, as were many Egyptians against their government's best advice, when the destruction of the Twin Towers became known, and at some point she even attempted to commit suicide.²⁶ This point was also addressed by the Dean of the Faculty of Law at Qatar

University, who wrote about his opposition to the kind of Islam that bred terrorists, his commitment to curricular reform in the Arab world, his criticism towards those who called the US counter-attack 'terrorism', and about his plea to eradicate 'all seeds of hatred, repulsion and fanaticism toward the other, towards women, towards those whose religion is different from ours.'[27]

Similarly, a Tunisian columnist, al-'Afif al-Akhdar, took to task those clerics who issued fatwas to incite to violence and to legitimize murder. He cited the instance when Tunisian military personnel had refused to participate in a coup against President Bourguiba before obtaining a fatwa permitting them to kill their fellow soldiers, and even the President if necessary, and Gannouchi's Deputy himself issued that ruling from his prison cell. The author determines that the connection between the fatwa and terrorism lies in the fact that the religious ruling 'unleashes the terrorist's sadism and instinct for murder. It frees him from all moral restraints and shrivels what remains of his conscience. It also releases him from any sense of guilt.' He says that while the fatwas of the previous decades were secret, like the organizations who issued them, it has now become fashionable for famous sheikhs to make them public and boast about them, and various religious authorities use the media to publicize their competition amongst themselves permitting the killing of individuals, groups, or even nations. Worse, there were fatwas that were announced after the murder was committed. For example, Gannouchi himself legiti-mized the murder of President Sadat 12 years after the deed, thus leaving open the possibility of permitting the murder of other political leaders. In another example, Saudi Sheikh al-Hawali issued a fatwa that the rulers of the Northern Alliance in Afghanistan were Unbelievers because they supported the United States against the Taliban government, for any support for Unbelievers against Muslims, even if only verbal, constitutes blatant heresy and hypocrisy. The fatwa said that the 11 September disaster was strictly a justified response to the Clinton Administration's missile attack on al-Qa'ida bases in Afghanistan following the bombing of the US Embassies in East Africa in 1998.[28]

This rather strange ruling means, as has been corroborated by Hamas attacks against Israel, that only Muslims can target what they regard as legitimate goals, but when the victims retaliate against them, that constitutes a trigger for further Muslim retributions. In other words, the non-Muslim must submit to

Muslim attacks; simply absorb and duck until he has got what he deserved at the hands of Islamic justice, while any reprisal on his part would be considered a new 'provocation' or 'aggression' deserving of Muslim violent response. That is the reason why the Saudi sheikh justified the attack on the Twin Towers, due to their corrupt role as the world 'centre of money laundering', and on the Pentagon, which 'Gore Vidal had himself called "Hell and a nest of Satans"'. Attacks on those targets was thus legitimate in Muslim terms, and even more so as a retaliation for the US missile attack. He also condemned those in the Islamic world 'weeping and expressing sorrow and pain over the American victims', arguing that they were all combatants, because they supported their regime ('may Allah not multiply such regimes!!!' said he, the champion of Saudi democracy), and in their case, he ruled that it was even permissible to kill the non-combatants among them, such as the aged, the blind and the *dhimmis*: all Americans without exception. The author remarks that it was such rulings, which were endorsed by other Muslim clerics, such as the eminent Sheikh Qardawi, which gave license to the Hamas to eliminate Israeli civilians indiscriminately under the pretext that they were 'combatants'. He wrote that 'fanaticism and hatred for anyone who is different, removes the lobe of logic from the brain of the fanatic'.[29]

Nor does the 'lobe of logic' function when it comes to discussing ways to eradicate hatred from Muslim writings that generations of Muslims are raised upon. *Al-Jazeera* television convened a panel of Muslim educators and writers to discuss reform in religious education in the Muslim world. All but one participant, who significantly lives in Washington, denied that there was any need for reform and turned the tables on the Americans by accusing them of all the ills of the Muslim world. The panel began with a survey of the situation which posited that, in view of the US struggle against 'what she calls terrorism', she has undertaken to 'engineer societies in order to dry up the sources of opposition to Western hegemony'. The author of the survey, *Al-Jazeera* reporter Hassan Ibrahim, remarked that the 'black scenario feared by the Islamists of the 1970s that the West might try to tamper with the Qur'an, has now become an open Western policy'. The input of the participants reflects both the adamance of the Muslims to reform what they hold as truth, and their innate propensity to accuse others of their ills. Some admitted that though they accepted the need to amend technicalities, such as giving precedence to comprehension of texts over repetition and memorizing, they totally refuted the selective approach of the West to texts they considered as arousing hatred and bigotry. They claimed that if the United States wished to dry up the sources of terrorism, it ought to begin at home and tackle first the Arab–Israeli conflict, the Third World debt, and the gaping cultural and economic gulf between the North and the South. On the other hand, they maintained that any attempt to 'wipe out Islamic identity, upon which one billion Muslims worldwide consent, can only trigger a new confrontation between the arrogant West and an East that is still stuck in the lowest reaches of development'.[30]

Other participants in the panel accused the West of seeking to penetrate the 'depth of our conscience, into the way we teach...That is done not in order to fight terrorism, but to brainwash us and to control us spiritually, culturally and economically.' They claimed that Western interest in population growth in the Third World was geared to neutralize the only edge it has over the West, and that is demography. They made the case that the phenomenon of violence and terror is a product of the West, as reflected in their colonial conquests, in their world wars, in their use of weapons of mass destruction, and their refusal to conform to limitations for the protection of the environment. They contended that there was no call for violence in Islam, and that US deeds in Vietnam, like the deeds of other Western and Zionist governments, evinced more violence than had ever been known in Islam. The upturn in the debate occurred when Majdi Khalil, a former Egyptian now residing in the United States, took the floor. He lashed out at the takeover by political Islam of the educational systems of the Islamic world, comparing the 3,000 madrasas in Pakistan in 1978 with the 39,000 today. He said that although Israel pursued political violence today, there was not a single case where a Jew blew himself up in New York or London...and at any rate, there were fewer Jews altogether in the world today (some 17 million) than there were terrorists among the one billion-strong Muslim population. He asserted that a wall of concrete surrounded the Islamic world which prevented democracy, globalization, development and modernity from getting in, and emphasized that the pretexts advanced by the Muslims for this state of affairs were so scanty and shallow that no serious forum could accept them. He said that all those who pretend to speak in terms of science or medicine, that is, medicine according to the

Prophet of Islam, cannot seriously expect to be heard at any gathering in London or New York.[31] He said:

> The Muslim Brothers are the source of all trouble in Egypt and the world, in combination with Saudi Arabia and Pakistani Islam of the Mawdudi brand. That trio – the Muslim Brothers, the Wahhabis and Mawdudi – are the source of all disasters that have befallen the Muslim world. In Egypt, since the times of the King and then Sadat, a great deal was invested in Muslim education. Faculties of education were erected and deans were appointed, all among the Brothers' membership. Two million graduates are churned out every year from religious schools, who studied religion for 20 years…What can they do for society? Do we need two million sheikhs a year? They teach topics that belong to the seventh century. Pakistan churns out four million of them annually, and in Saudi Arabia 70 per cent of the graduates of higher education are likewise. We do not need all these quantities, and I am opposed to the contents of their schooling too, which talk against the homeland[32] and accuse people of heresy…
>
> It is true that the West acted violently during the Crusades, but now it no longer practices religious violence…Religious violence today is only practiced by Islam. Political Islam advocates holding texts in one hand and a gun in the other. The education they talk about is no education at all; it is a hate-club…It is education against everything, against modernity, against science. When modernity was Islamized, a distorted system was created, like a Mongoloid child suffering with Downs Syndrome. We do not oppose religious education per se, but the religious education that breeds hatred, encourages fighting others and their thoughts, advocates fanaticism, racism and isolationism and borders on metaphysics, accuses intelligent people of heresy, and opposed modern science…
>
> The basic textbook in our faculties of education, 'The Fundaments of Education', says, for example, that Christianity emanates from Judaism, but that Judaism is not a faith…On page 15 of that book, they say that Jesus never existed, and that Christianity was full of pagan ideas that were drawn from the trinity of gods in ancient Egypt. Not only are others accused of heresy, but these books are full of repulsion from nationalism…and they contain nothing but Islam at the

expense of Egyptian, Arab and human identity... If this is the system of education, which calls upon its followers to kill others, and is not much different from the Terrorism Manuals that were found in the Afghani caves, do the others not have the right to interfere and clamour for its reform? And I am not talking only about education, but also about free communication and democracy. It is the absence of this trinity which created the atmosphere of terrorism, therefore if there are reforms, they must apply to all three.[33]

Nothing exemplifies the internal intellectual strife that tore the Muslim world apart in the aftermath of 11 September better than the conspiracy theories that were rife at the time and thereafter. Indeed, in addition to the usual fabricated stories about the use of depleted uranium by the Americans against the Kosovars, or the 'massacres' that are, or were, allegedly committed against Muslims, or the accusations of poisoning wells, lands and innocent people that are hurled regularly against Israel, the Twin Towers disaster afforded novel opportunities for imaginations to work overtime and make up all manner of unfounded stories. The comments of two Saudi columnists on the fantasy-ridden stories of an Islamist Egyptian journalist, Fahmi Huweidi, go a long way in opening a window on the conspiracy theories which haunt much of the Muslim world. While Huweidi presented his stories in Saudi papers, notably in *al-Watan* daily,[34] the Saudi columnists responded in Egyptian papers. To Huweidi's allegation that it was 'probable' that extremist US militias carried out that horrendous attack, Hamad al-'Isa retorted that it was unthinkable that the Egyptian writer did not as much as mention that the fatwa calling for the murder of US civilians had been issued in 1996 by an 'Afghani' Arab, presumably Bin-Laden himself. To Huweidi's claim that the Arabs could not have concocted that attack due to its complex and sophisticated planning and execution, al-'Isa answered that it was Arabs who had tried to blow the Towers up in 1993, that Arabs knew how to fly aeroplanes and how to mount Islamikaze operations in Southern Lebanon and in Palestine. He also insisted that it was the Arabs who invented hijacking and the blowing up of civilian aeroplanes in the 1970s: a method they only abandoned when they realized that it had failed dismally.[35]

Countering Huweidi's exultation over that barbaric attack, al-'Isa said that the terrorists' success was due to the good and peaceful

American people's civilized treatment of anyone who went to the United States legally, and was allowed to tour freely everywhere, including the White House and the FBI Buildings, even if he wore a Muslim fundamentalist attire. He drew attention to the fact that Arab and Muslim preachers were free to curse the United States on its own home soil without being harmed. He also denounced Huweidi's call for an international investigative committee to find out what happened on 11 September on the grounds that, due to the United States' superb judicial system, it was well able to investigate itself and to protect the rights of the accused. He also ridiculed Hizbullah television, which had claimed that the '4,000 Israelis who worked at the World Trade Center and were absent on the day of the attack' had 'demonstrated that it was the Mossad who carried out that crime'.[36] Another Saudi columnist, al-Nkidan, also published a scathing critique of Sheikh Huweidi, whom he otherwise venerated as an 'enlightened' cleric, and other Muslim conspiracy theorists, accusing them of marketing absurdities and nonsense that were no better than those of the 'Qandahar cave-dwellers'. He also lambasted 'modern Arab thought which was collapsing under the weight of delusions, since it lacked the rationality or critical spirit required for Arab and Islamic societies today and in the future'.[37] He thoughtfully concludes:

> Most of the Arab and Muslim commentators have not eliminated the possibility of conspiracy in one way or another. Naturally, the conspirator is always Israel; alternatively the finger is pointed at the Jews. If it seems inconceivable logically and in the light of events that this catastrophe was perpetrated by the Zionist movement or that Jewry had a hand in it, we tend to stress the Jewish influence on decision-making and public opinion, or even their control over the American business and financial community. These claims appear somewhat convincing, but there remains an important point to notice, and that is that American society is democratic and open and there is no way of hiding the truth from it to please anyone, even if it concerns Israel itself…
>
> Throughout history, there has not been one single case of proof of the veracity of the assumptions underpinning this conspiracy theory. But Arab thought has remained enamoured of it…The truth is that we are not capable of formulating and interpreting of events, and therefore we recycle this idiotic

culture, the same improbable and stupid theory...Despite the changes in the Arab world, and in the world around us, the Arab citizen still does not have a complete character that could enable him to independently impose on the Arab rhetoric his own position regarding events...In conclusion, do any of us remember the Protocols of the Elders of Zion? They too spoke of a Jewish conspiracy against the world, even though no one in his right mind in the world today can view them as the truth.[38]

To complete this part about internal strife and targeting the enemies from within, one has to mention the Christian minorities within the Islamic world, which, when they exist, are dwindling in numbers in the face of the rising numbers of Muslim fundamentalists who make their lives untenable and oblige them to emigrate to the West; and until they do that they are universally suspected of collaborating with their co-religionists in the outside world. Already, in the early 1980s, Jean-Pierre Peroncel-Hugoz, the *Le Monde* correspondent in Cairo, raised the issue in his reports about the terror and pogroms that the Muslim fundamentalists of Egypt were sowing among the Christian Copts, which caused him to be expelled from the country by the Sadat regime.[39] This has not since let up: quite the contrary. With the rise of Muslim fundamentalism, the attitude to the Christians is no longer a matter of communal bigotry or inter-faith rifts, but has grown into an ideological and doctrinal affair where dialogues have become virtually impossible. A young fundamentalist sheikh in Kafr Kanna, near Nazareth, did not mince his words:

> My words may sound harsh to proponents of Arab nationalism who regard the solution of the problem in national terms, while I regard it in Islamic terms...Jerusalem and Palestine, which had warmly embraced 'Umar [the caliph], Khalid [the Arab General] and Saladin, cannot embrace Archbishop Capucci or George [Habash], because she was a loyal spouse...The absence of her true spouse does not mean that he died...He will return with passion and longing.[40]

In other articles of the Muslim Movement in Israel, Hanna Siniora, one of the spokesmen of Palestinian nationalism in the West

Bank, and a Christian, was charged with having 'warned America against the rise of Islamic fundamentalism', and for 'having maintained contacts with Jewish personalities in the Jewish entity'. It was also claimed that the 'New Crusade' in Palestine had been fostered by people like Butrus Ghali, a Copt and, for a time, the Minister of State for Foreign Affairs in Egypt, and later the Secretary General of the United Nations, and Clovis Maqsud, a Christian and delegate of the Arab League in the United Nations, who 'pretended to speak in the name of the Muslims'.[41] Attacks against, and condemnation of, Christians are also often heard in mosques, in sermons, and in publications of the Muslim Movement. On the eve of the Al-Ad'ha Festival of 1996, a leaflet was distributed in the Muslim community of Umm al-Fahm which accused local youth of improper behaviour 'mimicking that of Jewish and Christian Unbelievers'.[42] In an interestingly lopsided way, it was a commentator for the Hamas who demanded, in response to the BBC 'Panorama' programme aired in June 2001, in which Prime Minister Ariel Sharon of Israel was, once again, falsely accused of the Sabra and Shatila massacres, that the Christian forces in Lebanon who had committed the massacres with their own hands be tried.[43] It is not the case that Hamas was suddenly overcome by a bout of remorse and an urge to redress justice, but it was an occasion to settle accounts with the Lebanese Christians once Sharon had been indicted anyway in the eyes of the world, even if falsely.

The Christian holy cities of Bethlehem and Nazareth slipped under Muslim dominion, not only by the relentless power of demography, which turned the millennial Christian majority into a minority, but also by the systematic terrorizing of the Christians. In Bethlehem, where the Muslim population grew by 80 per cent under the Palestinian Authority, which purports to defend the Christians and protect their Holy Places, the tragedy of the Muslim takeover became evident when, in April 2002, 200 Palestinian gunmen burst into the Church of the Nativity and fortified themselves within its walls as the Israeli army entered the city in search of terror activists who had wrought Islamikaze havoc on the civilian population of Israel during the preceding month. The stand-off ended when the leaders of the gunmen were deported to Europe and Israeli troops withdrew as a result, but it is feared that both this precedent of taking Christian Holy Places hostage and then releasing them at a price, and the fact that the Church is built as a fortress, which may always attract people who seek asylum, or simply flee from justice, will lend further impetus to the Islamization of the city and the rapid evacuation of its remaining Christians, except for the monks and clerics of various denominations who assure the upkeep of the holy places. Consequently, Christian pilgrims will depend even more than before on the goodwill of Palestinian gunmen who are neither willing to, nor capable of, safeguarding free access there. The Churches, and especially the Vatican, fearing that any protest or firm stand might endanger what little Christianity remains, and boosted by their representatives who are Arab for the most part, will tend to appease the violators of their sanctuaries rather than oppose them, something that, in the long run, will by necessity contribute to their own demise.

In Nazareth, which has been under Israeli rule since 1948, the demographic balance was already shifting towards the Muslims during the 1948–49 war, as thousands of Muslim refugees flocked from adjoining Arab villages to the safety of the town. Over the years, it was the hub of Arab nationalism in Israel, the centre of Arab politics and intellectual life, and the hotbed of all major parties and trends among Israeli Arabs. For most of those years, the city was run by the Communist Party in its various guises, until the local elections of 1998 from which, for the first time, the Islamists emerged victorious and won the majority of seats in the local municipal council, though the Mayor remained a former Communist Christian (probably the last). Then things began to go awry. The new majority of the City Council announced its support for the construction of a mosque on the plaza of the Basilica of the Annunciation, on a patch of land which was not theirs. The Christians were infuriated, but due to considerations of domestic Israeli politics, successive Israeli governments yielded in part to the Muslim demands, thereby causing a wave of protest, including from the Pope himself. Only then did the Sharon government decide to backtrack, to halt the actual laying of the foundations of the mosque, and to oppose in court the Muslims' plea to proceed with their gigantic construction plan. While the end of the affair is not yet in sight, it is evident that the Muslim insistence on building their mosque at that particular place is more of a political and religious statement than anything else. On the walls of the temporary mosque that the Muslims have established in the open air, pending the permanent construction, a huge sign is posted, advertising Sura CXII of the Holy Qur'an: 'Say, He is God, One ... who has not begotten, and has not been begotten, and equal to him is not anyone', a denial and rejection of the Father–Son relationship in the Trinity, right there where it had all begun.

THE UNITED STATES: THE ULTIMATE REPRESENTATIVE OF WESTERN EVIL

Targeting the United States as the ultimate, the most potent symbol of power and the cultural and technological hub of the West, is one of the driving and mobilizing forces of the Islamikaze doctrine and praxis. For not only have the Islamikaze spotted the United States' weak points, emanating from her democracy, freedom and openness, and learned how to hit at them, taking advantage of her generosity, naivety, hospitality and concern for others, but they have also developed the harrowing means and Satanic thinking required to lead their struggle in a ruthless, cruel and totalitarian way, in a war to the finish. The United States is not only perceived as a counter-example that challenges Islamic civilization, but as a military, economic and political power that bars the way before the universal takeover by Islam, which is proclaimed as the shining future of all humanity. Christianity, which is perceived as the culture of the great rival, is often derided and reviled to make it a legitimate prey of Islamikaze attacks. And, once again, the harshest criticism of the United States and the West (and Israel for that matter) emanates from their two supposedly closest allies: Egypt and Saudi Arabia; as if the surest recipe for the United States to be attacked were to offer protection and military hardware to its 'friends' or to shower them with aid to prop up their economic prosperity. The explanation for this, of course, is that the closer the United States gets to a Muslim ally, the more 'dangerous' and 'threatening' it is perceived as by its detractors, namely the fundamentalists who wish to uproot its cultural challenge. Arab attacks on the United States and the West are not always factual and positional, and often sink to the personal vilification of leaders, to lies and delusions and to blasphemy and verbal cruelty that say more about the speaker than his intended target.

Dr 'Adel Sadeq, Chair of the Arab Psychiatrists Association and himself the Head of Psychiatry at the Ein Shams University in Cairo, wrote an open letter to President Bush entitled 'Class is Not Over Yet, Stupid!' It is important to begin our anti-American journey with him, not only because he is known as a wholehearted supporter of Islamikaze attacks, but also due to the recognition he has enjoyed throughout the Arab world and by Egypt, which awarded him its State Prize in 1990, but would certainly jail him if he dared to direct even a fraction of his libelous insults against his own President. Excerpts from that open letter serve to illustrate the state of mind of this psychiatrist, highly respected in the Arab world:

> Though you invest a lot in improving yourself, you are not successful in doing so because you are stupid and understand nothing of what is happening in the world. Stupidity and idiocy are synonyms, and if you do not like the word 'stupid', you are an evil person with an ugly soul...I equate your stupidity with mercilessness and inhumanity, and swear that I knew you were stupid long before it became known to the entire world, and long before your cronies admitted it...Your face reminds me of the face of those who frequent a clinic of the mentally retarded. Your gaze is mindless and unfocused... Your facial expressions are out of sync with the matter being discussed and your tone of voice is completely divorced from the content of your words, a salient characteristic of the mentally retarded...The IQ of stupid people ranges from 90 to 110, and according to my personal judgment, based on 35 years of psychiatrist experience, your IQ is 110, and I challenge anyone who thinks otherwise...
>
> Don't you understand, stupid, that Israel does not want peace and that Sharon is a criminal?...Don't you understand, stupid, that the interests of your country are in great jeopardy because of your complete bias towards Israel?...Don't you understand, stupid, that anyone who dies for the liberation of his homeland is a martyr?...Don't you understand, stupid, that when an 18-year-old girl blows herself up, this means that her cause is right, and that her people will be victorious sooner or later? I do not imagine, stupid, that you will understand anything from this article, as advisors hide thoughts of this kind from you, and you will go on thinking you are smart. This means that class is not over yet, you stupid idiot, you basest man in the world.[44]

Insults apart, this expert psychiatrist also found an explanation for the Islamikaze, and reviled President Bush and the Western state of mind, 'which is incapable of understanding the soul of the youth who sacrifice themselves [contrary to conventional wisdom] because they love life'. He said that people who do not have the concepts of honour and self-sacrifice offer 'stupid explanations to them which emanate from sheer ignorance'. However, he insists, since Arab and Muslim culture is one of sacrifice, loyalty and honour, it was Bush who was mistaken when he said that the Palestinian girl who blew herself up was in fact 'killing the future', while in fact 'she died so that others would live'. He, the enlightened psychiatrist and the student of Western learning, matching and even surpassing the most obscene of the obscurantist clerics in cruelty and denial of the right of children to pursue their lives and future away from the threat of death, wrote:

> When the martyr dies a martyr's death, he attains the height of bliss... As a professional psychiatrist, I say that the height of bliss comes with the end of the countdown: ten, nine, eight, seven, six, five, four, three, two, one. And then you press the button to blow yourself up. When the martyr reaches 'one' and then 'boom', he explodes and then senses himself flying, because he knows for certain that he is not dead... It is a transition to another, more beautiful world, because he knows very well that within seconds he will see the light of the Creator. He will be at the closest possible point to Allah... None in the West sacrifices himself for his homeland. If his homeland is drowning, he is the first to jump ship. In our culture it is different...
>
> In the West they have lost the ability to understand the situation... According to my professional assessment, they have lost their faculties. They do not understand what is happening. They see the Islamikaze as a strange breed of people... As far as they are concerned, life is sex, love and money. So they tell you 'It is someone committing suicide, a drug addict, someone in despair.' That is a mistake!!! Someone committing suicide hates life and considers it a burden. They want to impose the term 'suicide' on them, but they are not suicidal, rather people who sacrifice their souls.[45]

The Egyptian government weekly, *al-Ahram*, turned on its head President Bush's dubbing of Iran, Iraq and North Korea as the 'Axis of Evil', and termed the trio of the United States, Israel and

Turkey as the 'True Axis of Evil'. It declared that for the Arabs and Middle Easterners in general, the emerging security pact between these three countries held woeful consequences. It also added that while Ankara and Washington were finalizing their joint plot against Iraq, they were also co-ordinating a joint strategic military, economic and political blockade on Teheran, and castigated Turkey for 'relinquishing its traditional loyalties and historic commitments' to the Arab and Islamic worlds to promote its national interests. According to the author of this article, the co-ordination of these efforts brought about the encirclement of the Arabs from the north by Turkey, and Israel from the south via Eritrea and Ethiopia, and therefore the bolstering of Arab links with Iran was called for. He revealed that while Egypt, Saudi Arabia and Syria were inching towards closer ties between themselves, they were also creating a new Egyptian–Syrian–Iranian-Gulf axis to confront the Turkish–Israeli alliance.[46] That meant that beyond the façade of the 'support' that Saudi Arabia and Egypt have been lending to the United States in its fight against terrorism and in building a 'coalition' for that purpose, they are in fact preparing another coalition and another front to resist together, at best, to counter actively, at worst, US efforts.

Condemnations of the United States in the establishment Arab and Muslim press, some of which we have abundantly documented throughout this book, either attack it on religious grounds, or for reasons emanating from its power that they cannot equal, or its cultural achievements which they cannot match, or its economic clout on which they so depend, or its political influence to which they have to submit. There also seems to be an innate envy of Western prosperity amidst freedom, which is typical of the bourgeois middle class in the United States, which they cannot emulate, much to their chagrin and shame, due to the limitations that their faith imposes on them on both scores. This creates an enormous pool of enmity, jealousy, envy and frustration for their inability to reach out to it and partake of its bounty. This in turn produces a fountainhead of either self-aggrandizement and one-upmanship, seeking to prove their spiritual 'superiority' above Western materialism, or justifying and rationalizing their inferiority by accusing the West of arrogance, aggression, injustice, colonialism, imperialism and material greed while they, as it is well known, have never conquered any country, spoiled any people, suppressed any minority, vied for any wealth or oppressed any living creature.

Furthermore, in doing that, they reject Western values and ways of life, discard Western-style democracy and human rights while claiming, at the same time, that they have mastered them, in their own way, before the West and better than it has done, and are applying them, and they attempt to persuade world opinion that they pursue modern goals and have never really entertained any lust for world dominion under Islam. They are using Western academics, whom they feed financially and spiritually, to defend those causes and theses which never had any basis in the first place, but were nevertheless made fashionable by the oppressive, vindictive and politically correct post-modernist scholarship.

After 11 September, the no-nonsense US press, unlike its European counterpart, which sought 'sophisticated' interpretations and hidden motives, asked the requisite straightforward questions and sought explanations to them. In consequence, the Saudi and Egyptian perpetrators of those horrors were taken to task, together with their supposedly 'moderate' and 'friendly' governments and the culture that bred them. The Arab backlash was not slow in coming. The US media were accused of 'tyranny' and of having become a tool of incitement against Arab culture, which they presented to their readers as 'ugly', while at the same time they failed to comprehend that the 'other people of the world act according to rules that do not regard liberties as a licence for the outburst of instincts or for reducing human beings to anonymous numbers under the hegemony of capitalism'. The Arabs also complained that while it was they who still wished to reach the average Americans to explain to them their cause, the US media produced the obstacles that prevented that communication between peoples from taking place by 'leaning towards Israel, depicting the Arabs as barbarians who are enslaved by their sexual and material greed, and controlled by their backward beliefs'.[47] Another writer accused the US press of their 'mad attack against Egypt and Saudi Arabia', thus 'casting doubts on the feasibility of building a bridge of trust between America and the Arab people'. He lambasted not only those attacks on the Arabs, but particularly their 'interference in Arab domestic affairs, by claiming that the curricula in the Arab world bred terrorist ideas', and demanding that the Muslims 'ought to exclude Qur'anic texts from their mosques due to their incitement against Unbelievers'.[48]

An Arab author set out to 'demonstrate' that it was Western curricula which were training terrorists who later spread 'corruption and oppression' around the globe. He 'quoted' from a book entitled 'The Mission', which was allegedly published in Britain and distributed throughout the world, and which included a chapter depicting a scenario whereby terrorists would hijack a plane and crash it into a nuclear plant. The fear of such a scenario has caused the Americans to test it by crashing into a nuclear site in order to test the impact. He also claimed that following the discussion of biological warfare in that book, the Americans 'spread anthrax over the southern tip of Manhattan, which killed over 600,000 people, namely half of those who were contaminated'. He came to the conclusion that those who perpetrated the Twin Towers and the Pentagon horrors took their idea from that book, with one variation: instead of crashing into a nuclear plant, they chose to destroy buildings of commercial and military significance in order to hurt US prestige. He sums up: 'After this quick survey of the curricula in the United States and Britain, would the American press still claim that it is others' education rather than theirs, which breeds terrorism?' It is evident, in his eyes, that the terrorist manuals published in the West were just 'waiting for someone to use them', and warned that 'those who lived in glass houses should beware of pelting rocks on others' houses'.[49] This is what a mainstream, government-controlled paper had to say in Saudi Arabia. Another columnist warned that the 'pressures to revise religious curricula in our schools will be counter-productive', because in the past those very curricula had trained the best religious minds in the country, who learned from them a tradition of tolerance and humanity 'the like of which has never emerged in any other religion throughout history'. Hence his ominous conclusion that the reform of this 'tolerance', in the extreme, system of education 'might leave a spiritual vacuum which might cause many of us to seek alternatives'.[50]

Other writers derided the US alternatives that could be adopted, for example, establishing a US television network in Arabic, where:

> The Great Mufti Rumsfeld will appear, or Sheikh Graham and Preacher Ross, who would pronounce fatwas for Muslim youth on Islamic affairs...This channel would only show programmes that conform to the Islamic Shari'a, such as Muslim Hollywood films, the Muslim Cowboys, Islamic striptease, Muslim alcohol, and the tolling of church bells in accordance with the Muslim time frame.[51]

When the Saudi King's niece, Princess Banya, was arrested in Orlando, Florida for having beaten her maid, the press coverage of that affair was also understood as an element of 'Saudi-bashing' by the US media. The Saudis decried what they viewed as 'American insistence on distorting her relations with Arab and Islamic countries, especially Saudi Arabia, in spite of the latter's effort to cultivate normal relations with Washington'. An editorial commented that:

> America, which has attained the world record of homicides, rapes, and violent attacks of all sorts round the clock, America that has sunk herself in a world war against terrorism, and has been seeking ways to revive her battered economy since 11 September, all her security apparatus, her official machinery and her media are no longer interested in anything beyond vain attempts to call the attention of the press, including the Arab media, to the arrest of the Saudi princess as if Bin-Laden himself was about to be arrested... The American media are not interested any longer in distinguishing between friend and foe, due to the control of the media and of some senior positions by the Jews. Things have gotten to the point where the Israeli interest has superseded American interests. At any rate, the only way to explain this phenomenon is to regard it as part of the continuing campaign to discredit Saudi Arabia, in addition to the hundreds of our youth who were incarcerated in American prisons without indictment... The Americans had better understand that our patience is wearing thin.[52]

Let us admit it, there is a confrontation between the West and the world of Islam... The onslaught against Islam is part of the aftermath of the 11 September events... This is a conflict triggered by the strong who are trying to rob people of their will, to exercise terror against the holy places of others and expropriate their resources. Western governments have embraced double standards: they are trying to appease the Muslim world by declarations, but at the same time they adopt security legislation and a public conduct via the media to launch broadsides against everything Arab or Muslim. They forget how the world has suffered from the worst kinds of tyranny and exploitation, how Britain conducted herself in China and India, Spain in the Philippines and South America, Holland in Indonesia and the French in Africa and in the Arab homeland, which show that Western culture did not shrink from that sort of conduct...

Even the advanced Asian countries are subjected to the same discriminatory behaviour because they do not have the same European and American genes. Even within their own cities they marginalize the Blacks, the Asians and the Latinos, because they are considered as alien. Suffice it to recall what happened to the Japanese in America after Pearl Harbor; they were concentrated in one prison and they treated them horribly, even though they had American citizenship. The migration of millions of Blacks and Asians to Europe and to America is the fruit of Colonialism... which will not relent until an end is put to Western hegemony over everything non-Western...[53]

America is trying to make us abrogate the most valuable tenet of our faith, that is jihad against the aggressors and usurpers of rights. In one stroke they attempt to overturn Allah's decree, to justify their incitement and terror... Their generals become war criminals out of their own volition, they murder prisoners of war and people who gave up their arms. What kind of culture is that? That is the basest of all cultures.[54]

It would be a mistake for us to embrace the western notions of liberty, human rights and equality between nations... Because those who led two world wars in the name of greedy ambitions, racism, elimination of other cultures and the claim of racial supremacy... give us reason to believe that an eternal roadblock is standing erect between us and the West.[55]

Columnists on behalf of the regimes in place are not the only opinion-makers in the Islamic world, just as matters relating to the United States or the West in general are not decided only by clerics, whatever the impact of their preaching in their societies. To the extent that there exist public opinion makers other than imams and other men of religion and representatives of the rulers, a certain leeway exists in the press, as long as the persona of the ruler is not accused, attacked or de-legitimized. Within those boundaries, Arab columnists are free to launch broadsides against the West and Israel, and when reproached, they cynically invoke the principle of 'freedom of the press', which is well understood in the West and difficult to refute, but is manipulated in Arab and Muslim countries to attack their external enemies without risking much in terms of the government backlash, as long as the criticism reflects popular consensus. It would be instructive to dwell on some of those attacks in the mainstream, and often state-owned, press which lambasted the United States, her policy and especially her policy-makers. When President Bush made his State of the Union speech, where he characterized certain countries as the 'Axis of Evil', he was abused and compared to Shylock, an honour usually reserved for Israeli leaders in that press.[56] A columnist in the Egyptian government daily, *Al-Ahram*, for example, said that 'President Bush used language no different from Bin-Laden in his videotapes',[57] while the editor of the London-based daily, *al-Quds al-'Arabi*, compared Bush to Hitler under the abusive title: 'A Rash and Vulgar President'. Here are some 'pearls' from that article:

> The American President...presented himself in his State of the Union address as a leader thirsty for bloodshed and for declaring war on half the world to satisfy a sense of vengeance and in submission to the sick Israeli incitement that stems from the interests of the Hebrew State, even if satisfying these interests comes at the expense of the destruction of the entire world...The triangle of evil that he cited does not pose any danger to the interests of the United States, but it does put in jeopardy Israel's aspirations for expansion...
>
> Bush's fiery address reminds us of the speeches of the Nazi, Adolph Hitler. His threatening of Iran and Iraq reminds us of Hitler's threatening Poland and Czechoslovakia. For this reason the whole world must act to stop him...before he drowns in destructive wars that will make the First and Second World Wars look modest...With these idiotic threats, President Bush accomplished the miracle of bringing Iraq and Iran closer together...He created a global front against the unjustified policy of fear that he leads. Iraq and Iran are not the Taliban...They have advanced weaponry and the cultural experience of thousands of years in the depths of history...
>
> If the American President has lost his wits because of the acts of one man such as Bin-Laden, the leader of an organization whose members do not exceed a few hundred, what state would he be in should he face an alliance of Iran, Iraq, North Korea, Syria, Hamas, Islamic Jihad and Hizbullah, as all of which have a rich history of struggle, wars and 'frightening' experience in carrying out operations abroad?

The US President is playing with fire. He is like an unbalanced man given a rifle, about to go into the street and start shooting at passers-by. Therefore, the intelligent people of the world must hasten to stop him, to take away his gun before it is too late...

I admit to feeling pain and disappointment when I saw the representatives of the American people applauding Bush and lending support to his threats which will lead to great losses of their electorate, and will lead their country into bankruptcy and perhaps even collapse... The 'Axis of Evil' in the world is not Iran, Iraq and North Korea, it is America and Israel.[58]

Besides the direct threat to the United States and the humiliation of its President from whose hand countries like Egypt feed, the above writer unwittingly enumerates the list of terror countries and movements and posits them as a natural opposition to the United States. So do many other writers and columnists in Egypt, Saudi Arabia and many other 'friendly' and 'moderate' Arab countries. Similarly, other senior US officials, especially the Vice-President, the Secretaries of State and Defense, and the National Security Adviser are attacked personally, once again along the ancient tribal lines by which demeaning the persona of the enemy equates to diminishing his ability to cause harm. After Secretary Powell left at the end of his visit to the Middle East in April 2002, the Palestinian News Agency (WAFA) published an editorial headlined 'The American Mailman', where it was asserted that 'Powell did nothing, because he was completely committed to the Israeli point of view and did not deviate from it... Israeli withdrawals should have taken place if the American President, Powell himself, and Miss Genius Condoleezza had kept their word'.[59] During the same visit, President Assad vowed once again to support Islamikaze acts of terror, 'because hundreds of millions of Muslims supported them',[60] and his demonstrating students shouted: 'Powell, Go Home !!!, Syria will not surrender, the Intifadah will continue!!!'[61] In response to Powell's visit to calm tempers, the Lebanese stressed that Hizbullah's firing across the line was not terrorism. He was greeted by a series of demonstrations and calls of 'Death to America!!', 'Death to Israel!!', and 'The Lebanese People does not welcome Powell!!!'. Two Lebanese attorneys demanded that the Attorney General arrest the US Secretary of State, regardless of his diplomatic immunity, or deport him because he 'had carried out crimes against humanity and participated in the murder of civilians and military personnel and in destroying civilian infrastructures in Lebanon...and because he seeks to restrict the right of the Lebanese resistance to bring about liberation'.[62]

During the same visit, Powell was due to meet President Mubarak, but the latter snubbed him and sent his Foreign Minister to the meeting instead. The editor of the government daily, *al-Akhbar*, read much into that conduct, and under the title 'No to Powell's Provocation and to the Clear American Bias', did not mince his words, unlike the diplomatic 'previous engagements' and 'ill-disposition' that were resorted to by the diplomats involved. He said that President Mubarak did the right thing in cancelling the meeting, in his capacity as a statesman, national and pan-Arab leader, to express the fact that 'the President is too great to listen to more runaround and provocation, and to solutions based on the overt and obvious bias in favour of Israeli aggression'. He emphasized that the Palestinian acts of Islamikaze are not terrorism but resistance, while it was Washington who 'terrorized everyone who criticizes the crimes of Israel, accusing them of anti-Semitism born of Hitlerian Nazism, stand idly by, even supporting the Nazi crimes of Israel which surpass every kind of Nazism the world has ever known'.[63] The same Egyptian columnists who castigated Powell for condoning 'Nazi crimes', and even supporting them, urged the Palestinians in no uncertain terms, to increase their Islamikaze operations against Israel by 'expanding their suicide bombings and intensifying the violence of their attacks against anything Jewish'. Secular writers of this sort lend credence to 'all Muslim clerics...who have stated that these operations lead to Paradise, and that the martyrs do not die but go on living with Allah'. The columnist concludes that

> If America and Israel view these acts as terrorism, that is their business...but the world of Allah will be supreme. Woe betide the aggressors and the sinners who gnaw at both dead and living flesh. Their punishment is Hell and they will reach its fire in both this world and the world to come.[64]

An Egyptian opposition paper went one step further when it declared that Condoleezza Rice was only 'suited to work in a night club or to make her bed in the heart of the jungle'. The abuse against her as a woman, a Black, and a US official, takes us to the darkest crevices of Arab and Muslim repulsion against US policy. The columnist of the critique stated clearly:

> Within days Condoleezza Rice became the most famous woman in the world when President Bush appointed her as his top adviser. She does not flinch from calling Palestinian President Arafat a leader of terror. By the same token, she has shown her great hatred of the Islamic world by declaring her full support for the Zionist terror entity. She even said that the blood-shedder, the terrorist Ariel Sharon is a man of peace and a veteran warrior...
>
> This woman has damaged the world of the Blacks, which produced many distinguished individuals...like Martin Luther King...Nelson Mandela...Muhammed Ali and other fighters and men of honour...Some have called her an insolent woman, like the dangerous anaconda snake that attacks anyone in its path. She is only suited to work in a nightclub or make her bed in the jungles and forests of Brazil, as a predatory woman...
>
> Behind every American President stands a woman who raises him to heaven or casts him down to the abyss...Ronald Reagan made no political decision without fortune teller Joan Quigley. This relationship became scandalous when the American press described her as responsible for the mental retardation that afflicted Reagan...The President was most famous for his scandals with women, and he fell in love with the childish Jewess Madeleine Albright, the Secretary of State. He would make no approval without the permission of that woman, who became notorious for her short garments that often caused embarrassment when she met political dignitaries. She too, in the end, followed the same path, describing the Palestinian resistance as terror...
>
> These are bad examples of women who rule America. We thank Allah that there are no similar women in our Arab world, otherwise our lives – we men – would be absolute hell and we would become prisoners to the declarations of Condoleezza Rice and the other vulgar women.[65]

Thus, in view of the pervasiveness of the clerics' fundamentalist decrees in the secular media and public opinion, attention must also be paid to what is said in the mosques, especially after the Friday prayer, which is usually attended by the top brass of the country and in which the political sermon (*khutba*) is approved *a priori* by the authorities. Namely, what is expressed in those sermons, and certainly in a tightly controlled country such as Saudi Arabia, often reflects official thinking or trial balloons that rulers and officials dare not release directly, for fear of the Western backlash. There, the preachers (*khatib*) have no compunction about expanding on the inter-cultural struggle between Islam and the West, which they view as a continuous and eternal contention for the soul and the leadership of the human race. The very compulsive and repetitive references to the West in these sermons is evidence of the apologetic nature of the Muslim arguments, and to the lack of self-confidence they evince in the face of the approaching confrontation between the two cultures. At any rate, those clerics who are versed in the art of heaping all the blame on others and exonerating themselves of any wrongdoing find it easy to accuse the West of terrorism, corruption, lack of values and aggression, and congratulate themselves for the purity and compassion of the Islamic *umma* and the bright future that awaits it, in contrast to the sinking and decaying Western civilization. For example:

> The most noble civilization that humankind has ever known is our Islamic one. Western culture today is nothing more than the product of its contacts with our own in Andalusia and elsewhere. The reason for the bankruptcy of Western culture is its dependence on a material approach and its detachment from religion and values, which have brought about the misfortune of humankind, the growing number of suicides due to emotional problems, and to moral deviations...
>
> Western culture has failed to lead man to happiness and stability...One nation alone is capable of reviving world civilization, and that is the Islamic *umma*. No decent man in the world can deny that no other civilization has been so compassionate to other humans, or created more sublime values, or rules with more justice than Islam...While the imaginary cultures have been sinking in the marshes of materialism and crossing moral crises, our Islamic *umma* is the only one worthy of taking over the reins of leadership and riding the horse of pioneering and world dominion...

When this happens, our *umma* will not use its cultural progress to exploit other peoples, exhaust their resources and damage their honour; it will not use technological innovation to spread secularism and support terror; it will not tap military technologies to menace the security of other peoples and countries or to mount wild and barbaric campaigns, and will not use its media to misinform public opinion... This is the nature of the Islamic message which undertakes the burden to rescue humankind, and to bring happiness to those lost in the dark tunnels of oppression and misfortune.[66]

And so, on and on, many preachers throughout the Muslim world sing the praises of Islam and predict the imminent demise of the West and its values, more often than not implying justification for any act taken against the West, which is sinking into decay in any case, and whose sinful existence must be put to an end by Islam, the Saviour of humankind. Other preachers deprecate Western culture, which:

...has contributed nothing of value to humanity, save a fake and base civilization... which harms human rights and freedoms while proclaiming them, discriminates between races, colors genders and languages, and has developed technologies of mass destruction in order to annihilate human kind, and invented deceit and cheating.[67]

But perhaps permissiveness has become the most negative aspect of Western society in the eyes of the puritanical Muslims. Homosexuality, which in most Muslim countries is considered a crime, is imputed by some preachers to the 'brothers of monkeys and pigs [that is, the Jews], for whom, as for the Unbelievers, this is a normative pattern of conduct'. The UN Secretary General was attacked for 'bringing together Jews and Christians, thus pushing people to the abyss', and at the same time that he campaigns to arrest the spread of AIDS, he 'advocates permissiveness that allows the spread of that disease'. He was accused of allowing prostitution and 'spreading disgusting customs of homosexuality that is called "sexual deviation", and even convened a conference of those people to encourage them to enter into marriages of the third kind'.[68] One official Saudi daily even predicted the end of the United States, when Islam will prevail. He insisted that 'those being

mowed down in Palestine are Martyrs to their cause, dignity, land
and religion, the morons in Washington notwithstanding'. He
compared Bush to Caligula the Roman and counselled 'Condo-
whatever Rice' to bring him some of those history books to read
and learn from. He challenged Bush's authority to speak for the
Palestinians when he issued his negative judgement on Arafat,
because while the Palestinians were ready to fight and die for
Arafat, he contended, no one would die for Bush. He promised that
while Bush and the United States would vanish into oblivion, the
Arabs and Muslims, who are pure and ancient, would survive,
exactly as the Arab palm and olive trees would outlive US nuclear
power. He saw that engraved in the Holy Scripture which stated 'In
God We Trust.'[69]

The question of permissiveness is linked to the status of women
who, when liberated and Westernized, become, for those Muslim
fundamentalists, the worst and most dangerous agent of social
disruption. The discussion of women in the sermons of the clerics is
not anecdotal, as it sometimes appears in Western discourse, when
a sudden interest is taken in Saudi women under their oppressive
veils, who are banned from driving or from strolling the streets
unaccompanied, or the occasional stoning of women for adultery,
but a constant theme of concern in Muslim society, especially
among the clerical milieus who fear that emulation of the 'corrupt'
and permissive ways of women in the open Western societies might
wreak havoc on their traditional social order. This is so because for
the Muslim conservatives, the very interference of the West in the
rights of women in the Muslim world is seen as a sure sign of its
determination to ruin the Muslim social order by hitting at its soft
underbelly. One sheikh, for example, said 'the woman, being a
double-edged sword, can be turned into the most dangerous
weapon of mass destruction', hence her being a target of most plots
against the social order of the *umma*, it being understood that the
woman possesses many characteristics that can either build or
destroy the entire Muslim community. The West, which is often
labelled as the 'enemy of Islam', is accused of using the women, the
weakest link in the Muslim social chain, in order to detach Muslims
from their faith. The West appears under the guise of compassion
and protection of the rights of women, and many Muslim women
were led astray, due to their ignorance of Islam, which regards the
woman as the equal and partner of man, and allocates to women
rights and duties that 'concord with their nature and character'.

Their nature and character are, of course, determined by those same clerics who say explicitly that 'permitting women to go out to the streets and rub shoulders with men, and talk with persons who are not their protectors in public, and even expose parts of their bodies that are forbidden, leads to destruction and shame'.[70]

Incidentally, the Jews take the brunt of those accusations, maybe due to their close proximity to the Muslims in Palestine, and they are considered as the agents of the Western drive to corrupt Muslim women. There are numerous quotations from Muslim sources during the sermons of clerics which 'corroborate' Jewish corruption with regard to women. For example, they say that the first crime committed by the biblical Children of Israel was to let their women go out adorned with jewelry, with a view to rousing *fitna* (internal strife), and they were therefore punished by Allah.[71] Another preacher remarked that one could detect the clear link between the Western campaign against the 'modesty and morality of Muslim men and women, and the Jewish schemes to destroy their humanity and make them look like beasts, namely naked and exposed'.[72] Preachers draw lessons from other cultures, like those of the Greeks and the Romans which collapsed, in their view, due to 'the corruption of women in their midst'. They contend that while at the inception of those ancient civilizations women were 'modest, protected and cared about their housework, both the Greeks and the Romans were successful and built vast empires, but when their women engaged in make up and frequenting clubs and public places, those civilizations were doomed'. They infer from that example that since the enemies of Islam wish it to collapse irretrievably, they have decided to target the corruption of Muslim women. They find solid 'proof' for their contention in the form of the irrefutable Protocols of the Elders of Zion, and therefore they conclude that the 'enemies of Muslim women are the Jews, the Christians, the "hypocrites", the secularists, and the utilitarian types that flock in their wake'.[73]

Imputing to the Jews, the 'sons of Satan', the schemes to derail the Muslim woman from her traditional modesty[74] does not tell the whole story. Western women, in themselves, are to blame, for they heed the false ideas current in the West regarding the protection of women's rights, which in fact are calculated to 'push them to a sinful freedom'. According to this interpretation by the preachers, this kind of free conduct of women in the West has generated societies where 'crime is their hobby, adultery their entertainment, and murder a form of expressing anger'. This is no coincidence, in their view, in societies where 'the number of illegitimate children surpasses the numbers of those originating from legal intercourse', where women, even when married, 'do what they wish', where juvenile girls know and do more than adult married women, and where 'ideological garbage is diffused through the media and satellite television'. They view as horrifying the sight of women 'going out of the house when they please, where they please and without permission of their husbands'. Even more horrible is the fact that 'in some households, it is the woman who establishes the rules', so much so that in many Western countries the women have grown 'masculine'. Thus, their men are emasculated to such an extent that, except for their external appearance, there is nothing left of their masculinity.[75] Some clerics view Western women as a 'cheap commodity which presents herself naked or half naked to please the men', especially when they serve as maids in houses, clerks in offices, nurses in hospitals, stewardesses on flights and in hotels, teachers in men's classes and actresses in movies and on television. They castigate men also for using feminine voices on radio as singers or announcers. The gloomy consequence in the eyes of those clerics is that since there are more women than men in the West, but the number of wives was unwisely limited to one, all the rest were earmarked for corruption and debauchery.[76]

Muslim preachers, who are the main shapers and controllers of public opinion in conservative Muslim societies, compare thus between the 'corruption' of Western women and the chastity and purity of their Muslim counterparts:

> Western women travel without supervisors and live as strangers among strangers. Thus, the enemies of Allah and of humanity have denied their unfortunate women all the fortunate components of life which make them happy, as well as their social rights, so as to condemn them to a life of corruption and destruction. And despite all these crimes, they claim that they defend women's freedom ... Men have become like animals of prey who treat cruelly the weaker [women], while men regard their women like wild cats ... Even Sylvester Stallone said that he had all reasons to hate women ... Thus, women's lot in Islam is far superior to that of Western women, and certainly to that of Indian women who have to be incinerated alive when their husbands die, or Chinese women

whose husbands are allowed to bury them alive ...

The West makes hollow statements regarding human rights for women by making them the equals of men, but when they left their house they were consumed by the lie of this freedom. Public corruption grew and spread as a result, not only to bordellos but also to hotels ... dance clubs, or even on the open highway. It is no longer strange there when fathers copulate with their daughters and brothers with their sisters ...

One of the mistakes committed by women is that under the pretext of fatigue, or because they wish to provoke their partners, they refrain from joining them when they are summoned to bed ... By doing so, the woman expresses ignorance, because she robs her husband of his greatest right and puts herself in jeopardy, because it is written that when a man summons his wife and she refuses, she is cursed by the Angels until she recants. Another mistake regards the service of the husband. When she fails in her duties to her husband by disregarding his needs in cooking, washing and cleaning etc., that may be attributed to sheer laziness, and this is serious enough in itself. Service to her husband is her right and duty. Muslim women ought to treat their husband well and serve him, and this will make the husband happy and create happiness in the family ...

Another mistake is to allow into the house anyone that has been banned by her husband. Husbands have the right to bring into the house only people they like, and women have to obey. The woman is not allowed to bring in anyone not to his liking, even if it is her relatives ... When her husband marries more wives, some women behave with extreme jealousy, ignorance and stupidity.[77]

Evidently, by setting the high standards of the obedient Muslim woman, even when she is one of four, up against the deficient morality of the Western woman, not only are Muslim women warned not to fall into the Western trap, but the West in general is told to keep off the virtuous Muslim wives and not try to incite them to abandon their faith and submissive status. Conversely, Muslims are constantly warned by the mosque preachers against the Unbelievers' lures and customs, and urged not to follow them. Particularly targeted are the 'People of the Book', namely Christians and Jews, who are credited with/accused of elaborating the trappings of Western culture that have become so attractive to the world in general and Muslim countries in particular. The inference is clear: if the Scriptuaries are inherently corrupt and the enemies of Allah, and actively seek to undermine Muslim societies and subvert Allah's, that is Muslim , values, then no Muslim should have any compunction about, or recoil from, destroying them. One of those sermons states:

> Two communities constitute the camp of the Unbelievers, and they will continue to be at its base, until Allah causes their collapse and elimination in the long run: Jews and Christians. These are the two most important communities in the camp of Infidels, that same camp which bred hatred of Allah's Prophets and Messengers and waged war against them. Since Moses ... and until Muhammed, the Seal of Prophets, the Jews and the Christians have persisted in their opposition to the Prophets and in sustaining the camp of blasphemy...
>
> When the Prophet Muhammed was dispatched to his mission, the camp of blasphemy declared war on his message, and those two communities, especially the Jews, stood at the focus of that war, and will continue to constitute the two pillars of war and conflict between Faith and Blasphemy to eternity... Only then will the conflict end, when Jesus, the son of Mary will come back, smash the Cross and eliminate it from the face of the earth, and will kill the one-eyed false Messiah who is awaited by the Jews.[78] Until then our conflict with the Christians and Jews will continue, with highs and lows, sometimes we win and sometimes we lose.
>
> The Jews are those 'who have earned Allah's anger', and the Christians are those 'who were led astray'.[79] The Qur'an has depicted the Jews as a nation accursed by Allah, because they drew his anger, so much so that he turned some of them into pigs and monkeys.[80]

The treatment of Christianity and Judaism as inextricably evil religions, which reflect the satanic nature of the West and in turn shape it, does not preclude attacks on either of them separately. While the attitude towards Jews and Judaism will be dealt with in detail in the next chapter, some of the harsh words reserved for Christianity will be discussed here. One preacher in 'moderate' Saudi Arabia had this to say about Christianity:

Today we shall talk about one of the distorted religions, a faith that deviates from the Straight Path, about a false religion and those whom Allah has described as 'having been led astray'. We shall examine their faith and survey their history which is full of hatred, contempt and wars against Islam and Muslims...In that distorted religion that has many adepts around the world, one can see how the Christians deviate from the Path by their very belief in the Trinity, which means that God consists of three in one: the Father, the Son and the Holy Spirit. When we look at their ancient books and religion for references endorsing this concept, we find nothing...

Christians believe that Jesus was nailed to the Cross while he was crying: 'Oh, God why did you forsake me?' [while Muslims believe that he was saved from the Cross by Allah]... Despite all these deviations, many Muslims are led to believe Christian claims to love, tolerance, serving the poor and disabled and other slogans that have no substance. Based on this, we still see people among us who endeavour for a rapprochement between us and them, as if the differences between us were minor and could be removed by convening those politically motivated meetings...

Oh Believers, the hearts of the Crusaders who despised us are still beating in their chests, the weapons they used against us are still in their possession, the hatred that blinded them when they came to us as colonialists and conquerors is still brewing in their hearts. Their hostility to us is deeply entrenched in their faith.[81]

One of the basic tenets of Islam is that there is the choice only between Islam and heresy, and there is no way to Paradise and to avoid Hell but following our Prophet and joining Islam. Any other option leads to Hell...In view of this, how can anyone claim that Christianity, Judaism and Islam constitute equal ways to get to Allah?...All the appeals for the unity of the monotheistic faith...[are] no more than a false claim and a hollow slogan...because that means that there is no longer the difference between Muslim and heretic...If this accursed idea were to be implemented, it would lead Muslims to the lowest reaches of Hell, because it would posit groups of Infidels as being correct, allow Believers to join Christianity and Judaism shamelessly, abrogate the differences between

Muslims and heretics, namely between Truth and lie, and turn Islam into the like of the false religions. This would be something that would facilitate the penetration of the Christian Mission into the lands of Islam.[82]

In other sermons, Muslim preachers attacked the Pope for his 'arrogant' appeal, during his visit to Syria, to the different religions to live in harmony together, maintaining that such an appeal actually meant unity between them, while in fact the Pope and those who appealed for harmony were the:

> ...heirs of the Inquisitions which administered the worst torture to Muslims, and of the Crusader campaigns to the Muslim East where thousands of Muslims were made prisoners, and they led the massacres in Bosnia, Kosovo, Indonesia and Chechnya, something that put in doubt the compassion of those murderer wolves.

The message of the Pope's visit, it was said, was that, not content with usurping Muslim lands, he also wished to rob Muslims of their faith, so that they lose both this and the next world. Thus, conclude the preachers, there can be no rapprochement or understanding or co-existence between Islam and Christianity, as long as the latter defame Allah by claiming that Jesus is His son.[83] Incidentally, this is such a sensitive aspect of Islam's rejection of Christianity that the Muslim squatters who set out to build a mosque in the plaza of the Church of the Annunciation in Nazareth[84] pasted a sign on the plaza displaying the Sura of the Qur'an, which proclaims that God neither begets nor is begotten.[85] Due to the hopelessness of converting the Scriptuaries to the human values of Islam, some preachers conclude, there is no point in listening to all the peace initiatives, Security Council Resolutions or prayers for peace because 'wild beasts cannot become human, and they cannot produce anything but wildness'.[86] Jews and Christians are further accused not only of heresy, but also of disbelief in the Messengers who were sent to them, hence their innate inability to distinguish between good and bad, truth and lie. The Unbelievers, it is claimed, did not even believe in Moses and Jesus, and had they believed, they would have embraced Islam, because all previous prophets had forewarned their peoples of the coming of Muhammed and the obligation to believe in him.[87]

Even the credit given to Jewish and Christian, that is Western, scientists who have invented useful tools that the Muslims can benefit from, such as electricity, or the close relations that the Prophet had entertained with some Jews in Medina, are skewed by the preachers in such a way as to become a liability. The Jews, whom the Prophet had counted on, violated their alliance with him, therefore they were deservedly punished by killing, slavery and confiscation of their property. One of them reminds his audiences that any non-Muslim who wishes to live among Muslims was still welcome, provided he paid the *jizya*, that is, the poll-tax which guaranteed Jews and Christians the *dhimmi* status that was discussed in Chapter 2. Because that subordinate status demonstrated the prevalence of the Muslims and of their rule, it negated any possibility of equality between Islam and its rivals religions. The other traditional limitations of Islam on the *dhimmis*, what have come to be known as the 'Umar Regulations, were also invoked by a present-day preacher, as if they were modern legislation and not the vestiges of medieval obscurantism. Because not permitting the Christians to build or even repair their churches and monasteries in Muslim lands, as the preacher emphasizes, something that has been enforced in Saudi Arabia today, is a sign that Islam reigns supreme, so no other faith may dwell in equality side by side with it. Preachers advanced more demands, as in years past, as a condition to allow Christians and Jews to live in Islamdom, as if there were long lines of Westerners seeking to enter the domain of oppression. They are obliged:

> ...to feed in their churches Muslim passers-by for three days, to stand up when Muslims seek a seat, not to imitate Muslims in their dress and speech, not to ride horses, not to wear a sword or any other kind of weapon, not to sell wine, not to toll the churches' bells, not to raise their voices in prayer, to shave their forehead to make them recognizable, not to incite against Muslims, not to beat Muslims...If they violate these conditions, they enjoy no protection any longer.[88]

When one considers that in the Christian West and Israel, which they so demean and are so set against, and which they accuse of oppression and arrogance, they are not obliged to feed anyone, least of all Christians, in their mosques, and are certainly allowed to repair existing mosques and build new ones on any spot they want and can afford; are encouraged to imitate local speech, dress and way of life, as an encouragement to integrate within the host society; can ride horses like any other citizens; are inducted into the local armies, where they wear weapons; sell and buy freely what they wish; call for prayers at all hours of day and night, often disturbing entire neighbourhoods and violating statutory limitations on noise emission; incite at will against the cultures and countries which generously gave them asylum; and on top of all this, are often taken care of by the host welfare services, without any need for protection money, humiliation or gross discrimination, one wonders who is the arrogant oppressor. In the Muslim order of things, they deserve all the goodies, they can demand equality from the West due to their inherent superiority, and in the name of the democracy that they despise, they can curse, kick and accuse their benefactors, they can impose their own ways of life in violation of others' rights, and still label their hosts as arrogant and oppressors. That is the only way for them to demonstrate that Muslims cannot violate any non-Muslim law, because that law is invalid in the first place, and the only restrictions that are moral and valid are those imposed on non-Muslims when their misfortune brings them to Muslim lands. This conceptually huge gap in the value of people and cultures, with one supreme and the other despised, is what feeds the fundamentalists, who are then prepared to resort to violence in order to make the desirable, in their eyes, supreme, and the Western undesirable disappear.

One of the perverse effects of this total negation of the West and its Christian infrastructure has been the aid that some Christian minorities among the Arabs have been rendering to their Muslim persecutors, accounting for the fact that many of them feel they are primarily Arab. During the takeover by Palestinian gunmen of the Church of the Nativity in Bethlehem, and the subsequent siege by Israeli troops in April–May 2002, Father Musalem, who heads the tiny Latin Church in Gaza, called upon the Church to launch a war 'crueller than the Crusades' against Israel for having besieged the Nativity, not against the Muslims who took it over. He urged the Christian world to 'Save Jesus', and derided it for raising heaven and earth for the Buddha statues that were destroyed by the Taliban regime in Afghanistan while Bethlehem, which should have counted much more for them, left them indifferent. He exploded at world Christianity on Palestinian television, and in front of Muslim clerics from the Palestinian Ministry of *Waqf*, to the delight of his predominantly Muslim audience:

You are loathsome!!! You are contemptible!! You are cowards!! because you cannot carry the message of Jesus in your hearts. The message of Jesus is one of love, sacrifice, mercy, life and manhood, and these Christians in the world have no mercy, no compassion, no manliness, no sacrifice. I do not mean only towards us but even towards the Jews. As not only the Jews kill us – we also kill them, because we are in a war of self-defence...

We – and I say this brutally, because he who remains silent is Satan – are facing the filthy Christians of the West...We hear that the US Congress is demanding that Bush unleash Israel to slaughter the Palestinians. What kind of Christian is this? This is not Christianity, this is not even paganism, this is Christianity of the jungle. Our New Testament is not their New Testament, our Jesus is not their Jesus, our Nativity is not their Nativity and our peace is not their peace. I will say still more: our God is not their God...[89]

The Western Christians, stripped of their love, tolerance, truth and justice in their hearts, must cast away their New Testament. The New Testament and Christianity have nothing to do with those Christians. If I were the head of the church where President Bush worships, and he came to pray, I would bar him from entering, because he has renounced the Church's moral standards.[90]

Other Christian clerics, such as Bishop Alex of the Roman Orthodox Bishopric of Gaza, or Coptic priest Marcus Aziz in Egypt – both persecuted and dwindling minorities in a sea of hostile Muslim fundamentalism – trod the same line of self-flagellation, apparently to prove their loyalty to their people rather than to their faith, by claiming that the Western Churches are not truly Christian. The former said that since love and harmony existed only in embattled Palestine, the true Holy Land, Western Christianity must be false in consequence, for no one who had no tolerance in their hearts could be named Christian.[91] The Coptic priest, whose Church in the West, especially in the United States, Canada and Australia, is the main guarantor of survival for his home-grown and down-trodden Christianity,[92] addressed a letter to Bush under the heading 'Are you Christian or Crusader?', in which he derided Israel for 'drugging the leaders of Christian countries, especially those who belong to no religion and do not know the road to Heaven', and for manipulating those leaders 'like marionettes, to destroy their religion'. He claimed that it was Israel who planted in their hearts hatred and rage towards the Arabs and the Muslims, like Bush, the father, who attacked Iraq, and now his son attacking Afghanistan. He equated those Christian leaders to wolves seeking to kill the flock, and dramatically concluded with a statement of loyalty to his persecutors, a typical *dhimmi* who is beaten by his Muslim lord but is grateful for the beating:

> We, Christians of the East, who in the past refused to stand by the Crusaders and stood by our Muslim brethren, are also opposed to the negative deeds of the Western governments biased in favour of Israel, despite its arrogance and even though it damages the holy sites... We say to Bush, during your term, Jesus' name is disgraced by the attacks on the holy places. Are you a Christian, Mr Bush? I doubt it. Perhaps you are a Crusader. God alone knows.[93]

Others, like the Coptic scholar Dr Babawi, attacked Bush under the title 'Judas is Back'. He accused Christian leaders, notably Bush, of betraying Jesus, selling out the Messiah for their own private interests and in order 'not to anger the Zionist lobby in America'. He warned that if the Church of the Nativity is reduced to rubble, it would be Bush's fault, because he is considered the head of all Christian rulers. He is dubbed the modern Judas because he will have sold Jesus for 'Jewish votes'.[94] More ominously, the Egyptian-dominated Arab League, whose Secretary General is the former hard-line Egyptian Foreign Minister, Amr Mussa, and where Saudi Arabia also plays a dominant role, lends credence to the conspiracy theories which accuse the US establishment of having itself concocted the 11 September tragedy for its own obscure reasons.

On 8 April 2002, the Arab League's Zayed Centre for Co-ordination and Follow Up hosted a lecture by French author Thierry Meyssan, who has been promoting the idea that the United States military was behind the 11 September disaster.[95] More to the point, however, is the official publication by the League of the summary of that guest lecture. It said, *inter alia*, that:

- Both Congress and the United States media covered up the truth by not investigating events;

- It was not reported that the White House's Old Executive Building was bombed, as was a third building in Manhattan;
- Bin-Laden's involvement was a myth that defied analysis, since he was a previous CIA agent who was visited by the head of the CIA in a Dubai hospital in July (2001);
- The 1,200 detainees held in the United States knew nothing of the attacks and their names are kept secret so that they cannot be charged;
- The US military – to further its interest and hegemony over the world – was responsible for the attack;
- It is a possibility that the attacking aeroplanes of 11 September were remote-controlled. For two hours before the attack, waves from a homing device were recorded transmitting from, and interfering with transmission from, the Twin Towers, and such a device could be used to direct aeroplanes. If the planes were remote-controlled, no hijackers were needed, thus the passenger lists were fake.[96]

The same report of the League was given prominence in the official *Saudi Gazette*, titled 'US Military Officials Behind 11 September Attacks', and detailed Meyssan's proposal that a United Nations committee be established to find 'those really behind 11 September, and until this happens, all US military operations, including any against Iraq or Iran should be considered illegal'. The *Gazette* cited Meyssan as stating that 'those who masterminded the operations were US terrorists'; that since the presidential communication codes were deciphered, it proved that at least one of the masterminds was an insider; and that US participation in the plot was possible due to the precedent of 1961, when 'the American Command planned attacks against American citizens'.[97] Another columnist from the United Arab Emirates seconded his colleague's interest in the affair, citing Meyssan's reference to the list of the kidnappers shown in the airline document, where 'only three passengers were identified on Flight 11 and two on Flight 93', as casting doubt on the entire story of the hijacking, and concluding that 'it is ridiculous enough to believe the story of the passport that was found in the debris of the World Trade Center amid such horrible fire and smoke'.[98] This technique of criticizing by quoting others in order to escape direct self-incrimination is too transparent to fool anyone; it is too reminiscent of one telling anti-Semitic jokes to avoid being suspected oneself of anti-Semitism. Those famously democratic states of Egypt, Saudi Arabia and the Gulf know very well how to excise from their press any open criticism of their autocratic rulers, and how to hide behind the spurious argument of 'freedom of the press' when they wish to publish material that does not accord with their stated policies.

There are also explicit, direct attacks and threats in the Muslim media against the United States, from a 'declaration of war' by Egypt's Al-Azhar clerics, threats by the Hamas of using anthrax and other non-conventional weapons against the United States, to pledges to target Americans in the Middle East. All this is connected, as might be expected, to the 'horrors that America conducts in various parts of the world':

> Oh, we Nation of Islam! We are all targeted by our enemy... Why should we not unite, therefore, around the cry 'There is no God but Allah and Muhammed is the Messenger of Allah', and fight our enemy?... Entering into an alliance with the Americans is *ridda*[99]... The Afghan opposition must not collaborate with the Americans, they must stand with their countrymen and fellow Muslims, otherwise Allah and his angels will curse them[100]... If the enemy sets foot on the lands of Islam, he must be fought. In this case, a man must set out for jihad without the permission of his father, a woman without the permission of her husband, a debtor without the permission of his lender, and the slave without the permission of his master. Islam urges us to set out on jihad for the sake of Allah until we accomplish one of two things: martyrdom or victory.[101]
>
> Terrorism is a modern term. In Islam, the meaning of terrorism is intimidation, not all intimidation is forbidden by religious law... In the modern age, when different kinds of oppression and persecution emerged, some ethnic groups in almost every country were stripped of their rights. When they insisted on their rights, the despotic regimes rejected them, and the oppressed and persecuted people found no other way to express themselves but by means of rebellion... Hence the so-called terrorism against America, who is the one that killed and was killed... It was completely successful in sowing hatred and loathing in the hearts of people of the entire world by means of its policy of double standards,

especially regarding Islamic and Arab affairs...In Timor, the stronger [Indonesian] side was Muslim, so America went berserk and mobilized all the international institutions to defend the non-Muslims [in East Timor]...In contrast, it allows Israel to slaughter Palestinians and to destroy the mosques...After all this America still wants Allah to give her security, yet it is the one that attacked herself by angering the world...

What America has done in Afghanistan is the worst kind of international terrorism. America has refused to seek a precise definition of international terrorism, after which every state could have sought the terrorists within its own jurisdiction. But that the United States should carry out that mission by herself...a thousand times no!! Even if present Muslim regimes support America, they are only passing clouds... Stability is in the hands of peoples...What America is doing now is terror waged against the weak...the forces of tyranny deserve to be defeated.[102]

Accusing Islam and Muslims of terrorism is mistaken, because Muslims as a nation are a symbol of peace in the world, and the Muslim nation has never attacked a neighbouring nation...There is a huge difference between terrorism and jihad in terms of words, leadership and war. War is conducted on behalf of a nation...and not on the decision of an individual. What the Palestinians are waging is jihad in accordance with Islamic law, aimed at defending the Islamic holy places. What the Afghani people are doing in response to the aggression is also a jihad that is legitimate according to religious law.[103]

Muslims must declare a jihad. We all must prepare for jihad against America, because the strikes will reach even us. What America and the West have done is an international crime...a great crime against humanity. This is a war against Islam...We have no choice but to declare our own position: Are we with Islam or with Bush? The answer will determine the fate of the Muslim nation in the new century.[104]

Not only the Muslim establishment in Egypt emitted these sounds of hostility towards the United States and the West, but also the press, citing, amongst others, some eminent Islamists. One article threatened the United States with chemical, biological and nuclear weapons, and with attacks against Americans working in the Middle East. The author even described the number of US victims in the New York and Washington horrors as 'minuscule', even if it should amount to 50,000 in the final analysis, and seemed delighted that 'the white Christian man could also scream, suffer pain, bleed and die'. He found it ridiculous to cry over two destroyed buildings, while the United States 'destroyed entire countries and obliterated cities from the face of the earth'. He admitted that he saw majesty in the death of those thousands of Americans, and that he cried in front of his television set as he was watching the horror. But not out of sympathy for the victims, rather out of 'fear from Allah the Powerful, the Avenger, the Victor, the Precious, the Just. How He takes the tyrants just when they think they rule the earth and are capable of confronting Him.' He thought that the lessons of martyrdom that have been imparted to the world, and where Islam 'was the teacher of the martyrs', will make the United States indefensible, once the 'ambulatory human bombs could cause at any time a train and a truck to collide, set a gas station alight and set off chemical, biological, and even nuclear bombs'. He vowed that, as he had repeatedly predicted in the past, more Islamikaze operations have become inevitable, as a response to US oppression and tyranny, until the United States totally collapsed from within, just like the Soviet Union.[105]

A Western-educated Hamas leader, who specialized in writing open letters to world leaders and resonating events, this time addressed his 163rd message to anthrax, praising it for having sown terror in the hearts of 'the lady of arrogance, tyranny and boastfulness' who 'terrorizes and horrifies the world with fear', and pledged that the fear of anthrax would continue to expand and counselled it to 'enter their air and the water faucets from which they drink and the pens with which they draft their conspiracies'. He urged the anthrax to 'turn the bodies of the tyrants into matches burning slowly and gradually, so they understand that the truth belongs to Allah and that they should give rights to those entitled to them'.[106] This inhuman rhetorical cruelty, which equals the wildest and most barbaric words ever uttered by humans with regard to their kind, was not an isolated case. For example, Arab circles described the incarceration of al-Qa'ida prisoners in the US base in Guantanamo as 'worse than the Nazi treatment of their prisoners', an Egyptian columnist even comparing Guantanamo to Auschwitz and the arrest of al-Qa'ida and Taliban people to the trumped up condemnation of Dreyfus.[107] An author for the Hamas *Risala* castigated the United States' historical record that not only wiped out Hiroshima and Nagasaki, but also its own Presidents Lincoln and Kennedy, and caused the assassination of Martin Luther King and Malcolm X, and the extermination of children in Iraq. He singled out Dick Cheney and his 'girl-friend', Condoleezza Rice, and turned the situation around by turning the Arabs into the victims of the United States, not the other way around.[108]

Egyptian media accused the United States of dropping 'genetically altered food' into Afghanistan, specifically in areas full of land mines, in order to cause more Afghan civilian casualties, all under the cover of bringing food aid to the population, and lambasted the US media for their 'deranged attack' on Egypt for daring to question the false Arab accusations.[109] Even the leaders of the jihad army in Indonesia pledged to target US interests in their country and to act against the Christians in the eastern part of the country.[110] A Jordanian physician, the former Head of the Jordanian Doctors' Association, attacked Condoleezza Rice for her criticism of the treatment of women in the Arab world, and asserted that women in the United States were more humiliated than in Saudi Arabia, citing the cases of Hillary Clinton, 'whose husband served her all kinds of degradation and humiliation, to the point where she was forced to lie in front of the cameras to defend him and his perverted relationships', and of President Nixon, who 'beat his wife and tore her eye retina'. This author, who had nothing to say about the harems, the polygamy and the slavery that is still practised in parts of the Muslim world, also attacked US television and trappings of modernity, such as 'hamburgers, Cola and Marlboro', and claimed that US women are raped and harassed, even in the US armed forces, when the generals 'rape their women between one bombing and another of Iraq and Afghanistan'.[111] Al-Qa'ida activist, Abu 'Ubeid al-Qurashi summed up the situation by promising that the superiority of Islam over the West, that has been proved on 11 September, would be maintained due to the basic differences between them which are in Islam's favour:

1. No form of surveillance can provide early warning or permit rapid decision-making. Even the Echelon satellite surveillance system, which cost billions of dollars … did not manage to stop the 19 mujahedin wielding knives.
2. The Americans' marketing of the war is totally inefficient. The

United States could not even find an acceptable name for the campaign. Neither 'Crusader War', 'Absolute Justice', nor 'Infinite Justice' allowed the US propaganda apparatus to overcome the feelings of hatred for America. They could not even remove internal American qualms.

3. The Islamic nation is struggling against globalization, and it continues with its negative attitude towards Western rhetoric and explanations. The Westerners' rage increased once it became clear to them that Muslims could use the same computers that they made, without espousing the same values. Against all their assessments, Islamic culture cannot be shattered by technology.

4. The West ignores the power of faith. Western civilization, which is based on the information revolution, cannot distance the Muslims from the Qur'an. The Book of Allah brings to the hearts of the Muslims a faith deeper than all the utopian descriptions and than the fallacies of the tyrannical Western propaganda machine.

5. Symbols never lose their value. Sheikh Bin-Laden has become a symbol for the repressed from the four corners of the earth – even for non-Muslims.

6. The Western propaganda machine's size did not keep it from being defeated by Sheikh Bin-Laden with what resembled a judo move. The aggressive Westerners became accustomed to observing the tragedies of others – but on September 11 the opposite happened.

7. There are data attesting to the importance of the Munich operation[112] in the history of the resistance movement, and the extent of its influence on the entire world. It is known that direct consequences of the operation were that thousands of young Palestinians were roused to join the *Fidayeen* organizations... The number of organizations engaging in international 'terror' increased from a mere 11 in 1968 to 55 in 1978. Fifty-four per cent of these new organizations sought to imitate the success of the Palestinian organization – particularly the publicity the Palestinian cause garnered after Munich... This increase in activities will no doubt recur, particularly if we take into account that the New York raid was a political, economic and military disaster for the United States, ten times greater than that of the Munich operation... It will gradually give rise to an all-out struggle against the American Crusader which, if it

continues to spread, will strike at the heart of the United States.[113]

NOTES

1. That was the official end of the Ottoman Empire, when it was defeated during World War I and modern Turkey emerged, together with other independent nations which declared their independence. It has become a basic element of faith among practically all Muslim fundamentalist movements to call for the re-establishment of the universal Muslim caliphate as the panacea for the ills of Muslim countries.
2. J. Post (ed.), *The Qaeda Training Manual: Military Studies in the Jihad Against the Tyrants*, published as Vol. 14, No. 1 of *Terrorism and Political Violence*, London: Frank Cass, Spring 2002. p. 17.
3. *Al-Ayyam* ((Yemen), 8 August 1999. See *MEMRI*, No. 72, 16 October 2001.
4. *Christian Science Monitor*, 27 September 2001, ibid.
5. www.al-bab.com/yemen/hamza/hamzal/htm, ibid.
6. Ibid. That website disappeared after the 11 September disaster in New York. See *MEMRI*, ibid.
7. Ibid.
8. Ibid.
9. Ibid.
10. Ibid.
11. *Al-Ayyam* (Yemen), 11 August 1999. *MEMRI*, ibid.
12. *Al-Quds al-'Arabi* (London) 21 July 2001. *MEMRI*, ibid.
13. *The Observer* (London) 13 August 1995. *MEMRI*, No. 73, 3–4 October 2001.
14. CNSNews.com , 24 May 2000.
15. See *Middle East Intelligence Bulletin*, November 2000; Irfan Hussein, 'The Battle for Hearts and Minds', *Dawn Weekly*, 6 October 2001; and *Periscope Daily Defense News Capsules*, 4 September 1996, *MEMRI*, ibid.
16. *Le Monde*, 9 September 1998, ibid.
17. Literally catastrophe, but the term is used for the Arab defeat by Israel in the 1948 War, and has come to symbolize all the Arab defeats since.
18. *Al-Sharq al-Awsat* (London), 8 May 2002.
19. See Chapter 3.
20. *Al-Sharq al-Awsat*, 10 May 2002.
21. IRNA (Iranian News Agency), 1 May 2002.
22. *Kayhan*, 14 April 2002; IRNA, 19 April 2002; *Kayhan*, 17 April 2002, and *Al-Risala*, 11 April 2002.
23. *Al-Quds al-'Arabi* (London), 23 January 2002.
24. *Al-Quds al-'Arabi*, 7 October 2001.
25. *Al-Hayat* (London), 19 January 2002. *MEMRI*, No. 334, 23 January 2002.
26. *Akhbar-al-Yawm* ((Egypt), 29 December 2001. See *MEMRI*, No. 329, 11 January and, No. 330, 11 January 2002.
27. *Al-Raya* (Qatar), 6 January 2002; see also *Al-Sharq al-Awsat* (London), 28 September 2001 and 25 October 2001. All in *MEMRI*, No. 337, 29 January 2002.
28. *Al-Hayat* (London), 13 January, 2002.
29. Ibid.
30. Ibid.
31. Ibid
32. Fundamentalist Muslims shun the modern nation-state in favour of re-establishing the caliphate, which ought to encompass all Muslims.
33. *Al-Jazeera* television (Qatar), 17 December 2001.

34. *Al-Watan* (Saudi Arabia), 18 and 25 September 2001. See *MEMRI*, No. 294, 31 October 2001.
35. *Al-Qahira* (Egypt), 23 October 2001. *MEMRI*, ibid.
36. Ibid.
37. *Al-Sharq al-Awsat*, 25 October 2001, ibid.
38. Ibid.
39. J.-P. Peroncel-Hugoz, *The Raft of Muhammed*, New York: Paragon Press, 1988. (First appeared in French, under the title *Le Radeau de Mahomet*, Paris: Lieu Commun, 1983.
40. *Al-Sirat* (Israel), 7 November 1987. Cited in R. Israeli, *Green Crescent Over Nazareth: The Displacement of Christians by Muslims in the Holy Land*, London: Frank Cass, 2002, p. 57.
41. Ibid.
42. See R. Israeli, *Muslim Fundamentalism in Israel*, London: Brassey's, 1993, pp. 38–48 and 67.
43. *Al-Risala* (the Hamas weekly in the Palestinian Authority), 21 June 2001. *MEMRI*, No. 232, 22 June 2001.
44. *Hadith al-Madina* (Egypt), 23 April 2002, cited in *Al-Quds al-'Arabi* (London) 23 April 2002. See *MEMRI*, No. 30 April 2002.
45. *Iqra'* television (Saudi Arabia and Egypt), 24 April 2002.
46. www.ahram.org.eg/weekly, 7–13 March 2002. *MEMRI*, No. 355, 14 March 2002.
47. *Al-Riyadh* (Saudi Arabia), 27 November 2001.
48. *Al-Jazeera* (Saudi Arabia), 10 December 2001.
49. Ibid.
50. *Al-Watan* (Saudi Arabia), 10 December 2001.
51. Ibid. See also *Al-Watan*, 10 November 2001.
52. *Al-Watan*, 20 December 2001.
53. *Al-Riyad*, 2 December, 2001.
54. *Al-Watan* (Saudi Arabia), 10 November 2001.
55. *Al-Riyad*, 18 December 2001.
56. See R. Israeli, *Peace is in the Eye of the Beholder*, Berlin and New York: Mouton 1985, esp. Chapter 4.
57. *Al-Ahram*, 2 February 2002. *MEMRI*, No. 341, 5 February 2002
58. *Al-Quds al-'Arabi*, 1 February 2002. See *MEMRI*, No. 341, 5 February 2002.
59. WAFA, 17 April 2002.
60. *Al-Hayat* (London), 16 April 2002. *MEMRI*, No. 92, 26 April 2002.
61. *Al-Mustaqbal* (Lebanon), 16 April, 2002, ibid.
62. *Al-Hayat* (London), 16 April 2002.
63. *Al-Akhbar*, 18 April 2002.
64. *Al-Gumhuriyya* (Egypt), 17 April 2002.
65. *Al-Usbu'* (Egypt), 20 May 2002. *MEMRI*, No. 385, 31 May 2002.
66. www.alminbar.cc/alkhutab/khutbaa.asp?mediaURL = 5473. 1 February 2002.
67. Ibid. = 5505, 22 April 2002.
68. Ibid. = 4341. No date is mentioned.
69. *Saudi Gazette*, 8 April 2002. *MEMRI*, No. 381, 16 May 2002.
70. See n. 68 , 12 December 1999.
71. Ibid. See Sura XVII, verse 4.
72. Ibid. = 1620, 5 June 1999, *MEMRI*.
73. Ibid. = 1628, 22 May 1999; and Ibid. = 2699, 13 June 1998, *MEMRI*.
74. Ibid.
75. Ibid. 4096. No date.
76. Ibid. = 1069. No date.
77. Ibid. = 1633, 1 May 1999; and = 4461, 4 September 1999, *MEMRI*.
78. This is, in a nutshell, the essence of Muslim eschatology and the place Jesus ('*Isa* in the Qur'an) is to play at the end of time, when both Christianity and Judaism will be annihilated and Islam will emerge triumphant.
79. This is the verbatim text of the Opening Sura of the Qur'an, whose conventional interpretation refers it to Jews and Christians respectively. See Verse 7 of the Opening Sura.

80. www.alminbar.cc/alkhutab/khutba.asp?media URL = 1220. No date. *MEMRI*, Survey of Sermons, Part II (Hebrew).
81. Ibid. = 1455, 13 September 1997.
82. Ibid. = 4 141, 11 May 2001.
83. Ibid.
84. See R. Israeli, *Green Crescent over Nazareth: the Displacement of Christians by Muslims in the Holy Land*, Frank Cass, 2002.
85. Sura 112:3.
86. Ibid.
87. Ibid. = 2761, 12 September 2000.
88. Ibid. = 4068. No date.
89. Palestinian television, 22 April 2002. *MEMRI*, No. 93, 1 May 2003.
90. *Al-Quds* (Palestinian Authority), 24 April 2002, ibid.
91. *Al-Quds* 24 April 2002.
92. For details, see J.-P. Peroncel-Hugoz, *The Raft of Muhammed*.
93. *Al-Maydan* (Egypt) 22 April 2002; cited by *Al-Quds* (London), 24 April 2002. Both in *MEMRI*, No. 93, 1 May 2002.
94. *Al-Quds al-'Arabi* (London), 29 April 2002, ibid.
95. Th. Meyssan, *The Appalling Fraud*. The author was invited by the Arab League Think Tank to promote his thesis and his book in one of its prestigious forums, exactly as most Arab regimes are in the habit of inviting and promoting Sho'ah deniers, such as Roger Garaudy of France. Previously, illustrious speakers at that Centre were celebrities such as Al Gore, James Baker and Neil Bush, the US President's brother.
96. www.zccf.org.ae/LECTURES/E2_lectures/e201.htm. See *MEMRI*, No. 383, 23 May 2002. Similar reports in the Arab and Muslim press, supporting the conspiracy theory and/or attributing the misdeed to Jews/Israelis/Zionists, were already mentioned above. See also *MEMRI* Special Reports 6 and 270.
97. *Saudi Gazette*, 10 April 2002. See *MEMRI*, No. 383, 23 May 2002.
98. *Khaleej Times*, 9 April 2002, ibid.
99. *Ridda* is apostasy and punishable by death in Islam.
100. www.lailatalqadr.com, the website of Al-Azhar University, the heart of the Muslim establishment in the Arab world, citing Sheikh Abu al-Hassan, the Head of Al-Azhar's Religious Ruling (fatwa) Department, 11 October 2001. *MEMRI*, No. 296, 2 November 2001.
101. Ibid., 18 October 2001.
102. Ibid., 15 October 2001.
103. Ibid., 22 October 2001.
104. Ibid., 11 October, 2001.
105. *Al-Sha'b* (Egypt), 23 September 2001. *MEMRI*, No. 280, 3 October 2001.
106. *Al-Risala* (Palestinian Authority), 1 November 2001. *MEMRI*, No. 297, 6 November 2001.
107. *Al-Liwa* (Lebanon), 21 February 2002. See also Margaret Wente, 'Atrocities in Guantanamo and other Fruit Loops Tales', in *Globe and Mail* (Toronto), 22 January 2002.
108. *Al-Risala* (Palestinian Authority), 13 September 2001.
109. *Al-Ahram* and *Al-Akhbar* (Egypt), 16–19 October 2001. *MEMRI*, No. 292, 26 October 2001.
110. *Al-Hayat* (London) , 19 March 2002. *MEMRI*, No. 359, 25 March 2002.
111. *Al Quds al-'Arabi* (London), 7 December 2001. *MEMRI*, No. 312, 2001.
112. Reference is made to the Munich Olympic games of 1972, when a gang of Palestinian terrorists murdered many of the participating Israeli athletes and sowed terror and panic in the Olympic camp. See, for details, John Cooley, *Black September: the Story of the Palestinian Arabs*, London: Frank Cass.
113. *Al-Ansar* (online publication), 27 February 2002. *MEMRI*, No. 353, 12 March 2002.

8. The Jews, Zionism and Israel:
An Evil Unto Itself

One would have expected that Israel, a tiny country compared to the vast power of the West, would not have attracted so much scorn, drawn so much hatred and carried so much weight in the Muslim fundamentalist discourse, almost equal to the satanic West. Many explanations are possible, notably that Israel is not only considered part and parcel of that hated Western world, but in some ways its vanguard and a dagger in the heart of the Muslim world. Secondly, unlike other Western countries which are remote, to which one is not obliged to travel, and whose ways one is not obliged to emulate, Israel's proximity forces the Muslims, especially those directly involved in the Arab–Israeli dispute, to face her on an almost daily basis, interact with her, respond to her challenges and take cognizance of her. True, the West is present everywhere in the Muslim world, in one way or another, but its presence as a guest or a partner can be ejected physically and rejected spiritually, while Israel's presence is political, permanent, independent and sovereign. Thirdly, the State of Israel is the state of the Jews and of the Zionists and therefore cannot be better than the sum total of its components; and since the Jews are looked down upon by Arabs, and Zionism is considered evil and racist, there is an incentive for the Muslims to eradicate it. Finally, there is pure resentment born out of jealousy: the startling success of the Jewish State is a thorn in the side for the Muslim environment, for not only did it succeed in acting against the expected stereotypical image of the 'cowardly and wretched' Jew, but in doing so it exposed the helplessness, hopelessness and backwardness of the Muslim world.

THE DEEPLY INGRAINED ANTI-JEWISH SENTIMENT

The sources of anti-Jewish, anti-Israeli and anti-Zionist sentiment in the Muslim world have been dealt with extensively in many scholarly writings.[1] Here, suffice it to recapitulate the main layers of this attitude: firstly, the deeply ingrained negative stereotypes of Jews in the Muslim sources, those labelled 'descendants of dwarfs and monkeys' both in the Holy Qur'an itself, which sometimes lumps together the Scriptuary Peoples, namely Christians and Jews, and sometimes singles out the Jews, and in Hadith literature, where vast portions are devoted to the denigration of the Jews. Secondly, the Christian anti-Semitic themes of the Blood Libel, the Protocols of the Elders of Zion and the world Jewish conspiracy were imported, lock stock and barrel, by Christian Arabs in the nineteenth century, into the already existing vast arsenal of anti-Jewish recriminations and grievances against the Jews. Thirdly, when Zionism heralded the return of Jews to their homes in Palestine, the Arab and Muslim resistance to that idea wove together all these anti-Jewish and anti-Zionist stereotypes into a powerful fabric of political and military opposition. And when the State of Israel was founded in 1948, and the fears of the Arabs and the Muslims became a reality, new waves of anti-Semitism, this time translated into anti-Zionism and anti-Israelism, erupted, following the fortunes of the Arab–Israeli conflict. Every time the dispute rose to new summits, for example, after the Palestinian Intifadah and the 11 September horrors, the Arabs and Muslims lashed out mercilessly at the Jews, Israel and Zionism, while during the rare periods of tranquility and conciliation, those eruptions were likely to subside. This chapter will deal almost exclusively with the events following 11 September.

In an article published in the establishment *al-Ahram*, an enlightened Coptic scholar, Dr Babawi, lambasted the US Congress for not stopping 'Israel's artillery attacks on the Nativity and Al-Aqsa mosque', and urged American Muslims and Copts to demonstrate against 'madman Sharon, who began to behave like a madman after he was hit in his sensitive place by a bullet during the 1948 War, which left him with only one testicle', something which has affected him psychologically, and he has become a 'crazy psychopath using power to hide his weak point'.[2] The Bishop of the Assyrian Church in Lebanon said that although the leaders of the Christian world today are not Jewish, they are led by Jews, whose faith is the 'enemy of God, of the people and of Christianity'. He cites Jesus as having said to the Jews: 'You are the sons of Satan, and you do the will of your father Satan', to which they answered 'No, we are not the sons of Satan, we are the sons of Abraham.' He replied: 'Had you been the sons of Abraham you would be acting in accordance with the acts and precepts of Abraham. Therefore, you are the sons of Satan.'[3] This deep hatred for the Jews, coming from Christian Arabs who ought logically to have common cause against the overwhelming majority of the Muslims in the East, defies logic and is often exploited by Muslim fundamentalists and others to prove the universal disgust for the Jews. Many of the anti-Jewish stereotypes among the Muslims are imported from Western Christianity, while others are Muslim-made, but they liberally borrow from each other, through the intermediary of the Eastern Christians in the Arab world who master both cultures and traditions, including anti-Semitism, and who have not been reformed by the recent far-reaching concessions made to Judaism by the Catholic Church. Moreover, during the Aqsa Intifadah, which has pushed to the forefront of Palestinian existence the Islamikaze martyrs, some Christians found a similarity between them and Christ's martyrdom. A few quotes from Christian–Arab clerics and intellectuals will illustrate these points:

> We kneel before the Palestinian people in the Nativity. He starves and thirsts, but he is steadfast. These words were not born in a vacuum. The one who said 'I am hungry' when he was on the Cross was our Lord Jesus himself…Our Palestinian people in Bethlehem died like a crucified martyr, on the rock guarded by the Israeli soldiers armed from head to toe who have no compassion, love, life or tolerance…The Jew has a principle from which we suffer and which he tries to impose on people: the principle of the Gentiles. To him, the Gentile is a slave. They give the Palestinians working in Israel only a piece of bread, and tell them: 'This piece of bread that you eat is taken from our children, and we give it to you so you will live as free men in your land, but as a proletariat and slave in Israel, to serve us.' The Protocols of the Elders of Zion are based on this principle, and anyone who reads the Protocols feels that we are in this period with the Jews…
>
> The Church, the Pope, the Christians and the New Testament clearly state that, according to Christian belief, the ones who killed Jesus are the Jews, and there is no way to deny or renounce this…The Jews are the ones who killed Jesus; after him they killed the Christians, and after them the Muslims. Now they are again killing both Muslims and Christians. Throughout history we have seen that the Jews

persecuted the Christians at the beginning of the Church, and now again, they are persecuting the Church, and Islam ... As is known throughout the world, even in our time, they always accuse the Christians ... The case of Pope Pie XII is bad enough. They accuse him of terrible things ... They attack the Church because the Pope was not as strict as they wanted in protecting Jews from Nazism – while the Jews found shelter only in the Church and with Christian families.[4]

Jews have been inextricably linked to the Christians in Muslim imagery, in the depiction of the two faiths that are, in Muslim eyes, inimical to Islam and seeking its destruction. Therefore, as we have seen above, whether it is an attack against the West, or accusing the West of acts of barbarism and the like, Jews and Christians are lumped together, since they share that same verse in the Opening Sura of the Holy Qur'an.[5] The same senior psychiatrist, Dr Adel Sadeq, cited above, who attacked President Bush and 'Western ignorance' of the Arab and Muslim psyche, reserves an even harsher scenario for Israel, a totalistic and politicidal[6] war to the finish that knows no concession or compromise and which, if heeded, should signal the escalation of the Arab–Israeli dispute. His message is chilling:

The message to Israel is that we will not cease ... It is very important to convey this message ... The child who threw a stone in 1993 today wraps himself in an explosive belt. Some Israeli politicians take this into account, and say to themselves: 'This was will never end.' As long as there is a single Palestinian left, the war will not end ... What is happening now indicates one thing: Israel will not exist for ever. We as Arabs must know that this war will not end. The conflict will continue. This conflict is not over land alone ... This war will not end, and anyone who deludes himself that there will be peace must understand that Israel did not come to this region to love the Arabs or to normalize relations with them. Anyone who thinks that peace will come, either now or in the future, has limited historical vision. Either we will exist or we will not exist. Either the Israelis or the Palestinians – there is no third option ...

There are no Israeli civilians. They are all plunderers. History teaches this. I am completely convinced that the psychological effect [of the Islamikaze] on the Israeli usurper will be his realizing that his existence is temporary...They have become completely convinced that their existence in the region is temporary...Remove the Apache from the equation, leave them one on one with the Palestinian people with the only weapon being dynamite, then you will see all the Israelis leave, because among them there is not even one Israeli man willing to don a belt of dynamite...

On the strategic level, there must be a pan-Arab plan to reach our goal. The goal of all of us is to liberate Palestine from the Israeli aggressors. To use words that some people no longer like to use today: 'We will throw Israel into the sea.' There is no middle ground. Co-existence is total nonsense... The real means of dealing with Israel directly is those who blow themselves up. According to what I see in the battle arena, there is no other way by the pure, noble Palestinian bodies. This is the only Arab weapon there is, and anyone who says otherwise is a conspirator. I regret having to use these terms, but Arab politicians and journalists who condemn this *fida'i* movement are trying to impose such ideas on us to appease the West...The Palestinian body is the only means in this battle.[7]

If this is what an educated scientist has in store for Israel, and what the television serving Egypt and Saudi Arabia, the supposedly 'moderate' and 'peaceful' countries, has to say, then one wonders whether any accommodation is possible between the parties, or whether the identification of the Jews and Israel as a permanent enemy of the Arabs and Muslims is something immutable that makes them the strategic target whatever the circumstances. We shall see in the following pages that not only is Israel identified as an enemy, but also Jews and Zionism. The vilification of all three, and the total rejection of any amicable settlement with any of them, are what makes them intractable in the eyes of the Arabs and Muslims. Moreover, Israel is conceived as the long arm of the West in the midst of the Arab and Muslim worlds, in order to facilitate their demise, and world Jewry, by means of the world Zionist movement, as the predominant satanic power which reaches its tentacles to all corridors of political and economic power so as to undermine Western societies from within and take over the world.[8] As such, they have to be fought first, and put, as they indeed are, at the forefront and top priority of the Muslim struggle against the West. Heads of the Islamist movement, and certainly the Islamikaze groups, from Bin-Laden's al-Qa'ida to Sheikh Yassin of the Hamas, from Sheikh Tantawi of the al-Azhar to the field operatives in the name of Allah all over the globe, have subscribed to this doctrine and are pursuing it to the best of their ability.

Once again, Saudi Arabia and Egypt, the supposed mainstays of moderation, pro-Western partnership and sources 'of peace initiatives' in the Middle East, are also the most venomous sources of not only anti-American pronouncements, but also of blatant anti-Semitism. Once again, these are not occasional and sparsely spread preachings by obscurantist fanatics, or frustrated and deprived individuals, but the systematic teachings crystallized by politicians clerics, professionals, intellectuals, opposition diehards and strategists, who shape public opinion, and are in turn shaped by it. How much more so in the Muslim fundamentalist writings, some of which we have perused before, and which in themselves have an impact on non-Muslim writings in this regard. At the heart of the Egyptian establishment and consensus, for example, is the weekly *October* – founded and directed by one of the most notorious anti-Semites in the Arab world, and a close associate of President Anwar Sadat: the Christian, Anis Mansur[9] – which published the following opinions on Jews by a retired general, Hassan Sweilem. This is straight from the platform of the Hamas and the Protocols of the Elders of Zion:

> Throughout history, since Emperor Justinian and down to Hitler, Europe's rulers had been trying to rid themselves of the acts of violence, barbarism, corruption, conflict mongering, and other deeds that Jews were, and are still, in the custom of performing in European societies... like, for example, their domination of monetary systems, treasuries, banks and commercial monopolies, which has caused widespread bankruptcy and economic destruction. They also diffuse drugs, prostitution, trade of women as sexual slaves, and alcohol. They have also monopolized the gold and precious stone trade, paid bribes to rulers and extorted them throughout history...
>
> The Jews stood behind wars and internal strife, and that caused European rulers to expel them and kill them. For example, the Crusader armies, passing along the Rhine basin on their way east, massacred them and burned their houses as

an act of repentance to their God. When the Crusaders entered Jerusalem, they collected the Jews in a synagogue and burned them alive. Their kin in Russia suffered a similar fate... They were expelled from France, England, Germany, Hungary, Belgium, Slovakia, Austria, Holland and finally from Spain, after they underwent the Inquisition trials for their conspiracy to penetrate Christian society like a Trojan horse... The Jewish conspiracy to take over Europe generated civil revolutions, wars and internal strife... The Cromwell revolution failed in 1649 England, following the Jewish conspiracy to drag England into several wars in Europe... Then the French Revolution broke out, which the Jews had planned, based on the first conference of their rabbis and interest-loaners that had been convened by the first Rothschild in 1773 in order to take over all the world resources... That 'conference' adopted 24 Protocols, among which was the 'uprooting of the belief in God from the hearts of the Gentiles, distracting peoples by distributing among them literature of heresy and impurity, destruction of the family and the eradication of all morality'.[10]

And so on and so forth *ad nauseam*, evincing the primitive, delusive and bigoted minds of the writers and of those who facilitated or allowed those utterings to gain 'respectability' by being published in a truly respectable magazine. The Jews were 'credited' in that article with putting Napoleon on the throne and then of causing his demise, of the 1775 war between England and the nascent United States of America, of establishing the Bank of America in 1881 with a view to controlling the wealth of the fledgling United States, and then of kindling the fire of the American Civil War. He told the story of how the Protocols were written by a 'German rabbi in 1770, financed by Rothschild', again in order to 'destroy all governments and religions, spread anarchy and revolutions, kindle wars, take over the wealth of nations, spread corruption among the youth, and control rulers by implanting in their governments Jewish ministers and advisers'. This sick mind goes on: the Jews ordered the start of World War I, and got the United States involved by spreading the rumour that an American ship had been sunk by the Germans. During that war, they prepared the ground for the rise of both communism and Nazism, as a follow-up to the work done by the Jews, Marx and Engels, half a century earlier, when they circulated the

Communist Manifesto in London. Eventually, communism and Nazism took over power and came to confront each other, 'exactly as the Jews had planned'. World War II erupted due to the limitations imposed by the Allies on Germany in Versailles, by order of the Jews, thus inciting the Germans to revolution and bringing about the rise of Hitler. The Jews also brought about the fall of the Ottoman Empire and they were to reap the fruit thereof by concentrating all wealth in their hands.[11]

The Jewish conspiracy was not the only irrational narrative that the writer was deluded enough to believe. He also found that the very roots of Zionism went back to that plot, as the Jews had already tried to build a settlement in Suez in 1903. Even Chaim Weizmann's credit for having extracted the Balfour Declaration from the British in 1917 due to his contribution as a chemist to the British war effort, the author attributes to 'secrets that Weizmann had stolen from Russian scientists'. The Europeans let the Jews go to Palestine, not because they had sympathy for them, but in order to 'rid themselves of the Jewish cancer that threatened to choke them on all sides', for they could not find any other country to absorb the 'poisoned human garbage called the Jews'. Thus, Britain permitted the Jews to take over Palestinian lands by facilitating their attacks on Palestinians and by letting Jewish gangs receive weapons from Europe. It was the Jews who spread false rumours about Germany's defeat in World War I and ruined the German economy, spread anarchy in Germany by introducing communism, and even tried to murder Bismarck. Hitler wanted to collaborate with the British in thwarting the Jewish menace in Europe, but they outsmarted him when they appointed their agent, Winston Churchill, as the British Prime Minister. He even tells us that Hitler set up a special research institute to study the 'roots of Jewish corruption and rot', and how they could be cured of that disease so as to arrest their menace to humanity. But when he gave up on remedying their incurable diseases, he began to restrict and neutralize them.[12]

Nor does this extraordinary material, which also included the claim that the Jews caused the economic crisis of the great depression in order to pave the way for World War II,[13] fall on deaf ears in Egypt, where it is cultivated in a horrendously assiduous and repetitive fashion. It is replicated and repeated as mantras of conventional wisdom and documented history, and almost no decent intellectual, researcher, scientist, let alone politician or cleric, ever dare contradict or question the validity, rationale, veracity and authenticity of its details. Forged citations, made-up 'facts', fake sources, trumped-up accusations and all manner of calumniations, which in civilized countries result in prosecution and prison sentences, are current in the Muslim world, and not only among the fundamentalists. This is not only a matter of re-inventing history as a propaganda tool, but its propagators begin to believe in their own inventions, and others, who stand in awe before the military, religious or political authority of the fakers, copy from them without criticism and spread their venom worldwide. For example, the calumniations we have just seen were concocted in Christian Europe over the centuries, then imported to the Middle East by Christian Arabs who wished to raise their stature in the eyes of their fellow Arabs, then copied by Muslim Brothers such as Sayyid Qut'b,[14] then adopted, almost verbatim, by the Hamas Charter, which was published in early 1988,[15] until they became common knowledge that needs neither corroboration nor reference. This is the reason that so many distorted, fanatical and obscure minds emerge in the Arab and Muslim world, where almost no one is interested in facts, and where young children are educated to believe in those fallacies. The innocent, misguided and ignorant common people, who have no way to know, and are imbued, generation after generation, by this culture of lies and hatred, grow up, naturally, steeped in it and unlikely to be convinced otherwise. They make the human raw material for the Islamikaze.

Saudi clerics, who usually deride Arab nationalism and pan-Arabism, insist that there is no way to defeat the 'monkeys and pigs', that is, the Jews, unless they embrace the road of jihad. They say that as long as the Palestinians and other Arabs fight for their fields and orchards, namely their material belongings and false nationalism, they will not achieve much, and therefore they ought to go back to their Islamic faith and fight in its name. They counsel their audiences to learn from the ways of the Jews:

> They [the Arabs] are not prepared to confront the people of the Bible, the people of Israel, with an Islamic battle. While the Jews are escaping to their religion and find in it a source of unity and force, those [Arabs] are running away from their Islam... The Jews had fought continuously against our Prophet Muhammed... does anyone imagine that they would yield to people who still fight for their watermelons, land, mountains, wells, olive trees and orange groves?[16] We have to

cluster around those who are talking about the Islamization of the conflict...If we said that the problem is Arab, there are among them Christians, Unbelievers and Socialists. What do all these have to do with Al-Aqsa Mosque?[17]

We have to realize that our defeats by the Jews are due to the fact that we did not let the Islamic *umma* confront them...These were defeats of Arab regimes which did not wave the banner of Islam...Should our lost [sons] revert to the truth, then the Jews shall return to their wretchedness and humiliation that they were condemned to [by the Holy Book]. Then, nothing can rescue the Jews, when the ignorant wake up, they will never see victory as long as they profess mistaken notions, heretic curricula, and humiliating peace.[18]

The decisive solution of the conflict must be through Intifadah and jihad for Allah, not for Arab nationalism or for the Arab Homeland. The Islamic *umma* knows that that the Holy Land will not be resolved by...negotiating at the table with the Unbelievers. The only solution is to emulate the example of the Prophet in what he did to the Jews when they violated the agreements. The only solution lay with the words of the Prophet to the Jews: 'I brought slaughter upon you.' The solution with them is not peace and harmony, for jihad, not peace is the solution...It is secularism that surrendered to Judaism and Christianity, threw away its weapons and retreated, not Islam. For Islam has not been defeated by Judaism and Christianity in the ideological campaign that it has been prevented from engaging.[19]

The Islamic *umma* is sitting with its enemy to discuss peace, agreements and treaties...The Jews themselves do not forget their hatreds, and they are spreading around their lie about the Holocaust and claim that Hitler killed 6 million Jews in gas chambers. In spite of the fact that this is a pure lie, they turned it into an essential part of their pains and propagate it through their powerful propaganda machine so as to blackmail the nations of the world. They received huge compensations from the Germans, and now accuse all the Holocaust deniers as anti-Semites and incite the world against them...Jews have always bitten all the hands that were extended to them in peace, they have always violated all the agreements they signed, they betrayed the Prophet, they betrayed the Ottoman Empire and caused its demise, they violated all their contemporary treaties, from Oslo to Sharm al-Sheikh.[20]

One is then puzzled and circumspect when Saudis propose peace to the Jews through the international media, while in the thick of their mosques and in their press they promote jihad, politicide, massacres and genocide against them, using the precedent of their Prophet, and vilify them to a degree that even should they change their mind, they would have a very difficult time in convincing their citizenry, which has been systematically exposed to this venom, to suddenly alter course. Because as they see it, it is untenable that a 'handful of monkeys and pigs should torture 1 billion Muslims; therefore, there is no escaping jihad and education to jihad'.[21] One of the mosque preachers concluded in no uncertain terms that:

> This matter is historical, legal and ideological. It is impossible to make peace with the Jews under any circumstances, and no alliance or treaty can be signed with them, in spite of those among us who believe otherwise... and who are themselves Jewish like the Jews. We cannot hide from Jewish evil or wickedness. They are impure creatures and satanic scum. They are the helpers of Satan, and, together with other Unbelievers and polytheists, the true reason for the misfortunes of humanity. Satan will lead them to Hell and to their unfortunate end. Jews are our enemies and hatred towards them dwells in our heart. Jihad against them is our ritual... Muslims must educate their children to jihad. This is the benefit we can draw from this situation: educate our children to jihad and hatred towards the Jews, the Christians and the Unbelievers, and the kindling of the spirit of jihad in their souls. This is what we need now.[22]

Incidentally, those preachers of peace-loving Saudi Arabia urge their people to cultivate courage in their children by telling them the stories of Muslim war heroes, including children who followed their fathers to the battlefields and 'finished off the wounded enemies, and that is a proof of their courage'.[23] This is not education to terror, insist those preachers, because this is only the Qur'anic 'intimidation', which is permitted by Islamic law against hypocrites, seculars and rebels, and cannot be considered an aggression or injustice towards anyone, and is solely intended to 'elevate the Word of Allah and spread His religion'. In other words, anything sanctioned by the Qur'an is *ipso facto* 'kosher' and cannot be disputed or challenged on human, legal or moral grounds. Just use the right word, 'intimidation' instead of 'terror', and you have made it into the fold of the human race. The preacher clarifies this point:

> What they call 'terror' in the media, is in fact jihad in the path of Allah. Jihad is the apogee of Islam, and some jurists regard it as the sixth Pillar of the faith.[24] Jihad, whether it is invoked for protecting the lands of Islam such as Chechnya, the Philippines and Afghanistan, or for propagating the Faith, constitutes 'terror' for the enemies of Allah. While the *mujtahid*, sets out to gain martyrdom, or to achieve victory and bring back spoils of war, for the enemies of Allah he is a terrorist... Therefore, the Faithful must not use this term, for otherwise Allah's anger might be upon him on the Day of Judgement... Jihad is part of our faith, and the word 'terror' is only used to de-legitimize this blessed and powerful element of our faith...
>
> The use of the term 'terror' [by the Unbelievers] is also calculated to discredit the important principle of '*al-wala' wal-bara'* by which is meant support for other Believers, be they Arabs or otherwise. For there is no difference for us between an Arab or non-Arab Believer, and the non-Arab Believer is preferable to a corrupt Arab. People must know that they owe loyalty to other Believers, and hostility to the Infidels who are the enemies of Allah. We love whom Allah loves and hate whom Allah hates. Muslim blood is safeguarded, because Muslim blood is superior to the Infidel's blood. It is forbidden to kill a Muslim for a prize... These are some expressions of our principles, which are considered as terror by the Westerners.[25]

And how does one determine those whom Allah hates? Of course the Qur'an, which is the word of God, and other sources of the faith, such as the Sunna of the Prophet, are the sole and ultimate guide. Thus, the Jews (and the Christians for that matter) who are labelled as enemies of Allah cannot extricate themselves from that sealed fate, unless they embrace Islam, and until then jihad must be waged against them by 'intimidation', never mind that others see that as 'terror'. At any rate, that act is considered a legal, even compulsory, jihad, which by definition leads to martyrdom, and is in any case the quintessence of Islam, in the eyes of the Saudi (and other) fundamentalists. The only remaining question, once the enemies of Allah have been identified, is how and to what extent to discredit and vilify those enemies of Allah so as to make them a legitimate target for the Believers. In this regard, a mix of secular, historical, 'logical', religious, analogical, or simple outbursts of atavistic and unexplained hatred are mobilized from the vast arsenal of Arab and Islamic anti-Semitism to crystallize such a despicable picture of the Jews, Zionists and Israel as to make them 'attractive', indeed irresistible, targets for the Muslim fundamentalist wrath and ingrained desire for vengeance. It suffices to follow the outpouring of rage by millions of Muslim demonstrators in the streets of all Arab and Western capitals following the eruption of the Intifadah of 2000, with the attendant burning of Israeli flags and local Jewish synagogues, the abuses hurled at Israel, Jews and Zionists during those violent demonstrations and on the hundreds of Muslim internet sites, and the utter disrespect they evince towards Jewish values and Holy Places, to realize the depth of that hatred, which culminated in Durban during the summer of 2001.

ENCOURAGING ANTI-SEMITISM

The most immediate concern of Muslims around the world after 11 September was how to absolve themselves of the accusations pointed at them, arising from the fact that the much publicized horrors were all linked to an Islamic act of terror, masterminded and performed by Muslims, mainly Saudis and Egyptians, who paradoxically benefited from US generosity more than others. One of the ways to do that was to build, as is their wont, a plausible conspiracy theory which can be appended to the well-known world Jewish conspiracy. Therefore, on the morrow of those attacks, 'explanations' started burgeoning throughout the Muslim world, suggesting that Jews stood to 'gain' the most from that attack, and therefore it could arguably be imputed to Jews, Zionists, the Israeli Mossad and so forth, producing as 'proof' the assumption that most workers at the Twin Towers who were Jewish absented themselves from work on that day. This theory, which gained wide currency in the Arab and Muslim world, was upheld by the prisoner Yassin, who had been arrested in the United States following the first attempt against the Trade Center in 1993, and then released to go back to his sponsors in Baghdad. In an interview aired on US television in early June 2001, Yassin, who was interviewed in his Iraqi jail, recounted quite candidly and as a matter of course that his gang had first planned to hit the Jewish neighbourhoods of Crown Heights and Williamsburg in Brooklyn, and then shifted their attention to the Twin Towers when they 'realized' that those were 'better' targets.[26]

As far as one can gauge from the state of mind of those mentally disturbed sub-humans, it was not only their inexplicable, and inconceivable to any civilized person, yearning to kill as many Jews as possible – something that they have been practicing as a serial orgy of murder against Israelis day in, day out – that was at stake, but also their eagerness to promote anti-Semitism by 'showing' that it was unsafe to befriend Jews, live in their neighbourhoods or work in their company. In other words, by demonstrating that Jews in general were a liability, dangerous and to be avoided, enough local anti-Semites in the United States and elsewhere would appear to make them also dispensable and disposable. This also accords with the conventional wisdom in the United States which claims that Jewish immigrants to the United States have succeeded in integrating into, and in turn contributing to, US society at large, and their success, which has been translated into their advantageous political, economic, intellectual and cultural status, has attracted much hatred, born out of jealousy, from other less fortunate immigrant minorities, notably Arabs, Muslims and Blacks. Incidentally, well before 11 September, and in connection with the exportation of the Palestinian Intifadah, following October 2000, to all Arab and Muslim communities in the Western democracies, hundreds of acts of intimidation, abuse, attacks, arson and destruction have been launched by those communities against the older and most established Jewish congregations in their localities. Though those attacks spanned the entire world, from Australia to Lithuania, and from South Africa to Canada and the United States, they were particularly vicious in France, Britain and Germany, and were calculated as much to discredit Israel as to threaten local Jews in those countries.

An Israeli journalist who was out to interview the imam of the Shihab-a Din Mosque in Nazareth, which has raised a controversy in its own 'right',[27] encountered a rather militant stance on his part

in the aftermath of 11 September, despite the fact that he grew up in
Israel, knew the Jews well, and nevertheless was swept, like his
peers in many parts of the world, by the magic of the conspiracy
that was essentially anti-Semitic, but lumped together all the
enemies of Islam: domestic, Western and Israelis:

> You Westerners do not understand anything. Those people [in
> Afghanistan] want to be *shahids*, and even if they are faced by
> a tank or an aeroplane, they are stronger because there is
> nothing in the world stronger than a *shahid* who is not afraid
> to die ... There are many ethnic groups in the United States ...
> Why did you blame only the Muslims? Aren't there Japanese,
> Chinese, Blacks, Jews? Tell me, aren't there any Jews? [The
> moment Jews were mentioned, says the interviewer, the
> surrounding group of Muslims lit up. They nodded fervently
> as if they had reavealed a secret that they kept deep inside].
> Why haven't they blamed it on the Jews?
>
> I will tell you why. Four thousand Jews did not go to work
> that day, and do you think this was a coincidence? The Jews
> want the Americans to do the killing, because you [the Jews]
> want them to be your stick against the Muslims ... [one
> participant shouted] Bush and Hitler are the same
> thing! ... You can write that, but do not mention my name!!!
>
> In America itself, many groups want to topple the regime,
> because it is in the hands of the Jews ... The world is facing a
> situation that will divide people into two camps: one that
> wants Islam and the other who doesn't, the good are those
> who seek justice and mercy, the believers in Islam ... Islam will
> defeat its opponents. There is no point to the life of anyone
> who will not convert to Islam ... Islam is the greatest gift that
> Allah has given to men. The Prophet came into the world to
> complete the work of Moses and Jesus, and his coming
> presaged the end of the role of the other religions. Thus,
> anyone who does not board the train of Islam is in serious
> trouble and anyone who wants to be secure in his life, and also
> after his death, must convert to Islam. In the end, there will be
> only one religion left – Islam ...
>
> But before Islam succeeds and conquers the world, the
> Americans and Israelis will do all they can to spoil the
> celebration ... Before Islam spreads its wings over the earth, the
> Muslims will rise up in their own countries ... and depose their

> corrupt leaders...who are fated to disperse to the four winds
> like desert dust...and put an end to their submissiveness to
> their American overlord.[28]

What is rather shocking is the fact that after 11 September and
the accusations hurled in the United States at the Arabs in general,
the Saudis in particular, for the overwhelming part of their
nationals in the horror, Saudi spokesmen and media, while
attempting to mitigate Western furor against them, at the same time
stepped up their campaigns of hatred against Jews and Israel, as if
purposely avoiding American wrath by shifting and channelling
their unrelenting hostility towards the Zionist target which could
not retaliate. Typical to these reactions is a dissertation of bigotry,
shamelessly titled 'The Culture of Hatred', that appeared in the
official *al-Riyadh*:

> When a particular culture is characterized by negative traits
> such as aggression, piracy, racism, or any other repulsive term,
> it must be hated by the other societies, except for those
> societies that share the very same traits. This is a natural
> reaction...On the other hand, when the hatred takes root in a
> particular society towards another society or nation [that is,
> Western 'hatred' for the nation of Islam] for its beliefs, for its
> way of life, or because it cannot come to terms with particular
> traditions and customs – this cannot be accepted!
>
> For example, one cannot be amazed by the hatred of most of
> the nations of the world for the 'Zionist entity', because of its
> history, replete not with human achievements but with
> barbaric massacres, deceit and evil conscience. Hatred
> towards them is on the rise among the Arabs in particular
> because of what they suffer from the occupation of the Arab
> state of Palestine, the catastrophes, the cruelty and the
> injustice that are known to all. For this reason, Arab infants,
> before they reach the age of self-humiliation and submission,
> suckled hatred of the Zionist enemy with their mothers' milk,
> and this hatred cannot be uprooted despite the talk about false
> peace agreements...However warm the kisses, however firm
> the handshakes, their hearts are full of hatred, their souls are
> full of rage, and their eyes glance away with loathing at the
> sight of the flag of the Zionist enemy flying in the heart of
> Arab capitals...

Men of honour want to rip up the flag, to dirty it on the ground. They want to expel these foreigners [Israelis and Jews] who came to our land, so that our Palestinian brothers will live on their land in peace and security...I am in no way preaching hatred or praising it as a way of human behaviour. But the hated individual or society must examine themselves so as to understand why it is this way, since no society or individual can be hated in such a way for no reason...I will give you an example of how hatred for the Zionist entity takes root in the soul of the Arabs...I once attended an international conference on road accidents in the military, held in Paris. With me was my colleague...whose mood changed when he was informed that a man who stood next to us...was a transportation officer of the detested Zionist entity...My colleague raged, swearing that he would not stand next to this criminal, talk with him or enter the hall in which he was sitting...He did not calm down until I swore to him that I did not know the citizenship of that man, because he was in the company of officers from all over the world, and I myself was incapable of standing next to someone whose hands were dripping with the blood of innocent Arabs...

These are our enemies, and our hatred towards them is rooted in our souls, and the only thing that can remove it is their departure from our lands and the purification of their defilement of our Holy Places.[29]

These repulsive statements of hatred towards Jews not only are not much different from classic and millennial European anti-Semitism, but they also use, in addition to the Muslim rationale that we have examined above, the perennial themes borrowed from the West, like the Protocols of the Elders of Zion, the Blood Libel, the Jewish conspiracy, and, more recently, following the trend, Jewish terrorism as incorporated in the Jewish State. It might seem paradoxical that the hatred of Jews, so disgustingly and unabashedly expressed in Arab and Muslim media, is but an expression of 'hesperophobia', that is, fear, and then hate, of anything Western,[30] and Israel is considered essentially Western. The paradox lies in the Arabs/Muslims borrowing the vocabulary of European prejudice against the Jews at a time when they wish to attack not only the Jews or Israel but also the West in general. The leading government newspaper in Egypt, and most prestigious daily in the Arab world, *al-Ahram*, integrated all these themes in an article prior to 11 September, under the telling title 'Israel: The Plague of our Time and a Terrorist State', lumping together Jews, Zionists and Israel into a fabric of complaints, fears, biases, prejudice, bigotry and plain, uncontrollable hatred:

> What do the Jews want? Read the Ninth Protocol of the Elders of Zion. It says 'We have limitless ambitions, inexhaustible greed, merciless vengeance, and hatred beyond imagination. We are a secret army whose plans are impossible to understand using honest methods. Cunning is our approach, mystery is our way. The way of the Free Masons, in which we believe, cannot be understood by those among the Gentiles who are stupid pigs... In order to destroy the Gentiles' industry, we create scalping and raise the prices of basic commodities and raw materials. We control the stock market, distribute drugs, and create chaos among the blue-collar workers. We persecute any wisdom among Gentiles... We spread disputes, conflicts and hatred between peoples by using harmless organizations such as the Rotary and Lyons Clubs and the Jehovah's Witnesses. We seek out and feel what is going on in other people's minds and hearts... We are not talking about harmless organizations here, but about channels of tracking and watchful eyes in every town. The blind public does not notice our methods since they are too busy indulging in their pleasures and lusts...'.
>
> The ultimate goal of the Free Masons is to destroy the world and build it anew according to Zionist policy so that the Jews can control the world... and destroy other religions. Their goal is that there won't be any other religion but the religion of Moses, no other law but that of Moses, and no other book except for the Torah... The eye at the head of the pyramid displayed on the American dollar is the sleepless eye of the Free Masons. On the other side of the dollar it is written in Latin 'The new world order', which translates to globalization and its disasters. It seems like all of their plans are coming to realization. They have fulfilled what they were planning for a long time...
>
> For them, all people are beasts and cattle created for them to ride and govern. These are the Gentiles, riff-raff which God has created for them so they could lead them, exploit them and suck their blood. The destruction of the Church, the

destruction of the Aqsa Mosque, the destruction of the Dome of the Rock, the destruction of the Church of the Holy Sepulchre, are all part of their goals and dreams. The Jewish Karl Marx, using his communism and Marxism...actually destroyed the Church in Eastern Europe...

In the Talmud, the soul of the Jew is considered as part of the spirit of God, as the son is part of his father. Every soul that is not Jewish is an evil soul...Their Paradise is this world's paradise and no one but the Jews should enter its gates. As for the rest of the people, their place is in Hell somewhere between the tar and the fire. The property of the Christians is considered by the Jews as theirs or like property without owners. It is permissible for the Jew to deceive the Gentile who is a non-Jew...Despite the fact that the Torah contains a thousand pages, it makes no mention of resurrection, Judgement Day or the hereafter...The Jews erased from their Bible anything that has to do with the Hereafter and turned this world into everything they care about...

The same forgery happened with Zionist history regarding Jerusalem, which is presented as the eternal capital of the Jews...and this is despite the fact that Jerusalem, Urshalim, is the ancient name of al-Quds, which is a Palestinian Cana'anite name. King Solomon is the one who had ownership over Jerusalem in order to destroy his rivals, and he is the one who built the [Jewish] Temple...

The Kings of Israel and Judea never displayed any kind of reverence for the Jewish Temple in their internal strifes. Furthermore, they plundered it during every invasion or retreat. Moses died without setting his foot on the land of Palestine, the land around which the Zionist dream revolves...

Israel today is composed of 13 million Ashkenazi Jews who came from Germany, and Sephardi Jews who came from Spain and Eastern Europe [*sic*], and they are in fact more European, Slavic or Aryan than Semites. Their ethnic affinity is completely disconnected from the Torah–Semitic origin they claim to be part of...they are vestiges of peoples and nations who have no identity but that of blackmail, theft and robbery of property and land, with the help of overwhelming American support and suspicious European silence...

Islam is not the problem...Israel is, because she is radical, racist, follows religious blindness and is the plague of our time and a terrorist state...The dilemma is now to be or not to be, there is no middle ground; either death or life with all the risks involved. Allah wishes for this clash to happen, as nothing in this world happens without his knowledge or will...I tell our Arab brothers: death is inevitable, don't die dishonourably... Servants of Allah, hurry up and fulfil your duty...Disgrace will not add a single day to your lives, while courage will not take away a single moment from them. The end is eternal life in Heaven or in Hell. There is no middle ground.[31]

The abysmal ignorance of the writer, in this most prestigious of the Arab papers, without anyone in the editorial office to correct the basic facts about Israel's population and its composition, and the chilling repetition of the Protocols of the Sages of Zion, that Russian forgery of the turn of the twentieth century that was brought to trial in the West on three occasions and failed to stand any test of authenticity, is an insult to the readership of that otherwise highly regarded medium. But that is, unfortunately, what the readers of the Arabic press are fed, day in day out, in the service of discrediting the Jews and increasing anti-Semitism. Moreover, the trumped-up 'citations' from the Talmud, that no one took the trouble to verify, are often repeated and perpetuated as 'genuine', resulting in 'educating' the young Arab generation to intellectual dishonesty and irrational hatred; worse, it blunts scientific curiosity, rigorous methodology and research pursuits that are undiluted by fantasy and wishful thinking. But apparently, Jew- and Israel-bashing are more important than truth, and vindictiveness and humiliation of the enemy more expedient than fact, history, reality and soul-searching.

The most efficient tool at the hands of Arab anti-Semites to ally to them the Christian world is still the Blood Libel, which in its crude version accuses Jews of spilling Christian blood on the eve of the Jewish Passover for the manufacture of the Matza bread. In its derivative versions, Jews are also accused of poisoning wells, spreading the plague, and in more modern terms, of using depleted uranium against the Palestinians, of distributing poisoned sweets to, or injecting HIV-positive virus into, Palestinian children, or of diffusing an aphrodisiac chewing gum to arouse the sexual appetites of Muslim women in order to corrupt them. While the Blood Libel has virtually disappeared in the Christian establishment of the Western world, it is still being cultivated in Arab and Islamic circles and is often sponsored by the governments in place, who in any case do nothing to eradicate it.

The civilized world was shocked when a Saudi 'scholar', Dr Umayma al-Jalahma, of King Faysal University in Dammam, purported to write about the Jewish holiday of Purim, which is based on the Book of Esther in the Bible, with delirious detail that only a mentally sick and unbelievably cruel person could produce, and which is probably unsurpassed in the millennial annals of the Blood Libel against Jews. The great 'innovation' is that the classic Blood Libel, which is usually connected with Passover, was now switched to Purim, and that the new 'revelation' was published in the Saudi government Daily, *Al-Riyadh*.[32] In the author's words:

> I chose to speak about the Jewish Holiday of Purim, because it is connected to the month of March. This holiday has some dangerous customs that will, no doubt, horrify you, and I apologize if any reader is harmed because of this...During this holiday, the Jew must prepare very special pastries, the filling of which is not only costly and rare – it cannot be found at all on international markets. Unfortunately, this filling cannot be left out, or substituted with any alternative serving the same purpose. For this holiday, the Jewish people must obtain human blood so that their clerics can prepare the holiday pastries. In other words, the practice cannot be carried out as required if human blood is not spilled...
>
> Before I go into details, I would like to clarify that the Jews' spilling human blood to prepare pastry for their holidays is a well-established fact, historically and legally, all throughout history. This was one of the main reasons for the persecution and exile that were their lot in Europe and Asia at various times. This Holiday of Purim begins with a fast, on 13 March, like the Jewess Esther who vowed to fast. The holiday continues on 14 March, during which the Jews wear carnival-style masks and costumes and over-indulge in drinking alcohol, prostitution and adultery. This holiday has become known among Muslim historians as the Holiday of Masks...
>
> Who was Esther and why the Jews sanctify her and act as she did, I will clarify in my next article...Today I would like to tell you how human blood is spilled so that it can be used for their pastries...For this holiday, the victim must be a

mature adolescent who is, of course, a non-Jew, namely a Muslim or a Christian. His blood is taken and dried into granules. The cleric blends these granules into the pastry dough, they can also be saved for the next holiday. In contrast, for the Passover slaughtering, about which I intend to write later... the blood of Christian and Muslim children under the age of 10 must be used, and the cleric can mix the blood into the dough before or after dehydration...

Let us now examine how the victim's blood is spilled. For this, a needle-studded barrel is used. This is a kind of barrel, about the size of the human body, with extremely sharp needles set in on all sides, which pierce the human body from the moment he is placed in the barrel... These needles do the job, and the victim's blood drips from him very slowly. Thus, the victim suffers dreadful torment – torment that affords the Jewish vampires great delight as they carefully monitor every detail of the blood-shedding with a pleasure and love that are difficult to comprehend...

After this barbaric display, the Jews take the spilled blood in the bottle set in the bottom, and the Jewish cleric makes his co-religionists completely happy on their holiday when he serves them the pastries in which human blood is mixed... There is another way to spill the bood: the victim can be slaughtered like a sheep, and his blood collected in a container. Or, the victim's veins can be slit in different places, letting his blood drain from his body. The blood is very carefully collected by the rabbi, the chef who specializes in preparing this kind of pastry. The human race refuses even to look at the Jewish pastries, let alone prepare them and consume them.[33]

That article was retracted by the editor following a worldwide outcry and the US protests which resulted, but the fact remains that it was published, with 'precise' and sickening detail that adds to its credibility in the eyes of the uninformed, and it would certainly not have been retracted had it not been for the protest. Moreover, the dangerous trend of hatred that the author exhibited when addressing her avid readers points to the receivability of her messages and perhaps to the 'academic' garbage she imparts to her university students. The anger it caused has generated the breaking of the thermometer, but the fever was not removed, if one is to judge by the vast quantity and variety of the materials included in this book, and that author's demand in another article that was not retracted, based on the founding fathers of the United States, Washington and Franklin, that the United States should expel its Jews.[34] However, the most notorious (due to the identity of its author) case of Blood Libel, which has become *cause célèbre* among the Arabs, is the oft-quoted book by Syrian Defence Minister, Mustafa T'las, published first in 1983 and then as a more 'scientific' 'doctoral dissertation' in 1986. Both versions were based on the 1840 Damascus Blood Libel, when the Jewish community was accused of having murdered a Christian priest, Thomas al-Kabushi, and his aide, for the purpose of preparing Yom Kippur pastries. Apart from the pathetic ignorance of the writer, who does not know that on Yom Kippur the Jews fast, and therefore could not eat pastry, or that the original Blood Libel was connected with the unleavened Matza bread which the Jews eat solely on Passover, or that the Jews go to great lengths to avoid eating blood of any sort as part of their meticulous dietary laws, the T'las account is horrendous in itself. This was not the first time that Arabic papers invoked the Blood Libel – Egyptian mainstream dailies had done so before – [35] but T'las' vitriol, from such a high official who would not dare publish without the approval of his President, another notorious, virulent anti-Semite, not only serves as a back-up to European anti-Semites who avidly use his garbage for their own propaganda,[36] but establishes a model for other Arab Jew-haters to follow.

In the new 1986 version, the photograph of the murdered priest is reproduced, with the inscription 'Murdered by the Jews'. On the jackets of both versions the mind-boggling picture of a person is represented with his throat cut and the running blood being collected in a large bowl. In the first edition, it is a gang of Jews who commit the murder, while in the later version, a Jewish Menorah performs the throat cutting itself. This 'scientific study' links this horrible 'crime by the Jews' to the 'directives of the Jewish religion' without specifying any reference, as 'laid out in the Talmud', without saying where, but concludes that 'these directives encompass destructive distortions emanating from the fervent hatred of the Jews towards humanity and all religions without exception'. The book then describes all the network of worldwide pressures and briberies effected by influential Jews of that time, such as Moses Montefiore, in order to gain the release of the 'culprits'. T'las' introduction to the latest version of his book, written by the perpetrator of the Hama Massacre (1982), when 20,000 Muslim Brothers of his countrymen were slaughtered by the armed forces that he commanded, ended on the gloomy note of that inhuman butcher:

> The event of 1840 was repeated time and again in the twentieth century, when the Zionists committed horrendous crimes in Palestine and Lebanon, which have shaken decent people everywhere. But every time the media, political and financial influence of the Zionists succeeded in mitigating that anger and distracting public opinion away from those crimes. And instead of punishment, they got rewarded by huge amounts of financial aid and vast arsenals of frightening armaments...
>
> The murder [of Father Thomas] had happened in Damascus, the city of tolerance and peace, exactly as other crimes had occurred in other places around the world. How could that happen at a time when the Jews constitute a minuscule minority in the midst of the societies where they live? How could those societies ignore that hatred-laden minority?... It is possible that the atmosphere of tolerance that was ushered in by the Muslim Arabs was what had allowed the Jews to live in total freedom in Muslim Arab countries. The Jews know those countries very well, but they surrounded themselves with mystery so that the Muslims knew nothing about them. No wonder, then, that Damascus was thoroughly shaken by that harrowing crime, but it soon learned the truth about them. Every mother would thenceforth warn her children: 'Beware not to wander far away from the house, lest the Jew would seize you, put you in his bag, slaughter you and collect your blood for the *Matza of Zion* [the title of T'las' book].' Generation after generation they bequeathed that warning regarding the 'treacherous Jews'.
>
> In the meantime a state was created for the Jews in al-Sham,[37] but Jewish hatred did not disappear, and the rules of the Talmud, with their sanctioning of all manner of distortions and crimes, continue to govern their hatred-laden attitude towards humanity... Anyone who follows daily events in the Occupied Territories understands beyond any doubt that what is termed as 'Zionist racism is nothing but the contininuous and 'improved' implementation of the Talmudic tenets... In publishing this book it was my intention to throw some light on some secrets of the Jewish religion, by describing their

deeds, their blind and repulsive fanaticism towards their faith and the implementation of the Talmudic teachings, which had been written by their Diaspora Rabbis and in so doing they have distorted the tenets of their own faith, namely Mosaic Law, as certified in the Baqra Sura of the Qur'an, verse 79.[38]

Aside from the Blood Libel, the Protocols of the Elders of Zion, which will be discussed in more detail below, are the most 'popular' hoax which took root among the Arabs and Muslims, exactly as it had taken root in European anti-Semitism in the twentieth century. Many Arab writers, including 'intellectuals' and 'scientists', in their primitive attempts to justify their hatred of Israel and the Jews, using anything that comes their way without criticism, examination or test of logic, refer to the Protocols as a fact of history and make extensive use of them. The period of Ramadan, a month of fasting and spiritual reckoning, is also one of intellectual output, geared to satisfy the masses of Muslims that gather in their families for physical and spiritual self-denial and abstention during the day, and collective orgies of food and entertainment after the sun sets. In those family gatherings after the fast, new television series are aired, which capture the attention of the populace. In series of that sort, inaugurated in the past, one created in the Gulf States vilified Prime Minister Sharon in person when showing him drinking Arab blood, in line with the Blood Libel. The Ramadan after 11 September, which occurred in December 2001, was the propitious occasion for Arab television stations, including in 'moderate' Egypt, to launch the 'Horseman Without a Horse', a horrendous anti-Semitic series based on the Protocols, which was described thus by the popular weekly *Roz al-Youssuf*:

> For the first time, the series' writer courageously tackles the 24 Protocols of the Elders of Zion, revealing them and clarifying that they are the central line that still, to this very day, dominates Israel's policy, political aspirations, and racism... The series' first scene is set in 1948, after the retreat of the four Arab armies and the Zionist invasion of the land of Palestine. From this point, there is a flashback to the mid-nineteenth century... The idea of exposing the Protocols in a drama series took shape in the director's mind as a result of two events: the first was the London Convention [*sic*] that he considered the greatest single calamity ever to affect the Arab region. That

convention, he claimed, was the work of three Zionist rabbis, promoters of the Zionist idea, who concocted an elaborate plot according to which Palestine would be annexed to Egypt, and Britain would subsequently conquer Egypt and hand Palestine over to the Zionists... This is, he said, what sparked his desire to investigate the Zionist idea, which existed years before the London Convention, but emerged only at the first Zionist Congress in Basel, Switzerland, at which the Jews began to appear as the Zionist organization; previously, they had been active only in associations and large institutions throughout the world...

The second reason was a book by Egyptian writer al-'Aqqad on the Zionist movement, where he claimed that in order to examine whether the Protocols were an invention as the Jews claimed, one had to trace the implementation of the 24 Protocols. Thus, if we find that some of them have come to pass, we must expect the rest also to be valid. The director of the series followed that advice and found that 19 of the 24 Protocols had already been put into practice... The director said that by means of the series he was able to expose all the 24 Protocols that have been implemented to date, in a dramatic, comic, historic, national, tragic and romantic manner... Here are some quotes from the Protocols, which were implemented: 'We will act to establish a state to be a superpower that will rule the world, we will damage its morality with pornography, prostitution and drugs, and we will corrupt the world of the Gentiles.' 'We must choose someone corrupt [to head that state], and when he resists us we will expose him.' The director noted in this context that we should remember what happened to President Clinton and to other Presidents throughout history...

The series will also reveal 'advice', reportedly taken from the Protocols, such as 'Feed a dog, but not a Muslim or a Christian', and 'Kill a Muslim or a Christian and take his house as your house and his land as your land'. The director also raised questions such as 'How can a country like America collaborate with the Jews when it is familiar with the Protocols' directives against it?'[39]

These fantasies and their like, when they are concocted by a stupid individual or a racist bigot, would be set aside with a condescending smile for the distorted mind which created them. But when brought together by an artist, whose methods of investigation are questionable, who yields to injurious and groundless stereotypes against his fellow men under the guise of artistry, and who diffuses his utter nonsense to millions of watchers who assume that their respectable director did the necessary historical investigations to uphold what he claims as history, and all that is praised in the mainstream press of the major Arab country which made peace with Israel, one wonders whether all participants in that farce are out of their minds, lack basic intelligence and sense of criticism, or are so blinded by their hatred that they take the book of one of their anti-Semitic writers as gospel and base on it a scandalous series that UNESCO should be the first to come out and condemn. Probably it is a mixture of all that, which casts doubts on the solidity of historical research in general in that culture of lies and fantasies that no one dares to come out against. It also poses a big question mark over the ability of those societies, where wishful thinking overrides fact, and where a television series which purports to 'clarify' and 'teach' in fact adds to the blindness and bigotry of its audience, to pull their people out of their obscurantism into the modern and real world.

ENCOURAGING VIOLENCE AGAINST JEWS AND ISRAEL

While we have seen, above, the extent and the depth of the Muslim clerics' and columnists' commitment to, and support of, Islamikaze attacks against the West, or the 'enemies of Allah' in general, and analysed in detail the Palestinian *modus operandi* against Israel, it would be instructive here to focus on the anti-Jewish motivations that make the Islamikaze tick and their supporters act. A Palestinian woman, for example, who was interviewed about her son who went on an Islamikaze mission, besides repeating the requisite mantra of the religious obligation to sacrifice oneself in jihad, for the sake of Allah, and her duty to encourage him, as she did with her other sons, on this endeavour since he was seven years of age, unabashedly admitted that when he set out for his operation, she prayed Allah to 'give her', namely that her son would kill ten Israelis, and Allah 'granted her request' when her son 'realized his dream and murdered ten Israeli soldiers and settlers'. She added chillingly that 'Allah honoured him even more, in that there were many more Israelis wounded', and that when she heard of it she began to cry in joy: 'Allah is the greatest!', and she prayed and thanked Allah 'for the success of the operation'. She also said that young people began to fire guns into the air out of joy over that success, because 'this is what we had hoped for'. She concluded her harrowing interview by stating that:

> After the Martyrdom operation, my heart was peaceful for Muhammed. I encouraged all my sons to die a martyr's death, and I wish this often for myself. After all this I prepared myself to receive the body of my son, the pure *shahid*, in order to look upon him one last time and accept the well-wishers who came to us in large numbers and participated in our joy over Muhammed's martyrdom.[40]

Similarly, after the horrendous Islamikaze attack on the discotheque in Tel Aviv in June 2001, where 21 teenagers perished, the family of the perpetrator went into a public orgy of joy and celebration that was so callous that the foreign journalist who covered it was dumbfounded. He reported that the neighbours hung on trees pictures of the dead terrorist holding seven sticks of dynamite, spray-painted graffiti on their walls reading '21 [Israelis killed] and counting', and arranged flowers in the shapes of hearts and bombs to display on their front doors. That meant that jubilation was more or less universal, not only the martyr's family feast. 'I am very proud of what my son did and, frankly, a bit envious', the 54-year-old father of the terrorist declared to the press. 'I wish I had done the bombing, my son has fulfilled the Prophet's wishes. He has become a hero. Tell me, what more could a father want?' The goal of those killers, as gauged in the many interviews that the correspondent of *USA Today*, Jack Kelly, carried out, was 'to kill and injure as many Jews as possible, in the hope that Israel will withdraw from the West Bank and Gaza'. By doing that, they were 'promised financial stability for their families, eternal martyrdom and unlimited sex in the after-life', and even if they cannot attain their goal, the casualties they inflict on Israel are sufficient justification for their ordeal.[41] The journalist saw Hamas kindergartens sporting signs 'The Children of the Kindergartens are the *Shahids* of Tomorrow', and he was assured by a senior Hamas leader in the West Bank that when he walked the streets of his community, young children went to him and begged him to 'conduct another bombing to make us happy!' 'I cannot disappoint them', retorted the sheikh, 'they won't have to wait for long.' That group claimed, during the months preceding 11 September, that tens of thousands of youth were ready to follow in the footsteps of the martyrs and become martyrs themselves. 'We like to grow them', said the sheikh, 'from kindergarten to universities.'[42]

In that culture of death, the US reporter saw signs, at both the Najah University in Nablus and the Islamic University in Gaza, declaring that 'Israel has nuclear bombs, we have human bombs'. An 11-year-old student in Gaza was so determined to kill that he declared to the reporter: 'I will make my body a bomb that will blast the flesh of the Zionists, the sons of pigs and monkeys, I will tear their bodies into small pieces and cause them more pain than they will ever know.' In response, his classmates chanted in unison 'Allah Akbar!!!' ('Allah is the Greatest' – the war cry of the Muslims). The class teacher cried out in return: 'May the virgins give you pleasure!!!' The school principal, who was present, smiled and nodded his approval.[43] Certainly, this deeply ingrained faith in martyrdom, which begins at kindergarten and prepares the candidate to act when he reaches adulthood or even adolescence, goes a long way to dismissing the economic rationale for this kind of murderous operation, since a child is certainly not aware of his poverty when he is poor, nor of the opportunities that await or do not await him when he grows up. To impute these horrendous acts to economic reasons is not only false factually, but is condescending inasmuch as it suggests that for a passing economic or financial bounty one would give up eternal life and bliss in the hereafter. That is the reason why pious Muslims without criminal records are recruited for the Islamikaze self-sacrifice, and are then reminded during their training and indoctrination of Israel's 'illegal occupation', 'harsh treatment of the Palestinians' and the 'Prophet's call for Muslims to wage jihad against the Infidels'. The sheikh cited approvingly: 'Kill the Idolaters wherever you find them!!!'[44]

In return for martyrdom, Hamas tells the youths that their families would be financially compensated, their pictures would be posted in schools and mosques, and they will earn a special place in Heaven. As part of the heavenly regime, the youth are promised unlimited sex with 72 virgins, who are described in the Qur'an as 'beautiful like rubies, with complexions like diamonds and pearls', and the 'martyrs and the virgins shall delight themselves, lying on green cushions and beautiful carpets'. There is enough to kindle the imagination of any sexually deprived youth in a reputedly puritanical society which shuns and condemns pre-marital sex. And yet, the youth has to perform the supreme act of self-sacrifice to get there, inspired by his burning belief that he will. In other words, religious fervour, doctrinal motivation, fame, social and family approval and the promises of the afterlife are the name of the game, not economic expediency or feelings of vengeance, which are merely auxiliary and may help the hesitant to walk the extra inch and make the fateful decision of martyrdom. A Hamas youth leader, himself merely 16, confided to the US reporter: 'I know my life is poor compared to Europe or America, but I have something awaiting me that will make all my suffering worthwhile. Most boys cannot stop thinking about the virgins',[45] and there is no doubt that some sex-maniacs may be mainly lured by those prospects, but there is also no doubt that the absolute devotion to God that is instilled in the trainees for Islamikaze, the promise to live thereafter in the close vicinity of Allah as martyrs and their desire to leave in their wake as many dead Jews as they possibly can, take precedence over the sexual lust involved, though the latter cannot be totally dismissed. The obstacle of fear, not of death but of losing one's life, is partly overcome when the recruit is taken to a cemetery where he is told to prepare himself by lying between graves for hours, wearing a white hooded shroud that is normally used to cover bodies for burial. Then the recruit is taken to a safe house where a video is made where he states his consent to become a martyr out of his devotion to Islam, and a photograph is also prepared to be reproduced for distribution throughout the land.[46]

Islamikaze bombings have been the Palestinians' weapon of choice, and they had staged over 100 of them by June 2002, resulting (together with shooting incidents since October 2000) in the death of over 500 Israelis (compared with 1,500 among the Palestinians), 75 per cent of whom were civilians (compared with 45 per cent among the Palestinians) and 30 per cent women (only 5 per cent in the Palestinian camp). On the Israeli side, many young people, women and elderly people were murdered because discotheques, restaurants, buses and cafes were targeted where these groups of civilian non-combatants tend to cluster, while the many Palestinian children hit were either armed, or sent on Islamikaze missions, or otherwise engaged in combat zones instead of being kept at schools or at home, and were therefore incidentally, never purposely, injured or killed. Moreover, to increase the impact among the non-combatants, nails and bolts are included in the bombs. In one case, a woman who was hit at the Passover Seder in Netanya (27 March 2002), which resulted in 29 dead and 140 injured civilians, had 40 nails in her legs and arms which caused her extensive bleeding and concussion, and might have caused her death had they been lodged in her skull or any of her internal organs.[47]

An Egyptian columnist, as another example of encouraging violence against Israel, followed and preceded by many others, specifically urged the Islamikaze to step up their operations against the Jews, and called upon volunteers to join them. His imagination is gruesome in its detail and inhumanity:

> With every blow struck by Al-Aqsa Intifadah, my conviction grows stronger that I, and all those who are of the same mind, have been right all along, and I am still right in my belief that the despised racist Jewish entity will be annihilated. Contrary to others, however, I am not ashamed to speak about driving them into the sea, to hell or to the trash heap they deserve...I maintain, and Allah is my witness, that the annihilation and defeat of the Israelis, after which they will not rise up again, does not require all these things. All that it requires is to concentrate on acts of martyrdom, or what is known as the 'strategy of the balance of fear'...
>
> Let us do some mathematical calculations: 250 Palestinians have signed up for martyrdom operations, and it is not impossible to raise this number to 1,000 throughout the Arab world...that is, one *fida'i* out of every 250,000 Arabs. The average harvest of each act of martyrdom is 10 dead and 50 wounded. Thus, 1,000 acts of martyrdom would leave the Zionists with at least 10,000 dead and 50,000 wounded. This is double the number of Israeli casualties in all their wars with the Arabs since 1948 [*sic*].[48] They cannot bear this. There is also the added advantage, not noted by many, of the negative Jewish emigration, which, as a result of the 1,000 martyrdom operations, will come to at least 1 million Jews, followed by the return of every Jew to the place whence he came...
>
> I am signing myself up as the first martyr from Egypt and declare that I am ready to commit an act of martyrdom at any moment. I will place myself under the command of Mr Hassan Nasrallah [Head of Hizbullah], the Hamas, Islamic Jihad or

any other jihad movement...Never in my life have I asked Allah for money, honour or power. All I have asked, all I ask, all that I will ask, is that Allah allow me to become a *shahid* and grant me the honour of reaping as great a harvest as possible of Israeli lives.[49]

If these words of encouragement for Palestinian violence against Israel are expressed in Egypt, how much more so when we look at the hub of Muslim terrorism and violence – Iran. It turns out that representatives of the Islamic Jihad, the Hamas and the Palestinian Authority met in Iran to ask for financial support for their campaign of violence against Israel, and that the Iranian leadership promised them funds to 'cover the expenses of recruiting young Palestinians for suicide operations'. In this context, the Islamic Jihad was assured by the Iranians that its own operational budget would no longer depend on, or be channelled through, Hizbullah in Lebanon, but would be independent.[50] The Islamic Jihad leader, who denied in public any patronage of Iran over his organization, nevertheless threatened both Israel and the United States of his imminent Islamikaze acts, while Hizbullah television repeatedly makes references to Khomeini's speeches to justify its animosity against Israel and to rationalize the need to annihilate it:

If America is the one to divide the world into the camps of good and evil, and if it puts the Palestinian people and its jihad fighters on the evil side, claiming that the martyrs are evil, then we say: 'Allah, make us all evil, make us all anger America and blow up in the heart of this cursed Zionist entity'...America, the West and any country of the world, has no moral right to decide whether a Palestinian has the right to blow himself up...or not. Why isn't America objecting when someone American or European contributes millions of dollars for cats or dogs? We are the owners of our souls...No one has the right to object to us giving away our souls and turning them into human bombs for a cause we consider more important and more sacred than our lives...[51]

All of Palestine is plundered. There is no difference between the 1948 [lost] territories and the 1967 ones. I ask the Muslims, why are you fighting over the River Jordan when all Palestine is plundered?...Israel's danger is not limited to Palestine...It spreads to the whole region. Imam Khomeini said: 'The goal of this virus [Israel] that was planted in the heart of the Islamic world, is not only to annihilate the Arab nation... The danger is to the whole Middle East... and the solution is in annihilating the virus. There is no other treatment... The Islamic states and the Muslims should initiate the annihilation of this den of corruption [Israel] in every possible way. It is permitted to use charity money for that purpose'. Imam Khomeini led the way... President Khatami upholds the same position despite international pressures...

The struggle against Israel is no picnic. It demands great sacrifices, and when I see a mother saying goodbye to her son, awaiting his return as a *shahid*, I know that the Palestinian people is a people of jihad warriors and it will surely win... We have to maintain the Iranian–Syrian–Lebanese–Palestinian axis... Our enemy cannot counter us when we are united.[52]

In other publications, the entire Muslim *umma* is called upon to unite in order to face the combined US and Israeli threat, which Iran terms 'state terrorism' against the pure souls of Muslims. The Arabs are urged not to accept any European or US mediation in the Middle East, because 'they are all Zionists', but at the end, exactly as the Crusaders had been extirpated from the land after their 88-year occupation of Jerusalem, the Jews would also have to go before that long. The Iranian writer calls upon the Muslim world to aid the Palestinians with arms and armies and to revive the spirit of jihad.[53] These statements are not only emitted by Muslim extremists, but by mainstream Muslims almost everywhere, in total disregard of, and in stark contradiction to, the repeated Qur'anic injunctions, namely the very word of Allah himself, calling 'His people', the Children of Israel, to 'Enter the Holy Land which Allah hath assigned unto you'.[54] Then, 'We settled the Children of Israel in a beautiful dwelling place, and provided for them sustenance of the best',[55] and 'Dwell securely in the Land of Promise'.[56] All those divine appeals notwithstanding, Muslim fundamentalists encourage the use of violence against Jews and Israelis in order to evict them from the Land of Israel. Muslim Brothers, who are prohibited in Egypt from political activity, mounted a chilling 'exhibit' at Al-Azhar University in Cairo amidst their student demonstration of support for the Palestinians, where they presented to the public eight members of their *Tanzim al-*

istishhadiyyin (the Organization of the Martyrs– Islamikaze) who are trained for martyrdom actions inside Israel. Sheikh Yassin, the Head of the Hamas, delivered a cellular-phone speech to the crowd of 1,000 Muslim students from his home in Gaza, while the eight masked men, who placed black cloth over their heads and wore red stripes around their foreheads with the inscription: 'Jihad is our Path', were demonstrating their fighting skills. After the half-hour performance, under the supervision of the police, who surrounded the campus precisely in order to prevent such events, the would-be martyrs removed their disguise and melted into the crowds to avoid arrest. One of them was interviewed by the correspondent of *al-Mustaqbal*, the Lebanese daily that is owned by Prime Minister al-Hariri, and he vowed to 'surrender his soul for the cause of the Muslim Palestinian people'. He said that his group's training and indoctrination are all directed against the Israeli enemy, and reiterated his support for the Fat'h organization of the PLO, the Hamas and Islamic Jihad.[57]

A Saudi columnist reproduced a disturbing 'discussion' he had with a friend, following a sermon he heard from his preacher in the mosque, advocating the killing and annihilation of Christians and Jews alike, making their children orphans and their wives widows. Here are excerpts of that dialogue, as reconstituted by the columnist who was opposed to those horrendous propositions, but found it nevertheless necessary to inform his readers of the controversy. One may only conjecture how many more dialogues or debates of that sort go on in Islamic societies unreported; worse, who knows how many sermons of incitement against Jews and Christians go unopposed or undebated? One may even suspect that if that dialogue never took place, it was used as a heuristic device by the author to raise that issue, which must have been on his and others' minds:

A. [those words of incitement] amount to heresy...
B. So you support [Christians and Jews?]. If so, the words of Allah apply to you which say 'Whoever supports them – belongs to them'.
A. The Prophet did not call for the annihilation of the People of the Book, but for their righteous behaviour. He urged us to hold a dialogue with them.
B. But the People of the Book of our day are not the People of the Book of the time of the Prophet. Those of our day have

associated other Gods with Allah [the Christians who believe in the Holy Trinity], and have introduced into their religion things that Allah has not commanded [the Jews who have introduced precepts not acceptable to Muslims]. In addition they fought us and drove us out of our homes.

A. But they were like that in the days of the Prophet too…Despite that, he called for dialogue with them… Christians and Jews are our guests and are protected by the pacts we give them to protect their safety. The Prophet's recommendation to his army was not to kill their infants, old men and women, or priests in their place of solitude, or uproot their trees or dry their wells.

B. But civilians in Western societies pay taxes which support the policies of their governments against the Muslims.

A. Nobody can avoid taxes, even not the Muslims living in those societies.

B. The Prophet had decreed one month for the annihilation of the Infidels of the Quraysh, because they captured and tortured some Muslims.

A. That was a limited response to a specific act, as 'no blame attaches to those who exact due retribution after they have been wronged'.

B. Had the Christians and Jews not been impure, then Allah would not have ordered them driven out of the Arabian Peninsula. 'Umar ibn al-Khattab carried that order out when he drove the Jews out of Khaybar.

A. Then why didn't the Prophet drive them out of Yemen and Najran too? The Prophet waged war against the Jews and drove them out from Medina to Khaybar. They persisted in their enemity towards the Muslims who could not feel safe with them. Reason dictated that they be driven out of fortified Khaybar to Tabuk, which is still in Arabia…The Prophet died as his shield was guarded by a Jew…The Prophet visited a Jew who was on his deathbed and called on him to convert to Islam…He finally died as a Muslim…This could not have happened unless the relations with the other parties were humane and neutral. Therefore, a preacher with a heart full of animosity towards the believers of other religions cannot persuade them that Islam is a religion of mercy and tolerance… Allah, do not punish us for the deeds of these idiots.[58]

Under the title 'Allah, Annihilate the Jews!!!', another Saudi columnist seems to rather agree with the preacher whom the previous author sees as a fool. Dr al-Nahari, and his colleague, Abdallah al-Ka'id, did not mince their words:

> Since I learned about America and Israel...I have been imploring Allah [during] every Friday [prayer], to annihilate the Jews, who have sown corruption on earth, as well as anyone who supports them, including, of course, their foremost supporter – America...Since the appearance of conflict in Islamdom, we urge Allah to support our Muslim brethren – in Palestine, Afghanistan, Chechnya and the Balkans. Before that, we urged Allah to support the Muslims in Somalia and in Bosnia...On all occasions we prayed to Allah to return Al-Aqsa to the Muslims, and to shudder the earth under the feet of the Jewish usurpers who have killed the old, children and women...but every time the tyranny of the Jews has prevailed and they have continued to kill mercilessly... Not because they are Israel, but because America is there, who voices slogans of human rights but at the same time provides Israel with weapons, ammunition and money in order to kill Palestinians...I have often asked myself why Allah does not respond to our prayers, and the answer is that we have committed the sin of betrayal and killing of other Muslims, something that Allah has rightly prohibited. We plot against each other and collaborate with the enemies of Islam in order to harm Muslims and their countries.[59]

> One should not wonder why most people of the world hate the Zionist entity, due to its history that is replete not with human achievements, but with barbarous massacres, deception and evil...For that reason, Arab babies have absorbed that hatred with the milk of their mothers, and that hatred cannot be removed in spite of those fake peace treaties...Our hearts are full of hatred, our souls with wrath, and our eyes are repulsed by the sight of the Zionist flag which is hoisted in some Arab countries...Men of honour want to tear those flags apart and soil them with dust. They want to oust those aliens who came to our lands, so that our Palestinian brethren can live in peace like all others...These are our enemies, and our hatred towards them is so deeply

rooted that the only thing that can remove it is that they evacuate our land and the Holy Places be purified from their scum. Is there anyone who can reproach us for our hatred of the Zionist usurpers and their supporters?[60]

The Arab strategy of incitement to violence, and of continuous and relentless violence against Israel, was chosen as a strategy to drain little Israel's limited resources and manpower and force her into submission. Some of them can already see the fruit of their strategy looming on the horizon. Faruq Qaddumi, the 'Foreign Minister' of the PLO, who did not accept Oslo and remained in Tunis, made such predictions from the safety of his exile:

> Sharon is the last bullet in the Israeli gun. If he is defeated, the countdown will begin for the end of Israel, because that state was established through coercion historically, and will come to its end as the USSR and Yugoslavia have...The Palestinian resistance will continue, but we have to ensure not to hurt Palestinian security and to reduce our casualties... Resistance is not a conventional war. It is based on surprise in time and place. In this war we need to incite the public 20 hours [a day] and fight perhaps for two hours. [Hamas and Islamic Jihad] have suspended their activities for a while, because guerilla warfare is like trade: as Mao Zi-dong has said, 'We deal when it is profitable, but we suspend trade when we lose'...We have condemned the terror [of 11 September] against America, but those events constituted a lesson to the Americans. This is the first time that Arab names have become familiar to Americans, and have caused them to reconsider their policies and examine the true reasons of terror.[61]

VILIFYING THE JEWS, ISRAEL AND ZIONISTS

Knowing the particular sensitivity of the Jewish people to Hitler and his Nazi regime, Arabs and Muslims often turn the victims of Nazism, that is, the Jews, into Nazis themselves, and their leaders into replicas of Hitler. Suffice it to scan through the platform of the Hamas and writings by many fundamentalist and non-fundamentalist Muslims to realize the recurrence of this comparison, which is clearly calculated not only to discredit Israel by vilifying it, but also by warning the West, especially the United States, who 'condones Israel's acts', to steer clear of the new 'Nazi' country. Under the heading 'Hitler of the Year 2002', for example, a columnist in the respectable *al-Hayat* lambasted Sharon as Hitler, and Israel's actions in the Palestinian territories as 'Nazism'. In order not to sound like a promoter of hyperbole, the author produces 'proof', a figment of his imagination, to 'corroborate' his 'findings'. He assures his readers that Israel has 'revived concentration camps like Hitler's', 'assassinated Arafat's guards after they were captured' and 'imposed a terrorist conquest upon the Palestinian people'. He implied that, just like the Nazis, the Israelis set buildings of innocent civilians alight, deprived citizens of water and electricity. Thus, he said, when 'American stupidity converges with Israeli barbarism, the world has to beware of a new Nazi Hitlerism'.[62] In a slightly different vein, a venomous female columnist from Egypt made an appeal to Hitler, the 'Brother who had done it':

> They [the Jews] are accursed in Heaven and on Earth. They are accursed from the day they were created and their mothers bore them. They are accursed because they killed the Prophets: they murdered the Prophet John the Baptist... Allah also cursed them because they argued with and resisted his words of truth, deceived the Prophet Moses and worshipped a calf they created... These accursed people are a catastrophe for the human race. They are the virus doomed to a life of humiliation and wretchedness until the Day of Judgement. They are accursed because they repeatedly tried to kill the Prophet Muhammed... they tried to mix poison in his food, but Providence saved him from their crimes... Allah cursed them because they carried out the crime against peaceful Palestinians in Sabra and Shatilla...
>
> They are accursed, they, their fathers and their forefathers... because they burst into the Al-Aqsa mosque with their defiled filthy feet and violated its sanctity. They are accursed because they are the plague of the human race of all times. Their history was always stained with treachery and lying. Historical documents prove it... Thus the Jews are accursed, the Jews of our time, those who preceded them and come after them, if any Jews come after them... Since their birth, the Jews have amassed hatred and hostility towards Islam... They have always laid traps for the Muslims, woven crimes and

conspiracies against them and are biased in favour of their enemies and occupiers... They always try to warp and distort everything fair and beautiful. Basically, they are bathing in moral ugliness, debasement and degradation. If only Allah could curse them more, to the end of all generations! Amen.[63]

Al-Jazeera television, perhaps the most attentive Arab network to burning issues of interest to Arabs and Muslims in general, initiated a debate, in May 2001, entitled 'Is Zionism Worse than Nazism?', in itself injurious to Jews and Israel. The talk-show, which presumptuously labelled itself 'scientific', was hosted by Dr al-Qassem and Dr Hayat 'Atiya, a self-styled 'researcher' on Zionism and a follower of the notorious French Sho'a denier, Roger Garaudy, who also translated his vicious book into Arabic. The debate was aired as a result of the anti-Semitic vitriol of President Assad of Syria on the one hand, and the manifesto signed by 14 Arab intellectuals denouncing the planned international conference of deniers of the Holocaust in Beirut, on the other. The liberal and courageous Tunisian intellectual, 'Afif al-Akhdar, balanced out the venomous 'Atiya. All participants certainly understood that the very positing of the opening question, which compared Zionism to Nazism, had no other purpose than to libel Israel, but no one opposed it. All of them were aware that the 1975 UN Resolution that had dubbed Zionism as a 'form of racism' had subsequently been cancelled by the United Nations in 1991, and therefore was anachronistic and did not relate to the peace process that was still the main point of reference of the contending parties in the Middle East. Nevertheless, 'Atiya found it necessary to draw the 'similarities' between Zionism and Nazism as a matter of course, evincing her abysmal ignorance of the topic she pretended to 'research'. She 'found' that both movements were characterized by racism and expansion of territory out of a sense of superiority over other surrounding peoples. But she failed to show any Zionist equivalent (because it does not exist) to the systematic annihilation of the Jews (and others) by the Nazis.[64] This is possibly the reason why she and other Sho'a deniers attempt to diminish the numbers of exterminated Jews, in order to make the comparison between Zionists and Nazis more palatable.

Zionism has amassed in the Jewish State people from over 100 countries, from the dark black Jews of Ethiopia to the blond Ukrainian Jews; the widest possible gamut of people under the same national roof and hardly something that could be even remotely called 'racism', certainly not by Arab countries who prohibit, by law, Jews from inhabiting, or even entering their territories. There is no Jewish 'race', except in the sick minds of the Nazis and their followers today, while the Nazis promoted their Aryan theories. That bigoted Arab–Christian 'researcher' should have also known that the Zionists bought with money every piece of land where they settled prior to the foundation of the State of Israel (1948); that they could not 'expand' by force even if they wanted to, because a foreign power (Britain) was ruling the land; that it was Zionist Israel who accepted the UN Partition Plan in November 1947, and it was the Arabs who invaded Israel's allotted territory, not the other way around; and that after the establishment of Israel, all public land (80 per cent in the Middle East system) was duly and legally inherited by the state from the British Mandatory Power, exactly as the latter had inherited it from the defeated Ottoman Empire. She also approvingly cited some author who 'found' that the 'roots of Nazi expansionism were in the Book of Joshua', and 'similarities' between *Mein Kampf* and the Pentateuch.[65] This slight to the Judeo-Christian Holy Book, by a Maronite who shares in that heritage, sounded like a *dhimmi* mode of behaviour towards a dominant Islamic culture, which had sentenced to death many Rushdies for broadcasting Satanic verses in the Holy Qur'an, and hardly needs to be discussed.

Even the Tunisian intellectual, who distanced himself from 'Atiya's gratuitous venom, was not forceful in denouncing the comparision between Zionism and Nazism on historical and moral grounds. He preferred to cite diplomatic reasons for his dissent, fearing that the Arabs would lose the world arena if they persisted in their internationally unacceptable positions against the Jews and Zionism. 'Atiya accused him and other Arab intellectuals of 'appeasing' Western opinion, while she 'told the truth' in denouncing the 'collaboration between Zionists and Nazis' and the 'support by the Jews of the Nuremberg Laws'. Liberal al-Akhdar succumbed and finally recognized the 'commonality between Nazism and Zionism', but he emphasized that all national movements who focused on the centrality of the ethnic group, like the Jews in their 'Chosen People' concept, or the Islamists who claim that they are 'the greatest nation delivered to mankind', suffered from the same racism, and that only nations who gave up national narcissism attained higher degrees of civilization. Even when the programme's host, Dr al-Qassem, suggested that the infamous 1975

UN Resolution should be revived, al-Akhdar's retort was that it 'was not politic' to do so now, because Israel was internationally accepted as not being a Nazi-like state. But 'Atiya persisted, claiming that comparing Zionism to Nazism constituted a 'psychological blow' to the West, who is so sensitive to Nazism, and therefore should be pursued in order to demean Christianity and Zionism.[66]

At the peak of the programme, Robert Faurisson, another infamous French Sho'a denier, was brought on the line. He asserted that since historical revisionism was the most dangerous weapon against Zionism, it had to be pursued. He encouraged the Arabs to defend Palestine not by guns and shells, but by exposing the 'greatest lie of the twentieth and twenty-first centuries', that is the Holocaust, and that would prove to be the 'nuclear weapon of the poor'. Al-Akhdar tried to mitigate the debate by asserting that it was wrong for the Arabs to uphold Nazism and blame the Jews, while most Germans today rejected Nazism. But both 'Atiya and the moderator interrupted and lambasted him for his dissent from the consensus among Arab intellectuals who justified Holocaust denial. 'Atiya took out a large picture of an Arab child – who was incidentally killed during the Palestinian Intifadah – on which it was inscribed in red: 'The murderers of the Prophets are the murderers of the innocent.' And, totally disregarding the sustained and deliberate massacres of Jewish children in buses and restaurants by her own terrorist kin, screamed to the cameras: 'This is the Holocaust...There is no Jewish Holocaust!!! There is only a Palestinian Holocaust!!!' The programme's host, before he summed up the internet poll on the programme which showed that 84.6 per cent of his Arab viewers thought that Zionism was worse than Nazism, and 'greeted the Zionists for exceeding the Nazis', gratuitously cited a writer for the *Al-Jazeera* website who wrote:

> Sons of Zion, whom our God described as the descendants of apes and pigs, will not be deterred unless there is a true Holocaust that will exterminate all of them at once, along with the traitors, the collaborators, the scum of the *umma*.[67]

In February 2000, Israeli Minister of Regional Co-operation, Shimon Peres, probably the most outspoken and influential champion of peace in the region, delivered a speech at the Davos Conference in Switzerland, where he mentioned that Israel did not wish to be the only 'island of prosperity and spot of cleanliness' in an ocean of poverty. The deluge of gutter language that was poured on him personally and as a Jew and an Israeli could not be considered, by any extent of normal imagination, as a logical or reasonable response to an innocent, well-meant and kind invitation to join regional development. The editor of *al-Akhbar* daily retorted that Israeli society was itself corrupt and racist, where black Jews from Ethiopia were discriminated against and lived under the poverty line, and therefore Israel had no lesson to teach others about fighting poverty. He interpreted the 'spot of cleanliness and progress' as 'no different from the spot on Monica Lewinski's skirt', or a Western spot on the Arab garb, which one day will be totally expunged by a new detergent'.[68] Incidentally, in the English version of that article, published the next day in the mainstream *Egyptian Gazette*, it is emphasized that the 'spot will be removed by a powerful Arab detergent'.[69] Nor does the Egyptian academic world shun that same language. Dr 'Abd-al-Wahhab, who published an encyclopaedic collection on 'Jews, Judaism and Zionism' and claimed that Zionism had invented the Jewish people in order to 'impose its ghetto mentality on the peoples of the world', has inspired and served as reference to many respectable academics and journalists in Egypt. One of them, a writer in the prestigious *al-Ahram*, cited the same words,[70] and the Cairo Centre for Political Studies convened a conference on 29–30 March 2000 to discuss that encyclopaedic, skewed 'masterpiece'.

Anti-Semitic stereotypes are rife, especially in cartoon form in the Egyptian and other Arab press. In one of them which appeared in the opposition *Al-Ahali*, a crooked-nosed Jew, holding a blood-dripping dagger, carries on his back a bag of spoils with the inscription 'the Arab Lands', and on his head, the double symbols of Zionism and Nazism, like inseparable Siamese twins. A separate hand holds a torch and projects a strong beam of light on the pictured miserable Jew, and is identified as the 'Arab press', that famous fortress of investigative reporting which has revealed the 'truth' about the Jews and Israel. The cartoon appeared after a protest that the Israeli Ambassador in Cairo lodged with the authorities there about the wild attacks against Israel in the Egyptian press, and the caption explains that the hideous Jew in the cartoon is none other than 'the Israeli Ambassador who had launched a hysterical broadside on the Egyptian press'.[71] Anti-Semitic stereotypes naturally link, in the eyes of Jewish detractors, the atavistic deficiencies of the Jews with what has been currently happening in Israel. An *al-Ahram* columnist enumerates all acts of Israeli corruption, and finds in them the 'decisive proof' of al-Masir's Jewish Encyclopaedia, described above, that links together Jews and Zionism. Both, says he, are 'greedy, lusting for money and devoid of morality'. The Israeli personality is imbued with those qualities, and therefore they:

> ... would drag their feet before anyone negotiating with them, cheat, refuse to give up anything in their possession until they are forced to do so, and even then only after they have caused confusion and chaos and spread around lies and false pretences regarding the right to rule that God has allotted them.[72]

The Jewish conspiracy, which draws its inspiration from the Protocols of the Elders of Zion, also occupies a prominent place in the Arab press in general, punctuated by an Islamic twist in Muslim fundamentalist literature, as in the Hamas Charter already discussed above. In cartoons, the Jewish octopus extends its tentacles in all directions in order to suck the blood and the water of the Arabs and to reach all the corridors of power in the world.[73] Thus any international conference, symposium or convention that is not to the Arabs' liking, such as the World Conference of Demography or the GATT Agreements, has been described by the Arab press as a Western attempt to control the Third World, headed by the United States, which is itself 'guided by a Zionist gang who wishes to manage world affairs from the corridors of the White House, with the aim of causing destruction and chaos'.[74] Other Arab media explained that Jews schemed to take over Canada and such countries in Europe as Sweden.[75] Jews are also accused of forging their history. When the David Irwing trial was unfolding before a court of law in London in 2000, the Egyptian public showed no interest in the human and Holocaust aspects thereof, but as a launching pad against Zionism and the Jews, it served the Arab purpose. Irwing, the notorious Holocaust denier, was seen as a victim of world Zionism, which 'terrorized the world press in order to prevent the publication of his books'.[76] The Jews were accused of exploiting their political, financial and media power to 'continue to spread their lies about the Holocaust and silence all those who reveal their lies to the world'.[77]

After the outbreak of the Intifadah in late 2000, the escalating Palestinian vitriol against Israel, which among other manifestations included the parade of a donkey in Ramallah, wearing a swastika on its forefront and a Jewish prayer shawl on its body, and the burning of Jewish Holy Sites in Nablus and Jericho, inspired other Arabs who were not directly involved, like the Egyptians, especially after Sharon was elected to the Israeli Premiership. A new wave of viciousness erupted, which in effect did not wish to accomplish any-thing except for hurting the feelings of their rivals and perversely drawing satisfaction therefrom. An editor of the weekly *al-Usbu'*, for example, described a dream he had had, in which he was delegated by the Egyptian government to serve as the bodyguard of Ariel Sharon on his official visit [also in the dream] to Cairo. The scene of the dream, starting with a pig, which is quite abhorrent to the Jews (and Muslims for that matter), begins at the airport:

> After a short while, the pig landed; his face was diabolical, a murderer; his hands soiled by the blood of women and children; a criminal who should be executed in the town square. Should I remain silent as many others did? Should I guard this butcher on my homeland's soil? All of a sudden I forgot everything: the past and the future, my wife and children, and I decided to do it. I pulled my gun and aimed at the cowardly pig's head. I emptied all the bullets and screamed: 'Blood vengeance for the [Egyptian] POW's!, Blood vengeance for the martyrs.' The murderer collapsed under my feet. I realized the meaning of virility, and self-sacrifice. The criminal died. I stepped on the pig's head with my shoes and screamed from the bottom of my heart: 'Long Live Egypt!, Long Live Palestine! Jerusalem will never die, and never will the honour of the nation be lost!' I kept screaming at the top of my lungs until my wife put her hand on me. I woke up from this most beautiful dream and decided not to surrender to humiliation.[78]

These sorts of reports and commentaries have dominated the Arab scene over the past few years, the peace process notwithstanding. This has been the direct way for the Arabs, and other Muslims, to vent their frustrations against Israel, regardless of whether she evacuates Arab territories, makes concessions for peace or shows her interest in regional co-operation. For Israel can do no good: if she refuses to give in, she is greedy and obstinate, and if she does, it is only because Arab power has prevailed upon her. If she refuses to co-operate with the Arabs, it is due to her racism, arrogance and alien character, but when she does, she is accused of economic imperialism. When she fails it is because of her innate wretchedness and the curse that Allah has brought upon the Jews, but when she makes some stunning breakthrough, that is because she is the client of the United States, and so on and so forth. The above sample of hateful attacks against the Jews in the Arab press is only the tip of the iceberg, while the main body remains submerged under the water, unexposed to the scrutiny of the public, except for those whose duty or interest it is to follow those events and analyze them periodically. The Israelis in particular, who have had their fill of the conflict and want to see or hear nothing that disturbs their sweet dreams of peace, remain curiously and dangerously unaware of this continuous litany of visceral hatred towards them, two decades after the bells of peace had tolled in their naive ears. People of Western background have difficulty in realizing that when they mean well, it does not necessarily signify that their interlocutors reason similarly; and when their neighbours use terms like democracy, tolerance, civil rights, freedom, peace, justice, lies, truth, fairness, concessions and negotiations, this does not necessarily mean that they conceive of those notions in the established Western fashion.

Therefore, in this Kafkaesque world where there is no cause and effect; when you achieve peace it does not mean reconciliation; when you wage hostilities that is not called war; when you massacre civilians that is not terrorism; when you make concessions, that does not mean that you cannot go back on them once you have achieved your goals; and when you pledge something it obliges you only as long as this is convenient to you, one could not expect much of these 'peace' deals. The infrastructure of anti-Israeli and anti-Jewish hatred, jealousy, helplessness, contempt, and a total misapprehension of Israeli society that the Arabs and Muslims evince, has been so deeply ingrained in their consciousness for so many centuries, and more so with the onset of the Arab–Israeli conflict, where Jews have showed their mettle for the first time and tackled them on a par, that it is hard to devise any way of turning things around. The peace process, if anything, has not mitigated these sentiments. Quite the contrary, it has woven together all those elements of hatred into a powerful fabric, which it is difficult to imagine starting to fray at the edges, unless the Muslim world first decides and then delves into a deep, courageous and determined process of soul-searching, from kindergartens, to the media and to the academic world. It is difficult to see how all this might happen in the foreseeable future.

These incriminating materials in the Arab and Islamic press, with regard to Jews, Israel and Zionism, do not need much research or commentary according to one's political convictions, wishful thinking, and the surrounding pressures of political correctness. They are so steady, all-encompassing, omnipresent, repetitive, prevalent and diffuse in all aspects of Arab and Islamic society, over many years, in war and in peace, that no one can avoid encountering them, they being the infrastructure of education and socialization in those societies. Worse, there is no known serious attempt made by the governments of those countries to mitigate these dangerous trends, therefore no one could venture any educated guess as to whether and when they might be uprooted. Quite the contrary, the fact that the hierarchy in those countries turns a blind eye, or may even be blinking with approval, is by necessity interpreted as official backing of these atrocious utterings. In turn, these writings, especially those emanating from Egypt, which is considered the cultural hub of the Arab world, are appreciated and widely read and cited and find currency in the rest of the Arab and Muslim world. Therefore, it is not enough to raise the consciousness of the civilized world to these hateful norms of human conduct, it is also imperative to arouse the conscience of those who care and those who can turn things around.

Much of the blame for this state of affairs lays at Israel's door, inasmuch as, in order not to 'rock the boat of peace', it did not deploy the requisite efforts to make any negotiations or concessions conditional on substantial steps by the Arab governments to control these waves of hatred. Camp David I did not put an end to the vilification of Israel and the Jews by the Egyptian media, in spite of President Sadat's commitment to embrace such a policy, starting with school textbooks where these ideas are systematically inculcated. In the Oslo and Wye Agreements, repeated and emphatic obligations were imposed on the Palestinians in this regard, only to see them frustrated by the tenacious reality.[79] But Israel, instead of taking firm steps as it did when Haider's party came to power in Austria, has adopted an inexplicably lenient attitude towards the Arabs it wants to appease and to sign peace with: something that has encouraged them to pursue their anti-Semitic attacks when they realize what concessions they could get for their unrelenting pressures on the Jewish State. This caving in by Israel is not appreciated in the Arab world as a strategy on her part to avoid conflict and to promote dialogue, but either as a silent confirmation of their irrefutable calumnies which Israel must live with, or as a lever to squeeze more concessions from her under the threat of more scorn and libel. They look at Israel, smile under their moustaches and wonder about how reluctant and shy the Jews can be in defence of their national and personal pride in the face of the most outrageous attacks against them.

In 1999, a Jewish girl in Hebron dared to insult local Muslims by offending them and their faith with a poster she drew. As in any society which lives by the rule of law, she was considered by Israeli police as committing an offence and was duly arrested, indicted and jailed for a term of a few months. The Muslims took that step as a matter of course, because their faith does not bear denigration, even if it is done by individuals and not government-sponsored. If their insults of the Jews were to be judged by the same civilized criteria, most of their intellectuals, journalists and spiritual and political leaders should be serving prison terms now: but they do not, in spite of the fact that they not only attack Jews on their own whim, but often represent the official anti-Semitic policy of their societies and governments. The result is that there is nothing to stop their abuses of the Jews and Israel, and as Israel routinely disregards those daily and repetitive abuses, encouragement for more builds up in their minds. Worse, as the treatment of these issues is differentiated, namely that the Arabs can say what they wish about Jews and Israel in the name of freedom of expression, while Jews are restricted by their own laws, there is no escaping the conclusion that in Arab eyes, Islam reigns supreme and remains untouchable, while Judaism is an open target.

In the context of the Palestinian Intifadah, with its corollary of sustained anti-Jewish and anti-Israeli propaganda and the vast amounts of libel and scorn poured upon the Jews and Israel in all Arab media, which go unheeded for the most part, the Arabs and Muslims have often raised the threshold of their libellous attacks. In 1983, they mounted the huge hoax which claimed, against all evidence, and with European, UN and Red Cross support, that Israel had 'poisoned school girls in the West Bank',[80] and since it was not refuted by anyone except Israel, the Palestinian delegate to the UN Commission on Human Rights, a Dr Nabil Ramlawi, accused Israel of injecting the AIDS virus into Palestinian children, again without anyone asking for substantiation.[81] Following that calumny, which again was not challenged by anyone, Arafat declared, during the Intifadah, that Israel used uranium-depleted bullets against the Palestinians, distributed poisoned sweets to Palestinian children, and all manner of nonsense of that sort. No wonder, then, that after 11 September and the onset of the Anthrax panic in the United States, the Arabs, specifically the 'moderate' Egyptians, and in their government-sponsored scientific journal, *al-'Ilm* (Science) to boot, turned the tables on the West and accused the United States and Israel of the most hideous war-crimes, including the use of non-conventional weapons of mass-destruction. Reading is believing:

> The cases of anthrax infection in the United States emerged simultaneously with the beginning of the US war against Afghanistan. News coming from Afghanistan mentions symptoms of a strange disease...causing fever, headaches and haemorrhaging...This brought us back to the discovery of a biological weapons factory in the Ural Mountains in Russia, by the American espionage apparatus... However, the Russians exposed American activities in this destructive field, as well as the death of American scientists who worked in the germ industry...Scientists from 52 universities are collaborating with the Pentagon in preparing for biological war...The United States also contracted several universities abroad, including in Israel. The missiles that the United States supplied to NATO are equipped with biological warheads. These things were approved by the White House...
>
> According to a report by Dr Joseph of UNESCO, Korea, China and Vietnam were attacked with biological weapons... It was not the first such incident. The Allies [of World War II] have a well-known history of germ industry. After World War II broke out, British Prime Minister Churchill received a secret letter from his scientific adviser, who asked him to request anthrax microbes from the Americans...to use against the Germans, because it was an effective weapon that annihilated people and farm animals in large numbers...Finally, it was decided to manufacture biological weapons in Britain instead of importing anthrax bombs from the United States...

The European colonialists gave the Indians in America smallpox. During the American Civil War, both sides used such methods as polluting water sources with animal corpses...In the modern age, biological weapons were first used when Bulgaria secretly joined Austria to fight Serbia. In the summer of 1949, cholera spread throughout Egypt following the establishment of the State of Israel in 1948. Egyptian documents indicate that the disease originated from Israel. When Japan began its experiments in the field, it injected prisoners with viruses of plague, anthrax, small pox and cholera. Three thousand prisoners died...Plague was scattered from aeroplanes during the Sino-Japanese War of 1940–42. In 1944, these epidemics spread to the border of the Soviet Union; a year later, Japan used the microbes against Mongolia...

The United States used germs against Vietnam, North Korea and China...Biological weapons research is being conducted by Israeli universities. Prior to the October War (1973), they injected birds with germs and released them above Jordan, Palestine and the Suez Canal...the United States and Israel keep biological weapons at American bases; if they were to be used, they would destroy half the population of the area under attack. Some of this weaponry makes women miscarry...the United States took over the state of Ottawa [*sic*] to conduct experiments there with deadly biological weapons. It is possible that the urge for vengeance will push the United States to test its advanced biological weapons on a real enemy, to find out how extensive the effect is...

Also, Jewish tourists infected with AIDS, are travelling around Asian and African countries with the aim of spreading the disease... It is no coincidence that the United States is the only member of the United Nations that has not signed the agreement on punishment for the collective annihilation of people...Israel continues to use germ warfare to destroy the Palestinian people on its occupied land, while it challenges the international community...A number of doctors have said that mad cow disease developed in Britain because of animal feed containing dead laboratory animals, including mice and pigs. After these were added to the artificial feed for sheep and cows, mad cow disease appeared.[82]

If this unbridled campaign of smearing the West and Israel or emanates from the heart of the Egyptian 'scientific' establishment, then what can other, less scientific, propagandists be expected to say, not to mention the self-discredit that 'scientists' are bringing upon themselves in the service of their rulers? The representative of Al-Azhar University in the United States, who also serves as the imam of the Islamic Center in New York, Muhammed Jami'a, was interviewed after 11 September following his hurried return to his Egyptian homeland because he was 'subjected to persecution' in the United States, as 'were all Muslims and Arabs' after the Twin Towers. He complained that Muslims no longer felt safe to send their wives for shopping or their children to schools, nor would they even go for medical help, because some 'Jewish doctors in a certain hospital have poisoned the bodies of Muslim children who subsequently died'. All this was generated, he claimed, by the bad image that was imputed to the Muslims by the 'Zionist media', who labelled Islam a 'religion of terror'. He also asserted that while he was arguing with a group of Americans who came to his house to harass him, he 'realized that everyone knew that Jews and Zionists stood behind these ugly deeds, but lacked the courage to say so in public'. He emphasized that the Americans 'knew that Zionists control everything, including political decision making, the media and the major financial and economic centres, but they were aware that whoever would dare to speak up would be accused of anti-Semitism'. His campaign of vilification of the Jews reached new heights when he smeared them as the evil actor behind the New York and Washington disasters:

> The Jews are as described in the words of Allah: 'They spread corruption on earth.' We know that they have always violated agreements, unjustly killed the Prophets and betrayed faith... You see tham at all times diffusing corruption, blasphemy, homosexuality, alcohol and drugs. They are responsible for strip-tease, homosexual and lesbian clubs everywhere, in order to impose their hegemony and colonialism over the world...Now they are riding on top of world powers, they always look for the hegemonic power of the day and establish a system of co-existence with it...They also rode on top of the German power, but Hitler eliminated them because they betrayed him and violated their treaty with him...We have seen those Zionists broadcasting on the BBC, merely one hour

after the events, that the Arabs, especially the Palestinians, were jubilating over the death of the Americans. They broadcast, in fact, an old video dating from 1991 during the Gulf War when Iraq was invading Kuwait, [as if it were a live reaction of the Palestinians to the New York events] but Allah undid their plot when a Brazilian professor proved that the video was faked... Those people have ready-made scenarios for everything and they are capable of fabricating events to their benefit... Unfortunately, this made the Americans hate anyone Arab or Muslim. What do you expect when, at first, everyone thought about 50,000 dead while the Arabs were celebrating? Of course, you want vengence. This is what the Jews plotted, and they used the Arabs as their victims...

All signs point in the direction of the Jews, because they are the only ones able to plan such an act. First, it was found that the automatic pilots of the aeroplanes were neutralized prior to the flights, which proves that the control towers had been taken over; secondly, the black boxes were empty of any information, and that cannot be done unless so programmed beforehand; thirdly, the United States has the strongest intelligence services in the world – the CIA and the FBI... it does not stand to reason that anyone could have infiltrated the United States without being detected; fourthly, it is Jews who control all decision making in the airports and in the sensitive foci of the White House and the Pentagon; fifthly, America has provided so far no shred of convincing evidence linking Osama Bin-Laden and al-Qa'ida to the events...

All these considerations taken together point out that only the Jews were able to concoct such an act... I told US officials that the American people will never identify the true enemy who hit it at its heart unless it wakes up first and stops accusing Arabs and Muslims... Immediately after the event, 30 per cent of the American people woke up and realized that they were the victims of a mammoth deception on the part of the Jews, who presented to them the Arabs and Muslims as a nation of barbars and blood-thirsty people... The American people has realized that mysterious hands have been playing with its fate. I have heard from many Americans who visited me at the Islamic Center that they had been deceived by the Jews, therefore they came to express their solidarity with Arabs and Muslims...

In America news spread about the 4,000 Jews who did not report to work on that day in the Twin Towers, and about the arrest by police of groups of Jews who were celebrating in the streets during the events...But that news was immediately silenced, and since the Jews control the media, they could silence them so as to prevent the American people from knowing. Had the American people known, they would have done to the Jews what Hitler did...The 30 per cent of Americans who understood the deception demonstrated in Washington and New York and called upon the US government to act with logic and not to launch war without first finding the culprits and arresting the Jews who are the true criminals...

I hope the Americans do not listen to the Zionists who want to destroy the world...I endorse President Mubarak's call to behave with logic before the blood of the innocent is spilled...An American attack on Afghanistan would be tantamount to terror, as it has already happened in Iraq and Palestine... If that war is resumed, the scenario of US terrorism against Arabs and Muslims will be repeated. This will not be a third world war, it will be the end of oppressive America. I regard America as a second 'Ad,[83] because America has the same character as 'Ad: it has skyscrapers and large factories therefore Allah will apply to the second 'Ad the fate of the first, once they also became arrogant with their power, but Allah will take His vengence...The turn-up in all this is that the Americans have become aware of Islam, after they discovered the Jewish deception...Allah has foiled the plot of the Jews who tried to distort the image of the Muslims, and shown the Americans the truth. Therefore, I think that Muslims can expect a brilliant future in the United States of America.[84]

DENYING THE HOLOCAUST

One of the favourite pastimes of the Arabs and Muslims is to deny the Holocaust and to sponsor all the Holocaust deniers in the world as heroes. One can assume that they do not do it out of concern for historical truth, but in order to vindicate their long-standing accusations of the Jews (and Christians for that matter) that they had forged their history and, worse, their Holy Scriptures. Regarding the Holocaust, the Jews are accused of 'using organized terrorism to cultivate that legend and turned it into a fact which ties down the hands of historians'.[85] The Jews are also accused that their forgery of history is constantly refuted by 'scientific articles which have proven that there have never been any gas chambers, or have revised downwards the figures of the dead in them'.[86] The Arab press produced abundant 'documentation' to back its accusations.[87] Some papers even claimed that the Jews, far from being harmed by World War II, on the contrary profited from it, for had Japan and Germany won the war, the Jews 'could not have continued to blackmail the world with their lies'.[88] Even when some dissenting voices in the Arab world denounced the denial of the Holocaust, they did it for utilitarian reasons – fearing that Arabs who denied the horrors of the Nazis could find themselves aligned with the racists and anti-Arab elements in Europe[89] – not out of a moral consideration which flatly condemned the Nazi evil. Others, while acknowledging the Holocaust, dug up all manner of rationalizations to justify it. The notorious Egyptian anti-Semite, Anis Mansur, for example, wrote on the sensitivity of the Jews to their loss of lives during their 'barbaric acts against the Palestinians', which was due to their small numbers, compared to the Arabs and Muslims. But he also asserts that if it were not for their escalating numbers of casualties, it would have become clear to the world that what happened to the Jews in Germany, Poland and Russia was justified. It is not true that all Jews want peace. There is a suicidal sect among them that does not desire to live. Thus, they kindle the people's hatred and hostility, and as a result, the people turn against them. Although there are many intelligent people among them, they use their intellect to devise new ways for people everywhere to hate them and unite against them:

> Because megalomania overwhelms the Jewish people, they do not bow their heads in order to survive; they prefer to surface behind the steering wheels of the leadership in Europe and the United States, in order to arouse the world's sympathy... They were in the shadows, in the rear lines and in the dark alleys before the establishment of the State of Israel. They prefer an Israel surrounded by enemies to a ghetto that no one has heard of. There are sects in Israel which view the Jewish State as a heretic one. They believe the Israelites deserve to be tortured, and that what Hitler did to

the Jews in the West is an appropriate punishment for their mistreatment of Oriental Jews.[90]

The author does not seem to be the least bothered by the fact that the Holocaust preceded the 'mistreatment' in Israel of the Oriental Jews by European Jews, since their encounter happened mainly in Israel after the Sho'a, nor by what denying the Holocaust and then explaining the reasons for it does to his credibility. It is also a fascinating projection onto the enemy of one's own faults, as, at the time when Islamikaze bombings were coming to their peak in the Muslim world and they were boasting that their edge over the West emanated from their desire to die, he should accuse Israeli sects of wishing to die: something that has never been identified or detected in the Jewish world. In any case, the author was certain that, as the Jews in Israel were no longer able to countenance the 'stones and artillery' of the Arabs, they would be forced to emigrate to their countries of origin, and concluded that the Jews were 'forced' to stay in their country in a state of high alert and eternal readiness, which unites their otherwise diverse skin colours, religions, schools of thought and social strata. For, without it, 'nothing would remain from Israel, except for the clerics, the elderly, the sick and Sharon'.[91] This pathetic explanation, by someone who considers himself, and is viewed by others, as a leading intellectual in Egypt, was aimed at clarifying to his readership the embarrassing fact that this odd Jewish State has been quite successful in spite of all its built-in deficiencies. As has happened before, by swearing at Jews and Israel, this kind of hateful writing is supposed to provide relief for the otherwise inexplicable distinction of democratic, prosperous and ingenuous tiny Israel, against the background of the surrounding authoritarian, backward, corrupt and poor Arab countries. In all evidence, these Arab writers would rather pull down the Jewish State that exposes their own frailties by comparison than learn from it to increase their Gross National Product twenty-fold.

Other writers, who also deny the Holocaust, have all manner of 'authorities' to refer to and cite repeatedly, *ad nauseam*:

> With regard to the fraud of the Holocaust...many French studies have proven that they are a fabrication, a lie and a fraud. That is a plot that was tailored, using several fake photos completely unconnected with the truth...Hitler himself,

whom they accuse of Nazism...is completely innocent of the charge of false holocaust...The entire matter, as many French and British scientists and researchers have determined, is no more than a huge Israeli plot aimed at extorting the German government...But I personally, and in light of this imaginary tale, am saying to him [Hitler] from the bottom of my heart, 'If only you had done it, brother, I wish it really happened, so that the world could sigh in relief, without their evil and sin.'[92]

This cacophony of anti-Semites was joined by Abu Mazem, the moderate, Western-educated and soft-spoken deputy of Arafat in the Palestinian establishment, who also became a denier of the Sho'a, in his 1982 'doctoral' dissertation for Moscow's Oriental College, that was published two years later in Arabic[93] for his avidly anti-Jewish audiences. There he joined the Holocaust deniers, whose assumptions have been consistently destroyed in courts in the West, in raising doubts about the existence of gas chambers, in reducing the numbers of Jewish victims to 'less than one million', as if that number were not chilling enough, and in claiming that the Zionist movement had a stake in convincing world public opinion that the number of victims was higher so as to achieve 'greater gains' after the war when the time came to 'distribute the spoils'. He accused the West of having 'concealed a basic partner in crime', that is the Zionist movement, and 'demonstrated' the commonality of interests between the Nazi regime and the Zionist leadership and the 'convergence of the interests and the fundamental similarity between the two movements' theories'. The point was to 'prove' that it was Zionism which 'conspired against the Jewish people and collaborated with the Nazis to annihilate it', but he fell short of explaining who would be left as the constituency of the Zionists if Jews were exterminated. Probably guided by the oppressive atmosphere of Moscow during the Cold War, and the constraint to please his dissertation supervisors, he lambasted the West for having 'locked up details, facts and crimes that they did not want to exist', and in the end they 'charged the Nazi leaders with all the crimes that were committed during the war, and relentlessly hunted down those still alive even though the crimes were committed long ago'.[94] As if crimes of genocide could be pardoned if the criminals hid away for long enough, or the hunt to bring them to justice was difficult and prolonged.

Besides castigating the West for the way it dealt with the war criminals in 'half-truths', Abu Mazem lambasted it for 'neglecting the other half', that is the 'truth' about the Jews. He lumped together all the dead of the war, the Germans with their victims, and enumerated the Nazi 'sacrifices' that amounted to 10 million, as compared with 20 million Soviets and 10 million Yugoslavs, Poles and others, totally disregarding the systematic annihilation of Jews (and gypsies, for that matter), who were, in fact, the only peoples not 'killed' in combat, but simply singled out for extermination, not for resisting the Germans or fighting them, but simply for being what they were. He refers to the 'claims that were announced about the Jewish victims after the war', specifying that the figure of six million was vastly exaggerated and might have amounted to 'less than one million'. He also accused Zionism of having created that fictitious figure in order to raise more sympathy for the Jews worldwide. He cited the 'famous Canadian author, Roger Delarom', who is so famous that his identity is hard to ascertain, as discarding the figure of six million because it 'had never been proven'. He even accused Zionism of having produced the figure of 12 million Jewish victims, that is, two-thirds of world Jewry on the eve of the war, 'but then the number decreased sharply to six million'. He contends that 'the number further decreased to four million, as the Germans could not have killed or exterminated more Jews than there were in the world at the time'. He does not account for the fact that the Jewish people counted 18 million among its membership before the war and that only 12 million remained. Instead, he quotes, or rather dishonestly misquotes in order to account for his 'fictitious millions', the American historian Paul Hilberg, whom he cites (on p. 670) as saying that the number of killed Jews was less than a million, while Hilberg's *The Destruction of European Jews* in fact reported that in the decade between 1935 and 1945, the Jewish people lost one-third of its number, dropping from 16 to 11 million: namely five million were killed during the war and the resulting deportations and massacres.[95]

This obsession with the numbers, which is more elaborate in the Arabic version of the book and less developed in the original dissertation in Russian, found its basis in the author's accusation that the Zionist movement 'attempted to describe how the Jews were murdered in concentration camps and gas chambers', while disregarding two fundamental points: one, that 'many of the Jews in the camps remained alive and were rescued by the Zionists' (the same Zionists that we were told had concocted their extermination) in order to send them to Palestine; and many of them were saved by the Soviet Union, when two million of them were sent to Central Asia. Secondly, he claims that the killed Jews did not only perish in concentration camps, but many of them died in battle, through starvation or disease that had struck all Europe, and that concentration camps had housed those other than the Jews. He cites the notorious Jew-hater and Holocaust denier, the Frenchman, Robert Faurisson, who had repeatedly denied that gas chambers were intended to kill people and repeated the fallacy that they were only used to 'incinerate bodies in order to control the spread of disease'. Abu Mazen concludes his 'study', which would not have earned him a doctorate anywhere in the civilized world other than the then Soviet Union, by smearing the Zionist movement thus:

> It takes little effort to prove the truth about World War II... However, there is another aspect of the truth that remains shrouded in mystery, like the other side of the moon...How could anyone reasonable believe that the institutions of the Zionist movement that arose to defend the 'Jewish peoples' cause' then became a cause of Jewish annihilation? History taught us that Nero burned Rome, but he was insane, and his insanity relieved him of responsibility...There are also leaders who betrayed their country and their people and sold them to their enemies. But they are few, and they alone bear responsibility for their actions. Therefore, a popular, public movement's conspiracy against its own 'people' is astonishing and demands an in-depth and meticulous examination...
>
> When discussing declared Zionist ideas...one finds that they believe in the purity of the Jewish race – as Hitler believed in the purity of the Aryan race...and the movement calls for...a decisive solution to the 'Jewish problem' in Europe via immigration to Palestine. Hitler also called for this and carried it out...The Zionism movement maintains that anti-Semitism...is the basic motive for immigration, therefore if anti-Semitism did not exist it would have had to be invented, and if that flame dies away it must be fanned... These ideas provide a general dispensation to every racist in the world, most prominently to Hitler and the Nazis to treat the Jews as they wish, as long as this includes immigration to Palestine...

An Arabic proverb says: 'When differences arise between thieves, the theft is revealed'...This is what happened with the Zionist movement. When the Labour Party ruled Israel, it refused the Revisionists their share, and so the latter began to expose the facts and rend the curtain of falsehood. However, in the heat of the argument over the roles of the Labourites [in conspiring with the Nazis], they forgot to speak of the role they played, which was no different from the role of others. Then came a third side and revealed the positions of all.[96]

From denying the Holocaust, or diminishing its horrors, to accusing the Jewish victims of Nazism for having conspired with it against their own people, the road is short to defending Hitler against the 'offences' caused him by the Jews and their supporters. Following Western and Israeli protests to the Egyptian government regarding the unbridled support for Hitler that is current in the Egyptian and Arab press in general,[97] the government daily, *al-Akhbar*, relented for a while, but could not contain its irresistible fascination with Hitler for long and soon reverted to it with a vengeance. This time, a cleric from Al-Azhar University, Mahmoud Khadhr, entitled his contribution 'In Defence of Hitler', and used the occasion to attack not only Israel and the Jews, but also the hated West:

Hitler and many of his ministers took their own lives so that they would not have to see the faces of the old ape, Churchill, and the big bear, Stalin, who would sentence them to death with no one to defend them...Each one of them had the right to a defence...but Hitler's executioners took this right away and attributed to him crimes that he committed and that he did not commit...I do not know what would have happened to Churchill, Roosevelt and De Gaulle, had Hitler won. Perhaps the crimes for which they deserve the death sentence would have been much worse than all that Hitler has done...

But all of Hitler's crimes and infractions were forgotten, except for the crime that was exaggerated and blown completely out of proportion, thanks to the insistence of world Zionism to continue to stoke the fire. The reason for this was the emotional need of the Sons of Jacob to extort Germany and to eat away at its resources. It is amazing that the Westerners, who are entitled to their own thinking, confirming or denying anything, including the existence of the Prophets of Allah, cannot address the 'Jewish question', or more precisely the false Holocaust, whose numbers and scope they have exaggerated until it has reached the level of the merciless destruction of six million Jews, only because Hitler saw them as an inferior race unworthy of living next to the Germanic race, which must rule the world...

Anyone who knocks on this door is accused of the most horrible things, and is tried in all Western courts for anti-Semitism... for two reasons: one is due to Zionist control of thinking in the world and the degree of oppression of thought by the Zionist propaganda apparatus in those nations. No one can oppose this oppression for fear of going to prison or having his livelihood or reputation threatened... The second is the fear that the lies of Zionism would be exposed if the subject of the Holocaust is investigated by facts and the logical conclusions are drawn...

The first dubious fact is the number of six million Jews who were burnt in the gas chambers. Did they have families, children who demanded compensation, or did Zionism see itself as the only heir? If we assume that every person had an average of five family members, this would bring the number of Jews affected to 30 million. It is certain that many Jews escaped before the ship sank, that many of them survived, despite the so-called extermination and burning. This would mean that the number of Jews in Germany was 60 million, although the total number of Germans has never reached this many... Even if we cross off one zero from the six million and are left with a tenth of this number, it would still seem exaggerated and would have to be investigated.[98]

It is difficult to imagine that this writer did not know the number of Germany's population during the war, or that most of the exterminated Jews were not Germans but rather Polish, Baltic or Soviet, or that entire Jewish families, often over three generations, were decimated, therefore leaving no heirs behind. All these harrowing manipulations of unsubstantiated numbers are pages taken from the books of Sho'a deniers and have no other purpose than to diminish its dimensions and accuse the Jews of its inflation. A follow up of that line of thought would be to show that Hitler had no reason to exterminate so many Jews, therefore he did not, in fact. But deniers of the Sho'a, including Arabs and Muslims, are caught in the contradiction of both diminishing its numbers in order to relegate the whole horror to a 'footnote in history', as Jean-Marie Le Pen would have it, while at the same time explaining and exploding the 'threat' that Jews posed to the Germans, hence the 'imperative' to eliminate them. The Egyptian Islamist in question falls into the same trap of incoherence when he begins justifying the mass-killing that he initially denied:

> No one can ask why Hitler punished the Jews. The reason had nothing to do with that broken record called anti-Semitism. If Hitler were an anti-Semite, why was this mentioned only after World War II was declared? In the period in which Hitler built Germany and prepared it for war in order to regain what it had lost during World War I, he could have expelled this undesirable race from Germany and planted it in South Africa or anywhere else in the world. Did Hitler attack the Jews, or did their crime deserve even more?
>
> The Zionists were a Fifth Column in Germany, and they betrayed the country that hosted them, in order to realize their aspirations. This had to be exposed, and indeed Hitler discovered that the Zionists were spies for the Allied Powers. Inevitably, he was enraged and took revenge on them for this great betrayal. Both the Zionist movement and the Allied Powers had an interest in keeping this matter a secret, so that people would not know that the Zionists were punished for helping the Allied Powers, for their betrayal and for stabbing Hitler in the back...
>
> Even [post-war] Germany and the government set up by the Allied Powers could not tell the truth, although they knew it, bcause it was under the influence of the Allied Powers, and because defeated nations must pay. Thus, the Zionist movement took control over the subject from Europe and the United States, and has easily made laws with which they try anyone who wants to raise the subject. Even historians can research any subject except for this forbidden one. Furthermore, the influence of the Zionist oppression has reached some Arab countries, who prevented the meeting of two conferences of historians who want to investigate the subject and expose the truth. The conference was delayed more than once, but some of Egypt's main journalists

promised to host this conference, and we hope that it will succeed in exposing the secrets surrounding this subject...

We denounce racial discrimination and the persecution of any person on the basis or religion, race or colour, anywhere in the world. Those who yell about false persecutions that allegedly occurred half a century ago must not ignore the persecution of others, their expulsion from their houses and their lands, and the confiscation of their property. They should not commit those crimes that they claim were committed against them... Likewise, Germany should pay compensation to the victims of mines that were planted in the Western Desert [in Egypt], and compensation for the land that lay untouched for half a century as a result, before it pays compensation for false crimes that have no proof except for false and misleading claims.[99]

NOTES

1. See N. Stillman, *The Jews of Arab Lands*, Philadelphia, PA: Jewish Publication Society of America, 1979; Bernard Lewis, *The Jews of Islam*, Princeton, NJ, 1984; Bat Ye'or, *The Dhimmi*, Madison, WI: Fairleigh Dickinson University; Robert Wistrich, *Muslim Anti-Semitism* (American Jewish Committee Report, 2002); Joseph Bodansky, *Islamic Anti-Semitism* Tel Aviv: Ariel Centre in Israel, 1999; and R. Israeli, *Peace is in the Eye of the Beholder*, *Poison: Modern Manifestations of the Blood Libel*, Lanham, NY: Lexington Books, 2002, and *Arab and Islamic Anti-Semitism*, Position Paper of the Ariel Research Centre.
2. *Al-Ahram*, 25 April 2002.
3. *Al-Manar* television (Lebanon–Hizbullah), 24 April 2002.
4. Palestine television, 22 April 2002; see also *Al-Watan* (Egypt), 21 April 2002; *Al-Maydan* (Egypt), 22 April 2002; and *Al-Manar* television (Hizbullah–Lebanon), 24 April 2002, *MEMRI*, ibid.
5. See Chapter 7, n. 79.
6. 'Politicide' is a term coined by the late Yehoshovat Harkabi to designate the killing of a state or polity.
7. *Iqra'* television (Saudi Arabia and Egypt), 24 April 2002. *MEMRI*, No. 373, 30 April 2002.
8. See for example, The Charter of the Hamas, that Islamic movement which has been the leader of Islamikaze deployment and activism in the Muslim world, particularly Article 22. See 'The Charter of Allah: the Platform of the Islamic Resistance Movement', in R. Israeli, *Fundamentalist Islam and Israel*, Lanham, NY and London: The University Press of America, 1992, pp. 147–8.
9. For some of his harrowing calumniations against the Jews, see R. Israeli, *Peace, is in the Eye of the Beholder*.
10. *October*, 17 June 2001.
11. Ibid.
12. Ibid.
13. Ibid.
14. Sayyid Qut'b was a great luminary of the Muslim Brothers in Egypt until he was executed by the Nassarite regime in 1966 for having plotted against the government.

His book, *Our Campaign Against the Jews*, one of the most chilling anti-Semitic manifestos in history, became a reference that is revered by most Muslim fundamentalist movements.

15. For the full text of the Charter, see R. Israeli, *Fundamentalist Islam and Israel*, ch. 7.
16. www.alminbar.cc/alkhutab/khutbaa.asp?mediaURL=1216. No date. *MEMRI*.
17. Ibid. = 3095. No date.
18. Ibid. = 5530, 22 March 2002.
19. Ibid. = 5478. No date.
20. Ibid. = 4367, 22 October 2000.
21. Ibid. = 3094. No date.
22. Ibid. = 3095. No date.
23. Ibid. = 5477. No date.
24. The Five Pillars (*arkan*), i.e. the fundamental tenets of Islam, are the *shahadah*, that is, the vow that there is no God but Allah and Muhammed is His Messenger; the *salat*, or prayer five times a day; the *sawm*, that is, the fast during the month of Ramadan; the *zakat*, or paying of alms; and the *haj*, that is, the holy pilgrimage in Mecca. Some puritanical currents in Islam, like the Wahhabiyya in Saudi Arabia, add jihad as the sixth *rukn*, to emphasize the obligation of every Muslim individual to it (*fard 'ayn*), while in the mainstream of Islam it is considered the duty of the community (*fard kifaya*) that is left to the discretion of the rulers and jurists of each generation.
25. Ibid. = 5387, 6 October 2001.
26. Leslie Stahl, in '60 Minutes', CBS News, June 2002.
27. For details, see R. Israeli, *Green Crescent over Nazareth: The Displacement of Christians by Muslims in the Holy Land*.
28. *Ha'aretz*, 28 September 2001.
29. *Al-Riyadh* (Saudi Arabia), 22 November 2001.
30. The term was admirably used by John Derbyshire, who borrowed it from political scientist Robert Conquest, in his 'Hesperophobia: On Blaming the Jews', *National Review Online*, 13 September 2001.
31. *Al-Ahram*, 23 June 2001. *MEMRI*, No. 238, 9 July 2001.
32. *Al-Riyadh* (Saudi Arabia), 10 March 2002. A second part was published on 12 March which purported to 'explain' the story of the Book of Esther. *MEMRI*, No. 354, 13 March 2002.
33. Ibid.
34. *Al-Riyadh*, 2 March 2002. *MEMRI*, No. 357, 21 March 2002. See also *Al-Sharq al-Awsat* (London), 12 March, 20 March, and 25 March 2002. Anti-Semitic statements were supposedly made by Franklin during a recess of the Constitutional Convention of the founding fathers, and recorded by Charles Cotesworth Pinckney, the delegate from South Carolina, who recorded them in his diary. The statements were cited in *A Handbook on the Jewish Question*, a book of anti-Semitic propaganda published in 1935 by Nazi Germany. See *MEMRI*, No. 362, 5 April 2002.
35. See, for example, *Al-Ahram*, 28 October 2000, or *Al-Akhbar*, 20 October 2000 and 25 March 2001. See also *MEMRI* Special Dispatches 150, 201 and 354.
36. See, for example, the website of the revisionist historians who deny the Sho'a, *Worldwide Revisionst News*, http://64.156.139.229/vcotc/rituamord/id39m.htm. According to this site, T'las' book was first published in Arabic in 1968, and an English version of it appeared in 1991.
37. Al-Sham is the Arabic for Damascus and also the Province of Damascus in the Islamic Empire, which also included Palestine. This emphasis by T'las that the State of Israel was founded in al-Sham underscores Syria's standing claim to Palestine, where neither Israel nor Palestine (or Lebanon for that matter), are recognized as separate units independent from Syrian rule.
38. At the conclusion of his introduction, T'las warned of repeating the 'disastrous mistake make by President Sadat', which led to his assassination, when he compromised the integrity of his country by making peace with the Satan–Israel.
39. *Roz al-Youssuf* (Egypt), 17 November 2001. See also *Al-'Alam al-Yaum* (Egypt), 4

October 2001.

40. *Al-Sharq al-Awsat* (London), 5 June 2002. *MEMRI*, No. 391, 19 June 2002.
41. *USA Today*, 26 June 2001.
42. Ibid.
43. Ibid.
44. Ibid.
45. Ibid
46. For other aspects of preparing for a martyrdom bombing, see Amos Harel and Omer Barak, 'Portrait of the Terrorist as a Young Man', *Ha'aretz* (Israel), 23 April 2002, where a captured terrorist recruiter, commander and dispatcher from Israeli Operation Defensive Shield (April 2002) spoke candidly with Israeli journalists, albeit in the presence of Israeli Security Services who had arrested the man, interrogated him and put some restrictions on what he could say in the interview.
47. Data collected from the International Policy Institute for Counter Terrorism at the Interdisciplinary Centre in Herzliya, and published by Sylvana Foa, *The Village Voice*, 5–11 June 2002.
48. In fact, the number of Israeli casualties in the Arab–Israeli conflict since 1948 has long surpassed 20,000, that is the double the author's estimate.
49. *Al-Usbu'*, (Egypt), 28 May 2001. *MEMRI*, No. 224, 4 June 2001.
50. *Al-Sharq al-Awsat* (London), 8 June 2002.
51. Ibid.
52. *Al-Manar* television, (Hizbullah–Lebanon), 2 June 2002.
53. *Al-Kayan* (Iran), reported by the Iranian News Agency (IRNA), 7 May 2002. *MEMRI*, No. 379, 16 May 2002.
54. Sura 5, verse 21.
55. Sura 10, verse 93.
56. Sura 17, verse 104.
57. *Al-Mustaqbal* (Lebanon), 19 March 2002.
58. *Al-Hayat* (London), 21 October 2001. *MEMRI*, No. 295, 1 November 2001.
59. *Al-'Ukadh* (Saudi Arabia), 22 November 2001.
60. *Al-Riyadh* (Saudi Arabia), 22 November 2001.
61. *Al-Hayat* (London), 12 December 2001.
62. *Al-Hayat* (London), 1 April 2002.
63. *Al-Akhbar* (Egypt), 29 April 2002. *MEMRI*, No. 375, 2 May 2002. Similar virulence was shown by the editor of the same establishment paper, 19 December 2001.
64. *Al-Jazeera* television, 15 May 2001. *MEMRI*, No. 225, 6 June 2001.
65. Ibid.
66. Ibid.
67. Ibid.
68. *Al-Akhbar*, 2 February 2000.
69. *Egyptian Gazette*, 3 February 2002.
70. *Al-Ahram*, 13 February 2000.
71. *Al-Ahali*, (Egypt), 5 April 2000.
72. *Al-Gumhuriyya* (Egypt), 7 December 1999.
73. *Al-Wafd* (Egypt), 7 March 2000; and *Al-Ahram*, 25 March 2000.
74. *Al-Wafd*, 27 March 2000.
75. Al-Ahram, 20 March 2000 and 17 May 2000; *Al-Wafd*, 4 April 2000; and *al-Gumhuriyya* (all Egyptian), 12 February and 5 March 2000.
76. *Al-Ahram*, 25 January 2000.
77. *Al-Akhbar*, 11 May 2000.
78. Al-Usbu' (Cairo), 12 February 2001, cited by *Al-Quds al-'Arabi* (London), 13 February 2001. *MEMRI*, No. 188, 22 February 2001.
79. See R. Israeli, 'Education, State Building, and the Peace Process: Educating Palestinian Children in the Post-Oslo Era', *Journal of Terrorism and Political Violence*, January 2000.
80. See R. Israeli, *Poison: Modern Manifestations of the Blood Libel*.

81. Ibid. Especially pp. 65–6 and 106–8.
82. *Al-'Ilm*, (Egypt), November 2001. *MEMRI*, No. 322, 28 December 2001.
83. In Islamic history, 'Ad and Thamud were Arab tribes in Arabia who were completely annihilated following their reneging the Path of Allah.
84. www.lailatalqadr.com/stories/p5041001/shtml. *MEMRI*, No. 23, 4 October 2001. The same accusations against Jews were uttered by a member of the Saudi Shura Council, Dr Ahmed al-Twijri, on *Al-Jazeera* television, 12 June 2002.
85. *Al-Wafd*, 13 February 2000; *Al-Ahram*, 19 April 2000; and the *Egyptian Gazette*, 20 April 2000.
86. *Al-Ahram*, 30 December, 1999.
87. See, for example, *Roz al-Youssuf*, 28 January 2000, pp. 61–3.
88. *Al-Hayat*, 31 January 2000; *Al-Akhbar*, 26 January 2000; *Al-Ahram*, 18 April and 17 May 2000; *The Egyptian Gazette*, 17 April 2000; and so on.
89. *Al-Ahram*, 19 April 2000. See also *Al-Ahrahm al-'Arabi*, 6 May 2000.
90. *Al-Ahram*, 13 February 2001. *MEMRI*, No. 188, 22 February 2001.
91. Ibid.
92. *Al-Akhbar* (Egypt), 29 April 2002. *MEMRI*, No. 375, 2 May 2002.
93. Published as *Secret Ties between the Nazis and the Zionist Movement Leadership*, Amman: Dar Ibn Rushd, 1984.
94. Ibid. See *MEMRI*, No. 95, 30 May 2002.
95. Ibid.
96. Ibid.
97. See R. Israeli, *Peace is in the Eye*, pp. 33–4, 231, 326.
98. *Al-Akhbar*, 27 May 2001. *MEMRI*, No. 231, 20 June 2001.
99. Ibid.

9. The Western War Against Islamikaze

While for an ideological war, the like of which Islam has felt impelled to launch on the West, there was a need for us to understand the doctrine before we could identify its enemies, the counter-war of defence has no doctrine and no goals, political, economic or ideological, except for defeating the aggressors and thwarting their schemes. Much like the great ideological wars of the twentieth century, first of Fascism and Nazism against liberal democracy, and then the Cold War that pitted communism against capitalism, during which it was the democratic West that defended itself against totalitarianism until the latter was defeated, it is incumbent upon the West today to stand up to the new challenge of the Islamic onslaught and rout it, not to 'understand' it, cajole it, appease it, come to terms with it, and certainly not to yield to it, let alone capitulate before it. Except that two definitions must be made: what is terrorism, and who is the terrorist, namely who exactly is the enemy that the West (and Israel for that matter) are facing; and who is the aggressor and how must he be dealt with in order to defeat terrorism?

Rivers of ink (and blood) were spilled trying to answer these questions on either side of the divide. The West has repeatedly, and rightly, stated that it has no quarrel with Islam as such, not because Islam is 'a religion of peace', as the superficial and irresponsible cliché goes; in fact, we have seen that, judged on its own terms and ideology, it is not; but because, in order to avoid an all-encompassing civilizational battle that no one should be interested in, it is essential to define those manifestations of Islam which are actively and aggressively anti-Western, for example, the fundamentalists among them; to attempt to isolate them from the mass of Islam, which is not practically interested in or able to wage war against the West for now, even though it may evince a varying degree of emotional support for the Islamikaze totalitarian war; and seek ways to prevail on the culprits without causing much collateral damage to the others. Moreover, after the terrorists are overwhelmed, the regimes who back them toppled, their caches and lines of logistics destroyed, their finances confiscated and their doctrine proven bankrupt, a tremendous effort must be deployed worldwide to re-educate, Westernize and reshuffle, if that is possible, the structures of Islamic societies which are infected by terrorism today.

The issue of who is the terrorist is even more perplexing, since although it is raised for the most part by, or under, autocratic regimes, and is for the most part directed against Western democracies, there is no agreement on its definition. Arab and Muslim countries, for example, in their quest to justify Palestinian terrorism, claim that it is a legitimate way to battle against 'Israeli occupation', and since they do not possess weapons that match those of mighty Israel, it is understandable that they use what they have and what has proved efficient in combat. Most of the civilized world, however, which defines terrorism by its means, not by its ends, cannot find any justification for the indiscriminate killing of non-combatant civilians even if the cause of the terrorists is *prima facie* justified. Due to this world of difference between the worldviews of the terrorists and their prospective victims, and the varying degree to which one values life and would go to great lengths to protect it and punish its violation, while the other boasts his desire to die and attaches more importance to the afterworld than to this life, the choice is either to submit to the Muslim terrorists or to enforce on them the views of civilizations, by education and conviction if possible, by coercion and force if necessary. Because when the Islamic world, and not only the fundamentalists in its midst, cries and moans against the 'aggression, arrogance, exploitation and state terrorism pursued by the West', what can the West do except uphold its principles and defend them when necessary?

And so we are faced with a Kafkaesque world where all Muslim conquests, occupations and expansions are 'the will of Allah' and therefore justified and pre-ordained, while those of the West are corrupt and evil by definition and therefore liable to counter-attack and defeat. Any Muslim attack on non-Muslims, whether in Kashmir, Palestine or the United States, is dubbed an act of 'self-defence' of Muslim territory or of Muslim values and ideals, while anyone standing up to that attack, be it Israel, the United States or India, is the terrorist and the aggressor. Muslim wars against others are justified as jihad in the path of Allah, and the self-immolating terrorists in that endeavour are praised as heroes and martyrs, who supposedly observe the 'generous and humane' rules of war of Islam, while anything the non-Muslims do in their own defence is 'criminal, inhumane, brutal, a war crime, murderous, calamitous and contrary to Muslim Law'. For the Muslims, it is the West who has to 'understand' the motives behind the Muslim acts of horror, 'change its policies and ways', reverse its pacts and obligations, because ultimately 'the future belongs to Islam', which will prevail and expand the world over; but the Muslims have nothing to learn from others, least of all from the 'corrupt and materialistic West', which is doomed to decay and demise in any case, let alone from the Jews, the 'descendants of apes and pigs', who are earmarked for annihilation. The Muslims can incite against the West and their perceived enemies, can foment hatred, bigotry, call for murder and elimination of others, but woe to anyone who dares to utter a word of criticism against Islam, the Prophet of Allah, the Islamic legal system that he has bequeathed, or encourage reform in the world of Islam to meet the requirements of the modern age.

These two trends of thinking which do not meet – and there are not even many points of contact between them – should be left each to its own devices. The world of Islam is not likely to adopt democracy as we know it, because it is not open to such a regime, and seeking to democratize it would be like sending a blind person into a dark room to look for a black cat which is not there. The world of Islam, with all its 56 countries, has proven unable to adopt democracy, except for the border case of Turkey, which has tried but did not emerge from that experience with flying colours. In our lifetime there were three military takeovers there, admittedly with a return to democracy each time, but under the open and supervising eye of the armed forces. When democratically-elected Erbakan, the Head of the Muslim Refah Party, served as Prime Minister (1996–98), the military could not wait to oust him in the name of 'safeguarding the Attaturk heritage'; they finally did and outlawed his party. A democracy under the aegis of the military is by definition not a democracy. The rest of the Muslim world is composed either of absolute monarchies of various degrees of 'democratic leeway', from obscurantist Saudi Arabia to more 'open', 'constitutional monarchies', such as Morocco and Jordan; from 'republican monarchies' where the absolute ruler designates his heir, usually his son, like Iraq, Syria, Libya and perhaps also

Egypt; from military juntas, which took over by force, like Pakistan, to military rules that are perpetuated via rigged 'elections', such as in Algeria, the Yemen and Tunisia; from erratic 'democracies' such as Indonesia, to chaotic regimes like Somalia and the Balkans; from fundamentalist Muslim rule like in Iran, the Sudan and the Taliban, to the corrupt and self-perpetuating regimes in Central Asia; and from openly supporting terror, like Syria, Iraq and Iran, to the latent terrorists of the Balkans, the Sudan and Saudi Arabia.

No one should assume that democracy is suitable for everyone, for every people cultivates the regime it deserves and it understands. When the Iranians could no longer stand the Shah's regime, they rebelled against it and forced their mighty King of Kings to abdicate and flee for his life. Thus, the Muslims, who are not accustomed to Western democracy, can change their oppressive regime for another, within the perimeters of what they conceive as legitimate or acceptable, even if, in our eyes, it lacks the legitimacy of election by the people. Legitimacy lies elsewhere in those regimes, either via claimed descent from the family of the Prophet, like the Kings of Morocco and Jordan, or by assuming religious titles, such as the 'Curator of the Two Holy Places' for the King of Saudi Arabia and the 'Curator of the Al-Aqsa Mosque' for the King of Jordan, and now Arafat, who presumes to be the Curator of the Holy Places, of Islam and Christianity, in the Holy Land. The others seek legitimacy in the sheer inertia of hereditary power, monarchical or republican (Saudi Arabia, the Gulf States, Jordan, Morocco, Syria, Libya, Iraq), or in the sheer power of inertia of military regimes which replace each other in succession (Pakistan, Syria, Iraq, Libya, the Yemen), or by being recognized by their fellow Arabs and Muslims, and by the Great Powers. Certainly, the game of democracy is being played to satisfy the appearances, 'elections' are held without opposing candidates being permitted to run (Egypt, Iraq, Syria, Libya), or those 'elected' in fact practice rule for life (Mubarak, Assad, Qaddafi, Arafat, Saddam and so on). When 'parliaments' are allowed to be 'elected' they must be 'loyal', that is, rubber-stamps to the regime in place; the monarch or autocrat retains the right to disband them at will, and often governs by fiat or emergency rules, which give him virtually unlimited powers.[1]

When rulers lack legitimacy, and this is the situation in virtually all Muslim countries, the regimes must impose their autocratic government, thus denying the basic requirements of democracy though they continue to advertise their 'democratic' system. They are encouraged to persist by the Western democracy which would rather have them in power, under the illusion of 'moderation' that it attaches to them, than having to face the fundamentalists among them who are the opposition to the regimes, unless they are the government themselves (like in Iran, Sudan and, until recently, the Taliban in Afghanistan, who have not yet had their final say). In this state of affairs, the Islamist opposition – such as the Hamas, the Hizbullah, the Muslim Brothers and other Muslim fundamentalist groupings, which for the most part are banned from government (Egypt, Jordan, Tunisia, Algeria, Turkey) – can acquire the legitimacy their governments lack, and wait in the aisles for the opportunity to take over power, as did the fundamentalists in Iran, Afghanistan and the Sudan. Since the latter are dreaded by the West, which would rather support the illegitimate governments in place, the West is therefore considered as 'meddling in internal Islamic affairs', and is popularly hated in consequence as 'aggressive' and 'arrogant', as are its 'puppet regimes' that it supports against popular will (Egypt, Jordan, Pakistan, Morocco, Turkey and so forth). In other words, the West is not only facing the wrath of the Islamists in the international arena, but also on the domestic front in every Muslim country where it sustains a local illegitimate government. The grim consequence is that the 'alliances' that the West likes so much to cultivate in the Muslim world are, by definition, not only temporary, but also detrimental in the long run to Western interests, and only serve to postpone the showdown.

RAISING THE CONSCIOUSNESS OF THE WESTERN PUBLIC

Many in the West like to cite truly moderate clerics and statesmen in the world of Islam, such as Sheikh Palazzi, the imam of the Muslim Mosque in Rome (who is contested by other Italian Muslims), or the Dean of the Department of Shari'a Law at Qatar University, who has come out in favour of Western-style Islamic reforms, especially in the school curricula, or Presidents Mubarak and Musharraf and Kings Hussein and Hassan, who have opted for dialogue with the West and are enjoying the US protective shield domestically and internationally. These rulers and clerics are so afraid of US retribution, on the one hand, and of the wrath of their publics, on the other, that they prefer, for now, to ride out the storm holding on to the lesser of the two evils. But, among the masses of the Muslim world, it is the radical Sheikh Qardawi and his peers who condone Islamikaze attacks; columnists who cannot hide their jubilation at the sight of the collapsing Twin Towers or the ripping apart of corpses of Israeli children by Palestinian martyr-bombers; or politicians and journalists who defy the United States and challenge Western culture, that enjoy the most popularity. And the more they are oppressed by their regimes, who wish to avoid the embarrassment of public celebration in front of Western television cameras, the more they are provoked to hate the West for its interference in their internal affairs, and to despise their governments as spineless 'lackeys' who cannot stand up to the West.

For better or for worse, then, the West must consider the Islamic world at large as an area of potential conflict and prepare its public opinion for it. A number of knowledgeable and courageous scholars and columnists, like Bernard Lewis, Victor Hansen, Fouad Ajami, Daniel Pipes, Thomas Friedman, Benny Morris, Martin Kramer and Sheikh Palazzi, to name only a few, have come out with extensive analyses that defy the stifling political correctness that has paralyzed Western political thinking in the past generation, and have provided enriching insights to the bewildered public opinion of the post-11 September era. Perhaps the bluntest of them all, and the most assiduous critique of radical Islam, is Daniel Pipes, who lashed out at the present state of paralysis among the governing elite, which unsuccessfully attempted to disconnect between Islam and the acts of terror, and counselled the need to 'Fight Militant Islam, Without Bias'. He pointed out that the problem at hand was not the religion of Islam as such, but the totalitarian ideology of Islamism, which prods Muslims to hold power, and when they do, to apply their Shari'a Law and enforce it through the state apparatus.[2] However, beyond the 10–15 per cent of Islamists that Pipes discerns in the Islamic world, with the rest 'fearing and loathing them', according to him, there is a vast silent portion of Muslims who sympathize, if not with militant Islam, then at least with its horrendous acts of terror, as the profuse statements and demonstrations of jubilation among Muslim intellectuals, professionals, columnists and the masses attested to in the aftermath of 11 September, and, on a daily basis, following every horrendous Islamikaze act which leaves Israeli civilians ripped apart, killed, or maimed for life.

Citing Nobel Prize winner, Mahfuz, as an adept of anti-Islamism, as Pipes rightly does, does not prove that his ideas or antipathies are sufficiently widespread to make a difference. Similarly, quoting the Tunisian Minister of Religious Affairs, Chebbi, as relegating Islamists to the 'garbage can', or Algeria's Interior Minister, who condemns without reserve the violence, murder and rape that the Islamists wreak on his country,[3] is equivalent to letting Mubarak express the anti-Islamic sentiment in his country. For in all those cases, the illegitimate rulers and some intellectuals, who are themselves threatened by the Islamists and therefore cannot speak highly of them, do not represent public opinion in general, to the extent that there is one. The facts are much more sombre and sad: when public opinion was free to express itself in Algeria, it gave the majority to the Islamists (1992), until the present illegitimate rulers, represented by their Interior Minister, took over; and after 11 September, the jubilation in the Egyptian press, which represented, and in turn shaped, popular opinion, had to be silenced by Mubarak, who feared for his standing *vis-à-vis* the United States. The sentiment in his country can be better gauged by the horrendous opinions of Sheikh Tantawi of Al-Azhar, by no means an Islamist, an appointee of Mubarak who as the Head of the Islamic establishment that Pipes calls 'traditional' – that is, quiescent and subservient to the rulers – who publicly and repeatedly approves of the Islamikaze martyrdom attacks, explicitly against Israel, but implicitly against all the rest, too. In other words, the fact that Mubarak and Tantawi condemned the 11 September horrors in order to placate the Americans, but at the same time Tantawi condones, even encourages, the same sort of attacks against Israel, points more to an expedient political double language than to a 'moderate' religious conviction that emanates from 'traditional Islam'. A thief is a thief whether he steals for you or from you.

President Bush, who did not buy the misnomer of 'suicide bombing', which would imply that the horrors in New York and elsewhere in the world were the deeds of a deranged and irresponsible few, went to the root of the issue when he declared in plain language that they were simple murderers, terrorists and homicide bombers. He pledged that not only would he go after them, but also destroy their bases and 'smoke them out of their holes', and consider their supporters and those who sheltered them as terrorists themselves, and bring them to justice (that is, trials in America) or justice to them (that is, physical destruction). The whole US operation in Afghanistan, and other operations that are in the pipeline and due to be launched – once the American arsenals, depleted in the years of complacency under Clinton, are replenished – are geared to respond to that challenge. He also established the Department of Internal Security, toughened the measures against terrorist organizations, including freezing the funds of their front charity associations, tightened the control of Muslim suspects in America, acquiesced to the arrest of many of them, is currently and routinely extending the list of acknowledged terrorist organizations, most of them Islamic, and urging his reluctant allies in the West to follow suit. He also pursues Muslim terrorists in other parts of the world, such as the Middle East, South-East Asia, South Asia and the Balkans, sends intelligence and military aid to those battling against them, and practically gives a free rein to Israel to battle and eliminate the terrorist threats that jeopardize her very existence.

Although the President's popularity has dramatically risen since the traumatic day of 11 September, in spite, or because, of the fact that he has practically put his country onto a war footing, he has been bogged down both by human rights and leftist groups who clamour for the terrorists' rights and against the all-out war in Afghanistan and the planned wars ahead, and the restrictions on civil liberties and arrests without trial which have become imperative since the crisis set in. He has also made some ill-considered, impulsive declarations that have complicated the situation, not eased it, notably the 'Crusade' he declared against terrorism and his statement that 'those who are not with us are against us'. For the West, the notion of 'Crusade' conjures up the medieval memories of an all-out war, where Christendom set out to defend its values which were being threatened by invading Islamdom along the very frontier of Europe in the Iberian Peninsula and Sicily, or were being endangered in its Holy Places by Saracen or 'Mohammedan' domination. Since then, those memories have been laid to rest, except for their temporary revival, in a purely Western context, when Ike Eisenhower launched his 'Crusade in Europe' in the last century not against Islam, but against European Fascism and Nazism. Bush made it clear that the United States would use all its power to pursue terrorists everywhere, 'smoke them out of their holes', search for them in their bases and destroy them and punish the countries which sheltered them or assisted them. If it were not for the US arsenals, depleted during the years of complacency under Clinton, the war would have expanded, sooner rather than later; he would have urged unity throughout the West under his leadership, as if he were a new Richard the

Lionheart or a Saint Louis of old, trying to drag endeavour into his reluctant European allies.

For the Muslim world, the revival of the crusade concept by a fervently Christian President, and his declaration of what sounded like total war against Islamdom – first in Afghanistan and then in Iraq, and then Allah knows where – evokes the ancient memories of an aggressive and arrogant West who invaded its territories and occupied them until it was expelled. Already, the Islamists have regarded the Gulf War of 1990–91 as an invasion of Islamic Holy Sites by the West, this time not in Palestine, but in the heart of the land of the two foremost Muslim Holy Sites – Mecca and Medina – hence the urgency to remove Western forces and the acts of terrorism that have ensued against the US servicemen in the Arabian Peninsula. The US President, who in his country and in the West may be regarded as battling today's equivalent of the medieval Isma'ili Assassins – those fanatic Muslims who wrought havoc and terror in the Middle East as today's Islamikaze now do the world over – is seen by Muslims, especially the fundamentalists among them, as a rogue President, bent on destroying Islam, not merely the 'terrorists' in its midst. Their response is also medieval, and is geared to seeking and identifying the new Saladin who will deliver the *coup de grâce* to present-day Crusaders, be they Americans, Europeans or Israelis. During the Gulf War, this was Saddam Hussein, who alone stood up to the Americans and their allies; today that honour belongs to Bin-Laden. Hence the tremendous sense of relief and joy that shuddered the length and breadth of the Muslim world when the Twin Towers collapsed, and the awaited end of Western 'arrogance' seemed close at hand.

The US President also erred when he let a number of Muslim leaders off the hook by urging them to choose whether they were with the United States or against it. Knowing the stakes, almost all of them declared that they were with America, while continuing at the same time to harbour terrorism (like Syria, Lebanon, Pakistan, Iran and the like); to aid it (like Iran, Saudi Arabia and Iraq); or practice it (like the Palestinians, the Pakistanis in Kashmir and the Hizbullah in Lebanon). But since those countries made their declarations of 'support' for the United States – though all of them continued to 'condemn' the acts of terror against civilians, not the terrorist organizations who committed them and took responsibility for them, and some of them not even that – they thought they had passed the US Administration's test and were thenceforth exonerated from any blame or punishment. Terrorism for them became some kind of natural calamity that one could do nothing to prevent, and most Muslim countries that were linked to terrorism in one way or another were content to pursue their dual standards, say one thing and do another, confident that their 'vow of allegiance' to the United States stood firm in the way between their deeds and US retribution. This did not last long; the US Adminsitration realized its mistake and shifted the test from mere words to actual deeds, and inevitably had to lengthen the list of terrorist organizations.

Some writers have contributed to raising public awareness of terrorism and its goals by exposing it and countering the arguments of the Muslims and their leftist supporters who conveniently imputed its 'root reasons' to US foreign policy: specifically favouring Israel, on the one hand, in its struggle against the Arabs and Muslims, and for clamping down on Saddam Hussein, on the other hand, thus 'bringing hunger and destruction to innocent Iraqi children'. Other false pretences of Muslim terrorists, such as the 'purity of their struggle', their 'defensive stance in the face of Western aggression', and good intentions in their quest to Islamize the entire world, have also been exposed, stripped bare, dismissed and ridiculed by many a writer who woke up to the harsh reality of Muslim terrorism and its worldwide schemes against Western civilization. Stanley Kurtz of the *National Review*, for example, asserted that mere changes in US foreign policy 'won't placate the terrorists', because 'it is America itself that the terrorists envy and hate – our freedom, our power, our prosperity', and therefore America was left with little alternative besides 'the use of diplomacy, finance and force to bring the terrorists and the nations that harbour them to heel'. He contended that had the first attempt against the Twin Towers succeeded in 1993, some 200,000 people could have perished, and the price of pleading with Sheikh 'Umar abd-al-Rahman to desist would not have been this or that concession by Israel to the Arabs, but the sacrifice of Israel's very existence, and the suspension of US aid to his home country, Egypt, so that he could return there 'Khomeini-like, to stand at the head of a fundamentalist Muslim state'.[4]

David Makovsky, of the *Baltimore Sun*, made the point that since the Americans hurriedly left Lebanon in 1983, when 241 US servicemen were blown up in the first declared jihad against the West in the contemporary Middle East, Islamic militants saw this as a 'vindication that suicide bombing was religiously sanctioned as well as being deadly effective', but it took another 18 years and the deadly horror of 11 September to 'galvanize America to action, resolving it to the idea that terrorism must be eradicated'. He added that the 'campaign was not only just about Bin-Laden, but confronting an ideology that justifies killing in the name of religion'. Therefore, he saw the essence of the battle not in getting the leaders and clerics of the Middle East to denounce the perpetrators of 11 September, but to 'discredit this revived ideology and make it clear to their faithful that Islam does not sanction the wanton killing of innocents'.[5] Judging from the voluminous literature of incitement still in vogue in the Muslim world today, including in countries that are close 'allies' of the United States, and especially the open contribution of the clerics and many columnists to that literature of hate and encouragement and praise of the Islamikaze martyrs, one realizes that Makovsky's expectations are yet to be fulfilled. Fouad Ajami, the incisive and insightful expert on the Middle East, himself of Lebanese extraction, explains why:

> America is off to an Eastern campaign, and we should not be surprised if we found ourselves almost alone. It is in a big non-American world that we must track the trail of terror that has tormented us for a good part of a difficult decade. We shall carry our gear and our desire for justice to hardened lands, places that may not yield the 'smoking guns' that the sceptics will demand to see...Few friends, we may find, can endure the fury of anti-American mobs and the burden of walking with us in broad daylight...There are leaders out there, and a watchful crowd, pleased that we have been humbled. We should not be surprised if by the lights of that vast region we never get it right, if in Karachi and Cairo and Ramallah, we shall be second-guessed at every turn...
>
> Others will tell us that we could have been spared this great pain had we listened to local laments...or had our shadow not lain across their world. When the missiles are fired into Afghanistan, we should be ready for the wrath of the city crowds and for the sudden interest in Afghan welfare that men and women in the Arab and Muslim lands will come to express...The Arabs tell us that all would have been well...had we cast Israel adrift, had we known where our true 'interest' lay. But nothing could be further from the truth. A

deeper anti-Americanism grips Arab and Muslim lands. It has been America's fate to be caught in the crossfire of a war over Islam itself, a war between privilege and wrath, between the secular powers in the saddle and a nativist-pious opposition from below.[6]

An editorial in the *Washington Post* lashed out at the false pretences of Mubarak's regime, which is 'politically exhausted and morally bankrupt', for his double-talk of support for the United States, his benefactor at a time when he and his Foreign Minister 'encouraged state-controlled media and clerics to promote the anti-Western, anti-modern and anti-Jewish propaganda of the Islamic extremists'.[7] Just to wake up to the realization that the 'trusted' ally of the United States in the Middle East – whose armies conducted annual manoeuvres with the Americans in his Western Desert, and whose economy was kept afloat by the $2 billion that the United States poured into its coffers – was in fact a broken reed that could not be counted on in times of strife, was one of the greatest after-shocks that the United States experienced after the shock of 11 September. And then it also woke up to the nauseating and insultingly primitive accusations throughout the Islamic world, trying to impute that horrendous massacre to a 'Jewish plot', so as to deflect public criticism from them. We have already seen the variety of Arab papers who espoused the idea with as much delight as the act itself, but we have to accept that belief in the Blood Libel has expanded into other lands of Islam as well. Robert Hardman of *The Spectator*, tells a harrowing story from Pakistan, another Muslim dictatorship thought to be an American 'ally':

> This week's blazing bazaar in Quetta, running street battles in Peshawar, and effigies of burning Bushes up and down the land, have all been incited by a small collection of mullahs who are thoroughly enjoying their sudden prominence. In a land controlled by a military oligarchy for two years, they are now the only civilian politicians regularly appearing on the front pages...The relatively moderate voices...attract little attention compared with the battle cries of men like Fazlur Rahman...or Azam Tariq – fringe figures who have become the strident new voice of opposition to the General and the West. These are the jihadmongers, they are a small minority...

but Iran's ayatollahs remain a sobering reminder of what a small, well-organized fundamentalist clique can do...

'Why is no one investigating the Jews?' Mr Rahman demands as we start to discuss the New York atrocities. 'They produced a list of names of Muslims on those planes and yet they turn out to be alive. Why is here no list of all the Jews on the plane? And why did 4,000 Jews not turn up for work on the day of the attacks? And why did Sharon cancel his visit to New York that day? And how come all the camera crews who filmed the crashes were Jewish? The Jews committed those attacks !'

Where is the evidence for this extraordinary Jewish conspiracy theory', I ask. 'We have our own sources', he says grandly. Rahman leads his own wing of the fundamentalist Jamiat ulama-e-Islam Party, the nearest thing to a Taliban fan club in this part of the world... He has between two and three million supporters, and his own private police force. He has been preaching his conspiracy theories across Pakistan for the best part of a month, and millions believe him.[8]

If, indeed, millions follow Rahman and believe his preaching, then how can Hardman tell us that he represents a 'small minority'? The 'balanced' Western reporting, which did not allow the reporter to cross the boundaries of political correctness on the morrow of the atrocities, impelled him to exonerate Islam in general, disregarding his own evidence of the widespread Muslim disturbances in Pakistan and of the fabrication of the Jewish plot, and the chorus of 'death to the Infidel!', which was shouted by the surrounding crowd during that interview. The United States also became aware, through a report by Ken Silverstein, that the powerful Pakistani Interservices Intelligence Agency (ISI), which has been collaborating with the CIA for years, had also backed the Taliban and trained them as its close allies, even as the massacres in the US Embassies in East Africa (1998) and on the USS *Cole* (2000), both related to al-Qa'ida, were being planned and executed; that it had participated as a full partner in the drug trafficking of the Taliban; and that it had sponsored some of the terrorist attacks in Kashmir against India. Many ISI officers were slated as 'deeply hostile to the West', to the point that an anonymous person who knew them closely (presumably a CIA operative) was quoted as commenting that 'If the ISI is going to be our eyes and ears in Afghanistan, we better watch our back.'[9]

And what of Saudi Arabia, for years the central pillar of US policy in the Middle East? The shift in Saudi policy and public opinion, as shaped by the official press, was brought to public attention in the West by a whole series of investigative reports. Joshua Teitelbaum, in *The New Republic*, posited that the inter-Arab ambiance and the improvement of Saudi relations with Iraq did not permit the Saudis to follow the US course any longer, especially as the Islamic opposition in the country was becoming more vociferous about the presence of US troops on Saudi soil.[10] There have also been reports on the House of Sa'ud, the Wahhabis, the oil wealth of Arabia, Saudi financial backing of terrorism, including the rewarding of Islamikze bombers,[11] and the ridicule that was widespread in the US press when the Saudi prince attempted to buy the good will of the American public, after he had slighted US foreign policy by presenting a US$10 million cheque to a dismayed Mayor Giuliani; which was consequently rejected by the proud mayor.[12] Fouad Ajami, on his part, commented in his scathing critique of Sandra Mackey's new book on Saddam's Iraq that it was the continued US presence on Saudi soil, occasioned by the fact that the United States had failed to dismantle Saddam's regime during the Gulf War – making it imperative for the United States to remain in close control of Iraqi air space – that had unleashed the fury of 11 September.[13] His commentary, especially his suggestion that the Iraqis of Baghdad and Basra would welcome the Americans as liberators, as the Afghans did in Kabul, certainly helped prepare the ground for the upcoming air-strikes against Iraq, once Saddam has been identified as the obstacle to security and stability in the Gulf, and as the indirect culprit of the events of 11 September.

Then came Martin Kramer's epoch-making study, which exposed the crippling political correctness of the Middle East studies discipline in the United States, which for years had played down the threat of extremist Islam, 'helping to lull America into complacency'. He lashed out at MESA, the Middle East Studies Association of North America, which, with the help of scholars and experts such as Edward Said, Richard Bulliet, Joel Beinin and others, dismissed the 'conspiracy to blow up buildings, sabotage commercial airlines and poison water supplies as highly exaggerated stereotyping' and denounced US policy in the Middle East as an imposition of a 'neo-liberal, repressive *Pax Americana*', or as a 'world hegemonic discourse of Western cultural imperialism'. He lamented the skirting, by MESA, of the word 'terrorism', even after the horrors of the Twin Towers, and for its treating the acts of war of the terrorists as felonies which required merely bringing the culprits to justice (what culprits, one might add? They are dead!!) rather than pursue their war-mongering operators who vie for mass-killings. He came to the conclusion that part of the problem, not of the remedy, were those academics whose institutions of higher learning were being subsidized by the US government precisely in order to prepare the nation, not to lull it, and urged the US Congress not to allocate 'one more penny for this Empire of Terror'.[14]

Other authors awoke to the link between the stepped-up Palestinian Islamikaze attacks against Israel and the 11 September attacks, once they agreed that, in principle, they were alike, though the scale of the act and the number of victims varied enormously. Or perhaps not. For, taking into account the numbers of deaths and respective population size, the 100 Islamikaze bombings against Israel, in which more than 500 innocent Israelis have been murdered, are equivalent, multiplied by a factor of 50, to 25,000 in America. Furthermore, the most horrendous acts, where restaurants and buses have been blown up by Palestinians, have accounted for 20 victims each (in the case of the Pesach Seder massacre in Netanya the number climbed to 29), that is, proportionately, 1,000 people killed, and many more maimed, in each of those chilling acts of terror. During the month of March 2002 alone, over 100 Israelis were massacred by terrorists, namely the equivalent of 5,000 in America, or the total amount of US casualties in both New York and Washington and on board the crashed planes. Thomas Friedman of the *New York Times*, under the telling title 'Suicidal Lies', took the Palestinians to task for imposing on all of civilization a new form of warfare, using 'suicidal bombers – strapped with dynamite ...to achieve their political goals', and to create a balance of power with the Israelis. He refutes as a lie the conventional wisdom which has claimed that the Palestinians used this strategy out of 'desperation, stemming out of Israeli occupation', for the simple reason that many other desperate people did not strap explosives onto their bodies to express their discontent. He castigated the Palestinians for having elected Islamikaze acts as a strategy, and warned that if such a strategy is allowed to work in Israel, then the entire civilized world will eventually be threatened by terrorists who might strap nuclear weapons around themselves, and that was the reason that the entire world should adopt the necessary measures to see that strategy defeated.[15]

This powerful message, which makes the entire civilized world responsible for seeing to it that Islamikaze terrorism comes to an end as a legitimate tool of struggle, not only connects the Palestinians to the events of 11 September, in which the same deadly tactics were used, but also warns that the West cannot disengage from Israel and leave her to her own devices, because her wars are the West's. Michael Gove of *The Times* warns, moreover, not to press Israel to settle with the Palestinians under the shadow of terrorist Islamikaze attacks, because that 'democracy's salient which evil means to overwhelm', like the Falklands 20 years ago and Czechoslovakia 63 years ago, and is the testing field for Western resolution by those who:

> ...live by violence and feast on weakness...prosecuting their claims by force of arms, directed against the innocent in their sights, and solicit international pressure for a 'peace plan' to satisfy their manufactured grievances. These plans, hybrids bred from the spores of aggression and watered by the sweat of fear, poison any contested ground in which they take root. They bind and weaken the innocent prey, confirm the calculation of the evil that democracy is too decadent to resist, and eventually embolden the wicked in their ambition for total conquest...The lesson of Czechoslovakia was a simple one: evil must not prosper if yet greater violence is to be averted...Now history asks us again...what we have learnt. Painfully little it seems. For in Israel, evil rolls the dice, and the West hands over the chips...
>
> The moral logic of self-defence, intuitively grasped across the West after 11 September, licenses a nation under such attack to seek out, punish and disable those responsible. But the West today seeks to circumscribe, hedge around or deny morality in Israel's 'peace plans'...Each of these 'peace plans' rewards terror by ratifying the gains secured by violence and reinforcing the message that the West is too weak to resist aggression. The terrorist calculation which Western sponsors of these plans fail to realise...is brutally simple. For Arafat and his allies in Hamas, and for his sponsors from Riyadh to Baghdad, the loss of Palestinian life is irrelevant. The indifference of the leaders of the Intifadah to the death of their people was articulated by Arafat...with his call for 'martyrs by the millions.[16]

Gove's conclusion is that any diplomatic settlement imposed on Israel as a result of the current wave of terror will have secured a better forward base for the terrorists' stated goal of exterminating Israel, and would 'advertise to the world what al-Qa'ida hoped to establish on 11 September: that suicide bombing, if prosecuted for long enough, will work'. But the spectre of a Muslim defeat of the West, and the specific vows of Muslim *reconquista*, do not hover over Israel alone: they touch the very heart of Europe also, notably the Iberian Penisnsula and Southern France. Alexander Rose of the *New Republic* cites Bin-Laden as pledging that 'the tragedy of Andalusia would not be repeated in Palestine' and that 'Palestine cannot be allowed to become Jewish'. That means not only that the memory of the loss of Muslim power in the Iberian Peninsula is still alive in the minds of Muslims, but that it serves as a historic lesson. Muslims had succumbed not due to Christian fortitude, they maintain, but to the evils of factionalism among Muslims along clannish lines, which allowed their Christian rivals to take advantage of their disunity and weakness and conquer them. To this day, writes Rose, the Muslim rulers who allied themseves alongside Christian princes to oust their dynastic rivals are reviled in Islamic history. The parallel that Bin-Laden posits is therefore a warning to the pro-Western Arab regimes of the Middle East not to 'sell out' to the United States and her peace plans,[17] lest the Andalusia tragedy is repeated. Moreover, it appears, according to Rose, that Bin-Laden regarded the Andalusia antecedent as a 'shorthand for Islamizing the world, or at least for forcibly restoring the imperial glories and religious dynamism of Islam's earlier centuries'. Spain, to his mind, had been treacherously ripped from the hands of its rightful owners, and 'humiliatingly remained gripped in the talons of the Christians'.[18] Therefore, both must be reclaimed, and history must be reversed on both scores.

Some commentators went to the root of the matter by exposing to the Western public the false pretensions of the Arabs and Muslims when justifying or rationalizing the acts of terror of which they were accused. To the claim of some terrorist leaders that they resembled the American founding fathers, as regards their morality, tactics and goals, Victor Hanson retorted in a scathing rebuttal in the *National Review* that 'Suicide Bombers are not akin to our founding fathers'. He described that claim as 'Goebbels-like gibberish, since few took seriously Bin-Laden's infantile references to the *Reconquista* of Crusader kingdoms, or his half-baked Nietzchean pontification about strong and weak horses'. He also lambasted the Palestinians' 'history lessons... that are presented ... on our newscasts and in our papers as serious paradigms that seek to prove not only the righteousness of their cause, but often a purported natural affinity with the American experience itself'. He feared the 'danger that distortions about the past, if repeated often enough, can take on the guise of orthodoxy'. He also lamented the comparison of the Israelis to the imperialistic and militarily preponderant British, and the weak and idealistic Palestinians to the American freedom-fighters of 1776. He asserted that not only was the analogy false, but also offensive to the American nation, for in spite of occasional atrocities on both sides of the American War of Independence, Americans did not blow up Loyalist American women and children, or dynamite Tory churches – much less 'had agents in London been shooting British schoolgirls in their beds'. 'The Palestinians have streets named after murderers', he added, and 'give bounties to those who butcher women at work and in their sleep; the Continental Congress did not'. He also stressed that before Palestinians drew any analogies, they should make sure that they had a legislative council that could make laws like in the fledgling United States, or a Washington that was not a dictator like Arafat.[19]

Hanson particularly lashed out at the Palestinians for their easy invocations of 'genocide' and the Holocaust, in association with Israeli incursions into Jenin and other nests of terrorism, especially in the undiscerning European press which had forgot the Nazi horrors generated by their countries and were now prone to swallow these insulting and fallacious parallels. The point is that no comparison can be made between the Nazi's systematic murder of millions of Jews – a daily 10,000 of them at Auschwitz – with 70 Palestinians who were killed during a battle in Jenin. He condemned the Palestinians for being wicked in their shameless efforts to invoke the Nazis to denigrate Holocaust survivals, and spurious in their equation of industial murder on a continental scale with the minimal collateral damage at war'. It was Saddam Hussein, he emphasized, who came closest to the Nazis, because he compelled the Israelis to wear gas masks, not the other way around, and he annihilated thousands of Iraqis using gas. He also thought that Arafat comparing Jenin to Stalingrad was preposterous, as the latter cost millions of lives and lasted through years of hunger, battles and untold misery, compared to the brief and mostly uneventful Jenin battle, following which international aid was quick to arrive and relieve the needy. He also contended that the Palestinians were spreading their fallacies about the Israeli 'occupation', that was launched in 1967 and was at the root of the Palestinian problem, while in fact it was a besieged and attacked Israel which responded by destroying and taking over the military emplacements from which it was being viciously harrassed. Therefore, he totally questions the credibility of Arab spokesmen who 'cannot vote, speak freely or criticize their government or religion in their papers', and attributed much of the blame to the allies of the Arabs, who are well entrenched in the universities and media. 'The former', he said, 'spread fabrications', but only after they had been manufactured by the latter.[20]

In a similarly courageous eye-opener, in a previous article, Hanson determined that in spite of Israel's readiness to offer concessions, the rhetoric of destroying Israel 'remain much more ubiquitous than the gospel of co-existence' in the Arab world. He said that while Arafat was negotiating peace outwardly, he continued to 'scream jihad and Infidels, as he praised suicide bombers as martyrs and heroes and promised the capture of Jerusalem'. Dismissing the Palestinian, and other Arab and Muslim grievances regarding the 'root causes' of their terrorist activities, he asserts that 'much of the matter is simply pure anti-Semitism and the power of oil'. He says that those two themes are central in the many angry letters he receives daily from critics, and concludes that much of the issue is psychological and arises because the:

> Jewish State is right smack in the Middle of the Arab world – and by every measure of economic, political, social and cultural success thriving amidst misery. Without oil, without a large population, without friendly countries on its borders, without vast real estate, and without the Suez Canal, it somehow provides its citizenry with a way of life far more humane than what is found in Syria, Iraq, Lebanon, Jordan or Egypt. Yet, the world listens to the Palestinians' often duplicitous leadership – despite the corrupt nature and the murderous past history of the Arafat regime – because its sponsors sell a good part of the globe's oil. And to risk their wrath, one would have to support a few million Jews, not hundreds of millions of, say, British, Swedes or Italians... And so, we do not give a damn over millions of innocents else-where butchered over millions of acres each year worldwide,

but instead focus on what the Palestinians lost while attempting to destroy their neighbours.[21]

These articles by prominent American and other columnists certainly helped the public understand that the spurious Muslim and Arab claim that should the Palestinian issue be resolved, that is, should Israel be abandoned by the West and the Palestinians vindicated, then the 'root reasons' of terrorism would have been addressed. Because the public began to understand that, in the sarcastic words of French writer Alexandre Del Valle, 'After 11 September, it is enough to dissociate oneself from Bin-Laden, to be considered moderate'.[22] The Palestinians did superficially dissociate themselves from Bin-Laden, while they continued to practice his teachings and his acts of martyrdom, but that was enough for some Western media to shift the responsibility for murders, those of Americans in New York, as those of Palestinians in Jenin, to the Jews. However, when Del Valle saw and read tracts distributed by Muslims at the Place de la Republique in Paris crying 'Mort aux Juifs!!!' (Death to the Jews!!!), unqualified racist appeals to exterminate Jews for what they are, then he and others understood that the Jews in Palestine, otherwise known as Israelis, as well as others, were earmarked for destruction, and that was the real issue, not Muslim terrorism. Del Valle cites the *Gud Magazine* of the extreme right in France which, in association with the Islamists, praised the Nazi–Palestinian alliance of World War II; this had been geared to eliminate the Jews of Palestine and facilitate the rise of a totally Arab state in Palestine, headed by the Mufti of Jerusalem, on their ashes.[23]

The American public did not need reports from Paris to awaken to the reality of hatred for Jews and Israelis in some Western circles, since it has been exposed to its own home-grown haters in the United States itself, not only those among its allies such as Israel. For example, a pro-Palestinian march at San Francisco State University, one of many, was reported in April 2002, in which the marchers distributed leaflets on campus which depicted a can bearing a photograph of a mutilated baby with the legend: 'Palestinian children meat – Slaughtered according to Jewish rites under American license.' A counter-rally on campus by pro-Israelis met with heckling and slogans, such as 'F*** the Jews', 'Jews, go back to Russia!', and even 'Too bad Hitler did not finish the job'. At the University of Colorado at Boulder, there was a wave of highly abusive graffiti daubed around the campus, bearing the same message: 'Zionazis', as well as others. The anti-Semitic abuse that was publicized in the United States included telephone death threats to Jewish institutions, such as Hillel, on campuses, or curses and spitting at pro-Israelis who distributed leaflets. At Carnegie-Mellon University in Pittsburgh, there were reports of a swastika being painted on the Hillel Centre, and hostile reactions hurled at Jews who wore skullcaps. Though most of the anti-Jewish and anti-Israeli activity is perpetrated by Muslim students, the most fanatical strongholds of anti-Semitism are on the West Coast of the United States, especially around Berkeley and San Francisco, where the phenomenon is not restricted to Muslims. These areas breed American-born students who are also America-haters, and their hatred for Israel is a consequence of their hatred for their own country against which they rebel, once they label themselves as revolutionaries, socialists and the like.[24]

Melanie Phillips, a columnist for the *Daily Mail*, expressed her protest at a world where terrorists are protected while the Jews are blamed. She said that while the Israelis were the victims of terror, they were being portrayed as 'cold-hearted, fascist thugs'. Apparently, she had become so alarmed at the firestorm of anti-Israeli and anti-Jewish hatred blazing out of the British media that she felt the need to publish a full-page article telling her readers that 'The Jewish Faith is Not an Evil Religion'. She put the question in all its horror:

> Not evil? Why should anyone think such a vile thing? After all, aren't the Jews in Isreal the victims of terror? Aren't they being blown to bits by suicide bombers who are deliberately targeting elderly Holocaust survivors at Passover Seders and children in pizza parlours? Haven't they suffered casualties that would be equivalent in Britain to 4,000 dead and many thousands injured since the Intifadah began?

Her answer is that Israel 'had committed a heinous crime, that of seeking to defend herself against the attempt to annihilate it, and for its effrontery, a torrent of lies, distortions, libels, abandonment of objectivity, and the substitution of malice and hatred for truth is pouring out of the British and European media and Establishment'. She condemned the double standards, twisted history and hate-imbued moral blindness in the analysis of the situation which 'defied belief'. Her summation is frightening:

The question is whether the West will stand shoulder to shoulder with Israel in its war against terror or whether it will side with terror against it. At present the signs are ominous. The leitmotiv of the State of Israel, forged after the world looked the other way from the Holocaust, is 'never again'; and if they are destroyed, the Jews, as ever, will be to blame.[25]

The outrage occasionally expressed by journalists and columnists, who cannot stand the distortion of facts and events and who refuse to submit to the prostitution of the profession of journalism, is largely due not only to the moral judgement of those courageous individuals, but also to the exposure and availability of the Arabic press to them which would have been otherwise inaccessible, due to language and inter-cultural difficulties of communication between the Western and Arab worlds. Bringing Arab thinking to the Western media and policy-makers, translated into English and often annotated from its original Arabic, and undistilled for Western audiences, has been the crucial contribution of *MEMRI* (the Middle East Media Reports), and its founder and director, Yigal Carmon. This has raised Western consciousness to the essence of terror and its supporters and distributors. For when an official Saudi medium tells the Americans that their media is controlled by the Jews as part of their 'conspiracy to rule the world, as spelled out in their Protocols of the Elders of Zion'[26] – few Americans would have been made aware of this insult, to Jews and Americans alike, if it were not for *MEMRI* – one can comprehend the extent of its impact on the awakening of the West to the realities of the world. Similarly, when such a close 'ally' of the United States as Mubarak, in an interview with an Arab daily, practically justifies the Islamikaze acts of violence by the Palestinians as being 'their only weapons', and puts the blame on Israel and Prime Minister Sharon for daring to act in self-defence;[27] or when he blames the Jewish Lobby in the United States for mounting an attack against Egypt and Saudi Arabia in the West; or when he condemns 'dictatorship in Israel' while boasting his own 'democracy';[28] few in the West would have been aware of this 'politically correct' interview with the Arab press, which would have caused derision in the Western press, had it not been for *MEMRI*.

MEMRI has also been responsible for making the West aware of the rare, but nonetheless noteworthy, eruptions of Arab self-criticism. Who would have known of the Dean of the University of Qatar, repeatedly cited in this book, who demanded reform in the Saudi curricular system, or of the Tunisian columnist who opposed the comparison between Zionism and Nazism, if not for *MEMRI*'s translations? A liberal columnist in the London-based Arabic daily *al-Hayat* blamed both 'fanatic Zionists' as well as 'Muslim jurists who justify the murder of Jews', as well as 'Arab media people who shape public opinion', for the new outbreak of anti-Semitism in the Arab world. He nevertheless finds four differences between Arab anti-Semitism, which he considers dangerous and deserving to be battled against, and classical European anti-Semitism:

1. Arab anti-Semitism does not deal with legends and myths, like the crucifixion of Jesus, the Blood Libel and well-poisoning, but with the practical issue of the Palestinian conflict.
2. The Muslim heritage does not deal with the Jews harshly or bitterly, unlike the Christians; the Prophet had defeated the three Jewish tribes in the Arabian Peninsula, and the Jews did not murder him, therefore enlightened Islam did not raise the issue of Islam *versus* Judaism.
3. While European anti-Semitism started at the grassroots and seeped upwards, in Islam it seeps down from the 'backward and defeated rulers'.
4. Arab anti-Semitism often merges with feelings of ethnic loyalty, in a world divided between Sunnites, Shi'ites, Christians, Kurds, Berbers and so on.

Evidently, this 'liberal' Arab was wrong on all four counts, as we have clearly seen: because Arabs have been accusing the Jews of all the faults that Christian anti-Semitism has laid at their door; Muslim heritage continues to lambast them for their relations with the Prophet and for a genealogy which relates them to 'apes and pigs'; there is widespread hatred among the masses of Arabs; and Jews have been singled out, in the most vicious terms, in spite of the ethnic divisions in the Arab and Islamic worlds. Nevertheless, he finds 'fault' in Arab anti-Semitism in the sense that, compared to Nazism, it does not possess the same qualities of 'functional modernism and the sense of order' that characterized the Nazis, nor the racist ideological commitment of European anti-Semitism. His summation is quite remarkable:

Our anti-Semitism is absolutely devoid of culture and is totally stupid, even when it is uttered by glamorous politicians and journalists, who evince insensitivity and misunderstanding towards racism in our history...Even in Durban we committed the mistake of dubbing 'racist' those who sought shelter [from the Holocaust], and confused the racist acts perpetrated by Israel and the 'racist' nature of Zionism...We simply suffer from ignorance and bad education and do not have the ability to distinguish between modern journalism and the danger of writing only our impressions [without thorough investigation]. We look out of the window, dislike what we see, express our solidarity with the Palestinians and curse the Jews...and then return to our deep slumber. To the ignorance of our journalists we have to add the fact that they operate within nationalized media, they were not accustomed to freedom of expression, and they chose the easiest way of pleasing their rulers...Our anti-Semitism becomes even more disgusting when it is devoid of any humanitarian and political aid to the Palestinians and is confined to cursing the Jews.[29]

John Derbyshire dealt with the destructiveness of 'hesperophobia', which literally means 'hatred of the West', but is somehow pointedly directed by the Arabs towards the Jews,[30] as if they were the quintessence of the West, or perhaps as what psychologists would term 'displaced aggression' towards the weak while the actual message is directed towards the strong that cannot be directly threatened or defied. He compared the armies of the West during the Gulf War, which were 'swift, deadly, efficient...under the command of elected civilians at the head of a robust, elaborate constitutional structure', while all the Arabs could show was a 'shambling, ill-nourished, shapeless rabble, led by a mad gangster despot'. Those were the enemies during that war, while the 'good Arabs' who were on the side of the United States were 'cowering in their plush-lined, air-conditioned bunkers being waited on by their Filipino servants, while we did their fighting for them'. And since the final body count was 134 Westerners dead, compared to 20,000 Arabs or more, the 'superiority of one culture over another has not been so starkly demonstrated since a handful of British wooden ships beat the Celestial Empire in the Opium War'. He sees the hesterophobia as a result of the bitterness towards the West, hence the Palestinian Islamikaze attacks against shopping malls or

Sbarro's outlets, themselves examples of Western culture, rather than on Jewish schools, synagogues or religious settlements. Israeli culture being Western puts anti-Semitism in the category of hesterophobia. Therefore, he urged full-fledged support for Israel, because:

> ... Israel's culture is ours. She is part of the West. If she goes down, we have suffered a defeat, and the howling, jeering forces of barbarism have won ... You do not have to be Zionist, or even Jewish, to support Israel ... you just have to think straight. You just have to understand that the war between civilization and barbarism is being fought today just as it was fought at Chalonnes and Tours, at the gates of Kiev and Vienna, by the Hoplites at Marathon and the Legions on the Rhine ... and the thing about war is, you have to take sides, and close your eyes to your allies' imperfections ... There is no other choice. What happened [on 11 September] was not, or not only, an act of anti-Americanism, anti-Israelism or anti-Semitism. It was more than anything else ... an act of hesperophobia.[31]

These voices of reason and integrity, which would have perhaps passed unnoticed, like faint stars, if it were not for the dark skies in the background, were joined by the witty and scathing comments of George Will, of the *Washington Post*, who this time took Europe to task for its general attitude towards Israel and the Jews, which allowed *La Stampa*, a supposedly liberal daily, to publish a cartoon depicting the infant Jesus in a manger, menaced by an Israeli tank and saying: 'Don't tell me they want to kill me again'. He also criticized the British press and intelligentsia for being 'toxic' and cited Ron Rosenbaum who, in his book *Explaining Hitler*, noted the scandal of European leaders supporting the Palestinian right of return, that is the right to 'eliminate the state that was created in response to European genocide, when so many Europeans are still living in homes stolen from Jews they helped to murder'. Following Ruth Wisse, he contended that Hitler's Reich had failed, all right, but his anti-Semitism, which had vowed to destroy European Jewry had not. Quite the contrary, he stresses that anti-Semitism has never been stronger in world affairs since the end of World War II, and the United Nations, the main embodiment of lessons learned from the war, has become the instrument of lending legitimacy to the anti-Semites' war against the Jewish State that was founded by the survivors of that war. Despite the current assertion that should Israel change her conduct, anti-Semites would be mollified, Will determines, again following Wisse, that anti-Semitism is not directed against the behaviour of the Jews but against their very existence, and concludes that although Israel contains just one thousandth of the world population, it holds all the hopes for the continuation of the Jewish experience as a portion of the human narrative.[32]

Numerous other American writers, who were incensed by the attacks against Israel and accusations against the Jews, tended to lump together Americans and Israelis, in defence of both. David Gelernter, of the *Weekly Standard*, explained the clear affinity between the first American settlers and the first returning Jews in Palestine – both of European extraction – and determined that the United States and Israel belonged, in the final analysis, to those who painstakingly built them. That is the reason, he says, that the Europeans and other 'experts' on Americans and Jews who did not live through similar experiences could not understand that affinity, and wrongly asserted that it was Jewish influence in the United States which determined the extraordinary intimate relationship between the two countries.[33] Charles Krauthammer, on his part, while dubbing Arabs and Muslims as 'Haters of Civilization', noticed the euphoria in fundamentalist circles immediately after 11 September, and before the United States overcame its disarray and launched the counter-attack, when one leader of the Hamas urged President Bush to convert to Islam as the 'only solution'. This seemed bizarre to the author, because American society 'was taught tolerance from the cradle [and Americans] visit each other's churches for interdenominational succour and solidarity'. A few days later, Bush was denounced by al-Qa'ida as the Head of the Infidels, signalling that what was to come would not be a war with social, economic or political roots, but would be one of fanaticism versus civilization itself. He said that the 'new enemy was heir to the malignant ideologies of the twentieth century. Its nihilism, its will to power, its celebration of blood and death, its craving for the cleansing policy that comes only from eradicating life and culture, radical Israel itself, is heir, above all, to Nazism.' The antecedent of the destruction of the Bamyan Buddhas should have been the signal for the upcoming horror of the Twin Towers, he implied, inasmuch as both were meant to 'obliterate beauty and greatness, elegance and grace. These artifacts represented civilization embodied in stone and steel. They had to be destroyed.'[34]

David Brooks, in his long dissertation in the *Weekly Standard*, imputes the joint European–Arab hatred of the United States and Israel to their bourgeoisophobia (a term borrowed from Gustave Flaubert, who signed his letters Bourgeoisophobus), as the 'bourgeois' form the quintessence of these two hated societies and cultures, Americans and Jews having 'emerged as the great exemplars of undeserved success. 'They are the money-mad Molochs of the earth, the vulgarizers of morals, corrupters of culture, and proselytizers of idolatrous values.' They practice 'conquest capitalism, overrunning poorer nations and exploiting weaker neighbours in their endless desire for more and more'. In the eyes of those who hate them, both nations 'thrive because they are spiritually stunted. In their obliviousness to things holy in life, their feverish energy, their injustice, their shallow pursuit of power and gain, that allow them to build fortunes, construct weapons, and play the role of hyperpower.' They are hated, he contends, exactly as French intellectuals of the 1830s hated bankers and traders and rose to destroy them, out of the same sense of unjust inferiority. Today's haters are not only intellectuals but also 'suicide bombers' who are taught in madrasa as to exercise hatred and violence. Like them, 'Europeans burn with humiliation, because they know, deep down, that both America and Israel possess a vitality and heroism that their nations once had but no longer do.' Therefore, he believes that the Palestinian conflict, which once was a local dispute about land, has been been transformed into a great cultural showdown, and new battle-lines are forming.[35]

Brooks sees a wide array of bourgeoisophobes taking shape: Arafat guerilla socialists, Hamas' Islamic fundamentalists, anti-globalist leftists, US anti-colonial multiculturalists and the BBC's Oxbridge mediacrats, who all 'focus their diverse rages and resentments on this one conflict'. They have no strategy for victory, nor a joint command, but they have their 'nihilistic rage, their envy mixed with snobbery, their suicide bombs and terror attacks – and above all, a burning sense that the rising, vibrant and powerful peoples of America and Israel must be humiliated and brought low'. He remarks that the Manichean divide between 'the successful who are hideous, and the bourgeoisophobes, who are spiritually pristine', brings the latter to conclude that the world is diseased, that it rewards the wrong values, the wrong people and the wrong abilities.

Thus, the bourgeoisophobes 'soon settle on the Americans and the Jews as the two chief objects of their ire, because no country has ever succeeded like America, and no people in the European experience ever achieved such sustained success as the Jews'. He finds that the six characteristics of bourgeois society that are the most hated by Muslim fundamentalists (the city, mass media, science and technology, prudence and safety, liberty, and liberation of women)[36] were the 'pillars of meritocratic capitalist society, practiced most assertively by countries like America and Israel'. He admits that Europeans are themselves bourgeois, but they nevertheless distrust the United States and Israel, who represent a:

> ...particularly aggressive, and to them unbalanced strain of bourgeois ambition. No European would ever acknowledge the category, but America and Israel are heroic bourgeois nations. The Israelis are driven by passionate Zionism to build their homeland and make it rich and powerful. Americans are driven by the Puritan sense of calling...and the special mission to spread our way of life around the globe.[37]

That is the reason, in his judgement, why the entire Arab world, and much of the rest of the world, is obsessed with Israel, and many people in many lands define themselves in opposition to the United States. Similarly, while the Islamic extremists 'regard us as lascivious hedonists, in a backhanded way they acknowledge both our freedom and happiness'.[38]

Certain voices among the Arabs in general, Arab–Americans in particular, who reject the anti-American consensus and choose to side with their country are important in raising the American people's awareness of the new threats and challenges facing it. Chief among them has been Fouad Ajami who, from his prestigious academic chair at Johns Hopkins University, adds the clout of his knowledge and the authority of his experience as a former Lebanese to his instinctive and rare loyalty to the country that not only gave him shelter but also catapulted him to international prominence. Some of his scathing remarks about Arab politics, beyond his learned and perceptive books about the world of delusion of the Arab rulers, have been cited above. However, less famous Arab Americans also feel the need to call their fellow Arabs and Muslims to task, not only in the US press in order to alleviate the sometimes unjust suspicions raised about them, but, more importantly and significantly, in the

Arabic press abroad. The London-based *al-Hayat* published a
selection of Letters to the Editor, one of them from Zuheir Abdullah
from the United States, where he essentially castigated the Arabs,
and especially their media, for following a delusive and destructive
course. He identified three phases that were actually watersheds in
the development of that press over the past 60 years:

1. The broadcasts of Yunis al-Bahri from the Arabic station in
    Berlin under the Nazis, in which he instigated the Arabs to act
    against the West and Britain, and lauded Hitler, Nazi Germany
    and the Axis Powers. He comments that though the Arabs were
    the lowest in the ladder of Nazi racism, the Arabs used to
    cluster around radio receivers and avidly swallow the
    incitements.
2. Ahmed Sa'id from Cairo's 'Voice of the Arabs', who gained a
    mass following among the Arabs due to his curses of Arab
    moderate leaders and the West. He considers this demagogy to
    be the underlying reason why moderate Arab regimes in Iraq
    and Libya eventually succumbed, to be replaced by 'tyrants
    and fascist parties under whose burden the Arab world has
    been still suffering.' After the 1967 defeat, the influence of the
    'Voice of the Arabs' receded when the masses realized that they
    had been pushed into a war for which they were ill-prepared.
3. The present phase of *al-Jazeera* televison, whose reporter in
    Kabul has become the spokesman for the Taliban. He has been
    in the habit of reporting the civilian casualties in order to raise
    sympathies for them, but concealing the military defeats of the
    Taliban and overlooking the massacres they perpetrate. He has
    also failed to report the joy of the inhabitants in those areas
    liberated from the Taliban, but nevertheless have attracted the
    third generation of the Arabs. However, with the fall of the
    Taliban *al-Jazeera* came to an end just as the demise of the Nazis
    and then of the Arabs in 1967 brought to an end the media
    heroes that accompanied them.

Abdullah concluded, nevertheless, that the new generation of
Arabs had learned nothing from the experiences of their
predecessors. For with the onset of Ramadan, other Arab stations
began to air television series that were imbued with hatred, on
topics such as the Crusades of one millennium ago; a subject which
is revived as if they were happening today. However, while the

media in the civilized world has encouraged the mending of fences between warring nations, like France and Germany or Japan and Russia, the Arab media continues to educate for incitement and hatred, licks the wounds of the past, and encourages young people to commit suicide and to kill people they know nothing about, just because they are members of other nations and religions.[39] This self-criticism by an Arab who has tasted the delights of Western culture naturally sounds like music in the ears of Westerners, and is therefore considered as credible and 'Faithful' as the biblical 'wounds of a friend'.[40] It also encourages Westerners in their belief that there must be something wrong with the Arabs, if some of their own kin admit it: even more so when such words come from an Arab national, like the Kuwaiti, Ahmed al-Baghdadi, who audaciously and innovatively lashes out at the Arabic press for focusing on Israeli deeds but overlooking what is happening in the Arab world itself. This from someone who had been condemned to one-month's imprisonment in October 1999 in a Kuwaiti court of law for 'insulting Islam' by claiming that the Prophet had failed to convert non-Muslims to Islam.[41] He 'conceded' to his readership that Prime Minister Sharon had 'committed acts of murder and terror against the Palestinians', but, and this is his point, he stressed that no Israeli official had ever terrorized his own society, because the:

> Zionist entity does not terrorize its intellectuals and writers and does not throw them into prisons ... We have to be honest towards our enemies, as our Qur'an prescribes, and recognize that the governments of the Israeli entity are elected democratically, while no elected Prime Minister is to be found in the entire Arab and Muslim world.[42]

In comparison with Mubarak's empty bravado, when he boasted of his own 'democratic system' while Israel was ruled by 'tyrants', Baghdadi's analysis is nothing short of revolutionary with regard to the Arab world. However, he also falsely claimed that Arabs and Muslims did not usually terrorize others, until 11 September, when a 'group of *shahids* killed 7,000 innocent people; but they did terrorize their own people'. Even as he was skimming over the sustained campaign of Muslim terrorism against Israel and Jews abroad in the previous two decades, he could not help enumerating the sins of his own people and culture:

1. The Arab world alone permitted the publication of fatwas which indicted and condemned people to death, while no such verdict has been issued by any Christian cleric since the Middle Ages. He sarcastically suggested giving a Nobel Prize to the Muslims for their 'invention that permitted the survival of such verdicts which [were retribution] against people of dissenting opinions.'
2. The prosecution of Arab intellectuals in courts of law, their indictments of heresy, and in consequence the verdicts that destroyed families when a spouse was ordered to abandon his or her 'heretic' partner. This exists only in the Islamic world. Is this not terrorism?
3. Our intellegence apparatuses have cut short the lives of hundreds of politicians, intellectuals and clerics. The Zionist entity has never acted likewise against its citizens, he contended. Is this not terrorism?
4. The phenomenon whereby any security apparatus, in all Arab and Muslim countries, can arrest people or to cause them to disappear, does not exist in the West or in Israel. Is not that terror?
5. Iraq alone has been a never-ending story of terror against her people and neighbours.
6. The Afghans had led a quiet and healthy life, albeit with their internecine wars, until the Arabs and Muslims arrived and introduced them to the circle of terror and hell, for which they pay the price today.
7. Who hijacked a Kuwaiti aeroplane and killed the Kuwaitis onboard? Was it not the pious Hizbullah?
8. The Palestinian Arabs were the first to invent the hijackings of planes and the terrorizing of peaceful passengers. Is this also not terrorism?
9. The Arabs and Muslims have no competitors: they are the masters of terrorism against their own citizens, and their terrorism often extends to other innocent people in the world with the support of some of their clerics.

He concluded that the Muslims were now paying the price for terrorism by being humiliated in the eyes of the entire civilized world. They are rejected everywhere: in restaurants, on aeroplanes and buses, and one cannot blame the West for that, because all the governments and people of the Muslim and Arab world are 'lying with regard to terror'. He claimed that while they are proclaiming Islam as the 'religion of peace and fraternity', Al-Azhar University students launch demonstrations against *Banquet for Sea Weeds*.[43] He said that the:

> ... ignorance of our nation provokes laughter in the world. The Muslim and Arab worlds are the only ones where prisons are full of intellectuals whose only sin was that they wrote ... For the past 500 years, no writer or intellectual has been murdered in the heretic West, while the indictment and death warrants issued by clerics in the Arab and Islamic worlds are cheap. And since the people and governments observe their silence, it means that they agree to these ways... Now is the day of reckoning. Nothing goes without retribution, and the account is longer than the beards of all the Taliban put together. The West's message to the Arab and Islamic worlds is clear: either you improve your ways, or else.[44]

THE RISING DANGER OF DOMESTIC ISLAM IN THE WEST

Until 11 September 2001, the Islamic world was not considered dangerous; Saudi Arabia was considered the 'best friend and ally' of the West in the Gulf; and the essentially Islamic struggles taking place in Bosnia, Kosovo, Palestine, Chechnya, the Philippines or Kashmir were regarded as so remote, incomprehensible and irrelevant to Western culture that few bothered to look these names up in world maps, let alone deepen their knowledge about them. But, as of 11 September, not only did these names began to resound clearly in the minds of ordinary people in the West who had been unaware of them, but many rushed to read the Qur'an and works about Islam, or to visit Islamic centres in the West, in a quest to understand what makes that faith tick; and it is believed that not a few even asked to join the ranks of the Believers. So, in a small measure, the 'Islam rush' was due not to an 'invading' foreign Islam that one needed to know and understand – as with the growth of literature about the Japanese during World War II – but to the shocking realization that the 'enemy' emerged from within. After all, those 19 Islamikaze who committed the atrocity of 11 September were, for the most part, asylum seekers in the United States; many of them were naturalized Americans, who had studied in US schools, become familiar with US openness and democracy, and were expected to conduct themselves loyally to their country. The fact that they did not, and that their common denominator was the Islamic faith, took the Americans by surprise and made them feel that a fifth column was growing in their midst, especially when it turned out that their operators, in this case al-Qa'ida, had organized them, given them orders, trained them and financed them from the outside.

And suddenly it occurred to the Americans that the events of 1993, when the first attempt against the Twin Towers was made by Sheikh abd-a-Rahman and his group – also asylum-seekers who had been generously sheltered by the United States – was not an isolated misdeed by misguided criminals, but one link in a long, uninterrupted and well-planned chain of operations by fundamentalist Islam against its host culture of the West. In other words, they had come to the United States not to seek refuge as they declared, capitalizing on the naiveté and good intentions of their hosts, but had infiltrated the West in order to build bases and to mount attacks against their benefactors. Then, of course, most Muslims became suspect, especially those of Arab and other Mediterranean origins; many of them were arrested, others left hurriedly for their countries of origin, while the rest lived in fear of public anger against them. Even black Muslims in America, who have in the past aligned themselves with their fellow Muslims in other parts of the world and have embraced their political positions, at least rhetorically, now felt threatened by a backlash from the alarmed public. Suddenly, new restrictions were imposed on incoming Arabs and Muslims, more specifically if they were Egyptian, Saudi or Afghani, in spite of their outcry about the 'collective punishment' imposed on the many because of the criminal few. But they were reminded that they were the first to impose collective punishment on the entire world, when they invented the hijackings that forced all of us to go through humiliating security checks which invaded our privacy and drove up the costs of travelling.

In Western Europe, Australia and Canada – the main targets of legal and illegal immigration from Muslim countries – the same strictures on further immigration from those countries have been imposed, as these societies woke up to the fact that some Muslim immigrants did not move to the Western democracies just to improve their lot or to work and provide for their families who stayed behind, but that an entire scheme lay behind their move which would revolutionize the status of entire Muslim communities in the United States and Europe: from being asylum seekers, political refugees and foreign workers, to being a real social and security liability. For, while many of them are grateful for their new home and go about their business, the political activists among them pressure the others to take a stand on current affairs of concern to other Muslims, encourage them to demonstrate, even violently, against their new compatriots and in favour of their original ones, and strive to increase their numbers and make a dent in local demography and politics. Hence, every wave of legal or illegal immigrants is assisted by those who have already settled in the land and been absorbed, and who, under the humanitarian excuse of 'family reunion', brings entire clans in their wake. If they constituted negligible minorities, no one would be overly concerned about their impact, cultural or political, on their host countries. However, in view of their fast growth, due to both high birthrates and increasing immigration, they have become numerous enough – between five per cent (in Sweden and Britain) (and 10 per cent) (in France and Belgium), aided by their extraordinarily low median age (most under the age of 20) – to alter the demographic balance further and faster in the years to come.

Had these minorities aspired to assimilate into their host societies and just become French, Swedes or Spaniards, peacefully and individually following their cult of Islam as a personal endeavour, no one would even notice. But as the communities grow larger they also grow more vociferous and violent, for the most part, and, no longer happy to be absorbed into their societies as individuals, they begin to claim group rights and to justify their often violent behaviour by their right to differ from the overwhelming majority. Many minorities have been absorbed by these countries over the centuries, especially the immigration-oriented among them, such as Canada, the United States and Australia, but seldom has a minority clung to its original roots in an effort to force the host-majority to yield to its will. For example, the Poles, Irish, Germans, Japanese and Jews who flocked to the United States or to Australia willingly and wholeheartedly hoisted the Stars and Stripes or the Union Jack, sang 'America the Beautiful' and 'God Save the Queen', and participated in the fighting forces of their adoptive countries in times of war. Now, Arab youth in France and in Israel refuse to sing the anthems of their countries and demand that their ethnic heritage be recognized in their school curricula, even if it contradicts the local national ethos, and think that they have the right to rip apart the national consensus and the basic values that hold the country together. Again, were it not for Muslim spokesmen who proclaim their blueprint for infiltrating Western societies in order to subvert them from within and take them over, one would tend to believe that these manifestations of recalcitrance among Muslim youth in their countries of absorption were merely pangs of assimilation and demonstrations of passing displeasure with their living standards or with the prevailing discrimination against them.

Worst of all are the violent methods which these groups are often seen resorting to, beyond the expected levels in any migrant and less affluent society. In Western Europe, the populations are terrified by the high rate of crime which is linked, according to statistics, with the immigrant Muslim population. You can hear recurrent complaints by Europeans who 'feel like strangers in their countries', and fear to use public transportation in certain areas or at certain late hours. Entire urban areas have brought the Muslim marketplaces into European cities, with their attendant voices, sights and smells, much to the disgust of many, though also to the delight of some, who would still laud cultural diversity if it were not for the attendant atmosphere of violence and fear; ugly sights of vandalism and littering in the heart of European cities previously famous for their neatness and public order; noises emanating from public squabbles or muezzin calls for prayers from mosques in otherwise tranquil neighbourhoods; the Muslims who squat for the Friday prayer in front of the most Italian of Christian churches in the heart of Florence or other cities; police forces that dare not enter Muslim-inhabited neighbourhoods for fear of battling violent criminals and drug dealers; and, most importantly, the oppression that many feel from their inability to air their concerns in public for fear of being accused of racism or political incorrectness.

Right-wing political parties in the West have learned to tap these concerns and to strengthen themselves politically, because they dare to voice in public what liberals and left-wingers consider taboo. And so, paradoxically, the liberals and socialist parties, who had been lenient towards immigration and had thus increased their constituencies when the new immigrants were naturalized and allowed to vote, find themselves impoverished when their original European constituents turn their backs on them. This has happened in France, Spain, Italy, Australia and the Netherlands, and is likely to happen next in Germany and Great Britain if they do not tighten their restrictions on immigration into their respective territories. In the meantime, those who have immigrated – including Muslim fundamentalists who admit in public their aspirations to subvert their benefactor states – have no qualms about milking the generous welfare systems which have absorbed them or of using the tax-payers' money, which was earned by the hard work of the local populations, to cultivate a whole sub-culture of parasitic dependence on state allowances which build up hatred against their naive hosts. Thus, rapid breeding – in order for their community to grow demographically and strengthen its electoral influence, so as to allow it to demand more funds and allocations – has become a way for these immigrants to exert political pressure and achieve political goals. The children they have are taken care of by the host states, as is their housing, education, health, unemployment benefits, pensions and minimum income, which free them to work for their unpublicized goals, such as sabotage and terrorism in the United States, building up caches of weapons in Europe, increasing Muslim proselytization in both, and demonstrating for their fellow Arabs and Muslims around the world.

Muslim diasporas in the West, having acquired political power through sheer numbers, have also been attempting to dislodge from their advantageous positions the older and more established, though far less numerous, for the most part, Jewish communities. By doing so, they wish to eliminate the 'Jewish influence' on the local governments and thereby shift the traditional political sympathies of the West from Israel to the Arabs. Again, these would seem acceptable and legitimate ways of political lobbying current in any open, liberal political system, except that the Muslim populations do not, in the main, fulfil the two conditions that go hand in hand with political protest: they do not act for the interest of their host countries rather than against it; nor do they refrain from violence and the breaking of the law. However, the immigrants do not seem to have internalized and digested these restrictions and values at the same pace that they have mastered the list of benefits they could get from their countries of shelter. On the first count, we have seen that many naturalized Muslims – for example, the perpetrators – of the New York and Washington atrocities, did not hesitate to act against their hosts who showered them with benefits; and many other Muslims, who have sought shelter in Europe and Australia, devote their time not to melting into their new environment by implementing its rules, but to cultivating their separate identity and building enclaves of Islam in their host countries and to their detriment. For example, far from accepting their new countries' Middle Eastern policies, or anti-terrorist struggles, they protest against them, often violently.

The second count, of using violence, which is usually shunned in democratic societies, raises even more concern in Western societies because it ultimately hurts public order and the core of their value systems. Since the outbreak of the October 2000 Palestinian Intifadah, thousands of violent demonstrations by Muslim immigrant populations have unfolded from Montreal to Sydney, from Sao Paulo to Durban, from Oslo to Rome (apart from the usual anti-Jewish and anti-Israeli demonstrations that exploded throughout the Arab and Islamic world). Anti-Israeli demonstrations are certainly legitimate, but when they involve the public burning of Israeli and US flags in the streets of those Western countries which are basically allies of Israel and the United States, or when both consulates and embassies in both these countries are pelted with rocks, or when effigies of the leaders of the United States and Israel – who are often personal friends, and certainly political allies of the local leaders – are burnt and abuses hurled at them, this is the limit that the rule of law, of which the Muslim immigrants seem to be unaware or oblivious, cannot permit. Indeed, few local Westerners have participated in these acts, and conversely, no Jews have responded by committing the same acts against any Western or Arab/Muslim country with which their host country maintains relations. What is more, although Jewish communities worldwide have rallied around Israel, they have done so with dignity and full respect for the law, and have not allowed harm to be committed either against their country of citizenship, or against the violent crowds of Muslims and their supporters.

The most distressing aspect of these outbursts of violence has been that Western countries have been turned, by their Muslim communities, into violent arenas where the Middle Eastern conflict has been exported and replayed. Not content with attacking Israeli and US symbols in most Western capitals and large cities, those hooligans who terrorized the down-town areas of their places of residence turned to brutal and cruel onslaughts on the local Jewish communities, thus signalling to the world that Jews and Israel were to be equated and that anti-Semitism meant also anti-Zionism. The worst hit were the Jewish communities in France, Britain and Germany, where hundreds of Jewish synagogues, cemetaries, schools and other institutions have been torched or otherwise desecrated, Jewish adults have been attacked on their way to worship, and children on their way to school; all that under the open eyes of the local police, who apparently did not dare to intervene forcefully for fear of the politically correct politicians on the eve of elections. One can only imagine what would have happened if a mosque or a church were likewise burned, or non-Jewish worshippers or children attacked and harmed. Other places, too, have experienced the full extent of this pogrom, which in many circles was reminiscent of the infamous *Kristallnacht* of 1938: in South America – Brazil and Venezuela; in North America and especially in Canada; in Australia – Canberra, Melbourne and Sydney; and in Europe – Russia, the Ukraine, the Baltic states, Belgium and Spain, France, Germany and Britain in particular, knew the horror and the shame of these anti-Semitic attacks, mostly but not exclusively, orchestrated by the Muslim communities, for in some places, local anti-Semites were also at work, separately or in conjunction with the Muslims.

The outcome of all this is that the Muslim communities in the Western democracies have shown that they can act in unison to undermine public order, to pose a real threat to national security, and to harm their fellow citizens, Jewish and otherwise; this means that they can organize and demonstrate in the same fashion in their host countries whenever they judge an issue is important enough to them, or that the local authorities are too lenient or reluctant to face up to them. Polls organized in the United States after the 11 September attacks found that Americans overwhelmingly tied Islam and Muslims to these terrible events; 68 per cent of them approved of randomly stopping people who might fit the profile of suspected terrorists; 83 per cent of Americans favoured stricter controls on Muslims entering the country; 58 per cent wanted tighter controls on Muslims travelling on planes or trains; 35 per cent of New Yorkers favoured establishing internment camps for individuals that the authorities identified as being sympathetic to terrorist causes; and 31 per cent of all Americans favoured detention camps for the Arab-Americans, as a way of preventing terrorist attacks in the United States.[45] This means that the threatened populations found themselves ahead of their authorities, which were much more cautious in drastically limiting civil rights, and they were prepared, to a great extent, to replay the unfortunate experience of the internment of Japanese-Americans in World War II. It stands to reason that if, and when, more major acts of terror unfold in the West, the latter will find itself compelled to curtail civil liberties and take radical measures against the Muslim minorities in its midst. Then, the very moderate measures taken by Israel against its demonstratively hostile Muslim minority, which had come under scathing criticism from the pre-11 September world, will look incredibly generous and even bordering on criminal neglect.

So, we observe two contradictory trends in the West: on the one hand, Muslim minorities decry their 'persecution and humiliation' following the 11 September events; but, on the other hand, they themselves, or other Muslims who are stunned by the outcome of events, either defy their countries of refuge or boast of their own numbers and their vision of ultimately taking over. The North Africans of France, including the second and third generation of *beur*, as they call themselves, are either totally assimilated Frenchmen, or they whistle in contempt when they hear the 'Marseillaise' sung or see the French colours hoisted. They congregate around Muslim fundamentalist leaders and adhere to all sorts of shady Islamic organizations, some of which work under the cover of 'charity' associations, mostly financed by Saudi Arabia or by violent groups bent on underground activity, the clandestine collection of weapons for 'rainy days', and training their fellow-Muslims for acts of terrorism; all supported by Iran and its agents. The same trends are identifiable in the rest of Europe: England, France, Germany, Benelux and the Balkans.[46] Before 11 September, Muslims of foreign extraction in the United States were beginning to realize their electoral power and were determined to use it, *inter alia* in order to influence the US government to reduce its support for Israel. At the same time, however – as reported by eminent investigative reporter Steven Emerson in his extraordinary eye-opening television documentary 'Jihad in America' – evidence was mounting of weapons training and secret training fields for radical Muslims in the United States in general and in New Jersey in particular. These revelations, which came on the heels of the 1993 attempt against the Twin Towers and the Holland and Brooklyn Tunnels, and which brought about the arrest, indictment, trial and imprisonment of Egyptian Sheikh abd-al-Rahman and his group, did not raise the requisite levels of alarm and alert in Washington, and no severe measures were taken to tackle the situation and perhaps avert a second Twin Towers disaster.

Already, one year prior to this disaster, the *Boston Globe* ran an extremely pertinent and almost prophetic article on the Muslims of America, who then numbered six million but were growing fast due to a combination of high birthrate, immigration of more Muslims and internal conversion to Islam. However, when reporter Michael

Paulson visited the mosque in Dearborn, Michigan – which was led by Iraqi-born Imam Qazwini, who was urging his congregants to vote and take part in the system in order to leave their impact on it – he noticed a group of male students who disagreed with their imam, claiming that he 'was usurping the authority of Allah and proposing an un-Islamic action that cannot be justified by the Qur'an'. Their explanation, offered by 25-year-old Danny Agemi, a marketing major at the University of Michigan, was no less perplexing: 'God forbids any Muslim from participating in the legislation of a non-Islamic state'. This young man then positioned himself by the entrance gate and distributed leaflets calling voting 'treason against Islam' and citing verses of the Qur'an as evidence for his position that voting was a sin. The reporter observed that 'Most Muslim Americans were newcomers and relatively new to this country and inexperienced in the ways of democracy, and many were frustrated that neither political party seemed supportive of their interests.'[47] But for a young man versed in American education and benefiting from its bounty to incite his fellow citizens to abstain from voting seems a rather extremist step that requires exploration, especially as other Muslim-Americans, who cannot identify with the preponderant Judeo-Christian culture, respond by saying 'To hell with the rest, we are going to keep to our own' – as Hassan Jaber, Deputy Director of the Arab Community Center in Dearborn, was quoted as saying. He indeed confirmed that 'You still see mosques here that do not encourage the movement of political activism – they see it as betraying their culture and religion, and as threatening their purity; although these are in the minority.'[48]

Indicative of the Muslim disaffection found by Paulson in Dearborn, which reflected, to his mind, the situation in the entire country, was their disengagement from the election process because they either were not yet citizens, and therefore could not vote, or they thought it was useless or wrong to vote. Among those who did vote, many gave their voices to Ralph Nader, the Green Party nominee, because 'He was Lebanese-American and was neither Bush or Gore'. The Muslims of Dearborn perpetuated their culture and faith outwardly by maintaining restaurants, clinics and shops by their kin, which is legitimate and understandable, but also by sporting signs in Arabic, a rather strange sign of aloofness. One store-keeper, of Lebanese extraction, said he would vote for Bush, because Gore had appointed a Jewish candidate as his Vice-President. But, on the other hand, many mosques organized voter registration drives, Muslim delegates went to both presidential conventions in 2000, and affluent Muslims contributed to political parties and candidates. A Muslim leader, Zahid al-Bukhari, said that the political debate among the Muslims was 'slowly and steadily tilting in favour of the notion that Muslims are there, they are citizens, and voting is part of their responsibility for the welfare of society'. An American-Muslim, a researcher at the University of North Carolina, conducted a survey in which he found that in 89 per cent of the mosques, Muslims were in favour of participating in the elections. However, the minority of Muslims who disapprove of voting are doing so vociferously, according to Paulson, therefore their voice is heard. Apart from their Islamic reservations, for which they find support in the Qur'an, they are also reluctant to vote for candidates who support Israel, support abortion rights or who supported an embargo against Iraq.[49]

When, in the 2000 election campaign in the United States, a Muslim cleric agreed to deliver a prayer at the Republican national convention, a newsletter was circulated in Muslim cafés in Michigan condemning the 'Muslim blessing of child-killers'; which referred to the US Republican Party support for the embargo against Iraq. Similarly, an electronic bulletin board put out by the Muslim Student Association,[50] in which a debate was conducted over voting, an opponent of the proposition wrote that 'once you enter the process, you agree to play by their rules, and from there on you become another begging minority'.[51] This argument, which is similar to others voiced by other Muslim fundamentalists – both in Muslim-majority entities such as the Palestinian Authority, where the Hamas refused to participate in the elections of 1995 in order not to lend legitimacy to the Oslo process, and in non-Muslim majorities, like Israel, where many of its Muslims refuse to vote – indicates the choice of the fundamentalists to create their own enclaves in non-Muslim territory rather than partake in un-Islamic legal systems. There were numerous Muslims in the United States who expressed to Paulson their 'envy, admiration and hostility towards Jews' and towards the Jewish Lobby in the United States, and admitted that they were inspired by their example of how to lobby, to be organized, to flood newspapers with letters and to approach politicians.[52] Envy and admiration are not only legitimate, but they can be very powerful driving forces for change and self-improvement. But hostility towards the successful raises the suspicion that David Brooks, who was quoted above, may have been right in his theory of bourgeoisophobia. But all this was before 11 September 2001.

Like other watersheds in history, 11 September seems to have sharpened these controversies among the Muslims. The integrationists were certainly vindicated in their conviction that Muslims in the United States ought to show their patriotism and go with the mainstream, but one suspects that isolationists, too, those who elected their detached Muslim enclaves, part of which had bred the terrorists that produced the horror, also hardened their positions in view of what they perceived as the impending collapse of the United States, or the stepped-up persecution of Muslims in the land, or the promise of unprecedented interest in, and mass-conversion to, the faith of Islam. Ironically, much of the success of proselytization in the United States has been imputed by Muslims to the messages of tolerance by the US government and the local authorities following 11 September. The leader of the Muslim fundamentalists in Israel, Sheikh Ra'id Salah, who had urged President Bush to convert as a 'solution to all problems', capitalized on the reports coming from the United States about the success of the Muslim drive there, and reiterated that message in a rally of his followers in the Galilee:

> Oh, people of the West, we say to you: we are the masters of the world and we are the repository of all good, because we are the 'best people, delivered to mankind'.[53] We do not hesitate. Oh Bush and Blair; we invite you to Islam, enter Islam, you and your peoples.[54]

Sheikh Ra'id's appeal, which sounded amusing to many Westerners, was taken very seriously by fundamentalist Muslims around the world, and was based on the many optimistic reports emanating from the United States, during the deep disarray after the Twin Towers events. 'Alaa Bayumi, the Director of Arab Affairs at the Council of American–Islamic Relations (CAIR): wrote in the London-based *Al-Hayat* that:

> ...non-Muslim Americans are now interested in getting to know Islam. There are a number of signs: libraries have run out of books on Islam and the Middle East... English translations of the Qur'an head the American best-seller list... The Americans are showing increased willingness to convert to Islam since 11 September... Thousands of non-Muslim Americans have responded to invitations to visit mosques, resembling the waves of the sea, one after another. All this is

happening in a political atmosphere that, at least verbally, encourages non-Muslim Americans' openness towards Muslims in America and in the Islamic world, as the American President has said many times in his speeches.[55]

Other Muslim spokesmen knew more details: Nihad 'Awad, the Chairman of CAIR, told a Saudi daily that 34,000 Americans had converted to Islam after 11 September, the highest rate in the United States to date;[56] Dr Walid al-Fatihi, an instructor at Harvard Medical School, sent a letter to an Egyptian journal attesting that 'from the first day, the media began to insinuate that Muslim and Arab hands were behind this incident'. He told how he was on line from his clinic to the Islamic Center in Boston, which convened an emergency meeting and decided to hold a blood drive and to contact the Red Cross to organize it, and the media were invited to cover the event, in the hope it would stem the anti-Muslim tide. He said that on that day, when Muslims found themselves attacked on all sides, they tried to prove their humanity, but Muslim proselytizing 'in the name of Allah' was thought to have been set back 50 years. On 15 September, the doctor said, he went to the largest church in Boston to represent Islam at the conference that was attended by all the notables in town, and he was moved by the sermon from the priest who defended Islam, after which he read a statement from the Islamic Society of Boston which condemned the 'incident' and explained the 'sublime tenets of Islam'. Then, he said, 'the entire church burst into tears upon hearing the passages of the Word of Allah'. Then he continued his account:

> One said to me: 'I do not understand the Arabic language, but there is no doubt that the words you said are the words of Allah.' As she left the church weeping, a woman put a piece of paper in my hand with the inscription: 'Forgive us for our past and our present. Keep proselytizing to us.' Another man stood at the entrance to the church, his eyes teary, and said: 'You are just like us, you are better than us.'[57]

It is very difficult to ascertain the veracity of the report from this respectable instructor of medicine, who was so swept away by the emotion his presence caused among civilized Christians who listened to his message that he forgot to mention that, since he read the translated verses from the Qur'an in English, his audience did not have to understand Arabic. He may have wondered about what would have happened to Christians or Jews in his native country had any of them blown up a block of buildings in Cairo. He could not help invoking his good fortune at being a Muslim in the United States, instead of a Christian or a Jew in Egypt, and thanked Allah for that difference. Nonetheless, he so imisconstrued the tolerance with which he was treated – compared to that which he and his compatriots would have meted out to Christians or Jews in his own country that he totally misunderstood his hosts' comments, misquoted some, and probably made up others, in his zeal to show his countrymen back home the wonders that the verses of Allah could effect on Unbelievers. This was part of the process of denial in the after-shock of the incredible horror of 11 September, the other part being the pretence that Islam became more, not less, popular, after the event. Otherwise, how could the Muslims in the United States justify to themselves and rationalize to others, the mass arrests of their kin, their thorough search in the airports, the hurried departure of some of them from the country, their fear of going out or sending their children to school that some Muslims have attested to; and, above all, the obsessive and sickening need to 'prove' that it was all the Jews' doing?

Fatihi's report, which was not borne out by all US writers, some of them Muslims themselves, whom we have cited above lashing out at Islam and the culture of violence it bred, did not end there. He further wrote:

> On 16 September, the Islamic Center of Boston...issued an open invitation...We did not expect more than 100 people, but to our surprise more than 1,000 came, among them the neighbours, the university lecturers, members of the clergy and even the leaders of the priests from the nearby churches who invited us to speak of Islam. All expressed solidarity with Muslims. Many questions flowed to us. Everyone wanted to know about Islam and understand its precepts...Of all questions, not a single one attacked me; on the contrary, we saw the eyes of the people filling with tears when they heard about Islam and its sublime principles...Many had heard about Islam before through the biased media. That day, I was invited again to participate in another meeting in the church, and again I saw the same things. On Thursday, a delegation of 300 students and lecturers from Harvard visited the Muslim

centre...accompanied by the American Ambassador to Vienna. They sat on the floor of the mosque, which was full to capacity. We explained the precepts of Islam and defended it from any suspicion promulgated by the media. I again read to them from the verses of Allah, and their eyes filled with tears. The audience was moved and many asked to participate in the weekly lessons for non-Muslims held by the Islamic Center...

On 21 September, the Muslims participated in a closed meeting with the Governor of Massachussetts, where a discussion was held about introducing Islam into the curriculum, to inform the American people and fight racism against Muslims arising from the American people's ignorance regarding the religion...Measures to examine implementation of this goal were agreed upon...These are only some of the examples of what happened in Boston and in many other American cities during these days. Proselytizing in the name of Allah has not been undermined, and has not been set back 50 years, as we thought during the first days after 11 September. On the contrary, the 11 days that have passed are like 11 years in the history of proselytizing in the name of Allah. I write to you today with the absolute confidence that over the next few years, Islam will spread in America and in the entire world, Allah willing, much more quickly than it has spread in the past, because the entire world is asking 'What is Islam?'.[58]

Reading these rosy words of self-aggrandizement, one is amazed by the gross exaggerations in the report, by someone who should have known better, and by the duplicitous language he used to depict to his fellow Arabs back home what he would not have dared to say in public in the United States: such as what sounds like the perverse running of Americans into the arms of their tormentors; the selective readings from the Qur'an for his Western listeners; the Muslim blueprint for proselytizing in the United States and turning it Muslim; and what later transpired as an attack on Israel, Zionism and the Jews. He seems to have interpreted US compassion, openness and will to learn as proof of its leanings towards Islam and as a hopeful sign of a speedy conversion of the United States to Islam. For he knew that, while in many Islamic countries Christian or other religious proselytization is forbidden, in the United States and the rest of the West it is widespread; however, he mistook that as US 'submission' to the militant Muslim message. He also knew that, while in Islam there is no will or openness to know about others, for there is only one absolute Truth and a constant denigration of other faiths as a result, the West is curious, open and keen to understand what made others tick, certainly after the trauma of 11 September. However, he misinterpreted this as a consequence of the awe-inspiring teachings of Islam, of which the West suddenly became cognizant under the impulse of the tragic circumstances. Fatihi might have read to his listeners the ambivalent passages in the Qur'an which speak of the universal message of Allah, of understanding between people, of the generosity of Islam towards others (once they have accepted its precepts), and of the proposition that 'there is no compulsion in faith'; but he should have also assumed that his academic guests were smart enough to open English translations of the book and read for themselves the harrowing encouragement of *shahids*, the promises of jihad against the Infidels and the ensuing rewards in Paradise, the denigration of other faiths, and the warnings not to befriend non-Muslims.[59]

Even assuming that Fatihi experienced the encounters he described, he based his views on his meetings with Bostonian intellectuals, some of whom would rather blame their country than be regarded as bigots by their academic colleagues on the left, and he wrongly extrapolated from that a picture of all the United States and its grassroots (who evinced the utmost hospitality towards Islam), and an exaggerated and often unjustified one at that. His reports of American Christians crying upon hearing Qur'anic verses have a historical context, since this is part of the Islamic narrative when recounting the ethos of Muslim proselytizing. This narrative comes from the tradition of the Prophet's invitation to the Christian community of Najran, in the southern Arabian Peninsula, to visit the mosque. As tradition has it, when the Christians were exposed to the verses of the Qur'an, they burst into tears and converted to Islam.[60] Fatihi presented his analysis as if he and his Muslim congregants were under attack from Americans, not the other way around, and therefore well-wishers and decent individuals among the otherwise evil Americans came to the Islamic Center to apologize and to show compassion. His most perplexing remark, however, made it sound as if he were privy to some obscure Muslim master-plan to Islamize the United States over the long run, and he took encouragement from the fact that, compared to 'the past 50 years', no setback was noticed in the process of Muslim proselytization in the country; quite the contrary, he seemed confident that the entire United States, with the 'help of Allah', would come to succumb to Islam. Some time later, having become the much-in-demand troubadour of the *One Thousand and One Night's* stories of the success of Islam in the United States, during its worst hours, Fatihi, who was apparently bored with his medical pursuits at Harvard, wrote another article, where he revealed his true motives:

> Despite the attacks of distortion coordinated by the Zionist lobby, to which it has recruited many of the influential media, there are initial signs that the intensive campaign of education about Islam has begun to bear fruit. For example, the rate of converts to Islam since 11 September has doubled... There is solidarity with Muslims on the part of many non-Muslims in American universities. For example, dozens of non-Muslim American women students at Wayne State University... have put on veils as a symbol of identification with the Muslim women students at the university and in other universities of America. For this reason, the Jewish institutions have begun to contact Muslim institutions and have called on us to hold dialogues and cooperate with them. They are afraid of the outcome of the Islamic–Christian dialogue through the churches, the mosques and the universities...
>
> There are many signs of change [for the worse] in Christian–Jewish relations, as a result of the openness toward Islam and the beginning of an Islamic–Christian dialogue. NPR [radio], for example, broadcast an even-handed programme on Palestine and the suffering of the Palestinian people; as a result, Jewish–Zionist donors in the United States called for their donations to be withdrawn from the station. This annoyed the station; in response, it intensified its coverage of Muslim–American affairs and the Palestine problem... One of the most important topics was an interview with several young women at American universities who recently converted to Islam through the Islamic Society of Boston. They hold advanced degrees from universities in Boston, such as Harvard, and they spoke of the power and greatness of Islam, of the elevated status of women in Islam, and why they converted to Islam. The programme was broadcast several times across the entire United States...
>
> This, the Muslim community in the United States in general, and in Boston in particular, have begun to trouble the Zionist

lobby. The words of the Qur'an on this matter are true: 'They will be humiliated wherever they are found, unless they are protected under a covenant with Allah, or a covenant with another people. They have incurred Allah's wrath and they have been afflicted with misery. That is because they continuously rejected the Signs of Allah and were after slaying the Prophets without just cause, and this resulted from their disobedience and their habit of transgression.'[61] The Great Allah spoke words of truth. Their covenant with America is the strongest possible in the United States, but it is weaker than they think, and one day their covenant with America will be cut off.[62]

So much for the ecumenical spirit of humanity, love and generosity of Islam which, if read in the original verses of the Qur'an, or even in English translation, can bring any decent person to tears of despair, not so much from that 'divine' message which might be obsolete, but from the tenacity of men and women in reading and believing one thing and telling others another, as if it were not open for everyone to read for themselves; and as if seen through the blinding spectacles of the Believers, the wrong can be righted and the evil straightened. However, unlike Fatihi, who only saw wrong in others and congratulated himself on the out-pouring of emotions for the verses of the Qur'an, another Muslim-American, Dr Muqtedar Khan, of Adrian College in Michigan and of Indian descent, took the Muslim world in its entirety to task when he addressed an open letter to his fellow Muslim-Americans, after duly paying lip service to Israel-bashing:

> What happened on 11 September will forever remain a horrible scar on the history of Islam and humanity, for no matter how we condemn this act...the fact remains that the perpetrators of this crime against humanity have indicated that their actions are sanctioned by Islamic values...Muslims have been practising hypocrisy on a grand scale. They protest against the discriminatory practices of Israel but are silent against the discriminatory practices in Muslim states. While acknowledging the ill-treatment of the Palestinians by Israel, I must remind you that Israel treats its 1 million Arab citizens with greater respect and dignity than most Arab nations treat their own citizens...Today, Palestinian refugees can settle and become citizens of the United States, but in spite of all the

tall rhetoric of the Arab world and Qur'anic injunctions [Sura 24:22], no Muslim country except Jordan extends this support to them...

Have we ever demanded international intervention or retribution against Saddam for gassing Kurds, against Pakistan for slaughtering Bengalis, against Saudis for abusing the Shi'as, against Syria for the massacre at Hamah? We condemn Israel not because we care for the Palestinians; we don't. We condemn Israel because we hate 'them'. Muslims love to live in the United States, but also love to hate it. Many openly claim that the United States is a terrorist state, yet their presence here is testimony that they would rather live here than anywhere else...As an Indian Muslim, I know for sure that nowhere on earth, including India, will I get the same sense of dignity and respect that I have received in the United States. It is time that we acknowlege that the freedoms we enjoy in America are more desirable to us than superficial solidarity with the Muslim world. If you disagree – then prove it – by migrating to whichever Muslim country you identify with...

The culture of hate and killing is tearing away at the moral fabric of Muslim society. In the pursuit of the inferior jihad [of violence and war], we have sacrificed the superior jihad [of spiritual striving]. It is time we faced these hypocritical practices and struggled to transcend them. It is time that American Muslim leaders fought to purify their own lot...While encouraging Islam to struggle against injustice... Allah also imposes strict rules of engagement...he also encourages Muslims to forgive Jews and Christians if they have committed injustices against us...Islam has been hijacked by hate and calls for murder and mayhem...Bin-Laden has become a phenomenon – a cancer eating away at our moral foundations. Yes, the United States has played a role in the creation of Bin-Laden, but it is we who have allowed him to grow and gain such a foothold. It is our duty to police our world. It is our responsibility to prevent our people from abusing Islam. We should have made sure that 11 September had never happened...

Islam is not about defeating Jews, or conquering Jerusalem, or competing with the American Jewish lobby for power over American foreign policy. It is about mercy, values, sacrifice and duty. Above all, it is the pursuit of moral perfection...

The worst exhibition of Islam happened on our turf. We must take responsibility to undo the evil it has manifested. This is our mandate, our burden but also our responsibility...I hope that we will now rededicate our lives and our institutions to the search for harmony, peace and tolerance. Let us be prepared to suffer injustice rather than commit injustices...If we wish to convince the world of the truth of our message, we cannot even be equal to others in virtue, we must excel, and we must be more forgiving, more sacrificing.[63]

In the United Kingdom, the situation was not judged any better by columnist Jonathan Stevenson, who wrote on 'Britain's New Terrorist Problem' in the *Wall Street Journal* (European edition). He reminded his readers – if need there was, in light (or rather obscurity) of the subversive activity of Sheikh Bakri and his like that went ignored and unpunished – that 11 out of the 19 Islamikaze hijackers of 11 September had stayed in the United Kingdom during the few months preceding the horror; he also mentioned that Abu Hamza al-Masri, who acted from Finsbury Park in London and was wanted in the Yemen for terrorism, had called for a jihad against Western Infidels, but his call remained unheeded by the authorities. He gave an account of several of the hijackers, of their training and shelter in Britain; and, as British law of evidence did not permit their extradition, they were permitted to thrive: fund-raising, purchasing property, publishing and proceeding without scrutiny. He also observed that since the 1970s, Britain had concentrated on the terrorist threat of the IRA and, thinking it could 'wean the IRA away from terrorism by allowing them full expression of their agenda', thought it could also 'carry its non-confrontational policy over to al-Qa'ida and other Islamic groups that subscribe to its grand strategy'. But he concludes that since negotiable objectives did not fit that strategy, unlike with the I.RA, and since Bin-Laden simply wanted to 'debilitate the US and its allies through violence', that counter-terrorism measures did not work. Only after 11 September did London wake up and outlaw 21 terrorist front organizations – 16 of them Islamic – but it remained, all the same, a staging and logistics centre for al-Qa'ida. Over 100 British Muslims had joined the Taliban in Afghanistan, and at least 500 British Muslims have received military training at terrorist groups in Afghanistan since 1996.[64]

THE EMERGING BLUEPRINT FOR WESTERN SELF-DEFENCE

When it is the stated purpose of Muslim fundamentalists to Islamize not only their own societies, which is strictly their own business, but also their Western host societies, must the Western democracies wait for demography and proselytization to run their course, or can they do anything to arrest the trend? Certainly, the Muslim minorities would brand as 'racist' any attempt in that direction, posing the very 'innocent' question of 'What is wrong if the United States or Europe should become democratically Muslim?' Nothing is wrong in principle, except that while Western democracy and tolerance allow Islam to prosper, proselytize, expand, immigrate and become part of their societies, it is a unilateral flow, as long as most Muslim countries do not allow, and are not attractive enough for reciprocity. Moreover, while Muslims preserve their 'bastions' of Islam in their purity, as in Saudi Arabia, the Sudan and Iran, Western democracies are told to dissolve, to alter their Christian values that are not acceptable to Islam, and to give up, ultimately, their traditions of democracy in favour of totalitarian Islam, although it is those very traditions which afford Islam a foothold on Western soil. Has a political and cultural (never mind religious) tradition the right to preserve itself against an evident Muslim onslaught, in the face of the pressing and mounting waves of both militant Islam, which does not hide its goals, and Muslim immigration, especially illegal, to Western countries?

There are admittedly many Muslims who live in the West and are content, as a minority, to accept the culture, values and way of life of the majority. Many North African intellectuals and others, who have found their way to Europe, have integrated into their new societies and seek nothing other than integration into the system as fully fledged Europeans. In the United States, too, American Muslims, whom Pipes labels 'integrationists', are patriotic Americans and Muslims at the same time. There is, however, a growing trend, especially among Muslim immigrants and converts, which rejects Western civilization and strives to replace it by a Muslim order. However, it is difficult to know what percentage of the population this represents. We have seen, above, the cases of Sheikhs al-Bakri's and al-Masri's virulence against the very British system that sheltered them and from whose hand they eat, and the phenomenon of a Sho'a denier who converted to Islam and now serves Islam's purposes in France and around the world. The case of Cat Stevens, the popular British pop-singer who became

Yussuf Islam and contributed much of his fortune to the Islamic Movement in Israel, became particularly relevant in the 1980s.[65] After the events of 11 September, the case of Richard Reid, another British citizen who converted to Islam, became Abdel Rahim, the 'shoe-bomber', and tried to blow up an airline but was foiled – came to the attention of the world.[66] There must be numerous other converts who did not come to public prominence and have remained quietly anonymous.

These Islamists, who are for the most part immigrants, and sometimes local converts, want to transform Western societies within which they dwell into Muslim ones, run according to Muslim precepts, because they consider the latter superior to the former. A former Muslim chaplain at Yale Unversity, someone who supposedly absorbed something of US values in one of the intellectual bastions of the United States, was quoted by Pipes as saying that: 'Muslims cannot accept the legitimacy of the existing American order since it is against the orders and ordainments of Allah...The orientation of the Qur'an pushes us in the exact opposite direction.'[67]

A word of commentary is needed here, to awaken the public to the danger posed to Western systems by this sort of thinking from someone who has made it to the summit of US society and benefited from its bounty. His dismissal relates to the very foundation of democracy, which in Western thinking posits the sovereignty of the people who, through their elected representatives, control the legislative process. This is the concept that Islamists reject lock, stock and barrel, because to claim sovereignty, which is Allah's, and Allah's alone, amounts to blasphemy; and since He has already dispensed to humanity the most perfect of legal codes, the Qur'an, it constitutes a second blasphemy to pretend to better it. Pipes rightly and incisively points out that the debate within the Islamist camp in the United States (and elsewhere in the West for that matter) is not about the desirability of Islamizing US society – that is a foregone conclusion – but about the pace of that transformation: gradually, through conversion, or in one stroke through a traumatic act of violence, as in the events of 11 September. He cites integrationist Siddiqi, of Pakistani origin, as advocating mass conversion over time, and the blind, convicted Sheikh abd-al-Rahman, who proposed conquest of the land from the American Infidels.[68]

Once again, it is not the elusive, apparently the majority, of the integrationists who will determine the outcome of this debate, but the purposefulness, the single-mindedness and the burning conviction and devoted activism of the Islamists, backed by the sympathy of the masses. People's imagination is much more likely to be carried by acts of daring and promises of sweat and blood than by cajoling assurances of a good, but remote and uncertain, future. Passion is impatient, and the Islamists in the United States and in Europe, being the most active and militant, also provide the leadership and the initiative for their Muslim communities in the mosques, Islamic centres, publications, websites, schools and organizations that they control and raise money for (from Saudi Arabia, the Gulf States, Libya and the like). Pipes also makes the point that it is the Islamists, being the most vociferous, rather than their quietist and law-abiding rivals, who get recognition from the authorities (in the United States, they were visited by the President and invited to the White House after 11 September). Therefore, Pipes advisedly proposed several immediate screening and supervisory measures to be taken to curtail prospective terrorist activity in the United States.[69] It might be noted that should the squeamish, hesitant and disunited Europeans adopt similar measures, they might also reduce the growth of Islamic terrorism in their midst. However, judging from the discord among European leaders, in the attempt at their June 2002 Conference in Spain to co-ordinate their restrictions on illegal immigration (including infiltrating Muslim fundamentalist elements) into the European continent, one tends to be rather pessimistic.

However, the emergency measures adopted in the United States, Israel and the West cannot be maintained in the long run, because not only are they untenable in terms of civil liberties, they also demand a long-term state of alert that can wear out innocent citizens who must pay the collective price for their leaders' incompetence and lack of political foresight and courage in tackling a dangerous situation that has been in the making for years, but which they chose not to confront. Hence the need to draw up a new policy, not a stop-gap, of re-educating the public: re-organizing the state institutions to deal with the enemy from within and without imposing new immigration limitations; surveillance of potentially subversive groups; of repatriation to their countries of origin of inciters and promoters of violence; of new legal systems to deal firmly and swiftly with subversive elements; of tests of allegiance to the host countries which absorb Muslim immigrants and of resoluteness in battling the terrorists and their helpers, both in Western countries and overseas in their bases if necessary. President Bush has already singled out the candidates for Western retaliation, like the countries in the 'Axis of Evil', and has already raised the concerns of the rest of the Western countries who wish to avoid confrontation, hoping to continue to buy the 'goodwill' of terrorist organizations by allowing them to operate on their soil with impunity. However, the terrified public in those countries has understood what its governments refuse to see, namely that the permissive policies of the past, which have allowed hundreds of thousands of potential terrorists to flock in unchecked, can no longer be pursued; that the cities, towns and neighbourhoods of Western Europe must be made safe once again and re-Westernized; and that the grounds lost to the hordes of terrorists, by domestic oversight and blind 'liberalism', or oblivious 'multi-culturalism', which have hitherto served the purposes of politicians to whom the new immigrants felt obliged on election day, must be recovered.

The Western public in Australia, Europe and the United States has already rewarded its tougher politicians, who have spoken out against unbridled immigration, by electing right-wing parties and wiping out socialists, and this trend seems to have taken hold in the entire West, with their last vestiges battling the rear-guard retreat – even as Cherie Blair and Jack Straw of Britain were showing 'compassion for the bombers' and 'understood' their 'despair'.[70] Just imagine if everyone who was in despair in the world were shown compassion in his mass killing of others – the world population would rapidly diminish. However, writers, historians, diplomats, commentators, professionals, columnists and other opinion-makers have already been hard at work suggesting various remedies which, if they do not amount to a blueprint as yet, at least suggest the contours thereof. Back in 1990, Bernard Lewis, the great luminary of Middle Eastern Studies, wrote about the quandry of modern Islam, whereby traditional 'dignity and courtesy towards others turned into an explosive mixture of rage and hatred', impelling goverments to 'espouse kidnapping and assassination and try to find, in the life of their Prophet, approval and indeed precedent for such an action'.[71] Now, the most urgent question has become how to tame that rage. He suggested, for example, that the removal of Saddam in Iraq, just like the Taliban demise in Afghanistan, might reveal an existing infrastructure that could facilitate the edging of that country toward a softer, more democratic way. He made the observation that the countries of the Middle East can be divided into three types: those with an anti-American government and pro-American people; those with governments considered pro-American in which anti-American hostility runs rampant; and those in which both government and people are pro-American. He enumerates Iran and Iraq as belonging to the first group, where the people look to Americans as liberators, as in Afghanistan. To the second group belong Egypt and Saudi Arabia, and Lewis emphasizes that it was no accident that the majority of the hijackers of 11 September came from these two countries. The fury in these people is directed as much against the United States as it is towards their own governments which are its protégés.[72]

The third category in Lewis' typology is the countries where both government and people are pro-American: for example, Turkey and Israel, where democracy seems to make the difference. But, against the voices which advise democratization as a panacea, Lewis warns that democracy is 'dangerous', and a 'strong medicine', and has to be administered in small and measured doses, otherwise the patient can be killed. He says that democracy, which is an Anglo-Saxon way to conduct affairs, does not necessarily suit others. For example, he fears that free and democratic elections in the Arab world, without a gradual maturation, might produce an end-result like the rise of Hitler in Germany through a democratic process. However, he believed that the fall of either Iran or Iraq, the two partners in Bush's 'Axis of Evil', would probably facilitate the fall of the other, and that both 'liberated' countries might make peace internally and with Israel, which would remove the motivation for currrent terrorism. Their lead will be followed by Egypt and Jordan, which already have peace treaties with Israel, but have great difficulty in applying them due to popular hostility. He also believed that the loss of their radical supporters would mollify the Palestinians, who would also embrace democracy not only after the horrifying experience of the tyrannical and corrupt Arafat regime, but mainly by reason of the positive and inspiring encounter with their Israeli neighbours.[73] Fouad Ajami, by comparison, appears much less optimistic. He believes that it was the oppressive regimes in the Arab and Muslim world (which decimated the fundamentalists in their own land), on the one hand, and the openness of the West (which afforded them money, shelter and freedom of movement), on the other, which gave rise to the fundamentalist Muslim bases of insurgency in Western lands. Those groups 'were sure of America's culpability for the growing misery in their lands, and they were sure that the regimes in Saudi Arabia and Egypt would fall if they could force the United States to cast its allies adrift'.[74]

But Ajami also noted that the 'more pro-American the regime, the more anti-American the political class and the political tumult', therefore US aid to the Egyptian regime, for example, did not dampen the mood in the Egyptian press or blunt popular fury against the United States, something that accords with Lewis' typology of Middle Eastern regimes and peoples. Hence the 'sense of glee and little sorrow among the upper-class Egyptians' after 11 September, and the revelation that 'there were no genuine friends of America to be found in a curiously hostile, disgruntled land'. Therefore, he believes that it is erroneous to claim that it was Arafat's Intifadah which had caused the anti-American rage of 11 September. And since the United States could abandon neither the oil lands nor the Israeli–Palestinian imbroglio, he envisioned a vast war inaugurating the wars of the twenty-first century, in which:

> ... friends and sympathizers of terror will pass themselves off as constitutionalists and men and women of the civil society. They will find shelter behind pluralist norms while aiding and abetting forces of terror. They will be chameleons good at posing as America's friends, but never turning up when needed. There will be one speaking to Americans, and another letting one's populations know that the words are merely a pretence. There will step forth informers, hustlers of every shade, offering to guide the foreign power through the minefields and alleyways. America, which once held the world at a distance, will have to be willing to stick around eastern lands. It is both heartbreaking and ironic that so quintessentially American a figure as George W. Bush ... far removed from the complications of foreign places, must be the one to take his country on a journey into so alien, so difficult, a world.[75]

In Britain, immediately after 11 September, people were gripped by fear and began to prepare for the next terrorist attack, which many thought might be in London. Shops began to sell gas masks and protective suits for biological, chemical and even nuclear attacks, and a banker who worked in a skyscraper on the Canary Wharf business section bought a parachute. The authorities in London have updated the procedures for mass-evacuation, and those in charge of the underground railway system are readying it to again fill the function of shelters as in World War II. London, the capital of the most important ally of the United States, was thought to be next in line by John Stevens, the Metropolitan Police Commissioner, who is also in chage of the fight to oppose terrorism. Planning to counter terrorism, to oppose 'fanatics who are totally indifferent to the sanctity of life, and have few compunctions about how many people they kill', as Prime Minister Tony Blair put it, then became a very tangible matter.[76] On the surface of it, Bin-Laden had attained his goals: to sow panic in the West and to force it not only to squander its resources and energies on defensive measures, but also to be passive and wait for the next strike which the Islamikaze might deliver at any time and any place of their choice. However, the panic did not discourage the British, nor did it intimidate them into submission. The London police have been on terrorist alert, many more patrol the streets than ever before in peacetime, and security guards were posted in strategic areas, such as the Stock Exchange, telephone switchboards, water pumps and electric power grids; passenger planes were prohibited from overflying the centre of London, and regressive emergency legislation to compel everyone in Britain to carry an ID card was proposed.

What is more important, security experts admitted that Britain had been a safe haven for terrorist networks for too many years, due to its liberal immigration policy, the many breaches at border crossing stations, the rigorous consideration shown for individual rights, the legislation that made extradition difficult, and the large Muslim population – about two million, according to some estimates. They also realized that the links between Arab sheikhs and businessmen and the Home and Foreign Offices had, for years, allowed work permits to be liberally distributed, with the depleted police force rarely carrying out spot checks in streets, on trains or other land transport. London has also served as an international centre of financial services, investments and transactions for Muslim companies and organizations, which often use straw men to launder money in the service of terrorist groups. No wonder, then, that 11 of the 19 terrorists who carried out the attacks on 11 September had spent some time in London before proceeding to their targets, and the fear is rife that more cells of Bin-Laden might still be operating clandestinely. The British distinguish between 'mouths' and 'brains' in these organizations, the former being extremist propaganda groups, such as the *Muhajirun*, headed by

Muhammed al-Bakri, who was cited above, which, though under surveillance, are still active in recruiting Believers and disseminating hate literature, especially against homosexuals and the Jews, Israel and the United States. The 'brains' are smaller, compartmentalized underground groups, whose people keep a low profile.[77] Now the British might have to adjust their categorization and add a third group, that of active terrorists, if and when the first major act of terror is carried out in Britain.

Over the past decades at least, the British have been warned by many quarters about their overly permissive policy towards sheltering terrorists, which was originally devised and carried out by the same Jack Straw who was then Home Secretary and is now the Foreign Secretary, notably after the Islamist 'mouths' and 'brains' of the Gama'at in Egypt, who massacred tourists, found shelter in Britain.[78] Now the realization is spreading in Britain that, though it was warned by its own security experts about its complacency, and by other intelligence services of impending attacks, it failed to understand the mechanisms and way of thinking of the Muslim terrorists. The failure is mainly due to successive governments who authorized the lax policies, resisted their tightening, and put aggressive data-gathering and analysis low on their scale of priorities, following recent scandals affecting the MI6 Intelligence Agency and the incompetence of MI5, which is responsible for countering domestic security risks, when arresting suspect Muslims and bringing them to justice. However, the main problem has been the legal protection that Britain has offered to terrorist suspects, and which is skilfully exploited by the Islamist networks. Even Islamists who have made statements in support of Bin-Laden, or of toppling Western regimes, were treated leniently by the courts, probably under the mistaken belief that the distance between words of incitement and action was much greater than it actually was. The absurdity of these proceedings reached the point where courts refused to extradite foreign criminals, who were requested by their governments, for 'fear for their lives', and allowed them to endanger the lives of British citizens and British security. Now, Britain is ready to re-think its policies, after a cell of terrorists based in Britain was caught at an advanced stage of planning to attack and decimate all members of the European Parliament in Strasbourg, France.[79]

Martin Kramer – while optimistically believing that the hideous video, released in mid-December 2001 by Bin-Laden's people in confirmation of his part in the horror, would 'silence all those in the

West who claim that the war against terror could be a case of mistaken identity' – maintains that the Arab and Muslim public opinion, which is 'ritually sceptical of American claims', will continue doubtful and attempt denial. He brings to public attention the three categories of public opinion in the Arab world in this regard: those who decided long ago that it was the Israeli Mossad who engineered 11 September, and no evidence would change their minds; the admirers of 11 September, who are celebrating these horrors; and those who admit Muslim culpapility but deny Bin-Laden's role in it. But, he says, as 'Arab journalists and intellectuals are notoriously impervious to evidence', some of them could, after the release of that video, use it as 'a ladder to climb down from the fence, and as ammunition against their critics'. He emphasizes that the Taliban must have known of the plot and its execution, and therefore it was right for the United States to remove them from power, in spite of the scepticism that continued to cloud the judgement in many Islamic and Arab circles. He justifies the war against terrorism and supports victory as its aim, if only to restore the feeling of awe toward the United States after 'years of its erosion by irresolution'.[80]

Tom Friedman, harrowed by the same video in which Bin-Laden was boasting of his 11 September 'success', while a Saudi sheikh at his side was reporting of 'positive response' in Saudi mosques, assured his readers that Bin-Laden was 'finished' by his self-indictment, but there were 'thousands of other fawning sheikhs still out there who sympathize with his religious totalitarianism', and he called upon the Americans to 'design a strategy to change their minds'. Because, he said, the question to ask is not which country comes next after the defeat of the Taliban, but how could the United States bring about the delegitimation espoused by Bin-Laden, 'who kept invoking Allah while discussing a mass murder'? He naively urged Muslim leaders to come up with a new language and leadership that could reform Islam and make it compatible with the modern age. He called to task President Bush who, upon the release of that horrendous video, announced his missile shield programme. It is not a shield that was needed, contends Friedman, because 'without religious tolerance and pluralism, no wall will be high enough and no missile shield accurate enough to protect America from the new wave of human missiles launched by some unidentified sheikh or his students'.[81] But he does not tell us how to go about the reforms, that Muslims alone can initiate and enforce, as they would not allow any foreign power, let alone the United States, dictate to them a new curriculum, or new and unfamiliar rules of tolerance that are foreign to their faith, and that often stand in stark contradiction to it and would only increase their anger and resistance.

In fact, the lonely voice of the moderate and reasonable Sheikh al-Ansari, Dean of Shari'a at Al-Qatar University – from which country the radical Sheikh Qardawi has been operating and spreading his fundamentalist, acrimonious and uncompromising anti-Western venom around the Islamic world – has been heard and broadcast. He, indeed, expressed fear that since 11 September, 'mutual misunderstanding, evil thought, suspicions and distortions between East and West, had built an unhealthy atmosphere that fostered ... the rise of the right in the West ... and the rise of extremist movements in Arab and Islamic societies', and urged the Arabs to reform. But his phrase about the 'mutual misunderstanding' sounds as if the West, too, had committed some horror in the Islamic world; and as if the 'misunderstanding' was the result, not the cause, of the Twin Towers events. Thus, instead of unconditionally disparaging and condemning the horror and its authors, as a first *sine qua non* step towards normalization between the two cultures, he lectures the West, the victim of terror, to redress the 'misunderstanding' of which it is not the author. He selectively cites a verse of vague tolerance towards others, but does not explain to us why the terrorists heeded other aggressive and intolerant verses of the same Qur'an, not the one he chose to soothe the West.[82] He interprets this verse as 'forbidding the imposition of a single culture, idea, regime or faith on the entire human race', and insists that jihad 'is a means of preserving the right of pluralism and variety, and guaranteeing freedom of choice for all, because diversity is considered natural and universal truth'.[83] If any authority in the Islamic world took that lofty principle of freedom of choice seriously, it would have enforced it domestically before announcing it to the world. Therefore, it stands as an empty sermon to soothe the West, and nothing more, while the jihad of the Islamikaze, which the author does not condemn, is being pursued. Unfortunately for al-Ansari, and certainly for the West, Qardawi's message has much more resonance in the Muslim world than his, even if he were sincere and carried influence among his co-religionists.

Rosemary Righter attacked the Europeans for their criticism of the United States' counter-attack in Afghanistan, and then elsewhere, and was full of praise for the US stand for the entire West. She said that Saddam shared the goals of the fundamentalists in evicting the United States from the Middle East, and that Europe should be aware that, of the hijackers and killers of the Twin Towers, 11 had spent time in Britain, while others had plotted in Genoa, Hamburg, Milan, Manchester and Paris, because 'this hostile conspiracy found in European cities and suburbs a general welcome, space, privacy and financial support that is completely chilling'. She also castigated the United States' critics and triumphalists in Europe, whose view was shared by many Arabists there, who could not hide their pleasure at seeing 'arrogant and bloody America finally getting it in the neck'. She asked: 'would there have been as many armchair fatalists if Piccadilly Circus or Montmartre had been levelled on a crowded Saturday night?', and answered: 'My necessary tentative answer is "Yes, quite probably", for one reason: Britain and France, Europe's only credible military powers, could not have taken the war to the enemy unless NATO declared the attack on American soil to be an assault on all.' Only Tony Blair understood that, to her mind, and that is the reason he would not retreat from the position of all-out support for the United States in its policies against Iraq. For the United States' power, and especially its will to project it, have exposed not only Europe's vulnerability and the hollowness of the EU pretensions for military self-sufficiency, but have also demonstrated how vital is US power for their security. She concluded that the rise in anti-Americanism in Europe, and its corollary – anti-Israel prejudice – 'tended to distort the political prism through which Britain's national interest was seen', and called upon the Conservatives in Britain to lend Bush their support.[84]

Similarly, analysts such as Matthew Levitt and Daniel Pipes express favour for US counter-attacks, not only against Iraq, but also against other areas where terror is rife, such as Georgia, where 'some 1,500 Chechen guerillas and dozens of Arab and Afghan fighters are reportedly hiding among as many as 8,000 Chechen refugees in the Pankisi Gorge area'.[85] Dennis Ross, the Middle East expert and negotiator, when called upon to give his opinion to the House Committee on International Relations, put his emphasis on the Palestinian issue, on which he is a specialist; but he had some interesting insights into the US war on terrorism. He called for a 'change in America's mindset', since the attack of 11 September was on civilization itself. He said that the war on terrorism had a psychological aspect to it and that terrorism must be discredited and deligitimized, and urged the United States to use all the instruments in its arsenal: intelligence and law-enforcement, and financial, diplomatic and military pressure. He said that, in the Middle East in particular, it was essential to apply that approach, because terrorism there was 'too often treated as legitimate', Islamikaze bombers were considered martyrs and heroes, instead of monsters, and children were recruited for human destruction and the killings they carried out celebrated. He called to task Arab leaders for 'using their media as safety valves, designed to release anger and appease extremist sentiments', and declared that, instead, they must condemn all forms of terrorism without reserve. He warned that if the Arabs did not act in that direction, they 'should not expect American intervention in the Arab–Israeli peace', and that this should be a condition for the United States maintaining any relationship with Arafat and his circle. He also blasted the Palestinian leadership for lying to its people on the progress of their peace talks with Israel, for accusing the Israelis for the obstacles in the process and for not reporting on the concessions they proposed, so that the Palestinian public was led astray, believing that their leadership were taking the necessary measures towards peace while the Israelis proscrastinated: something that legitimized acts of terror and Islamikaze.[86]

Americans in particular, with some lone European and Arab voices participating, also made an effort to wage their war against terrorism on the media level. In reply to the outpouring of incitement against the United States in the Arab press, which came to Western attention as detailed in the first section of this chapter, came a furious reaction from scholars, journalists and columnists, who counter-attacked, exposing Arab duplicity, ungratefulness and cultivation of hatred, as they had never done before when those very same scandalous lies were directed 'only' at Israel and the Jews and no one else. William Black, a Professor at the University of Texas, is one learned example of the hundreds of incensed Americans who emailed *al-Ahram Weekly* and aired their grievances. He refuted the false attacks of the Arabs against the United States' arrogance or support for Israel as the root reasons for the massive acts of terror in New York and Washington, and exposed Bin-Laden's lies:

> In fact, none of those things motivated Bin-Laden...He has made it abundantly clear that what lit his fuse was the presence of Infidels, 'defiling Holy Arabia'...Our soldiers do

not defile a country by defending it...and it is a myth to call all Arabia 'holy'...whatever policy we followed with regard to Israel, Bin-Laden would still have wished to engage in mass murder of Christians and Jews ('crusaders' in his argot)...He wants the restoration of the universal caliphate, the recovery of all lands ruled by Muslims, and the mass murder of those who stand in the way of such restoration – including women and children...What caused the terrorists to act as they did? It was hate, that hate was very carefully taught...

If the Americans knew more about the response of the Arab and Islamic world to the acts of terror against the United States, they would be vastly more upset...If they read your newspaper, they would be furious. Americans have no idea that the leading theory among Egyptians is that the Jews did it and that tens, perhaps hundreds, of millions of Muslims believe this grotesque lie. Americans have no idea that one of your frequent columnists intimates that US security services crashed the planes into the buildings. Your columnists rant about purported anti-Arab columnists in the United States, but their vituperation and lack of concern for the facts vastly exceeds US columnists...The absence of introspection in too wide a segment of the Egyptian intelligentsia is demonstrated every week by your columnists who blame the problems of the Arab and Islamic world on the West...The real issue is Israel...our 'blind', absolute support for Israel. Indeed, the Egyptians know this better than others, for the United States helped stop Israel in 1956 and provided both carrots and sticks to Egypt and Israel to bring about the return of Egyptian lands and the peace treaty...My concern is not the columnist, but his students who are being taught fantastic bigoted conspiracy theories as if they were political science...When students are taught to believe absurdities, the world suffers.[87]

A Colonel Kaiser wrote to *al-Ahram Weekly* that, while he held respect for the honest and forthright, even when he disagreed with them, he found despicable the slick, the propagandist, the hypocrite and the 'liar, masquerading as a wise one'. He said that while 'even the jihad, "American is Satan" crowd were still honest in their presentation', the English version of the paper in question amounted to 'a pseudo-intellectual pretence, trying to imitate a journal of free thought', whose 'unsophisticated readers are the only ones to be fooled by it'. He ridiculed the paper's 'snide comments', threats and advice to the United States to put 'its house in order instead of chasing a bunch of terrorists', and vowed that America would do both and totally 'eliminate each and every one of this putrid scum... The first change will be in our immigration policy, and then in our oil policy.' He concluded:

> This is all we hear from the Islamic community in America: Oh me, oh my, somebody gave me a dirty look, America is awful, oh yeah, 6,000 people were just murdered... you write an article about the poor Egyptian taxi-drivers who will lose money because of reduced tourism, boo hoo. I'll use one of my grandson's favorite responses, when he hears or reads something extremely dumb: 'duh'.[88]

Sara Welsh wrote to the editor that Egypt, which was pampered by aid from the United States, did not have the human decency to show it a friend's support in a time of crisis, and that the Egyptian readers who were lamenting the fate of the Palestinians under the Israelis could not care less about the many more Kurds who were slaughtered by Iraq. She also called the Egyptians to task for pointing fingers at the United States after the attack on the Twin Towers instead of condemning the fanatics of their own religion who had been wreaking havoc around the world. Andrew Hunter of Britain also exposed the double standards of the columnists of the *Weekly*, who shed tears over the Palestinian victims but not over Israelis, and demanded that the Arabs should stop ascribing only 'the basest motives to other countries and people', and advised the columnists to describe the West's motives for imposing sanctions over Iraq, or for its conduct in other conflicts, rather than ascribe genocidal tendencies to it. He also accused *al-Ahram* of racist writing. Jonathan Bonder, of McGill University, blasted the editor for putting the blame on 'others', while depicting the terrorists as 'eternally helpless victims with no recourse but revenge, as if the intentional killing of the enemy's innocents would serve to make the oppressed's lives better. I fear that such words are part of a constant tendency among... much of the Arab world to blame without accepting responsibility'. Tom Knox of Florida wrote:

> Several things became self-evident. First, Arabs in general... are quite prejudiced. There is very little tolerance in your

society...No wonder many of us here in the United States feel that we are talking to people still in the eleventh century. Join the twenty-first century and enjoy diversity! It is not a slap at the face of Islam to be Buddhist, Protestant, Christian or Jewish...Second, for all the problems with the Israelis...they pale in the face of the genocide Islamics have practiced on themselves over the past 25 years...Now let us look at Africa and the starving populations and AIDS crisis there. Where is Islam? The United States is there spending billions to keep these people alive, many of them Muslims...During the past ten years, the trend has been to cut back on military spending and to spend more on humanitarian/economic development all over the world.[89]

Another reaction to the *al-Ahram Weekly* article 'The Giant's Feet of Clay',[90] in which the United States was debased and blamed, was generated by Professor Wes Lundburg from Minnesota. He condemned the 'tone of celebration that this Giant has been brought down', and accused the Egyptian author of 'contributing to this lack of dialogue and understanding between people of different backgrounds', and called upon the journal to join him in the business of educating people by 'responsible education and reporting'. Another reader of that article, Douglas Bevins, was 'appalled by the article which spoke of America getting its "comeuppance" and the rage of the disenfranchised "coming home to roost" in the form of a huge mass murder of Americans'. He emphasized that the United States did not have clay feet, but rather clay friends: 'If what we got is seen as "comeuppance" by you, then you are not our friend...I, for one American, count you as a friend of our murderous enemy and not of America.' Mike Innarone asked the scathing question:

If it is truly believed that terrorism is wrong, why have the imams and leaders of Islam not demanded that the acts cease and that the perpetrators be dealt with by any authority? They did not, America will. Your readers can either join us, stand aside or be part of the problem we will deal with. It is all about choices.[91]

A psychologist from Tennessee, Meg Ewers, deplored the psychology of hate that the Arabs cultivated, and which reflected a 'psychology of avoiding waking up to one's own responsibility for one's own inner evils'. And finally, Ron Reilly of Pennsylvania offered his own analysis:

> It is wonderful how the internet can disseminate and illuminate your ridiculous pack of lies to those you abuse with those lies...It must be embarrassing for you when the Taliban have fallen and the Afghani people are celebrating in the streets playing music, shaving their beards, and dancing...I do not understand how those images which are all over the free world press, did not make it to you. But this would, of course, contradict the many lies you spread about America committing genocide in Afghanistan...
>
> Dictatorship...that is the kind of government you have. Egypt – a dictatorship with one third of the population illiterate and getting a $2 billion a year handout from the United States. Do your readers know that? Even before 11 September, the bags of wheat in the warehouses of Afghanistan came from America. I swear I did not see even one that said Egypt...I do not care that your country hates us, but I do care that we give money to liars and people who hate us. There is a movement now to stop this foolishness. I am writing my congressmen and senators tonight and providing links to your articles as I have already done with Fox News Network. Fox News is currently doing a story on the Muslim countries that we provide aid to that hate us...
>
> By the way, as far as the evidence against Bin-Laden is concerned, why do you act so stupid? Have you read the fatwa he issued in 1998 to kill all Americans? It is not exactly a confusing message, so why are you confused? His camps trained over 20,000 terrorists in the last several years. Do you think these people took the training to make pizzas?[92]

NOTES

1. For this discussion, see R. Israeli, 'Western Democracies and Islamic Fundamentalist Violence', *Journal of Terrorism and Political Violence*, January 2001.
2. Daniel Pipes, 'Fighting Militant Islam, Without Bias', *City Journal*, Autumn 2001, http://www.city-journal.org/html/11 4 fighting militant.html
3. Ibid.
4. *National Review* (USA), 3 October 2001.
5. *Baltimore Sun* (USA), 30 September 2001.

6. *US News and World Report*, Commentary, 8 October 2001.
7. *Washington Post*, 12 October 2001.
8. *The Spectator*, 13 October 2001.
9. Slate.com, 9 October 2001.
10. *The New Republic*, 22 October 2001.
11. See 'Washington Misled: Saudi Arabia's Financial Backing of Terrorism', *Jerusalem Issue Brief*, Jerusalem Centre for Public Affairs, Vol. 1:23, 6 May 2002.
12. See, for example, *The Spectator*, 22 September 2001.
13. Fouad Ajami, 'The Reckoning: Iraq and the Thief of Baghdad', *New York Times*, 19 May 2002.
14. M. Kramer, commenting on his book *Towers on Sand: The Failure of Middle Eastern Studies in America*, *Wall Street Journal*, 15 November 2001.
15. *New York Times*, 31 March 2002.
16. *The Times*, 2 April 2002.
17. *The New Republic on Line*, 10 October 2001.
18. Ibid.
19. *National Review*, 21 May 2002.
20. Ibid.
21. *National Review*, 18 March 2002.
22. Alexandre Del Valle, 'Islamophobie ou reductio ad Hitlerum?' *Le Figaro* (Paris), 28 May 2002.
23. Ibid.
24. Yair Sheleg, 'American-born Haters of the US and Israel, Spring up on Campus', *Ha'aretz*, 18 June 2002.
25. *The Spectator* (Britain), 20 April 2002.
26. *Al-Watan* (Saudi Arabia), 8 and 9 December 2001, a two-instalment article enitled: 'The Jewish Sense of Superiority in the World', *MEMRI*, No. 321, 27 December 2001. The reader will have noticed that much of the material used for this book draws from *MEMRI* dispatches.
27. *Al-Safir* (Lebanon), 7 December 2001.
28. Ibid. Another aproximate version of this interview appears in *Al-Hawadith* (Lebanon) and was cited by Zvi Bar'el, *Ha-Aretz* (Israel), 2 November 2001.
29. *Al-Hayat* (London), 12 December 2001. *MEMRI* (Hebrew), undated.
30. *National Review on Line*, 13 September 2001.
31. *National Review on Line*, 13 September 2001. See also Dore Gold, 'Israel is not the Issue: Militant Islam and America', *Jerusalem Viewpoints*, Jerusalem Centre for Public Affairs, *MEMRI*, No. 463, 1 October 2001; and Efraim Karsh, 'Israel's War', *Commentary*, 9 April 2002.
32. George Will, 'Final solution, Phase 2', *Washington Post*, 2 May 2002.
33. David Gelernter, 'A Nation Like Ours: Why Americans Stand with Israel', *Weekly Standard*, 20 May 2002.
34. *New York Post*, 16 October 2001.
35. *Weekly Standard*, 15 April 2002.
36. This typology is cited from Avishai Margalit and Ian Buruma, 'Occidentalism', that was published in the *New York Review of Books* some time earlier.
37. See n. 35.
38. Ibid.
39. *Al-Hayat* (London), 21 December 2001. *MEMRI*, No. 37 (Hebrew), undated.
40. Proverbs: 27:6.
41. After the death of the Prophet (AD 632), most of the tribes of Arabia that had converted to Islam as a personal oath of allegiance to him reneged upon learning about his passing away. It became incumbent upon his successor, the first Caliph Abu Bakr, to fight the bloody and cruel 'Ridda Wars' (The Wars of Apostasy), when the tribes were subjugated, one after the other, at a terrible human price.
42. *Akhbar al-Yaum* (Egypt), 3 November 2001.
43. This book by the Syrian writer Khaydar Khaydar, which was published in 2000 in

Cairo, 18 years after it was completed, incited a demonstration of Al-Azhar students who were incited by the Muslim Movement in Egypt. See *MEMRI*, No. 37 (Hebrew), undated.

44. *Akhbar al-Yaum* (Egypt), 3 November 2001. See *MEMRI*, No. 42.
45. See Daniel Pipes, 'Fighting Militant Islam, Without Bias', *City Journal*, Autumn 2001, http://www.city-journal.org/htm/41/fighting militant.html.
46. For a basic survey of Muslims in Western Europe, see the now somewhat dated work of Gilles Keppel, *La Revanche de Dieu*.
47. Michael Paulson, 'Muslims Eye Role at US Polls', *Boston Globe* (Boston), 23 October 2000. The article is headlined on p. A1, an indication of its importance in the eyes of the editor, but its bulk appears on p. A12.
48. Ibid.
49. Ibid.
50. www.msa-dearborn.org, ibid.
51. Ibid.
52. Ibid.
53. Qur'an, Sura 3:111.
54. *Sawt al-Haqq wal-Huriyya* (Israel), 26 October 2001, *MEMRI*, No. 301, 16 November 2001.
55. *Al-Hayat* (London), 11 November 2001. *MEMRI*, ibid.
56. *Al-Ayyam* (London), 12 November 2001. *MEMRI*, ibid.
57. *Al-Ahrah al-'Arabi* (Egypt), 20 October 2001. *MEMRI*, ibid.
58. Ibid.
59. See, for example, Suras 5:51, 2:191, 9:123, 9:5, 8:65, 9:29, 9:3, 9:14, 5:10, 9:28, 2:193, 14:17, 5:34, 22:19–22, 22:9, 25:68, 48:29, and more.
60. See also *MEMRI* Dispatch 41, 2 August 1999.
61. Sura 3:113.
62. *Al-Hayat* (London), 11 November 2001. *MEMRI*, No. 301, 16 November 2001.
63. From an article published in the *New York Post*, 19 October 2001. See http://nypost.com/seven/10192001/postopinion/opedcolumnists/34049.htm
64. *Wall Street Journal, Europe*, 15 November 2001. See also article by Jocelyne Cesari, in *MSANEWS*, 6 June 2000, who drew a wide background of the situation of the Muslims in Western Europe.
65. See R. Israel, *Muslim Fundamentalism in Israel*.
66. *Jerusalem Post*, 4 January 2002.
67. Pipes, 'Fighting Militant Islam'.
68. Ibid.
69. Ibid.
70. *Associated Press*, cited by *Ha'aretz* (Israel), 20 June 2002.
71. 'The Roots of Muslim Rage', *Atlantic Monthly*, September 1990.
72. In an interview to Saul Singer, *Jerusalem Post* (Israel), 5 April 2002, p. B2. See also 'How did the Infidels Win?', *National Post*, 1 June 2002.
73. Ibid.
74. *Foreign Affairs*, November/December 2001.
75. Ibid.
76. Sharon Sadeh, 'London Bridge is Falling Down', *Ha'aretz*, 30 September 2001.
77. Ibid.
78. R. Israeli, 'Muslim Fundamentalist Violence and the Western Democracies', *Journal of Terrorism and Political Violence*, Fall, 2001.
79. See n. 75.
80. *National Review*, 14 December 2001. See an opposing view by Alan Dershowitz, *National Post*, 15 December 2001.
81. *New York Times*, 17 December 2001.
82. Oh, people, we have created you male and female, and we have made you peoples and tribes, in order to make it easier for you to know each other. Indeed, those Allah honours most are those among you who are the most righteous (Sura 49:13).

83. *MEMRI*, No. 386, 5 June 2002.
84. *The Spectator*, March 2002, http://www.spectator.co.uk
85. See Updates from AIJAC (The Australian-Israel and Jewish Afairs Council) 03/02 #10, 22 March 2002.
86. Ibid.
87. *Al-Ahram Weekly* (Egypt), 11–17 October and 8–14 November 2001. *MEMRI*, No. 306, 30 November 2001.
88. Ibid.
89. Ibid.
90. 8–14 November 2001.
91. See n. 86.
92. Ibid.

10. Conclusions and Prospects

This is a very hard state of affairs to digest, let alone live with. The way Islamic ideology gave rise to the Islamikaze, and more so the way Islamic society rose to the defence of the Islamikaze following their acts, first against Israel and then against the United States (and the rest of the West for that matter, had many of their schemes not been foiled), leaves little room for optimism in the Western world regarding a quick accommodation with the Muslim world. Conversely, in the Muslim camp, which has generally taken great delight in seeing Israelis and Americans murdered *en masse*, there is a feeling of great shock and consternation in the face of the vigorous US and Israeli – and to a lesser and more hesitant extent also European – resolute counter-attacks which have been seriously blunting the Islamists' triumphalism and eroding their enthusiasm and popular support. Whatever the outcome of this confrontation, whether it takes a military form or the shape of a 'clash of civilizations', two seemingly contradictory elements are at work which might mitigate the situation and make this world livable, after all. On the one hand, it is hard to see if and how Islamic ideology, based on the Islamic discourse as delineated in Chapter 2, can or will change, if we bear in mind that almost all attempts at Westernization, modernization, democratization, liberalization and other imported concepts, to the world of Islam in the past century, have ended in dismal failure and bred more, not less, frustration, hatred and estrangement from the West.

On the other hand, however, we have observed in the past a pragmatic Islam that counsels its adherents to avoid the humiliations of ensuing defeats; the precedent being set by the *Hudaybiyyah Pact* in the times of the Prophet, who had himself set an example of accommodation with the enemy, temporary as it might be, when Islam was too weak to assert itself as master. That means that whenever Islam faces a resolute opponent, ready to take to the battlefield if attacked or abused, it will usually back down, prolong the *hudna* (armistice) with the enemy indefinitely and allow itself and the enemy a breath of respite. The first lesson for the West, therefore, is to return to the ancient Roman dictum of *para bellum* (prepare for war), to be perceived as strong and invincible, and to be ready to act with decisive force when the power of deterrence has failed to maintain peace. It now appears that Western complacency – born out of the end of the Cold War, the unchallenged power of the United States and the lowering of the standards of alertness and provision of the US armed forces during the Clinton Administration (1992–2000) and, especially, the lack of resoluteness in the US response to the 1998 terrorist attacks in Africa – had given the Islamists, Bin-Laden among them, the impression that the United States had lost the will to resist, and therefore it was time to strike. The Islamists also came to the conclusion that their cultivation of the Islamikaze as a form of warfare, as demonstrated by the Hizbullah Lebanese and the Hamas Palestinians against Israel; the opening of the training camps in Afghanistan, which allowed them to prepare the cadres necessary to fulfil their schemes; the easy penetration of the naive West by their operatives and networks; and the indifference, if not encouragement, evinced by the West towards their spectacular 'successes' in field tests of their new strategy in Israel, more than indicated that no one would dare to resist them.

For its part, the West has been naively convinced that if only it could cultivate its relations with the Arabs and Muslims, trade with them, enrich them with its dominant culture, teach them about its ideas, innovations, technology and modernity, help them to develop, admit their students to its best institutions of learning and open itself up to them and their religion and culture, sign alliances with them, collaborate with them and show goodwill towards them, that they would respond in kind. In fact, many of the Muslim fundamentalist luminaries, such as Sayyid Qut'b of Egypt and Hasan Turabi of the Sudan, know the West well, took degrees in its institutions, and then wrote the most vituperative attacks against it from their position of 'knowledge'. Was it because they hated that West that they could not imitate and which they could not resemble? Or perhaps they were afraid of the viable alternatives it offered to Muslims? We are talking, in other words, about two worlds apart, separated by an unbridgeable cultural gap: the one, modern, open, tolerant, advanced, well-meaning, law-abiding, democratic, orderly, eager to live and let live, oriented toward progress and the future, accepting and self-confident to the point of running the risk of self-destruction by generously allowing into itself Muslim elements bent on terrorizing it; the other, narrow-minded, bigoted, jealous, backward, lawless, bent on restoring past glory, intolerant of others and other ideas, tyrannical in rule, unable to accept and include, suspicious and paranoid, taking shadows of things as the things themselves, vengeful and vindictive, prone to humiliation and shunning exposure to shame, and ready to waive its own life and to take down with it its Western enemy.

It would be necessary to discuss the component elements of this yawning gap which no policy, 'understanding' or declaration can bring together. All the cajoling, the courting, the 'compromises', the concessions and the 'agreements' of the past were taken by the Muslim world in general, and the fundamentalists in particular, to mean that the West was weak, decadent, soft and decaying, and that if only the Muslims kept pushing, it would collapse under the weight of its own imperfections. All the West can hope for, therefore, is not to adopt a policy line that would be acceptable to the Muslim fundamentalists, for nothing short of surrender to their absurdities will do; but, instead, to delineate clear lines beyond which Muslim aggression will find a determined, united and resolute West, ready to fight for its values and the very survival of its culture. It is not a foreign policy towards the Muslim world that the West needs, only foreign relations with it, and readiness to react, strongly and massively, when it feels threatened. After all, the battle against Islamikaze terrorism, the only brand of terrorism that has been systematically sustained, protected, sponsored, justified, idealized, defended and idolized by a wide array of peoples, countries and cultures that come under the heading of Islam, is not only a military or economic or territorial confrontation, but a clash between two world views, creeds and approaches to life (and death).

THE CONTOURS OF THE CONFRONTATION

This is a confrontation because, unlike Western culture which, at least in theory, agrees to co-exist with others, even when they are weaker, the Islamic world shows respect towards, and at the same time feels humiliated by, the stronger – technologically, militarily, economically and culturally. The frustration at their inability to match up to the strong, especially since they were themselves the strong of yesteryear, makes the Muslims eager to destroy the bearers of strength rather than try to raise themselves to their level. Frustration generates shame, and aggression is used to displace that shame. Several areas of comparison may be suggested which point out the differences between the two cultures, and which have been substantiated by the numerous quotes in the above chapters.

The Attitude Towards Human Life and Death

While Islam does not permit suicide of the faint-hearted individual who runs away from the difficulties of life, and enjoins him to face up to his fate and count on Allah, the Muslim fundamentalist champions have found a way to sanctify death as 'martyrdom', and to idolize it to such an extent as to turn it into a desirable pursuit, sanctioned by Allah, Islam, the precedents of the Prophet and his *tabi'un* (followers). Gradually, following in the footsteps of the medieval *fida'iyun*, the revived idea of sacrifice and ideal of suffering under the Khomeini Revolution, its application in the Iran–Iraq War and then by Hizbullah in Lebanon against the United States and Israel; and then through the adoption of the idea by extremist Muslim radicals, such as Hamas and Islamic Jihad, it developed as a popular, effective and universal strategy of warfare among other Muslim fighters, epecially the Palestinian nationalists of the Tanzim and the Aqsa Brigades in their Intifadah against Israel. Finally, Muslim women and children were brought into the widening circle of Islamikaze which, though still limited to hundreds, although potentially appealing to thousands, finds wide support among tens of thousands of clerics, columnists, political leaders and professionals, including some considered 'enlightened' by Islamic standards; and hundreds of thousands, if not millions, cannot contain their sympathy and adulation for them and express it openly in public. For this reason, one can no longer speak exclusively of the war declared by militant Islam against the West, but of a growing circle of support among the Muslim public in general for the radicals, especially when they can show positive results to their credit. The most harrowing and callous aspect of this attitude to human life has been the dragging of teenagers and women, by Palestinians and Hizbullah, into their relentless battles of terrorism against Israel.

This attitude to human life has other dark aspects to it, both internal, within the Muslim community, and *vis-à-vis* the enemy. During the Intifadah of the Palestinians, or the insurgency of the Islamic Groups in Algeria, for example, we have seen the widespread slashing of throats of other Arabs/Muslims just for belonging to the 'other camp', or for suspicion of 'collaboration with the enemy', be it domestic or external. There is no concern for human life, for the families of the murdered, or for the destructive impact on the minds of innocent civilians and children who grow up to accept, as a matter of course, the use of mass murder and hanging in public squares before their eyes, which blunts their human sentiments. This is accompanied by a masochistic display of wounds and blood, and sadistic lynching, abuse of the bodies of the dead, dragging the bodies through the streets, and the chants of the onlooking crowds, who appear maddened by this orgy of cruelty, violence and inhumanity. Funerals for their own favourite dead, for example, for those who died in combat, or as a result of targeted elimination by their enemies, or of the remains of Islamikaze bodies, are also accompanied by shoutings, shooting into the air, huge processions where the body of the dead is seized by the uncontrollable crowds and tossed from hand to hand, with vows of vengeance for the life of the departed martyr and for his replacement by the many others who will volunteer in his footsteps, and the like. Compare that to the funerals of the victims of terrorism in the United States or Israel, which are silent and dignified, intimate and inward-looking, and you have one of the keys to comprehending the difference between the two cultures.

If this is the situation with regard to Muslims *vis-à-vis* Muslims, how much more so when foreign enemies are concerned. We have seen the chilling scenes of the indiscriminate blowing up of unsuspecting civilians in restaurants and cafés; the cold-blooded murder of passengers on buses, aeroplanes and at check-in counters; the shooting of passersby in streets; and the shooting of hostages, on a scale and with a frequency unknown in other times and other cultures, save that of the Nazis. What is more harrowing is the jubilation of the masses of Muslims in support of such massacres, and the 'learned' rationalizations that many clerics, intellectuals and public opinion-makers produce to justify them. But that is not all: enemies can be abducted, killed, murdered, tortured, and jailed indefinitely, and no information about them is given to the families, no access to them is allowed to the Red Cross or anyone else, and expensive prices are extorted for just releasing any piece of news about their whereabouts or their putative fate. No other culture in modern memory has behaved so cruelly, so inhumanely and so obtusely with captured enemies and their loved ones. They know the sensitivity and concern in the West for human life, therefore they exploit this to the maximum, either by keeping silent, thus raising the price of the extortion, or by hiding behind non-governmental organizations, such as the Hizbullah in Lebanon or the Hamas in Palestine or the Islamic Jihad in Syria, in order to escape responsibility. We have also witnessed, live on television, attackers tearing Israeli soldiers to pieces with their bare hands and then the boastful exhibition of the blood-soiled hands before an approving public seized by inhuman frenzy and demanding more cruelty. We have seen Israeli teenagers ambushed by Arabs and left, lying in the open, their skulls appallingly crushed by rocks. The worst part of all this is that when the Arab authorities are confronted with these inhumane situations, they 'condemn' acts of 'murder of innocent civilians on all sides', as if there were two sides to this story, and as if these were natural calamities without murderers who could be identified, called to task and prosecuted.

This callousness in the attitudes of Muslims towards their victims is supplemented by the horrendous re-enactment of scenes of murder, as if they were sublime human experiences worth replaying and memorizing, and models to educate their public and for their young generation to emulate. This, of course, goes a long way to demonstrate how cold-bloodedly these murders are planned, rather than being the spur-of-the-moment act of 'frustration' by some ill-fated or 'desperate' Palestinian or al-Qa'ida member. For, when the scene of an Israeli café or a paper model of an Israeli bus is carefully and meticulously reconstructed in a public place at the heart of an Arab or Muslim city, flying limbs of Israeli children, dripping with blood, are hung around as part of the scene, explosions are re-played and sounds of dying victims are amplified for the impact of their despair – and all this to the frenzied cries of joy of the assembled masses, including children – then something is decidedly sick in the psyche of this society. If no amount of explanation or justification can excuse the horrible acts of murder themselves, where the murderers become hallowed martyrs, how much more so the sheer madness of reproducing those acts, time and again, like a tape being replayed in slow motion to satisfy the sadism of its producers. There are reports of Nazi murderers who delighted in projecting onto screens, to private audiences, their 'feats' of mass murder, but even they did not stoop so low as to screen them, let alone replay them in detail, for the general public. Only now do we understand that these re-enactments are the outcome and extension of the terrible *ta'zia* ceremonies widely celebrated by the Shi'ites during the 'Ashura Day, when the Believers relive the suffering of Hussein in Karbalah by inflicting pain and injuries on their own bodies. But while the Shi'ites exhibit a masochistic sense of identification with their own kin, out of their own volition and without inflicting pain or damage upon others, the Hamas scenes express their hatred towards, and sadistic joy at, the suffering of their enemies.

An additional menace that threatens to descend on the civilized world is the fundamentalists' threat to use non-conventional weapons for mass extermination, as if the mass-killings by the usual mechanical means were not sufficient to quench their thirst for blood. Palestinians and the Hizbullah are known to have experimented with gas and poisons which are contained in the shells and bombs they use against Israeli civilians. The most sure sign of what is to come is when they begin, as part of the process of projection, to impute to their enemy what they themselves plan to do. The massacres that they perpetrate or plan against others, which for them are permitted and to be expected, become in their minds the 'crimes, atrocities and massacres' that the enemy have or will carry out, and as they have been experimenting with gas and poison, they spread the rumours about Israeli use of depleted uranium in the Territories, 'like NATO in Kosovo'; or the distribution of 'poisoned sweets' and the 'HIV-positive virus' among Palestinian children. This means that before they use these materials for mass killings, they wish to impress on the minds of the world the idea that they were not first and that they only responded to the 'massacres' carried out by Israel with US connivance. The eyes of the Arab world were longingly and hopefully directed to Saddam Hussein, in expectation of the arsenal he would deliver against the United States and Israel when the US attack began. No public voice was heard in the Muslim world attempting to dissuade him from that folly, for any moral reason (for example, with a view to restricting the loss of human lives), and not even for the practical reason of avoiding a holocaust of his people. For if the Twin Towers were a 'big success' for them, so much more so the lesson that Saddam was about to teach the West. Hamas and al-Qa'ida, as well as Egyptian fundamentalists, have been adding their voices to those in Iran[1] who threaten Israel and the West with the poisoning of their waters or with infecting them with viruses.[2] It is hard to see who will be left to be brought under Muslim dominion, in accordance with the fundamentalists' dream, if and when the nuclear, chemical and biological annihilation of the enemy is completed.

Intolerance Built into the Culture

Bernard Lewis has made the point that, unlike other civilizations, which are essentially regional, Islam and Christianity have, by their very pattern of expansion, become both universal – and exclusive in the sense that they consider themselves the 'fortunate recipients of God's final revelation to mankind, and therefore [it is] their duty to bring it to the rest of humanity'; and so the clash between them becomes inevitable.[3] However, while Western culture has forsaken the use of violence to spread its message, and pursues it by ways that the Muslims regard as devious (for example, through the pop culture of jeans, fast food, music and coca-cola, television, cinema, alcohol and so forth), militant Islam and its supporters do not shun violence, as the Islamikaze phenomenon has dramatically shown. In other words, the humanistic idea of 'tolerance of the Other' in European culture, which has come to mean that the Other is accepted as is, without value judgements, has become predominant, and has paved the way to the free market of ideas that prevails in the West today. This thinking has not only permitted the renouncing of the use of force, at least in principle, for spreading Christianity, democracy, free trade and other Western ideas, but has also allowed Islam and other creeds to compete on European turf – without Europeans ever suspecting that the competition would ultimately concern the turf itself. Moreover, since the West accepted the idea of separating the Church from the modern secular state, faith has become the domain of the individual, while the public arena has been made impervious to it. In the Islamic world, practically all the 'secular' governments, which for the most part lack legitimacy, must pay lip service to the Islamists, at times by even including them in their governments. Even so, the Islamists appear as the most popular claimants on power, and if allowed to operate as political parties, can often show their mettle and gain access to government. Therefore, no Muslim territory can be made neutral towards other faiths, and the frequent use of violence against them goes a long way to prove that, day in, day out.

Furthermore, Muslim radicals regard the defeat of their own illegitimate governments as a prelude to their restoration of the universal caliphate of all Muslims, and therefore treat the Western governments who protect, aid and sponsor the dictators in place as the direct enemy of the Muslims. From their point of view, then, not only is Western culture despicable in its own 'right' and faulty due to its own deficiencies, but it invaded their turf in order to subvert it and undermine it from within, until it falls off like a ripe fig. It is the West that came to them, not they to it. This creates a paradox, nevertheless, for while Muslim fundamentalists decry the Western cultural invasion, which is 'worse', in their eyes, than the physical invasions of the medieval Crusades, they and their less militant co-religionists at the same time fill the queues in front of US, Australian and European Embassies and Consulates across the world to gain entry visas into those bastions of Western values that they love to hate. Some explain their quest as a simple wish to study in the West, especially value-free technical professions which are not 'soiled' by Western thinking, ignoring the fact that Western learning and protracted sojourns in the West by necessity will have an impact on them, to the point that they could ultimately elect to stay and become Western. Others wish from the start to improve their economic lot by immigrating to the West, but once they get there they congregate around their kin and provide fertile grounds for Muslim fundamentalist *da'wa* (Call, Mission). Still others, such as Sheikhs Bakri and al-Masri in Britain, have migrated to the West as 'refugees', because there was no other place left as a safe haven for them in their countries of origin, and the West was generous enough to accommodate them.

Paradoxically, it is the latter who place themselves at the forefront of Muslim fundamentalism in the West and who, benefiting from the hospitality and social welfare arrangements in their host-countries, recruit local converts or already naturalized Muslims for training abroad, for indoctrination at home and for activities in the Path of Allah. It is they, who are tolerated by societies against whom they are operating ideologically, who are the least tolerant towards their hosts. Their objective is loud and clear: to Islamize their host societies and let Islam take them over. If, until now, it was the integrationists – who wished to assimilate into society, fit into its political, economic and social institutions and become part of it culturally if not religiously – who made an impact the penetration of Muslim fundamentalism into the West has begun to turn these trends around. More and more Muslims 'rebel' against their host cultures and demand, as fully fledged citizens, that their culture be recognized as a component of the national make-up, that state symbols (for example, the cross in Scandinavian national flags) be altered to become inclusive, and that mosques, foreign Muslim languages and Muslim education should be subsidized by the State. In France, following the scandal aroused by François

Bayrou, the Education Minister in the 1970s, when he refused to allow veiled Muslim women into the secular education system of the state (*l'affaire du foulard*), young French Muslims, the sons of immigrants from North Africa (*beurs* in local parlance), frequently boo the 'Marseillaise' when it is played on football fields prior to the matches.

All this emanates not only from the absolute conviction of the Muslims that Allah's message to them, being the most recent, is also the most 'updated', as it were, but also that their way to Allah is the only valid one. However, in contrast to Christianity, the other universal monotheistic religion which claims the same, the Muslims do not preclude the use of force to enforce their beliefs and to 'save the Infidels from themselves', by their own volition if possible, by violence if necessary. Therefore, when they speak of 'tolerance', they mean some sort of temporary measure of accommodation towards the Infidel, who clearly embraces an inferior creed, until Islam is strong enough to prevail. The miscalculation of al-Qa'ida on 11 September, and before and after that of the Hamas and the Islamic Jihad, was that Western societies, including Israel, were so ripe for their demise that a shocking trauma, or a series of smaller but frequent and consistently growing blows, would ultimately overwhelm the enemy. Thus, everytime the enemy responds more forcefully, or in more unconventional ways than expected according to this view – like the United States in Afghanistan or the Israelis in the West Bank – they cry 'foul play!'. This is not how the enemies of Islam are supposed to behave; their very resistance to their subjugation by Islam is regarded as 'blasphemous' for its failure to recognize the will of Allah, and their retaliatory strikes against Islam are seen as 'signs of distress and despair' which augur their approaching end. Hence the stepped-up activities to speed up that process and bring it to its conclusion. This point of view does not recognize the right of the attacked, 'for the sake of Allah', to self-defence. The Muslims can expand, conquer, kill, enslave, dominate and rule, for the entire universe is theirs to be included in *Dar al-Islam*, but woe to those who resist that 'noble' process entrenched in the Will of Allah; those who do are decried as 'aggressors', 'killers of civilians and children', 'arrogant' and perfomers of 'massacres'.

Thus, any hideous attack upon Western enemies, even when it involves innocent lives, as in the case of the Twin Towers, is 'inevitable' and 'blessed' and 'well-deserved' and a 'great success', and causes masses to jubilate and writers to sing its praise throughout the Muslim world, while every retaliation is lamented, condemned and blasted as 'unjustified', 'out of proportion', 'cruel', 'wanton massacre' and 'proof', if proof were needed, of the enemy's inherent evil. The idea of fair play, of attack and counter-attack and, in consequence, of casualties inflicted on both parties to a conflict, is misunderstood in Muslim circles. Even the issue of aggressive and defensive warfare is foreign to them, because the Muslim definitions of warfare do not follow the accepted objective norms prevailing in the West, but abide strictly by the subjective rules drawn by Muslim jurists who have formulated Muslim political theory and international relations.[4] According to these rules, any attack by non-Muslims on Muslims is inherently illegal and immoral, and therefore it is incumbent upon all Muslims to assist their co-religionists, regardless of what they did to provoke the attack. Conversely, any Muslim attack, on the West, for example, since it can be justified as a defensive war against the Infidel, or as an act of self-defence against the spiritual invasion of the West, or as a battle to repulse the enemy from *Dar al-Islam* (for example, Palestine, Andalusia and Southern France), is *eo ipso* a just war that all Muslims are called upon to support it. In other words, once a war against the enemy had been entitled 'jihad', and any of the latter examples justifies a jihad, the arena is wide open for war. Guerilla warfare, or Islamikaze, terrorism and the like, are means of warfare that are hallowed by Islam, with all the attendant ideological and doctrinal elaborations.

The West has no standing in these definitions and what it says or thinks does not matter, because the Islamic position is Allah-inspired and Shari'a-dictated, which means that it is beyond discussion, compromise, debate or concession. External wars in the West are considered quantitative issues (over territories, interests, assets), and when they are terminated, compromise, concessions and negotiations are discussed until an agreement emerges; and when it does, it is binding on the parties who signed the treaty, cease-fire or convention. In Islam the wars are qualitative (over ideas, doctrines, 'justice', 'redress of wrongs'), are never terminated until the victory of Islam and the imposition of its rule, and when an 'agreement' is signed under duress (for example, after a military defeat) it always derives from the precedent of *hudaybiyyah* that was established by the Prophet. The agreement is therefore temporary (*hudna* = armistice), and it is to be violated at the first opportunity, when Muslims feel they have regained superiority, or have found new forms of warfare that the enemy is unable to counter (such as the Islamikaze). *Sulh* (peace-cum-reconciliation) can be concluded only under the terms of a *Pax Islamica*, when the non-Muslim has accepted the hegemony of Islam and submitted to its rule.[5] This is the reason why Muslim authorities in Egypt and Saudi Arabia justified the Camp David Accords of 1977, as well as the Oslo Accords of 1993, in terms of a temporary, *hudaybiyyah*-like truce which is open-ended and reversible, if and when the circumstances so allow. Like the Prophet's precedent, these 'agreements' were only necessary to extort concessions from the enemy, but once they are made and cashed, they no longer necessarily bind.

This worldview, where rules of war and peace do not apply equally to the belligerents, and clearly benefit the Muslims, while they are expected to obligate only the non-Muslims, is the very reason why the Muslims see themselves free to violate their 'agreements', and they constantly accuse their adversaries of 'violating all agreements and commitments', and they themselves face no reproach because they had never expected to live up to their 'commitments' in the first place, while their adversaries, who were truly obliged by them, were expected to keep to them to the letter. Thus, when the Palestinians, for example, committed themselves in Oslo (another *hudaybiyyah*, in the words of Arafat), without reserve or qualification, to end terrorism and violence in general, not to introduce into their territory any category of forbidden weapons, to maintain their armed forces at agreed levels and under one command, to put an end to incitement against Israel and the Jews and to arrest terrorists and pursue them to justice or extradite them, as a prerequisite to receiving more territory from Israel and to advancing the peace process, they only remembered the Israeli part of the agreement and, when not fulfilled, they heaped all the blame on Israel, while their consistent violations of their main commitments did not matter. They became accustomed, with the Rabin government, to being able to break their commitments, while Israel, for fear of arresting the 'peace process', was to swallow all violations and proceed with its one-sided concessions; and so it happened. But when a new Israeli government came in, which made further Israeli concessions in accordance with the peace accords, contingent upon Palestinian parallel implementation, they cried 'foul play!' once again, and that brought the process to an end.

Intolerance based on a concept of superiority, whereby the superior does not have to conform like the inferior, is apparent also in the daily conduct in the Muslim world towards other religions. There are numerous instances in which Christian churches have been burned down in Egypt and Indonesia, and synagogues have been attacked and destroyed by Palestinians (notably the Joseph Tomb in Nablus and the Jewish Synagogue in Jericho during the Intifadah), and by Muslims, throughout the Western world since the outbreak of the Palestinian 'insurgency' in late 2000, but the occasions are rare when Muslim mosques are attacked by anyone anywhere. The Muslims do not take this, and the fact that they can build their mosques anywhere in the West, as an indication of Western tolerance and acceptance of the Other, but as a sure sign that no one dares to resist Islamic expansion while they, in their countries of origin, can curtail or totally prevent the construction of any Christian, let alone Jewish, house of prayer. Muslims can be the inhabitants of any country in the world, including the Christian world and Israel, on whose doors they knock for immigration or 'right of return', and still label those countries 'racist' for not completely surrendering to their will, but Jews and Christians are severely restricted in various areas of the Muslim world. That suggests to them, once again, that while the whole universe is their domain as of right, other faiths are not, by their very nature, entitled to the same rights in the lands of Islam.

No country in the West sees its citizens following the same shameful scenes, current in the Muslim world, where US and Israeli flags, and the effigies of their leaders, are burned ritually as a matter of routine; save when Muslim communities in the West practice the same ritual. However, the burning of Arab or Muslim flags or effigies is an unknown phenomenon in the West or in Israel. Once again, the inability of the Muslim world to accept the national symbols of others as the equal of theirs is striking, especially at a time when the West respects theirs as a matter of course. This, far from awakening the consciousness of the Muslims to their own intolerance, in contrast with the publicly advertised and exhibited Western tolerance towards them, on the contrary has confirmed them in their belief in the hegemony of their faith and symbols which no one dares to challenge, at a time when Muslims openly challenge with impunity other creeds and symbols. This has encouraged the Muslim communities in the West and in Israel to demand the right to construct their mosques, or to perform their Friday rituals, in places known as holy sites to other faiths. On Temple Mount in Jerusalem, they built their mosques on a site that they knew was the holiest for the Jewish creed, they have transformed many churches and synagogues into mosques during their conquests and expansion, and turned every occupied land into a *waqf* (Holy Endowment) that cannot revert to non-Muslims.[6] But woe to anyone who dares to turn a mosque into another house of prayer, or to occupy land that is, or was, Muslim, for that is intolerable. More recently, new challenges arose when Muslims began illegally constructing their mosque on the grounds of, and in defiance of, the Basilica of the Annunciation in Nazareth; to kneel for the Friday prayers near the main cathedral of Florence; and to deny any historical rights to the Jews over Temple Mount, thereby declaring to Christianity and to Judaism, in Lewis' memorable words: 'Your time has passed. Now we are here. Move over.'[7]

This is not exactly tolerance. Significantly, the verse from the Qur'an that Bernard Lewis mentioned in connection with the inscription in the Dome of the Rock – that is: 'He is God, He is One. He does not beget, He is not begotten', which was meant to reject the basic dogma of Christianity about God and His Son when the Muslims took over Jerusalem in the seventh century – was also inscribed on the temporary tent-mosque in front of the Basilica, which awaits the building of the permanent mosque, and obviously has the same intention and meaning. Coupled with the denial of Jewish rights on Temple Mount, this signifies, in the eyes of the Muslims, that they indeed intend to supersede both Judaism and Christianity, as Islam has taught them of old. Hence the Muslim hatred of the construct 'Judeo-Christian tradition', which they regard as having been relegated to a passing episode in history once the Seal of the Prophets had dispensed to humanity the latest divine message. 'Your time has passed. Now we are here' is not only the statement of a factual chronological sequence, but also a declaration of mastery, dominance, hegemony and exclusivity, backed by the will and the power to make it happen in the real world. For a creed that was designed by Allah to replace all others and to bring all humanity under its aegis cannot be expected to tolerate other faiths, let alone competitors for the same world constituency.

The Eternal Victims
In stark contradiction to the dreams of world dominion that they entertain, Muslims tend, at the same time, to regard themselves as eternal victims of the West, which they hate and want to displace, but whose help they need and implore, and they rationalize this

contradiction by the plots and conspiracies constantly woven around and against them, as if the West had no other concerns than them, or could not do very well without their lacrymose complaints. First, and most important, for them is the need to explain to themselves and to the world why and how they, who had pioneered civilization and sciences in medieval times, and had caused Europe to tremble and fear from their successive mighty empires, found themselves, without preparation, warning or transition, at the bottom of the hierarchy of world powers as the modern era dawned. For a shamed society like theirs, it is difficult, even impossible, to take responsibility for their deeds and to devise a policy of adaptation that could help them pull out of the quagmire, for that would amount to admitting the deficiencies of their culture, the stifling restrictions of their faith, the pipe-dreams of their leaders and the insufficiencies of their social systems. Thus, rather than admit their inabilities and seek succour elsewhere, it is easier to project their own ill-will on others, to disguise their jealousies and bigotry as 'revivalism', and to accuse the all-powerful West, the colonizer and imperialist of yesteryear, of all their ills, including their demise, suffering and backwardness, the population explosion, dictatorial rule, corruption, and so on. They do not want to recall that when they were the powerful, the conquerors, the colonizers and the imperialists, they did not stop for one moment to ask themselves what they were doing with the conquered peoples and civilizations which they gradually decimated.

Arabs and Muslims have resources, human and mineral, a great tradition of learning and a vast ambition to restore themselves to where they were before they began slipping in the modern era. However, their self-inflicted deficiencies in government, economics and antiquated social structure do not permit them to take off. Perhaps most stifling of all is their array of dictatorships of all sorts: monarchical and republican, one-party and military juntas, rulers who were never elected and self-imposed Presidents-for-life. Illegitimate rule spawns corruption, helplessness and hopelessness; and the near non-existence of civil society and non-governmental organizations and voluntary associations with the necessary clout to fill in when the government is deficient, make change nigh on impossible. Uncontrollable poverty and population explosion are hardly the requisite processes to arrest these trends. When allowed to intervene, Islamists often step in to fill the gap, but they are closely monitored, or harnessed to the regime's goals, and therefore their attempts are often circumscribed and cause them to become part of the problem instead of the solution. In this state of affairs – in which the Western world, and Israel on their doorstep, advance and increase the gap between themselves and the poor Muslim world – a glaring gap that is observed daily on television screens and in neighbouring Israel and people find refuge in self-victimization: it is not their fault, it is the fault of others. This state of mind is aided in those societies by the dependence of the ordinary individual on his corrupt government for food subsidies, for employment, for education and social services, for development and for his well-being. However, the governments are incompetent, illegitimate and bent on staying in power, and they lack a blueprint for resolving the ever-growing problems of their countries and societies.

Paradoxically, the stronger the regimes become, by virtue of the modern weaponry which affords them a superior power of enforcement, the more disaffected the populations, who sense that their government's interests are not their own: all the more so, since the maintenance of the rulers in their place is often made possible by their Western 'allies', who provide the money, the economic aid, the weapons and the food that keep this explosive situation from getting worse and blowing up in the West's and the regimes' faces. Another paradox develops: because they are dispossessed, unemployed and hopelessly classified as have-nots, the masses in these countries are not only victims of their rulers and Western 'allies', and therefore are 'entitled' to demand that both provide for their needs, but the more they receive to sustain themselves and ascertain their survival, the more humiliated they become because of that dependence, the more enraged they are by it, and the more violence-prone, as this is the only way to air their ever-increasing frustration. In other words, the West and the local governments, who are held jointly responsible for the poverty and frustration of which the masses are the victims, are not only expected to alleviate the burden of the impoverished and the disadvantaged, but when they do so, they are all the more resented and likely to become the targets of the frustration. A no-win situation. A case in point: Bin-Laden is no less enraged against the United States and Israel than against his own Saudi government, which is sustained by its alliance with the United States. If it is so with a Saudi system which is not needy, and a Bin-Laden who is not impoverished, how much more so with other Arabs and Muslims where both government and people are in dire poverty?

The eternal victim also believes not only that everyone owes him everything, and they themselves are exempted from any self-strengthening effort, but also that they can use violence to redress their ills. So, for example, Palestinians who have been living on handouts and sacks of flour from the United Relations Relief and Works Agency (UNRWA) for the past 50 years – and their population in the squalid refugee camps has quadrupled in that period – believe it is the duty of the world to continue to feed them indefinitely. They have children and the West has to take care of them. They have resisted all attempts at resettlement in their host countries, which are also Arab and Muslim but prefer to leave the refugee problem seething and the refugees dependent on the world's goodwill for survival. Arab and Muslim do not want to force the refugees to take up a constructive life and end their refugee status, because a refugee has the kudos of ultimate victimhood, and they are not about to relinquish it. What is more, the United States, and the other Western countries that bear the brunt of the UNRWA budget, are also the most hated and threatened by the Muslim fundamentalists who feed from their hands. If they had learned, if they had been willing to learn, from Western nations and Israel, how to absorb refugees on their own and put them onto a productive track, rather than to encourage them in the mentality of the eternal victim, much of the bitterness and frustration which engenders violence and terrorism could have been avoided. This is not only a matter of money or of development (Bin-Laden and Saudi Arabia being the ultimate example), but a matter of culture. If one is educated not to accept any handouts, to stand on one's own two feet and help oneself, to shed the feeling of victim and to be proud of a self-made and self-sustaining livelihood, then dignity is restored, the humiliation effaced or diminished, and the paralyzing jealousy and stifling apathy replaced by aspiration, ambition and striving.

No wonder then that among Palestinians, some 80 per cent have been found to support terrorism, which is for them, without doubt, the 'right' of the eternal victim to both avenge his situation and to have it redressed. How exactly, they do not say, unless they think – as part of their delusions that we shall address below – that they can bring the West to submission. It is also no wonder that al-Qa'ida, the Hamas, Hizbullah and the rest rationalize their wild terrorism as 'retaliation' for their humiliation and victimhood by the strong, the arrogant and the powerful who have turned them into victims. Therefore, while their terrorism is to be 'understood' in their eyes, and justified as the cry of the desperate victim, as Mrs Blair or Minister Straw have themselves intimated, any Western counter-attack or defensive act must be construed as 'aggression' against, and 'massacre' of, the eternal victim. For every one of their orgies of death one must seek the 'roots' and comprehend the 'reasons', and address the 'causes' – for example, with every burning of a church or a synagogue; although if a mosque is hit, or children are hurt accidentally, that is 'desecration' and 'blasphemy'. For this reason, they do not recognize the difference between intentional damage and collateral casualties: it is the result that counts, no matter what the intention of the enemy planners may have been. The United States and Israel are always arrogant 'children-killers', 'heretics', aggressors and performers of massacres. Americans 'kill' Iraqi children by 'preventing food and medicaments from reaching them', even if it is Saddam who preferred to purchase weapons or compensate the families of the Palestinian Islamikaze rather than import food and drugs for the sick. The dead corpses of the Iraqi children are there for display; if they are clearly the victims, then the Americans are their killers.

Thus, a reversal of roles is effected, whereby the West and Israel become the 'terrorists' and the Muslims the victims thereof; it is the West who terrorizes the Muslim world and is arrogant and condescending towards it, and the Muslims merely act in self-defence. Hence the failure of Muslim countries, including in their Kuala Lumpur Conference of June 2002, as well as in other international forums, to accede to the Western definition of terrorism which is, in essence, 'the use of violence against innocent civilians for political goals'. They refuse to relinquish the mantle of victimhood to others, therefore terrorism is what is done to them, not what they do to others. They struggle at all international forums to show that the Palestinians and Hizbullah cannot be considered terrorists, whatever they do, because they fight for 'liberation' from 'occupation'. Many of them also rationalize the Twin Towers horror as 'liberation' from the choking US tutelage; or as a 'message' to the 'real terrorist', which is the United States (or Israel, for that matter); or as a 'lesson' to the arrogant; or as a new 'mode of warfare' against the threatening and aggressive West; or as the 'desire for death' by the audacious Islamikaze martyrs, which counterbalances the 'desire for life and comfort' of the cowardly and decadent West. This is also the reason why they remind the United States of its own 'terrorist attacks' against Hiroshima and Nagasaki, proof that what matters is not what is done and to whom, but who does it. Victims of the world, unite, if, of course, the United States or Israel are the authors of your misery.

Other victims, such as those Americans murdered on 11 September, or the Indians obliterated in Kashmir, or the Israelis who are blown apart in pizza parlours, or on the bus, are not victims in the eyes of the Muslim fundamentalist, or, increasingly in the eyes of ordinary Muslims, who are also the perpetrators of this terror in all these cases. Other victims do not deserve compassion, because they 'had brought that upon themselves', or better, 'have concocted it themselves' in conjunction with the CIA or the Jews or the Mossad. The wide acceptance of these theories of conspiracy, including among intellectuals and opinion-makers, as we have noticed above, add to the universal sense of victimhood that is rampant in the Islamic world. Another important corollary of this attitude is that, while in the Judeo-Christian tradition martyrs are usually the victims of external aggression inflicted on them in the pursuit of their faith, in Islam it is the perpetrator of the aggression, who also immolates himself in the process, who becomes the Islamikaze martyr. In other words, the martyr is not he who suffers death or torture or misery on his way to martyrdom, since he chose that course avidly and advisedly; the martyr must kill in order to gain his place in the hierarchy of martyrdom. This dramatic shift in definition, from those who were killed in battle or by accident and thereby became martyrs in classical Islam, to the Islamikaze intentional mass-killing of others in order to go to Paradise and enjoy the 72 virgins promised by the Qur'an, baffles the West today.

Self-Delusion, Fantasy and the Real World

The proverbial Arab love of words, to the point of ecstasy, has been studied by scholars, such as Gibb and Patai, and been found to relate to the strength of the Arabic idiom, as exemplified in the Qur'an, as well as in the ancient Arabic poetry of the time of the *Jahidiyya* and in the subsequent Arab and Muslim literature. The ability of the word to move people and to incite them to action, a key element in the training of the Islamikaze, is supplemented by a rich world of fantasy, which defies rational analysis, and in which wishful thinking replaces facts, mantra-like slogans supersede policy ('Jerusalem will be liberated by one million *shahids*'; 'if the Israelis do not like it, they can drink the waters of the Gaza Sea/the Dead Sea'), and the unpleasant is denied as if it did not exist (no

Muslims were involved in the Twin Towers murders: the Israelis/ Jews did it). For that reason, commitments are ignored as if they had never been undertaken (for example, smuggling in weapons by Palestinians, arresting terrorists); promises are forgotten the moment they are made (to stop incitement and terrorism); slogans are coined and repeated (Israelis inject HIV-positive viruses into Palestinians; Oslo is an example of *hudaybiyyah*); propaganda and incitement thrive (the *Karine A* and *Santorini* weapons smuggling never took place; Israelis and Americans are child-killers); boasting of one's exploits (Egyptian democracy is more authentic than Israel's) and denigrating the enemy are rife (the Jews are cowardly, the descendants of monkeys and pigs); lies are made up to cover up deficiencies (Palestinians economic suffering is due to Israel's policies, not to terrorist activities by the Palestinians); and denial is exercized when one is faced with facts (no *Karine A*; no blowing up of the Twin Towers). History is invented (Palestinians are the descendants of Cana'anites); false analogies are made (between Palestinian leaders and the founding fathers of America); facts are denied (the Holocaust; or involvement in terrorism); and self-embellishment and self-aggrandizement are sought (the future belongs to Islam; the West's demise is imminent) for consolation. Palestinian and other Arab and Muslim textbooks for children tell the entire story with such eloquence that not much needs to be added.[8] But enough examples will be cited, especially in connection with Islamic terrorism, the incitement to it, and praise for it after the acts of murder, to illustrate the main assumptions of this chapter.

Each of these fantasies undergoes several stages. First, the fabrication of a web of lies that bears no relation to facts, and which Muslims think, if repeated often enough, becomes a reality in which they themselves begin to believe, even when they cannot prove it. Because no rules of evidence apply to these stories, and what matters is the manufacturing of 'facts' and their diffusion through their own societies and across the world, Muslims swallow the stories, not suspecting that hoaxes of such dimensions could be invented. They also believe, however, that even if the Israelis or the Americans did not 'do it', it is likely that they would, because it is in their nature. A classic case in point is the Blood Libel against the Jews, which we see being repeated by the Minister of Defence in Syria, and reiterated by nearly all Muslim media, without criticism. In the same vein, the Palestinian delegate at the Commission of Human Rights in Geneva, of all places, can stand up and accuse the

Israelis of injecting the AIDS virus into Palestinian children; and Arafat can lambast the Israelis for spreading poisoned sweets to kill Palestinians; and the Saudis and Egyptians can claim that Israel has distributed an aphrodisiac which increases the sexual appetite of women in order to corrupt their morals, or that the Israeli armed forces have used depleted uranium bullets to harm the Palestinians. During the battles of Jenin in April–May 2002, for example, a Palestinian father was produced on television cameras, crying and weeping for his nine children who had 'perished' before his eyes and whom he 'had seen with his own eyes' under the rubble. A very horrible and heart-rending experience indeed, except that all nine children were fortunately found safe and sound. Perhaps the most chilling hoax to be fabricated by the Palestinians, and actively supported by all Arabs and Muslims and passively accepted by much of the European press, was the 'Poison Affair' of 1983, when the Israelis were accused of 'poisoning Palestinian schoolgirls in Jenin', and then in other areas of the West Bank, with a view to 'sterilizing them before their age of reproductive activity', thus 'battling against Palestinian demography'. These accusations were made throughout the world press, and even when it was proved that the 'poisoning' was a case of mass hysteria – what the medical profession recognizes as 'hyper-ventilation' – the accusations did not recede.[9] Any accusation is considered valid, and when the accuser is not held responsible for providing evidence, accusations and libel become cheap and no one is held to account.

Self-delusion operates on other levels as well. Convinced of the righteousness and exclusivity of their Islamic universal message, the Islamists cannot understand why the West and Israel pursue them, why they do not allow them follow the Path of Allah with impunity, or why they wage war against them. For the message of Allah is clear and unambiguous; it declares the Jews monkeys, it forbids Muslims to befriend Jews and Christians,[10] enjoins the Muslims to 'kill Unbelievers wherever we find them',[11] to 'murder them and treat them harshly',[12] 'fight and slay the Pagans, seize them, beleaguer them, and lie in wait for them in every stratagem'.[13] So why do the Infidels behave the way they do? That word of Allah was intended to be against them, and they cannot deny or resist it, because Allah Himself said it, and it is written, word for word, in His Divine Message – the Holy Book which applies to all humanity. They also believe that Allah and His Messenger had announced that it was acceptable for Muslims to go back on their promises and obligations with Pagans and make war on them whenever Muslims find themselves strong enough to do so;[14] or that Allah has taken away the freedom of belief from all humanity and relegates those who do not believe in Islam to Hell,[15] calls them 'untouchable and impure',[16] and orders His followers to fight the Unbelievers until no other religion except Islam is left;[17] and more. Then why should they spare non-Muslims, make any agreement with them, or honour any of their commitments to them?

The hard-core Islamists are therefore shocked that the West fights back and resists them, instead of submitting to them and recognizing that Islam is their only salvation. We have seen appeals to President Bush to convert to Islam and astonishment at his procrastination about doing so. They cannot comprehend how and why the Westerners are failing to see the light and do not hurry into the fold of Islam. In their world of delusion, they already see 'thousands of Americans' repenting for their previous obtuse misunderstanding of Islam, and their 'being reduced 'to tears when they listen to the Words of the Qur'an recited to them'. Their worldview, which cannot accept a plurality of creeds, also cannot understand why they, the disseminators of the good of Allah and his message, should be held in low esteem and feared and persecuted by the West. All they did on 11 September was to fulfil the Word of Allah:

> For them [the Unbelievers], garments of fire shall be cut and there shall be poured over their heads boiling water, whereby whatever is in their bowels and skin shall be dissolved and they will be punished with hooked iron rods.[18]

Unbelievers will not only have to live in 'disgrace in this life, but at the Day of Judgement He shall make them taste the penalty of burning'.[19] To have precipitated the Day of Judgement upon the victims of that massacre was therefore not aberrant, just the early fulfilment of the Word of Allah.

Then, the stage of denial sets in, when the Muslims realize the outrage and havoc that their delusions have impelled them to commit. Be it acts of terror against Israel, the *Karine A* weapon smuggling, or the 11 September horror, they first of all deny they ever carried out, intended, knew or participated in those acts; while at the same time paradoxically displaying unrestrained jubilation about them. In this stage of denial, they wish both to dissociate themselves from the atrocities they have committed and to 'enjoy' their results at the same time. For example, the first major terrorist act against Israel, committed at the height of the Oslo euphoria in mid-1994, in which 21 young Israelis perished, was immediately denied by Arafat, who 'had no knowledge' of it, and as 'proof' of innocence, he denounced the 'act'. In an interview given to Israeli media, he speculated that it must have been the 'deed of the Israeli services' who 'were interested in wrecking the Oslo agreements'. Why wreck them, when the Rabin government which signed them was in power, and was full of goodwill, lenient towards Palestinian violations, and eager to show to a suspicious constituency in Israel that they 'worked'. Arafat did not explain. His conspiracy theory and strong sense of denial was stronger than any rational consideration he might have invoked. When the *Achille Lauro* was hijacked by Palestinians in the Mediterranean in 1986 and an American citizen on board was murdered and callously tossed into the sea, the hijackers retired to Port Said, where they were arraigned. However, President Mubarak denied that he had any knowledge of the mastermind of that terrorist act, while the same time that he gave this terrorist shelter in his country. The affair of the ship *Karine A* which, in early 2002, was seized by the Israeli Navy in the Red Sea, and was found to be illicitly carrying weapons to the Palestinians under the command of one of Arafat's associates, was claimed by Arafat and the Palestinian Authority as an 'Israeli plot'. Then, when presented with the facts, and with the shipment of weapons exposed to world media, Arafat said that he 'had no knowledge of it personally'; only when he was confronted with the documents that he had personally signed had he no choice but to apologize to President Bush.

In the aftermath of 11 September, similar patterns of behaviour were detected in the Muslim world. In spite of displays of uncontainable joy, Muslims from Pakistan to America, from Egypt to Afghanistan, denied that any Muslim could 'commit such horror', because it was patently against 'the compassion and tolerance of Islam', and verses were cited in support of this contention: for example, Islam 'was opposed to compulsion in faith', or to the execution of 'innocent civilians', unless they challenged Islam or 'humiliated it'. They also contended that an act of terror of such proportions could not possibly have been planned, let alone executed, by any Muslim state or organization, thus exonerating themselves in advance, even if that implied an admission of their incompetence in carrying out operations of such a scale. Even as the evidence was being gathered and divulged of al-Qai'da involvement, and demands were mounting for the group's indictment, Muslims continued to insist that 'unless America provided decisive and undisputed evidence for Muslim involvement', it was wrong on the part of the West to 'smear the entire Muslim world', which was 'opposed to terrorism', on account of the 'yet unproven' deeds of the few. The roles were therefore reversed once again: the Muslims, who needed no evidence for their delusions, and never stopped to reflect on the irrationality of their accusations against the West and Israel, suddenly found themselves being scrupulous about 'evidence' when the accusations were laid at their door. They also found themselves pledging that should any evidence emerge of Muslim involvement, the culprits ought to be pursued with 'Muslim justice', and dealt with according to Muslim legal procedures; which meant, in effect, exonerating Muslims altogether.

But the facts kept pressing at the door, and as the Muslim claims of 'innocence' had become ludicrous in the eyes of world opinion, the next stage, of projection and laying the blame on others, began. As in those cases where Israelis were accused by Palestinians of 'provocations'; in organizing terrorism against their own citizens in order to blame the 'innocent and peace-loving Palestinians'; or of concocting the *Karine A* arms-smuggling in order to smear the Palestinians' 'impeccable reputation' for being 'law-abiding' and having 'respect for its commitment' – so the Muslim world orchestrated a campaign blaming others for the evils of 11 September. First, it was claimed by Muslims in Egypt and Pakistan, that the United States and Saudi Arabia, or the Jews, the CIA or the Israeli Mossad 'did it', with countless 'indications' showing, successively or simultaneously, either or all of these theories. Again – becoming suddenly meticulous about 'data gathering' and the provision of 'conclusive evidence' – they began to fabricate piecemeal, fantastic stories about Israelis or Jews who 'had been forewarned and evacuated the premises of the Twin Towers prior to the blast'; or about the takeover of control towers by 'suspect elements', also presumably Jewish, who 'collaborated with the hijackers'; or about other hoaxes. All of which never cease to raise our admiration for the boundless imagination of their inventors. Indeed, Muslim day-dreaming is unlimited, and 'imagination' soon becomes their 'reality'; they do not seem to share the Western concept of the 'imaginative' differing from the 'real' and they appear bent on the 'imaginary', which seems to fill their world and to satisfy their emotions.

In this Kafkaesque world of the unreal, only non-Muslims are supposed to sin, and therefore anything projected onto them is either true, or could be true, even if it is not proven. This is the foundation of the vicious and sustained campaigns of denigration and diminishment of the West and the Jews in Muslim circles, countries and societies: which we commonly call incitement and which is the pre-requisite for terrorism against the West. Incitement often involves delegitimization of the enemy, making it look corrupt and decadent, an inherent enemy of Islam and Allah, and therefore deserving of annihilation through terror. To that end, any means is justified, even the invention of lies and false quotations from non-existent sources, such as the 'citation' by Palestinians in their textbooks of passages that have never existed, which 'prove' the Jewish conspiracy, the 'evil' of the Jews and their ill-intentions against Islam and the rest of humanity; or the ritual repetition of the Blood Libel as a fact of history; or liberal quotations from the forged Protocols of the Elders of Zion as true documents; and so forth. It seems amazing to us that they care so little for the truth, as long as it serves their goals of libelling Israel and the West, and even less about educating their children with falsehoods and training them to take imaginary texts as 'quotes'.[20] In May 2002, when the Israeli armed forces launched their Defensive Shield Operation against terrorist bases in Jenin – an operation which was led extremely carefully as regards to civilians – the Palestinians immediately shouted: 'Foul play!' They had just conducted a series of murderous attacks against Israeli civilians, and blown up 100 of them within one week, including during the Passover Seder, where entire families had been wiped out (29 killed in all), and that was considered by the Palestinian public as a matter of routine; but when Israel decided to rout the bases of terror from the West Bank, accusations of 'massacres' began immediately, echoed by the Arab and Muslim press (and also by the European press, and the numbers of 'massacred' people kept increasing, reaching the peak of 3,000, according to Saeb Arekat, the Chief Palestinian negotiator. Then it turned out that 'only' 50 Palestinians had been killed in that centre of terror, and for the most part amid very heavy fighting. In short, there was no massacre.

Similarly, when the Americans opened up their counter-attack against the Taliban, and thoughtfully attempted not to harm civilians, as far as possible, in the process – and even dropped significant quantities of food to sustain them during the fighting – it was the stories of 'massacres' of 'innocent civilians', 'poisoning of the dropped food parcels', the 'intentional bombing of schools and food depots', the 'cruel arrest of Taliban POWs' and their transport to Guantanamo, where they were treated 'inhumanely' like 'the Nazis would', that dominated the Arab and Muslim reporting of the operation, and not the intentional atrocities, committed by the Taliban themselves and their supporters. For the Arab and Muslim audiences in both cases, the intention was not to report a balanced truth, where the evils and motivations of both parties were recounted, and where the sequence of cause and effect had to be explained concerning the horrendous terrorist attacks against civilians which had to be avenged and rooted out; only the 'callous and senseless American and Israeli aggressive attacks against civilians', committed without reason or cause, just to satisfy the evil instincts of Bush and Sharon, were reported. For Arab and Muslim audiences, vilifying, debasing, calumniating and libelling their enemies was the only way to deligitimize them as inhuman predators, so as to pave the way for future additional terrorist attacks against them. This sort of projection on to the enemy not only permits his delegitimization and encourages more attacks against him, but also, more significantly, exposes the hidden dreams of what the Muslims would do to the Americans and the Israelis if they could. Projection-cum-incitement, therefore, reveals to the West what fate awaits it, should the Muslim world win this confrontation. Was it not the Secretary General of the Arab League, 'Azzam Pasha, who declared, on the day the Arab armies invaded nascent Israel in 1948 in order to eliminate it, that a 'massacre would ensue that the world had not seen since the Mongols'? He meant a massacre of the Jews, just as the Muslim terrorists mean and implement today, but not piecemeal – in one fell swoop.

Thus, Americans and Israelis, in their reprisals carried out in self-defence, have espoused the strategy of saving civilian lives to the greatest extent possible, and would rather fight surgically instead of blanket-bombing entire cities or population centres, at the risk of their own casualties. Muslim terrorists act differently. Their stated aim is to maximize civilian casualties in the enemy's ranks, as evidenced in the attack on the Twin Towers and in the massive explosions in crowded civilian places in Israel, where nails and bolts are added to the bombs for maximum effect, and sometimes poisonous substances are tucked into the bombs. In other words, while the West operates with considerable restraint placed on its forces, for fear of their devastating impact, terrorists use their power to its greatest extent; something which leads to the fear in the West that the terrorists would not hesitate to use unconventional weapons if they could lay their hands on them. That is precisely the West's Achilles heel, which is tied in with its concern for human life, due process of law and restraint in use of power, which the Muslim terrorists, who are not shackled by those limitations, seek to exploit and attack. To make that happen, roles are once again reversed: 'We are not the terrorists!!!, You are!!!', they shout at the West. For what Muslim martyrs do in terms of wanton killing is not only justified because it is in the Path of Allah, but by delegitimizing the West as a terrorist itself, the fight against it is called for, and to be fought by all means available to the Muslims: precisely those that the West has restrained itself from using.

Pathological Anti-Semitism
Perhaps not since Nazi Germany has such vitriol been poured on the Jews *per se*, not only on Israelis and Zionists, as has been the case in the past few years. We have seen nauseating examples of anti-Semitic attacks in the high echelons of Arab politics, not only in intractable Syria, but even in the Egyptian mainstream press, which shamelessly recounts its lies and fabrications as 'history', and avidly 'quotes' from the Protocols of the Elders of Zion, which never really existed, and recounts with a sadistic delight, that can only match its joy at the carnage at the Twin Towers, the Blood Libels of which Jews have been accused. There is not one voice to stand up to the calumniators and intercede to stop this orgy of hatred. All one has to do is to rummage through the hundreds of hate sites that are fed by Muslims and Arabs across the world to realize the width and depth of anti-Semitic sentiment in the Muslim world. There has also never been any society since the Nazis which so boasted of its hate towards the Jews as Muslim society today. Its preachers denigrate and humiliate them, incite against them, justify massacres against them, and associate them with the United States and the evil West. The reason for this new outburst of hatred, which has also been manifested throughout the democratic West, where Jewish and Muslim communities live side by side, is perhaps that Jews represent the successful middle class which has made the West prosperous. For the Muslims, it is painful to admit that Jews have succeeded where they

have failed, and their jealousy in this regard cannot be contained or suppressed. They console themselves with their prophecies about the 'cowardly' Jews, who at the end of the day will run away and hide from the Muslims who will seek their destruction.

There is no need, as some advise, for Israel (and the West, for that matter) to undergo any soul-searching or to dig up the 'reasons' (there must be reasons, right?) for this hatred, anymore than there was such a need when the Jews were made the scapegoats of the Nazis, and were murdered for what they were, with the burden of the 'guilt' accruing to them. If anything needs to be investigated, it is the sick minds of the anti-Semites, today and of old, but this does not seem to be the moment, although some of the character traits of the Muslims which make them so prone to accuse others in general should be enumerated. Given that the Muslims and Arabs are so fond of Hitler and of citing him, and that they miss no opportunity to analyse 'scientifically' the 'reasons' for his victimization of the Jews – and they naturally find the Jews themselves guilty – then words such as 'reason' and 'cause' have been depleted of their meanings, and one is dragged into the realm of the incomprehensible. However, in addition to this, the Holocaust which the Jews were supposed to have brought upon themselves is vehemently, and again 'scientifically', denied, and the Jews are relegated to the role of 'Nazis' in their dealings with the Palestinians. Such a web of lies, presumptions, pretences, denials and contradictions, could only be created by the modern Arab and Muslim mind. In any case, the delegitimization of the Jews, Israel (their state), and Zionism (their movement of national liberation), is so thorough, total and irreversible, as to turn them into the target of the coming Islamikaze massacres, which they deserve.

By making their hatred of Jews so pathologically inseparable from Jewish physiology, the Muslims immunize themselves against any human compassion. Otherwise, it is hard to understand how crowds would jump for joy in Palestinian and Egyptian streets, at the sight of Jewish children blown to pieces, or entire families wiped out in one stroke of madness. They have turned so obtuse and cruel where Jewish victims are concerned, that it is necessary to remind them, from time to time, that they are evil to pursue civilians and murder them in streets, restaurants and buses. Even more evil are those who rejoice with them, and they must be excluded from the human race. If the Muslims call their massacres jihads, and their murderers martyrs, that does not mitigate their crime; on the contrary, it discredits the faith that motivates them and the God in Whose name they act. But the Muslim fundamentalists' judgement is blunted by hatred, to the point that they can no longer differentiate between good and evil, human or inhuman. They support the evil of the indiscriminate killing which is dictated by their blind hatred, even though they risk being consumed by its fire. They have no use for facts (for example the Holocaust), nor respect for values (the mass murders they commit without hesitation), nor concern for the victims. Because only they, the fighters of jihad, who are awaited in Paradise, count, and anyone who stands in their way should be eliminated. They blame their own plight onto the Jews and accuse the Jews of causing their backwardness, oppression and poverty; and impute to Zionism the 'oppression of freedom' from which they themselves suffer. Only a twisted mind beyond repair can accuse the Jews of the Twin Towers massacre, begin to believe it, and then come to the conclusion that because of the 'Jewish failure' to achieve their goals, the 'future of Muslims in America looks bright'.[21]

Muslim Lessons and Blueprint

Muslim fundamentalists have drawn several lessons from their understanding of the present state of affairs and prepared a blue-print for their confrontation with the West, which in its gradually emerging details has proven quite popular with the Muslim masses in general, who are in no mood for compromise or 'understanding' or spreading ecumenical messages. The belief in Allah's blessing on their venture has become so deeply rooted in their hearts that they feel no fatigue or fear and do not recoil from implementing their plan, even if, or precisely because, there seem to be difficulties and obstacles along the road. For Allah had tested many of His followers in the past, and He ultimately made them victorious, as one of His many names (al-Nasser, the Victorious) indicates; and modern Muslims want victory and nothing less. They are equipped with the requisite faith, zeal and enthusiasm, as the acronym of Hamas (The Islamic Resistance Movement) points out; are boundlessly devoted to Allah, as their various Hizbullah (Party of God) groups profess; are determined to pursue their *da'wa* (Mission, Call) the world over, as many of their organizations call themselves and their organs; are intent to wage a merciless jihad (Holy War) if their 'peaceful' message of surrender is not heeded by their enemies, as their recurrent attacks against the United States and Israel evince, and as the name of many of their associations, 'Islamic Jihad', remind us;

and they are all co-ordinated by the main base (al-Qa'ida), physically and spiritually, which trains the candidates for Islamikaze, finances their operations, plans their schemes and initiates the time and place of their spectacular strikes. In the meantime, they are acquiring the skills of double-talk: soothing, anaesthetizing the enemy and manipulating the media, as if their innate propensity for lying, fabricating, pipe-dreaming, bigotry, hatred, violence, terrorism, calumniating others, rationalizing, denying, projecting their own deficiencies and deluding themseves were not sufficient. The main components of this blueprint can be summarized as follows:

1. The West must be defeated, or at least weakened, frightened and put on the defensive. For not only does it corrupt the Muslim world with its debauchery, innate corruption, alliances with Muslim countries and its valueless societies; but also purely by posing an alluring alternative to the young Muslims, with its permissive way of dress, co-educational schools, music, pornography, mixed dancing and frolicking, alcohol, technology and Western movies, it threatens the future generation of Muslims. Naturally, the fundamentalists, with the acquiescing silent support of many conservative Muslims, dread the prospect of seeing their societies slip from their grip and supervision, therefore they enlist for their endeavour any Allah-fearing Muslim, though not necessarily of their affiliation, who is concerned, like them, about the rapid drift of the young towards modernity and the West.

2. A first step towards this goal is to cultivate the rift between pro-Arab and pro-Muslim Europe, on the one hand, and 'Zionist-controlled America', on the other. Thus, while both belong to the evil West, it is imperative to go easy on Europe at first, due to its assistance, both directly to the Muslim world, and indirectly by diminishing the United States' power and keeping it in check. This policy has proved a success, for the time being, inasmuch as the European Council has been openly favouring the Palestinians over the Israelis, in spite of US misgivings; and the Muslims have succeeded in drawing Europe onto their side in the Balkans (Bosnia, then Kosovo, then Macedonia), and dragging with it the US forces who have implemeted the joint European–Muslim design in Europe.

3. Europe's turn will come after the United States is driven out of the game and Israel is eliminated. Muslim fundamentalists

speak about their *reconquista* of Europe, first of the territories that used to be under Muslim rule in the Iberian Peninsula and southern France (what they call Andalusia), and then the rest of the continent. The first signs of these ambitions begin to emerge in speech and in writing, as shown above, and are also present among North African immigrants, legal and illegal, who are aware of the historical reversals they have suffered. Already, in the 1980s, when former Gaullist French Prime Minister, Michel Debre, was made aware of the school curricula in Algeria and announced on the first page of a Parisian daily: 'The Danger Comes From the South', little response or concern was shown by his fellow Frenchmen or Europeans. Indications of such schemes, indeed a foretaste of them, came to the attention of the Europeans on 12 September, when several major Islamic terrorist strikes were foiled in Paris, Strasbourg, Bruxelles and other locations. Al-Qa'ida bases and undercover lodges already exist in practically every European capital, and the time will come when they will be activated.

4. Preparations for the showdown in Europe has included both testing public opinion as regards the Muslim *reconquista*, first of the Spanish vestiges of their colonial rule in North Africa (Ceuta and Melilla) and then some disputed islands in the Mediterranean; and also increasing the numbers of Muslims who migrate to Europe – legally if possible, and illegally if necessary – in order to hasten their taking up of political rights individually, and then beginning to claim cultural and political group rights. The 20 million Muslims of Europe today, varying from five to over ten per cent of the population of each country, has already made an impact on domestic politics: both due to immigration and, more importantly, to the high birthrate among them, which drives up the proportionate numbers of Muslim childen now, and will drive up their absolute numbers when they come of age for elections.

5. Jews (and by inference, Israel and Zionism), have to be eliminated, as Bin-Laden, the Hamas and the Hizbullah have vowed, because their sins are numerous: they humiliated the Prophet and betrayed him, therefore they cannot be trusted; they have invaded the lands of the Muslims in Palestine and established their hated Zionist state which, in effect, tore off a valuable piece of *Dar al-Islam* and turned it into *Dar al-Harb*, which requires jihad to reclaim it; they constitute a Western

society in the Muslims' midst, thereby aiding at close range the Western scheme to corrupt Islamic society and undermine it from within; they have 'desecrated' the holy places of Islam in Jerusalem; they control the corridors of power in the United States, such as commerce, the media, financial centres, right to the very heart of the White House, as described in the Protocols of the Elders of Zion; and, most dangerous of all, they act as the US agent in the Middle East, hence their close links to Washington, to an extent that makes it hard to determine who is subservient to whom. Therefore, the Jews are targets not only in their own state – Israel – but worldwide, as the frequent attacks against them throughout their world diasporas, since October 2000, have demonstrated.

6. Above all – the cherry on the cake – the United States of America, due to its military and economic power, not only dominates the West and leads it, determines its agenda and enforces it, but also battles Islam into submission, protects Israel and serves its purposes, produces and disseminates the decadent sub-culture that arouses the wrath of Islam, and is the first model of imitation for the youth everywhere, including the Muslims. If the United States, the 'Great Satan', as another fundamentalist – Khomeini – called it, cannot be reduced to submission, at least it can battered, threatened, humiliated and weakened, to the extent that not only will it no longer be able to protect its citizens and its interests around the world, but that its many allies, primarily Israel, Europe and the illegitimate Muslim rulers it sustains, will no longer trust her and depend on her. It is also singled out by the Islamists for being the only power that can, and is, willing to effectively block the fulfilment of their schemes and the implementation of their pipe-dreams. Hence the hatred for the United States, first and foremost, which is proclaimed in the slogans and propaganda statements of the fundamentalists, and displayed in the massive acts of terror against it.

7. Finally, pending the anticipated Muslim victory, much long-term groundwork is needed, which the Muslim radicals whole-heartedly support and initiate, and even push Muslim govern-ments and individuals to help finance. The list is long: recruiting new converts in the West; lending financial support to families of the Islamikaze martyrs; raising monies, either from 'charitable organizations' in the West itself, to be used against it, or from donor states and individuals (Saudi Arabia and Bin-Laden, for

example); building mosques, Islamic Centres and madrasas in Washington, Paris, Stockholm and London, and elsewhere in those unsuspecting countries (ostensibly for the Muslim populations of the West, but diverting their use to conversion programmes, indoctrination and the diffusion of hate propaganda and recruitment of trainees for Islamikaze purposes); strengthening Islamic education in already Muslim countries on the periphery, such as Indonesia, South and Central Asia; and raising Muslim consciousness among the Muslim minorities in Nepal, Thailand, Israel, India, Europe and the United States. It is the fruit of such endeavours which ripened in the madrasas of Pakistan as the Taliban, in the religious schools of Qum, in Iran, as the Hizbullah, in the opium fields in Afghanistan as the Islamikaze terrorists, and in the mosques of Europe and the United States, as the planners and executors of 11 September.

What they cannot do today, they will try tomorrow. Like a burglar in a hotel, they will try to force open any door which offers little or no resistance, but will recoil when the alarm is activated, the door is steel-reinforced and its lock armoured, or when security personnel are on the alert and ready to interfere, immediately and resolutely, regardless of the risk of confrontation or the dangers of casualties and damage which might ensue. This general formula suggests what can assiduously and meticulously be done over the long term in order to foil the hideous designs of radical Islam against both the West and those of its own societies which have not yet run completely beserk.

THE CHALLENGE TO THE WEST

Contrary to what is advocated by some Muslim apologists in the West, who offer leniency for, and their 'understanding' of, the radicals to an exasperating limit; and regardless of whether they are motivated by their naiveté, ignorance, goodwill or sheer wishful thinking, or a hidden agenda; it is time to call a spade a spade, to stop playing into the hands of the terrorists and being manipulated by them, to stand up tall and determined, and fight back, as President Bush has taught all of us. For a plan of war to succeed, one must first of all understand the motives and convictions of the enemies, something that we have tried to accomplish in this book. Then one must assess the enemy's war-plan and try to foil it, as a prerequisite to counter-attack and victory. This, too, has been addressed in the previous pages of this chapter. We shall now attempt to develop ideas for counter-measures, taking into account that certain things, like verses from the Qur'an, or commonly accepted interpretations thereof, cannot be altered, and if they were, that this would only create more outrage and havoc. Secondly, in spite of the funda-mentalists' perception that their war against the West is total and perpetual, until it succumbs, the West, or any civilized society for that matter, cannot gear itself, nor educate its young, to such a grim prospect of permanent war. Thirdly, it is not the business of the West to educate others, to look for 'enlightenment' where it does not exist, or to determine one-sidedly scales of values that ought to apply universally.

Taking these premises as a starting point, one can then devise some sort of accommodation by co-existence – not by changing others to please us, or adapting ourselves to please them, for their choices, like ours, must be respected if we wish others to respect our choices. This is possible as long as they do not interfere with our choices or do not try forcibly to change them or to force their choices on us. In other words, it is a *modus vivendi* with others that the West has to choose over a *modus operandi* against them, as long as the live-and-let-live formula is accepted on both sides and neither tries actively to undermine the other. However, unfortunately, the test of whether this rule is respected has to remain subjective and within the domain of each party, as the present international organizations have shown us that politicking often takes precedence over decency and fairness. We must also be aware that conflicts of opinion, which might erupt into armed conflicts, will remain the constant characteristic of international relations in the foreseeable future. This means that, though politics of consensus remain a preferred course of action, the West has to be prepared to go its way alone, when it considers that its vital civilizational, economic, and perhaps existential, interests are at stake. The present rifts, suspicions, jealousies and bitterness between rich and poor countries and societies, Western and non-Western, Northern and Southern, developed and under-developed, and their struggles over resources, environment, immigration, social justice, population growth and standard of living, will not only deepen, but will create coalitions of the disadvantaged, against which the West will find itself outnumbered and outvoted at any international forum. That is already very much the case.

The West has tried over the past century, and especially after decolonization in the past half century – with the help of the emerging modernized elites in the liberated colonies, one must say – to introduce its own modern values of democracy, liberalism, human rights, peace for its own sake, free choices, education, development, technology, accountability in government, and an improving standard of living. The results were far from spectacular, save in a few exceptions, and in any case, in the 56 countries that define themselves as 'Muslim' today, with their population of over one billion (and growing), spanning two continents, the total failure is resounding. Yes, the perennial model of Turkey is cited, but since Westernization was enforced there brutally, rather than being allowed to grow organically from within by consensus, its coarse joints are still visible almost a century later, and when permitted, the reaction of the fundamentalists erupts to the surface. In other words, the West should try to pursue its dictated 'reforms' in Islamic countries, as it has been trying to do in the Palestinian Authority at the beginning of the new millennium, it will not get very far, because reforms adopted as a result of foreign pressure are doomed to fail under the internal counter-pressures of the Islamists. In consequence, it is not new reforms that the West should demand or expect in Muslim (or other non-Western, for that matter) countries as prerequisites to dealing with them, but the fulfilment of two conditions: renouncing the use of force externally, and granting human rights domestically.

The West, for its part, cannot attain credibility if it only insists on the enforcement of these conditions separately. For example, it cannot, on the one hand, detach itself from the domestic politics in Muslim countries, but, on the other hand, interfere in internal struggles for power between Islamists and others. It is its business to declare that it refuses to deal with a certain regime, for example, because of violations of human rights, but it is not its business to decide which regime should hold power, or how it should behave domestically or externally, or whether it is illegitimate or not, so long as it does not resort to violence. We have seen that current US support for illegitimate rulers in the Muslim world has only augmented popular resentment against both. If the United States does not ally itself with violators of human rights (though it does not interfere in their policies), then it cannot simultaneously treat those who own oil differently. This is laughable, and no one in the Islamic world would take it seriously. Let the peoples of the Islamic world struggle for their own form of government; they will emerge, at the end, with the order (or the chaos) they deserve, or that is best suited to them, or that they are prepared to suffer. If and when they reach the end of the road with a government, like the Shah's regime in Iran, then let them rise up, struggle and come up with a new arrangement, all on their own. And their 'choice' must be respected by the West, whether it is Islamic, monarchical, military or otherwise. In view of the results of that internal struggle, the West might decide to deal or not to deal with the emerging order, and only when it shows clear indications of using violence (conventional or non-conventional), or of resorting to terrorism against Western targets or interests, or against others who are allies of the West and whom it is interested to protect, will the trouble-making ruler encounter the unified resolve of the West, deployed to defend civilization from havoc.

In these terms, stability is a fetish that no longer has a place in the new world. Would we have preferred the continued 'stability' of the 'Empire of Evil' over the instability that followed its demise, until things finally took shape there (for now)? Or the 'stability' of the 1,000-year Reich over the instabilities and horrors of the war which ended that evil reign of the Nazis? Or do we prize the 'stability' of stagnant economies over the social mayhem and instability that rapidly growing societies may incur? Similarly, buying 'stability' in the Muslim world, at the price of perpetuating corrupt rulers and illegitimate regimes that the West supports, is not necessarily a superior choice over some domestic political struggle which may shake up those societies until something acceptable to them emerges. In the same vein, massive military and economic aid by the West, to those countries it judges 'vital' to its interests, does not necessarily serve that purpose in the long run: we have seen in our generation the Western-supported Shah of Iran, and the monarchies in Egypt, Iraq and Libya, crumble, and with them, Western influence, and the transfer of weaponry and funds from the West to the hands of its enemies. That very same process could happen tomorrow in Egypt, Saudi Arabia, Jordan, Pakistan and elsewhere in the Muslim world, where Islamists are waiting in the wings for their local illegitimate rulers to falter, or for US aid to be suspended. In the meantime, all that the United States and the West are getting out of these heavy investments is the strengthening of the illegitimate rulers they protect, by handing them more lethal power to maintain their rule, thereby causing the pressures of anti-American resentment to build up and ultimately explode in their faces.

This hands-off policy *vis-à-vis* the Muslim world will not necessarily harm Western interests. Certainly, the West needs oil, but the Muslims are no less interested in selling it than the Westerners are in buying it: they cannot drink it or turn it to any other use without bringing disaster upon themselves. Quite the contrary, if the West decides that the track record of the Muslims on human rights is unsatisfactory, it can also punish them by reducing its purchases of oil from them and increasing them from others. If the present corrupt sheikhs, who immorally and illicitly appropriate for themselves the legendary wealth of their kingdoms, decide to launch hostile boycotts against the West in order to strangle it economically, then perhaps the West can help the people of those countries seize their wealth, rid themselves of their exploiters, and put the income to a better and fairer use than financing the obscene debauchery of the princes, who have no more legal and moral rights over the resources of their country than all the rest of their fellow-citizens. There is nothing more just, democratic, fair and indisputable that the West can help create, and the fear of that happening alone will insure the unhampered flow of oil; and if it should happen, no one, save for the princes, would shed a tear.

However, the predicament of the West will not be solved by a hands-off policy towards the Muslim world. Enough fundamentalist rogues will remain in the midst of Islamdom to concoct plots, violence and acts of terror, the bitter foretaste of which we have all shared on 11 September. A unified West must devise a long series of long-term measures, both defensive and offensive, aimed at learning to co-exist with the Muslim world in good neighbourliness, with mutual respect if possible, in rough stand-off if necessary, where boundaries are drawn, the lines are clear, the rules of the game honoured, and their violation swiftly avenged. However, if terrorism or other kinds of violence are unleashed against the West, its citizens, its allies or its interests, then measures will have been rehearsed to contain the situation and prepare for combatting it. These measures must cover: prevention and deterrence; punishment and reward; coping and eradication.

Rules of Co-existence
Co-existence between the West and the Muslim world, if not peaceful then at least non-belligerent, cannot exist or last unless a system of

unilateral measures of self-defence has been adopted by the West and advertised and made clear to all. Also, a system of reward and non-lethal punishment should be put into place, a menu for every Muslim country or organization to choose from if it elects to enjoy Western 'goodies'. Neither action requires any agreement on the part of the Muslim countries, although both assume a united and uniform policy among Western countries. Those Muslim countries which are willing to participate in the effort – those who have either already proved they can be accepted by the West, or will do so in the future by fulfilling various criteria specified by the West – can enjoy the fruits. These include: a certain per capita income; a certain GNP judged necessary to maintain Western norms; a regime of liberal democracy – elected, with pacific transfer of power, accountable, apersonal, non-hereditary; a free press; transparency of government; human rights and freedoms; free enterprise; freedom of property; free transaction of real estate and funds; freedom to create in the arts, the humanities and literature, and protection of one's creation; and a strong and independent judiciary to oversee all this. Such countries that would be accepted into the Alliance of Western and Democratic States (AWADS) – at the centre of which will be the United States, Canada, Australia and Western Europe – can sponsor other applicants as they prove their adaptability to its rules and their willingness and capacity to live by, and up, to them. This system may sidetrack the chaotic situation in the United Nations today, where politics and shifting majorities, composed of dictatorships for the most part, determine the moral and other standards of behaviour in this world body. Durban 2001 should remain for ever a warning on the level of hatred and bigotry to which the United Nations today is capable of stooping.

AWADS will announce that it is united in the fight against terror, but it is open not only to co-operation with Muslim countries who so desire it, as long as they meet the two criteria of renouncing violence externally and enhancing human rights domestically, but would even consider co-opting them into the organization if they were to wean themselves from terror and develop political systems acceptable to AWADS. Thus, without threats, recriminations, forced reforms and all the rest, a powerful incentive is introduced into the international arena for change, the Western way, if a country so elects; or it can choose to stay in the putrid marsh of UN politics. The West will then determine whom to receive into AWADS, and once there, what sort of obligations each country has to meet, proportionate to its strength, population and wealth. This would be in contrast to the universality of the United Nations, which permits any group of evil terrorist countries, such as Algeria, Syria and Sudan, can determine the agenda and resolutions of, for example, the Commission on Human Rights in Geneva. Handing over public order and morality to the heads of the mafia is not exactly the most efficient way to achieve peace and equity. It is important to emphasize that to find the most horrendous incitement, libel and hatred, one does not need to search out the fundamentalists' discourse. It is there across the board: in mainstream and opposition newspapers, among both the general populace and students and intellectuals, in official chanceries, and in Arab and diplomatic missions abroad.[22]

Before anything else, however, an iron-clad definition of terror has to be adopted unilaterally and announced by AWADS, as there is no chance that Muslim countries would agree to any Western definition, or abide by it. For them, things are clear: the United States and Israel are terrorists, while the Arabs and Muslims are either 'freedom fighters', or they 'fight back' out of 'frustration' and 'despair'.[23] Even should the West agree unanimously on the formula of the State Department, there will remain the problem of which are the states that support terror and that President Bush pledged to also regard as terrorists. For example, Lebanon's government does not support terror openly, but it lets the Hizbullah operate in its territory, in conjunction with Iran and Syria who do support it. Also, consider Saudi Arabia and Egypt, who are supposed to be aligned with the Americans, not only for fear of their wrath, but mainly because they are themselves are threatened by the domestic terrorism which jeopardizes their regimes. However, while they do not strictly encourage terror or give it shelter, Saudi Arabia does finance the Hamas and Islamic centres around the world which spawn terror, and both it and Egypt have permitted such a high level of home-grown incitement and hatred against the West and Israel, including that in their state-controlled media, that it is doubtful whether they can be exempted from responsibility. We have already seen the furious rank-and-file US reactions to the incitement found in the press of these 'allies', but those who lodged the protests were unaware of the venomous anti-Western and anti-Jewish sermons in the Saudi mosques, and of the violent student demonstrations in Egyptian universities, where not only was support voiced for the Palestinian Islamikaze, but horrendous scenes of the massacres of Israeli civilians were re-enacted on campus while the police looked on.

Thus, only after having arrived at an internally agreed formula, tight enough not to let anyone slip through – and being aware that even though the West did not declare war on Islam, Muslim fundamentalists did vow to wage war on the United States and Israel – can AWADS then announce its rules of engagement with the Muslims, and the rest of the world, for that matter:

1. Immigration from Muslim countries to AWADS will be strictly curtailed, in view of the Muslim undergrounds that have been festering in the past years in Europe and the United States, due to the extremely liberal policies of the West, which have been abused, right and left, by terrorist Muslim organizations. Control must not be left to those countries from which immigration originates. Not only are they unwilling to stem the tide of the *reconquista* of Europe and of Muslims settling in all continents but, even had they been willing to stem immigration, their chaotic and corrupt systems would be incapable of implementing the decision. Therefore, only stringent defences around AWADS countries, interception of illegal immigrants and their repatriation without ceremony, and expulsion from their territory of operatives who assist them, will slow down the invasion.

2. Immigration, tourism and study by Muslim aliens in the West will be allowed only to nationals of those Muslim countries which themselves allow an equivalent unhampered flow of Western immigrants, students and tourists, without discrimination towards other races, faiths or nationalities.

3. Economic aid, food grants, technical assistance, health and education, and development projects outside AWADS will only be offered centrally by the organization if certain conditions are met by the applicants/recipients, such as: accountability; progress in democratization and human rights; a tangible effort in population control; renouncement of force in dealing with others; monitoring and taking steps against their centres of incitement in the media and the mosques; and the like. The centralised choice of programmes by the organization will not only eliminate the current competition between member-states, which generates a waste of funds and a disruption of priorities, but will also act as a positive incentive to candidates for aid to make domestic improvements in order to qualify.

4. No military assistance or sales of weapons will be permitted by AWADS to non-member states, experience having shown that

armed dictators are more lethally equipped to perpetuate their brutality and to divert their national wealth to undesirable ends. AWADS will also announce that any weapons-manufacturing third party, which sells or transfers weapons to those regimes, will itself be disqualified from dealings with AWADS members.

5. Muslim assistance, especially by Saudi Arabia for building mosques and other Muslim institutions in the West, and their continued funding thereafter, will be made contingent upon parallel permission to build religious institutions for other faiths in Muslim countries, including the Arabian Peninsula, and on the contributor and the recipient's commitment that no incitement and no hatred would be propagated therein.

6. Import to the West of Muslim cultural assets – in the form of books, movies, art shows and exhibits, perfoming art groups, missionaries and clerics, newspapers or tapes – will only be allowed from countries that allow a free flow of the same Western assets into their territories, and forbid, by law, the dissemination of hate, and act upon that law.

Rules of Confrontation

AWADS ought to be the main world body to fight terrorism, when the rules of peaceful engagement have been violated, or in preparation for such an eventuality. The struggle against terror is a continuous, never-relenting process, involving governments and populations, overt and covert means, punitive and preventive measures, legal and political, diplomatic and military initiatives, national and international efforts, education of the population to help avert catastrophe and to deal with it when it strikes. Morale, combat tactics and an overall strategy, intelligence-gathering and analysis, and sometimes plain luck or perceptive intuition can make the difference between disaster and relief. If AWADS does not establish, lead and operate an integrated system of this sort, the world efforts against terrorism will remain diffuse, unco-ordinated and inefficient; every country, organization and intelli-gence machine will remain suspicious of the others and jealous to preserve its own gathering networks and analysis staff, and every operational unit will continue to put its reputation and glory over the general good of the Western world. The very joining of AWADS should be a sign by its members that they are willing to surrender some national pride and resources for the sake of eradicating terrorism and neutralizing its causes. It is understood that the West has little patience for the tremendous waste in human power and resources which terrorism forces on it collectively by compelling it to spend so much energy and attention on prevention and surveillance. However, it is a challenge to the West to show to the terrorists that their goal of sapping Western strength until the West submits will not happen. As we have said before, a succession of three dichotomic concepts will have to be addressed: prevention and deterrence, punishment and reward, coping and eradication.

Prevention and Deterrence

When AWADS is established, with its goals stated and the necessary resources, chains of command, operational tools and organizational frameworks welded together, these in themselves will signal to the Muslim terrorists that the West has taken decisive steps to eradicate terrorism, and will no doubt act as a deterrent and preventive measure. But the list of necessary actions is only beginning: preventive arrests of suspects worldwide, not only in the United States; concerted intelligence efforts to penetrate terrorist circles, by all the means that human, electronic and communications intelligence can afford; stringent monitoring of AWADS countries' borders, tighter visa control, eviction of students orginating from countries which support terrorism, and more difficult access for those who are from dubious countries; a blanket prohibition of the use of weapons and explosives by non-governmental agencies; outlawing operations and fund-raising for terrorist, or otherwise 'charitable', Muslim organizations and freezing/confiscating their funds; a total ban on importing foreign money to build mosques for Muslims in AWADS countries, or on financing their activities, unless the same is allowed to other faiths in Muslim countries. Also, the special forces trained to battle terrorism or to curtail its activities should be given high visibility, and the AWADS budgets for that purpose should be advertised, both to explain to its own population the burdens it is asked to bear, and also for the sake of deterring prospective terrorists, who should know that they face an impregnable wall if they want to penetrate AWADS countries, and if they did succeed, that their bodies would be returned to their homelands in bags, with a great fanfare to deter others. Select, pre-emptive operations could also be held against terrorist bases prior to the terrorists setting out for action against the West or its allies.

Punishment and Reward

Deterrence only works when it is a credible and devastating force of punishment (not revenge, as the Muslims would have it) ready to be unleashed every time an identifiable act of terrorism is perpetrated. Naturally, since the Islamikaze themselves are likely to perish in their own blasts, the rapid detection of their sponsors, dispatchers, financers, supporters and trainers is crucial for swift and deadly retribution. No terrorist organization should escape unscathed by hiding under the apron of its sponsor state: just like Afghanistan (Taliban), so Lebanon (the Hizbullah), Jordan and the Palestinian Authority (the Hamas), Palestine (the Tanzim and Aqsa Brigades), or Damascus (the Islamic Jihad), should all be aware that any terrorist activity emanating from their territory would bring destruction and devastation to them. This is the only way, apart from military strikes, to make these countries responsible for eradicating terrorism in their midst or to signal to them that they cannot escape economic and political pressure to conform, unless they relent. Conversely, if those authorities battle terrorism themselves, which for them may amount to domestic insurgency which they are unable to control, as in the Philippines, AWADS should step in to help, to generously allocate equipment, funds and expertise, and to assist the self-purging society to take its steps even towards joining AWADS itself, if it meets the requirements.

Coping and Eradication

While total eradication of terrorism is apparently impossible, bringing it to manageable levels, as in the 1960s, is quite feasible, if the pressure on terrorist organizations keeps escalating to the point that the terrorists own societies would have to eject them from their midst. The irony may be that, while Muslim countries may be willing and able to adopt the requisite steps to eradicate terror, if only to allow their regimes to survive, it may be that European countries themselves, who for years had allowed al-Qa'ida bases to thrive on their turf, would have difficulties in invoking the necessary legal and political steps to wipe out would-be terrorists in their lands. In any case, no programme of long-term eradication is possible if the citizenry of AWADS is not taught to cope with the new situation in the long haul. It is not only a matter of patience in long security lines, alertness to suspicious people or parcels, precautionary steps on entering a building or exiting from it, vigilance in urban areas against terrorist mischief under the cover of darkness;

but also training to be calm in the face of adversity and not to panic, how to assist the injured after a blast, how to isolate an endangered area, to identify non-conventional blasts, to self-inject antidotes and to self-administer treatment, how to evacuate oneself and others to hospital, and how to placidly accept additional outlays that are not usually anticipated. A well-prepared, well-rehearsed and determined citizenry has proven, as in the unfortunate case of Israel, that it can not only reduce the panic and face up to the disaster, but also act as a deterrent in the final analysis, when the terrorist enemy knows that his initial scheme of sowing terror and fear had been *a priori* aborted.

These measures seem harsh, even inhuman and undemocratic, to the squeamish and faint-hearted among us. But they are needed by democracies to defend themselves in this hour of emergency. Other optimistic minds believe that by explaining and apologizing, the West's righteousness shall prevail and the bad spirits that have been threatening all of us shall be soothed and mitigated. Still others are expecting 'other interpretations' of Islam to emerge, which will be more enlightened, accommodating and modern. Such interpretations do exist, but as part of the underground: they are based more on apologetics than on moral grounds, and their authors have been attacked, killed, maimed or disgraced. The masses of Arabs are not exposed to free speech and to liberal media with contradicting opinions, they are subjected to the uniform and repetitive messages of hate and illusion that are hammered daily into their heads in the form of incitement, therefore they do not know any better. No enlightenment can be expected to emerge from a conservative Islam, which does not even display a human compassionate response to victims of terrorist massacres, and no liberal Muslim individuals would have the courage, let alone the power and stamina, to enforce their dissenting marginal views on the terrifyingly deluded and incited masses. Therefore, the West has no choice but to go all the way, all alone, in thinking, planning and implementing its measures of self-defence and survival.

In the 1960s, at the height of the Cultural Revolution in China, the heir-apparent to Mao, Lin Biao – who was later to die in a mysterious air-'crash' over Mongolia amidst rumours that he was trying to defect to the Soviet Union – developed a 'theory' which applied the class struggle to international relations. He said that as in the process of the Chinese Communist Revolution, whereby the peasants from the countryside assaulted the bastions of capitalism in the cities, so, in the future, would the peasants from the rural areas of the world (Asia, Africa and Latin America) launch an attack on the rich urban areas of the world (North America and Europe), thereby playing the final chord of the world Communist Revolution and takeover. That dream, like the pipe-dreams of the Muslims on world-domination, did not materialize, but there are enough world causes around, like globalization and the environment, which are propped up by day-dreamer leftists, anarchists and anti-capitalists, who might join up with the down-trodden Muslims, or be exploited by them in their drive to try once again to bring down the Western world. Terrorism is their tool, and anti-terrorism is the only way to contain them and then defeat them and their allies; objections of squeamish intellectuals notwithstanding

After the 11 September atrocities, the celebrated American social theorist, Mark Lilla, was interviewed on his recently published book, *The Reckless Mind: Intellectuals in Politics*, where he expounded his hypotheses on how Western intellectuals and writers ended up justifying communism, Fascism and other tyrannies: for example, Sartre with Maoism and Heidegger with Nazism. He explained that both European and American intellectuals have been attracted by tyranny, the former due to their temptation to return to some 'pre-modern idyll' and the elimination of bourgeois capitalism after they were disillusioned by secularity, democracy, capitalism and other trappings of modernity; the latter, out of 'ignorance and a naive optimism about human nature', and therefore they have all 'flirted with tyrants who promised radical alternatives to modern life and heaped contempt on those who engaged in meliorist reforms of that life'. Cases in point today, we might add, are Arafat, Bin-Laden, Saddam Hussein, Khomeini and other tyrants who pose as revolutionary innovators, and are often considered heroes by Western intellectuals, who would 'understand' their 'reasons', tolerate their terrorism and tyranny, suffer their whims and threats, and absorb silently the evils they inflict on their societies and neighbours rather than resist and combat them with resolution. To those, Lilla has these immortal words of wisdom and warning:

> We Americans find it easy to assume that political cut-throats are just misunderstood delinquents, and that their tyrannical practices are expressions of cultural differences we should tolerate. To reach such statements today about fascists,

Stalinism, the East Bloc, the Third World dictators is quite chilling. Our own modern and democratic and bourgeois convictions are so strong that we have trouble grasping political phenomena not governed by our rules... The misunderstanding is bred of American optimism and provinciality. Americans take legitimacy for granted, so they fail to take seriously the illiberal and antimodern implications of certain modern ideas they glean from translations and domesticate into English... Certainly, there has been a fascination with 'purifying' violence and terror in twentieth century intellectual life, as we see in the works of Sorel, Merleau-Ponty and Foucault, but it is also true that certain terroristic acts have woken people up, ending their illusions and their romanticizations of the 'Other'. I think here of the Cambodia Massacres, the Munich Olympics [in which Israeli athletes were murdered by Palestinian terrorists].[24]

American intellectuals and their like-minded European counterparts will wake up eventually, and rise in defence of their cherished values and assets, but only after they sense that their home turf and the freedoms they take for granted are directly and imminently threatened. But what of the mainstream of intellectuals in the Islamic world, who toe the line of their clerics instead of standing up to them? If Allah has it all in hand, and contradicting His spokesmen on earth amounts to heresy, then they might come to accept the trials and tribulations of the present as part of the path they must follow in order to achieve the anti-Western goals they seem to have embraced. And, since they have proven their propensity to lay the blame on others rather than delve into their psyche in search of solutions for their predicament, the process of change in their midst, if it should occur, would be prolonged, tortuous and painful. In the meantime, only a unified and firm stand in the West, based on positive incentives, on the one hand, and clear deterrents, on the other, might trigger that change.

NOTES

1.   Former President Rafsanjani spoke of using a nuclear bomb against Israel. See Iran News (English), *Kayhan* (Farsi) and *Al-Wifaq* (Arabic), 15 December 2001. *MEMRI*, No. 325, 3 January 2002. See also *Al-Sha'b* (Egypt), 23 September 2001.
2.   Al-Qa'ida Spokesman, Suleiman Abu Gheith, in an article titled 'In the Shadow of

the Lances', and also Ayman al-Zawahiri's article in *Al-Mujahedin*. For both, see *MEMRI*, 12 June 2002.

3. Bernard Lewis, 'How did the Infidels Win?', *National Post*, 1 June 2002.
4. For the most comprehensive and authoritative study to date, see Majid Khadduri, *War and Peace in Islam*, Baltimore, MD: Johns Hopkins University Press, 1969.
5. See Moshe Sharon, 'Hudna and Sulh in Islam' (Hebrew), *Nativ*, Summer 2002.
6. See repeated references to this in the Charter of the Hamas.
7. Lewis, 'How Did the Infidels Win?'
8. See, for example, Raphael Israeli, 'Identity and State-Building: Educating Palestinian Children after Oslo', *Journal of Terrorism and Political Violence*, Spring 2002.
9. See Israeli, *Poison: Modern Manifestations of a Blood Libel*.
10. Qur'an, Sura 5:51.
11. Sura 2:191.
12. Sura 9:123.
13. Sura 9:5.
14. Sura 9:3.
15. Sura 5:10.
16. Sura 9:28.
17. Sura 2:193.
18. Sura 22: 19–22.
19. Sura 22:9.
20. For example, see Israeli, 'Identity and State-Building'.
21. See, for example, Itamar Marcus, 'Islam's Mandatory War Against Jews and Israel in Palestinian Authority Religious Teaching', *Studies on Palestinian Culture and Society*, Study No. 4, 2 July 2001. By Palestinian Media Watch, Jerusalem; and James Cox, *USA Today*, 28 September 2001.
22. Note, for example, the virulent anti-Semitic terms with which Assad of Syria spoke about Israel during the visit of the Pope in Damascus, the Blood Libel that is promoted by his Defence Minister, or the statement by the Saudi Ambassador to London in support of the Islamikaze martyrs.
23. Regarding the heated debates in the Arab world on the definition of terrorism, see *Al-Hayat* (London) 25, 28, 29 September and 1 October 2001; *Al-Ba'th* (Syria), 1 October 2001; *Tishrin* (Syria), 3 October 2001; *Syria Times* (Syria), 2 October 2001; *Al-Safir* (Lebanon), 25 and 27 September 2001. All in *MEMRI*'s *Terror in America* Dispatch 18 (Hebrew), no date.
24. Interview by Eric Alterman, The *New York Times*, 10 November 2001.

Bibliography

ARAB AND MUSLIM MEDIA (WRITTEN AND ELECTRONIC)

Afaq Arabiyya, Egypt
Akhbar al-Yaum, Kuwait
Al-Ahali, Cairo
Al-Ahram, Cairo
Al-Ahram al-Arabi, Cairo
Al-Ahram Weekly, Cairo
Al-Ahrar, Egypt
Al-Akhbar, Egypt
Al-'Alam al-Yaum, Egypt
Al-Ansar (online)
Al- Arabi, Egypt
Al-Ayyam, Palestinian Authority
Al Ba'th, Syria
Al-Dustur, Jordan
Al-Gumhuriyya, Cairo
Al-Hawadith, Lebanon
Al- Hayat, London
Al-Hayat al-Jadida, Palestinian
  Authority
Al-'Ilm (scientific journal), Egypt
Al-Islam wa-Filastin (Islam and
  Palestine), Nicosia and then
  London
Al-Istiqlal, Weekly of Islamic
  Jihad in Gaza
Al-Jazeera Television, Qatar
Al-Kayhan, Iran
Al –Liwa', Lebanon
Al-Maidan, Cairo
Al-Manar, Hizbullah Television
  in Lebanon
Al-Mujahidin
Al-Mustaqbal, Beirut
Al-Qahira, Egypt
Al-Quds al-Arabi, London
Al-Ra'i, JordanQatar
Al-Raya,Qatar

Al-Risala (Hamas), Gaza
Al-Riyad, Saudi Arabia
Al-Safir, Lebanon
Al-Sha'b, Egypt
Al-Sharq al-Awsat, London
Al-Sirat, Israel
Al-'Ukadh, Saudi Arabia
Al-Usbu', Egypt
Al Usbu' al-Adabi (The Literary
  Weekly), Damascus
Al- Wafd, Cairo
Al-Watan, Saudi Arabia
Al- Watan al-Arabi, London
Al-Wifaq, Iran
Cassettes (video and audio of
  the Hamas), Palestinian
  Authority
Hadith al-Madina, Egypt
Iqra' Television, Saudi Arabia
IRNA (Iranian News Agency),
  Teheran
Khaleej Times, United Arab
  Emirates
Kul al-Arab, Israel
Leaflets distributed by Hamas
  and Islamic Jihad
Middle East Times
Palestinian Broadcasting
  Authority from Ramallah.
Roz al-Yussuf, Egypt
Saudi Gazette, Saudi Arabia
Sawt al-Haqq wal-Huriyya, Israel
Sawt al Umma, Egypt
Syria Times
Tishrin, Syria
WAFA (Palestinian News Agency),
  Palestinian Authority

ISRAELI MEDIA (WRITTEN AND ELECTRONIC)

Ha'aretz, Tel Aviv
IsraelTelevision Channel I,
    Jerusalem
Jerusalem Post, Jerusalem
Kol Ha'ir, Jerusalem
MEMRI (*Middle East Media*
Reports) [in Hebrew]: most of
the translations in the book
are based on *MEMRI*; I am
indebted to them immensely
Middle East News Online
Nativ, Sha'arei Tikva

INTERNET SITES AND PUBLICATIONS

Al-Ansar (online)
CNSNews.com
http://artsweb.bham.ac.uk/
    bmms/sample issue
http://www.city-journal.org/
    html/114fighting
    militant.html
http://dsc.discovery.com/
    news/briefs/20010/910/
    abroad.html
htpp://post.com/seven/10192
    001/postopinion/opedcolum
    nists/34049.htm
National Review Online
Online Journalism Review
Middle East News Online
WorldNet Daily.com
Worldwide Revisionist News:
    http://64.156.139.229/vcotc
    /rituamord/id39m.htm
www.ahram.org.eg/weekly
www.al-bab.com/yemen/
    hamza1.htm

www.alminbar.cc/alkhutab/kh
    utba.asp?mediaURL=5473
www.almuhajiroun.com/
    islamictopics/islamicissues/
    jihad.html
www.almuhajiroun.com/press
    _releases/index.html
www.geocities.com/al-
    ansar.index.html
www.geocities.com/ircc/
    women/comment.htm
www.lailatalqadr.com
www.lailatalqadr.com/stories/
    p5041001/shtml
www.lailatalqadr.com/stories/
    p4040401.shtml
www.msa-dearborn.org
www.obm.clara.net/
    shariacourt/fatwas/fs.html
www.terrorism.com/_trcctforu
    m5/000004b5.htm
www.zccf.org.ae/Lectures/E2/
    e201.htm

WESTERN MEDIA

AFP (*French News Agency*), Paris
AP (Associated Press)
Asian Age Magazine, New York
Atlantic Monthly, New York
Baltimore Sun, Baltimore
BBC News, London
Boston Globe, Boston
CBS News, New York
CBS, June 2002; Stahl, Leslie,
    '60 minutes'

Christian Science Monitor, Boston
City Journal, New York
CNSNews.com
Commentary, New York
Daily Mirror, London
Daily Telegraph, London
Dawn Weekly
Executive Intelligence Review,
    Washington
FBIS, Washington
FBIS, http://199.221.15.211/
Foreign Affairs, New York
Globe and Mail, Toronto
The Guardian, London
Il Giornale, Milan
Intelligence Newsletter, London
La Republica, Italy
Le Figaro, Paris
Le Monde, Paris
Los Angeles Times, Los Angeles
Mail on Sunday, USA
Marine Corps Gazette, USA
MEMRI (*Middle East Media
    Reports*) [in English],
    Washington: especially the
    series 'Terror in America',
    which began on 11 September
    2001; most of the translations
    in the book are based on
    theirs, for which I am
    indebted
The Mercury, London
Middle East Intelligence Bulletin,
    Washington

MSANEWS,
    http://www.nsanews.com
National Post, Washington
National Review Online, New
    York
The New Republic, New York
The New York Times, New York
*The New York Times Review of
    Books*, New York
The Observer, London
Online Journalism Review,
    internet
Parameters, New York
*Periscope Daily Defense News
    Capsules*, New York
Survival, New York
Survival, http://
    survival.oupjournals.org
The Radical, New York
The Radical,
    www.theradical.com
The Spectator, London
The Times, London
The Village Voice, New York
The Wall Street Journal, New York
USA Today, New York
US News and World Report, New
    York
Washington Post, Washington
Weekly Standard, New York
WorldNetDaily.com, internet
Worldwide Revisionist News,
    New York

ARTICLES

Ajami, Fouad, 'The Reckoning: Iraq and the Thief of Baghdad', *The New York Times* (19 May 2002).

Alterman, Eric, 'Interview with Mark Lilla', *The New York Times* (10 November 2001).

Atawna, Muhammed, 'Shari'a and Politics in Saudi Arabia: Siyyasa Shar'iyya as a Mechanism to Stabilize Saudi Society and Government', *Jama'a,* Vol. 8 (2000) [Hebrew].

Bailey, Clinton, 'A Note on the Bedouin Image of *'adl* as Justice', *Muslim World*, Vol 66, No. 2 (1976).

Buruma, Ian and Margalit, Avishai, 'Occidentalism', *The New York Review of Books* (17 January 2001), p. 4.

Cesari, Jocelyne, 'Muslims in Western Europe', *MSANEWS* (6 June 2000).

Cox, James, 'On Palestinian Education to Terror', *USA Today* (28 September 2001).

Conquest, Robert, 'Hesterophobia: On Blaming the Jews', National Review Online, 13 September 2001.

Del Valle, Alexandre, 'Islamophobie ou reductio at Hitlerum', *Le Figaro* (28 May 2000).

Dershowitz, Alan, 'On the Bin Laden Tape', *National Post* (15 December 2001).

Foa, Sylvana, 'Data on Terrorism from the International Policy Institute for Counter Terrorism', *The Village Voice* (5–11 June 2002).

Friedman, Thomas, 'Suicidal Lies', *The New York Times* (31 March 2002).

Gelernter, David, 'A Nation like Ours: Why Americans Stand with Israel', *Weekly Standard* (20 May 2002).

Goulding, V., 'Back to the Future, With Asymmetric Warfare', *Parameters* (Winter 2001–2002), pp. 21–30.

Gove, Michael, 'Spare Us More Middle East Peace Plans', *The Times* (2 April, 2002).

Hammes, Colonel Thomas, 'The Evolution or War: the Fourth Generation', *Marine Corps Gazette* (September 1994).

Harel, Amos and Barak, Omer, 'Portrait of the Terrorist as a Young Man', *Ha'aretz* (23 April 2002).

Hussein, Irfan, 'The Battle for Hearts and Minds', *Dawn Weekly* (6 October 2001).

Israeli, Raphael, 'Islamikaze and their Significance', *Terrorism and*

Political Violence, Vol 9, No. 3 (Autumn 1997), pp 96–121.

——, 'Education, Identity, State-Building and the Peace Process: Educating Palestinian Children in the Post Oslo Era', *Terrorism and Political* Violence, Vol. 12, No. 1 (Spring 2000), pp. 79–84.

Karsh, Efraim, 'Israel's Wars', *Commentary* (9 April 2002).

Kramer, Martin, 'Commenting on *Ivory Towers on Sand*: The Failure of Middle Eastern Studies in America', *The Wall Street Journal* (15 November 2001).

Lewis, Bernard, 'The Roots of Muslim Rage', *Atlantic Monthly* (September 1990).

——, 'How did the Infidels Win?', *National Post* (1 June 2002).

Lind, Captain W. *et al.*, 'The Changing Face of War: Into the Fourth Generation', *Marine Corps Gazette* (October 1989).

Paulson, Michael, 'Muslims Eye Role at US Polls', *Boston Globe* (23 October 2000).

Pipes, Daniel, 'Fighting Militant Islam, Without Bias', *City Journal* (Autumn 2001).

Sadeh, Sharon, 'London Bridge is Falling Down', *Haaretz* (30 September 2001).

Sharon, Moshe, 'Hudna and Sulh in Islam', *Nativ* (Summer 2002) [Hebrew].

Sheleg, Yair, 'American-Born Haters of the US and Israel Spring up on Campus', *Ha'aretz* (18 June 2002).

Singer, Paul, 'Interview with Bernard Lewis', *Jerusalem Post* (5 April 2002).

Wente, Margaret, 'Atrocities in Guantanamo and other Fruit Loop Tales', *Globe and Mail* (Toronto) (22 January 2002).

Will, George, 'Final Solution, Phase 2', *Washington Post* (2 May 2002).

BOOKS

Abu Mazen, *The Secret Ties between the Nazis and the Zionist Movement Leadership* (Amman: Dar Ibn-Rushd, 1984) [Arabic].

Akad, Med (ed.), *The Martyrs*, Series A, No. 6 (Amsterdam, 1955).

Algar, Hamid, *Islam and Revolution* (Berkeley, CA, University of CA Press: 1981).

Ayud, Mahmoud, *Redemptive Suffering in Islam* (The Hague, 1978).

Bat Ye'or, *The Dhimmi* (Madison and London: Fairleigh Dickinson University Press, 1985).

——, *The Decline of Eastern Christianity under Islam* (Madison and London: Fairleigh Dickinson University Press, 1996).

Bodansky, Joseph, *Islamic Anti-Semitism* (Tel Aviv: Ariel Center, 1999).

Cooley, John, *Green March, Black September: The Story of the Palestinian Arabs* (Frank Cass: London, 1973).

Eklund, Ragnar, *Life Between Death and Resurrection According to Islam* (Uppsala: Brill, 1941).

Gold Dore, *Israel is not the Issue: Militant Islam and America. Jerusalem Viewpoints* (Jerusalem: Jerusalem Center for Public Affairs, 2001).

——, *Washington Misled: Saudi Arabia's Financial Backing of Terrorism. Jerusalem Issue Brief* (Jerusalem: The Jerusalem Center for Public Affairs, 2002).

Goldziher, Ignaz, *Muhammedanische Studien* (Hildesheim: George Olm, 1961).

Handbook on the Jewish Question (Germany, 1935).

Hatina, Meir, *Palestinian Radicalism: The Islamic Jihad Movement* (Tel Aviv University: Tel Aviv University, 1994) [Hebrew].

Hodgson, Marshall, *The Venture of Islam*, 3 Vols (Chicago, IL: University of Chicago, 1974).

Hodgson, S.G., *The Order of Assassins* (The Hague, 1955).

Ibn abi-'Isam, *Kitab al-Jihad* [The Book of Jihad], 2 Vols (al-Madina, 1989).

Ibn Khaldun, *The Muqaddimah: An Introduction to History*, 3 Vols (Princeton, NJ: Princeton University, 1958).

Israeli, Raphael, 'The Charter of Allah: The Platform of the Islamic Resistance Movement', in Y. Alexander (ed.) *The 1988–9 Annual of Terrorism* (Amsterdam: Martinus Nijhoff, 1990), pp. 99–134

——, 'Western Democracies and Islamic Fundamentalist Violence', in David Rapoport *et al.* (eds), *The Democratic Experience and Political Violence* (London: Frank Cass, 2001), pp. 79–94.

——, *Peace is in the Eye of the Beholder* (Berlin and New York: Mouton Press, 1985).

——, *Fundamentalist Islam and Israel* (Lanham and New York: University Press of America, 1993).

——, *Muslim Fundamentalism in Israel* (London: Brassey's, 1993).

——, *Arab and Islamic Anti-Semitism*, Policy Paper (Tel Aviv: Ariel Center of Policy Research, 2001).

——, 'Western Democracies and Islamic Fundamentalist Violence' in *The Democratic Experience and Political Violence*, David Rapaport and Leonard Weinberger (eds), Special issue of *Terrorism and*

Political Violence, Vol. 12, Nos 3 and 4 (London: Frank Cass, 2001), pp. 160–73.

——, *Green Crescent over Nazareth: The Displacement of Christians by Muslims in the Holy Land* (Frank Cass, London, 2002).

——, *Poison: Modern Manifestations of the Blood Libel* (Lanham, MD: Rowman and Littlefield, 2002).

Keppel, Gilles, *La Revanche de Dieu* (Paris: Presses Universitaires, 1994).

Khadduri, Majid, *War and Peace in Islam* (Baltimore, MD: Jons Hopkins University Press, 1969).

Kodansha Encyclopedia of Japan (Tokyo and New York: Kodansha, 1983).

The Koran (Harmondsworth: Penguin, 2003).

Kramer, Martin (ed.), *Protest and Revolution in Shi'ite Islam* (Tel Aviv: Hakibbutz Hameuhad, 1987).

Kramer, Martin, *Ivory Towers on Sand: The Failure of Middle Eastern Studies in America* (Washington, DC: The Washington Institute for Near East Policy, 2001).

Lewis, Bernard, *The Assassins* (New York: Basic Books, 1968).

——, *The Jews of Islam* (Princeton: Princeton University Press, 1984).

Marcus, Itamar, 'Islam's Mandatory War against Jews and Israel in Palestinian Authority Religious Teaching', Palestine Media Watch, Studies on Palestinian Culture and Society, Special Report No. 37 (Jerusalem: Palestine Media Watch, 2001).

O' Shaughnessy, Thomas, *Muhammed's Thoughts on Death* (Leiden: Brill, 1969).

Peroncel-Hugoz, J., *The Raft of Muhammed* (New York: Paragon Press, 1988).

Post, Jerry (ed.), *The Qaeda Training Manual: Military Studies in the Jihad against the Tyrants* (London: Frank Cass, 2002).

Qira'a fi Fiqh al-Shahada [Readings in Islamic Martyrology] (Nicosia/London: Filastin al-Muslima, n.d.).

Qut'b, Sayyid, *Ma'rakatuna ma'a al-Yahud* [Our War against the Jews], 7th edn (Beirut, 1986).

Sivan Emanuel, *Muslim Radicals* (Tel Aviv: Am Oved, 1985) [Hebrew].

Solnick, Aluma, 'The Joy of the Mothers of Palestinian Martyrs', *MEMRI*, No. 61 (25 June 2001).

Stillman, Norman, *The Jews of Arab Lands* (Philadelphia, PA: Jewish Publication Society, 1979).

Taheri, Amir, *The Spirit of Allah* (Tel Aviv: Am Oved, 1986) [Hebrew translation].

Weissbrod, Amir, *Turabi: A Spokesman of Radical Islam* (Tel Aviv: Tel Aviv University, 1999) [Hebrew].

Wensick, A.J. 'The Oriental Doctrine of the Martyrs', in Med Akad (ed.), *The Martyrs*, Series A No. 6 (Amsterdam, 1955).

Wistrich, Robert , 'Muslim Anti-Semitism. American Jewish Committee Report (New York: AJC, 2002).

Index

Balkans, 38, 189, 316, 348, 352, 383,
    444 (*see also* Bosnia and Kosovo)
Baltic, 339, 382
Baltimore Sun, 354–5
Bamyan, 370
Bangladesh, 65
Bank of America, 287
Banya, Princess, 253
Barak, Prime Minister Ehud, 201
Barakat, Halim, 214
Barbars, 214, 251, 260, 275, 284,
    331, 369; American, 182, 214;
    Jewish, 181, 214, 286, 296, 316,
    318, 333
Basel, 306
Basilica of Annunciation, 128, 246,
    267, 428
Baset, abd-al-'Oudeh, 215
Basra, 358
Bat Ye'or, 48
Bayrou, Francois, 424
Bayumi, 'Ala', 386
BBC, 153, 245, 330, 371
Beirut, 192, 319
Beit Lid, 109
Belgium, 53, 287, 378, 382
Ben-Gurion Airport, 3
Berbers, 367
Bengal(i), 393
Berkeley, 365
Berlin, 50, 373
Bet Hanun, 16
Bethlehem, 245, 269, 283
Bevins, Douglas, 409
Bhutto, Prime Minister Benazir, 82
Beinin, Joel, 358
BENELUX, 383 (*see also* Belgium
    and Holland)
Bible, 49, 262, 333; Book of Esther,
    301; Book of Joshua, 320; New
    Testament, 46, 99, 270, 283; Old
    Testament, 46, 298–9;

Pentateuque / Torah, 320; People
    of the, 289 (*see also dhimmi*)
Bilal, Muhammed, 196
Bin-Laden, Osama, 6–7, 11, 19, 23,
    25–6, 28, 30, 34, 36, 41, 45, 52,
    54, 56, 61, 75, 79, 80–1, 84, 86,
    108, 124–6, 128, 130, 136–7, 139,
    144–5, 149–50, 154, 167, 174ff.,
    185–6, 192, 196–9, 226, 229–30,
    237, 242, 253, 255–6, 272, 277,
    286, 331, 353, 355, 361, 364,
    393–4, 401, 403, 406–7, 410, 416,
    430–1, 445–6, 459
Birmingham (England), 194–5
Bishara, Dr Ahmed, 142
Bismarck, Chancellor, 288
Black, William, 406
Black community, 14, 20, 37, 254,
    258, 294–5, 319, 322, 377
Black Sea, 167
Blair, Cherie, 398, 432
Blair, Prime Minister Tony, 194,
    386, 401, 405
blasphemy / heresy / apostasy,
    140–1, 177, 193, 201–3, 223,
    229–30, 233, 238, 241, 246, 265–7,
    273, 287, 290, 314, 330, 375–6,
    396, 424–5, 432, 460
Blood Libel, 56, 67, 153, 228, 282,
    297, 300–5, 356, 367, 434, 439,
    441; Damascus, 303–4
Bnai Brith, 56
Bonder, Jonathan, 408
Bosnia, 81–2, 267, 316, 376, 444
Boston, 58–9, 387, 389-90; Islamic
    Center, 58–9, 387–9; Muslim
    Association, 58, 60, 391
Boston Globe, 383
Boulder, University of Colorado
    at, 364–5
bourgeoisie, 459
bourgeoisophobia, 371–2, 385